CONTENTS

PREFACE

This text examines today's most important moral problems. The emphasis is on critical reasoning by leading moral philosophers.

The tenth edition has twenty new readings and five new or refocused chapters. The new topics are "Financial Crisis," "World Poverty and Hunger," "Vegetarianism" (in combination with animal rights), and "Assassination." There are many new Problem Cases on issues such as illegal immigrants, health care, the government bailout, and assassinating Americans.

Abortion, euthanasia, the duty to die, capital punishment, same-sex marriage, animals, war, terrorism, and torture continue to be topics of vital interest. The ethical theories provide a basic theoretical background for the readings; many of them assume or apply a moral theory such as utilitarianism, Kant's theory, Rawls's theory, or natural law theory.

The choice of the particular readings for each topic was influenced by a variety of considerations. First, there was an attempt to find readings of high quality. All of the readings have been previously published. Some of the readings are considered to be classics, such as Judith Jarvis Thomson's "A Defense of Abortion" and Peter Singer's "Famine, Affluence, and Morality." Other readings were chosen for their historical importance; for example, the Supreme Court decisions on abortion and capital punishment. There was an attempt to balance the readings, to allow different and conflicting points of view to be expressed. Thus, in the chapter on abortion, we include a variety of viewpoints, ranging from John T. Noonan's strict pro-life position to Mary Anne Warren's radical pro-choice view. The readings also were chosen to be read together; they respond to one another as in a conversation. This is well demonstrated in the abortion chapter, where the articles can be read as replying to one another.

Suitability for students was another important consideration. The book is intended to be an introductory-level textbook that can be read and understood by most college or junior college students. But finding the right level is difficult, as most practicing teachers know. No doubt some students will find the book too easy, and others will say it is too hard. For those who want it or need it, several student aids have been provided:

1. *Chapter Introductions.* With the exception of the first chapter, on ethical theories, each chapter introduction is divided into three sections: factual background, the readings, and philosophical issues. The emphasis on factual background continues with the tenth edition; a diligent attempt has been made to provide accurate

and up-to-date information on each topic. Next, there are brief summaries of the readings, emphasizing how they respond to each other, and finally a short discussion of the main philosophical issues.

2. *Reading Introductions.* An author biography and a short summary of the author's main points precede each reading.

3. *Study Questions.* Two types of study questions follow each reading. First, there are rather detailed and pedestrian review questions that test the student's grasp of the main points in the reading. These are intended for students wanting or needing help in following the text. They can be read either before or after studying the reading, or both. (Students should read the material at least two times.) Second are more difficult discussion questions that probe deeper into the reading. They are aimed at the student who has understood the reading and is ready to discuss it critically.

4. *Problem Cases.* The Problem Cases at the end of each chapter require the student to apply the arguments and theories in the chapter to hard cases, either actual or hypothetical. This case-study method, as it is called in law schools and business schools, can produce lively discussion and is a good way to get the students to think about the issues. The Problem Cases also can be assigned as short paper topics or used for essay tests.

5. *Suggested Readings.* Instead of going to the library, I have come to rely on the Internet for information, mainly using Google as my search engine. For factual information, I include a few websites. But the Internet is not yet a substitute for printed books and articles, which still constitute most of the annotated suggestions for further reading.

In revising the book for the tenth edition, I have benefited from the help and support of many people. Wall Street impresario Harry Forsyth explained the financial industry. I had weekly discussions on current affairs with Myron Anderson, George Yoos, Lee Davis, Jim Lundquist, Dick Corliss and Balasubramanian Kasi. As always, Elena White provided invaluable support. I am grateful to the following reviewers for their thoughtful advice and criticisms:

Mary Whall, University of Alabama at Birmingham; Robert Micallef, Madonna University; Matt Zwolinski, University of San Diego; Benjamin Gorman, York College of Pennsylvania; Shin Kim, Central Michigan University; Donald L. Batz, Scott Community College; Mark T. Nelson, Westmont College; Brian Barnes, University of Louisville; Gene Kleppinger, Eastern Kentucky University; Caleb Miller, Messiah College; Shawn Kaplan, Adelphi University; Todd Thompson, Randolph Community College; Paul Greenberg, Tulane University School of Continuing Studies; Barbara Solheim, William Rainey Harper College; Jill Hernandez, University of Texas at San Antonio; Heimir Geirsson, Iowa State University; George Schedler, Southern Illinois University; John M Gulley, Winston Salem State University; David Phillips, University of Houston; Kerry Edwards, Red Rocks Community College; Ron Martin, Lynchburg College; Shaun Miller, Weber State University; Richard Sumpter, Baker University; Ronald Novy, University of Central Arkansas; Eugene Mills, Virginia Commonwealth University; Gaile Pohlhaus, Miami University; Ramona Ilea, Pacific University; Michael Bollenbaugh, Northwest Christian University; Ernani Magalhaes, West Virginia University; Tammie Foltz, Des Moines Area Community College; Meredith Gunning, Northern Essex Community College; Jonathan D. Gainor; Harrisburg Area Community College; Mary Lyn Stoll, University of Southern Indiana; Darci Doll, Central Michigan University; Sarah Conrad, University of North Texas.

CHAPTER ONE

Ethical Theories

INTRODUCTION

This chapter presents the basic moral theories that are the background for the subsequent readings in the book. For the sake of discussion, we can divide the theories into six main types: theory of the right, theory of the good, virtue theory, rights theory, social contract theory, and feminist theory.

Theory of the Right

A theory of the right tries to tell us what is morally right and what is morally wrong. Such a theory is obviously relevant to the moral problems investigated in this book, such as abortion, euthanasia, capital punishment, and war and terrorism.

Theories of the right are usually subdivided into two types: teleological and deontological. Teleological theories focus on consequences; they can be said to be forward looking. Deontological theories do not do this but, rather, look backward at some nonconsequential feature, such as a motive or God's commands.

One popular teleological theory is *ethical egoism*, the view that everyone ought to act in his or her rational self-interest. This view is often defended by an appeal to psychological egoism, the thesis that, as a matter of fact, everyone does act in a self-interested way. But if this is so, then it is impossible for us to act unselfishly; all we can do is act selfishly. It seems to follow that ethical egoism is the only option available to us.

James Rachels attacks both psychological and ethical egoism. He argues that psychological egoism is false and confused. It is false because people do act unselfishly and in ways contrary to self-interest. It is confused because it fails to distinguish between selfishness and self-interest, it falsely assumes that every action is done either from self-interest or from other-regarding motives, and it ignores the fact that concern for one's own welfare is compatible with concern for the welfare of others.

As for ethical egoism, Rachels admits that it is not logically inconsistent and that it cannot be decisively refuted. However, he thinks there are considerations that count very strongly against it. Most people do care about others; genuine egoists who really do not care about others are rare. Also, saying that an action will benefit others is giving a complete and sufficient reason for doing it. No further reason need be given.

Perhaps the most famous and widely discussed teleological theory is *utilitarianism*. The standard formulation of this theory is presented by John Stuart Mill. The most basic principle of utilitarianism is the principle of utility, which Mill states as follows: "Actions are right in proportion as they tend to promote happiness, wrong as they tend to produce the reverse of happiness." But what is happiness? Mill's answer is that happiness (or what is good) is pleasure and the absence of pain. Here Mill adopts a standard theory of the good, called *hedonism*, the view that the good is pleasure. We will examine this theory and alternatives to it in the next section.

In considering the happiness or unhappiness (or the good or evil) produced, utilitarianism counts everyone equally. But who counts? The answer of Mill and his followers is radical and important: We should consider everyone and everything that is capable of suffering, including nonhuman animals. In Chapter 6, we see Peter Singer and others arguing that it is wrong to discriminate against animals. This is in sharp contrast to the conventional view (defended by John T. Noonan in Chapter 2) that only human beings count, or at least that human beings count more than nonhumans.

Unlike Kant (discussed later), Mill does not consider the motive for action to be relevant to the rightness or wrongness of the action. He notes that 99 of 100 of our actions are done from some motive other than duty, but this does not matter when it comes to judging the morality of the act. To use his examples, a person who saves someone from drowning does what is morally right, even if his motive is selfish—for example, the desire to be paid for his action. And a person who betrays a friend who trusts him does something wrong even if his motive is a moral one—for example, the desire to help another friend.

A standard objection to utilitarianism is that it can be used to justify acts that we suspect are morally wrong, such as lying. (See the Problem Case on lying at the end of the chapter.) It seems obvious that lying can sometimes have good consequences, for example, in social situations where telling the unvarnished truth will hurt people's feelings. In the reading, Mill suggests a reply to this objection. Even though the principle of utility is the fundamental principle of morality, in practice it needs to be supplemented by subordinate rules based on our experience and, indeed, the experience of all humankind. One of these practical rules is the one forbidding lying or deceiving others. Experience has shown that following this rule produces good consequences in the long run; so we would be wise to follow it most of the time, allowing for occasional exceptions. Mill admits that there is no practical rule of conduct that admits of no exceptions. An emphasis on moral rules rather than action results in a modified version of Mill's theory called *rule utilitarianism*. On this theory, an act is judged right or wrong by reference to the rule being followed. If the rule has good consequences, then the act is right, and if the rule has bad consequences, then the act is wrong. Mill's original theory is called *act utilitarianism* since it focuses on the act rather than the rule being followed by the act.

Now let us turn to the other main kind of theory of the right, deontological theory. One popular view is the *divine command theory* discussed by John Arthur. As Arthur explains it, the divine command theory says that an act is right if and because God commands it and wrong if and because God forbids it. According to this view, God is the source of morality because without God there would be no right or wrong. Just as a legislator enacts laws, God dictates and commands moral rules. According to Arthur, defenders of the divine command theory, such as F. C. Copleston, often add the claim that the objective difference between right and wrong rests on the existence of God as the foundation of morality. No doubt this theory is accepted by millions of religious people, but few philosophers are willing to defend it. One problem is that many philosophers think that morality can be founded on something other than God's commands, such as reason, human nature, culture, or natural senti- ments. Another objection is that "right" and "commanded by God" do *not mean* the same thing. People in other cultures—in Japan and China, for example—use moral concepts without understanding them as references to God's commands. It goes without saying that atheists will not accept the theory, but Arthur thinks that even theists should reject it because of the possibility that God might change the moral commands. This would be like a legislature changing the law. Suppose that tomor- row God commands us to be cruel. Because, according to the theory, something is right just because God commands it, cruelty is now morally right. Arthur thinks this is patently absurd. It is absurd to think that the greatest atrocities might be morally right if God were to command them. This point is similar to the famous question posed by Socrates in Plato's dialogue *Euthyphro*: Is something holy (or right) because God commands it, or does God command it because it is holy (or right)? As Arthur demonstrates in his discussion, this question raises some fundamental difficulties for the divine command theory. On the first alternative, morality seems arbitrary because God could command anything at all and make it right. On the second alter- native, God is not the source of morality after all because it seems that God has to discover what is right rather than legislating it.

Friedrich Nietzsche (see the Suggested Readings) launches a different sort of attack on the divine command theory and, indeed, on any moral theory or religion making obedience a virtue. He denigrates any such theory or religion as a "slave morality" because it emphasizes slave virtues such as obedience, humility, sympathy, and friendliness. Nietzsche thinks these slave virtues are contemptible; they are suitable only for weak and servile people. The noble person rejects them in favor of the "master morality," a morality that focuses on superior virtues such as power, strength, pride, vanity, and egoism.

An influential deontological theory in Christian thought is the *natural law theory* of Saint Thomas Aquinas. On this view, God created the world following a divine plan that Aquinas calls the "eternal law." According to this plan, everything in nature has a purpose; for example, eyes are designed for seeing and rain falls to nourish plants. The divine plan includes values; it includes a natural law that tells us what is right and what is good. This natural law can be discerned by humans using the natural light of reason, which humans have because they are made in the image of the rational God. The most basic precept of the natural law is the self-evident truth that one ought to do good and avoid evil. But what is good and what is evil? Aquinas equates goodness with what is in accord with natural inclinations and evil with that which is opposed by natural inclinations. For example, humans have a basic natural inclination to preserve life and avoid death. This implies that actions that preserve life are right and those that do not, such as abortion, suicide, euthanasia, capital punishment, and war, are wrong. Another basic instinct is the animal inclination to engage in sexual intercourse. But since the natural purpose of sex is reproduction, nonreproductive sex such as masturbation is wrong.

Few people outside the Catholic Church appeal to natural law theory. One problem is that modern science does not explain things in terms of purposes or values. The eye was not designed for seeing; it is simply the result of a long period of evolution and natural selection, or at least that is the explanation given in biology. Rain does not fall to nourish plants. It falls because of the law of gravity. The laws of science merely describe what happens; they do not ascribe purposes or values to anything. Another problem is the equation of natural inclination with good and unnatural inclination with evil. Male humans have a natural inclination to be aggressive and to dominate females, but are these natural tendencies good? Feminists do not think so. Many people find celibacy to be unnatural, as it is opposed by natural desires, yet the Church teaches that total abstinence from sex is good, not evil. Finally, how do we know what the natural law says? Any rational person is supposed to be able to discern the natural law, but we find that rational people do not agree about values. Is it possible that some rational people are deceived when they try to discern the moral law? How can we be sure we are perceiving the true moral law, assuming there is such a thing? Even Catholics who accept natural law theory do not agree about everything. For example, some are pacifists who find war immoral, whereas others justify war using the just war theory. (For a discussion of pacifism and just war theory, see Chapter 9.)

Unlike Aquinas, David Hume denies that reason can tell us what is right and what is good. Hume argues that morality cannot be derived from reason. According to Hume, if you consider, for example, a case of intentional murder, you will find that the wrongness of murder is not found in your reasoning about objective facts or relations of ideas but simply in your sentiment, in your feelings of disapproval of murder. The view that moral judgments are based on subjective feelings of approval or disapproval is called *ethical subjectivism*. Strictly speaking, this is a view about the factual basis of morality, not a deontological theory that tells us what is right. Some philosophers call such a theory a *meta-ethical theory*. It tells us what morality is based on as a matter of fact, not what morality ought to be. In a famous passage, Hume suggests that it is a mistake to argue from "is" to "ought"—that is, to argue that because something is the case, that therefore it ought to be the case. But Aquinas seems to make this very mistake when he says that what is natural ought to be done; for example, that because reproductive sex is natural, it ought to be done. It should be noted that Hume did have a view about what ought to be done: He recommended following a sentiment of benevolence toward all humans. He did not, however, think that people ought to do this because they do have such a sentiment. The fact that people have such a sentiment only shows that acting benevolently is possible.

Hume's views are controversial. Some philosophers have maintained that arguing from "is" to "ought" is acceptable in some cases. For example, in the reading in this chapter, Mill claims that the only proof that can be given that happiness is desirable is that people desire it. Happiness is good because everyone wants it. Clearly, Mill is arguing from a fact to a value, but is this a mistake? Another problem with Hume's theory about morality is that it implies that people cannot be mistaken in their moral judgments. If moral judgments are just expressions of feeling, the equivalent of approving or disapproving of something, then as long as they are sincere, people cannot be mistaken when making a moral judgment. But it seems obvious that people like sadists or Nazis can be mistaken in their moral judgments. A related problem is that Hume's theory does not seem to give an adequate account of moral disagreements. If the abortion controversy amounts to different people having different feelings about abortion, with some approving and others disapproving, then they do not really have a substantive disagreement. They are not contradicting each other. They just have different feelings. This hardly seems like a satisfactory account of the disagreement. After all, both sides defend their position using arguments and reasoning. They appeal to facts. No doubt emotions play a role in the controversy, but it is not just about feelings.

A deontological theory that takes moral disagreements seriously is *ethical relativism*. Cultural ethical relativism is the view that what is right is whatever a culture says is right, and what is wrong is whatever a culture thinks is wrong. If our culture says that homosexuality is wrong, then it is wrong in our society. If ancient Greek culture said that homosexuality is right, then it was right in that society. But if what is wrong in one culture is right in another culture, if seems to follow that we cannot legitimately criticize cultures that do not share our moral beliefs and practices. We must be tolerant of other cultures no matter what they do, even if they practice human sacrifice or torture and kill people because of their race or religion.

In the readings, Mary Midgley illustrates the moral tolerance problem with a vivid example, the Japanese custom of trying out one's new samurai sword on a chance wayfarer. Although this seems obviously wrong from a Western moral perspective, can we justifiably criticize it? Midgley argues that we can and that cultural relativism, with its implication that we cannot criticize other cultures, is unacceptable. The basic problem with cultural relativism, Midgley argues, is that it results in a moral isolationism that forbids moral reasoning. It is essentially a program of immoralism that wants to put moralizing out of business.

Although she does not discuss it, Midgley's attack on cultural relativism also undermines individual relativism, the view that what is right or wrong is whatever an individual thinks is right or wrong. Sometimes this popular view is expressed in the slogan "Morality is just a matter of opinion," with the implication that one opinion is just as good as another. This view is vulnerable to the same objection that Midgley raises to cultural relativism. We can and do criticize the moral beliefs of other people. People can be mistaken or inconsistent in their moral beliefs. To rule this out is to forbid moral reasoning and its requirement of consistency.

Perhaps the most influential deontological theory is Immanuel Kant's theory. Kant believes that by pure reasoning we can discover one supreme moral principle that is binding on all rational beings. By "pure reasoning," he means reasoning that does not appeal to anything else, such as religious faith or popular opinion; it is like reasoning in geometry and mathematics. In Kant's view, the category of "rational beings" excludes animals (see his reading in Chapter 6); it includes not just human beings but also God and angels. The supreme moral principle uncovered by pure reasoning is called the *categorical imperative* because it commands absolutely, as distinguished from hypothetical imperatives that command only if you have certain desires.

Kant formulated the categorical imperative in several different ways, but commentators usually focus on two distinct versions. The first is that you should "act only on that maxim through which you can at the same time will that it should become a universal law." This principle gives you a way of deciding whether or not an act is wrong. You ask yourself what rule you would be following if you did something; this rule is the "maxim" of your act. If you are not willing to have this rule become a universal law that everyone follows, then the act is wrong. To take one of Kant's examples, suppose you want to borrow money and not pay it back. To get the money, you have to promise to pay it back even though you have no intention of doing so. The maxim of your act, then, would be something like this: "Whenever I believe myself short of money, I will borrow money and promise to pay it back, though I know that this will never be done." According to Kant, this maxim could never be a universal law because it contradicts itself. If everyone followed this maxim, then the very practice of promising would be impossible because nobody would believe a promise. These considerations show that such false promising is wrong.

Many philosophers have thought that this first formulation of the categorical imperative is problematic. One problem is that you can formulate the rule under which an act falls in different ways. Some of these rules could be made universal and others not. To go back to borrowing money, suppose you need to borrow money to pay for expensive cancer treatment to save your infant son's life. You do not have health insurance, and Medicaid will not cover the treatment. To get the money, you promise to pay it back even though you know you cannot do so. Now the maxim of your act is something like this: "Whenever I need money to save my baby's life, then I will borrow money from the bank and promise to pay it back, even though I know this will never be done because I will never have that much money." Would you be willing to have this be a universal law? If so, would it destroy the practice of promising?

Another objection attacks Kant's notion of perfect duty, the idea that there are duties that admit no exceptions. As we have seen, Mill does not believe we can find any moral rules or duties that have no exceptions. As Mill notes, one way exceptions arise is when there is a conflict between duties. Suppose, for example, there is a conflict between the duty not to lie and the duty not to harm others. A terrorist asks you for a loaded gun to use in killing innocent hostages. You know where there is a gun handy, but should you tell the truth? It seems obvious enough that you should not tell the truth in this case because the duty not to harm others overrides the duty not to lie. The notion of one duty overriding another is the basis of W. D. Ross's theory (discussed later).

Unlike Mill, Kant judges the morality of an act solely by its motive and not by its consequences. The only motive that counts morally is the "good will," which is willing an act simply because it is one's duty—the duty to obey the categorical imperative—and not because of any inclination or consequences produced by the act. It is not good enough to act in accordance with duty; one must act just because it is one's duty. The motive must be duty alone uncontaminated by any other considerations. But as a practical matter, how many acts would qualify as moral, given Kant's strict requirement? Mill claims that only one of a hundred acts is motivated by duty. Indeed, one may doubt that there are any acts not motivated by some inclination or some desired consequence.

Kant formulated the categorical imperative in a second way, which some commentators find more plausible. This second formulation, called the *formula of the end in itself,* recommends that you "act in such a way that you always treat humanity, whether in your own person or in the person of any other, never simply as a means, but always at the same time as an end." Treating others as a mere means is to engage them in an activity to which they could not, in principle, consent—for example, a deception. Treating people as ends in themselves requires that we not only treat them as mere means but also that we help them with their projects and activities. This imposes on us a duty to help or a duty of beneficence, but this duty is only imperfect. That is, it is a duty that cannot always be satisfied but always requires us to exercise judgment and discretion.

Kant's theory has had an important impact on three of the moral problems covered in the book. First, Kant is a stern defender of capital punishment. In the reading in Chapter 4, Kant condemns the "serpent-windings of utilitarianism" and insists that the only appropriate punishment for murderers is death. They must be paid back for their crimes, and the consequences of the punishment are irrelevant. Kant is one of the main sources of the retributive theory of punishment, which holds that guilty people should be punished and that the punishment should fit the crime.

Second, according to Kant, we do not have any direct duties toward animals. (See the Reading in Chapter 6.) We have only indirect duties based on the effect the treatment of animals has on the treatment of humans. We should not be cruel to animals because this makes us likely to be cruel to humans. Animals are not subjects of direct moral concern because they are not rational beings. Kant's view, then, stands in sharp contrast to the utilitarians such as Mill and Singer, who believe that animals do have the status of moral subjects who deserve moral consideration. Third, there is the abortion controversy. Kant does not discuss abortion, but it seems clear that fetuses are not rational beings, and thus, an implication of Kant's view is that they have no more moral status than animals. This is similar to the position that Mary Anne Warren takes in Chapter 2.

W. D. Ross (see the Suggested Readings) presents an important deontological theory that appeals to duty, like Kant, but is significantly different from Kant's theory. Ross claims that various features can make an act right, not just one, as in utilitarianism, Kant's theory, and the other theories we have discussed. Some of these features are backward looking—for example, the fact that we have made a promise or signed a contract in the past. Other features are forward looking—for example, the prospect of making someone happy or improving one's life in the future. Such considerations are the basis for our duty, but this duty can always be overridden by other duties. In Ross's terminology, these duties are prima facie (at first glance) in that they can be overridden by other moral considerations. The concept of prima facie duty is found frequently in writings on ethics. The basic idea is that there can be conflicts between prima facie duties such that we cannot satisfy them all. For example, we may be able to help someone only if we break a promise. We may be required to lie to save someone's life. In such cases, we can only make a judgment about what to do using moral intuition. Moral intuition is also supposed to reveal self-evident principles about duty that are more certain than judgments about particular acts. An example is the principle that "ought implies can"; that is, we ought to do something only if we are able to do it, and if we cannot do something, then we cannot have the obligation to do it. Because Ross appeals to moral intuition, his theory is often called *intuitionism*. It is also said to be a pluralistic deontology because it recognizes different types of duty.

Theory of the Good

A theory of the good tries to tell us what is good and what is bad. Teleological theories seem to require some theory of the good to evaluate consequences. We noted earlier that Mill accepts hedonism, the theory that the good is pleasure. Hedonism is usually defended by making two important distinctions. First, there is a distinction between intrinsic and instrumental value. Something has *intrinsic value* if it is good or bad in itself apart from its use or consequences. By contrast, something has *instrumental value* if it is good or bad depending on how it is used. Hedonists allow that things such as knowledge and beauty can be instrumentally good but insist that only pleasure is intrinsically good. Similarly, things such as ignorance and ugliness can be instrumentally bad, but hedonists claim that only pain is intrinsically bad.

Critics of Mill and hedonism argue, however, that other things besides pleasure can be intrinsically good—for example, unexperienced beauty that is not instrumentally good because no one experiences it. They also claim that things besides pain can be intrinsically bad—for example, the injustice of punishing an innocent person. Indeed, the fact that utilitarianism does not seem to give a satisfactory account of retributive or distributive justice is seen as a serious defect. This has led modern philosophers to formulate theories of justice that are independent of utilitarianism— for example, Rawls's theory of justice in the readings for this chapter.

Another criticism of hedonism (which can be found in the reading by Aristotle) is that pleasure is an appropriate goal for animals but not for humans. According to Aristotle, the highest good for humans is found in contemplation, because this involves the use of reason, and reasoning is what humans are naturally suited to do. The reply that Mill makes in the reading rests on the second distinction made by hedonists, a distinction between higher and lower pleasures. Roughly, higher pleasures involve the use of the intellect, whereas lower pleasures involve the senses. The higher pleasures are better than the lower pleasures, Mills argues, because the person who has experienced both will prefer the higher pleasures. Whether this is true or not is a matter of debate. In any event, Mill's view about the good life turns out to be not much different from Aristotle's view; on both views intellectual activities have a central role.

There are alternatives to hedonism. One is Kant's position that the only thing that is good without qualification is the good will, the desire to do one's duty for its own sake. By the way, Kant denied that pleasure is always intrinsically good. He thought that the pleasure of a wicked person is not good; for example, in Kant's view, the pleasure the sadist gets from torturing others is both instrumentally and intrinsically evil.

Another main source of alternatives to hedonism is religion. The monotheistic religions (Judaism, Christianity, and Islam) agree that the highest good involves God in some way. It might be obedience to God's will (emphasized in Islam), love of

God (recommended by Jesus), a mystical union with God in this life, or a beatific vision of God in heaven. Aristotle says that the highest good for humans is found in the contemplation of God. Although in this book we will not be concerned with religion as such, there is no doubt that religion has played an important role in ethics. Arthur discusses some of the connections between ethics and religion in the reading. We have already discussed the divine command theory, which is tacitly adopted in the monotheistic religions. (There are, of course, religions that do not worship God, such as Buddhism, Taoism, and Confucianism.) Other religious doctrines come up in various contexts. In Chapter 2, Noonan mentions *ensoulment*, the doctrine that the immortal soul enters the fetus (technically, the zygote) at the moment of conception. Traditionally, philosophers have defended our lack of moral concern for animals by maintaining that animals do not have souls (although it should be mentioned that in Hinduism and Jainism, animals are believed to have souls; indeed, some of them have the reincarnated souls of humans!).

Virtue Theory

Virtue theory is included in this chapter because it offers an important alternative to the theories that dwell on moral rightness and duty. The classical source of virtue theory is Aristotle. Aristotle makes several important points about virtues. First, there is a distinction between intellectual and moral virtue. Intellectual virtue involves the use of what is best in humans—namely, reasoning—and the highest form of reasoning is self-sufficient, pure contemplation of God. Moral virtues involve a mean between the extremes of excess and deficiency. This is sometimes called the *doctrine of the golden mean*. To use one of Aristotle's examples, courage is a mean between the excess of foolhardiness and the deficiency of cowardliness. Second, Aristotle claims that some actions do not involve any means but are always wrong. This is an important point, for if there are such actions, then it seems to follow that some of the theories we have just discussed are problematic. Consider, for example, the action of torturing a small child to death. It seems obvious that this is wrong even if a person or a culture believes it is right, even if God commands it, and even if it produces good consequences for others or the person doing the torturing. If so, then egoism, cultural relativism, the divine command theory, and utilitarianism all have a problem.

Some commentators argue that Aristotle gives us a theory about what to be rather than what to do; that is, the theory recommends certain moral traits of character rather than types of moral action. It switches our attention from principles and rules of conduct to ideal moral heroes such as Aristotle's person of moral wisdom, Plato's just person, Augustine's citizen of the City of God, or to actual moral saints such as Jesus, Confucius, the Buddha, and Saint Francis. Instead of trying to formulate and refine abstract rules of right conduct, the project is to imitate these moral heroes and saints.

Rights Theory

Many of the readings in the book do not appeal to virtues or duties but to rights. We find references to the rights of fetuses, newborn infants, the terminally ill, animals, and even the environment. Most often mentioned are the rights to life and liberty. But what exactly is a *right*? Joel Feinberg (see the Suggested Readings) explains personal rights in terms of claims; he calls them "claim-rights" and distinguishes them from other liberties, immunities, and powers. Consider the right most often discussed in the book, the right to life. On Feinberg's analysis, when people have a right to life, they have a legal claim-right to life such that they have no duty to relinquish their lives, and other people have a duty not to interfere with their lives. Notice that according to Feinberg's analysis, rights logically entail other people's duties, so in an indirect way, rights do include duties.

There is debate about the duties entailed by rights, which we can illustrate with the right to life. Does the right to life imply a duty of noninterference so that we respect this right by just leaving people alone? If so, then this right might be characterized as a negative right. Or does the right to life imply a duty to help others stay alive by giving them the necessities of life such as food, clothing, and medical care? If that is how we interpret it, then the right to life is a positive right, an entitlement, that requires positive action of others and not merely noninterference. (See the Problem Case about health care at the end of the chapter.)

Besides the rights to life and liberty, what other rights do people have? Again, this is a matter of debate and interpretation. In the United States, the Constitution gives citizens certain fundamental rights that they hold against other people as well as the government; these rights include the right to free speech, to a free press, to bear arms, and so on. Just how these rights are to be interpreted is the subject of legal debate. For example, does the right to bear arms give citizens the right to bear fully automatic weapons? (See the Problem Case about the Colt Sporter at the end of the chapter.)

A comprehensive list of rights can be found in the United Nations' Universal Declaration of Human Rights, which was approved unanimously by the UN General Assembly in 1948. It is presented as a common universal standard of human rights for all nations. The rights are to be granted irrespective of race, color, sex, language, religion, political or other opinion, national or social origin, property, birth, or other status. Among the basic rights are the right to life, liberty, and security of person. Article 5 says, "No one shall be subjected to torture or to cruel, inhuman, or degrading treatment or punishment." (See Chapter 10 for denials of this right.) Article 23 says, "Everyone has the right to work, to free choice of employment, to just and favourable conditions of work, and to protection against unemployment." If this is a positive right, then everyone is entitled to work at the job they choose under just and favorable conditions. Article 26 says, "Everyone has the right to education. . . . Technical and professional education shall be made generally available and higher education shall be equally accessible to all on the basis of merit."

Social Contract Theory

The traditional basis for moral rights is that they are created by God. John Locke and Thomas Jefferson talk about humans being endowed by their Creator with certain basic rights that are inalienable, that cannot be taken away by other people or the government. But most philosophers today do not want to make God the source of rights; they want a different foundation. The traditional secular view that is used to provide a foundation for rights is the *social contract theory* of Thomas Hobbes and Jean-Jacques Rousseau. According to this theory, it is in everyone's self-interest to live together in a society rather than alone in a state of nature. Life in a state of nature would be short, nasty, and brutish. To live in a society, though, people must agree to follow certain rules (don't steal, don't murder, etc.), and these rules imply corresponding rights. Every citizen tacitly makes such an agreement (the social contract) to get the benefits of living in society. Without this social contract, society would be impossible.

John Rawls's theory of justice is a type of social contract theory. We are asked to imagine what rules free, rational, and informed people would accept for a society. To make sure that the contractors are fair and unbiased, we are to imagine them operating under a "veil of ignorance" that hides from them personal facts such as their gender, race, and class. The rules such contractors would accept in the hypothetical original position, according to Rawls, are a principle giving people an equal right to liberty and a principle concerning social and economic inequalities.

Feminist Theory

Feminist theory has two features that distinguish it from the theories discussed so far. It emphasizes the moral experience of women, and it focuses on the subordination or oppression of women in the male-dominated society. As Hilde Lindemann explains it, *feminism* is a movement that is about the power or domination that men have over women, and feminist ethical theory analyzes this power and criticizes it. To do this, feminists must look at actual social practices as well as making suggestions for moral improvement. They discuss both abstract male theories and specific social practices such as mothering.

Feminist ethical theory is typically critical of the theories discussed so far, in that they ignore the experience of women and contribute to the oppression of women. For example, the emphasis on freedom we find in Mill, Rawls, Kant, and other male philosophers is of little help to poor and oppressed women who lack basic necessities such as food, shelter, and medical care. The justice perspective of Kant, Rawls, and other male philosophers is irrelevant to the experience of women who care for children. The experience of these women involves emotions such as love rather than reasoning about abstract principles such as the categorical imperative.

What is the feminist alternative to the male theories? In general, there is an appeal to the moral thinking of women rather than men. According to feminists such as Carol Gilligan and Nel Noddings, for example, women tend not to appeal to abstract rules and principles in the same way as men; rather, they appeal to concrete and detailed knowledge of the situation, and they are more likely to consider the personal relationships involved. According to Jean Grimshaw, (see the Suggested Readings) women do not share the male preoccupation with war, violence, and destruction. Sara Ruddick argues that the activity of mothering generates a concept of virtue that is the basis for a critique of the male values of contemporary life such as the militarism and constant warfare we see in the United States. Caroline Whitbeck argues that the practices of caring for others can provide an acceptable ethical model of mutual realization that is an alternative to the competitive and individualistic model we see in male-dominated society.

A problem with feminist ethical theory is that it seems to apply to the private world of domestic life, where women care for children and others, and not to the male-dominated public world of war, politics, and the market. Male theorists argue that when it comes to war and the market, the feminist ethic of care does not make sense. The very concept of war or the market precludes the sort of caring behavior recommended by feminists. Jean Grimshaw and others reply that there is really no clear distinction between the public male world of war and the market and the private female world of domestic relations. Women work outside the home, and men have a domestic role. Furthermore, the experience of women is a valuable source of criticism of the male-dominated public world of war and the market, and the basis for reform.

Egoism and Moral Skepticism

JAMES RACHELS

James Rachels (1941–2003) was university professor of philosophy at the University of Alabama at Birmingham, where he taught for twenty-six years. He was the author of *The End of Life* (1986), *Created from Animals* (1991), a collection of papers entitled *Can Ethics Provide Answers* (1990), and *The Elements of Moral Philosophy* (5th ed., 2006). *A Legacy of Socrates*, another collection of his papers, is forthcoming from Columbia University Press. During his career, he wrote 85 philosophy essays, edited 7 books, and gave about 275 professional lectures.

Rachels critically examines psychological egoism and ethical egoism, two popular theories used to attack conventional morality. *Psychological egoism* is the view that all human actions are self-interested. *Ethical egoism*, which is supposed to follow logically from psychological egoism, holds that all human actions morally ought to be self-interested. After examining two arguments used to defend psychological egoism, Rachels concludes that the theory is both false and confused. Even though he is unable to decisively refute ethical egoism, he argues that it has serious problems. Genuine egoists are rare, and it is just a fundamental fact about human nature that humans care about others and not only about themselves.

1. Our ordinary thinking about morality is full of assumptions that we almost never question. We assume, for example, that we have an obligation to consider the welfare of other people when we decide what actions to perform or what rules to obey; we think that we must refrain from acting in ways harmful to others, and that we must respect their rights and interests as well as our own. We also assume that people are in fact capable of being motivated by such considerations, that is, that people are not wholly selfish and that they do sometimes act in the interests of others.

Both of these assumptions have come under attack by moral sceptics, as long ago as by Glaucon in Book II of Plato's *Republic*. Glaucon recalls the legend of Gyges, a shepherd who was said to have found a magic ring in a fissure opened by an earthquake. The ring would make its wearer invisible and thus would enable him to go anywhere and do anything undetected. Gyges used

the power of the ring to gain entry to the Royal Palace where he seduced the Queen, murdered the King, and subsequently seized the throne. Now Glaucon asks us to determine that there are two such rings, one given to a man of virtue and one given to a rogue. The rogue, of course, will use his ring unscrupulously and do anything necessary to increase his own wealth and power. He will recognize no moral constraints on his conduct, and, since the cloak of invisibility will protect him from discovery, he can do anything he pleases without fear of reprisal. So, there will be no end to the mischief he will do. But how will the so-called virtuous man behave? Glaucon suggests that he will behave no better than the rogue: "No one, it is commonly believed, would have such iron strength of mind as to stand fast in doing right or keep his hands off other men's goods, when he could go to the market-place and fearlessly help himself to anything he wanted, enter houses and sleep with any woman he chose,

Source: James Rachels, "Egoism and Moral Skepticism," from *A New Introduction to Philosophy*, ed. Steven M. Cahn (Harper & Row, 1971). Reprinted with permission.

set prisoners free and kill men at his pleasure, and in a word go about among men with the powers of a god. He would behave no better than the other; both would take the same course."[1] Moreover, why shouldn't he? Once he is freed from the fear of reprisal, why shouldn't a man simply do what he pleases, or what he thinks is best for himself? What reason is there for him to continue being "moral" when it is clearly not to his own advantage to do so?

These sceptical views suggested by Glaucon have come to be known as *psychological egoism* and *ethical egoism* respectively. Psychological egoism is the view that all men are selfish in everything that they do, that is, that the only motive from which anyone ever acts is self-interest. On this view, even when men are acting in ways apparently calculated to benefit others, they are actually motivated by the belief that acting in this way is to their own advantage, and if they did not believe this, they would not be doing that action. Ethical egoism is, by contrast, a normative view about how men *ought* to act. It is the view that, regardless of how men do in fact behave, they have no obligation to do anything except what is in their own interests. According to the ethical egoist, a person is always justified in doing whatever is in his own interests, regardless of the effect on others.

Clearly, if either of these views is correct, then "the moral institution of life" (to use Butler's well-turned phrase) is very different than what we normally think. The majority of mankind is grossly deceived about what is, or ought to be, the case, where morals are concerned.

2. Psychological egoism seems to fly in the face of the facts. We are tempted to say: "Of course people act unselfishly all the time. For example, Smith gives up a trip to the country, which he would have enjoyed very much, in order to stay behind and help a friend with his studies, which is a miserable way to pass the time. This is a perfectly clear case of unselfish behavior, and if the psychological egoist thinks that such cases do

not occur, then he is just mistaken." Given such obvious instances of "unselfish behavior," what reply can the egoist make? There are two general arguments by which he might try to show that all actions, including those such as the one just outlined, are in fact motivated by self-interest. Let us examine these in turn:

A. The first argument goes as follows. If we describe one person's action as selfish, and another person's action as unselfish, we are overlooking the crucial fact that in both cases, assuming that the action is done voluntarily, *the agent is merely doing what he most wants to do.* If Smith stays behind to help his friend, that only shows that he wanted to help his friend more than he wanted to go to the country. And why should he be praised for his "unselfishness" when he is only doing what he most wants to do? So, since Smith is only doing what he wants to do, he cannot be said to be acting unselfishly.

This argument is so bad that it would not deserve to be taken seriously except for the fact that so many otherwise intelligent people have been taken in by it. First, the argument rests on the premise that people never voluntarily do anything except what they want to do. But this is patently false; there are at least two classes of actions that are exceptions to this generalization. One is the set of actions which we may not want to do, but which we do anyway as a means to an end which we want to achieve; for example, going to the dentist in order to stop a toothache, or going to work every day in order to be able to draw our pay at the end of the month. These cases may be regarded as consistent with the spirit of the egoist argument, however, since the ends mentioned are wanted by the agent. But the other set of actions are those which we do, not because we want to, nor even because there is an end which we want to achieve, but because we feel ourselves *under an obligation* to do them. For example, someone may do something because he has promised to do it, and thus feels obligated, even though he does not want to do it. It is sometimes suggested that in such cases we do the action because, after all, we want to keep our promises; so, even here, we are doing what we want. However, this dodge will not work: if I have promised to do something, and if I do not want to do it, then it is simply false to say that I want to keep my promise. In such cases we feel a conflict precisely because we do *not* want to do what we feel obligated to do. It is reasonable to think that Smith's action falls roughly into this second category: he might stay behind, not because he wants to, but because he feels that his friend needs help.

But suppose we were to concede, for the sake of the argument, that all voluntary action is motivated by the agent's wants, or at least that Smith is so motivated. Even if this were granted, it would not follow that Smith is acting selfishly or from self-interest. For if Smith wants to do something that will help his friend, even when it means forgoing his own enjoyments, that is precisely what makes him *un*selfish. What else could unselfishness be, if not wanting to help others? Another way to put the same point is to say that it is the *object* of a want that determines whether it is selfish or not. The mere fact that I am acting on *my* wants does not mean that I am acting selfishly; that depends on *what it is* that I want. If I want only my own good, and care nothing for others, then I am selfish; but if I also want other people to be well-off and happy, and if I act on *that* desire, then my action is not selfish. So much for this argument.

B. The second argument for psychological egoism is this. Since so-called unselfish actions always produce a sense of self-satisfaction in the agent,[2] and since this sense of satisfaction is a pleasant state of consciousness, it follows that the point of the action is really to achieve a pleasant state of consciousness, rather than to bring about any good for others. Therefore, the action is "unselfish" only at a superficial level of analysis. Smith will feel much better with himself for having stayed to help his friend—if he had gone to the country, be would have felt terrible about it—and that is the real point of the action. According to a well-known story,

this argument was once expressed by Abraham Lincoln:

> Mr. Lincoln once remarked to a fellow-passenger on an old-time mud-coach that all men were prompted by selfishness in doing good. His fellow-passenger was antagonizing this position when they were passing over a corduroy bridge that spanned a slough. As they crossed this bridge they espied an old razor-backed sow on the bank making a terrible noise because her pigs had got into the slough and were in danger of drowning. As the old coach began to climb the hill, Mr. Lincoln called out, "Driver, can't you stop just a moment?" Then Mr. Lincoln jumped out, ran back, and lifted the little pigs out of the mud and water and placed them on the bank. When he returned, his companion remarked: "Now, Abe, where does selfishness come in on this little episode?" "Why, bless your soul, Ed, that was the very essence of selfishness. I should have had no peace of mind all day had I gone on and left that suffering old sow worrying over those pigs. I did it to get peace of mind, don't you see?"[3]

This argument suffers from defects similar to the previous one. Why should we think that merely because someone derives satisfaction from helping others this makes him selfish? Isn't the unselfish man precisely the one who *does* derive satisfaction from helping others, while the selfish man does not? If Lincoln "got peace of mind" from rescuing the piglets, does this show him to be selfish, or, on the contrary, doesn't it show him to be compassionate and good-hearted? (If a man were truly selfish, why should it bother his conscience that *others* suffer—much less pigs?) Similarly, it is nothing more than shabby sophistry to say, because Smith takes satisfaction in helping his friend, that he is behaving selfishly. If we say this rapidly, while thinking about something else, perhaps it will sound all right; but if we speak slowly, and pay attention to what we are saying, it sounds plain silly.

Moreover, suppose we ask *why* Smith derives satisfaction from helping his friend. The answer will be, it is because Smith cares for him and

---

[2]Or, as it is sometimes said, "It gives him a clear conscience," or "He couldn't sleep at night if he had done otherwise," or "He would have been ashamed of himself for not doing it," and so on.

[3]Frank C. Sharp, *Ethics* (New York, 1928), pp. 74–75. Quoted from the Springfield (Ill.) *Monitor in the Outlook*, vol. 56, p. 1059.

wants him to succeed. If Smith did not have these concerns, then he would take no pleasure in assisting him; and these concerns, as we have already seen, are the marks of unselfishness, not selfishness. To put the point more generally: if we have a positive attitude toward the attainment of some goal, then we may derive satisfaction from attaining that goal. But the *object* of our attitude is *the attainment of that goal*; and we must want to attain the goal *before* we can find any satisfaction in it. We do not, in other words, desire some sort of "pleasurable consciousness" and then try to figure out how to achieve it; rather, we desire all sorts of different things—money, a new fishing-boat, to be a better chess-player, to get a promotion in our work, etc.—and because we desire these things, we derive satisfaction from attaining them. And so, if someone desires the welfare and happiness of another person, he will derive satisfaction from that; but this does not mean that this satisfaction is the object of his desire, or that he is in any way selfish on account of it.

It is a measure of the weakness of psychological egoism that these insupportable arguments are the ones most often advanced in its favor. Why, then, should anyone ever have thought it a true view? Perhaps because of a desire for theoretical simplicity: In thinking about human conduct, it would be nice if there were some simple formula that would unite the diverse phenomena of human behavior under a single explanatory principle, just as simple formulae in physics bring together a great many apparently different phenomena. And since it is obvious that self-regard is an overwhelmingly important factor in motivation, it is only natural to wonder whether all motivation might not be explained in these terms. But the answer is clearly No; while a great many human actions are motivated entirely or in part by self-interest, only by a deliberate distortion of the facts can we say that all conduct is so motivated. This will be clear, I think, if we correct three confusions which are commonplace. The exposure of these confusions will remove the last traces of plausibility from the psychological egoist thesis.

The first is the confusion of selfishness with self-interest. The two are clearly not the same.

If I see a physician when I am feeling poorly, I am acting in my own interest but no one would think of calling me "selfish" on account of it. Similarly, brushing my teeth, working hard at my job, and obeying the law are all in my self-interest but none of these are examples of selfish conduct. This is because selfish behavior is behavior that ignores the interests of others, in circumstances in which their interests ought not to be ignored. This concept has a definite evaluative flavor; to call someone "selfish" is not just to describe his action but to condemn it. Thus, you would not call me selfish for eating a normal meal in normal circumstances (although it may surely be in my self-interest); but you would call me selfish for hoarding food while others about are starving.

The second confusion is the assumption that every action is done *either* from self-interest or from other-regarding motives. Thus, the egoist concludes that if there is no such thing as genuine altruism then all actions must be done from self-interest. But this is certainly a false dichotomy. The man who continues to smoke cigarettes, even after learning about the connection between smoking and cancer, is surely not acting from self-interest, not even by his own standards—self-interest would dictate that he quit smoking at once—and he is not acting altruistically either. He is, no doubt, smoking for the pleasure of it, but all that this shows is that undisciplined pleasure-seeking and acting from self-interest are very different. This is what led Butler to remark that "The thing to be lamented is, not that men have so great regard to their own good or interest in the present world, for they have not enough."[4]

The last two paragraphs show (*a*) that it is false that all actions are selfish, and (*b*) that it is false that all actions are done out of self-interest. And it should be noted that these two points can be made, and were, without any appeal to putative examples of altruism.

---

[4]*The Works of Joseph Butler,* edited by W. E. Gladstone (Oxford, 1896), vol. II, p. 26. It should be noted that most of the points I am making against psychological egoism were first made by Butler. Butler made all the important points; all that is left for us is to remember them.

The third confusion is the common but false assumption that a concern for one's own welfare is incompatible with any genuine concern for the welfare of others. Thus, since it is obvious that everyone (or very nearly everyone) does desire his own well-being, it might be thought that no one can really be concerned with others. But again, this is false. There is no inconsistency in desiring that everyone, including oneself *and* others, be well-off and happy. To be sure, it may happen on occasion that our own interests conflict with the interests of others, and in these cases we will have to make hard choices. But even in these cases we might sometimes opt for the interests of others, especially when the others involved are our family or friends. But more importantly, not all cases are like this: sometimes we are able to promote the welfare of others when our own interests are not involved at all. In these cases not even the strongest self-regard need prevent us from acting considerately toward others.

Once these confusions are cleared away, it seems to me obvious enough that there is no reason whatever to accept psychological egoism. On the contrary, if we simply observe people's behavior with an open mind, we may find that a great deal of it is motivated by self-regard, but by no means all of it; and that there is no reason to deny that "the moral institution of life" can include a place for the virtue of beneficence.[5]

3. The ethical egoist would say at this point, "Of course it is possible for people to act altruistically, and perhaps many people do act that way—but there is no reason why they *should* do so. A person is under no obligation to do anything except what is in his own interests."[6] This is really quite a radical doctrine. Suppose I have an urge to set fire to some public building (say, a department store) just for the fascination of watching the spectacular blaze: according to this view, the fact that several people might be burned to death provides no reason whatever why I should not do it. After all, this only concerns *their* welfare, not my own, and according to the ethical egoist the only person I need think of is myself.

Some might deny that ethical egoism has any such monstrous consequences. They would point out that it is really to my own advantage not to set the fire—for, if I do that I may be caught and put into prison (unlike Gyges, I have no magic ring for protection). Moreover, even if I could avoid being caught it is still to my advantage to respect the rights and interests of others, for it is to my advantage to live in a society in which people's rights and interests are respected. Only in such a society can I live a happy and secure life; so, in acting kindly toward others, I would merely be doing my part to create and maintain the sort of society which it is to my advantage to have.[7] Therefore, it is said, the egoist would not be such a bad man; he would be as kindly and considerate as anyone else, because he would see that it is to his own advantage to be kindly and considerate.

This is a seductive line of thought, but it seems to me mistaken. Certainly it is to everyone's advantage (including the egoist's) to preserve a stable society where people's interests are generally protected. But there is no reason for the egoist to think that merely because *he* will not honor the rules of the social game, decent society will collapse. For the vast majority of people are not egoists, and there is no reason to think that they will be converted by his example—especially if he is discreet and does not unduly flaunt his style of life. What this line of reasoning shows is not that the egoist himself must act benevolently, but that he must encourage *others* to do so. He must take care to conceal from public view his own self-centered method of decision-making, and urge others to act on precepts very different from those on which he is willing to act.

The rational egoist, then, cannot advocate that egoism be universally adopted by everyone. For he wants a world in which his own interests

---

[5] The capacity for altruistic behavior is not unique to human beings. Some interesting experiments with rhesus monkeys have shown that these animals will refrain from operating a device for securing food if this causes other animals to suffer pain. See Masserman, Wechkin, and Terris, "'Altruistic' Behavior in Rhesus Monkeys," *The American Journal of Psychiatry,* vol. 121 (1964), 584–585.

[6] I take this to be the view of Ayn Rand, in so far as I understand her confusing doctrine.

[7] Cf. Thomas Hobbes, *Leviathan* (London, 1651), chap. 17.

are maximized; and if other people adopted the egoistic policy of pursuing their own interests to the exclusion of his interests, as he pursues his interests to the exclusion of theirs, then such a world would be impossible. So he himself will be an egoist, but he will want others to be altruists.

This brings us to what is perhaps the most popular "refutation" of ethical egoism current among philosophical writers—the argument that ethical egoism is at bottom inconsistent because it cannot be universalized.[8] The argument goes like this:

To say that any action or policy of action is *right* (or that it *ought* to be adopted) entails that it is right for *anyone* in the same sort of circumstances. I cannot, for example, say that it is right for me to lie to you, and yet object when you lie to me (provided, of course, that the circumstances are the same). I cannot hold that it is all right for me to drink your beer and then complain when you drink mine. This is just the requirement that we be consistent in our evaluations; it is a requirement of logic. Now it is said that ethical egoism cannot meet this requirement because, as we have already seen, the egoist would not want others to act in the same way that he acts. Moreover, suppose he *did* advocate the universal adoption of egoistic policies: he would be saying to Peter, "You ought to pursue your own interests even if it means destroying Paul"; and he would be saying to Paul, "You ought to pursue your own interests even if it means destroying Peter." The attitudes expressed in these two recommendations seem clearly inconsistent—he is urging the advancement of Peter's interest at one moment, and countenancing their defeat at the next. Therefore, the argument goes, there is no way to maintain the doctrine of ethical egoism as a consistent view about how we ought to act. We will fall into inconsistency whenever we try.

What are we to make of this argument? Are we to conclude that ethical egoism has been refuted? Such a conclusion, I think, would

be unwarranted; for I think that we can show, contrary to this argument, how ethical egoism can be maintained consistently. We need only to interpret the egoist's position in a sympathetic way: we should say that he has in mind a certain kind of world which he would prefer over all others; it would be a world in which his own interests were maximized, regardless of the effects on other people. The egoist's primary policy of action, then, would be to act in such a way as to bring about, as nearly as possible, this sort of world. Regardless of however morally reprehensible we might find it, there is nothing *inconsistent* in someone's adopting this as his ideal and acting in a way calculated to bring it about. And if someone did adopt this as his ideal, then he would not advocate universal egoism; as we have already seen, he would want other people to be altruists. So, if he advocates any principles of conduct for the general public, they will be altruistic principles. This would not be inconsistent; on the contrary, it would be perfectly consistent with his goal of creating a world in which his own interests are maximized. To be sure, he would have to be deceitful; in order to secure the good will of others, and a favorable hearing for his exhortations to altruism, he would have to pretend that he was himself prepared to accept altruistic principles. But again, that would be all right; from the egoist's point of view, this would merely be a matter of adopting the necessary means to the achievement of his goal—and while we might not approve of this, there is nothing inconsistent about it. Again, it might be said: "He advocates one thing, but does another. Surely *that's* inconsistent." But it is not; for what he advocates and what he does are both calculated as means to an end (the *same* end, we might note); and as such, he is doing what is rationally required in each case. Therefore, contrary to the previous argument, there is nothing inconsistent in the ethical egoist's view. He cannot be refuted by the claim that he contradicts himself.

Is there, then, no way to refute the ethical egoist? If by "refute" we mean show that he has made some *logical* error, the answer is that there is not. However, there is something more that can be said. The egoist challenge to our ordinary

---

[8]See, for example, Brian Medlin, "Ultimate Principles and Ethical Egoism," *Australasian Journal of Philosophy*, vol. 35 (1957), 111–118; and D. H. Monro, *Empiricism and Ethics* (Cambridge, 1967), chap. 16.

moral convictions amounts to a demand for an explanation of why we should adopt certain policies of action, namely policies in which the good of others is given importance. We can give an answer to this demand, albeit an indirect one. The reason one ought not to do actions that would hurt other people is: other people would be hurt. The reason one ought to do actions that would benefit other people is: other people would be benefited. This may at first seem like a piece of philosophical sleight-of-hand, but it is not. The point is that the welfare of human beings is something that most of us value *for its own sake*, and not merely for the sake of something else. Therefore, when *further* reasons are demanded for valuing the welfare of human beings, we cannot point to anything further to satisfy this demand. It is not that we have no reason for pursuing these policies, but that our reason *is* that these policies are for the good of human beings.

So: if we are asked "Why shouldn't I set fire to this department store?" one answer would be "Because if you do, people may be burned to death." This is a complete, sufficient reason which does not require qualification or supplementation of any sort. If someone seriously wants to know why this action shouldn't be done, that's the reason. If we are pressed further and asked the sceptical question "But why shouldn't I do actions that will harm others?" we may not know what to say—but this is because the questioner has included in his question the very answer we would like to give: "Why shouldn't you do actions that will harm others? Because, doing those actions would harm others."

The egoist, no doubt, will not be happy with this. He will protest that *we* may accept this as a reason, but *he* does not. And here the argument stops: there are limits to what can be accomplished by argument, and if the egoist really doesn't care about other people—if he honestly doesn't care whether they are helped or hurt by his actions—then we have reached those limits. If we want to persuade him to act decently toward his fellow humans, we will have to make our appeal to such other attitudes as he does possess, by threats, bribes, or other cajolery. That is all that we can do.

Though some may find this situation distressing (we would like to be able to show that the egoist is just *wrong*), it holds no embarrassment for common morality. What we have come up against is simply a fundamental requirement of rational action, namely, that the existence of reasons for action always depends on the prior existence of certain attitudes in the agent. For example, the fact that a certain course of action would make the agent a lot of money is a reason for doing it only if the agent wants to make money; the fact that practicing at chess makes one a better player is a reason for practicing only if one wants to be a better player; and so on. Similarly, the fact that a certain action would help the agent is a reason for doing the action only if the agent cares about his own welfare, and the fact that an action would help others is a reason for doing it only if the agent cares about others. In this respect ethical egoism and what we might call ethical altruism are in exactly the same fix: both require that the agent *care* about himself, or about other people, before they can get started.

So a nonegoist will accept "It would harm another person" as a reason not to do an action simply because he cares about what happens to that other person. When the egoist says that he does *not* accept that as a reason, he is saying something quite extraordinary. He is saying that he has no affection for friends or family, that he never feels pity or compassion, that he is the sort of person who can look on scenes of human misery with complete indifference, so long as he is not the one suffering. Genuine egoists, people who really don't care at all about anyone other than themselves, are rare. It is important to keep this in mind when thinking about ethical egoism; it is easy to forget just how fundamental to human psychological makeup the feeling of sympathy is. Indeed, a man without any sympathy at all would scarcely be recognizable as a man; and that is what makes ethical egoism such a disturbing doctrine in the first place.

4. There are, of course, many different ways in which the sceptic might challenge the assumptions underlying our moral practice. In this essay I have discussed only two of them,

the two put forward by Glaucon in the passage that I cited from Plato's *Republic*. It is important that the assumptions underlying our moral practice should not be confused with particular judgments made within that practice. To defend one is not to defend the other. We may assume—quite properly, if my analysis has been correct—that the virtue of beneficence does, and indeed should, occupy an important place in "the moral institution of life"; and yet we may make constant and miserable errors when it comes to judging when and in what ways this virtue is to be exercised. Even worse, we may often be able to make accurate moral judgments, and know what we ought to do, but not do it. For these ills, philosophy alone is not the cure.

⚜ REVIEW QUESTIONS

1. Explain the legend of Gyges. What questions about morality are raised by the story?
2. Distinguish between psychological and ethical egoism.
3. Rachels discusses two arguments for psychological egoism. What are these arguments, and how does he reply to them?
4. What three commonplace confusions does Rachels detect in the thesis of psychological egoism?
5. State the argument for saying that ethical egoism is inconsistent. Why doesn't Rachels accept this argument?
6. According to Rachels, why shouldn't we hurt others, and why should we help others? How can the egoist reply?

⚜ DISCUSSION QUESTIONS

1. Has Rachels answered the question raised by Glaucon, namely, "Why be moral?" If so, what exactly is his answer?
2. Are genuine egoists rare, as Rachels claims? Is it a fact that most people care about others, even people they don't know?
3. Suppose we define ethical altruism as the view that one should always act for the benefit of others and never in one's own self-interest. Is such a view immoral or not?

Religion, Morality, and Conscience

JOHN ARTHUR

John Arthur (1947–2007) was professor of philosophy and director of the Program in Philosophy, Politics, and Law at Binghamton University. He was the author of *Words That Bind* (1995), *The Unfinished Constitution* (1989), and the editor of *Morality and Moral Controversies* (2004).

Arthur discusses and rejects three ways morality has been thought to depend on religion: that without religious motivation people could not be expected to do the right thing; that religion is necessary to provide guidance to people in their search for the correct course of action; and that religion is essential for there even to be a right and wrong. Arthur then considers another conception of morality, suggested by John Dewey, which claims "morality is social." He concludes with some brief comments on the importance of these reflections for moral deliberation and for education.

Source: John Arthur, "Religion, Morality, and Conscience," from *Morality and Moral Controversies* (4th ed., ed. John Arthur, Prentice Hall, 1996), pp. 21–28. Reprinted with permission of the author.

My first and prime concern in this paper is to explore the connections, if any, between morality and religion. I will argue that although there are a variety of ways the two can be connected, in fact religion is not necessary for morality. Despite the lack of any logical or other necessary connection, I will claim, there remain important respects in which the two are related. In the concluding section I will discuss the notion of moral conscience, and then look briefly at the various respects in which morality is "social" and the implications of that idea for moral education. First, however, I want to say something about the subjects: Just what are we referring to when we speak of morality and of religion?

1. MORALITY AND RELIGION

A useful way to approach the first question—the nature of morality—is to ask what it would mean for a society to exist without a social moral code. How would such people think and behave? What would that society look like? First, it seems clear that such people would never feel guilt or resentment. For example, the notions that I ought to remember my parents' anniversary, that he has a moral responsibility to help care for his children after the divorce, that she has a right to equal pay for equal work, and that discrimination on the basis of race is unfair would be absent in such a society. Notions of duty, rights, and obligations would not be present, except perhaps in the legal sense; concepts of justice and fairness would also be foreign to these people. In short, people would have no tendency to evaluate or criticize the behavior of others, nor to feel remorse about their own behavior. Children would not be taught to be ashamed when they steal or hurt others, nor would they be allowed to complain when others treat them badly. (People might, however, feel regret at a decision that didn't turn out as they had hoped; but that would only be because their expectations were frustrated, not because they feel guilty.)

Such a society lacks a moral code. What, then, of religion? Is it possible that a society such as the one I have described would have religious beliefs? It seems clear that it is possible. Suppose every day these same people file into their place of worship to pay homage to God (they may believe in many gods or in one all-powerful creator of heaven and earth). Often they can be heard praying to God for help in dealing with their problems and thanking Him for their good fortune. Frequently they give sacrifices to God, sometimes in the form of money spent to build beautiful temples and churches, other times by performing actions they believe God would approve, such as helping those in need. These practices might also be institutionalized, in the sense that certain people are assigned important leadership roles. Specific texts might also be taken as authoritative, indicating the ways God has acted in history and His role in their lives or the lives of their ancestors.

To have a moral code, then, is to tend to evaluate (perhaps without even expressing it) the behavior of others and to feel guilt at certain actions when we perform them. Religion, on the other hand, involves beliefs in supernatural power(s) that created and perhaps also control nature, the tendency to worship and pray to those supernatural forces or beings, and the presence of organizational structures and authoritative texts. The practices of morality and religion are thus importantly different. One involves our attitudes toward various forms of behavior (lying and killing, for example), typically expressed using the notions of rules, rights, and obligations. The other, religion, typically involves prayer, worship, beliefs about the supernatural, institutional forms, and authoritative texts.

We come, then, to the central question: What is the connection, if any, between a society's moral code and its religious practices and beliefs? Many people have felt that morality is in some way dependent on religion or religious truths. But what sort of "dependence" might there be? In what follows, I distinguish various ways in which one might claim that religion is necessary for morality, arguing against those who claim morality depends in some way on religion. I will also suggest, however, some other important ways in which the two are related, concluding with a brief discussion of conscience and moral education.

2. RELIGIOUS MOTIVATION AND GUIDANCE

One possible role which religion might play in morality relates to motives people have. Religion, it is often said, is necessary so that people will DO right. Typically, the argument begins with the important point that doing what is right often has costs: refusing to shoplift or cheat can mean people go without some good or fail a test; returning a billfold means they don't get the contents. Religion is therefore said to be necessary in that it provides motivation to do the right thing. God rewards those who follow His commands by providing for them a place in heaven or by ensuring that they prosper and are happy on earth. He also punishes those who violate the moral law. Others emphasize less self-interested ways in which religious motives may encourage people to act rightly. Since God is the creator of the universe and has ordained that His plan should be followed, they point out, it is important to live one's life in accord with this divinely ordained plan. Only by living a moral life, it is said, can people live in harmony with the larger, divinely created order.

The first claim, then, is that religion is necessary to provide moral motivation. The problem with that argument, however, is that religious motives are far from the only ones people have. For most of us, a decision to do the right thing (if that is our decision) is made for a variety of reasons: "What if I get caught? What if somebody sees me—what will he or she think? How will I feel afterwards? Will I regret it?" Or maybe the thought of cheating just doesn't arise. We were raised to be a decent person, and that's what we are—period. Behaving fairly and treating others well is more important than whatever we might gain from stealing or cheating, let alone seriously harming another person. So it seems clear that many motives for doing the right thing have nothing whatsoever to do with religion. Most of us, in fact, do worry about getting caught, being blamed, and being looked down on by others. We also may do what is right just because it's right, or because we don't want to hurt others or embarrass family and friends. To say that we

need religion to act morally is mistaken; indeed, it seems to me that many of us, when it really gets down to it, don't give much of a thought to religion when making moral decisions. All those other reasons are the ones that we tend to consider, or else we just don't consider cheating and stealing at all. So far, then, there seems to be no reason to suppose that people can't be moral yet irreligious at the same time.

A second argument that is available for those who think religion is necessary to morality, however, focuses on moral guidance and knowledge rather than on people's motives. However much people may want to do the right thing, according to this view, we cannot ever know for certain what is right without the guidance of religious teaching. Human understanding is simply inadequate to this difficult and controversial task; morality involves immensely complex problems, and so we must consult religious revelation for help.

Again, however, this argument fails. First, consider how much we would need to know about religion and revelation in order for religion to provide moral guidance. Besides being aware that there is a God, we'd also have to think about which of the many religions is true. How can anybody be sure his or her religion is the right one? But even if we assume the Judeo-Christian God is the real one, we still need to find out just what it is He wants us to do, which means we must think about revelation.

Revelation comes in at least two forms, and not even all Christians agree on which is the best way to understand revelation. Some hold that revelation occurs when God tells us what he wants by providing us with His words: The Ten Commandments are an example. Many even believe, as evangelist Billy Graham once said, that the entire Bible was written by God using thirty-nine secretaries. Others, however, doubt that the "word of God" refers literally to the words God has spoken, but believe instead that the Bible is an historical document, written by human beings, of the events or occasions in which God revealed himself. It is an especially important document, of course, but nothing more than that. So on this second view, revelation is not understood as *statements* made by God but rather as His *acts*, such as leading His people from Egypt, testing Job, and sending His son as an example of the ideal life. The Bible is not itself revelation, it's the historical account of revelatory actions.

If we are to use revelation as a moral guide, then, we must first know what is to count as revelation—words given us by God, historical events, or both? But even supposing that we could somehow answer those questions, the problems of relying on revelation are still not over since we still must interpret that revelation. Some feel, for example, that the Bible justifies various forms of killing, including war and capital punishment, on the basis of such statements as "An eye for an eye." Others, emphasizing such sayings as "Judge not lest ye be judged" and "Thou shalt not kill," believe the Bible demands absolute pacifism. How are we to know which interpretation is correct? It is likely, of course, that the answer people give to such religious questions will be influenced in part at least by their own moral beliefs; if capital punishment is thought to be unjust, for example, then an interpreter will seek to read the Bible in a way that is consistent with that moral truth. That is not, however, a happy conclusion for those wishing to rest morality on revelation, for it means that their understanding of what God has revealed is itself dependent on their prior moral views. Rather than revelation serving as a guide for morality, morality is serving as a guide for how we interpret revelation.

So my general conclusion is that far from providing a short-cut to moral understanding, looking to revelation for guidance often creates more questions and problems. It seems wiser under the circumstances to address complex moral problems like abortion, capital punishment, and affirmative action directly, considering the pros and cons of each side, rather than to seek answers through the much more controversial and difficult route of revelation.

3. THE DIVINE COMMAND THEORY

It may seem, however, that we have still not really gotten to the heart of the matter. Even if religion is not necessary for moral motivation or guidance, it is often claimed, religion is necessary in another more fundamental sense. According to this view, religion is necessary for morality because without God there could BE no right or wrong. God, in other words, provides the foundation or bedrock on which morality is grounded. This idea was expressed by Bishop R. C. Mortimer:

> God made us and all the world. Because of that He has an absolute claim on our obedience . . . From [this] it follows that a thing is not right simply because we think it is. It is right because God commands it.[1]

What Bishop Mortimer has in mind can be seen by comparing moral rules with legal ones. Legal statutes, we know, are created by legislatures; if the state assembly of New York had not passed a law limiting the speed people can travel, then there would be no such legal obligation. Without the statutory enactments, such a law simply would not exist. Mortimer's view, the *divine command theory*, would mean that God has the same sort of relation to moral law as the legislature has to statutes it enacts: without God's commands there would be no moral rules, just as without a legislature there would be no statutes.

Defenders of the divine command theory often add to this a further claim, that only by assuming God sits at the foundation of morality can we explain the objective difference between right and wrong. This point was forcefully argued by F. C. Copleston in a 1948 British Broadcasting Corporation radio debate with Bertrand Russell.

> *Copleston:* . . . The validity of such an interpretation of man's conduct depends on the recognition of God's existence, obviously. . . . Let's take a look at the Commandant of the [Nazi] concentration camp at Belsen. That appears to you as undesirable and evil and to me too. To Adolph Hitler we suppose it appeared as something good and desirable. I suppose you'd have to admit that for Hitler it was good and for you it is evil.

---

[1]R. C. Mortimer, *Christian Ethics* (London: Hutchinson's University Library, 1950), pp. 7–8.

Russell: No, I shouldn't go so far as that. I mean, I think people can make mistakes in that as they can in other things. If you have jaundice you see things yellow that are not yellow. You're making a mistake.

Copleston: Yes, one can make mistakes, but can you make a mistake if it's simply a question of reference to a feeling or emotion? Surely Hitler would be the only possible judge of what appealed to his emotions.

Russell: . . . You can say various things about that; among others, that if that sort of thing makes that sort of appeal to Hitler's emotions, then Hitler makes quite a different appeal to my emotions.

Copleston: Granted. But there's no objective criterion outside feeling then for condemning the conduct of the Commandant of Belsen, in your view. . . . The human being's idea of the content of the moral law depends certainly to a large extent on education and environment, and a man has to use his reason in assessing the validity of the actual moral ideas of his social group. But the possibility of criticizing the accepted moral code presupposes that there is an objective standard, that there is an ideal moral order, which imposes itself. . . . It implies the existence of a real foundation of God.[2]

Against those who, like Bertrand Russell, seek to ground morality in feelings and attitudes, Copleston argues that there must be a more solid foundation if we are to be able to claim truly that the Nazis were evil. God, according to Copleston, is able to provide the objective basis for the distinction, which we all know to exist, between right and wrong. Without divine commands at the root of human obligations, we would have no real reason for condemning the behavior of anybody, even Nazis. Morality, Copleston thinks, would then be nothing more than an expression of personal feeling.

To begin assessing the divine command theory, let's first consider this last point. Is it really true that only the commands of God can provide

an objective basis for moral judgments? Certainly many philosophers have felt that morality rests on its own perfectly sound footing, be it reason, human nature, or natural sentiments. It seems wrong to conclude, automatically, that morality cannot rest on anything but religion. And it is also possible that morality doesn't have any foundation or basis at all, so that its claims should be ignored in favor of whatever serves our own self-interest.

In addition to these problems with Copleston's argument, the divine command theory faces other problems as well. First, we would need to say much more about the relationship between morality and divine commands. Certainly the expressions "is commanded by God" and "is morally required" do not *mean* the same thing. People and even whole societies can use moral concepts without understanding them to make any reference to God. And while it is true that God (or any other moral being for that matter) would tend to want others to do the right thing, this hardly shows that being right and being commanded by God are the same thing. Parents want their children to do the right thing, too, but that doesn't mean parents, or anybody else, can make a thing right just by commanding it!

I think that, in fact, theists should reject the divine command theory. One reason is what it implies. Suppose we were to grant (just for the sake of argument) that the divine command theory is correct, so that actions are right just because they are commanded by God. The same, of course, can be said about those deeds that we believe are wrong. If God hadn't commanded us not to do them, they would not be wrong.

But now notice this consequence of the divine command theory. Since God is all-powerful, and since right is determined solely by His commands, is it not possible that He might change the rules and make what we now think of as wrong into right? It would seem that according to the divine command theory the answer is "yes": it is theoretically possible that tomorrow God would decree that virtues such as kindness and courage have become vices while actions that show cruelty and cowardice will henceforth be the right actions. (Recall the analogy with a

---

[2]This debate was broadcast on the Third Program of the British Broadcasting Corporation in 1948.

legislature and the power it has to change law.) So now rather than it being right for people to help each other out and prevent innocent people from suffering unnecessarily, it would be right (God having changed His mind) to create as much pain among innocent children as we possibly can! To adopt the divine command theory therefore commits its advocate to the seemingly absurd position that even the greatest atrocities might be not only acceptable but morally required if God were to command them.

Plato made a similar point in the dialogue *Euthyphro.* Socrates is asking Euthyphro what it is that makes the virtue of holiness a virtue, just as we have been asking what makes kindness and courage virtues. Euthyphro has suggested that holiness is just whatever all the gods love.

Socrates: Well, then, Euthyphro, what do we say about holiness? Is it not loved by all the gods, according to your definition?
Euthyphro: Yes.
Socrates: Because it is holy, or for some other reason?
Euthyphro: No, because it is holy.
Socrates: Then it is loved by the gods because it is holy: it is not holy because it is loved by them?
Euthyphro: It seems so.
Socrates: . . . Then holiness is not what is pleasing to the gods, and what is pleasing to the gods is not holy as you say, Euthyphro. They are different things.
Euthyphro: And why, Socrates?
Socrates: Because we are agreed that the gods love holiness because it is holy: and that it is not holy because they love it.[3]

This raises an interesting question. Why, having claimed at first that virtues are merely what is loved (or commanded) by the gods, would Euthyphro contradict this and agree that the gods love holiness *because* it's holy, rather than the reverse? One likely possibility is that Euthyphro believes that whenever the gods love

something, they do so with good reason, not without justification and arbitrarily. To deny this and say that it is merely the gods' love that makes holiness a virtue would mean that the gods have no basis for their attitudes, that they are arbitrary in what they love. Yet—and this is the crucial point—it's far from clear that a religious person would want to say that God is arbitrary in that way. If we say that it is simply God's loving something that makes it right, then what sense would it make to say God wants us to do right? All that could mean, it seems, is that God wants us to do what He wants us to do; He would have no reason for wanting it. Similarly, "God is good" would mean little more than "God does what He pleases." The divine command theory therefore leads us to the results that God is morally arbitrary, and that His wishing us to do good or even God's being just mean nothing more than that God does what He does and wants whatever He wants. Religious people who reject that consequence would also, I am suggesting, have reason to reject the divine command theory itself, seeking a different understanding of morality.

This now raises another problem, however. If God approves kindness because it is a virtue and hates the Nazis because they were evil, then it seems that God discovers morality rather than inventing it. So haven't we then identified a limitation on God's power, since He now, being a good God, must love kindness and command us not to be cruel? Without the divine command theory, in other words, what is left of God's omnipotence?

But why, we may ask, is such a limitation on God unacceptable? It is not at all clear that God really can do anything at all. Can God, for example, destroy Himself? Or make a rock so heavy that He cannot lift it? Or create a universe which was never created by Him? Many have thought that God cannot do these things, but also that His inability to do them does not constitute a serious limitation on His power since these are things that cannot be done at all: to do them would violate the laws of logic. Christianity's most influential theologian, Thomas Aquinas, wrote in this regard that "whatever implies

---

[3]Plato, *Euthyphro,* trans. H. N. Fowler (Cambridge, MA: Harvard University Press, 1947).

contradiction does not come within the scope of divine omnipotence, because it cannot have the aspect of possibility. Hence it is more appropriate to say that such things cannot be done than that God cannot do them."[4]

How, then, ought we to understand God's relationship to morality if we reject the divine command theory? Can religious people consistently maintain their faith in God the Creator and yet deny that what is right is right because He commands it? I think the answer to this is "yes." Making cruelty good is not like making a universe that wasn't made, of course. It's a moral limit on God rather than a logical one. But why suppose that God's limits are only logical?

One final point about this. Even if we agree that God loves justice or kindness because of their nature, not arbitrarily, there still remains a sense in which God could change morality even having rejected the divine command theory. That's because if we assume, plausibly, I think, that morality depends in part on how we reason, what we desire and need, and the circumstances in which we find ourselves, then morality will still be under God's control since God could have constructed us or our environment very differently. Suppose, for instance, that he created us so that we couldn't be hurt by others or didn't care about freedom. Or perhaps our natural environment were created differently, so that all we have to do is ask and anything we want is given to us. If God had created either nature or us that way, then it seems likely our morality might also be different in important ways from the one we now think correct. In that sense, then, morality depends on God whether or not one supports the divine command theory.

4. "MORALITY IS SOCIAL"

I have argued here that religion is not necessary in providing moral motivation or guidance, and that the religious person should not subscribe to the divine command theory's claim that God

is necessary for there to be morality. In this last section, I want first to look briefly at how religion and morality sometimes *do* influence each other. Then I will consider briefly the important ways in which morality might correctly be thought to be "social."

Nothing I have said so far means that morality and religion are independent of each other. But in what ways are they related, assuming I am correct in claiming morality does not *depend* on religion? First, of course, we should note the historical influence religions have had on the development of morality as well as on politics and law. Many of the important leaders of the abolitionist and civil rights movements were religious leaders, as are many current members of the pro-life movement. The relationship is not, however, one-sided: morality has also influenced religion, as the current debate within the Catholic Church over the role of women, abortion, and other social issues shows. In reality, then, it seems clear that the practices of morality and religion have historically each exerted an influence on the other.

But just as the two have shaped each other historically, so, too, do they interact at the personal level. I have already suggested how people's understanding of revelation, for instance, is often shaped by morality as they seek the best interpretations of revealed texts. Whether trying to understand a work of art, a legal statute, or a religious text, interpreters regularly seek to understand them in the best light—to make them as good as they can be, which requires that they bring moral judgment to the task of religious interpretation and understanding.

The relationship can go the other direction as well, however, as people's moral views are shaped by their religious training and their current religious beliefs. These relationships are often complex, hidden even from ourselves, but it does seem clear that our views on important moral issues, from sexual morality and war to welfare and capital punishment, are often influenced by our religious outlook. So not only are religious and moral practices and understandings historically linked, but for many religious people the relationship extends to the personal level—to

[4]Thomas Aquinas, *Summa Theologica,* Part I, Q. 25, Art. 3.

their understanding of moral obligations as well as their sense of who they are and their vision of who they wish to be.

Morality, then, is influenced by religion (as is religion by morality), but morality's social character extends deeper even than that, I want to argue. First, of course, the existence of morality assumes that we possess a socially acquired language within which we think about our choices and which alternatives we ought to follow. Second, morality is social in that it governs relationships among people, defining our responsibilities to others and theirs to us. Morality provides the standards we rely on in gauging our interactions with family, lovers, friends, fellow citizens, and even strangers. Third, morality is social in the sense that we are, in fact, subject to criticism by others for our actions. We discuss with others what we should do, and often hear from them concerning whether our decisions were acceptable. Blame and praise are a central feature of morality.

While not disputing any of this, John Dewey has suggested another important sense in which morality is social. Consider the following comments about the origins of morality and conscience taken from an article he titled "Morality Is Social":

> In language and imagination we rehearse the responses of others just as we dramatically enact other consequences. We foreknow how others will act, and the foreknowledge is the beginning of judgment passed on action. We know *with* them; there is conscience. An assembly is formed within our breast which discusses and appraises proposed and performed acts. The community without becomes a forum and tribunal within, a judgment-seat of charges, assessments and exculpations. Our thoughts of our own actions are saturated with the ideas that others entertain about them. . . . Explicit recognition of this fact is a prerequisite of improvement in moral education.... Reflection is morally indispensable.[5]

So in addition to the three points I already mentioned, Dewey also wants to make another, and in some ways more important suggestion about morality's social character. This fourth idea depends on appreciating the fact that to think from the moral point of view, as opposed to the selfish one, for instance, demands that we reject our private, subjective perspective in favor of the perspective of others, envisioning how they might respond to various choices we might make. Far from being private and unrelated to others, moral conscience is in that sense "public." To consider a decision from the moral perspective requires envisioning what Dewey terms an "assembly of others" that is "formed within our breast." In that way, conscience cannot even be distinguished from the social: conscience invariably brings with it, or constitutes, the perspective of the other. "Is this right?" and "What would this look like were I to have to defend it to others?" are not separate questions.[6]

It is important not to confuse Dewey's point here, however. He is *not* saying that what is right is finally to be determined by the reactions of actually existing other people, or even by the reaction of society as a whole. To the contrary, what is right, and accords with the true dictates of conscience, might in fact not meet the approval of others. Conscience is "social" not in the sense that morality is determined by surveying what others in society think. Understood as the voice of an "assembly" of others within each of us, conscience cannot be reduced to the expected reaction of any existing individual or group. But what then does Dewey mean? The answer is that the assembly Dewey is describing is not an actual one but instead an hypothetical, "ideal" one; the actual "community without" is transformed into a "forum and tribunal within, a judgment

---

[5]John Dewey, "Morality Is Social," in *The Moral Writings of John Dewey*, rev. ed., ed. James Gouinlock (Amherst, NY: Prometheus Books, 1994), pp. 182–4.

[6]Obligations to animals raise an interesting problem for this conception of morality. Is it wrong to torture animals only because other *people* could be expected to disapprove? Or is it that the animal itself would disapprove? Or, perhaps, that duties to animals rest on sympathy and compassion while human moral relations are more like Dewey describes, resting on morality's inherently social nature and on the dictates of conscience viewed as an assembly of others?

seat of charges, assessments and exculpations." Only through the powers of imagination can we exercise our moral powers, envisioning with the powers of judgment what conscience requires.

Morality is therefore *inherently* social, in a variety of ways. It depends on socially learned language, is learned from interactions with others, and governs our interactions with others in society. But it also demands, as Dewey put it, that we know "with" others, envisioning for ourselves what their points of view would require along with our own. Conscience demands we occupy the positions of others.

Viewed in this light, God might play a role in moral reflection and conscience. That is because it is unlikely a religious person would wish to exclude God from the "forum and tribunal" that constitutes conscience. Rather, for the religious person conscience would almost certainly include the imagined reaction of God along with the reactions of others who might be affected by the action. So it seems that for a religious person morality and God's will cannot be separated, though the connection between them is not as envisioned by the divine command theory.

This leads to my final point, about moral education. If Dewey is correct, then it seems clear there is an important sense in which morality not only can be taught but must be. Besides early moral training, moral thinking depends on our ability to imagine others' reactions and to imaginatively put ourselves into their shoes. "What would somebody (including, perhaps, God) think if this got out?" expresses more than a concern with being embarrassed or punished; it is also the voice of conscience and indeed of morality itself. But that would mean, thinking of education, that listening to others, reading about what others think and do, and reflecting within ourselves about our actions and whether we could defend them to others are part of the practice of morality itself. Morality cannot exist without the broader, social perspective introduced by others, and this social nature ties it, in that way, with education and with public discussion, both actual and imagined. "Private" moral reflection taking place independently of the social world would be no moral reflection at all; and moral education is not only possible, but essential.

⚜ REVIEW QUESTIONS

1. According to Arthur, how are morality and religion different?
2. Why isn't religion necessary for moral motivation?
3. Why isn't religion necessary as a source of moral knowledge?
4. What is the divine command theory? Why does Arthur reject this theory?
5. According to Arthur, how are morality and religion connected?
6. Dewey says that morality is social. What does this mean, according to Arthur?

⚜ DISCUSSION QUESTIONS

1. Has Arthur refuted the divine command theory? If not, how can it be defended?
2. If morality is social, as Dewey says, then how can we have any obligations to nonhuman animals? (Arthur mentions this problem and some possible solutions to it in footnote 6.)
3. What does Dewey mean by moral education? Does a college ethics class count as moral education?

The Natural Law

SAINT THOMAS AQUINAS

Saint Thomas Aquinas (1225–1274) was one of the most important Christian philosophers. He was declared a saint in 1323, and in 1567 he was named an Angelic Doctor of the Roman Catholic Church, giving his teachings a special authority. Our reading is taken from his "Treatise on Law," which is Questions 90–97 of the *Summa Theologica*, a vast work containing 22 volumes.

Aquinas sees the world as the creation of a supremely rational being, God, who has made everything according to a divine plan, an eternal law governing everything. God rules the world according to the eternal law. This divine law gives everything a role or purpose: Eyes are designed for seeing; rain falls in order to nourish plants, and so on. Humans are made in the image of God; they are rational as God is rational, although to a lesser degree. Because they are rational, humans are endowed with the light of natural reason that enables them to discern the eternal law, which includes the natural law. The natural law is the moral law that tells us what is right and good. According to Aquinas, the most basic precept of the natural law is the self-evident truth that good ought to be done, and evil ought to be avoided. All the precepts of the natural moral law are derived from this fundamental principle. But what is good and what is evil? Aquinas goes on to say that because good is an end, all things to which humans have a natural inclination are good. He mentions three such natural inclinations: the inclination to preserve human life, animal inclinations for sexual intercourse, education of the young, and so on; and a general inclination to good, which includes knowing the truth, avoiding offense to others, and so on. Aquinas does not attempt to give an exhaustive list of the precepts of the natural law; presumably it is up to us to add to the list using the natural light of reason.

WHETHER THERE IS IN US A NATURAL LAW?

. . . A *Gloss* on *Rom*. ii. 14 (*When the Gentiles, who have not the law, do by nature those things that are of the law*) comments as follows: *Although they have no written law, yet they have the natural law, whereby each one knows, and is conscious of, what is good and what is evil.*

I answer that, As we have stated above, law, being a rule and measure, can be in a person in two ways: in one way, as in him that rules and measures; in another way, as in that which is ruled and measured, since a thing is ruled and measured in so far as it partakes of the rule or measure. Therefore, since all things subject to divine providence are ruled and measured by the eternal law, as was stated above, it is evident that all things partake in some way in the eternal law, in so far as, namely, from its being imprinted on them, they derive their respective inclinations to their proper acts and ends. Now among all others, the rational creature is subject to divine providence in a more excellent way, in so far as it itself partakes of a share of providence, by being provident both for itself and for others. Therefore it has a share of the eternal reason, whereby it has a natural inclination to its proper act and end; and this participation of the eternal law in the rational creature is called the natural law. Hence the Psalmist, after saying (*Ps*. iv. 6): *Offer up the sacrifice of justice,* as though someone asked what

Source: Saint Thomas Aquinas, *Treatise on Law, Summa Theologica,* in *Basic Writings of Saint Thomas Aquinas* (Volume 2, ed. Auton C. Pegis, Indianapolis: Hackett 1997, pp. 749–751). Reprinted by permission of the publisher.

the works of justice are, adds: *Many say, Who showeth us good things?* in answer to which question he says: *The light of Thy countenance, O Lord, is signed upon us.* He thus implies that the light of natural reason, whereby we discern what is good and what is evil, which is the function of the natural law, is nothing else than an imprint on us of the divine light. It is therefore evident that the natural law is nothing else than the rational creature's participation of the eternal law. . . .

WHETHER THERE IS HUMAN LAW?

. . . Now it is to be observed that the same procedure takes place in the practical and in the speculative reason, for each proceeds from principles to conclusions, as was stated above. Accordingly, we conclude that, just as in the speculative reason, from naturally known indemonstrable principles we draw the conclusions of the various sciences, the knowledge of which is not imparted to us by nature, but acquired by the efforts of reason, so too it is that from the precepts of the natural law, as from common and indemonstrable principles, the human reason needs to proceed to the more particular determination of certain matters. These particular determinations, devised by human reason, are called human laws, provided that the other essential conditions of law be observed, as was stated above. . . .

WHETHER THE NATURAL LAW CONTAINS SEVERAL PRECEPTS, OR ONLY ONE?

. . . As was stated above, the precepts of the natural law are to the practical reason what the first principles of demonstrations are to the speculative reason, because both are self-evident principles. Now a thing is said to be self-evident in two ways: first, in itself; secondly, in relation to us. Any proposition is said to be self-evident in itself, if its predicate is contained in the notion of the subject; even though it may happen that to one who does not know the definition of the subject, such a proposition is not self-evident. For instance, this proposition, *Man is a rational being,* is, in its very

nature, self-evident, since he who says *man*, says *a rational being*; and yet to one who does not know what a man is, this proposition is not self-evident. Hence it is that, as Boethius says, certain axioms or propositions are universally self-evident to all; and such are the propositions whose terms are known to all, as, *Every whole is greater than its part, and, Things equal to one and the same are equal to one another.* But some propositions are self-evident only to the wise, who understand the meaning of the terms of such propositions. Thus to one who understands that an angel is not a body, it is self-evident that an angel is not circumscriptively in a place. But this is not evident to the unlearned, for they cannot grasp it.

Now a certain order is to be found in those things that are apprehended by men. For that which first falls under apprehension is *being*, the understanding of which is included in all things whatsoever a man apprehends. Therefore the first indemonstrable principle is that *the same thing cannot be affirmed and denied at the same time,* which is based on the notion of *being* and *not-being:* and on this principle all others are based, as is stated in *Metaph.* iv. Now as *being* is the first thing that falls under the apprehension absolutely, so *good* is the first thing that falls under the apprehension of the practical reason, which is directed to action (since every agent acts for an end, which has the nature of good). Consequently, the first principle in the practical reason is one founded on the nature of good, viz., that *good is that which all things seek after.* Hence this is the first precept of law, that *good is to be done and promoted, and evil is to be avoided.* All other precepts of the natural law are based upon this; so that all the things which the practical reason naturally apprehends as man's good belong to the precepts of the natural law under the form of things to be done or avoided.

Since, however, good has the nature of an end, and evil, the nature of the contrary, hence it is that all those things to which man has a natural inclination are naturally apprehended by reason as being good, and consequently as objects of pursuit, and their contraries as evil, and objects of avoidance. Therefore, the order of the precepts of the natural law is according to the order of natural inclinations. For there is in man, first of all, an inclination to good in accordance with the nature which he has in common with all substances, inasmuch, namely, as every substance seeks the preservation of its own being, according to its nature; and by reason of this inclination, whatever is a means of preserving human life, and of warding off its obstacles, belongs to the natural law. Secondly, there is in man an inclination to things that pertain to him more specially, according to that nature which he has in common with other animals; and in virtue of this inclination, those things are said to belong to the natural law *which nature has taught to all animals,* such as sexual intercourse, the education of offspring and so forth. Thirdly, there is in man an inclination to good according to the nature of his reason, which nature is proper to him. Thus man has a natural inclination to know the truth about God, and to live in society; and in this respect, whatever pertains to this inclination belongs to the natural law: *e.g.,* to shun ignorance, to avoid offending those among whom one has to live, and other such things regarding the above inclination.

⚜ REVIEW QUESTIONS

1. Distinguish between the eternal law and the natural law. How are they related?

2. What are the precepts of the natural law? Specifically what should we do, and what should we avoid?

⚜ DISCUSSION QUESTIONS

1. Do you agree that everything in the world has a purpose? If so, can you discern it using reason alone?
2. Are all natural inclinations good? Why or why not?

3. Does the natural law tell you what to do in a particular situation? Explain your answer.

Morality Is Based on Sentiment

DAVID HUME

David Hume (1711–1776), the great Scottish philosopher and historian, wrote his most famous work, *A Treatise of Human Nature* (1739), before he was twenty-four years old. His other important philosophical work, the *Dialogues Concerning Natural Religion* (1779), was published posthumously.

Hume argues that moral judgments are not based on reason but on sentiment, feelings of approval or disapproval. According to Hume, reason deals with relations of ideas or matters of fact. But an examination of common moral evils reveals neither relations of ideas nor matters of fact, but only sentiment. He uses three examples to support his argument: incest, murder, and ingratitude. Why is it that incest in humans is wrong, while the very same action in animals is not? There is no difference in the relations of ideas or in the basic facts. The only difference

Source: From David Hume, *A Treatise of Human Nature* (1740), bk. 3, pt. 1, sec. 1; and *An Inquiry Concerning the Principle of Morals* (1751), app. 1.

is that we disapprove of incest in humans and not in animals. Hume finds this argument to be entirely decisive. Or consider a deliberate murder. Is the wrongness of murder to be found in any objective fact or any reasoning about relations of ideas? Hume thinks not. The wrongness is a matter of fact, but it is the fact that you disapprove of intentional murder. Examine the crime of ingratitude. Is the crime an observable fact? Is it found in relations of ideas? No, it is found in the mind of the person who is ungrateful; specifically, it is a feeling of ill-will or indifference. Hume's conclusion is that morality is determined by sentiment, not reasoning.

Those who affirm that virtue is nothing but a conformity to reason; that there are eternal fitnesses and unfitnesses of things, which are the same to every rational being that considers them; that the immutable measures of right and wrong impose an obligation, not only on human creatures, but also on the Deity himself: All these systems concur in the opinion, that morality, like truth, is discern'd merely by ideas, and by their juxtaposition and comparison. In order, therefore, to judge of these systems, we need only consider, whether it be possible, from reason alone, to distinguish betwixt moral good and evil, or whether there must concur some other principles to enable us to make that distinction.

If morality had naturally no influence on human passions and actions, 'twere in vain to take such pains to inculcate it; and nothing wou'd be more fruitless than that multitude of rules and precepts, with which all moralists abound. Philosophy is commonly divided into *speculative* and *practical;* and as morality is always comprehended under the latter division, 'tis supposed to influence our passions and actions, and to go beyond the calm and indolent judgments of the understanding. And this is confirm'd by common experience, which informs us, that men are often govern'd by their duties, and are deter'd from some actions by the opinion of injustice, and impell'd to others by that of obligation.

Since morals, therefore, have an influence on the actions and affections, it follows, that they cannot be deriv'd from reason; and that because reason alone, as we have already prov'd, can never have any such influence. Morals excite passions, and produce or prevent actions. Reason of itself is utterly impotent in this particular. The rules of morality, therefore, are not conclusions of our reason. . . .

But to make these general reflexions more clear and convincing, we may illustrate them by some particular instances, wherein this character of moral good or evil is the most universally acknowledged. . . .

I would fain ask any one, why incest in the human species is criminal, and why the very same action, and the same relations in animals have not the smallest moral turpitude and deformity? If it be answer'd, that this action is innocent in animals, because they have not reason sufficient to discover its turpitude; but that man, being endow'd with that faculty, which *ought* to restrain him to his duty, the same action instantly becomes criminal to him; should this be said, I would reply, that this is evidently arguing in a circle. For before reason can perceive this turpitude, the turpitude must exist; and consequently is independent of the decisions of our reason, and is their object more properly than their effect. According to this system, then, every animal, that has sense, and appetite, and will; that is, every animal must be susceptible of all the same virtues and vices, for which we ascribe praise and blame to human creatures. All the difference is, that our superior reason may serve to discover the vice or virtue, and by that means may augment the blame or praise: But still this discovery supposes a separate being in these moral distinctions, and a being, which depends only on the will and appetite, and which, both in thought and reality, may be distinguish'd from the reason. Animals are susceptible of the same relations, with respect to each other, as the human species, and therefore wou'd also be susceptible of the same morality, if the essence of morality consisted in these relations. Their want of a sufficient degree of reason may hinder them from perceiving the duties and obligations of morality, but can never hinder these duties from existing; since they must antecedently exist, in order to their being perceiv'd. Reason must find them, and can never produce them. This argument deserves to be weigh'd, as being, in my opinion, entirely decisive.

Nor does this reasoning only prove, that morality consists not in any relations, that are the objects of science; but if examin'd, will prove with equal certainty, that it consists not in any *matter of fact,* which can be discover'd by the understanding. This is the *second* part of our argument; and if it can be made evident, we may conclude, that morality is not an object of reason. But can there be any difficulty in proving, that vice and virtue are not matters of fact, whose existence we can infer by reason? Take any action allow'd to be vicious: Wilful murder, for instance. Examine it in all lights, and see if you can find that matter of fact, or real existence, which you call *vice.* In which-ever way you take it, you find only certain passions, motives, volitions and thoughts. There is no other matter of fact in the case. The vice entirely escapes you, as long as you consider the object. You never can find it, till you turn your reflexion into your own breast, and find a sentiment of disapprobation, which arises in you, towards this action. Here is a matter of fact; but 'tis the object of feeling, not of reason. It lies in yourself, not in the object. So that when you pronounce any action or character to be vicious, you mean nothing, but that from the constitution of your nature you have a feeling or sentiment of blame from the contemplation of it. Vice and virtue, therefore, may be compar'd to sounds, colours, heat and cold, which, according to modern philosophy, are not qualities in objects, but perceptions in the mind: And this discovery in morals, like that other in physics, is to be regarded as a considerable advancement of the speculative sciences; tho', like that too, it has little or no influence on practice. Nothing can be more real, or concern us more, than our own sentiments of pleasure and uneasiness; and if these be favourable to virtue, and unfavourable to vice, no more can be requisite to the regulation of our conduct and behaviour.

I cannot forbear adding to these reasonings an observation, which may, perhaps, be found of some importance. In every system of morality, which I have hitherto met with, I have always remark'd, that the author proceeds for some time in the ordinary way of reasoning, and establishes the being of a God, or makes observations concerning human affairs; when of a sudden I am surpriz'd to find, that instead of the usual copulations of propositions, *is,* and *is not,* I meet with no proposition that is not connected with an *ought,* or an *ought not.* This change is imperceptible; but is, however, of the last consequence. For as this *ought,* or *ought not,* expresses some new relation or affirmation, 'tis necessary that it shou'd be observ'd and explain'd; and at the same time that a reason should be given, for what seems altogether inconceivable, how this new relation can be a deduction from others, which are entirely different from it. But as authors do not commonly use this precaution, I shall presume to recommend it to the readers; and am persuaded, that this small attention wou'd subvert all the vulgar systems of morality, and let us see, that the distinction of vice and virtue is not founded merely on the relations of objects, nor is perceiv'd by reason. . . .

Examine the crime of *ingratitude,* for instance; which has place, wherever we observe good-will, expressed and known, together with good-offices performed, on the one side, and a return of ill-will or indifference, with ill-offices or neglect on the other: anatomize all these circumstances, and examine, by your reason alone, in what consists the demerit or blame. You never will come to any issue or conclusion.

Reason judges either of *matter of fact* or of *relations.* Enquire then, *first,* where is that matter of fact which we here call *crime;* point it out; determine the time of its existence; describe its essence or nature; explain the sense or faculty to which it discovers itself. It resides in the mind of the person who is ungrateful. He must, therefore, feel it, and be conscious of it. But nothing is there, except the passion of ill-will or absolute indifference. You cannot say that these, of themselves, always, and in all circumstances, are crimes. No, they are only crimes when directed towards persons who have before expressed and displayed good-will towards us. Consequently, we may infer, that the crime of ingratitude is not any particular individual *fact;*

but arises from a complication of circumstances, which, being presented to the spectator, excites the *sentiment* of blame, by the particular structure and fabric of his mind.

This representation, you say, is false. Crime, indeed, consists not in a particular *fact,* of whose reality we are assured by *reason;* but it consists in certain *moral relations,* discovered by reason, in the same manner as we discover by reason the truths of geometry or algebra. But what are the relations, I ask, of which you here talk? In the case stated above, I see first good-will and good-offices in one person; then ill-will and ill-offices in the other. Between these, there is a relation of *contrariety.* Does the crime consist in that relation? But suppose a person bore me ill-will or did me ill-offices; and I, in return, were indifferent towards him, or did him good-offices. Here is the same relation of *contrariety;* and yet my conduct is often highly laudable. Twist and turn this matter as much as you will, you can never rest the morality on relation; but must have recourse to the decisions of sentiment.

When it is affirmed that two and three are equal to the half of ten, this relation of equality I understand perfectly. I conceive, that if ten be divided into two parts, of which one has as many units as the other; and if any of these parts be compared to two added to three, it will contain as many units as that compound number. But when you draw thence a comparison to moral relations, I own that I am altogether at a loss to understand you. A moral action, a crime, such as ingratitude, is a complicated object. Does the morality consist in the relation of its parts to each other? How?

After what manner? Specify the relation: be more particular and explicit in your propositions, and you will easily see their falsehood.

No, say you, the morality consists in the relation of actions to the rule of right; and they are denominated good or ill, according as they agree or disagree with it. What then is this rule of right? In what does it consist? How is it determined? By reason, you say, which examines the moral relations of actions. So that moral relations are determined by the comparison of action to a rule. And that rule is determined by considering the moral relations of objects. Is not this fine reasoning?

All this is metaphysics, you cry. That is enough; there needs nothing more to give a strong presumption of false-hood. Yes, reply I, here are metaphysics surely; but they are all on your side, who advance an abstruse hypothesis, which can never be made intelligible, nor quadrate with any particular instance or illustration. The hypothesis which we embrace is plain. It maintains that morality is determined by sentiment. It defines virtue to be *whatever mental action or quality gives to a spectator the pleasing sentiment of approbation;* and vice the contrary.

We then proceed to examine a plain matter of fact, to wit, what actions have this influence. We consider all the circumstances in which these actions agree, and thence endeavour to extract some general observations with regard to these sentiments. If you call this metaphysics, and find anything abstruse here, you need only conclude that your turn of mind is not suited to the moral sciences.

♔ REVIEW QUESTIONS

1. According to Hume, how do morals have an influence on action?
2. Explain Hume's argument about incest.
3. What is Hume's point about "is" and "ought"?
4. How does Hume explain ingratitude?

♔ DISCUSSION QUESTIONS

1. Suppose I say, "I disapprove of abortion, but it is not wrong." Does this make any sense? Why or why not?
2. Some philosophers have claimed that arguing from facts to values is not always a mistake.

Can you construct an acceptable argument with a fact as a premise and a value as a conclusion? For example, what about Mill's argument that if something is desired, then it is desirable?

Trying Out One's New Sword

MARY MIDGLEY

Mary Midgley (b. 1919) taught philosophy at the University of Newcastle-upon-Tyne in England for twenty years and attained the rank of senior lecturer. She is the author of twelve books, including *Beast and Man* (1978); *Heart and Mind* (1981), from which our reading is taken; *Animals and Why They Matter* (1983); *Wickedness* (1984); *Evolution as a Religion* (1985); *Wisdom, Information and Wonder* (1989); *Science as Salvation* (1992); *The Ethical Primate* (1994); *Utopia, Dolphins and Computers* (2000); *Science and Poetry* (2001); *Myths We Live By* (2003); *The Owl of Minerva* (2005); and *The Essential Mary Midgley* (2005).

Midgley explains and attacks moral isolationism, the view of anthropologists and relativists that we cannot criticize other cultures we do not understand—for example, the traditional Japanese culture that had the practice of trying out a new samurai sword on a chance wayfarer. She argues that moral isolationism is essentially a doctrine of immoralism because it forbids any moral reasoning. Furthermore, it falsely assumes that cultures are separate and unmixed, whereas most cultures are in fact formed out of many influences.

All of us are, more or less, in trouble today about trying to understand cultures strange to us. We hear constantly of alien customs. We see changes in our lifetime which would have astonished our parents. I want to discuss here one very short way of dealing with this difficulty, a drastic way which many people now theoretically favour. It consists in simply denying that we can ever understand any culture except our own well enough to make judgements about it. Those who recommend this hold that the world is sharply divided into separate societies, sealed units, each with its own system of thought. They feel that the respect and tolerance due from one system to another forbids us ever to take up a critical position to any other culture. Moral judgement, they suggest, is a kind of coinage valid only in its country of origin.

I shall call this position 'moral isolationism'. I shall suggest that it is certainly not forced upon us, and indeed that it makes no sense at all. People usually take it up because they think it is a respectful attitude to other cultures. In fact, however, it is not respectful. Nobody can respect what is entirely unintelligible to them. To respect someone, we have to know enough about him to make a *favourable* judgement, however general and tentative. And we do understand people in other cultures to this extent. Otherwise a great mass of our most valuable thinking would be paralysed.

To show this, I shall take a remote example, because we shall probably find it easier to think calmly about it than we should with a contemporary one, such as female circumcision in Africa or the Chinese Cultural Revolution. The principles involved will still be the same. My example is this. There is, it seems, a verb in classical Japanese which means 'to try out one's new sword on a chance wayfarer'. (The word is *tsujigiri*, literally 'crossroads-cut'.) A samurai sword had to be tried out because, if it was to work properly, it had to slice through someone at a single blow, from the shoulder to the opposite flank. Otherwise, the warrior bungled his stroke. This could injure his honour, offend his ancestors, and even let down his emperor. So tests were needed, and wayfarers had to be expended. Any wayfarer would do—provided, of course, that he was not another

Source: Mary Midgley, "Trying Out One's New Sword," from *Heart and Mind* Reprinted by permission of the author.

Samurai. Scientists will recognize a familiar problem about the rights of experimental subjects.

Now when we hear of a custom like this, we may well reflect that we simply do not understand it; and therefore are not qualified to criticize it at all, because we are not members of that culture. But we are not members of any other culture either, except our own. So we extend the principle to cover all extraneous cultures, and we seem therefore to be moral isolationists. But this is, as we shall see, an impossible position. Let us ask what it would involve.

We must ask first: Does the isolating barrier work both ways? Are people in other cultures equally unable to criticize *us*? This question struck me sharply when I read a remark in *The Guardian* by an anthropologist about a South American Indian who had been taken into a Brazilian town for an operation, which saved his life. When he came back to his village, he made several highly critical remarks about the white Brazilians' way of life. They may very well have been justified. But the interesting point was that the anthropologist called these remarks 'a damning indictment of Western civilization'. Now the Indian had been in that town about two weeks. Was he in a position to deliver a damning indictment? Would we ourselves be qualified to deliver such an indictment on the Samurai, provided we could spend two weeks in ancient Japan? What do we really think about this?

My own impression is that we believe that outsiders can, in principle, deliver perfectly good indictments—only, it usually takes more than two weeks to make them damning. Understanding has degrees. It is not a slapdash yes-or-no matter. Intelligent outsiders can progress in it, and in some ways will be at an advantage over the locals. But if this is so, it must clearly apply to ourselves as much as anybody else.

Our next question is this: Does the isolating barrier between cultures block praise as well as blame? If I want to say that the Samurai culture has many virtues, or to praise the South American Indians, am I prevented from doing *that* by my outside status? Now, we certainly do need to praise other societies in this way. But it is hardly possible that we could praise them

effectively if we could not, in principle, criticize them. Our praise would be worthless if it rested on no definite grounds, if it did not flow from some understanding. Certainly we may need to praise things which we do not *fully* understand. We say 'there's something very good here, but I can't quite make out what it is yet'. This happens when we want to learn from strangers. And we can learn from strangers. But to do this we have to distinguish between those strangers who are worth learning from and those who are not. Can we then judge which is which?

This brings us to our third question: What is involved in judging? Now plainly there is no question here of sitting on a bench in a red robe and sentencing people. Judging simply means forming an opinion, and expressing it if it is called for. Is there anything wrong about this? Naturally, we ought to avoid forming—and expressing—*crude* opinions, like that of a simple-minded missionary, who might dismiss the whole Samurai culture as entirely bad, because non-Christian. But this is a different objection. The trouble with crude opinions is that they are crude, whoever forms them, not that they are formed by the wrong people. Anthropologists, after all, are outsiders quite as much as missionaries. Moral isolationism forbids us to form *any* opinions on these matters. Its ground for doing so is that we don't understand them. But there is much that we don't understand in our own culture too. This brings us to our last question: If we can't judge other cultures, can we really judge our own? Our efforts to do so will be much damaged if we are really deprived of our opinions about other societies, because these provide the range of comparison, the spectrum of alternatives against which we set what we want to understand. We would have to stop using the mirror which anthropology so helpfully holds up to us.

In short, moral isolationism would lay down a general ban on moral reasoning. Essentially, this is the programme of immoralism, and it carries a distressing logical difficulty. Immoralists like Nietzsche are actually just a rather specialized sect of moralists. They can no more afford to put moralizing out of business than smugglers can afford to abolish customs regulations. The power of moral judgement is, in fact, not a luxury, not a perverse indulgence of the self-righteous. It is a necessity. When we judge something to be bad or good, better or worse than something else, we are taking it as an example to aim at or avoid. Without opinions of this sort, we would have no framework of comparison for our own policy, no chance of profiting by other people's insights or mistakes. In this vacuum, we could form no judgements on our own actions.

Now it would be odd if Homo sapiens had really got himself into a position as bad as this—a position where his main evolutionary asset, his brain, was so little use to him. None of us is going to accept this sceptical diagnosis. We cannot do so, because our involvement in moral isolationism does not flow from apathy, but from a rather acute concern about human hypocrisy and other forms of wickedness. But we polarize that concern around a few selected moral truths. We are rightly angry with those who despise, oppress or steamroll other cultures. We think that doing these things is actually *wrong*. But this is itself a moral judgement. We could not condemn oppression and insolence if we thought that all our condemnations were just a trivial local quirk of our own culture. We could still less do it if we tried to stop judging altogether.

Real moral scepticism, in fact, could lead only to inaction, to our losing all interest in moral questions, most of all in those which concern other societies. When we discuss these things, it becomes instantly clear how far we are from doing this. Suppose, for instance, that I criticize the bisecting Samurai, that I say his behaviour is brutal. What will usually happen next is that someone will protest, will say that I have no right to make criticisms like that of another culture. But it is most unlikely that he will use this move to end the discussion of the subject. Instead, he will justify the Samurai. He will try to fill in the background, to make me understand the custom, by explaining the exalted ideals of discipline and devotion which produced it. He will probably talk of the lower value which the ancient Japanese

placed on individual life generally. He may well suggest that this is a healthier attitude than our own obsession with security. He may add, too, that the wayfarers did not seriously mind being bisected, that in principle they accepted the whole arrangement.

Now an objector who talks like this is implying that it *is* possible to understand alien customs. That is just what he is trying to make me do. And he implies, too, that if I do succeed in understanding them, I shall do something better than giving up judging them. He expects me to change my present judgement to a truer one— namely, one that is favourable. And the standards I must use to do this cannot just be Samurai standards. They have to be ones current in my own culture. Ideals like discipline and devotion will not move anybody unless he himself accepts them. As it happens, neither discipline nor devotion is very popular in the West at present. Anyone who appeals to them may well have to do some more arguing to make *them* acceptable, before he can use them to explain the Samurai. But if he does succeed here, he will have persuaded us, not just that there was something to be said for them in ancient Japan, but that there would be here as well.

Isolating barriers simply cannot arise here. If we accept something as a serious moral truth about one culture, we can't refuse to apply it— in however different an outward form—to other cultures as well, wherever circumstances admit it. If we refuse to do this, we just are not taking the other culture seriously. This becomes clear if we look at the last argument used by my objector—that of justification by consent of the victim. It is suggested that sudden bisection is quite in order, *provided* that it takes place between consenting adults. I cannot now discuss how conclusive this justification is. What I am pointing out is simply that it can only work if we believe that *consent* can make such a transaction respectable—and this is a thoroughly modern and Western idea. It would probably never occur to a Samurai; if it did, it would surprise him very much. It is *our* standard. In applying it, too, we are likely to make another typically

Western demand. We shall ask for good factual evidence that the wayfarers actually do have this rather surprising taste—that they are really willing to be bisected. In applying Western standards in this way, we are not being confused or irrelevant. We are asking the questions which arise *from where we stand*, questions which we can see the sense of. We do this because asking questions which you can't see the sense of is humbug. Certainly we can extend our questioning by imaginative effort. We can come to understand other societies better. By doing so, we may make their questions our own, or we may see that they are really forms of the questions which we are asking already. This is not impossible. It is just very hard work. The obstacles which often prevent it are simply those of ordinary ignorance, laziness and prejudice.

If there were really an isolating barrier, of course, our own culture could never have been formed. It is no sealed box, but a fertile jungle of different influences—Greek, Jewish, Roman, Norse, Celtic and so forth, into which further influences are still pouring—American, Indian, Japanese, Jamaican, you name it. The moral isolationist's picture of separate, unmixable cultures is quite unreal. People who talk about British history usually stress the value of this fertilizing mix, no doubt rightly. But this is not just an odd fact about Britain. Except for the very smallest and most remote, all cultures are formed out of many streams. All have the problem of digesting and assimilating things which, at the start, they do not understand. All have the choice of learning something from this challenge, or alternatively, of refusing to learn, and fighting it mindlessly instead.

This universal predicament has been obscured by the fact that anthropologists used to concentrate largely on very small and remote cultures, which did not seem to have this problem. These tiny societies, which had often forgotten their own history, made neat, self-contained subjects for study. No doubt it was valuable to emphasize their remoteness, their extreme strangeness, their independence of our cultural tradition. This emphasis was, I think, the root of moral isolationism. But, as the tribal studies themselves showed, even there the anthropologists were able to interpret what they saw and make judgements—often favourable—about the tribesmen. And the tribesmen, too, were quite equal to making judgements about the anthropologists—and about the tourists and Coca-Cola salesmen who followed them. Both sets of judgements, no doubt, were somewhat hasty, both have been refined in the light of further experience. A similar transaction between us and the Samurai might take even longer. But that is no reason at all for deeming it impossible. Morally as well as physically, there is only one world, and we all have to live in it.

⚜ REVIEW QUESTIONS

1. What is "moral isolationism"?
2. Explain the Japanese custom of *tsujigiri*. What questions does Midgley ask about this custom?
3. What is wrong with moral isolationism, according to Midgley?
4. What does Midgley think is the basis for criticizing other cultures?

⚜ DISCUSSION QUESTIONS

1. Midgley says that Nietzsche is an immoralist. Is that an accurate and fair assessment of Nietzsche? Why or why not?
2. Do you agree with Midgley's claim that the idea of separate and unmixed cultures is unreal? Explain your answer.

Utilitarianism

JOHN STUART MILL

John Stuart Mill (1806–1873) was one of the most important and influential British philosophers. His most important works in ethics are *On Liberty* (1859) and *Utilitarianism* (1861), from which the reading is taken.

Mill sets forth the basic principles of Utilitarianism, including the Principle of Utility (or the Greatest Happiness Principle) and the hedonistic principle that happiness is pleasure. He explains the theory by replying to various objections, and concludes with an attempt to prove the Principle of Utility.

The creed which accepts as the foundation of morals, Utility, or the Greatest Happiness Principle, holds that actions are right in proportion as they tend to promote happiness, wrong as they tend to produce the reverse of happiness. By happiness is intended pleasure, and the absence of pain; by unhappiness, pain, and the privation of pleasure. To give a clear view of the moral standard set up by the theory, much more requires to be said; in particular, what things it includes in the ideas of pain and pleasure; and to what extent this is left an open question. But these supplementary explanations do not affect the theory of life on which this theory of morality is grounded—namely, that pleasure, and freedom from pain, are the only things desirable as ends; and that all desirable things (which are as numerous in the utilitarian as in any other scheme) are desirable either for the pleasure inherent in themselves, or as means to the promotion of pleasure and the prevention of pain.

Now, such a theory of life excites in many minds, and among them in some of the most estimable in feeling and purpose, inveterate dislike. To suppose that life has (as they express it) no higher end than pleasure—no better and nobler object of desire and pursuit—they designate as utterly mean and groveling; as a doctrine worthy only of swine, to whom the followers of Epicurus were, at a very early period, contemptuously likened; and modern holders of the doctrine are occasionally made the subject of equally polite comparison by its German, French, and English assailants.

When thus attacked, the Epicureans have always answered, that it is not they, but their accusers, who represent human nature in a degrading light; since the accusation supposes human beings to be capable of no pleasures except those of which swine are capable. If this supposition were true, the charge could not be gainsaid, but would then be no longer an imputation; for if the sources of pleasure were precisely the same to human beings and to swine, the rule of life which is good enough for the one would be good enough for the other. The comparison of the Epicurean life to that of beasts is felt as degrading, precisely because a beast's pleasures do not satisfy a human being's conceptions of happiness. Human beings have faculties more elevated than the animal appetites, and when once made conscious of them, do not regard anything as happiness which does not include their gratification. I do not, indeed, consider the Epicureans to have been by any means faultless in drawing out their scheme of consequences from the utilitarian principle. To do this in any sufficient manner, many Stoic, as well as Christian elements require to be included. But there is no known Epicurean theory of life which does not assign to the pleasures of the intellect, of the feelings and imagination, and of the moral sentiments, a much higher value as

Source: John Stuart Mill, from *Utilitarianism* (1861), Chapters 12 and 17.

pleasures than to those of mere sensation. It must be admitted, however, that utilitarian writers in general have placed the superiority of mental over bodily pleasures chiefly in the greater permanency, safety, uncostliness, etc., of the former—that is, in their circumstantial advantages rather than in their intrinsic nature. And on all these points utilitarians have fully proved their case; but they might have taken the other and, as it may be called, higher ground, with entire consistency. It is quite compatible with the principle of utility to recognize the fact, that some *kinds* of pleasure are more desirable and more valuable than others. It would be absurd that while, in estimating all other things, quality is considered as well as quantity, the estimation of pleasures should be supposed to depend on quantity alone.

If I am asked, what I mean by difference of quality in pleasures, or what makes one pleasure more valuable than another, merely as a pleasure, except its being greater in amount, there is but one possible answer. Of two pleasures, if there be one to which all or almost all who have experience of both give a decided preference, irrespective of any feeling of moral obligation to prefer it, that is the more desirable pleasure. If one of the two is, by those who are competently acquainted with both, placed so far above the other that they prefer it, even though knowing it to be attended with a greater amount of discontent, and would not resign it for any quantity of the other pleasure which their nature is capable of, we are justified in ascribing to the preferred enjoyment a superiority in quality, so far outweighing quantity as to render it, in comparison, of small account.

Now it is an unquestionable fact that those who are equally acquainted with, and equally capable of appreciating and enjoying, both, do give a most marked preference to the manner of existence which employs their higher faculties. Few human creatures would consent to be changed into any of the lower animals, for a promise of the fullest allowance of a beast's pleasures; no intelligent human being would consent to be a fool, no instructed person would be an ignoramus, no person of feeling and conscience would be selfish and base, even though they should be persuaded that the fool, the dunce, or the rascal is better satisfied

with his lot than they are with theirs. They would not resign what they possess more than he for the most complete satisfaction of all the desires which they have in common with him. If they ever fancy they would, it is only in cases of unhappiness so extreme, that to escape from it they would exchange their lot for almost any other, however undesirable in their own eyes. A being of higher faculties requires more to make him happy, is capable probably of more acute suffering, and certainly accessible to it at more points, than one of an inferior type; but in spite of these liabilities, he can never really wish to sink into what he feels to be a lower grade of existence. We may give what explanation we please of this unwillingness; we may attribute it to pride, a name which is given indiscriminately to some of the most and to some of the least estimable feelings of which mankind are capable; we may refer it to the love of liberty and personal independence, an appeal to which was with the Stoics one of the most effective means for the inculcation of it; to the love of power, or to the love of excitement, both of which do really enter into and contribute to it: but its most appropriate appellation is a sense of dignity, which all human beings possess in one form or other, and in some, though by no means in exact, proportion to their higher faculties, and which is so essential a part of the happiness of those in whom it is strong, that nothing which conflicts with it could be, otherwise than momentarily, an object of desire to them. Whoever supposes that this preference takes place at a sacrifice of happiness—that the superior being, in anything like equal circumstances, is not happier than the inferior—confounds the two very different ideas, of happiness, and content. It is indisputable that the being whose capacities of enjoyment are low, has the greatest chance of having them fully satisfied; and a highly endowed being will always feel that any happiness which he can look for, as the world is constituted, is imperfect. But he can learn to bear its imperfections, if they are at all bearable; and they will not make him envy the being who is indeed unconscious of the imperfections, but only because he feels not at all the good which those imperfections qualify. It is better to be a human being dissatisfied than a pig satisfied; better to be Socrates dissatisfied than a fool satisfied. And if the fool, or the pig, are of a different opinion, it is because they only know their own side of the question. The other party to the comparison knows both sides.

It may be objected, that many who are capable of the higher pleasures, occasionally, under the influence of temptation, postpone them to the lower. But this is quite compatible with a full appreciation of the intrinsic superiority of the higher. Men often, from infirmity of character, make their election for the nearer good, though they know it to be the less valuable; and this no less when the choice is between two bodily pleasures, than when it is between bodily and mental. They pursue sensual indulgence to the injury of health, though perfectly aware that health is the greater good. It may be further objected, that many who begin with youthful enthusiasm for everything noble, as they advance in years sink into indolence and selfishness. But I do not believe that those who undergo this very common change, voluntarily choose the lower description of pleasures in preference to the higher. I believe that before they devote themselves exclusively to the one, they have already become incapable of the other. Capacity for the nobler feelings is in most natures a very tender plant, easily killed, not only by hostile influences, but by mere want of sustenance; and in the majority of young persons it speedily dies away if the occupations to which their position in life has devoted them, and the society into which it has thrown them, are not favourable to keeping that higher capacity in exercise. Men lose their high aspirations as they lose their intellectual tastes, because they have not time or opportunity for indulging them; and they addict themselves to inferior pleasures, not because they deliberately prefer them, but because they are either the only ones to which they have access or the only ones which they are any longer capable of enjoying. It may be questioned whether any one who has remained equally susceptible to both classes of pleasures, ever knowingly and calmly preferred the lower; though many, in all ages, have broken down in an ineffectual attempt to combine both.

From this verdict of the only competent judges, I apprehend there can be no appeal. On a question which is the best worth having of two pleasures, or which of two modes of existence is the most grateful to the feelings, apart from its moral attributes and from its consequences, the judgment of those who are qualified by knowledge of both, or, if they differ, that of the majority among them, must be admitted as final. And there needs be the less hesitation to accept this judgment respecting the quality of pleasures, since there is no other tribunal to be referred to even on the question of quantity. What means are there of determining which is the acutest of two pains, or the intensest of two pleasurable sensations, except the general suffrage of those who are familiar with both? Neither pains nor pleasures are homogeneous, and pain is always heterogeneous with pleasure. What is there to decide whether a particular pleasure is worth purchasing at the cost of a particular pain, except the feelings and judgment of the experienced? When, therefore, those feelings and judgment declare the pleasures derived from the higher faculties to be preferable *in kind,* apart from the question of intensity, to those of which the animal nature, disjoined from the higher faculties, is susceptible, they are entitled on this subject to the same regard.

I have dwelt on this point, as being a necessary part of a perfectly just conception of Utility or Happiness, considered as the directive rule of human conduct. But it is by no means an indispensable condition to the acceptance of the utilitarian stand; for that standard is not the agent's own greatest happiness, but the greatest amount of happiness altogether; and if it may possibly be doubted whether a noble character is always the happier for its nobleness, there can be no doubt that it makes other people happier, and that the world in general is immensely a gainer by it. Utilitarianism, therefore, could only attain its end by the general cultivation of nobleness of character, even if each individual were only benefited by the nobleness of others, and his own, so far as happiness is concerned, were a sheer deduction from the benefit. But the bare enunciation of such an absurdity as this last, renders refutation superfluous.

According to the Greatest Happiness Principle, as above explained, the ultimate end, with reference to and for the sake of which all other things are desirable (whether we are considering our own good or that of other people), is an existence exempt as far as possible from pain, and as rich as possible in enjoyments, both in point of quantity and quality; the test of quality, and the rule for measuring it against quantity, being the preference felt by those who in their opportunities of experience, to which must be added their habits of self-consciousness and self-observation, are best furnished with the means of comparison. This, being, according to the utilitarian opinion, the end of human action, is necessarily also the standard of morality; which may accordingly be defined, the rules and precepts for human conduct, by the observance of which an existence such as has been described might be, to the greatest extent possible, secured to all mankind; and not to them only, but, so far as the nature of things admits, to the whole sentient creation. . . .

I must again repeat what the assailants of utilitarianism seldom have the justice to acknowledge, that the happiness which forms the utilitarian standard of what is right in conduct, is not the agent's own happiness, but that of all concerned. As between his own happiness and that of others, utilitarianism requires him to be as strictly impartial as a disinterested and benevolent spectator. In the golden rule of Jesus of Nazareth, we read the complete spirit of the ethics of utility. To do as you would be done by, and to love your neighbor as yourself, constitute the ideal perfection of utilitarian morality. As the means of making the nearest approach to this ideal, utility would enjoin, first, that laws and social arrangements should place the happiness, or (as, speaking practically it may be called) the interest, of every individual, as nearly as possible in harmony with the interest of the whole; and secondly that education and opinion, which have so vast a power over human character, should so use that power as to establish in the mind of every individual an indissoluble association between his own happiness and the good of the whole; especially between his own happiness and the practice of such modes of conduct, negative and positive, as regard for the universal happiness prescribes; so that not only he may be unable to conceive the possibility of happiness

to himself, consistently with conduct opposed to the general good, but also that a direct impulse to promote the general good may be in every individual one of the habitual motives of action, and the sentiments connected therewith may fill a large and prominent place in every human being's sentient existence. If the impugners of the utilitarian morality represented it to their own minds in this its true character, I know not what recommendation possessed by any other morality they could possibly affirm to be wanting to it; what more beautiful or more exalted developments of human nature any other ethical system can be supposed to foster, or what springs of action, not accessible to the utilitarian, such systems rely on for giving effect to their mandates. . . .

The objectors to utilitarianism cannot always be charged with representing it in a discreditable light. On the contrary, those among them who entertain any thing like a just idea of its disinterested character sometimes find fault with its standard as being too high for humanity. They say it is exacting too much to require that people shall always act from the inducement of promoting the general interests of society. But this is to mistake the very meaning of a standard of morals, and confound the rule of action with the motive of it. It is the business of ethics to tell us what are our duties or by what test we may know them, but no system of ethics requires that the sole motive of all we do shall be a feeling of duty; on the contrary, ninety-nine hundredths of all our actions are done from other motives, and rightly so done, if the rule of duty does not condemn them. It is the more unjust to utilitarianism that this particular misapprehension should be made a ground of objection to it, inasmuch as utilitarian moralists have gone beyond almost all others in affirming that the motive has nothing to do with the morality of the action though much with the worth of the agent. He who saves a fellow creature from drowning does what is morally right, whether his motive be duty or the hope of being paid for his trouble; he who betrays the friend that trusts him is guilty of a crime, even if his object be to serve another friend to whom he is under greater obligations. But to speak only of actions done from the motive of duty, and in direct obedience to principle: it is a misapprehension of the utilitarian mode of thought to conceive it as implying that people should fix their minds upon so wide a generality as the world or society at large. The great majority of good actions are intended, not for the benefit of the world but for that of individuals, of which the good of the world is made up; and the thoughts of the most virtuous man need not on these occasions travel beyond the particular persons concerned, except so far as is necessary to assure himself that, in benefiting them, he is not violating the rights—that is, the legitimate and authorized expectations—of any one else. The multiplication of happiness is, according to the utilitarian ethics, the object of virtue; the occasions on which any person (except one in a thousand) has it in his power to do this on an extended scale—in other words, to be a public benefactor—are but exceptional, and on these occasions alone is he called on to consider public utility; in every other case, private utility, the interest or happiness of some few persons, is all he has to attend to. Those alone, the influence of whose actions extends to society in general, need concern themselves habitually about so large an object. In the case of abstinences indeed—of things which people forbear to do from moral considerations, though the consequences in the particular case might be beneficial—it would be unworthy of an intelligent agent not to be consciously aware that the action is of a class which, if practised generally, would be generally injurious, and that this is the ground of the obligation to abstain from it. The amount of regard for the public interest implied in this recognition is no greater than is demanded by every system of morals, for they all enjoin to abstain from whatever is manifestly pernicious to society. . . .

Again: defenders of utility often find themselves called upon to reply to such objections as this—that there is not time, previous to action, for calculating and weighing the effects of any line of conduct on the general happiness. This is exactly as if any one were to say that it is impossible to guide our conduct by Christianity, because there is not time, on every occasion on which any thing has to be done, to read through the Old and New Testaments. The answer to the objection is that there has been ample time, namely, the whole past duration of the human species. During all that time, mankind have been learning by experience the tendencies of actions, on which experience all the prudence as well as all the morality of life are dependent. People talk as if the commencement of this course of experience had hitherto been put off and as if, at the moment when some man feels tempted to meddle with the property or life of another, he had to begin considering for the first time whether murder and theft are injurious to human happiness. Even then, I do not think that he would find the question very puzzling, but at all events the matter is now done to his hand. It is truly a whimsical supposition that, if mankind were agreed in considering utility to be the test of morality, they would remain without any agreement as to what *is* useful, and would take no measures for having their notions on the subject taught to the young and enforced by law and opinion. There is no difficulty in proving any ethical standard whatever to work ill, if we suppose universal idiocy to be conjoined with it; but on any hypothesis short of that, mankind must by this time have acquired positive beliefs as to the effects of some actions on their happiness, and the beliefs which have thus come down are the rules of morality for the multitude, and for the philosopher, until he has succeeded in finding better. That philosophers might easily do this, even now, on many subjects, that the received code of ethics is by no means of divine right, and that mankind have still much to learn as to the effects of actions on the general happiness—I admit or, rather, earnestly maintain. The corollaries from the principle of utility, like the precepts of every practical art, admit of indefinite improvement and, in a progressive state of the human mind, their improvement is perpetually going on. But to consider the rules of morality as improvable is one thing; to pass over the intermediate generalizations entirely, and endeavor to test each individual action directly by the first principle, is another. It is a strange notion, that the acknowledgment of a first principle is inconsistent with the admission of secondary ones. To inform a traveler respecting the place of his ultimate destination is not to forbid the use of landmarks and direction posts on the way. The proposition that happiness is the end and aim of morality does not mean that no road ought to be laid down to that goal, or that persons going thither should not be advised to take one direction rather than another. Men really ought to leave off talking a kind of nonsense on this subject which they would neither talk nor listen to on other matters of practical concernment. Nobody argues that the art of navigation is not founded on astronomy, because sailors cannot wait to calculate the "Nautical Almanac." Being rational creatures, they go to sea with it ready calculated, and all rational creatures go out upon the sea of life with their minds made up on the common questions of right and wrong, as well as on many of the far more difficult questions of wise and foolish. And this, as long as foresight is a human quality, it is to be presumed they will continue to do. Whatever we adopt as the fundamental principle of morality, we require subordinate principles to apply it by; the impossibility of doing without them, being common to all systems, can afford no argument against any one in particular; but gravely to argue as if no such secondary principles could be had, and as if mankind had remained till now and always must remain without drawing any general conclusions from the experience of human life, is as high a pitch, I think, as absurdity has ever reached in philosophical controversy.

The remainder of the stock arguments against utilitarianism mostly consist in laying to its charge the common infirmities of human nature, and the general difficulties which embarrass conscientious persons in shaping their course through life. We are told that an utilitarian will be apt to make his own particular case an exception to moral rules and, when under temptation, will see an utility in the breach of a rule greater than he will see in its observance. But is utility the only creed which is able to furnish us with excuses for evil-doing, and means of cheating our own conscience? They are afforded in abundance by all doctrines which recognize as a fact in morals the existence of conflicting considerations, which all doctrines do that have been believed by sane persons. It is not the fault of any creed, but of the complicated nature of human affairs, that rules of conduct cannot be so framed as to require no exceptions, and that hardly any kind of action can safely be laid down

as either always obligatory or always condemnable. There is no ethical creed which does not temper the rigidity of its laws by giving a certain latitude, under the moral responsibility of the agent, for accommodation to peculiarities of circumstances and, under every creed, at the opening thus made, self-deception and dishonest casuistry get in. There exists no moral system under which there do not arise unequivocal cases of conflicting obligation. These are the real difficulties, the knotty points both in the theory of ethics and in the conscientious guidance of personal conduct. They are overcome practically with greater or with less success according to the intellect and virtue of the individual, but it can hardly be pretended that any one will be the less qualified for dealing with them, from possessing an ultimate standard to which conflicting rights and duties can be referred. If utility is the ultimate source of moral obligations, utility may be invoked to decide between them when their demands are incompatible. Though the application of the standard may be difficult, it is better than none at all; while in other systems, the moral laws all claiming independent authority, there is no common umpire entitled to interfere between them, their claims to precedence one over another rest on little better than sophistry, and unless determined, as they generally are, by the unacknowledged influence of considerations of utility, afford a free scope for the action of personal desires and partialities. We must remember that only in these cases of conflict between secondary principles is it requisite that first principles should be appealed to. There is no case of moral obligation in which some secondary principle is not involved and, if only one, there can seldom be any real doubt which one it is, in the mind of any person by whom the principle itself is recognized. . . .

OF WHAT SORT OF PROOF THE PRINCIPLE OF UTILITY IS SUSCEPTIBLE

It has already been remarked, that questions of ultimate ends do not admit of proof, in the ordinary acceptation of the term. To be incapable of proof by reasoning is common to all first principles; to the first premises of our knowledge, as well as to those of our conduct. But the former, being matters of fact, may be the subject of a direct appeal to the faculties which judge of fact—namely, our senses, and our internal consciousness. Can an appeal be made to the same faculties on questions of practical ends? Or by what other faculty is cognizance taken of them?

Questions about ends, in other words, question what things are desirable. The utilitarian doctrine is, that happiness is desirable, and the only thing desirable, as an end; all other things being only desirable as means to that end. What ought to be required of this doctrine—what conditions is it requisite that the doctrine should fulfil—to make good its claim to be believed?

The only proof capable of being given that an object is visible, is that people actually see it. The only proof that a sound is audible, is that people hear it: and so of the other sources of our experience. In like manner, I apprehend, the sole evidence it is possible to produce that anything is desirable, is that people do actually desire it. If the end which the utilitarian doctrine proposes to itself were not, in theory and in practice, acknowledged to be an end, nothing could ever convince any person that it was so. No reason can be given why the general happiness is desirable, except that each person, so far as he believes it to be attainable, desires his own happiness. This, however, being a fact, we have not only all the proof which the case admits of, but all which it is possible to require, that happiness is a good: that each person's happiness is a good to that person, and the general happiness, therefore, a good to the aggregate of all persons. Happiness has made out its title as one of the ends of conduct, and consequently one of the criteria of morality.

But it has not, by this alone, proved itself to be the sole criterion. To do that, it would seem, by the same rule, necessary to show, not only that people desire happiness, but that they never desire anything else. Now it is palpable that they do desire things which, in common language, are decidedly distinguished from happiness. They desire, for example, virtue, and the absence of vice, no less really than pleasure and the absence of pain.

The desire of virtue is not as universal, but it is as authentic a fact, as the desire of happiness. And hence the opponents of the utilitarian standard deem that they have a right to infer that there are other ends of human action besides happiness, and that happiness is not the standard of approbation and disapprobation.

But does the utilitarian doctrine deny that people desire virtue, or maintain that virtue is not a thing to be desired? The very reverse. It maintains not only that virtue is to be desired, but that it is to be desired disinterestedly, for itself. Whatever may be the opinion of utilitarian moralists as to the original conditions by which virtue is made virtue; however they may believe (as they do) that actions and dispositions are only virtuous because they promote another end than virtue; yet this being granted, and it having been decided, form considerations of this description, what *is* virtuous, they not only place virtue at the very head of the things which are good as means to the ultimate end, but they also recognise as a psychological fact that possibility of its being, to the individual, a good in itself, without looking to any end beyond it; and hold, that the mind is not in a right state, not in a state conformable to Utility, not in the state most conducive to the general happiness, unless it does love virtue in this manner—as a thing desirable in itself, even although, in the individual instance, it should not produce those other desirable consequences which it tends to produce, and on account of which it is held to be virtue. This opinion is not, in the smallest degree, a departure from the Happiness principle. The ingredients of happiness are very various, and each of them is desirable in itself, and not merely when considered as swelling an aggregate. The principle of utility does not mean that any given pleasure, as music, for instance, or any given exemption from pain, as for example health, is to be looked upon as means to a collective something termed happiness, and to be desired on that account. They are desired and desirable in and for themselves; besides being means, they are a part of the end. Virtue, according to the utilitarian doctrine, is not naturally and originally part of the end, but it is capable of becoming so; and in those who love it disinterestedly it has become so, and is desired and cherished, not as a means to happiness, but as a part of their happiness.

To illustrate this farther, we may remember that virtue is not the only thing, originally a means, and which if it were not a means to anything else, would be and remain indifferent, but which by association with what it is a means to, comes to be desired for itself, and that too with the utmost intensity. What, for example, shall we say of the love of money? There is nothing originally more desirable about money than about any heap of glittering pebbles. Its worth is solely that of the things which it will buy; the desires for other things than itself, which it is a means of gratifying. Yet the love of money is not only one of the strongest moving forces of human life, but money is, in many cases, desired in and for itself; the desire to possess it is often stronger than the desire to use it, and goes on increasing when all the desires which point to ends beyond it, to be compassed by it, are falling off. It may, then, be said truly, that money is desired not for the sake of an end, but as part of the end. From being a means to happiness, it has come to be itself a principal ingredient of the individual's conception of happiness. The same may be said of the majority of the great objects of human life—power, for example, or fame; except that to each of these there is a certain amount of immediate pleasure annexed, which has at least the semblance of being naturally inherent in them; a thing which cannot be said of money. Still, however, the strongest natural attraction, both of power and of fame, is the immense aid they give to the attainment of our other wishes; and it is the strong association thus generated between them and all our objects of desire, which gives to the direct desire of them the intensity it often assumes, so as in some characters to surpass in strength all other desires. In these cases the means have become a part of the end, and a more important part of it than any of the things which they are means to.

What was once desired as an instrument for the attainment of happiness, has come to be desired for its own sake. In being desired for its own sake it is, however, desired as *part* of happiness. The person is made, or thinks he would be

made, happy by its mere possession; and is made unhappy by failure to obtain it. The desire of it is not a different thing from the desire of happiness, any more than the love of music, or the desire of health. They are included in happiness. They are some of the elements of which the desire of happiness is made up. Happiness is not an abstract idea, but a concrete whole; and these are some of its parts. And the utilitarian standard sanctions and approves their being so. Life would be a poor thing, very ill provided with sources of happiness, if there were not this provision of nature, by which things originally indifferent, but conducive to, or otherwise associated with, the satisfaction of our primitive desires, become in themselves sources of pleasure more valuable than the primitive pleasures, both in permanency, in the space of human existence that they are capable of covering, and even in intensity.

Virtue, according to the utilitarian conception, is a good of this description. There was no original desire of it, or motive to it, save its conduciveness to pleasure, and especially to protection from pain. But through the association thus formed, it may be felt a good in itself, and desired as such with as great intensity as any other good; and with this difference between it and the love of money, of power, or of fame, that all of these may, and often do, render the individual noxious to the other members of the society to which he belongs, whereas there is nothing which makes him so much a blessing to them as the cultivation of the disinterested love of virtue. And consequently, the utilitarian standard, while it tolerates and approves those other acquired desires, up to the point beyond which they would be more injurious to the general happiness than promotive of it, enjoins and requires the cultivation of the love of virtue up to the greatest strength possible, as being above all things important to the general happiness.

It results from the preceding considerations, that there is in reality nothing desired except happiness. Whatever is desired otherwise than as a means to some end beyond itself, and ultimately to happiness, is desired as itself a part of happiness, and is not desired for itself until it has become so. Those who desire virtue for its own sake, desire it either because the consciousness of it is a pleasure, or because the consciousness of being without it is a pain, or for both reasons united; as in truth the pleasure and pain seldom exist separately, but almost always together, the same person feeling pleasure in the degree of virtue attained, and pain in not having attained more. If one of these gave him no pleasure, and the other no pain, he would not love or desire virtue, or would desire it only for the other benefits which it might produce to himself or to persons whom he cared for. . . .

✧ REVIEW QUESTIONS

1. State and explain the Principle of Utility. Show how it could be used to justify actions that are conventionally viewed as wrong, such as lying and stealing.
2. How does Mill reply to the objection that epicureanism is a doctrine worthy only of swine?
3. How does Mill distinguish between higher and lower pleasures?
4. According to Mill, whose happiness must be considered?
5. Carefully reconstruct Mill's proof of the Principle of Utility.

✧ DISCUSSION QUESTIONS

1. Is happiness nothing more than pleasure, and the absence of pain? What do you think?
2. Does Mill convince you that the so-called higher pleasures are better than the lower ones? What about the person of experience who prefers the lower pleasures over the higher ones?
3. Mill says, "In the golden rule of Jesus of Nazareth, we read the complete spirit of the ethics of utility." Is this true or not?
4. Many commentators have thought that Mill's proof of the Principle of Utility is defective. Do you agree? If so, then what mistake or mistakes does he make? Is there any way to reformulate the proof so that it is not defective?

The Categorical Imperative

IMMANUEL KANT

Immanuel Kant (1724–1804), a German, was one of the most important philosophers of all time. He made significant contributions to all areas of philosophy. He wrote many books; the most important ones are *Critique of Pure Reason* (1781), *Prolegomena to All Future Metaphysics* (1783), *Critique of Practical Reason* (1788), *Critique of Judgment* (1790), and *The Foundations of the Metaphysics of Morals* (1785), from which the reading is taken.

Kant believes that our moral duty can be formulated in one supreme rule, the categorical imperative, from which all our duties can be derived. Although he says that there is just one rule, he gives different versions of it, and two of them seem to be distinct. He arrives at the supreme rule or rules by considering the nature of the good will and duty.

Source: Immanuel Kant, "The Categorical Imperative" from *The Moral Law: Kant's Groundwork of the Metaphysic of Morals* (trans. H. J. Paton, New York: Barnes & Noble, 1948).

THE GOOD WILL

It is impossible to conceive anything at all in the world, or even out of it, which can be taken as good without qualification, except a *good will.* Intelligence, wit, judgment, and any other *talents* of the mind we may care to name, or courage, resolution, and constancy of purpose, as qualities of *temperament,* are without doubt good and desirable in many respects; but they can also be extremely bad and hurtful when the will is not good which has to make use of these gifts of nature, and which for this reason has the term "*character*" applied to its peculiar quality. It is exactly the same with *gifts of fortune.* Power, wealth, honour, even health and that complete well-being and contentment with one's state which goes by the name of "*happiness,*" produce boldness, and as a consequence often overboldness as well, unless a good will is present by which their influence on the mind—and so too the whole principle of action—may be corrected and adjusted to universal ends; not to mention that a rational and impartial spectator can never feel approval in contemplating the uninterrupted prosperity of a being graced by no touch of a pure and good will, and that consequently a good will seems to constitute the indispensable condition of our very worthiness to be happy.

Some qualities are even helpful to this good will itself and can make its task very much easier. They have none the less no inner unconditioned worth, but rather presuppose a good will which sets a limit to the esteem in which they are rightly held and does not permit us to regard them as absolutely good. Moderation in affections and passions, self-control, and sober reflexion are not only good in many respects: they may even seem to constitute part of the *inner* worth of a person. Yet they are far from being properly described as good without qualification (however unconditionally they have been commended by the ancients). For without the principles of a good will they may become exceedingly bad; and the very coolness of a scoundrel makes him, not merely more dangerous, but also immediately more abominable in our eyes than we should have taken him to be without it.

THE GOOD WILL AND ITS RESULTS

A good will is not good because of what it effects or accomplishes—because of its fitness for attaining some proposed end: it is good through its willing alone—that is, good in itself. Considered in itself it is to be esteemed beyond comparison as far higher than anything it could ever bring about merely in order to favour some inclination or, if you like, the sum total of inclinations. Even if, by some special disfavour of destiny or by the niggardly endowment of stepmotherly nature, this will is entirely lacking in power to carry out its intentions; if by its utmost effort it still accomplishes nothing, and only good will is left (not, admittedly, as a mere wish, but as the straining of every means so far as they are in our control); even then it would still shine like a jewel for its own sake as something which has its full value in itself. Its usefulness or fruitlessness can neither add to, nor subtract from, this value. Its usefulness would be merely, as it were, the setting which enables us to handle it better in our ordinary dealings or to attract the attention of those not yet sufficiently expert, but not to commend it to experts or to determine its value. . . .

THE GOOD WILL AND DUTY

We have now to elucidate the concept of a will estimable in itself and good apart from any further end. This concept, which is already present in a sound natural understanding and requires not so much to be taught as merely to be clarified, always holds the highest place in estimating the total worth of our actions and constitutes the condition of all the rest. We will therefore take up the concept of *duty,* which includes that of a good will, exposed, however, to certain subjective limitations and obstacles. These, so far from hiding a good will or disguising it, rather bring it out by contrast and make it shine forth more brightly.

THE MOTIVE OF DUTY

I will here pass over all actions already recognized as contrary to duty, however useful they may be with a view to this or that end; for about these the question does not even arise whether they could have been done *for the sake of duty* inasmuch as they are directly opposed to it. I will also set aside actions which in fact accord with duty, yet for which men have *no immediate inclination,* but perform them because impelled to do so by some other inclination. For there it is easy to decide whether the action which accords with duty has been done *from duty* or from some purpose of self-interest. This distinction is far more difficult to perceive when the action accords with duty and the subject has in addition an *immediate* inclination to the action. For example, it certainly accords with duty that a grocer should not overcharge his inexperienced customer; and where there is much competition a sensible shopkeeper refrains from so doing and keeps to a fixed and general price for everybody so that a child can buy from him just as well as anyone else. Thus people are served *honestly;* but this is not nearly enough to justify us in believing that the shopkeeper has acted in this way from duty or from principles of fair dealing; his interests required him to do so. We cannot assume him to have in addition an immediate inclination towards his customers, leading him, as it were out of love, to give no man preference over another in the matter of price. Thus the action was done neither from duty nor from immediate inclination, but solely from purposes of self-interest.

On the other hand, to preserve one's life is a duty, and besides this every one has also an immediate inclination to do so. But on account of this the often anxious precautions taken by the greater part of mankind for this purpose have no inner worth, and the maxim of their action is without moral content. They do protect their lives *in conformity with duty,* but not *from the motive of duty.* When on the contrary, disappointments and hopeless misery have quite taken away the taste for life; when a wretched man, strong in soul and more angered at his fate than fainthearted or cast down, longs for death and still preserves his life without loving it—not from inclination or fear but from duty; then indeed his maxim has a moral content.

To help others where one can is a duty, and besides this there are many spirits of so sympathetic a temper that, without any further motive of vanity or self-interest, they find an inner pleasure in spreading happiness around them and can take delight in the contentment of others as their own work. Yet I maintain that in such a case an action of this kind, however right and however amiable it may be, has still no genuinely moral worth. It stands on the same footing as other inclinations—for example, the inclination for honour, which if fortunate enough to hit on something beneficial and right and consequently honourable, deserves praise and encouragement, but not esteem; for its maxim lacks moral content, namely, the performance of such actions, not from inclination, but *from duty.* Suppose then that the mind of this friend of man were overclouded by sorrows of his own which extinguished all sympathy with the fate of others, but that he still had power to help those in distress, though no longer stirred by the need of others because sufficiently occupied with his own; and suppose that, when no longer moved by any inclination, he tears himself out of this deadly insensibility and does the action without any inclination for the sake of duty alone; then for the first time his action has its genuine moral worth. Still further: if nature had implanted little sympathy in this or that man's heart; if (being in other respects an honest fellow) he were cold in temperament and indifferent to the sufferings of others—perhaps because, being endowed with the special gift of patience and robust endurance in his own sufferings, he assumed the like in others or even demanded it; if such a man (who would in truth not be the worst product of nature) were not exactly fashioned by her to be a philanthropist, would he not still find in himself a source from which he might draw a worth far higher than any that a good-natured temperament can have? Assuredly he would. It is precisely in this that the worth of character begins to show—a moral worth and beyond all comparison the highest—namely, that he does good, not from inclination, but from duty. . . .

Thus the moral worth of an action does not depend on the result expected from it, and so too does not depend on any principle of action that needs to borrow its motive from this expected result. For all these results (agreeable states and even the promotion of happiness in others) could have been brought about by other causes as well, and consequently their production did not require the will of a rational being, in which, however, the *highest and unconditioned good* can alone be found. Therefore nothing but the *idea of the law in itself, which admittedly is present only in a rational being*—so far as it, and not an expected result, is the ground determining the will—can constitute that preeminent good which we call moral, a good which is already present in the person acting on this idea and has not to be awaited merely from the result.

THE CATEGORICAL IMPERATIVE

But what kind of law can this be the thought of which, even without regard to the results expected from it, has to determine the will if this is to be called good absolutely and without qualification? Since I have robbed the will of every inducement that might arise for it as a consequence of obeying any particular law, nothing is left but the conformity of actions to universal law as such, and this alone must serve the will as its principle. That is to say, I ought never to act except in such a way *that I can also will that my maxim should become a universal law.* Here bare conformity to universal law as such (without having as its base any law prescribing particular actions) is what serves the will as its principle, and must so serve it if duty is not to be everywhere an empty delusion and a chimerical concept. The ordinary reason of mankind also agrees with this completely in its practical judgements and always has the aforesaid principle before its eyes. . . .

When I conceive a *hypothetical imperative* in general, I do not know beforehand what it will contain—until its condition is given. But if I conceive a *categorical imperative*, I know at once what it contains. For since besides the law this imperative contains only the necessity that our maxim[1] should conform to this law, while the law,

as we have seen, contains no condition to limit it, there remains nothing over to which the maxim has to conform except the universality of a law as such; and it is this conformity alone that the imperative properly asserts to be necessary.

There is therefore only a single categorical imperative and it is this: "*Act only on that maxim through which you can at the same time will that it should become a universal law.*"

Now if all imperatives of duty can be derived from this one imperative as their principle, then even although we leave it unsettled whether what we call duty may not be an empty concept, we shall still be able to show at least what we understand by it and what the concept means. . . .

ILLUSTRATIONS

We will now enumerate a few duties, following their customary division into duties towards self and duties towards others and into perfect and imperfect duties.[2]

1. A man feels sick of life as the result of a series of misfortunes that has mounted to the point of despair, but he is still so far in possession of his reason as to ask himself whether taking his own life may not be contrary to his duty to himself. He now applies the test "Can the maxim of my action really become a universal law of nature?" His maxim is "From self-love I make it my principle to shorten my life if its continuance threatens more evil than it promises pleasure." The only further question to ask is whether this principle of self-love can become a universal law of nature. It is then seen at once that a system of nature by whose law the very same feeling whose function (*Bestimmung*) is to stimulate the furtherance of life should actually destroy life would

---

[1]A *maxim* is a subjective principle of action and must be distinguished from an *objective principle*—namely, a practical law. The former contains a practical rule determined by reason in accordance with the conditions of the subject (often his ignorance or again his inclinations): it is thus a principle on which the subject *acts*. A law, on the other hand, is an objective principle valid for every rational being; and it is a principle on which he *ought to act*—that is, an imperative.

[2]It should be noted that I reserve my division of duties entirely for a future *Metaphysic of Morals* and that my present division is therefore put forward as arbitrary (merely for the purpose of arranging my examples). Further, I understand here by a perfect duty one which allows no exception in the interests of inclination, and so I recognize among *perfect duties*, not only outer ones, but also inner. This is contrary to the accepted usage of the schools, but I do not intend to justify it here, since for my purpose it is all one whether this point is conceded or not.

contradict itself and consequently could not subsist as a system of nature. Hence this maxim cannot possibly hold as a universal law of nature and is therefore entirely opposed to the supreme principle of all duty.

2. Another finds himself driven to borrowing money because of need. He well knows that he will not be able to pay it back; but he sees too that he will get no loan unless he gives a firm promise to pay it back within a fixed time. He is inclined to make such a promise; but he has still enough conscience to ask "Is it not unlawful and contrary to duty to get out of difficulties in this way?" Supposing, however, he did resolve to do so, the maxim of his action would run thus: "Whenever I believe myself short of money, I will borrow money and promise to pay it back, though I know that this will never be done." Now this principle of self-love or personal advantage is perhaps quite compatible with my own entire future welfare; only there remains the question "Is it right?" I therefore transform the demand of self-love into a universal law and frame my question thus: "How would things stand if my maxim became a universal law?" I then see straight away that this maxim can never rank as a universal law of nature and be self-consistent, but must necessarily contradict itself. For the universality of a law that every one believing himself to be in need can make any promise he pleases with the intention not to keep it would make promising, and the very purpose of promising, itself impossible, since no one would believe he was being promised anything, but would laugh at utterances of this kind as empty shams.

3. A third finds in himself a talent whose cultivation would make him a useful man for all sorts of purposes. But he sees himself in comfortable circumstances, and he prefers to give himself up to pleasure rather than to bother about increasing and improving his fortunate natural aptitudes. Yet he asks himself further "Does my maxim of neglecting my natural gifts, besides agreeing in itself with my tendency to indulgence, agree also with what is called duty?" He then sees that a system of nature could indeed always subsist under such a universal law, although (like the South Sea Islanders) every man should let his talents rust and should be bent on devoting his life solely to idleness, indulgence, procreation, and, in a word, to enjoyment. Only he cannot possibly *will* that this should become a universal law of nature or should be implanted in us as such a law by a natural instinct. For as a rational being he necessarily wills that all his powers should be developed, since they serve him, and are given him, for all sorts of possible ends.

4. Yet a *fourth* is himself flourishing, but he sees others who have to struggle with great hardships (and whom he could easily help); and he thinks "What does it matter to me? Let every one be as happy as Heaven wills or as he can make himself; I won't deprive him of anything; I won't even envy him; only I have no wish to contribute anything to his well-being or to his support in distress!" Now admittedly if such an attitude were a universal law of nature, mankind could get on perfectly well—better no doubt than if everybody prates about sympathy and goodwill, and even takes pains, on occasion, to practise them, but on the other hand cheats where he can, traffics in human rights, or violates them in other ways. But although it is possible that a universal law of nature could subsist in harmony with this maxim, yet it is impossible to *will* that such a principle should hold everywhere as a law of nature. For a will which decided in this way would be in conflict with itself, since many a situation might arise in which the man needed love and sympathy from others, and in which, by such a law of nature sprung from his own will, he would rob himself of all hope of the help he wants for himself. . . .

THE FORMULA OF THE END IN ITSELF

The will is conceived as a power of determining oneself to action *in accordance with the idea of certain laws*. And such a power can be found only in rational beings. Now what serves the will as a subjective ground of its self-determination is an *end;* and this, if it is given by reason alone, must be equally valid for all rational beings. What, on the other hand, contains merely the ground of the possibility of an action whose effect is an end is called a *means.* . . .

Now I say that man, and in general every rational being, *exists* as an end in himself, *not merely as a means* for arbitrary use by this or that will: he must in all his actions, whether they are directed to himself or to other rational beings, always be viewed *at the same time as an end*. All the objects of inclination have only a conditioned value; for if there were not these inclinations and the needs grounded on them, their object would be valueless. Inclinations themselves, as sources of needs, are so far from having an absolute value to make them desirable for their own sake that it must rather be the universal wish of every rational being to be wholly free from them. Thus the value of all objects that can *be produced* by our action is always conditioned. Beings whose existence depends, not on our will, but on nature, have none the less, if they are non-rational beings, only a relative value as means and are consequently called *things*. Rational beings, on the other hand, are called *persons* because their nature already marks them out as ends in themselves—that is, as something which ought not to be used merely as a means—and consequently imposes to that extent a limit on all arbitrary treatment of them (and is an object of reverence). Persons, therefore, are not merely subjective ends whose existence as an object of our actions has a value *for us:* they are *objective ends*—that is, things whose existence is in itself an end, and indeed an end such that in its place we can put no other end to which they should serve *simply* as means; for unless this is so, nothing at all of *absolute* value would be found anywhere. But if all value were conditioned—that is, contingent—then no supreme principle could be found for reason at all.

If then there is to be a supreme practical principle and—so far as the human will is concerned—a categorical imperative, it must be such that from the idea of something which is necessarily an end for every one because it is an *end in itself* it forms an *objective* principle of the will and consequently can serve as a practical law. The ground of this principle is: *Rational nature exists as an end in itself.* This is the way in which a man necessarily conceives his own existence: it is therefore so far a *subjective* principle of human actions. But it is also the way in which every other rational being conceives his existence on the same rational ground which is valid also for me; hence it is at the same time an *objective* principle, from which, as a supreme practical ground, it must be possible to derive all laws for the will. The practical imperative will therefore be as follows: *Act in such a way that you always treat humanity, whether in your own person or in the person of any other, never simply as a means, but always at the same time as an end....*

⚜ REVIEW QUESTIONS

1. Explain Kant's account of the good will.
2. Distinguish between hypothetical and categorical imperatives.
3. State the first formulation of the Categorical Imperative (using the notion of a universal law), and explain how Kant uses this rule to derive some specific duties toward self and others.
4. State the second version of the categorical imperative (using the language of means and end), and explain it.

⚜ DISCUSSION QUESTIONS

1. Are the two versions of the categorical imperative just different expressions of one basic rule, or are they two different rules? Defend your view.
2. Kant claims that an action that is not done from the motive of duty has no moral worth. Do you agree or not? If not, give some counterexamples.
3. Some commentators think that the categorical imperative (particularly the first formulation) can be used to justify nonmoral or immoral actions. Is this a good criticism?

Happiness and Virtue

ARISTOTLE

Aristotle (384–322 B.C.E.) made important contributions to all areas of philosophy, including the formulation of traditional logic. Along with his teacher Plato, he is regarded as one of the founders of Western philosophy.

Aristotle argues that all human beings seek happiness, and that happiness is not pleasure, honor, or wealth, but an activity of the soul in accordance with virtue. Virtue is of two kinds: moral and intellectual. Moral virtue comes from training and habit, and generally is a state of character that is a mean between the vices of excess and deficiency. For example, Aristotle portrays the virtue of courage as a mean between the extremes of rashness (an excess) and cowardice (a deficiency). Intellectual virtue produces the most perfect happiness and is found in the activity of reason or contemplation.

Our discussion will be adequate if it has as much clearness as the subject-matter admits of, for precision is not to be sought for alike in all discussions, any more than in all the products of the crafts. Now fine and just actions, which political science investigates, admit of much variety and fluctuation of opinion, so that they may be thought to exist only by convention, and not by nature. And goods also give rise to a similar fluctuation because they bring harm to many people; for before now men have been undone by reason of their wealth, and others by reason of their courage. We must be content, then, in speaking of such subjects and with such premisses to indicate the truth roughly and in outline, and in speaking about things which are only for the most part true and with premisses of the same kind to reach conclusions that are no better. In the same spirit, therefore, should each type of statement be received; for it is the mark of an educated man to look for precision in each class of things just so far as the nature of the subject admits; it is evidently equally foolish to accept probable reasoning from a mathematician and to demand from a rhetorician scientific proofs.

Now each man judges well the things he knows, and of these he is a good judge. And so the man who has been educated in a subject is a good judge of that subject, and the man who has received an all-round education is a good judge in general. Hence a young man is not a proper hearer of lectures on political science; for he is inexperienced in the actions that occur in life, but its discussions start from these and are about these; and, further, since he tends to follow his passions, his study will be vain and unprofitable, because the end aimed at is not knowledge but action. And it makes no difference whether he is young in years or youthful in character; the defect does not depend on time, but on his living, and pursuing each successive object, as passion directs. For to such persons, as to the incontinent, knowledge brings no profit; but to those who desire and act in accordance with a rational principle knowledge about such matters will be of great benefit.

These remarks about the student, the sort of treatment to be expected, and the purpose of the inquiry, may be taken as our preface.

Let us resume our inquiry and state, in view of the fact that all knowledge and every pursuit aims at some good, what it is that we say political science aims at and what is the highest of all goods achievable by action. Verbally there is very

Source: Extracts from "Ethica Nicomachea," Volume 9 *Ethics,* translated by W. D. Ross in *The Oxford Translation of Aristotle* (Oxford University Press, 1925).

general agreement; for both the general run of men and people of superior refinement say that it is happiness, and identify living well and doing well with being happy; but with regard to what happiness is they differ, and the many do not give the same account as the wise. For the former think it is some plain and obvious thing, like pleasure, wealth, or honour; they differ, however, from one another—and often even the same man identifies it with different things, with health when he is ill, with wealth when he is poor; but, conscious of their ignorance, they admire those who proclaim some great ideal that is above their comprehension. Now some thought that apart from these many goods there is another which is self-subsistent and causes the goodness of all these as well. To examine all the opinions that have been held were perhaps somewhat fruitless; enough to examine those that are most prevalent or that seem to be arguable. . . .

Let us, however, resume our discussion from the point at which we digressed. To judge from the lives that men lead, most men, and men of the most vulgar type, seem (not without some ground) to identify the good, or happiness, with pleasure; which is the reason why they love the life of enjoyment. For there are, we may say, three prominent types of life—that just mentioned, the political, and thirdly the contemplative life. Now the mass of mankind are evidently quite slavish in their tastes, preferring a life suitable to beasts, but they get some ground for their view from the fact that many of those in high places share the tastes of Sardanapallus. A consideration of the prominent types of life shows that people of superior refinement and of active disposition identify happiness with honour; for this is, roughly speaking, the end of the political life. But it seems too superficial to be what we are looking for, since it is thought to depend on those who bestow honour rather than on him who receives it, but the good we divine to be something proper to a man and not easily taken from him. Further, men seem to pursue honour in order that they may be assured of their goodness; at least it is by men of practical wisdom that they seek to be honoured, and among those who know them, and on the ground of their virtue; clearly, then,

according to them, at any rate, virtue is better. And perhaps one might even suppose this to be, rather than honour, the end of the political life. But even this appears somewhat incomplete; for possession of virtue seems actually compatible with being asleep, or with life-long inactivity, and, further, with the greatest sufferings and misfortunes; but a man who was living so no one would call happy, unless he were maintaining a thesis at all costs. But enough of this; for the subject has been sufficiently treated even in the current discussions. Third comes the contemplative life, which we shall consider later.

The life of money-making is one undertaken under compulsion, and wealth is evidently not the good we are seeking; for it is merely useful and for the sake of something else. And so one might rather take the aforenamed objects to be ends; for they are loved for themselves. But it is evident that not even these are ends; yet many arguments have been thrown away in support of them. . . .

Let us again return to the good we are seeking, and ask what it can be. It seems different in different actions and arts; it is different in medicine, in strategy, and in the other arts likewise. What then is the good of each? Surely that for whose sake everything else is done. In medicine this is health, in strategy victory, in architecture a house, in any other sphere something else, and in every action and pursuit the end; for it is for the sake of this that all men do whatever else they do. Therefore, if there is an end for all that we do, this will be the good achievable by action, and if there are more than one, these will be the goods achievable by action.

So the argument has by a different course reached the same point; but we must try to state this even more clearly. Since there are evidently more than one end, and we choose some of these (e.g. wealth, flutes, and in general instruments) for the sake of something else, clearly not all ends are final ends; but the chief good is evidently something final. Therefore, if there is only one final end, this will be what we are seeking, and if there are more than one, the most final of these will be what we are seeking. Now we call that which is in itself worthy of pursuit more final than that which is worthy of pursuit for the sake of something else, and that which is never desirable for the sake of something else more final than the things that are desirable both in themselves and for the sake of that other thing, and therefore we call final without qualification that which is always desirable in itself and never for the sake of something else.

Now such a thing happiness, above all else, is held to be; for this we choose always for itself and never for the sake of something else, but honour, pleasure, reason, and every virtue we choose indeed for themselves (for if nothing resulted from them we should still choose each of them), but we choose them also for the sake of happiness, judging that by means of them we shall be happy. Happiness, on the other hand, no one chooses for the sake of these, nor, in general, for anything other than itself. . . .

Presumably, however, to say that happiness is the chief good seems a platitude, and a clearer account of what it is is still desired. This might perhaps be given, if we could first ascertain the function of man. For just as for a fluteplayer, a sculptor, or any artist, and, in general, for all things that have a function or activity, the good and the 'well' is thought to reside in the function, so would it seem to be for man, if he has a function. Have the carpenter, then, and the tanner certain functions or activities, and has man none? Is he born without a function? Or as eye, hand, foot, and in general each of the parts evidently has a function, may one lay it down that man similarly has a function apart from all these? What then can this be? Life seems to be common even to plants, but we are seeking what is peculiar to man. Let us exclude, therefore, the life of nutrition and growth. Next there would be a life of perception, but *it* also seems to be common even to the horse, the ox, and every animal. There remains, then, an active life of the element that has a rational principle; of this, one part has such a principle in the sense of being obedient to one, the other in the sense of possessing one and exercising thought. And, as "life of the rational element" also has two meanings, we must state that life in the sense of activity is what we mean; for this seems to be the more proper sense of the

term. Now if the function of man is an activity of soul which follows or implies a rational principle, and if we say "a so-and-so" and "a good so-and-so" have a function which is the same in kind, e.g. a lyre-player and a good lyre-player, and so without qualification in all cases, eminence in respect of goodness being added to the name of the function (for the function of a lyre-player is to play the lyre, and that of a good lyre-player is to do so well): if this is the case, [and we state the function of man to be a certain kind of life, and this to be an activity or actions of the soul implying a rational principle, and the function of a good man to be the good and noble performance of these, and if any action is well performed when it is performed in accordance with the appropriate excellence: if this is the case,] human good turns out to be activity of soul in accordance with virtue, and if there are more than one virtue, in accordance with the best and most complete.

But we must add "in a complete life." For one swallow does not make a summer, nor does one day; and so too one day, or a short time, does not make a man blessed and happy. . . .

We must consider it, however, in the light not only of our conclusion and our premises, but also of what is commonly said about it; for with a true view all the data harmonize, but with a false one the facts soon clash. Now goods have been divided into three classes, and some are described as external, others as relating to soul or to body; we call those that relate to soul most properly and truly goods, and psychical actions and activities we class as relating to soul. Therefore our account must be sound, at least according to this view, which is an old one and agreed on by philosophers. It is correct also in that we identify the end with certain actions and activities; for thus it falls among goods of the soul and not among external goods. Another belief which harmonizes with our account is that the happy man lives well and does well; for we have practically defined happiness as a sort of good life and good action. The characteristics that are looked for in happiness seem also, all of them, to belong to what we have defined happiness as being. For some identify happiness with virtue, some with practical wisdom, others with a kind of philosophic wisdom, others with these, or one of these, accompanied by pleasure or not without pleasure; while others include also external prosperity. Now some of these views have been held by many men and men of old, others by a few eminent persons; and it is not probable that either of these should be entirely mistaken, but rather that they should be right in at least some one respect or even in most respects.

With those who identify happiness with virtue or some one virtue our account is in harmony; for to virtue belongs virtuous activity. But it makes, perhaps, no small difference whether we place the chief good in possession or in use, in state of mind or in activity. For the state of mind may exist without producing any good result, as in a man who is asleep or in some other way quite inactive, but the activity cannot; for one who has the activity will of necessity be acting, and acting well. And as in the Olympic Games it is not the most beautiful and the strongest that are crowned but those who compete (for it is some of these that are victorious), so those who act win, and rightly win, the noble and good things in life.

Their life is also in itself pleasant. For pleasure is a state of *soul*, and to each man that which he is said to be a lover of is pleasant; e.g. not only is a horse pleasant to the lover of horses, and a spectacle to the lover of sights, but also in the same way just acts are pleasant to the lover of justice and in general virtuous acts to the lover of virtue. Now for most men their pleasures are in conflict with one another because these are not by nature pleasant, but the lovers of what is noble find pleasant the things that are by nature pleasant; and virtuous actions are such, so that these are pleasant for such men as well as in their own nature. Their life, therefore, has no further need of pleasure as a sort of adventitious charm, but has its pleasure in itself. For, besides what we have said, the man who does not rejoice in noble actions is not even good; since no one would call a man just who did not enjoy acting justly, nor any man liberal who did not enjoy liberal actions; and similarly in all other cases. If this is so, virtuous actions must be in themselves pleasant. But they are also *good* and *noble*, and have each of these attributes in the highest degree, since the good man judges well about these attributes; his judgment is such

as we have described. Happiness then is the best, noblest, and most pleasant thing in the world. . . .

Yet evidently, as we said, it needs the external goods as well; for it is impossible, or not easy, to do noble acts without the proper equipment. In many actions we use friends and riches and political power as instruments; and there are some things the lack of which takes the lustre from happiness, as good birth, goodly children, beauty; for the man who is very ugly in appearance or illborn or solitary and childless is not very likely to be happy, and perhaps a man would be still less likely if he had thoroughly bad children or friends or had lost good children or friends by death. As we said, then, happiness seems to need this sort of prosperity in addition; for which reason some identify happiness with good fortune, though others identify it with virtue.

For this reason also the question is asked, whether happiness is to be acquired by learning or by habituation or some other sort of training, or comes in virtue of some divine providence or again by chance. Now if there is *any* gift of the gods to men, it is reasonable that happiness should be god-given, and most surely god-given of all human things inasmuch as it is the best. But this question would perhaps be more appropriate to another inquiry; happiness seems, however, even if it is not god-sent but comes as a result of virtue and some process of learning or training, to be among the most god-like things; for that which is the prize and end of virtue seems to be the best thing in the world, and something godlike and blessed.

It will also on this view be very generally shared; for all who are not maimed as regards their potentiality for virtue may win it by a certain kind of study and care. But if it is better to be happy thus than by chance, it is reasonable that the facts should be so, since everything that depends on the action of nature is by nature as good as it can be, and similarly everything that depends on art or any rational cause, and especially if it depends on the best of all causes. To entrust to chance what is greatest and most noble would be a very defective arrangement.

The answer to the question we are asking is plain also from the definition of happiness; for it has been said to be a virtuous activity of soul, of a certain kind. Of the remaining goods, some must necessarily pre-exist as conditions of happiness, and others are naturally co-operative and useful as instruments. And this will be found to agree with what we said at the outset; for we stated the end of political science to be the best end, and political science spends most of its pains on making the citizens to be of a certain character, viz. good and capable of noble acts.

It is natural, then, that we call neither ox nor horse nor any other of the animals happy; for none of them is capable of sharing in such activity. For this reason also a boy is not happy; for he is not yet capable of such acts, owing to his age; and boys who are called happy are being congratulated by reason of the hopes we have for them. For there is required, as we said, not only complete virtue but also a complete life, since many changes occur in life, and all manner of chances, and the most prosperous may fall into great misfortunes in old age, as is told of Priam in the Trojan Cycle; and one who has experienced such chances and has ended wretchedly no one calls happy. . . .

Since happiness is an activity of soul in accordance with perfect virtue, we must consider the nature of virtue; for perhaps we shall thus see better the nature of happiness. . . .

Virtue, then, being of two kinds, intellectual and moral, intellectual virtue in the main owes both its birth and its growth to teaching (for which reason it requires experience and time), while moral virtue comes about as a result of habit. . . . From this it is also plain that none of the moral virtues arises in us by nature; for nothing that exists by nature can form a habit contrary to its nature. For instance the stone which by nature moves downwards cannot be habituated to move upwards, not even if one tries to train it by throwing it up ten thousand times; nor can fire be habituated to move downwards, nor can anything else that by nature behaves in one way be trained to behave in another. Neither by nature, then, nor contrary to nature do the virtues arise in us; rather we are adapted by nature to receive them, and are made perfect by habit. . . .

We must, however, not only describe virtue as a state of character, but also say what sort of state it is. We may remark, then, that every virtue or excellence both brings into good condition the thing of which it is the excellence and makes the work of that thing be done well; e.g. the excellence of the eye makes both the eye and its work good; for it is by the excellence of the eye that we see well. Similarly the excellence of the horse makes a horse both good in itself and good at running and at carrying its rider and at awaiting the attack of the enemy. Therefore, if this is true in every case, the virtue of man also will be the state of character which makes a man good and which makes him do his own work well.

How this is to happen we have stated already, but it will be made plain also by the following consideration of the specific nature of virtue. In everything that is continuous and divisible it is possible to take more, less, or an equal amount, and that either in terms of the thing itself or relatively to us; and the equal is an intermediate between excess and defect. By the intermediate in the object I mean that which is equidistant from each of the extremes, which is one and the same for all men; by the intermediate relatively to us that which is neither too much nor too little—and this is not one, nor the same for all. For instance, if ten is many and two is few, six is the intermediate, taken in terms of the object; for it exceeds and is exceeded by an equal amount; this is intermediate according to arithmetical proportion. But the intermediate relatively to us is not to be taken so; if ten pounds are too much for a particular person to eat and two too little, it does not follow that the trainer will order six pounds; for this also is perhaps too much for the person who is to take it, or too little—too little for Milo, too much for the beginner in athletic exercises. The same is true of running and wrestling. Thus a master of any art avoids excess and defect, but seeks the intermediate and chooses this—the intermediate not in the object but relatively to us.

If it is thus, then, that every art does its work well—by looking to the intermediate and judging its works by this standard (so that we often say of good works of art that it is not possible either to take away or to add anything, implying that excess and defect destroy the goodness of the works of art, while the mean preserves it; and good artists, as we say, look to this in their work), and if, further, virtue is more exact and better than any art, as nature also is, then virtue must have the quality of aiming at the intermediate. I mean moral virtue; for it is this that is concerned with passions and actions, and in these there is excess, defect, and the intermediate. For instance, both fear and confidence and appetite and anger and pity and in general pleasure and pain may be felt both too much and too little, and in both cases not well; but to feel them at the right times, with reference to the right objects, towards the right people, with the right motive, and in the right way, is what is both intermediate and best, and this is characteristic of virtue. Similarly with regard to actions also there is excess, defect, and the intermediate. Now virtue is concerned with passions and actions, in which excess is a form of failure, and so is defect, while the intermediate is praised and is a form of success; and being praised and being successful are both characteristics of virtue. Therefore virtue is a kind of mean, since, as we have seen, it aims at what is intermediate.

Again, it is possible to fail in many ways (for evil belongs to the class of the unlimited, as the Pythagoreans conjectured, and good to that of the limited), while to succeed is possible only in one way (for which reason also one is easy and the other difficult—to miss the mark easy, to hit it difficult); for these reasons also, then, excess and defect are characteristic of vice, and the mean of virtue;

For men are good in but one way, but bad in many.

Virtue, then, is a state of character concerned with choice, lying in a mean, i.e. the mean relative to us, this being determined by a rational principle, and by that principle by which the man of practical wisdom would determine it. Now it is a mean between two vices, that which depends on excess and that which depends on defect; and again it is a mean because the vices respectively fall short of or exceed what is right in both passions and actions, while virtue both finds and chooses that which is intermediate. Hence in respect of its substance and the definition which states its essence virtue is a mean, with regard to what is best and right an extreme.

But not every action nor every passion admits of a mean; for some have names that already imply badness, e.g. spite, shamelessness, envy, and in the case of actions adultery, theft, murder; for all of these and suchlike things imply by their names that they are themselves bad, and not the excesses or deficiencies of them. It is not possible, then, ever to be right with regard to them; one must always be wrong. Nor does goodness or badness with regard to such things depend on committing adultery with the right woman, at the right time, and in the right way, but simply to do any of them is to go wrong. It would be equally absurd, then, to expect that in unjust, cowardly, and voluptuous action there should be a mean, an excess, and a deficiency; for at that rate there would be a mean of excess and of deficiency, an excess of excess, and deficiency of deficiency. But as there is no excess and deficiency of temperance and courage because what is intermediate is in a sense an extreme, so too of the actions we have mentioned there is no mean nor any excess and deficiency, but however they are done they are wrong; for in general there is neither a mean of excess and deficiency, nor excess and deficiency of a mean.

We must, however, not only make this general statement, but also apply it to the individual facts. For among statements about conduct those which are general apply more widely, but those which are particular are more genuine, since conduct has to do with individual cases, and our statements must harmonize with the facts in these cases. We may take these cases from our table. With regard to feelings of fear and confidence courage is the mean; of the people who exceed, he who exceeds in fearlessness has no name (many of the states have no name), while the man who exceeds in confidence is rash, and he who exceeds in fear and falls short in confidence is a coward. With regard to pleasures and pains—not all of them, and not so much with regard to the pains—the mean is temperance, the excess self-indulgence. Persons deficient with regard to the pleasures are not often found; hence such persons also have received no name. But let us call them "insensible."

With regard to giving and taking of money the mean is liberality, the excess and the defect prodigality and meanness. In these actions people exceed and fall short in contrary ways; the prodigal exceeds in spending and falls short in taking, while the mean man exceeds in taking and falls short in spending. (At present we are giving a mere outline or summary, and are satisfied with this; later these states will be more exactly determined.) With regard to money there are also other dispositions—a mean, magnificence (for the magnificent man differs from the liberal man; the former deals with large sums, the latter with small ones), and excess, tastelessness, and vulgarity, and a deficiency, niggardliness; these differ from the states opposed to liberality. . . .

That moral virtue is a mean, then, and in what sense it is so, and that it is a mean between two vices, the one involving excess, the other deficiency, and that it is such because its character is to aim at what is intermediate in passions and in actions, has been sufficiently stated. Hence also it is no easy task to be good. For in everything it is no easy task to find the middle, e.g. to find the middle of a circle is not for every one but for him who knows; so, too, any one can get angry—that is easy—or give or spend money; but to do this to the right person, to the right extent, at the right time, with the right motive, and in the right way, *that* is not for every one, nor is it easy; wherefore goodness is both rare and laudable and noble. . . .

If happiness is activity in accordance with virtue, it is reasonable that it should be in accordance with the highest virtue; and this will be that of the best thing in us. Whether it be reason or something else that is this element which is thought to be our natural ruler and guide and to take thought of things noble and divine, whether it be itself also divine or only the most divine element in us, the activity of this in accordance with its proper virtue will be perfect happiness. That this activity is contemplative we have already said.

Now this would seem to be in agreement both with what we said before and with the truth. For, firstly, this activity is the best (since not only is reason the best thing in us, but the objects of reason are the best of knowable objects); and, secondly, it is the most continuous, since we can contemplate truth more continuously than we can do anything. And we think happiness

has pleasure mingled with it, but the activity of philosophic wisdom is admittedly the pleasantest of virtuous activities; at all events the pursuit of it is thought to offer pleasures marvellous for their purity and their enduringness, and it is to be expected that those who know will pass their time more pleasantly than those who inquire. And the self-sufficiency that is spoken of must belong most to the contemplative activity. For while a philosopher, as well as a just man or one possessing any other virtue, needs the necessaries of life, when they are sufficiently equipped with things of that sort the just man needs people towards whom and with whom he shall act justly, and the temperate man, the brave man, and each of the others is in the same case, but the philosopher, even when by himself, can contemplate truth, and the better the wiser he is; he can perhaps do so better if he has fellow-workers, but still he is the most self-sufficient. And this activity alone would seem to be loved for its own sake; for nothing arises from it apart from the contemplating, while from practical activities we gain more or less apart from the action. And happiness is thought to depend on leisure; for we are busy that we may have leisure, and make war that we may live in peace. Now the activity of the practical virtues is exhibited in political or military affairs, but the actions concerned with these seem to be unleisurely. Warlike actions are completely so (for no one chooses to be at war, or provokes war, for the sake of being at war; any one would seem absolutely murderous if he were to make enemies of his friends in order to bring about battle and slaughter); but the action of the statesman is also unleisurely, and—apart from the political action itself—aims at despotic power and honours, or at all events happiness, for him and his fellow citizens—a happiness different from political action, and evidently sought as being different. So if among virtuous actions political and military actions are distinguished by nobility and greatness, and these are unleisurely and aim at an end and are not desirable for their own sake, but the activity of reason, which is contemplative, seems both to be superior in serious worth and to aim at no end beyond itself, and to have its pleasure proper to itself (and this augments the activity), and the self-sufficiency, leisureliness, unweariedness (so far as this is possible for man), and all the other attributes ascribed to the supremely happy man are evidently those connected with this activity, it follows that this will be the complete happiness of man, if it be allowed a complete term of life (for none of the attributes of happiness is *in*complete).

But such a life would be too high for man; for it is not in so far as he is man that he will live so, but in so far as something divine is present in him; and by so much as this is superior to our composite nature is its activity superior to that which is the exercise of the other kind of virtue. If reason is divine, then in comparison with man, the life according to it is divine in comparison with human life. But we must not follow those who advise us, being men, to think of human things, and, being mortal, of mortal things, but must, so far as we can, make ourselves immortal, and strain every nerve to live in accordance with the best thing in us; for even if it be small in bulk, much more does it in power and worth surpass everything. This would seem, too, to be each man himself, since it is the authoritative and better part of him. It would be strange, then, if he were to choose not the life of his self but that of something else. And what we said before will apply now; that which is proper to each thing is by nature best and most pleasant for each thing; for man, therefore, the life according to reason is best and pleasantest, since reason more than anything else is man. This life therefore is also the happiest.

But in a secondary degree the life in accordance with the other kind of virtue is happy; for the activities in accordance with this befit our human estate. Just and brave acts, and other virtuous acts, we do in relation to each other, observing our respective duties with regard to contracts and services and all manner of actions and with regard to passions; and all of these seem to be typically human. Some of them seem even to arise from the body, and virtue of character to be in many ways bound up with the passions. Practical wisdom, too, is linked to virtue of character, and this to practical wisdom, since the principles of practical wisdom are in accordance with the moral virtues and rightness in morals is in accordance

with practical wisdom. Being connected with passions also, the moral virtues must belong our composite nature; and the virtues of our com posite nature are human; so, therefore, are the life and the happiness which correspond to these. The excellence of the reason is a thing apart; we must be content to say this much about it, for to describe it precisely is a task greater than our purpose requires. It would seem, however, also to need external equipment but little, or less than moral virtue does. Grant that both need the necessaries, and do so equally, even if the statesman's work is the more concerned with the body and things of that sort; for there will be little difference there; but in what they need for the exercise of their activities there will be much difference. The liberal man will need money for the doing of his liberal deeds, and the just man too will need it for the returning of services (for wishes are hard to discern, and even people who are not just pretend to wish to act justly); and the brave man will need power if he is to accomplish any of the acts that correspond to his virtue, and the temperate man will need opportunity; for how else is either he or any of the others to be recognized? It is debated, too, whether the will or the deed is more essential to virtue, which is assumed to involve both; it is surely clear that its perfection involves both; but for deeds many things are needed, and more, the greater and nobler the deeds are. But the man who is contemplating the truth needs no such thing, at least with a view to the exercise of his activity; indeed they are, one may say, even hindrances, at all events to his contemplation; but in so far as he is a man and lives with a number of people, he chooses to do virtuous acts; he will therefore need such aids to living a human life.

But that perfect happiness is a contemplative activity will appear from the following consideration as well. We assume the gods to be above all other beings blessed and happy; but what sort of actions must we assign to them? Acts of justice? Will not the gods seem absurd if they make contracts and return deposits, and so on? Acts of a brave man, then, confronting dangers and running risks because it is noble to do so? Or liberal acts? To whom will they give? It will be strange if they are really to have money or anything of

vhat would their temperate acts
...ise tasteless, since they have no
...e were to run through them
...ces of action would be found
...nworthy of gods. Still, every one sup-
...s that they *live* and therefore that they are
active; we cannot suppose them to sleep like
Endymion. Now if you take away from a living
being action, and still more production, what is
left but contemplation? Therefore the activity of
God, which surpasses all others in blessedness,
must be contemplative; and of human activities,
therefore, that which is most akin to this must be
most of the nature of happiness.

This is indicated, too, by the fact that the
other animals have no share in happiness, being
completely deprived of such activity. For while the
whole life of the gods is blessed, and that of men too
in so far as some likeness of such activity belongs
to them, none of the other animals is happy, since
they in no way share in contemplation. Happiness
extends, then, just so far as contemplation does,
and those to whom contemplation more fully
belongs are more truly happy, not as a mere concomitant but in virtue of the contemplation; for
this is in itself precious. Happiness, therefore,
must be some form of contemplation.

But, being a man, one will also need external
prosperity; for our nature is not self-sufficient for
the purpose of contemplation, but our body also
must be healthy and must have food and other
attention. Still, we must not think that the man
who is to be happy will need many things or great
things, merely because he cannot be supremely
happy without external goods; for self-sufficiency
and action do not involve excess, and we can do
noble acts without ruling earth and sea; for even
with moderate advantages one can act virtuously
(this is manifest enough; for private persons are
thought to do worthy acts no less than despots—
indeed even more); and it is enough that we
should have so much as that; for the life of the
man who is active in accordance with virtue will
be happy. . . .

REVIEW QUESTIONS

1. What is happiness, according to Aristotle? How is
   it related to virtue? How is it related to pleasure?
2. How does Aristotle explain moral virtue? Give
   some examples.
3. Is it possible for everyone in our society to be
   happy, as Aristotle explains it? If not, who cannot
   be happy?

DISCUSSION QUESTIONS

1. Aristotle characterizes a life of pleasure as suitable
   for beasts. But what, if anything, is wrong with a
   life of pleasure?
2. Aristotle claims that the philosopher will be
   happier than anyone else. Why is this? Do you
   agree or not?

A Theory of Justice

JOHN RAWLS

John Rawls (1921–2002) was the James Bryant Conant University Professor Emeritus at Harvard University. He was the author of *Political Liberalism* (1993), *Collected Papers* (1999), *Lectures on the History of Moral Philosophy* (2000), *Justice as Fairness: A Restatement* (2001), and *The Law of Peoples* (2001). Our reading is taken from his well-known book, *A Theory of Justice* (1971).

Rawls's theory states that there are two principles of justice: The first principle involves equal basic liberties, and the second principle concerns the arrangement of social and economic inequalities. According to Rawls's theory, these are the principles that free and rational persons would accept in a hypothetical original position where there is a veil of ignorance hiding from the contractors all the particular facts about themselves.

THE MAIN IDEA OF THE THEORY OF JUSTICE

My aim is to present a conception of justice which generalizes and carries to a higher level of abstraction the familiar theory of the social contract as found, say, in Locke, Rousseau, and Kant.[1] In order to do this we are not to think of the original contract as one to enter a particular society or to set up a particular form of government. Rather, the guiding idea is that the principles of justice for the basic structure of society are the object of the original agreement. They are the principles that free and rational persons concerned to further their own interests would accept in an initial position of equality as defining the fundamental terms of their association. These principles are to regulate all further agreements; they specify the kinds of social cooperation that can be entered into and the forms of government that can be established. This way of regarding the principles of justice I shall call justice as fairness.

Thus we are to imagine that those who engage in social cooperation choose together, in one joint act, the principles which are to assign basic rights and duties and to determine the division of social benefits. Men are to decide in advance how they are to regulate their claims against one another and what is to be the foundation charter of their society. Just as each person must decide by rational reflection what constitutes his good, that is, the system of ends which it is rational for him to pursue, so a group of persons must decide once and for all what is to count among them as just and unjust. The choice which rational men would make in this hypothetical situation of equal liberty, assuming for the present that this choice problem has a solution, determines the principles of justice.

In justice as fairness the original position of equality corresponds to the state of nature in the traditional theory of the social contract. This

---

[1]As the text suggests, I shall regard Locke's *Second Treatise of Government*, Rousseau's *The Social Contract*, and Kant's ethical works beginning with *The Foundations of the Metaphysics of Morals* as definitive of the contract tradition. For all of its greatness, Hobbes's *Leviathan* raises special problems. A general historical survey is provided by J. W. Gough, *The Social Contract*, 2nd ed. (Oxford, The Clarendon Press, 1957), and Otto Gierke, *Natural Law and the Theory of Society*, trans. with an introduction by Ernest Barker (Cambridge, The University Press, 1934). A presentation of the contract view as primarily an ethical theory is to be found in G. R. Grice, *The Grounds of Moral Judgment* (Cambridge, The University Press, 1967).

Source: Reprinted by permission of the publisher from *A Theory of Justice* by John Rawls, pp. 11–16, 60–65, Cambridge, Mass.: The Belknap Press of Harvard University Press. Copyright © 1971, 1999, by the President and Fellows of Harvard College. Footnotes renumbered.

original position is not, of course, thought of as an actual historical state of affairs, much less as a primitive condition of culture. It is understood as a purely hypothetical situation characterized so as to lead to a certain conception of justice.[2] Among the essential features of this situation is that no one knows his place in society, his class position or social status, nor does any one know his fortune in the distribution of natural assets and abilities, his intelligence, strength, and the like. I shall even assume that the parties do not know their conceptions of the good or their special psychological propensities. The principles of justice are chosen behind a veil of ignorance. This ensures that no one is advantaged or disadvantaged in the choice of principles by the outcome of natural chance or the contingency of social circumstances. Since all are similarly situated and no one is able to design principles to favor his particular condition, the principles of justice are the result of a fair agreement or bargain. For given the circumstances of the original position, the symmetry of everyone's relations to each other, this initial situation is fair between individuals as moral persons, that is, as rational beings with their own ends and capable, I shall assume, of a sense of justice. The original position is, one might say, the appropriate initial status quo, and thus the fundamental agreements reached in it are fair. This explains the propriety of the name "justice as fairness": it conveys the idea that the principles of justice are agreed to in an initial situation that is fair. The name does not mean that the concepts of justice and fairness are the same, any more than the phrase "poetry as metaphor" means that the concepts of poetry and metaphor are the same.

---

[2]Kant is clear that the original agreement is hypothetical. See *The Metaphysics of Morals*, pt. I (*Rechtslehre*), especially § 47, 52; and pt. II of the essay "Concerning the Common Saying: This May Be True in Theory but It Does Not Apply in Practice," in *Kant's Political Writings*, ed. Hans Reiss and trans. by H. B. Nisbet (Cambridge, The University Press, 1970), pp. 73–87. See Georges Vlachos, *La Pensée politique de Kant* (Paris, Presses Universitaires de France, 1962), pp. 326–335; and J. G. Murphy, *Kant: The Philosophy of Right* (London, Macmillan,1970), pp. 109–112, 133–136, for a further discussion.

Justice as fairness begins, as I have said, with one of the most general of all choices which persons might make together, namely, with the choice of the first principles of a conception of justice which is to regulate all subsequent criticism and reform of institutions. Then, having chosen a conception of justice, we can suppose that they are to choose a constitution and a legislature to enact laws, and so on, all in accordance with the principles of justice initially agreed upon. Our social situation is just if it is such that by this sequence of hypothetical agreements we would have contracted into the general system of rules which defines it. Moreover, assuming that the original position does determine a set of principles (that is, that a particular conception of justice would be chosen), it will then be true that whenever social institutions satisfy these principles those engaged in them can say to one another that they are cooperating on terms to which they would agree if they were free and equal persons whose relations with respect to one another were fair. They could all view their arrangements as meeting the stipulations which they would acknowledge in an initial situation that embodies widely accepted and reasonable constraints on the choice of principles. The general recognition of this fact would provide the basis for a public acceptance of the corresponding principles of justice. No society can, of course, be a scheme of cooperation which men enter voluntarily in a literal sense; each person finds himself placed at birth in some particular position in some particular society, and the nature of this position materially affects his life prospects. Yet a society satisfying the principles of justice as fairness comes as close as a society can to being a voluntary scheme, for it meets the principles which free and equal persons would assent to under circumstances that are fair. In this sense its members are autonomous and the obligations they recognize self-imposed.

One feature of justice as fairness is to think of the parties in the initial situation as rational and mutually disinterested. This does not mean that the parties are egoists, that is, individuals with only certain kinds of interests, say in wealth, prestige, and domination. But they are conceived as not taking an interest in one another's interests.

They are to presume that even their spiritual aims may be opposed, in the way that the aims of those of different religions may be opposed. Moreover, the concept of rationality must be interpreted as far as possible in the narrow sense, standard in economic theory, of taking the most effective means to given ends. I shall modify this concept to some extent . . . but one must try to avoid introducing into it any controversial ethical elements. The initial situation must be characterized by stipulations that are widely accepted.

In working out the conception of justice as fairness one main task clearly is to determine which principles of justice would be chosen in the original position. To do this we must describe this situation in some detail and formulate with care the problem of choice which it presents. . . . It may be observed, however, that once the principles of justice are thought of as arising from an original agreement in a situation of equality, it is an open question whether the principle of utility would be acknowledged. Offhand it hardly seems likely that persons who view themselves as equals, entitled to press their claims upon one another, would agree to a principle which may require lesser life prospects for some simply for the sake of a greater sum of advantages enjoyed by others. Since each desires to protect his interests, his capacity to advance his conception of the good, no one has a reason to acquiesce in an enduring loss for himself in order to bring about a greater net balance of satisfaction. In the absence of strong and lasting benevolent impulses, a rational man would not accept a basic structure merely because it maximized the algebraic sum of advantages irrespective of its permanent effects on his own basic rights and interests. Thus it seems that the principle of utility is incompatible with the conception of social cooperation among equals for mutual advantage. It appears to be inconsistent with the idea of reciprocity implicit in the notion of a well-ordered society. Or, at any rate, so I shall argue.

I shall maintain instead that the persons in the initial situation would choose two rather different principles: the first requires equality in the assignment of basic rights and duties, while the second holds that social and economic inequalities, for example inequalities of wealth and authority, are just only if they result in compensating benefits for everyone, and in particular for the least advantaged members of society. These principles rule out justifying institutions on the grounds that the hardships of some are offset by a greater good in the aggregate. It may be expedient but it is not just that some should have less in order that others may prosper. But there is no injustice in the greater benefits earned by a few provided that the situation of persons not so fortunate is thereby improved. The intuitive idea is that since everyone's well-being depends upon a scheme of cooperation without which no one could have a satisfactory life, the division of advantages should be such as to draw forth the willing cooperation of everyone taking part in it, including those less well situated. Yet this can be expected only if reasonable terms are proposed. The two principles mentioned seem to be a fair agreement on the basis of which those better endowed, or more fortunate in their social position, neither of which we can be said to deserve, could expect the willing cooperation of others when some workable scheme is a necessary condition of the welfare of all.[3] Once we decide to look for a conception of justice that nullifies the accidents of natural endowment and the contingencies of social circumstance as counters in quest for political and economic advantage, we are led to these principles. They express the result of leaving aside those aspects of the social world that seem arbitrary from a moral point of view.

The problem of the choice of principles, however, is extremely difficult. I do not expect the answer I shall suggest to be convincing to everyone. It is, therefore, worth noting from the outset that justice as fairness, like other contract views, consists of two parts: (1) an interpretation of the initial situation and of the problem of choice posed there, and (2) a set of principles which, it is argued, would be agreed to. One may accept the first part of the theory (or some variant thereof), but not the

---

[3]For the formulation of this intuitive idea I am indebted to Allan Gibbard.

other, and conversely. The concept of the initial contractual situation may seem reasonable although the particular principles proposed are rejected. To be sure, I want to maintain that the most appropriate conception of this situation does lead to principles of justice contrary to utilitarianism and perfectionism, and therefore that the contract doctrine provides an alternative to these views. . . .

A final remark. Justice as fairness is not a complete contract theory. For it is clear that the contract idea can be extended to the choice of more or less an entire ethical system, that is, to a system including principles for all the virtues and not only for justice. Now for the most part I shall consider only principles of justice and others closely related to them; I make no attempt to discuss the virtues in a systematic way. Obviously if justice as fairness succeeds reasonably well, a next step would be to study the more general view suggested by the name "rightness as fairness." But even this wider theory fails to embrace all moral relationships, since it would seem to include only our relations with other persons and to leave out of account how we are to conduct ourselves toward animals and the rest of nature. I do not contend that the contract notion offers a way to approach these questions which are certainly of the first importance; and I shall have to put them aside. We must recognize the limited scope of justice as fairness and of the general type of view that it exemplifies. How far its conclusions must be revised once these other matters are understood cannot be decided in advance. . . .

TWO PRINCIPLES OF JUSTICE

I shall now state in a provisional form the two principles of justice that I believe would be chosen in the original position. In this section I wish to make only the most general comments, and therefore the first formulation of these principles is tentative. As we go on I shall run through several formulations and approximate step by step the final statement to be given much later. I believe that doing this allows the exposition to proceed in a natural way.

The first statement of the two principles reads as follows.

> First: Each person is to have an equal right to the most extensive basic liberty compatible with a similar liberty for others.
>
> Second: Social and economic inequalities are to be arranged so that they are both (a) reasonably expected to be to everyone's advantage, and (b) attached to positions and offices open to all. . . .

By way of general comment, these principles primarily apply, as I have said, to the basic structure of society. They are to govern the assignment of rights and duties and to regulate the distribution of social and economic advantages. As their formulation suggests, these principles presuppose that the social structure can be divided into two more or less distinct parts, the first principle applying to the one, the second to the other. They distinguish between those aspects of the social system that define and secure the equal liberties of citizenship and those that specify and establish social and economic inequalities. The basic liberties of citizens are, roughly speaking, political liberty (the right to vote and to be eligible for public office) together with freedom of speech and assembly; liberty of conscience and freedom of thought; freedom of the person along with the right to hold (personal) property; and freedom from arbitrary arrest and seizure as defined by the concept of the rule of law. These liberties are all required to be equal by the first principle, since citizens of a just society are to have the same basic rights.

The second principle applies, in the first approximation, to the distribution of income and wealth and to the design of organizations that make use of differences in authority and responsibility, or chains of command. While the distribution of wealth and income need not be equal, it must be to everyone's advantage, and at the same time, positions of authority and offices of command must be accessible to all. One applies the second principle by holding positions open, and then, subject to this constraint, arranges social and economic inequalities so that everyone benefits.

These principles are to be arranged in a serial order with the first principle prior to the second. This ordering means that a departure from the institutions of equal liberty required by the first principle cannot be justified by, or compensated for, by greater social and economic advantages. The distribution of wealth and income, and the hierarchies of authority, must be consistent with both the liberties of equal citizenship and equality of opportunity.

It is clear that these principles are rather specific in their content, and their acceptance rests on certain assumptions that I must eventually try to explain and justify. A theory of justice depends upon a theory of society in ways that will become evident as we proceed. For the present, it should be observed that the two principles (and this holds for all formulations) are a special case of a more general conception of justice that can be expressed as follows.

> All social values—liberty and opportunity, income and wealth, and the bases of self-respect—are to be distributed equally unless an unequal distribution of any, or all, of these values is to everyone's advantage.

Injustice, then, is simply inequalities that are not to the benefit of all. Of course, this conception is extremely vague and requires interpretation.

As a first step, suppose that the basic structure of society distributes certain primary goods, that is, things that every rational man is presumed to want. These goods normally have a use whatever a person's rational plan of life. For simplicity, assume that the chief primary goods at the disposition of society are rights and liberties, powers and opportunities, income and wealth. . . . These are the social primary goods. Other primary goods such as health and vigor, intelligence and imagination, are natural goods; although their possession is influenced by the basic structure, they are not so directly under its control. Imagine, then, a hypothetical initial arrangement in which all the social primary goods are equally distributed: everyone has similar rights and duties, and income and wealth are evenly shared. This state of affairs provides a benchmark for judging improvements. If certain inequalities of wealth and organizational

powers would make everyone better off than in this hypothetical starting situation, then they accord with the general conception.

Now it is possible, at least theoretically, that by giving up some of their fundamental liberties men are sufficiently compensated by the resulting social and economic gains. The general conception of justice imposes no restrictions on what sort of inequalities are permissible; it only requires that everyone's position be improved. We need not suppose anything so drastic as consenting to a condition of slavery. Imagine instead that men forego certain political rights when the economic returns are significant and their capacity to influence the course of policy by the exercise of these rights would be marginal in any case. It is this kind of exchange which the two principles as stated rule out; being arranged in serial order they do not permit exchanges between basic liberties and economic and social gains. The serial ordering of principles expresses an underlying preference among primary social goods. When this preference is rational so likewise is the choice of these principles in this order.

In developing justice as fairness I shall, for the most part, leave aside the general conception of justice and examine instead the special case of the two principles in serial order. The advantage of this procedure is that from the first the matter of priorities is recognized and an effort made to find principles to deal with it. One is led to attend throughout to the conditions under which the acknowledgment of the absolute weight of liberty with respect to social and economic advantages, as defined by the lexical order of the two principles, would be reasonable. Offhand, this ranking appears extreme and too special a case to be of much interest; but there is more justification for it than would appear at first sight. Or at any rate, so I shall maintain. . . . Furthermore, the distinction between fundamental rights and liberties and economic and social benefits marks a difference among primary social goods that one should try to exploit. It suggests an important division in the social system. Of course, the distinctions drawn and the ordering proposed are bound to be at best only approximations. There are surely circumstances in which they fail. But it is essential to depict clearly the main lines of a reasonable conception of justice; and under many conditions anyway, the two principles in serial order may serve well enough. When necessary we can fall back on the more general conception.

The fact that the two principles apply to institutions has certain consequences. Several points illustrate this. First of all, the rights and liberties referred to by these principles are those which are defined by the public rules of the basic structure. Whether men are free is determined by the rights and duties established by the major institutions of society. Liberty is a certain pattern of social forms. The first principle simply requires that certain sorts of rules, those defining basic liberties, apply to everyone equally and that they allow the most extensive liberty compatible with a like liberty for all. The only reason for circumscribing the rights defining liberty and making men's freedom less extensive than it might otherwise be is that these equal rights as institutionally defined would interfere with one another.

Another thing to bear in mind is that when principles mention persons, or require that everyone gain from an inequality, the reference is to representative persons holding the various social positions, or offices, or whatever, established by the basic structure. Thus in applying the second principle I assume that it is possible to assign an expectation of well-being to representative individuals holding these positions. This expectation indicates their life prospects as viewed from their social station. In general, the expectations of representative persons depend upon the distribution of rights and duties throughout the basic structure. When this changes, expectations change. I assume, then, that expectations are connected: by raising the prospects of the representative man in one position we presumably increase or decrease the prospects of representative men in other positions. Since it applies to institutional forms, the second principle (or rather the first part

of it) refers to the expectations of representative individuals. As I shall discuss below, neither principle applies to distributions of particular goods to particular individuals who may be identified by their proper names. The situation where someone is considering how to allocate certain commodities to needy persons who are known to him is not within the scope of the principles. They are meant to regulate basic institutional arrangements. We must not assume that there is much similarity from the standpoint of justice between an administrative allotment of goods to specific persons and the appropriate design of society. Our common sense institutions for the former may be a poor guide to the latter.

Now the second principle insists that each person benefit from permissible inequalities in the basic structure. This means that it must be reasonable for each relevant representative man defined by this structure, when he views it as a going concern, to prefer his prospects with the inequality to his prospects without it. One is not allowed to justify differences in income or organizational powers on the ground that the disadvantages of those in one position are outweighed by the greater advantages of those in another. Much less can infringements of liberty be counterbalanced in this way. Applied to the basic structure, the principle of utility would have us maximize the sum of expectations of representative men (weighed by the number of persons they represent, on the classical view); and this would permit us to compensate for the losses of some by the gains of others. Instead, the two principles require that everyone benefit from economic and social inequalities. It is obvious, however, that there are indefinitely many ways in which all may be advantaged when the initial arrangement of equality is taken as a benchmark. How then are we to choose among these possibilities? The principles must be specified so that they yield a determinate conclusion. I now turn to this problem. . . .

⚜ REVIEW QUESTIONS

1. Carefully explain Rawls's conception of the original position.
2. State and explain Rawls's first principle of justice.

3. State and explain the second principle. Which principle has priority such that it cannot be sacrificed?

☙ DISCUSSION QUESTIONS

1. According to the first principle, each person has an equal right to the most extensive basic liberty as long as this does not interfere with a similar liberty for others. What does this allow people to do? Does it mean, for example, that people have a right to engage in homosexual activities as long as they don't interfere with others? Can people produce and view pornography if it does not restrict anyone's freedom? Are people allowed to take drugs in the privacy of their homes?

2. Is it po
   original
   ent from
   wouldn't
   wealth an
   bution? T.
   ism rather
   rational as

What Is Feminist Ethic

HILDE LINDEMANN

Hilde Lindemann is professor of philosophy at Michigan State University. She is the author of *An Invitation to Feminist Ethics* (2005) and, as Hilde Lindemann Nelson, *Damaged Identities, Narrative Repair* (2001). With James Lindemann Nelson, she wrote *Alzheimer's: Answers to Hard Questions for Families* (1996) and *The Patient in the Family* (1995). She is the editor of *Feminism and Families* (1997) and *Stories and Their Limits: Narrative Approaches to Bioethics* (1997). Most recently, she is the editor (with Marian Verkerk and Margaret Urban Walker) of *Naturalized Bioethics* (2008).

Lindemann begins by explaining feminism. In her view it is a social and political movement that is about the power men have over women in our society, and not about equality with men, the nature of women, or the difference between men and women. Various names are given to men's power over women: male dominance, patriarchy, the subjugation of women, and the oppression of women. Feminist ethics describes how this power works, criticizes it, and corrects it. Feminist normative theory analyzes actual social practices and determines if they are morally right or wrong. Feminist practical ethics focuses on specific topics such as marriage and employment.

WHAT IS FEMINISM?

What, then, is feminism? As a social and political movement with a long, intermittent history, feminism has repeatedly come into public awareness, generated change, and then disappeared again. As an eclectic body of theory, feminism entered colleges and universities in the early 1970s as a part of the women's studies movement, contributing to scholarship in every academic discipline, though probably most heavily in the arts, social sciences, literature, and the humanities in general. Feminist ethics is a part of the body of theory that is being developed primarily in colleges and universities.

Many people in the United States think of feminism as a movement that aims to make women the social equals of men, and this impression has been reinforced by references to feminism and feminists in the newspapers, on television, and in the movies. But bell hooks has pointed out in *Feminist Theory from Margin to Center* (1984, 18–19) that this way of defining feminism raises some serious problems. Which men do women want to be equal to? Women who are socially well off wouldn't get much advantage from being

...o are poor and lower ...ey aren't white. Hooks's ...re no women and men in the ...re poor, black, young, Latino/a, ...-bodied, upper class, down on their ...ve American, straight, and all the rest ...When a woman doesn't think about this, ... probably because she doesn't have to. And that's usually a sign that her own social position is privileged. In fact, privilege often means that there's something uncomfortable going on that others have to pay attention to but you don't. So, when hooks asks which men women want to be equal to, she's reminding us that there's an unconscious presumption of privilege built right in to this sort of demand for equality.

There's a second problem with the equality definition. Even if we could figure out which men are the ones to whom women should be equal, that way of putting it suggests that the point of feminism is somehow to get women to measure up to what (at least some) men already are. Men remain the point of reference; theirs are the lives that women would naturally want. If the first problem with the equality definition is "Equal to *which* men?" the second problem could be put as "Why equal to *any* men?" Reforming a system in which men are the point of reference by allowing women to perform as their equals "forces women to focus on men and address men's conceptions of women rather than creating and developing women's values about themselves," as Sarah Lucia Hoagland puts it in *Lesbian Ethics* (1988, 57). For that reason, Hoagland and some other feminists believe that feminism is first and foremost about women.

But characterizing feminism as about women has its problems too. What, after all, is a woman? In her 1949 book, *The Second Sex*, the French feminist philosopher Simone de Beauvoir famously observed, "One is not born, but becomes a woman. No biological, psychological, or economic fate determines the figure that the human female presents in society: it is civilization as a whole that produces this creature, intermediate between male and eunuch, which is described as feminine" (Beauvoir 1949, 301). Her point is that while plenty of human beings are born female,

'woman' is not a natural fact about them—it's a social invention. According to that invention, which is widespread in "civilization as a whole," man represents the positive, typical human being, while woman represents only the negative, the not-man. She is the Other against whom man defines himself—he is all the things that she is not. And she exists only in relation to him. In a later essay called "One Is Not Born a Woman," the lesbian author and theorist Monique Wittig (1981, 49) adds that because women belong to men sexually as well as in every other way, women are necessarily heterosexual. For that reason, she argued, lesbians aren't women.

But, you are probably thinking, everybody knows what a woman is, and lesbians certainly *are* women. And you're right. These French feminists aren't denying that there's a perfectly ordinary use of the word *woman* by which it means exactly what you think it means. But they're explaining what this comes down to, if you look at it from a particular point of view. Their answer to the question "What is a woman?" is that women are different from men. But they don't mean this as a trite observation. They're saying that 'woman' refers to *nothing but* difference from men, so that apart from men, women aren't anything. 'Man' is the positive term, 'woman' is the negative one, just like 'light' is the positive term and 'dark' is nothing but the absence of light.

A later generation of feminists have agreed with Beauvoir and Wittig that women are different from men, but rather than seeing that difference as simply negative, they put it in positive terms, affirming feminine qualities as a source of personal strength and pride. For example, the philosopher Virginia Held thinks that women's moral experience as mothers, attentively nurturing their children, may serve as a better model for social relations than the contract model that the free market provides. The poet Adrienne Rich celebrated women's passionate nature (as opposed, in stereotype, to the rational nature of men), regarding the emotions as morally valuable rather than as signs of weakness.

But defining feminism as about the positive differences between men and women creates yet another set of problems. In her 1987 *Feminism*

Unmodified, the feminist legal theorist Catharine A. MacKinnon points out that this kind of difference, as such, is a symmetrical relationship: If I am different from you, then you are different from me in exactly the same respects and to exactly the same degree. "Men's differences from women are equal to women's differences from men," she writes. "There is an *equality* there. Yet the sexes are not socially equal" (MacKinnon 1987, 37). No amount of attention to the differences between men and women explains why men, as a group, are more socially powerful, valued, advantaged, or free than women. For that, you have to see differences as counting in certain ways, and certain differences being created precisely because they give men *power* over women.

Although feminists disagree about this, my own view is that feminism isn't—at least not directly—about equality, and it isn't about women, and it isn't about difference. It's about power. Specifically, it's about the social pattern, widespread across cultures and history, that distributes power asymmetrically to favor men over women. This asymmetry has been given many names, including the subjugation of women, sexism, male dominance, patriarchy, systemic misogyny, phallocracy, and the oppression of women. A number of feminist theorists simply call it gender, and throughout this book, I will too.

WHAT IS GENDER?

Most people think their gender is a natural fact about them, like their hair and eye color: "Jones is 5 foot 8, has red hair, and is a man." But gender is a *norm*, not a fact. It's a prescription for how people are supposed to act; what they must or must not wear; how they're supposed to sit, walk, or stand; what kind of person they're supposed to marry; what sorts of things they're supposed to be interested in or good at; and what they're entitled to. And because it's an *effective* norm, it creates the differences between men and women in these areas.

Gender doesn't just tell women to behave one way and men another, though. It's a *power* relation, so it tells men that they're entitled to things that women aren't supposed to have, and it tells women that they are supposed to defer to men and serve them. It says, for example, that men are supposed to occupy positions of religious authority and women are supposed to run the church suppers. It says that mothers are supposed to take care of their children but fathers have more important things to do. And it says that the things associated with femininity are supposed to take a back seat to the things that are coded masculine. Think of the many tax dollars allocated to the military as compared with the few tax dollars allocated to the arts. Think about how kindergarten teachers are paid as compared to how stockbrokers are paid. And think about how many presidents of the United States have been women. Gender operates through social institutions (like marriage and the law) and practices (like education and medicine) by disproportionately conferring entitlements and the control of resources on men, while disproportionately assigning women to subordinate positions in the service of men's interests.

To make this power relation seem perfectly natural—like the fact that plants grow up instead of down, or that human beings grow old and die—gender constructs its norms for behavior around what is supposed to be the natural biological distinction between the sexes. According to this distinction, people who have penises and testicles, XY chromosomes, and beards as adults belong to the male sex, while people who have clitorises and ovaries, XX chromosomes, and breasts as adults belong to the female sex, and those are the only sexes there are. Gender, then, is the complicated set of cultural meanings that are constructed around the two sexes. Your sex is either male or female, and your gender—either masculine or feminine—corresponds socially to your sex.

As a matter of fact, though, sex isn't quite so simple. Some people with XY chromosomes don't have penises and never develop beards, because they don't have the receptors that allow them to make use of the male hormones that their testicles produce. Are they male or female? Other people have ambiguous genitals or internal reproductive structures that don't correspond in the usual manner to their external genitalia. How should we classify them? People with Turner's syndrome have XO chromosomes instead of XX. People with Klinefelter's syndrome have three sex chromosomes: XXY. Nature is a good bit looser in its categories than the simple male/female distinction acknowledges. Most human beings can certainly be classified as one sex or the other, but a considerable number of them fall somewhere in between.

The powerful norm of gender doesn't acknowledge the existence of the in-betweens, though. When, for example, have you ever filled out an application for a job or a driver's license or a passport that gave you a choice other than M or F? Instead, by basing its distinction between masculine and feminine on the existence of two and only two sexes, gender makes the inequality of power between men and women appear natural and therefore legitimate.

Gender, then, is about power. But it's not about the power of just one group over another. Gender always interacts with other social markers—such as race, class, level of education, sexual orientation, age, religion, physical and mental health, and ethnicity—to distribute power unevenly among women positioned differently in the various social orders, and it does the same to men. A man's social status, for example, can have a great deal to do with the extent to which he's even perceived as a man. There's a wonderful passage in the English travel writer Frances Trollope's *Domestic Manners of the Americans* (1831), in which she describes the exaggerated delicacy of middle-class young ladies she met in Kentucky and Ohio. They wouldn't dream of sitting in a chair that was still warm from contact with a gentleman's bottom, but thought nothing of getting laced into their corsets in front of a male house slave. The slave, it's clear, didn't count as a man—not in the relevant sense, anyway. Gender is the force that makes it matter whether you are male or female, but it always works hand in glove with all the other things about you that matter at the same time. It's one power relation intertwined with others in a complex social system that distinguishes your betters from your inferiors in all kinds of ways and for all kinds of purposes.

POWER AND MORALITY

If feminism is about gender, and gender is the name for a social system that distributes power unequally between men and women, then you'd expect feminist ethicists to try to *understand, criticize,* and *correct* how gender operates within our moral beliefs and practices. And they do just that. In the first place, they challenge, on moral grounds, the powers men have over women, and they claim for women, again on moral grounds, the powers that gender denies them. As the moral reasons for opposing gender are similar to the moral reasons for opposing power systems based on social markers other than gender, feminist ethicists also offer moral arguments against systems based on class, race, physical or mental ability, sexuality, and age. And because all these systems, including gender, are powerful enough to *conceal* many of the forces that keep them in place, it's often necessary to make the forces visible by explicitly identifying—and condemning—the various ugly ways they allow some people to treat others. This is a central task for feminist ethics.

Feminist ethicists also produce theory about the moral meaning of various kinds of *legitimate* relations of unequal power, including relationships of dependency and vulnerability, relationships of trust, and relationships based on something other than choice. Parent–child relationships, for example, are necessarily unequal and for the most part unchosen. Parents can't help having power over their children, and while they may have chosen to have children, most don't choose to have the particular children they do, nor do children choose their parents. This raises questions about the responsible use of parental power and the nature of involuntary obligations, and these are topics for feminist ethics. Similarly, when you trust someone, that person has power over you. Whom should you trust, for what purposes, and when is trust not warranted? What's involved in being trustworthy, and what must be done to repair breaches of trust? These too are questions for feminist ethics.

Third, feminist ethicists look at the various forms of power that are required for morality to operate properly at all. How do we learn right from wrong in the first place? We usually learn it from our parents, whose power to permit and forbid, praise and punish, is essential to our moral training. For whom or what are we ethically responsible? Often this depends on the kind of power we have over the person or thing in question. If, for instance, someone is particularly vulnerable to harm because of something I've done, I might well have special duties toward that person. Powerful social institutions—medicine, religion, government, and the market, to take just a few examples—typically dictate what is morally required of us and to whom we are morally answerable. Relations of power set the terms for who must answer to whom, who has authority over whom, and who gets excused from certain kinds of accountability to whom. But because so many of these power relations are illegitimate, in that they're instances of gender, racism, or other kinds of bigotry, figuring out which ones are morally justified is a task for feminist ethics.

DESCRIPTION AND PRESCRIPTION

So far it sounds as if feminist ethics devotes considerable attention to *description*—as if feminist ethicists were like poets or painters who want to show you something about reality that you might otherwise have missed. And indeed, many feminist ethicists emphasize the importance of understanding how social power actually works, rather than concentrating solely on how it ought to work. But why, you might ask, should ethicists worry about how power operates within societies? Isn't it up to sociologists and political scientists to describe how things *are*, while ethicists concentrate on how things *ought* to be?

As the philosopher Margaret Urban Walker has pointed out in *Moral Contexts*, there is a tradition in Western philosophy, going all the way back to Plato, to the effect that morality is something ideal and that ethics, being the study of morality, properly examines only that ideal. According to this tradition, notions of right and wrong as they are found in the world are unreliable and shadowy manifestations of something lying outside of human experience—something

to which we ought to aspire but can't hope to reach. Plato's Idea of the Good, in fact, is precisely not of this earth, and only the gods could truly know it. Christian ethics incorporates Platonism into its insistence that earthly existence is fraught with sin and error and that heaven is our real home. Kant too insists that moral judgments transcend the histories and circumstances of people's actual lives, and most moral philosophers of the twentieth century have likewise shown little interest in how people really live and what it's like for them to live that way. "They think," remarks Walker (2001), "that there is little to be learned from what is about what ought to be" (3).

In [another chapter] we'll take a closer look at what goes wrong when ethics is done that way, but let me just point out here that if you don't know how things are, your prescriptions for how things ought to be won't have much practical effect. Imagine trying to sail a ship without knowing anything about the tides or where the hidden rocks and shoals lie. You might have a very fine idea of where you are trying to go, but if you don't know the waters, at best you are likely to go off course, and at worst you'll end up going down with all your shipmates. If, as many feminists have noted, a crucial fact about human selves is that they are always embedded in a vast web of relationships, then the forces at play within those relationships must be understood. It's knowing how people are situated with respect to these forces, what they are going through as they are subjected to them, and what life is like in the face of them, that lets us decide which of the forces are morally justified. Careful description of how things are is a crucial part of feminist methodology, because the power that puts certain groups of people at risk of physical harm, denies them full access to the good things their society has to offer, or treats them as if they were useful only for other people's purposes is often hidden and hard to see. If this power isn't seen, it's likely to remain in place, doing untold amounts of damage to great numbers of people.

All the same, feminist ethics is *normative* as well as descriptive. It's fundamentally about how things ought to be, while description plays the crucial but secondary role of helping us to figure that out. Normative language is the language of "ought" instead of "is," the language of "worth" and "value," "right" and "wrong," "good" and "bad." Feminist ethicists differ on a number of normative issues, but as the philosopher Alison Jaggar (1991) has famously put it, they all share two moral commitments: "that the subordination of women is morally wrong and that the moral experience of women is worthy of respect" (95). The first commitment—that women's interests ought not systematically to be set in the service of men's—can be understood as a moral challenge to power under the guise of gender. The second commitment—that women's experience must be taken seriously—can be understood as a call to acknowledge how that power operates. These twin commitments are the two normative legs on which any feminist ethics stands.

Feminist ethics, then, is both descriptive and prescriptive. The belief that good normative theory requires a solid grasp of actual social practices isn't shared by all feminist ethicists, but it's reflected in enough feminist work to cause what seems to me to be a confusion. Flip back to the ethics road map, and look again at the distinction between normative ethics and practical ethics. In nonfeminist ethics, the division between these two branches of ethics can often be pretty sharp. *Normative ethics* tends to consist of ideal moral theory, with scant or no attention paid to specific social practices, whereas *practical ethics* uses principles extracted from that ideal theory and applies them to something concrete, like business. But when you try to apply the distinction between normative ethics and practical ethics to feminist ethics, you'll find it doesn't work very well, because feminist moral theory tends not to be ideal but instead is grounded in description. And that's what causes the confusion: Many people assume that because feminist ethics is practical, it's opposed to theory, and furthermore, that all feminist ethics is "applied" ethics.

A better way of looking at it, I think, is to see *feminist normative ethics* as moral theory that

arises out of actual social practices of all kinds and that in turn relies on those practices to help determine whether it's on the right track, while *feminist practical ethics*—for example, feminist bioethics—offers ethical analyses of specific social practices (like biomedicine). If you think of it that way, you can see that feminists aren't so much opposed to theory as dubious about certain kinds of theory-building and that, even at its most practical, feminist ethics retains its normative bite.

MORALITY AND POLITICS

If the idealization of morality goes back over two thousand years in Western thought, a newer tradition, only a couple of centuries old, has split off morality from politics. According to this tradition, which can be traced to Kant and some other Enlightenment philosophers, morality concerns the relations between persons, whereas politics concerns the relations among nation-states, or between a state and its citizens. So, as Iris Marion Young (1990) puts it, ethicists have tended to focus on intentional actions by individual persons, conceiving of moral life as "conscious, deliberate, a rational weighing of alternatives," whereas political philosophers have focused on impersonal governmental systems, studying "laws, policies, the large-scale distribution of social goods, countable quantities like votes and taxes" (149).

For feminists, though, the line between ethics and political theory isn't quite so bright as this tradition makes out. It's not always easy to tell where feminist ethics leaves off and feminist political theory begins. There are two reasons for this. In the first place, while ethics certainly concerns personal behavior, there is a long-standing insistence on the part of feminists that the personal *is* political. In a 1970 essay called "The Personal Is Political," the political activist Carol Hanisch observed that "personal problems are political problems. There are no personal solutions at this time" (204–205). What Hanisch meant is that even the most private areas of everyday life, including such intensely personal areas as sex, can function to maintain abusive power systems like gender. If a heterosexual woman believes, for example, that contraception is primarily her responsibility because she'll have to take care of the baby if she gets pregnant, she is propping up a system that lets men evade responsibility not only for pregnancy, but for their own offspring as well. Conversely, while unjust social arrangements such as gender and race invade every aspect of people's personal lives, "there are no personal solutions," either when Hanisch wrote those words or now, because to shift dominant understandings of how certain groups may be treated, and what other groups are entitled to expect of them, requires concerted political action, not just personal good intentions.

The second reason why it's hard to separate feminist ethics from feminist politics is that feminists typically subject the ethical theory they produce to critical political scrutiny, not only to keep untoward political biases out, but also to make sure that the work accurately reflects their feminist politics. Many nonfeminist ethicists, on the other hand, don't acknowledge that their work reflects their politics, because they don't think it should. Their aim, by and large, has been to develop ideal moral theory that applies to all people, regardless of their social position or experience of life, and to do that objectively, without favoritism, requires them to leave their own personal politics behind. The trouble, though, is that they aren't really leaving their own personal politics behind. They're merely refusing to notice that their politics is inevitably built right in to their theories. (This is an instance of Lindemann's ad hoc rule Number 22: Just because you think you are doing something doesn't mean you're actually doing it.) Feminists, by contrast, are generally skeptical of the idealism nonfeminists favor, and they're equally doubtful that objectivity can be achieved by stripping away what's distinctive about people's experiences or commitments. Believing that it's no wiser to shed one's political allegiances in the service of ethics than it would be to shed one's moral allegiances, feminists prefer to be transparent about their politics as a way of keeping their ethics intellectually honest.

⚜ REVIEW QUESTIONS

1. What is feminism according to Lindemann? Why isn't it about equality with men, the nature of women, or the differences between men and women?
2. How does Lindemann explain gender? What are the gender roles of women according to Lindemann? How does gender interact with other social markers like race and class?
3. According to Lindemann, how do feminist ethicists deal with gender and other social markers?
4. Why does Lindemann think that feminist ethics needs to describe how social power actually works?
5. Alison Jaggar says that feminist ethicists share two basic moral commitments. What are they?
6. How is feminist ethics related to feminist political theory in Lindemann's view?

⚜ DISCUSSION QUESTIONS

1. Simone de Beauvoir says that being a woman is not a natural fact, but a social invention that represents a woman as "only the negative, the not-man." Do you agree? Why or why not?
2. Should our society recognize the existence of "in-betweens" who are neither male nor female? If so, how should this be done?
3. Should the gender roles of women, such as being wives and mothers, be changed? If so, what roles should women play in our society?
4. Do you agree with the feminist view that women in our society are oppressed? If so, how are they oppressed and what should be done about it?

PROBLEM CASES

1. The Myth of Gyges' Ring

(The myth about Gyges is found in Book II of Plato's *Republic*. The story is told by Glaucon, who is having a argument with Socrates and his companions.) Gyges is a poor shepherd who one day finds a magic ring that makes the wearer invisible, so that the wearer can go anywhere and do anything undetected. Gyges uses the ring to his advantage. He goes into the royal palace, seduces the queen, murders the king, and seizes the throne. Just how he does all this is not explained; apparently, the ring has other powers besides making the wearer invisible.

Now suppose that there are two such rings. One is given to a wicked man and another to a virtuous man.

No doubt the wicked man will act like Gyges. He will commit crimes to gain wealth and power, and since he cannot be caught and punished, he will do this without being constrained by morality, by considerations of right and wrong. But what will the virtuous man do? Glaucon argues that the virtuous man will behave no better than the wicked man. If he can commit crimes like stealing and killing with no fear of punishment, then why wouldn't he do them? Why should he care about morality? Why should he worry about what is right and wrong?

How would you reply to Glaucon? Why should you care about morality if you can do whatever you want without getting caught and punished? Why be moral?

2. Lying

Many philosophers have held that lying is morally wrong. Kant thought that lying is "a crime of man against his own person" and should be avoided at all costs. Saint Augustine said that when regard for truth has broken down, then everything is open to doubt, and little by little, lies grow in size. In contrast, Nietzsche thought that "lying is a necessity of life" and is "part of the terrifying and problematic character of existence." Goethe asserted that lying is part of human nature; truth is not.

Certainly, lying seems to be very common in our society. As the saying goes, people tell lies in love and war. There are professions that seem to require lying, such as espionage agent and politician—or at least these people cannot stay in their professions very long if they tell the whole truth and nothing but the truth. Consider the list of public figures caught lying in recent years: Representative Gary A. Condit, Democrat of California,

lied about his affair with Chandra Ann Levy. President Bill Clinton lied under oath about his relationship with Monica Lewinsky and then argued that distorting the truth in testimony is not necessarily illegal. Edmund Morris, author of a so-called biography of President Ronald Reagan, lied about his participation in Reagan's life. Nobel Prize winner Rigoberta Menchu lied about her life in Guatemala. Historian Joseph J. Ellis lied about his heroic service in Vietnam. Jayson Blair, a *New York Times* reporter, wrote more than 600 articles with misleading information and false quotes. George W. Bush lied when he said (in his State of the Union speech) that Iraq had tried to buy yellowcake uranium from Africa to make nuclear weapons. Dick Cheney lied when he said there was no doubt that Saddam Hussein was building a nuclear device. The list goes on and on, with no end in sight. But is lying always wrong? Is it wrong to give people misleading information? Explain your view.

3. The Colt Sporter and Handguns

The Colt Sporter is one of the most popular semiautomatic assault rifles. A semiautomatic weapon fires one bullet with each pull of the trigger, as distinguished from a fully automatic weapon, which fires a stream of bullets with one trigger pull. Fully automatic weapons are banned by the federal government, but

semiautomatic weapons are legal in most states. In 1993, a Connecticut law banned thirty kinds of semiautomatic guns, including the Colt Sporter. The Sporter is made by Colt's Manufacturing Company, based in Hartford, Connecticut. Even though it looks just like the Colt-made M-16 (a standard military weapon), Colt officials say the Sporter is made for target practice and hunting. Furthermore, the Colt officials insist that people have a right to own and use rifles such as the Sporter. Critics claim that the Sporter can be converted into a fully automatic weapon and that it is used mostly in urban gang and drug shootings.

Do citizens have a right to own and use semiautomatic weapons? What about fully automatic weapons? What is your position?

Most gun owners have handguns, not semiautomatic or fully automatic weapons. It is estimated that private citizens in the United States own 70 million handguns. Those who support more gun control or even the elimination of all these guns point to statistics. Each year about 39,000 Americans are killed with guns: There are 19,000 suicides, 18,000 homicides, and some 2,000 people killed in gun accidents. In addition, there are about 40,000 injuries from accidents with

guns each year and probably millions of crimes committed using guns. By contrast, countries with strict handgun control have much lower rates of homicide. In 1990, eighty-seven people were killed by handguns in Japan, thirteen in Sweden, ten in Australia, and twenty-two in Great Britain.

Given these facts, why not have strict gun control in the United States? What would Mill say? How about Kant?

The opposition to gun control comes mainly from the National Rifle Association and its members. The NRA defends each person's right to own and use handguns in self-defense. It claims that the homicide statistics are inflated and that the most important statistic is that there are 645,000 defensive uses of handguns each year. As for accidental deaths and injuries, the NRA solution is to teach principles of safe weapon use. Do you agree with the NRA position? Why or why not?

4. A New Drug

Suppose you are a poor and uneducated person from Chicago. Your only chance for success in life is through athletics, particularly distance running. You have trained hard, and you have placed high in ten-kilometer and marathon races, but you have never won a major race. You need to be just a little faster to win. In one month, there is the Chicago Marathon, with a cash prize of $50,000 for the winner. There is a good chance that the winner will also get a lucrative endorsement contract with a major running-shoe company. A friend who is an athletic trainer tells you she has obtained a limited supply of a new drug that dramatically improves endurance by preventing the buildup of lactic acid in

the muscles. The drug is the result of genetic research on human growth hormones, and it has been tested on animals with no bad side effects thus far. It seems much safer and more effective than steroids or the human growth hormones used by some runners. Your friend offers you a month's supply of the drug. She assures you that it is not on the list of banned drugs and that it will not show up on drug tests—or at least the drug tests currently used. In return for giving you the drug, your friend wants $5,000, but only if you win the race and collect the $50,000 cash prize. If you do not win, you owe her nothing.

Should you take the drug? Why or why not?

5. Adultery

Adultery or extramarital affairs are common in our society. According to Alfred Kinsey's famous 1948 survey of sexual behavior, seven out of ten men had cheated on their wives. More recent research found that more than 20 percent of men and more than 10 percent of women had engaged in an extramarital affair. A short list of famous men who committed adultery would include Franklin Roosevelt, Dwight D. Eisenhower, John F. Kennedy, Ronald Reagan, Bill

Clinton, John Edwards, Eliot Spitzer, John Hagee, David Letterman, and Tiger Woods.

Is adultery morally wrong? No doubt most people think so. Promises are broken and people are harmed. But is it always wrong? For the sake of discussion, let's consider an imaginary case.

Billy Pilgrim is a famous Christian evangelist with a popular TV show called God Loves You (GLU). He is good-looking and an electrifying preacher, having converted thousands to the faith. He raises millions each year, and gives almost all of it away to help needy people in the United States and other countries. Volunteers who receive no money for their work run the God Loves You Foundation (GLUF) that administers the money. Billy himself lives very modestly in a two-room apartment with Milly, his wife of fifty years. They have no children because, as Billy says, "Everyone is God's child, and I want to care for everyone equally." In short, Billy is a model of Christian virtue and charity except for one weakness. For more than twenty years, Billy has carried on a secret extramarital affair with Jill, a secretary at GLUF. They get together infrequently, but these encounters are enormously fulfilling for both Billy and Jill because they are deeply and madly in love. The fact that they are doing something forbidden by their religion seems to make the affair all the more exciting. Sin is somehow very attractive to virtuous people. Of course Billy feels some pangs of guilt about his love affair, and he frequently asks God for forgiveness, which itself is gratifying in a strange way. In fact, this secret love is what makes it possible for Billy to be a model of virtue in the other parts of his life. Without this one sin, he could never be so good.

All things considered, is Billy's love affair morally wrong or not? Why or why not?

6. Health Care

The U.S. health care system is a patchwork of different programs. There are 10 million people who buy private insurance without any help from the government. There are 5 million military veterans who rely on government doctors and hospitals. There are 32 million retirees insured by Medicare, which is usually supplemented by private insurance. There are 37 million covered by Medicaid. There are about 8 million persons covered by the Federal Employees Health Benefits Program (FEHBP), which includes members of Congress. Finally, there are 153 million workers and their families who get government-subsidized private insurance from their employers.

Those who are uninsured and cannot pay their medical bills still go to the hospital, typically the emergency room, where they get expensive treatment. The hospital has to absorb the cost as bad debt. For example, in 2004, HCA, the nation's largest hospital company, set aside $5.9 billion to cover bad debts. This increases the cost of medical care for those who are covered by insurance or pay their bills.

Health care in the United States is very expensive and the cost is rising rapidly. According to Health Affairs, $7,498 was spent on each man, woman, and child in this country in 2007. For a person with a serious illness such as cancer, the cost of insurance can exceed $27,000 a year. The total spending on health care amounts to 16 percent of the U.S. gross national product and the cost is growing at a rate of 6.4 percent a year. By the year 2016, the cost of health care in the United States is projected to increase to $12,782 per person.

Compared to European countries, U.S. health care is inefficient and expensive. These countries provide universal health care for their citizens for about half what is spent in the United States. They spend an average of 8.4 percent of their gross national product on health care, whereas the United States spends 16 percent of its gross national product.

Various proposals have been made to reform U.S. health care. A conservative plan is to privatize health care for nonmilitary citizens; in this scheme, inefficient and wasteful government programs would be eliminated and the free market would be allowed to set the price of medical care. The result would be much lower taxes for individuals and more profit for companies, as firms would not have to pay for employee medical insurance. Doctors and hospitals would compete for patients in a free market and the result would be more efficient and better health care. People would be free to choose the doctors and hospitals they liked. They could buy private insurance or be "self-insured" (that is, be personally responsible for paying their medical bills).

The conservative plan may appeal to the rich who can afford health care or the healthy who do not need it, but what about people who are poor and sick or disabled? They would have to rely on charity. There could be free medical clinics for the needy, supported by generous donations from the rich. This assumes, of course, that the rich are willing to make the necessary donations. Also, there is a risk that charity will not do the job, and that some needy people will receive no medical care at all.

The basic objection to the conservative plan appeals to rights. Liberals believe that citizens of a rich country such as the United States have a positive right—an entitlement—to medical care. This implies that the federal government has a positive duty to provide health care to all U.S. citizens, and it is wrong to not do so. The basic liberal plan, then, is to mandate government health insurance for all U.S. citizens. This is called the "single payer system," to use the Clinton-era term. The government would be the single payer that insures everyone directly. President Clinton's proposal for universal health care went nowhere, but recently there have been attempts to revive it. One proposal is to extend the Medicare program to include everyone. Another proposal is to give citizens the same coverage as U.S. representatives and senators get in the federal FEHBP program. This program offers various health plans from which to choose, allows members of Congress to insure their spouses and dependents, has no preexisting-condition clauses, and does not deny coverage because of health problems. The government pays up to 75 percent of the premium, making it a "socialist" program.

The basic conservative objection to universal health care goes back to rights. In the conservative view, there are no positive rights in the sense of entitlements to goods or services such as food, clothing, education, or health care. The government has no obligation to provide these to citizens. To say otherwise is to embrace socialism and reject free market capitalism. Socialized medicine would result in the downfall of the private medical insurance system, it is claimed, and abolish for-profit medicine. The result, conservatives argue, would be inefficient, wasteful, and low-quality care. Liberals can reply that socialized medicine works well in European counties, so why can't it work in the United States? Furthermore, several government-supported programs are already in place: namely, Medicare, Medicaid, the Veteran's Administration, and the FEHBP program, as we have seen.

On March 21, 2010, the House of Representatives passed a health care bill that will produce major changes in the United States. The biggest change is providing health insurance coverage to 32 million citizens who do not have any because they cannot afford it or cannot get it. There will still be more than 20 million uninsureds, including illegal immigrants. About 16 million poor people will be added to the Medicaid roles, and coverage for poor people will be subsidized. Most insurance plans will be prohibited from placing limits on coverage and canceling policies of sick people. Children with preexisting conditions cannot be denied coverage, and in 2014, adults with preexisting conditions cannot be denied coverage. Dependent children up to age twenty-six will be eligible for coverage under their parent's plan. By an executive order, federal money provided by the bill cannot be used to pay for abortion.

Opponents of the bill complain that it costs too much; it will produce unaffordable levels of national debt. Defenders grant that the cost will be $938 billion over 10 years, but claim that the bill will reduce deficits by $143 billion in 10 years. Besides, they say, it will be even more expensive to do nothing. To help pay for the new coverage, rich families with an annual income of more than $250,000 will pay an additional 3.8 percent tax.

Another objection to the bill is that it requires most Americans to have health insurance and penalizes those who refuse to get it. This seems to be unwelcome government interference in private life—the government forcing people to buy something they do not want or need. At least 14 states are suing the government on the ground that this provision is unconstitutional. The argument is that even though the Constitution gives the federal government the authority to "regulate commerce," this does not mean that the government can mandate that individuals *must* buy something.

Still another complaint about the bill is that it provides health insurance to irresponsible people who do not deserve it. Why should healthy people be forced to help pay for the medical insurance of smokers, overeaters, and drug abusers?

Should people be required to have health insurance? Should U.S. taxpayers be forced to subsidize the health insurance of people who choose unhealthy lifestyles? State and explain your position.

Some conservatives object to the very idea of government-controlled health care. In their view, this amounts to socialism and as such is unacceptable. Do you agree? Why or why not?

The most basic issue about health care involves rights. Do individuals in a rich society such as the United States, which can afford to provide basic health care for its citizens, have a positive right to health care? Does the U.S. government have a moral obligation to provide this basic care?

⚜ SUGGESTED READINGS

James Rachels, *The Elements of Moral Philosophy,* 5th ed. (New York: McGraw-Hill, 2006), is a good introduction to the standard moral theories. *A Companion to Ethics,* ed. Peter Singer (Oxford, UK: Basil Blackwell Ltd., 1991), is a useful anthology that includes short articles on egoism, natural law theory, relativism, subjectivism, utilitarianism, Kantian ethics, virtue theory, and rights theory.

Joseph Butler makes the classical attack on egoism in *Fifteen Sermons upon Human Nature* (London, 1729). Ayn Rand explains and defends egoism in *The Virtue of Selfishness* (New York: Signet, 1964). In *Principles of Ethics: An Introduction* (Belmont, CA: Wadsworth, 1975), Paul W. Taylor argues that ethical egoism contains an inconsistency.

The Divine Command Theory of Ethics, ed. Paul Helm (Oxford, UK: Oxford University Press, 1979), contains several articles on the divine command theory. Robert M. Adams defends the theory in "A Modified Divine Command Theory of Ethical Wrongness," in *The Virtue of Faith* (Oxford, UK: Oxford University Press, 1987). Philip L. Quinn gives a sophisticated defense and explanation of the theory using deontic logic in *Divine Commands and Moral Requirements* (Oxford, UK: Clarendon Press, 1978). Kai Nielson, *Ethics without God* (Buffalo, NY: Prometheus Books, 1990), argues that ethics can exist without belief in God.

John Finnis, in *Natural Law and Natural Rights* (Oxford, UK: Clarendon Press, 1980), gives a sophisticated defense of natural law theory; basically, Finnis argues that following natural law is necessary for human flourishing. J. Budziszewski, *Written on the Heart: The Case for Natural Law* (Downers Grove, IL: InterVarsity Press, 1997), explains and defends natural law theory as it is found in Aristotle, Aquinas, and Locke. Anthony J. Lisska, *Aquinas's Theory of Natural Law: An Analytical Reconstruction* (Oxford, UK: Oxford University Press, 1998), argues that the problem with natural theory is its assumption that all humans have a common nature or essence.

James Baillie, *Hume on Morality* (London: Routledge, 2000), gives a clear and well-organized introduction to Hume's moral philosophy. J. L. Mackie, *Hume's Moral Theory* (London: Routledge & Kegan Paul, 1980), presents a classic discussion of Hume's views on morality. *The Is-Ought Problem,* ed. W. D. Hudson (New York: Macmillan, 1969), is a collection of papers on Hume's famous problem concerning reasoning from "is" to "ought."

Ethical Relativism, ed. John Ladd (Belmont, CA.: Wadsworth, 1973), has readings on cultural relativism. James Rachels criticizes cultural relativism and subjectivism in *The Elements of Moral Philosophy* (New York: Random House, 1993). William H. Shaw dismisses subjectivism as implausible and raises objections to cultural relativism in "Relativism and Objectivity in Ethics," in *Morality and Moral Controversies,* ed. John Arthur (Englewood Cliffs, NJ: Prentice Hall, 1981), 31–50. J. L. Mackie presents a subjectivist theory in *Ethics* (Harmondsworth, UK: Penguin, 1977). Gilbert Harman defends a version of relativism in *The Nature of Morality: An Introduction to Ethics* (Oxford, UK: Oxford University Press, 1977).

J. J. C. Smart defends utilitarianism and Bernard Williams attacks it in J. J. C. Smart and Bernard Williams, *Utilitarianism: For and Against* (Cambridge, UK: Cambridge University Press, 1973). *Utilitarianism and Beyond,* ed. A. Sen and Bernard Williams (Cambridge, UK: Cambridge University Press, 1973), is a collection of articles on utilitarianism. *Ethics,* ed. Peter Singer (Oxford, UK: Oxford University Press, 1994), has a selection of classical and modern readings on utilitarianism.

Kant's work on ethics is difficult. A good place to begin is his *Lectures on Ethics,* trans. Louis Infield (New York: Harper & Row, 1963). His ethical theory is developed in *Critique of Practical Reason,* trans. Lewis White Beck (New York: Bobbs-Merrill, 1956); *The Metaphysical Elements of Justice,* trans. John Ladd (New York: Bobbs-Merrill, 1965); and *The Metaphysical Principles of Virtue,* trans. James Ellington (New York: Bobbs-Merrill, 1964). For commentaries on Kant's moral philosophy, see H. J. Paton, *The Categorical Imperative* (New York: Harper & Row, 1967), and H. B. Acton, *Kant's Moral Philosophy* (New York: Macmillan, 1970).

W. D. Ross explains Aristotle's ethics in his *Aristotle* (New York: Meridian Books, 1959), ch. 7. John M. Cooper defends Aristotelian ethics in *Reason and the Human Good in Aristotle* (Cambridge, MA: Harvard University Press, 1975). For articles on virtue theory by classical and contemporary philosophers, see *Vice and Virtue in Everyday Life,* 3d ed., ed. Christina Sommers and Fred Sommers (San Diego: Harcourt Brace Jovanovich,

1993). James Rachels raises objections to virtue theory in *The Elements of Moral Philosophy* (New York: McGraw-Hill, 1993). Peter Geach discusses classical virtues such as courage in *The Virtues* (Cambridge, UK: Cambridge University Press, 1977).

Human Rights, ed. Ellen Paul, Fred Mill, and Jeffrey Paul (Oxford, UK: Blackwell, 1948), is a collection of articles on rights. Another anthology on rights is *Theories of Rights*, ed. Jeremy Waldron (Oxford, UK: Oxford University Press, 1984). Ronald Dworkin, in *Taking Rights Seriously* (Cambridge, MA: Harvard University Press, 1977), argues that the basis of rights in the Constitution of the United States is the Kantian idea of treating people with dignity as members of the moral community. Judith Jarvis Thomson, in *The Realm of Rights* (Cambridge, MA: Harvard University Press, 1990), develops a systematic theory of the nature and foundation of rights. John Locke's classical theory of God-given natural rights is found in his *Two Treatises* (1690). Joel Feinberg "The Nature and Value of Rights," *The Journal of Value Inquiry* 4 (1970): 243–257, demonstrates that rights are morally important by imagining a world where people do not have rights. In such a world, people could not make moral claims when they are treated unjustly, and as a result they would be deprived of self-respect and dignity.

The classical formulations of the social contract theory are Thomas Hobbes's *Leviathan* (1651), John Locke's *The Second Treatise of Government* (1690), and Jean-Jacques Rousseau's *The Social Contract* (1762).

Since it first appeared in 1971, Rawls's theory of justice has been widely discussed. One of the first books on the theory to appear was Brian Barry, *The Liberal Theory of Justice* (Oxford, UK: Oxford University Press, 1973). Another useful critical discussion is Robert Paul Wolff, *Understanding Rawls* (Princeton, NJ: Princeton University Press, 1977). The journal *Ethics* devoted its entire July 1989 issue to a symposium on developments in the Rawlsian theory of justice.

Feminist theory has been much discussed in recent years. A big anthology that covers the application of feminist theory to current issues such as affirmative action, abortion, reproductive technology, meateating, militarism, and environmentalism is *Living with Contradictions*, ed. Allison M. Jaggar (Boulder, CO: Westview Press, 1994). Another collection of readings on feminist theory and its applications is *Woman and Values*, 2nd ed., ed. Marilyn Pearsall (Belmont, CA: Wadsworth, 1993). For a comprehensive introduction to different feminist theories, see *Feminist Thought*, ed. Rosemarie Tong (Boulder, CO: Westview Press, 1989). Another comprehensive anthology is *Feminism and Philosophy*, ed. Nancy Tuana and Rosemarie Tong (Boulder, CO: Westview Press, 1995). This book covers liberal, Marxist, radical, psychoanalytic, socialist, ecological, phenomenological, and postmodern feminist perspectives. Jean Grimshaw, "The Idea of a Female Ethic," in Peter Singer, ed., *A Companion to Ethics* (Oxford, UK: Blackwell, 1991): 491–499, explains the development of the idea of a female ethic, starting with Mary Wollstonecraft, and ending with contemporary feminists such as Mary Daly, Carol Gilligan, Sara Ruddick, Nel Noddings, and Caroline Whitbeck.

CHAPTER TWO

Abortion

- **Introduction**
  - Factual Background
  - The Readings
  - Philosophical Issues

INTRODUCTION

Factual Background

Abortion is usually defined as the intentional termination of pregnancy. Although the term *fetus* is often used to describe the prenatal organism from conception to birth, the prenatal organism is, strictly speaking, an embryo until the eighth week and a zygote when it is a fertilized egg. In the future it may be possible to terminate pregnancy at any stage of development without causing the fetus to die; the fetus could be kept alive in an artificial womb. The decision to terminate pregnancy would then be separate from the decision about the life of the fetus. But given the present state of medical technology, the decision to terminate pregnancy before the fetus is viable is also a decision to kill the fetus or let it die.

In 2005, 1.21 million abortions were performed, down from 1.31 million in 2000. From 1973 through 2005, more than 45 million legal abortions occurred. In 2000, 21 out of every 1,000 women aged 15 to 44 had had an abortion, making it one of the most common surgical procedures. It is estimated that 46 million abortions occur worldwide each year; about 26 million of these abortions are legal, and about 20 million women have abortions in countries where abortion is restricted or prohibited by law. (For sources of statistics on abortion, see the Suggested Readings.)

In the United States, about 52 percent of the women obtaining abortions each year are younger than age 25, and about 20 percent of them are teenagers. Women who have never married obtain two-thirds of all abortions. Three-fourths of the women having abortions say that having a baby would interfere with work, school, or other responsibilities. About two-thirds say that they cannot afford a child. About 13,000 women have abortions each year because they become pregnant after rape or incest.

Before the U.S. Supreme Court decision in *Roe v. Wade* in 1973, the number of illegal abortions in the United States was 1.2 million a year. After the *Roe* decision made abortion legal, the number of abortions increased to nearly 1.5 million in 1990, and then started to decline. The latest figures show that the number of abortions in the United States continues to decline.

When performed by a qualified doctor, abortion is a reasonably safe procedure. Less than 1 percent of all abortion patients experience complications such as infection or hemorrhage requiring a blood transfusion. The risk of death from abortion increases with length of pregnancy, however, with 1 death for every 600,000 abortions at 8 or fewer weeks to 1 death per 8,000 at 20 or more weeks. But the risk of death from childbirth is ten times as high as that associated with all abortions.

The law has treated abortion differently at different times. As Justice Blackmun notes in the first reading, English common law did not treat abortion before "quickening" as a criminal offense. *Quickening*, which is the first movement of the fetus, usually occurs between the sixteenth and eighteenth weeks of pregnancy. This traditional view of abortion was widely accepted up to the mid-nineteenth century, but it was rejected in 1928, when Connecticut made abortion before quickening a crime.

Other states followed the example of Connecticut, and by the 1960s most states had laws restricting abortion. All fifty states and the District of Columbia, however, allowed abortion to save the life of the mother, and Colorado and New Mexico permitted abortion to prevent serious harm to the mother.

These laws restricting abortion were overturned by the Supreme Court in the landmark *Roe* decision in 1973. In the *Roe* case, the Court ruled that restrictive abortion laws, except in certain narrowly defined circumstances, are unconstitutional. In a companion case, *Doe v. Bolton* (1973), the Court held further that a state may not unduly burden a woman's right to abortion by prohibiting or limiting her access to the procedure. These decisions made abortion before viability legally available to women who could afford it and who could find a doctor willing to perform the procedure. It is not accurate to say, as critics do, that the Court legalized "abortion on demand." In fact, the Court has allowed a number of restrictions on the abortion right, as we shall see.

The decision has been very controversial, and it has been repeatedly challenged. Opponents of the decision have proposed to amend the Constitution with the Human Life bill, which affirms that human life begins at conception and that every human life has intrinsic worth and equal value under the Constitution. As Justice Blackmun notes in the reading, the Constitution says that the bearers of rights are "persons" and not "human lives."

A legal challenge to the decision was the case of *Webster v. Reproductive Health Services* (1989). In a 5-to-4 decision, the Court did not overturn *Roe* but upheld as constitutional certain restrictions placed on abortion by a Missouri law: namely, (1) banning the use of public funds for abortion and abortion counseling, (2) banning abortions in public hospitals and clinics, and (3) forbidding public employees to assist in the performance of an abortion.

The next challenge to *Roe* was the case of *Planned Parenthood v. Casey* (1992). In a complicated and controversial decision that left people on both sides of the issue unsatisfied, the Court again reaffirmed the essential holding of *Roe* that a woman has a right to get an abortion. However, it permitted states to impose further restrictions on abortion, provided they do not impose an undue burden on the woman. After this decision the Court indicated that it did not intend to reconsider its basic abortion stance. Now that we have new Justices in the Court, though, and given the ongoing controversy about abortion, it seems likely that the Supreme Court will revisit the abortion issue in the future.

Many states have passed laws banning partial-birth abortions, and in November 2003 President Bush signed into law the Partial-Birth Abortion Act Ban of 2003. (See the Problem Cases.) The law prohibits a specific abortion procedure technically called *intact dilation and evacuation*, which involves pulling the fetus out feet first and then crushing the skull to remove it. Defenders of the law claim that it prohibits a rare and unnecessary operation that amounts to killing a baby. Opponents of the law argue that it also prohibits a common procedure called *dilation and curettage*. Furthermore, they claim that the procedure is sometimes necessary to protect the life or health of the mother.

In April 2007, the U.S. Supreme Court ruled in a 5-to-4 decision (*Gonzales v. Carhart*) that the partial-birth ban is constitutional. Writing for the majority, Justice Anthony Kennedy found that the law does not impose an undue burden on the woman, and thus is not unconstitutional "under the precedents we here assume to be controlling," namely the Court's decisions in *Roe* and *Planned Parenthood*.

The Readings

With the exception of the excerpt from *Roe*, the readings are not concerned with the legal aspects of the abortion controversy, but instead concentrate on the moral problem of whether abortion is or is not morally wrong. There are at least three views of the matter: (1) the pro-life view, (2) the pro-choice view, and (3) moderate views.

The pro-life view is that abortion is morally wrong, or almost always morally wrong, because it is the killing of an innocent person, or at least a potentially innocent person. It seems more accurate to call this the "anti-abortion" view rather than a "pro-life" view, because defenders of this view are rarely in favor of preserving all life, including the lives of murderers or those engaging in an unjust war or, for that matter, the lives of innocent animals. Nevertheless, those who hold this view prefer the label "pro-life" rather than "anti-abortion," so this text continues to refer to it as the "pro-life" view.

The representatives of the pro-life view in the readings are Noonan and Marquis. Noonan argues that the humanity of the fetus gives it moral significance and makes abortion morally wrong. However, he also mentions some exceptions, namely the cases of ectopic pregnancy and cancer in the uterus. The most common form of ectopic pregnancy (where the fetus is not in the usual position) is tubal pregnancy; in this condition the zygote does not descend to the uterus but remains lodged in the fallopian tube. In this situation the mother will die if an abortion is not performed, and there is no hope for the survival of the zygote at the present stage of medical technology. Noonan grants that abortion is not wrong in this case, and so does Marquis, because he allows abortion to save the mother's life.

Marquis bases the moral status of the fetus on its potential to have a future life like ours rather than its biological humanity. On his view it is wrong to kill a being with a future as a person, and given the fact that the fetus has such a future, it is wrong to kill it. But Marquis grants some exceptions at the outset: cases of rape, abortion during the first fourteen days after conception, threat to the woman's life, and when the fetus is anencephalic (partially or completely lacking a brain). The reasons for granting the last two cases are clear. The anencephalic fetus will not have a future like ours and so it is not wrong to kill it. The pregnant woman is an actual person and it would be wrong to let her die to save a potential person. The first two cases present problems that Marquis does not want to address. During the first fourteen days, there is the argument (the twinning argument, explained below), that the fetus is not a single individual. As for abortion after rape, the fetus in this case has a future like ours—that is, a future as a person—and that is the property that makes abortion wrong according to Marquis. Thus, it seems inconsistent for Marquis to make an exception in the rape cases. In any event, given the number of these exceptions he allows himself at the outset, it is tempting to say that Marquis is really a moderate rather than strictly pro-life, but because his emphasis is on the claim that abortion is seriously wrong, I will put him in the pro-life camp.

It is worth noting that those adopting the pro-life view do not agree about when a human being with rights comes into existence. Marquis seems to put it at fourteen days because before that time, twinning can occur, producing more than one human being. At least, Marquis acknowledges that this twinning argument presents a serious problem for those saying that a single individual is created at conception. Noonan accepts the standard Catholic position that human life begins at conception, but this is not quite right. According to medical textbooks, DNA sets from the egg and sperm do not immediately merge. The complete genetic coding that is the result of the combination of the DNA from the egg and sperm does not exist until the ovum divides after it has been fertilized.

In addition, there is debate about when pregnancy begins. Not everyone agrees that conception is the start of pregnancy. Some doctors hold that pregnancy begins when the incipient embryo (or blastocyst), the small collection of developing cells, attaches itself to the wall of the uterus a week or two after conception. Before that, the mother is not really pregnant, because the embryo is not connected or hooked up to the mother but is just a free-floating speck in the womb. On this view, the death of the zygote or blastocyst, however it happens, does not count as an abortion.

Many defenders of the pro-life position speak of the fetus as a human *life* rather than as a human being or a person. For example, Sidney Callahan (see the Suggested Readings) claims that human life has intrinsic value from beginning to end, not because the life is conscious or has some other feature, but just because it is human. The burden of proof is on those who want to end life rather than those who want to continue life with pregnancy and birth. In particular, she argues that feminist attempts to justify abortion by appealing to women's rights (Judith Jarvis Thomson) or to the nature of personhood (Mary Anne Warren) do not work.

The pro-choice view is that abortion is morally permissible whenever the mother chooses it. It would not be accurate to call this the "pro-abortion" view, because those who hold it do not believe that every mother ought to have an abortion; they merely defend the option to have one. Perhaps it would be better to call it the pro-abortion-choice view, because defenders of this view certainly do not endorse any and all choices, including the choice to murder innocent adult humans. With these qualifications in mind, I will continue to refer to the view in question as "pro-choice."

Instead of viewing the fetus as a person with rights, or as a potential person, the pro-choice view defended by Mary Anne Warren in her essay adopts the Kantian view that only rational beings are persons with a moral status, and argues that because fetuses are not rational, self-conscious beings, they have no moral status, or at least not the moral status of persons. She takes seriously the fact that in the later stages of development the fetus resembles a person, and she seems to accept this as a reason for not killing it. Thus, she holds that an early abortion is preferable to a late one. But Warren's position is that in the early stages of development, when the fetus does not resemble a person, abortion should be permitted whenever the mother chooses it.

Those who defend the pro-choice view do not agree about infanticide. In a classic article (see the Suggested Readings), Michael Tooley argues that there is no moral difference between abortion and infanticide; both are morally acceptable in his view. Warren does not agree. She gives several reasons for making a moral distinction between abortion and infanticide. One important difference, she says, is that the fetus can pose a threat to the woman's life or health, whereas the newborn infant cannot pose such a threat because the mother can put it up for adoption or place it in foster care.

The Supreme Court decision in *Roe* and the reading by Judith Jarvis Thomson represent what I call the moderate view. Moderates agree in rejecting both the pro-life and the pro-choice views. Generally speaking, moderates are willing to morally allow abortions in some cases and not others, but they give different reasons for doing so.

Thomson does not think that a newly fertilized ovum is a person, and she rejects the slippery-slope argument for saying that the fetus is a person from the moment of conception. Still, she is not inclined to draw a dividing line in development of the fetus, a line demarking the point at which it becomes a person. Instead, she takes a different approach. Suppose we grant the conservative premise that the fetus is a person from the moment of conception. It does not follow, she argues, that abortion is never permitted. Take a case of rape, for example. The woman's rights, her right to self-defense, and her right to control her own body are strong enough to justify an abortion when pregnancy is due to rape. But a woman also has a duty of decency generated by a principle Thomson calls Minimally Decent Samaritanism, and this duty rules out abortion in some cases. To use Thomson's example, it would be indecent for a woman in her seventh month of pregnancy to get an abortion just to avoid postponing a trip abroad.

Elizabeth Harman (see the Suggested Readings) argues that the moral status of the early fetus is not determined by its intrinsic properties but by its actual future, and specifically by the Actual Future Principle, which says that an early fetus that becomes a person has a moral status, but an early fetus that dies while still an early fetus has none. Interestingly, she concludes that an early abortion is morally insignificant, but the decision to *fail* to abort is morally significant. Before failing to abort, a woman should deliberate seriously and recognize her responsibility for the creation of a person.

Harman seems to accept consciousness as a morally significant dividing line in the development of the fetus. The majority decision in *Roe* also takes a dividing-line position. That is, Justice Blackmun tries to draw a line in the development of the fetus before which abortion is justified and after which it is much harder to justify. Unlike Harman, Justice Blackmun adopts viability as a dividing line. *Viability* occurs when the fetus is capable of surviving outside the womb. Just when this occurs is the subject of debate. Justice Blackmun puts viability at the twenty-eighth week of pregnancy, but many doctors say it occurs at twenty-four weeks or perhaps as early as twenty weeks. In any case, Justice Blackmun holds that abortion is legal before viability but that after viability the state may impose restrictions or even proscribe it except when it is necessary to save the life or health of the mother.

Noonan objects to lines drawn separating what is a person and what is not a person when those lines are based in the development of the fetus. Such lines, he argues, are always arbitrary and inadequate. For example, viability is a shifting point. The development of artificial incubation will make the fetus viable at any time, even shortly after conception. Furthermore, the time at which the fetus is viable varies according to circumstances such as its weight, age, and race.

Opponents of dividing lines also use what are called slippery-slope arguments; that is, they argue that a line cannot be securely drawn at any point in the development of the fetus because such a line inevitably slides down the slope of development to conception. They insist that the only place to draw the line is at conception. Thomson rejects this argument as invalid. The conclusion does not follow. It is like arguing that because an acorn develops into an oak tree, therefore an acorn is an oak tree.

Noonan, Callahan, and many others insist that a human being or human life begins at conception. Mills does not agree. He argues that whether or not an adult human being was once a zygote, the adult did not begin at conception. On the one hand, if the adult was never a zygote, but came into existence at a later stage of development, then obviously the adult did not come into existence at conception. (As we have seen, Marquis seems to suggest that a determinate human being does not come into existence until fourteen days after conception.) On the other hand, if the adult was once a zygote, then the adult does not begin as a zygote but as an unfertilized egg. Mills emphasizes the biological fact that at conception the unfertilized egg is already there ready to be impregnated by the sperm and that once it is absorbed by the egg, the sperm ceases to exist. So, if the adult was once a zygote, the real beginning was the creation of the mother's unfertilized egg and not conception. This metaphysical conclusion has important implications for the morality of early abortions. Contraception and sexual abstinence kill the woman's egg just as much as zygotic abortion. Thus, if contraception and sexual abstinence are not seriously wrong, as Marquis and many others hold, then an early abortion is not seriously wrong either. If conception is not the beginning of a human life or human being, then it does not have the moral significance given it by pro-life advocates.

Philosophical Issues

Is a human life intrinsically valuable? Callahan thinks so, but not everyone agrees. An implication of Marquis's view is that a human life without a future like ours is not intrinsically valuable. For example, on his view it would not be wrong to kill a comatose or brain-dead human being who has no possibility of regaining consciousness.

Is anything with the complete human genetic code a person with a right to life? Noonan assumes this, but Warren holds that a being that is merely genetically human, e.g., a complete human cell, is not morally human, that is, a person with rights. Basically, the problem lies in determining who is a person with rights or who has a moral standing. The standard approach is to find a criterion for personhood—that is, some one feature, such a human genetic coding or consciousness or rationality—that is both a necessary and sufficient condition for being a person. Utilitarians say that that consciousness is the criterion for personhood or moral standing, whereas followers of Kant, such as Warren, hold that rationality is essential. (Warren adds five other features—sentience, emotionality, the capacity to communicate, self-awareness, and moral agency—but these seem to be built into the concept of rationality.) As we have seen, Noonan thinks that human genetic coding is the criterion for personhood.

Marquis argues that these criteria for personhood have scope problems, that is, they are either too broad or too narrow. Noonan's genetic criterion is too broad because it includes human cancer cells that are biologically human but not persons. Warren's rationality criterion, in contrast, is too narrow because it excludes from the class of persons infants, the severely retarded, and some of the mentally ill.

Jane English (see the Suggested Readings) makes a different objection to the search for a criterion of personhood. In her view, the search is doomed from the outset because the concept of *person* has fuzzy borders; that is, there are borderline cases in which we cannot say whether a living being is a person or not, and the fetus constitutes just such a case.

Marquis argues that the moral status of the fetus is not based on properties such as being human or being conscious, but rather on the potentiality of the fetus. If it has a future like ours, it is wrong to kill. Elizabeth Harman does not agree. In "The Potentiality Problem" (see the Suggested Readings), she takes the position that consciousness does give a being moral status, and this means that both cats and conscious babies have this status. But the potentiality of the nonconscious embryo does not by itself confer any moral status on the embryo. According to Harman's Actual Future Principle, it is the actual future of the fetus that determines its moral status. If the fetus dies in an abortion, then it has no actual future as a person, and it has no moral status at all. However, if the fetus does have an actual future as a person, then it does have a moral status as a subject of care and concern.

If we cannot conclusively determine the nature and moral status of the fetus, then how can we answer the moral question about abortion? Thomson's tactic is to shift the focus of debate from the status of the fetus to the rights of the pregnant woman. She argues that even if the fetus is a person with a right to life, it still does not follow that abortions are never justified. The right to life does not entail the right to control a woman's body, and this right as well as the woman's right to life and self-defense can justify abortion.

Callahan (see the Suggested Readings) grants that a woman has a moral right to control her own body in cases such as contraception and sterilization, but not in pregnancy—for then one's own body is not a single unit but is engendering another life. She also criticizes Thomson for relying on analogies that fail to apply. She objects that being pregnant is not analogous to being hooked up to a famous violinist's life-support system, or to anything else, for that matter.

Thomson's method is common in ethics: an appeal to moral intuitions in a particular case. She asks us what we would say or think in an imaginary case in which you are kidnapped by the Society of Music Lovers and connected to a famous but unconscious violinist who uses your kidneys to stay alive for nine months. She thinks it would not be morally wrong to disconnect from the violinist in this case even if this means that the violinist will die. Even though the violinist has a right to life, this does not entitle the violinist to use your kidneys. At least, those are Thomson's moral intuitions. The problem is that we cannot assume everyone will have the same intuitions, particularly when we are dealing with strange cases like this. When it comes to pregnancy, Callahan, for example, does not have the same moral intuitions as Thomson.

The most basic and difficult problem is formulating an acceptable principle about the wrongness of killing. Such a principle is needed not only in the abortion controversy but also in dealing with questions about euthanasia, capital punishment, killing of animals, and war. It is hard to find a moral principle about killing that does not have scope problems, that is not too broad or too narrow or subject to counterexamples. The principle that it is wrong to take an innocent human life is too broad because it makes it wrong to kill a human cancer cell, which is both human and living. The alternative principle that it is wrong to kill an innocent human being is too narrow; it does not seem to apply to the fetus in the early stages of development. This principle may also be too broad, as it rules out killing innocent human beings in war or in self-defense. The Kantian principle that it is wrong to kill persons or rational beings has similar problems; for example, it does not seem to apply to newborn infants or the retarded or the mentally ill.

Marquis's principle is that killing someone is wrong, in general, when it deprives her or him of a future like ours. This principle forbids killing someone because it inflicts on the victim the loss of a future containing valuable experiences, activities, projects, and enjoyments. However, this principle seems to have scope problems similar to those of the other principles about killing. It may be too broad because it seems to imply that killing nonhuman animals such as pigs is wrong, and this is very problematic in our meat-eating society. (See the discussion of animal rights in Chapter 6.) Marquis's principle may be too narrow as well, as it seems to imply that active euthanasia of those facing unhappy or meaningless lives, such as the mentally ill or severely retarded or the incurable diseased, is not wrong, and this is surely debatable.

Excerpts from *Roe v. Wade* (1973)

THE U.S. SUPREME COURT

Harry B. Blackmun (1909–1999) was an associate Justice of the U.S. Supreme Court. He was appointed to the Court in 1970 and retired in 1994.

Byron R. White (1917–2002) was appointed to the Supreme Court in 1962 and retired in 1993.

Source: U.S. Supreme Court, *Roe v. Wade*, 410 U.S. 113 (1973).

In the case of *Roe v. Wade*, a pregnant single woman challenged a Texas abortion law making abortion (except to save the mother's life) a crime punishable by a prison sentence of two to five years. ("Jane Roe" was a pseudonym for Norma McCorvey, a woman who now says she is pro-life.) By a 7-to-2 vote, the Court ruled that the Texas law was unconstitutional.

The reading includes excerpts from the majority opinion, written by Justice Blackmun, and from the dissenting opinion, written by Justice White.

After an interesting survey of historical views of abortion, Justice Blackmun argues that the abortion decision is included in the right of personal privacy. But this right is not absolute; it must yield at some point to the state's legitimate interest in protecting potential life, and this interest becomes compelling at the point of viability.

In his dissenting opinion, Justice White claims that the Court has no constitutional basis for its decision and that it incorrectly values the convenience of the mother more than the existence and development of human life.

It perhaps is not generally appreciated that the restrictive criminal abortion laws in effect in a majority of States today are of relatively recent vintage. Those laws, generally proscribing abortion or its attempt at any time during pregnancy except when necessary to preserve the pregnant woman's life, are not of ancient or even of common-law origin. Instead, they derive from statutory changes effected, for the most part, in the latter half of the 19th century.

ANCIENT ATTITUDES

These are not capable of precise determination. We are told that at the time of the Persian Empire, abortifacients were known and that criminal abortions were severely punished. We are also told, however, that abortion was practiced in Greek times as well as in the Roman Era, and that "it was resorted to without scruple." The Ephesian, Soranos, often described as the greatest of the ancient gynecologists, appears to have been generally opposed to Rome's prevailing free abortion practices. He found it necessary to think first of the life of the mother, and he resorted to abortion when, upon this standard, he felt the procedure advisable. Greek and Roman law afforded little protection to the unborn. If abortion was prosecuted in some places, it seems to have been based on a concept of a violation of the father's right to his offspring. Ancient religion did not bar abortion.

THE HIPPOCRATIC OATH

What then of the famous Oath that has stood so long as the ethical guide of the medical profession and that bears the name of the great Greek (460(?)–377(?) B.C.E.), who has been described as the Father of Medicine, the "wisest and the greatest practitioner of his art," and the "most important and most complete medical personality of antiquity," who dominated the medical schools of his time, and who typified the sum of the medical knowledge of the past? The Oath varies somewhat according to the particular translation, but in any translation the content is clear: "I will give no deadly medicine to anyone if asked, nor suggest any such counsel; and in like manner I will not give to a woman a pessary to produce abortion," or "I will neither give a deadly drug to anybody if asked for it, nor will I make a suggestion to this effect. Similarly, I will not give to a woman an abortive remedy."

Although the Oath is not mentioned in any of the principal briefs in this case or in *Doe v. Bolton, post*, p. 179, it represents the apex of the development of strict ethical concepts in medicine, and its influence endures to this day. Why did not the authority of Hippocrates dissuade abortion practice in his time and that of Rome? The late Dr. Edelstein provides us with a theory: The Oath was not uncontested even in Hippocrates' day; only the Pythagorean school of philosophers frowned upon the related act of suicide. Most Greek thinkers, on the other hand, commended abortion, at least prior to viability. See Plato, Republic, V, 461; Aristotle, Politics, VII, 1335b 25. For the Pythagoreans, however, it was a matter of dogma. For them the embryo was animate from the moment of conception, and abortion meant destruction of a living being. The abortion clause of the Oath, therefore, "echoes Pythagorean doctrines," and "[i]n no other stratum of Greek opinion were such views held or proposed in the same spirit of uncompromising austerity."

Dr. Edelstein then concludes that the Oath originated in a group representing only a small segment of Greek opinion and that it certainly was not accepted by all ancient physicians. He points out that medical writings down to Galen (130–200 C.E.) "give evidence of the violation of almost every one of its injunctions." But with the end of antiquity a decided change took place. Resistance against suicide and against abortion became common. The Oath came to be popular. The emerging teachings of Christianity were in agreement with the Pythagorean ethic. The Oath "became the nucleus of all medical ethics" and "was applauded as the embodiment of truth." Thus, suggests Dr. Edelstein, it is "a Pythagorean manifesto and not the expression of an absolute standard of medical conduct."

This, it seems to us, is a satisfactory and acceptable explanation of the Hippocratic Oath's apparent rigidity. It enables us to understand, in historical context, a long-accepted and revered statement of medical ethics.

THE COMMON LAW

It is undisputed that at common law, abortion performed *before* "quickening"—the first recognizable movement of the fetus *in utero*, appearing usually from the 16th to the 18th week of pregnancy—was not an indictable offense. The absence of a common-law crime for pre-quickening abortion appears to have developed from a confluence of earlier philosophical, theological, and civil and canon law concepts of when life begins. These disciplines variously approached the question in terms of the point at which the embryo or fetus became "formed" or recognizably human, or in terms of when a "person" came into being,

that is, infused with a "soul" or "animated." A loose consensus evolved in early English law that these events occurred at some point between conception and live birth. This was "mediate animation." Although Christian theology and the canon law came to fix the point of animation at 40 days for a male and 80 days for a female, a view that persisted until the 19th century, there was otherwise little agreement about the precise time of formation or animation. There was agreement, however, that prior to this point the fetus was to be regarded as part of the mother, and its destruction, therefore, was not homicide. Due to continued uncertainty about the precise time when animation occurred, or to the lack of any empirical basis for the 40–80-day view, and perhaps to Aquinas' definition of movement as one of the two first principles of life, Bracton focused upon quickening as the critical point. The significance of quickening was echoed by later common-law scholars and found its way into the received common law in this country.

Whether abortion of a *quick* fetus was a felony at common law, even a lesser crime, is still disputed. Bracton, writing early in the 13th century, thought it homicide. But the later and predominant view, following the great common-law scholars, has been that it was, at most, a lesser offense. In a frequently cited passage, Coke took the position that abortion of a woman "quick with childe" is "a great misprision, and no murder." Blackstone followed, saying that while abortion after quickening had once been considered manslaughter (though not murder), "modern law" took a less severe view. A recent review of the common-law precedents argues, however, that those precedents contradict Coke and that even post-quickening abortion was never established as a common-law crime. This is of some importance because while most American courts ruled, in holding or dictum, that abortion of an unquickened fetus was not criminal under their received common law, others followed Coke in stating that abortion of a quick fetus was a "misprision," a term they translated to mean "misdemeanor." That their reliance on Coke on this aspect of the law was uncritical and, apparently in all the reported cases, dictum (due probably to the paucity of common-law prosecutions for post-quickening abortion), makes it now appear doubtful that abortion was ever firmly established as a common-law crime even with respect to the destruction of a quick fetus. . . .

THE AMERICAN LAW

In this country, the law in effect in all but a few States until mid-19th century was the preexisting English common law. Connecticut, the first State to enact abortion legislation, adopted in 1821 that part of Lord Ellenborough's Act that related to a woman "quick with child." The death penalty was not imposed. Abortion before quickening was made a crime in that State only in 1860. In 1828, New York enacted legislation that, in two respects, was to serve as a model for early anti-abortion statutes. First, while barring destruction of an unquickened fetus as well as a quick fetus, it made the former only a misdemeanor, but the latter second-degree manslaughter. Second, it incorporated a concept of therapeutic abortion by providing that an abortion was excused if it "shall have been necessary to preserve the life of such mother, or shall have been advised by two physicians to be necessary for such purpose." By 1840, when Texas had received the common law, only eight American States had statutes dealing with abortion. It was not until after the War Between the States that legislation began generally to replace the common law. Most of these initial statutes dealt severely with abortion after quickening but were lenient with it before quickening. Most punished attempts equally with completed abortions. While many statutes included the exception for an abortion thought by one or more physicians to be necessary to save the mother's life, that provision soon disappeared and the typical law required that the procedure actually be necessary for that purpose.

Gradually, in the middle and late 19th century the quickening distinction disappeared from the statutory law of most States and the degree of the offense and the penalties were increased. By the end of the 1950s, a large majority of the jurisdictions banned abortion, however and whenever performed, unless done to save or preserve the life of the mother. The exceptions, Alabama and the District of Columbia, permitted abortion to preserve the mother's health. Three States permitted abortions that were not "unlawfully" performed or that were not "without lawful justification," leaving interpretation of those standards to the courts. In the past several years, however, a trend toward liberalization of abortion statutes has resulted in adoption, by about one-third of the States, of less stringent laws, most of them patterned after the ALI Model Penal Code, § 230.3.

It is thus apparent that common law, at the time of the adoption of our Constitution, and throughout the major portion of the 19th century, viewed abortion with less disfavor than most American statutes currently in effect. Phrasing it another way, a woman had a substantially broader right to terminate a pregnancy than she does in most states today. At least with respect to the early stage of pregnancy and very possibly without such a limitation, the opportunity to make this choice was present in this country well into the 19th century. Even later, the law continued for some time to treat less punitively an abortion procured in early pregnancy. . . .

Three reasons have been advanced to explain historically the enactment of criminal abortion laws in the 19th century and to justify their continued existence.

It has been argued occasionally that these laws were the product of a Victorian social concern to discourage illicit sexual conduct. Texas, however, does not advance this justification in the present case, and it appears that no court or commentator has taken the argument seriously. The appellants and *amici* contend, moreover, that this is not a proper state purpose at all and suggest that, if it were, the Texas statutes are overbroad in protecting it since the law fails to distinguish between married and unwed mothers.

A second reason is concerned with abortion as a medical procedure. When most criminal abortion laws were first enacted, the procedure was a hazardous one for the woman. This was particularly true prior to the development of antisepsis. Antiseptic techniques, of course, were based on discoveries by Lister, Pasteur, and others first announced in 1867, but were not generally accepted and employed until about the turn of the century. Abortion mortality was high. Even after 1900, and perhaps until as late as the development of antibiotics in the 1940's, standard modern techniques such as dilation and curettage were not nearly so safe as they are today. Thus, it has been argued that a State's real concern in enacting a criminal abortion law was to protect the pregnant woman, that is, to restrain her from submitting to a procedure that placed her life in serious jeopardy.

Modern medical techniques have altered this situation. Appellants and various *amici* refer to medical data indicating that abortion in early pregnancy, that is, prior to the end of the first trimester, although not without its risk, is now relatively safe. Mortality rates for women undergoing early abortions, where the procedure is legal, appear to be as low as or lower than the rates for normal childbirth. Consequently, any interest of the State in protecting the women from an inherently hazardous procedure, except when it would be equally dangerous for her to forgo it, has largely disappeared. Of course, important state interests in the areas of health and medical standards do remain. The State has a legitimate interest in seeing to it that abortion, like any other medical procedure, is performed under circumstances that insure maximum safety for the patient. This interest obviously extends at least to the performing physician and his staff, to the facilities involved, to the availability of aftercare, and to adequate provision for any complication or emergency that might arise. The prevalence of high mortality rates at illegal "abortion mills" strengthens, rather than weakens, the State's interest in regulating the conditions under which abortions are performed. Moreover, the risk to the woman increases as her pregnancy continues. Thus the State retains a definite interest in protecting the woman's own health and safety when an abortion is proposed at a late stage of pregnancy.

The third reason is the State's interest—some phrase it in terms of duty—in protecting prenatal life. Some of the argument for this justification rests on the theory that a new human life is present from the moment of conception. The State's interest and general obligation to protect life then extends, it is argued, to prenatal life. Only when the life of the pregnant mother herself is at stake, balanced against the life she carries within her, should the interest of the embryo or fetus not prevail. Logically, of course, a legitimate state interest in this area need not stand or fall on acceptance of the belief that life begins at conception or at some other point prior to live birth. In assessing the State's interest, recognition may be given to the less rigid claim that as long as at least *potential* life is involved, the State may assert interests beyond the protection of the pregnant woman alone.

Parties challenging state abortion laws have sharply disputed in some courts the contention that a purpose of these laws, when enacted, was to protect prenatal life. Pointing to the absence of legislative history to support the contention, they claim that most state laws were designed solely to protect the woman. Because medical advances have lessened this concern, at least with respect to abortion in early pregnancy, they argue that with respect to such abortions the laws can no longer be justified by any state interest. There is some scholarly support for this view of original purpose. The few state courts called upon to interpret their laws in the late 19th and early 20th centuries did focus on the State's interest in protecting the woman's health rather than in preserving the embryo and fetus. Proponents of this view point out that in many States, including Texas, by statute or judicial interpretation, the pregnant woman herself could not be prosecuted for self-abortion or for cooperating in an abortion performed upon her by another. They claim that adoption of the "quickening" distinction through received common law and state statutes tacitly recognizes the greater health hazards inherent in late abortion and impliedly repudiates the theory that life begins at conception.

It is with these interests, and the weight to be attached to them, that this case is concerned.

The Constitution does not explicitly mention any right of privacy. In a line of decisions, however, going back perhaps as far as *Union Pacific R. Co. v. Botsford*, 141 U.S. 250, 251 (1891), the Court has recognized that a right of personal privacy, or a guarantee of certain areas or zones of privacy does exist under the Constitution. In carrying contexts, the Court or individual justices have, indeed, found at least the roots of that right in the First Amendment, in the Fourth and Fifth Amendments, in the penumbras of the Bill of Rights, in the Ninth Amendment, or in the concept of liberty guaranteed by the first section of the Fourteenth Amendment. These decisions make it clear that only personal rights that can be deemed "fundamental" or "implicit in the concept of ordered liberty," are included in this guarantee of personal privacy. They also make it clear that the right has some extension to activities relating to marriage, procreation, contraception, family relationships, and child rearing and education.

This right of privacy, whether it be founded in the Fourteenth Amendment's concept of personal liberty and restrictions upon state action, as we feel it is, or, as the District Court determined, in the Ninth Amendment's reservation of rights to the people, is broad enough to encompass a woman's decision whether or not to terminate her pregnancy. The detriment that the State would impose upon the pregnant woman by denying this choice altogether is apparent. Specific and direct harm medically diagnosable even in early pregnancy may be involved. Maternity, or additional offspring, may force upon the woman a distressful life and future. Psychological harm may be imminent. Mental and physical health may be taxed by child care. There is also the distress, for all concerned, associated with the unwanted child, and there is the problem of bringing a child into a family already unable, psychologically and otherwise, to care for it. In other cases, as in this one, the additional difficulties and continuing stigma of unwed motherhood may be involved. All these are factors the woman and her responsible physician necessarily will consider in consultation.

On the basis of elements such as these, appellant and some *amici* argue that the woman's right is absolute and that she is entitled to terminate her pregnancy at whatever time, in whatever way, and for whatever reason she alone chooses. With

this we do not agree. Appellant's arguments that Texas either has no valid interest at all in regulating the abortion decision, or no interest strong enough to support any limitation upon the woman's sole determination, are unpersuasive. The Court's decisions recognizing a right of privacy also acknowledge that some state regulation in areas protected by that right is appropriate. As noted above, a State may properly assert important interests in safeguarding health, in maintaining medical standards, and in protecting potential life. At some point in pregnancy, these respective interests become sufficiently compelling to sustain regulation of the factors that govern the abortion decision. The privacy right involved, therefore, cannot be said to be absolute. In fact, it is not clear to us that the claim asserted by some *amici* that one has an unlimited right to do with one's body as one pleases bears a close relationship to the right of privacy previously articulated in the Court's decisions. The Court has refused to recognize an unlimited right of this kind in the past.

We, therefore, conclude that the right of personal privacy includes the abortion decision, but that this right is not unqualified and must be considered against important state interests in regulation.

We note that those federal and state courts that have recently considered abortion law challenges have reached the same conclusion.

Although the results are divided, most of these courts have agreed that the right of privacy, however based, is broad enough to cover the abortion decision, that the right, nonetheless, is not absolute and is subject to some limitations; and that at some point the state interests as to protection of health, medical standards, and prenatal life, become dominant. We agree with this approach.

Where certain "fundamental rights" are involved, the Court has held that regulation limiting these rights may be justified only by a "compelling state interest," and that legislative enactments must be narrowly drawn to express only the legitimate state interests at stake.

In the recent abortion cases, cited above, courts have recognized these principles. Those striking down state laws have generally scrutinized the State's interests in protecting health and potential life, and have concluded that neither interest justified broad limitations on the reasons for which a physician and his pregnant patient might decide that she should have an abortion in the early stages of pregnancy. Courts sustaining state laws have held that the State's determinations to protect health or prenatal life are dominant and constitutionally justifiable.

The District Court held that the appellee failed to meet his burden demonstrating that the Texas statute's infringement upon Roe's rights was necessary to support a compelling state interest, and that, although the appellee presented "several compelling justifications for state presence in the area of abortions," the statutes outstripped these justifications and swept "far beyond any areas of compelling state interest." Appellant and appellee both contest that holding. Appellant, as has been indicated, claims an absolute right that bars any state imposition of criminal penalties in the area. Appellee argues that the State's determination to recognize and protect prenatal life from and after conception constitutes a compelling state interest. As noted above, we do not agree fully with either formulation.

A. The appellee and certain *amici* argue that the fetus is a "person" within the language and meaning of the Fourteenth Amendment. In support of this, they outline at length and in detail the well-known facts of fetal development. If this suggestion of personhood is established, the appellant's case, of course, collapses, for the fetus' right to life would then be guaranteed specifically by the Amendment. The appellant conceded as much on reargument. On the other hand, the appellee conceded on reargument that no case could be cited that holds that a fetus is a person within the meaning of the Fourteenth Amendment.

The Constitution does not define "person" in so many words. Section 1 of the Fourteenth Amendment contains three references to "person." In nearly all these instances, the use of the word is such that it has application only postnatally. None indicates, with any assurance, that it has any possible pre-natal application.

All this, together with our observation, *supra*, that throughout the major portion of the 19th century prevailing legal abortion practices were far freer than they are today, persuades us that the word "person," as used in the Fourteenth Amendment, does not include the unborn. This is in accord with the results reached in those few cases where the issue has been squarely presented. Indeed, our decision in *United States v. Vuitch*, 402 U.S. 62 (1971), inferentially is to the same effect, for we there would not have indulged in statutory interpretation favorable to abortion in specified circumstances if the necessary consequence was the termination of life entitled to Fourteenth Amendment protection.

This conclusion, however, does not of itself fully answer the contentions raised by Texas, and we pass on to other considerations.

B. The pregnant woman cannot be isolated in her privacy. She carried an embryo and, later, a fetus, if one accepts the medical definitions of the developing young in the human uterus. See Dorland's Illustrated Medical Dictionary 478–479, 547 (24th ed. 1965). The situation therefore is inherently different from marital intimacy, or bedroom possession of obscene material, or marriage, or procreation, or education, with which *Eisenstadt* and *Griswold, Stanley, Loving, Skinner,* and *Pierce* and *Meyer* were respectively concerned. As we have intimated above, it is reasonable and appropriate for a State to decide that at some point in time another interest, that of health of the mother or that of potential human life, becomes significantly involved. The woman's privacy is no longer sole and any right of privacy she possesses must be measured accordingly.

Texas urges that, apart from the Fourteenth Amendment, life begins at conception and is present throughout pregnancy, and that, therefore, the State has a compelling interest in protecting that life from and after conception. We need not resolve the difficult question of when life begins. When those trained in the respective disciplines of medicine, philosophy, and theology are unable to arrive at any consensus, the judiciary, at this point in the development of man's knowledge, is not in a position to speculate as to the answer.

It should be sufficient to note briefly the wide divergence of thinking on this most sensitive and difficult question. There has always been strong support for the view that life does not begin until live birth. This was the belief of the Stoics. It appears to be the predominant, though not the unanimous, attitude of the Jewish faith. It may be taken to represent also the position of a large segment of the Protestant community, insofar as that can be ascertained; organized groups that have taken a formal position on the abortion issue have generally regarded abortion as a matter for the conscience of the individual and her family. As we have noted, the common law found greater significance in quickening. Physicians and their scientific colleagues have regarded that event with less interest and have tended to focus either upon conception, upon live birth, or upon the interim point at which the fetus becomes "viable," that is, potentially able to live outside the mother's womb, albeit with artificial aid. Viability is usually placed at about seven months (28 weeks) but may occur earlier, even at 24 weeks. The Aristotelian theory of "mediate animation," that held sway throughout the Middle Ages and the Renaissance in Europe, continued to be official Roman Catholic dogma until the 19th century, despite opposition to this "ensoulment" theory from those in the Church who would recognize the existence of life from the moment of conception. The latter is now, of course, the official belief of the Catholic Church. As one brief *amicus* discloses, this is a view strongly held by many non-Catholics as well, and by many physicians. Substantial problems for precise definition of this view are posed, however, by new embryological data that purport to indicate that conception is a "process" over time, rather than an event, and by new medical techniques such as menstrual extraction, the "morning-after" pill, implantation of embryos, artificial insemination, and even artificial wombs.

In areas other than criminal abortion, the law has been reluctant to endorse any theory that life, as we recognize it, begins before live birth or to accord legal rights to the unborn except in narrowly defined situations and except when the rights are contingent upon live birth. For example, the traditional rule of tort law denied recovery for prenatal injuries even though the child was born alive. That rule has been changed in almost every jurisdiction. In most States, recovery is said to be permitted only if the fetus was viable, or at least quick, when the injuries were sustained, though few courts have squarely so held. In a recent development, generally opposed by the commentators, some States permit the parents of a stillborn child to maintain an action for wrongful death because of prenatal injuries. Such an action, however, would appear to be one to vindicate the parents' interest and is thus consistent with the view that the fetus, at most, represents only the potentiality of life. Similarly, unborn children have been recognized as acquiring rights or interests by way of inheritance or other devolution of property, and have been represented by guardians *ad litem*. Perfection of the interests involved, again, has generally been contingent upon live birth. In short, the unborn have never been recognized in the law as persons in the whole sense.

In view of all this, we do not agree that, by adopting one theory of life, Texas may override the rights of the pregnant woman that are at stake. We repeat, however, that the State does have an important and legitimate interest in preserving and protecting the health of the pregnant woman, whether she be a resident of the State or a nonresident who seeks medical consultation and treatment there, and that it has still *another* important and legitimate interest in protecting the potentiality of human life. These interests are separate and distinct. Each grows in substantiality as the woman approaches term and, at a point during pregnancy, each becomes "compelling."

With respect to the State's important and legitimate interest in the health of the mother, the "compelling" point, in the light of present medical knowledge, is at approximately the end of the first trimester. This is so because of the now-established medical fact, referred to above, that until the end of the first trimester mortality in abortion may be less than mortality in normal childbirth. It follows that, from and after this point, a State may regulate the abortion procedure to the extent that the regulation reasonably relates to the preservation and protection of maternal health. Examples of permissible state regulation in this area are requirements as to the qualifications of the person who is to perform the abortion; as to the licensure of that person; as to the facility in which the procedure is to be performed, that is, whether it must be a hospital or may be a clinic or some other place of less-than-hospital status; as to the licensing of the facility; and the like.

This means, on the other hand, that, for the period of pregnancy prior to this "compelling" point, the attending physician, in consultation with his patient, is free to determine, without regulation by the State, that, in his medical judgment, the patient's pregnancy should be terminated. If that decision is reached, the judgment may be effectuated by an abortion free of interference by the State.

With respect to the State's important and legitimate interest in potential life, the "compelling" point is at viability. This is so because the fetus then presumably has the capability of meaningful life outside the mother's womb. State regulation protective of fetal life after viability thus has both logical and biological justifications. If the State is interested in protecting fetal life after viability, it may go so far as to proscribe abortion during that period, except when it is necessary to preserve the life or health of the mother.

To summarize and to repeat:

1. A state criminal abortion statute of the current Texas type, that excepts from criminality only a *lifesaving* procedure on behalf of the mother, without regard to pregnancy stage and without recognition of the other interests involved, is violative of the Due Process Clause of the Fourteenth Amendment.

   a. For the stage prior to approximately the end of the first trimester, the abortion decision and its effectuation must be left to the medical judgment of the pregnant woman's attending physician.

   b. For the stage subsequent to approximately the end of the first trimester, the State, in promoting its interest in the health of the mother, may, if it chooses, regulate the abortion procedure in ways that are reasonably related to maternal health.

   c. For the stage subsequent to viability, the State in promoting its interest in the potentiality of human life may, if it chooses, regulate, and even proscribe, abortion except where it is necessary, in appropriate medical judgment, for the preservation of the life or health of the mother.

2. The State may define the term "physician" as it has been employed in the preceding paragraphs of this Part XI of this opinion, to mean only a physician currently licensed by the State, and may proscribe any abortion by a person who is not a physician as so defined.

In *Doe v. Bolton, post*, p. 179, procedural requirements contained in one of the modern abortion statutes are considered. That opinion and this one, of course, are to be read together.

This holding, we feel, is consistent with the relative weights of the respective interests involved, with the lessons and examples of medical and legal history, with the lenity of the common law, and with the demands of the profound problems of the present day. The decision leaves the State free to place increasing restrictions on abortion as the period of pregnancy lengthens, so long as those restrictions are tailored to the recognized state interests. The decision vindicates the right of the physician to administer medical treatment according to his professional judgment up to the points where important state interests provide compelling justifications for intervention. Up to those points, the abortion decision in all its aspects is inherently, and primarily, a medical decision, and basic responsibility for it must rest with the physician. If an individual practitioner abuses the privilege of exercising proper medical judgment, the usual remedies, judicial and intra-professional, are available.

MR. JUSTICE WHITE, DISSENTING

At the heart of the controversy in these cases are those recurring pregnancies that pose no danger whatsoever to the life or health of the mother but are nevertheless unwanted for any one or more of a variety of reasons—convenience, family planning, economics, dislike of children, the embarrassment of illegitimacy, etc. The common claim before us is that for any one of such reasons, or for no reason at all, and without asserting or claiming any threat to life or health, any woman is entitled to an abortion at her request if she is able to find a medical advisor willing to undertake the procedure.

The Court for the most part sustains this position: During the period prior to the time the fetus becomes viable, the Constitution of the United States values the convenience, whim or caprice of the putative mother more than the life or potential life of the fetus; the Constitution, therefore, guarantees the right to an abortion as against any state law or policy seeking to protect the fetus from an abortion not prompted by more compelling reasons of the mother.

With all due respect, I dissent. I find nothing in the language or history of the Constitution to support the Court's judgment. . . . As an exercise of raw judicial power, the Court perhaps has authority to do what it does today; but in my view its judgment is an improvident and extravagant exercise of the power of judicial review which the Constitution extends to this Court.

The Court apparently values the convenience of the pregnant mother more than the continued existence and development of the life or potential life which she carries. . . .

It is my view, therefore, that the Texas statute is not constitutionally infirm because it denies abortions to those who seek to serve only their convenience rather than to protect their life or health. . . .

⚜ REVIEW QUESTIONS

1. Justice Blackmun discusses three reasons for the enactment of criminal abortion laws. Why doesn't he accept these reasons?
2. Where does the Constitution guarantee a right of privacy, according to Justice Blackmun?
3. Is the fetus a person in the legal sense, according to Justice Blackmun?
4. According to Justice Blackmun, when is the *compelling* point in the state's interest in the health of the mother?
5. When, according to Justice Blackmun, is the *compelling* point in the state's interest in potential life?
6. Explain Justice Blackmun's conclusions.
7. What are Justice White's objections?

⚜ DISCUSSION QUESTIONS

1. What is the right to privacy? Try to define it.
2. What do you think is properly included in the right to privacy, and what is properly excluded?
3. Do you think that the fetus has any legal rights or any moral rights? Defend your view.
4. Justice White complains that Justice Blackmun's opinion allows a woman to get an abortion "without asserting or claiming any threat to life or health" provided she is able to find a doctor willing to undertake the procedure. Do you think that women should be allowed to get such abortions? Explain your answer. Do you believe that doctors have any obligation to perform such abortions? Why or why not?

An Almost Absolute Value in History

JOHN T. NOONAN, JR.

John T. Noonan, Jr. (b. 1926), is a senior judge on the U.S. Court of Appeals for the Ninth Circuit (in San Francisco) and is professor emeritus of law at the University of California, Berkeley. He is the author of *Contraception* (1968); *The Morality of Abortion* (1970), from which our reading is taken; *Power to Dissolve* (1972); *Persons and Masks of the Law* (1975); *A Private Choice* (1979); *Bribes* (1984); *The Antelope* (1990); *The Lustre of Our Country* (1998); *Narrowing the Nation's Power* (2002); and *A Church That Can and Cannot Change* (2005).

Noonan begins with the question: How do you determine the humanity of a being? The answer he defends is what he says is the view of traditional Christian theology: namely, that you are human if you are conceived by human parents. This view is compared with other alleged criteria of humanity, such as viability, experience, feelings of adults, sensations of adults, and social visibility. Each of these is rejected as inadequate and arbitrary. In his defense of the traditional view, Noonan does not appeal to the medieval theory of *ensoulment*, that is, the theory that the soul enters the body at conception. Instead, he rests his case on the fact that at conception the fetus (or, strictly speaking, the zygote) receives the full genetic code of a human being. He assumes that anything with human genetic coding is a human being with rights equal to those of other humans. It follows that the fetus is a human being with rights from the moment of conception. Once this assumption has been granted, we can see that abortion is morally wrong except in the rare cases in which it is necessary to save the mother's life.

The most fundamental question involved in the long history of thought on abortion is: How do you determine the humanity of a being? To phrase the question that way is to put in comprehensive humanistic terms what the theologians either dealt with as an explicitly theological question under the heading of "ensoulment" or dealt with implicitly in their treatment of abortion. The Christian position as it originated did not depend on a narrow theological or philosophical concept. It had no relation to theories of infant baptism.[1]

It appealed to no special theory of instantaneous ensoulment. It took the world's view on ensoulment as that view changed from Aristotle to Zacchia. There was, indeed, theological influence affecting the theory of ensoulment finally adopted, and, of course, ensoulment itself was a theological concept, so that the position was always explained in theological terms. But the theological notion of ensoulment could easily be translated into humanistic language by substituting "human" for "rational soul"; the problem of knowing when a man is a man is common to theology and humanism.

If one steps outside the specific categories used by the theologians, the answer they gave can be analyzed as a refusal to discriminate among human beings on the basis of their varying potentialities. Once conceived, the being was recognized as man because he had man's potential. The criterion for humanity, thus, was simple and all-embracing: if you are conceived by human parents, you are human.

---

[1] According to Glanville Williams (*The Sanctity of Human Life*), "The historical reason for the Catholic objection to abortion is the same as for the Christian Church's historical opposition to infanticide: the horror of bringing about the death of an unbaptized child." This statement is made without any citation of evidence. As had been seen, desire to administer baptism could, in the Middle Ages, even be urged as a reason for procuring an abortion. It is highly regrettable that the American Law Institute was apparently misled by Williams' account and repeated after him the same baseless statement. See American Law Institute, *Model Penal Code: Tentative Draft No. 9* (1959), p. 148, n. 12.

The strength of this position may be tested by a review of some of the other distinctions offered in the contemporary controversy over legalizing abortion. Perhaps the most popular distinction is in terms of viability. Before an age of so many months, the fetus is not viable, that is, it cannot be removed from the mother's womb and live apart from her. To that extent, the life of the fetus is absolutely dependent on the life of the mother. This dependence is made the basis of denying recognition to its humanity.

There are difficulties with this distinction. One is that the perfection of artificial incubation may make the fetus viable at any time: it may be removed and artificially sustained. Experiments with animals already show that such a procedure is possible. This hypothetical extreme case relates to an actual difficulty: there is considerable elasticity to the idea of viability. Mere length of life is not an exact measure. The viability of the fetus depends on the extent of its anatomical and functional development. The weight and length of the fetus are better guides to the state of its development than age, but weight and length vary. Moreover, different racial groups have different ages at which their fetuses are viable. Some evidence, for example, suggests that Negro fetuses mature more quickly than white fetuses. If viability is the norm, the standard would vary with race and with many individual circumstances.

The most important objection to this approach is that dependence is not ended by viability. The fetus is still absolutely dependent on someone's care in order to continue existence; indeed, a child of one or three or even five years of age is absolutely dependent on another's care for existence; uncared for, the older fetus or the younger child will die as surely as the early fetus detached from the mother. The unsubstantial lessening in dependence at viability does not seem to signify any special acquisition of humanity.

A second distinction has been attempted in terms of experience. A being who has had experience, has lived and suffered, who possesses memories, is more human than one who has not. Humanity depends on formation by experience.

The fetus is thus "unformed" in the most basic human sense.

This distinction is not serviceable for the embryo which is already experiencing and reacting. The embryo is responsive to touch after eight weeks and at least at that point is experiencing. At an earlier stage the zygote is certainly alive and responding to its environment. The distinction may also be challenged by the rare case where aphasia has erased adult memory: has it erased humanity? More fundamentally, this distinction leaves even the older fetus or the younger child to be treated as an unformed inhuman thing. Finally, it is not clear why experience as such confers humanity. It could be argued that certain central experiences such as loving or learning are necessary to make a man human. But then human beings who have failed to love or to learn might be excluded from the class called man.

A third distinction is made by appeal to the sentiments of adults. If a fetus dies, the grief of the parents is not the grief they would have for a living child. The fetus is an unnamed "it" till birth, and is not perceived as personality until at least the fourth month of existence when movements in the womb manifest a vigorous presence demanding joyful recognition by the parents.

Yet feeling is notoriously an unsure guide to the humanity of others. Many groups of humans have had difficulty in feeling that persons of another tongue, color, religion, sex, are as human as they. Apart from reactions to alien groups, we mourn the loss of a ten-year-old boy more than the loss of his one-day-old brother or his 90-year-old grandfather. The difference felt and the grief expressed vary with the potentialities extinguished, or the experience wiped out; they do not seem to point to any substantial difference in the humanity of baby, boy, or grandfather.

Distinctions are also made in terms of sensation by the parents. The embryo is felt within the womb only after about the fourth month. The embryo is seen only at birth. What can be neither seen nor felt is different from what is tangible. If the fetus cannot be seen or touched at all, it cannot be perceived as man.

Yet experience shows that sight is even more untrustworthy than feeling in determining humanity. By sight, color became an appropriate index for saying who was a man, and the evil of racial discrimination was given foundation. Nor can touch provide the test; a being confined by sickness, "out of touch" with others, does not thereby seem to lose his humanity. To the extent that touch still has appeal as a criterion, it appears to be a survival of the old English idea of "quickening"—a possible mistranslation of the Latin *animatus* used in the canon law. To that extent touch as a criterion seems to be dependent on the Aristotelian notion of ensoulment, and to fall when this notion is discarded.

Finally, a distinction is sought in social visibility. The fetus is not socially perceived as human. It cannot communicate with others. Thus, both subjectively and objectively, it is not a member of society. As moral rules are rules for the behavior of members of society to each other, they cannot be made for behavior toward what is not yet a member. Excluded from the society of men, the fetus is excluded from the humanity of men.[2]

By force of the argument from the consequences, this distinction is to be rejected. It is more subtle than that founded on an appeal to physical sensation, but it is equally dangerous in its implications. If humanity depends on social recognition, individuals or whole groups may be dehumanized by being denied any status in their society. Such a fate is fictionally portrayed in *1984* and has actually been the lot of many men in many societies. In the Roman empire, for example, condemnation to slavery meant the practical denial of most human rights; in the Chinese Communist world, landlords have been classified as enemies of the people and so treated as nonpersons by the state. Humanity does not depend on social recognition, though often the failure of society to recognize the prisoner, the alien, the heterodox as human has led to the destruction of human beings. Anyone conceived by a man and a woman is human. Recognition of this condition

by society follows a real event in the objective order, however imperfect and halting the recognition. Any attempt to limit humanity to exclude some group runs the risk of furnishing authority and precedent for excluding other groups in the name of the consciousness or perception of the controlling group in the society.

A philosopher may reject the appeal to the humanity of the fetus because he views "humanity" as a secular view of the soul and because he doubts the existence of anything real and objective which can be identified as humanity. One answer to such a philosopher is to ask how he reasons about moral questions without supposing that there is a sense in which he and the others of whom he speaks are human. Whatever group is taken as the society which determines who may be killed is thereby taken as human. A second answer is to ask if he does not believe that there is a right and wrong way of deciding moral questions. If there is such a difference, experience may be appealed to: to decide who is human on the basis of the sentiment of a given society has led to consequences which rational men would characterize as monstrous.

The rejection of the attempted distinctions based on viability and visibility, experience and feeling, may be buttressed by the following considerations: moral judgments often rest on distinctions, but if the distinctions are not to appear arbitrary *fiat*, they should relate to some real difference in probabilities. There is a kind of continuity in all life, but the earlier stages of the elements of human life possess tiny probabilities of development. Consider, for example, the spermatozoa in any normal ejaculate: there are about 200,000,000 in any single ejaculate, of which one has a chance of developing into a zygote. Consider the oocytes which may become ova: there are 100,000 to 1,000,000 oocytes in a female infant, of which a maximum of 390 are ovulated. But once spermatozoon and ovum meet and the conceptus is formed, such studies as have been made show that roughly in only 20 percent of the cases will spontaneous abortion occur. In other words, the chances are about 4 out of 5 that this new being will develop. At this stage in the life of the being there is a sharp shift in probabilities, an

---

2. . . . Thomas Aquinas gave an analogous reason against baptizing a fetus in the womb: "As long as it exists in the womb of the mother, it cannot be subject to the operation of the ministers of the Church as it is not known to men" (*In sententias Petri Lombardi* 4.6 1.1.2).

immense jump in potentialities. To make a distinction between the rights of spermatozoa and the rights of the fertilized ovum is to respond to an enormous shift in possibilities. For about twenty days after conception the egg may split to form twins or combine with another egg to form a chimera, but the probability of either event happening is very small.

It may be asked, What does a change in biological probabilities have to do with establishing humanity? The argument from probabilities is not aimed at establishing humanity but at establishing an objective discontinuity which may be taken into account in moral discourse. As life itself is a matter of probabilities, as most moral reasoning is an estimate of probabilities, so it seems in accord with the structure of reality and the nature of moral thought to found a moral judgment on the change in probabilities at conception. The appeal to probabilities is the most commonsensical of arguments; to a greater or smaller degree all of us base our actions on probabilities, and in morals, as in law, prudence and negligence are often measured by the account one has taken of the probabilities. If the chance is 200,000,000 to 1 that the movement in the bushes into which you shoot is a man's, I doubt if many persons would hold you careless in shooting; but if the chances are 4 out of 5 that the movement is a human being's, few would acquit you of blame. Would the argument be different if only one out of ten children conceived came to term? Of course this argument would be different. This argument is an appeal to probabilities that actually exist, not to any and all states of affairs which may be imagined.

The probabilities as they do exist do not show the humanity of the embryo in the sense of a demonstration in logic any more than the probabilities of the movement in the bush being a man demonstrate beyond all doubt that the being is a man. The appeal is a "buttressing" consideration, showing the plausibility of the standard adopted. The argument focuses on the decisional factor in any moral judgment and assumes that part of the business of a moralist is drawing lines. One evidence of the nonarbitrary character of the line

drawn is the difference of probabilities on either side of it. If a spermatozoon is destroyed, one destroys a being which had a chance of far less than 1 in 200 million of developing into a reasoning being, possessed of the genetic code, a heart and other organs, and capable of pain. If a fetus is destroyed, one destroys a being already possessed of the genetic code, organs, and sensitivity to pain, and one which had an 80 percent chance of developing further into a baby outside the womb who, in time, would reason.

The positive argument for conception as the decisive moment of humanization is that at conception the new being receives the genetic code. It is this genetic information which determines his characteristics, which is the biological carrier of the possibility of human wisdom, which makes him a self-evolving being. A being with a human genetic code is man.

This review of current controversy over the humanity of the fetus emphasizes what a fundamental question the theologians resolved in asserting the inviolability of the fetus. To regard the fetus as possessed of equal rights with other humans was not, however, to decide every case where abortion might be employed. It did decide the case where the argument was that the fetus should be aborted for its own good. To say a being was human was to say it had a destiny to decide for itself which could not be taken from it by another man's decision. But human beings with equal rights often come in conflict with each other, and some decision must be made as to whose claims are to prevail. Cases of conflict involving the fetus are different only in two respects: the total inability of the fetus to speak for itself and the fact that the right of the fetus regularly at stake is the right to life itself.

The approach taken by the theologians to these conflicts was articulated in terms of "direct" and "indirect." Again, to look at what they were doing from outside their categories, they may be said to have been drawing lines or "balancing values." "Direct" and "indirect" are spatial metaphors; "line-drawing" is another. "To weigh" or "to balance" values is a metaphor of a more complicated mathematical sort hinting at the process which goes on in moral judgments. All the metaphors suggest that, in the moral judgments made, comparisons were necessary, that no value completely controlled. The principle of double effect was no doctrine fallen from heaven, but a method of analysis appropriate where two relative values were being compared. In Catholic moral theology, as it developed, life even of the innocent was not taken as an absolute. Judgments on acts affecting life issued from a process of weighing. In the weighing, the fetus was always given a value greater than zero, always a value separate and independent from its parents. This valuation was crucial and fundamental in all Christian thought on the subject and marked it off from any approach which considered that only the parents' interests needed to be considered.

Even with the fetus weighed as human, one interest could be weighed as equal or superior: that of the mother in her own life. The casuists between 1450 and 1895 were willing to weigh this interest as superior. Since 1895, that interest was given decisive weight only in the two special cases of the cancerous uterus and the ectopic pregnancy. In both of these cases the fetus itself had little chance of survival even if the abortion were not performed. As the balance was once struck in favor of the mother whenever her life was endangered, it could be so struck again. The balance reached between 1895 and 1930 attempted prudentially and pastorally

to forestall a multitude of exceptions for interests less than life.

The perception of the humanity of the fetus and the weighing of fetal rights against other human rights constituted the work of the moral analysts. But what spirit animated their abstract judgments? For the Christian community it was the injunction of Scripture to love your neighbor as yourself. The fetus as human was a neighbor; his life had parity with one's own. The commandment gave life to what otherwise would have been only rational calculation.

The commandment could be put in humanistic as well as theological terms: do not injure your fellow man without reason. In these terms, once the humanity of the fetus is perceived, abortion is never right except in self-defense. When life must be taken to save life, reason alone cannot say that a mother must prefer a child's life to her own. With this exception, now of great rarity, abortion violates the rational humanist tenet of the equality of human lives.

For Christians the commandment to love had received a special imprint in that the exemplar proposed of love was the love of the Lord for his disciples. In the light given by this example, self-sacrifice carried to the point of death seemed in the extreme situations not without meaning. In the less extreme cases, preference for one's own interests to the life of another seemed to express cruelty or selfishness irreconcilable with the demands of love.

⚜ REVIEW QUESTIONS

1. According to Noonan, what is the simple Christian criterion for humanity?
2. Noonan discusses five distinctions (starting with viability) used by defenders of abortion. Explain Noonan's critique of these distinctions.
3. State and explain Noonan's argument from probabilities.
4. What is Noonan's positive argument for saying that conception is "the decisive moment of humanization"?
5. In Noonan's view, why does the fetus have rights equal to those of other human beings?
6. According to Noonan, how do Christian theologians resolve conflicts of rights such as that between the mother's right to life and the fetus's right to life?
7. According to the traditional view defended by Noonan, in which cases does the fetus's right to life outweigh the mother's right to life?

⚜ DISCUSSION QUESTIONS

1. Consider the following objection to Noonan's claim that "a being with a human genetic code is a man." A human cell also is a being with a human genetic code, but obviously it is not a man in the sense of being a human being; therefore, Noonan's claim is false. How could Noonan respond to this objection?

2. Is it possible for a nonhuman being—for example, an angel or an intelligent alien being—to have rights equal to those of human beings? Defend your answer.

3. Noonan admits that abortion can be justified by appealing to the right of self-defense. Does this right justify an abortion in a case of rape? Why or why not?

A Defense of Abortion

JUDITH JARVIS THOMSON

Judith Jarvis Thomson (b. 1929) is professor emeritus of philosophy at Massachusetts Institute of Technology. She is the author of many articles and the following books: *Acts and Other Events* (1977); *Rights, Restitution, and Risk* (1986); *The Realm of Rights* (1990) (with Gilbert Harman); *Moral Relativism and Moral Objectivity* (1996); and *Goodness and Advice* (2001).

Thomson does not believe that the fetus is a person from the moment of conception, and she rejects the slippery-slope argument for saying this. The newly fertilized ovum is no more a person than an acorn is an oak tree. But suppose we assume, just for the sake of argument, that the fetus is a person with the right to life from the moment of conception. It does not follow, she argues, that abortion is never justified. She appeals to a series of imaginary cases, such as being kidnapped and plugged into a famous violinist, being trapped in a tiny house with a growing child, and having people-seeds growing in your carpet. Reflection on these cases shows that the right to life is only the right not to be killed unjustly; it does not entail the right to use your body or to live in your house. These cases are supposed to be analogous to cases of rape, threat to life, or when a woman has taken reasonable precautions not to get pregnant. Thomson does not, however, conclude that abortion is justified in any and every case. There is a moral requirement to be a Minimally Decent Samaritan (as Thomson puts it), and this makes a late abortion wrong if it is done just for the sake of convenience. To use her example, it would be wrong for a woman in her seventh month of pregnancy to get an abortion just to avoid the nuisance of postponing a trip abroad.

Most opposition to abortion relies on the premise that the fetus is a human being, a person, from the moment of conception. The premise is argued for, but, as I think, not well. Take, for example, the most common argument. We are asked to notice that the development of a human being from conception through birth into childhood is continuous; then it is said that to draw a line, to choose a point in this development and say "before this point the thing is not a person, after this point it is

Source: Judith Jarvis Thomson, "A Defense of Abortion," from *Philosophy & Public Affairs*, Vol. 1, No. 1 (Fall 1971). Reprinted by permission of Blackwell Publishing.

a person" is to make an arbitrary choice, a choice for which in the nature of things no good reason can be given. It is concluded that the fetus is, or anyway that we had better say it is, a person from the moment of conception. But this conclusion does not follow. Similar things might be said about the development of an acorn into an oak tree, and it does not follow that acorns are oak trees, or that we had better say they are. Arguments of this form are sometimes called "slippery slope arguments"—the phrase is perhaps self-explanatory—and it is dismaying that opponents of abortion rely on them so heavily and uncritically.

I am inclined to agree, however, that the prospects for "drawing a line" in the development of the fetus look dim. I am inclined to think also that we shall probably have to agree that the fetus has already become a human person well before birth. Indeed, it comes as a surprise when one first learns how early in its life it begins to acquire human characteristics. By the tenth week, for example, it already has a face, arms and legs, fingers and toes; it has internal organs, and brain activity is detectable.[1] On the other hand, I think that the premise is false, that the fetus is not a person from the moment of conception. A newly fertilized ovum, a newly implanted clump of cells, is no more a person than an acorn is an oak tree. But I shall not discuss any of this. For it seems to me to be of great interest to ask what happens if, for the sake of argument, we allow the premise. How, precisely, are we supposed to get from there to the conclusion that abortion is morally impermissible? Opponents of abortion commonly spend most of their time establishing that the fetus is a person, and hardly any time explaining the step from there to the impermissibility of abortion. Perhaps they think the step too simple and obvious to require much comment. Or perhaps instead they are simply being economical in

argument. Many of those who defend abortion rely on the premise that the fetus is not a person, but only a bit of tissue that will become a person at birth; and why pay out more arguments than you have to? Whatever the explanation, I suggest that the step they take is neither easy nor obvious, that it calls for closer examination than it is commonly given, and that when we do give it this closer examination we shall feel inclined to reject it.

I propose, then, that we grant that the fetus is a person from the moment of conception. How does the argument go from here? Something like this, I take it. Every person has a right to life. So the fetus has a right to life. No doubt the mother has a right to decide what shall happen in and to her body; everyone would grant that. But surely a person's right to life is stronger and more stringent than the mother's right to decide what happens in and to her body, and so outweighs it. So the fetus may not be killed; an abortion may not be performed.

It sounds plausible. But now let me ask you to imagine this. You wake up in the morning and find yourself back to back in bed with an unconscious violinist. A famous unconscious violinist. He has been found to have a fatal kidney ailment, and the Society of Music Lovers has canvassed all the available medical records and found that you alone have the right blood type to help. They have therefore kidnapped you, and last night the violinist's circulatory system was plugged into yours, so that your kidneys can be used to extract poisons from his blood as well as your own. The director of the hospital now tells you, "Look, we're sorry the Society of Music Lovers did this to you—we would never have permitted it if we had known. But still, they did it, and the violinist now is plugged into you. To unplug you would be to kill him. But never mind, it's only for nine months. By then he will have recovered from his ailment, and can safely be unplugged from you." Is it morally incumbent on you to accede to this situation? No doubt it would be very nice of you if you did, a great kindness. But do you *have* to accede to it? What if it were not nine months, but nine years? Or longer still? What if the director of the hospital says, "Tough luck, I agree, but you've now

[1]Daniel Callahan, *Abortion: Law, Choice and Morality* (New York, 1970), p. 373. This book gives a fascinating survey of the available information on abortion. The Jewish tradition is surveyed in David M. Feldman, *Birth Control in Jewish Law* (New York, 1968), Part 5, the Catholic tradition in John T. Noonan, Jr., "An Almost Absolute Value in History," in *The Morality of Abortion*, ed. John T. Noonan, Jr. (Cambridge, Mass., 1970).

got to stay in bed, with the violinist plugged into you, for the rest of your life. Because remember this. All persons have a right to life, and violinists are persons. Granted you have a right to decide what happens in and to your body, but a person's right to life outweighs your right to decide what happens in and to your body. So you cannot ever be unplugged from him." I imagine you would regard this as outrageous, which suggests that something really is wrong with that plausible-sounding argument I mentioned a moment ago.

In this case, of course, you were kidnapped; you didn't volunteer for the operation that plugged the violinist into your kidneys. Can those who oppose abortion on the ground I mentioned make an exception for a pregnancy due to rape? Certainly. They can say that persons have a right to life only if they didn't come into existence because of rape; or they can say that all persons have a right to life, but that some have less of a right to life than others, in particular, that those who came into existence because of rape have less. But these statements have a rather unpleasant sound. Surely the question of whether you have a right to life at all, or how much of it you have, shouldn't turn on the question of whether or not you are the product of a rape. And in fact the people who oppose abortion on the ground I mentioned do not make this distinction, and hence do not make an exception in case of rape.

Nor do they make an exception for a case in which the mother has to spend the nine months of her pregnancy in bed. They would agree that would be a great pity, and hard on the mother; but all the same, all persons have a right to life, the fetus is a person, and so on. I suspect, in fact, that they would not make an exception for a case in which, miraculously enough, the pregnancy went on for nine years, or even the rest of the mother's life.

Some won't even make an exception for a case in which continuation of the pregnancy is likely to shorten the mother's life; they regard abortion as impermissible even to save the mother's life. Such cases are nowadays very rare, and many opponents of abortion do not accept this extreme view. All the same, it is a good place to begin: a number of points of interest come out in respect to it.

1. Let us call the view that abortion is impermissible even to save the mother's life "the extreme view." I want to suggest first that it does not issue from the argument I mentioned earlier without the addition of some fairly powerful premises. Suppose a woman has become pregnant, and now learns that she has a cardiac condition such that she will die if she carries the baby to term. What may be done for her? The fetus, being a person, has a right to life, but as the mother is a person too, so has she a right to life. Presumably they have an equal right to life. How is it supposed to come out that an abortion may not be performed? If mother and child have an equal right to life, shouldn't we perhaps flip a coin? Or should we add to the mother's right to life her right to decide what happens in and to her body, which everybody seems to be ready to grant—the sum of her rights now outweighing the fetus' right to life?

The most familiar argument here is the following. We are told that performing the abortion would be directly killing[2] the child, whereas doing nothing would not be killing the mother, but only letting her die. Moreover, in killing the child, one would be killing an innocent person, for the child has committed no crime, and is not aiming at his mother's death. And then there are a variety of ways in which this might be continued. (1) But as directly killing an innocent person is always and absolutely impermissible, an abortion may not be performed. Or (2) as directly killing an innocent person is murder, and murder is always and absolutely impermissible, an abortion may not be performed.[3] Or (3) as one's duty to

---

[2]The term "direct" in the arguments I refer to is a technical one. Roughly, what is meant by "direct killing" is either killing as an end in itself, or killing as a means to some end, for example, the end of saving someone else's life. See note 5 for an example of its use.

[3]Cf. *Encyclical Letter of Pope Pius XI on Christian Marriage*, St. Paul Editions (Boston, n.d.), p. 32: "however much we may pity the mother whose health and even life is gravely imperiled in the performance of the duty alloted to her by nature, nevertheless what could ever be a sufficient reason for excusing in any way the direct murder of the innocent? This is precisely what we are dealing with here." Noonan (*The Morality of Abortion*, p. 43) reads this as follows: "What cause can ever avail to excuse in any way the direct killing of the innocent? For it is a question of that."

refrain from directly killing an innocent person is more stringent than one's duty to keep a person from dying, an abortion may not be performed. Or (4) if one's only options are directly killing an innocent person or letting a person die, one must prefer letting the person die, and thus an abortion may not be performed.[4]

Some people seem to have thought that these are not further premises which must be added if the conclusion is to be reached, but that they follow from the very fact that an innocent person has a right to life.[5] But this seems to me to be a mistake, and perhaps the simplest way to show this is to bring out that while we must certainly grant that innocent persons have a right to life, the theses in (1) through (4) are all false. Take (2), for example. If directly killing an innocent person is murder, and thus is impermissible, then the mother's directly killing the innocent person inside her is murder, and thus is impermissible. But it cannot seriously be thought to be murder if the mother performs an abortion on herself to save her life. It cannot seriously be said that she *must* refrain, that she *must* sit passively by and wait for her death. Let us look again at the case of you and the violinist. There you are, in bed with the violinist, and the director of the hospital says to you, "It's all most distressing, and I deeply sympathize, but you see this is putting an additional strain on your kidneys, and you'll be dead within the month. But you *have* to stay where you are all the same. Because unplugging you would be directly killing an innocent violinist, and that's murder, and that's impermissible." If anything in the world is true, it is that you do not commit murder, you do not do what is impermissible, if you reach around to your back and unplug yourself from that violinist to save your life.

The main focus of attention in writings on abortion has been on what a third party may or may not do in answer to a request from a woman for an abortion. This is in a way understandable. Things being as they are, there isn't much a woman can safely do to abort herself. So the question asked is what a third party may do, and what the mother may do, if it is mentioned at all, is deduced, almost as an afterthought, from what it is concluded that third parties may do. But it seems to me that to treat the matter in this way is to refuse to grant to the mother that very status of person which is so firmly insisted on for the fetus. For we cannot simply read off what a person may do from what a third party may do. Suppose you find yourself trapped in a tiny house with a growing child. I mean a very tiny house, and a rapidly growing child—you are already up against the wall of the house and in a few minutes you'll be crushed to death. The child on the other hand won't be crushed to death; if nothing is done to stop him from growing he'll be hurt, but in the end he'll simply burst open the house and walk out a free man. Now I could well understand it if a bystander were to say, "There's nothing we can do for you. We cannot choose between your life and his, we cannot be the ones to decide who is to live, we cannot intervene." But it cannot be concluded that you too can do nothing, that you cannot attack it to save your life. However innocent the child may be, you do not have to wait passively while it crushes you to death. Perhaps a pregnant woman is vaguely felt to have the status of house, to which we don't allow the right of self-defense. But if the woman houses the child, it should be remembered that she is a person who houses it.

I should perhaps stop to say explicitly that I am not claiming that people have a right to do anything whatever to save their lives. I think, rather, that there are drastic limits to the right of self-defense. If someone threatens you with

---

[4]The thesis in (4) is in an interesting way weaker than those in (1), (2), and (3): they rule out abortion even in cases in which both mother *and* child will die if the abortion is not performed. By contrast, one who held the view expressed in (4) could consistently say that one needn't prefer letting two persons die to killing one.

[5]Cf. The following passage from Pius XII, *Address to the Italian Catholic Society of Midwives*: "The baby in the maternal breast has the right to life immediately from God. Hence there is no man, no human authority, no science, no medical, eugenic, social, economic or moral 'indication' which can establish or grant a valid juridical ground for a direct deliberate disposition of an innocent human life, that is, a disposition which looks to its destruction either as an end or as a means to another end perhaps in itself not illicit. The baby, still not born, is a man in the same degree and for the same reason as the mother" (quoted in Noonan, *The Morality of Abortion*, p. 45).

death unless you torture someone else to death, I think you have not the right, even to save your life, to do so. But the case under consideration here is very different. In our case there are only two people involved, one whose life is threatened, and one who threatens it. Both are innocent: the one who is threatened is not threatened because of any fault, the one who threatens does not threaten because of any fault. For this reason we may feel that we bystanders cannot intervene. But the person threatened can.

In sum, a woman surely can defend her life against the threat to it posed by the unborn child, even if doing so involves [the child's] death. And this shows not merely that the theses in (1) through (4) are false; it shows also that the extreme view of abortion is false, and so we need not canvass any other possible ways of arriving at it from the argument I mentioned at the outset.

2. The extreme view could of course be weakened to say that while abortion is permissible to save the mother's life, it may not be performed by the third party, but only by the mother herself. But this cannot be right either. For what we have to keep in mind is that the mother and the unborn child are not like two tenants in a small house which has, by an unfortunate mistake, been rented to both: the mother *owns* the house. The fact that she does adds to the offensiveness of deducing that the mother can do nothing from the supposition that third parties can do nothing. But it does more than this: it casts a bright light on the supposition that third parties can do nothing. Certainly it lets us see that a third party who says "I cannot choose between you" is fooling himself if he thinks this is impartiality. If Jones has found and fastened on a certain coat, which he needs to keep him from freezing, but which Smith also needs to keep him from freezing, then it is not impartiality that says "I cannot choose between you" when Smith owns the coat. Women have said again and again "This body is *my* body!" and they have reason to feel angry, reason to feel that it has been like shouting into the wind. Smith, after all, is hardly likely to bless us if we say to him, "Of course it's your coat, anybody would grant that it is. But no one may choose between you and Jones who is to have it." . . .

3. Where the mother's life is not at stake, the argument I mentioned at the outset seems to have a much stronger pull. "Everyone has a right to life, so the unborn person has a right to life." And isn't the child's right to life weightier than anything other than the mother's own right to life, which she might put forward as ground for an abortion?

This argument treats the right to life as if it were unproblematic. It is not, and this seems to me to be precisely the source of the mistake.

For we should now, at long last, ask what it comes to, to have a right to life. In some views having a right to life includes having a right to be given at least the bare minimum one needs for continued life. But suppose that what in fact is the bare minimum a man needs for continued life is something he has no right at all to be given? If I am sick unto death, and the only thing that will save my life is the touch of Henry Fonda's cool hand on my fevered brow, then all the same, I have no right to be given the touch of Henry Fonda's cool hand on my fevered brow. It would be frightfully nice of him to fly in from the West Coast to provide it. It would be less nice, though no doubt well meant, if my friends flew out to the West Coast and carried Henry Fonda back with them. But I have no right at all against anybody that he should do this for me. Or again, to return to the story I told earlier, the fact that for continued life that violinist needs the continued use of your kidneys does not establish that he has a right to be given the continued use of your kidneys. He certainly has no right against you that *you* should give him continued use of your kidneys. For nobody has any right to use your kidneys unless you give him such a right; and nobody has the right against you that you shall give him this right—if you do allow him to go on using your kidneys, this is kindness on your part, and not something he can claim from you as his due. Nor has he any right against anybody else that *they* should give him continued use of your kidneys. Certainly he had no right against the Society of Music Lovers that they should plug him into you in the first place. And if you now start to unplug yourself, having learned that you will otherwise have to spend nine years in bed with him, there is nobody in the world who must try to prevent you, in order to see to it that he is given something he has a right to be given.

Some people are rather stricter about the right to life. In their view, it does not include the right to be given anything, but amounts to, and only to, the right not to be killed by anybody. But here a related difficulty arises. If everybody is to refrain from killing that violinist, then everybody must refrain from doing a great many different sorts of things. Everybody must refrain from slitting his throat, everybody must refrain from shooting him—and everybody must refrain from unplugging you from him. But does he have a right against everybody that they shall refrain from unplugging you from him? To refrain from doing this is to allow him to continue to use your kidneys. It could be argued that he has a right against us that we should allow him to continue to use your kidneys. That is, while he had no right against us that we should give him the use of your kidneys, it might be argued that he anyway has a right against us that we shall not now intervene and deprive him of the use of your kidneys. I shall come back to third-party interventions later. But certainly the violinist has no right against you that *you* shall allow him to continue to use your kidneys. As I said, if you do allow him to use them, it is a kindness on your part, and not something you owe him.

The difficulty I point to here is not peculiar to the right to life. It reappears in connection with all the other natural rights; and it is something which an adequate account of rights must deal with. For present purposes it is enough just to draw attention to it. But I would stress that I am not arguing that people do not have a right to life—quite to the contrary, it seems to me that the primary control we must place on the acceptability of an account of rights is that it should turn out in that account to be a truth that all persons have a right to life. I am arguing only that having a right to life does not guarantee having either a right to be given the use of or a right to be allowed continued use of another person's body—even if one needs it for life itself. So the right to life will not serve the opponents of abortion in

the very simple and clear way in which they seem to have thought it would.

4. There is another way to bring out the difficulty. In the most ordinary sort of case, to deprive someone of what he has a right to is to treat him unjustly. Suppose a boy and his small brother are jointly given a box of chocolates for Christmas. If the older boy takes the box and refuses to give his brother any of the chocolates, he is unjust to him, for the brother has been given a right to half of them. But suppose that, having learned that otherwise it means nine years in bed with that violinist, you unplug yourself from him. You surely are not being unjust to him, for you gave him no right to use your kidneys, and no one else can have given him any such right. But we have to notice that in unplugging yourself, you are killing him; and violinists, like everybody else, have a right to life, and thus in the view we were considering just now, the right not to be killed. So here you do what he supposedly has a right you shall not do, but you do not act unjustly to him in doing it.

The emendation which may be made at this point is this: the right to life consists not in the right not to be killed, but rather in the right not to be killed unjustly. This runs a risk of circularity, but never mind: it would enable us to square the fact that the violinist has a right to life with the fact that you do not act unjustly toward him in unplugging yourself, thereby killing him. For if you do not kill him unjustly, you do not violate his right to life, and so it is no wonder you do him no injustice.

But if this emendation is accepted, the gap in the argument against abortion stares us plainly in the face: it is by no means enough to show that the fetus is a person, and to remind us that all persons have a right to life—we need to be shown also that killing the fetus violates its right to life, i.e., that abortion is unjust killing. And is it?

I suppose we may take it as a datum that in a case of pregnancy due to rape the mother has not given the unborn person a right to the use of her body for food and shelter. Indeed, in what pregnancy could it be supposed that the mother has given the unborn person such a right? It is not as if there were unborn persons drifting about the world, to whom a woman who wants a child says "I invite you in."

But it might be argued that there are other ways one can have acquired a right to the use of another person's body than by having been invited to use it by that person. Suppose a woman voluntarily indulges in intercourse, knowing of the chance it will issue in pregnancy, and then she does become pregnant; is she not in part responsible for the presence, in fact the very existence, of the unborn person inside her? No doubt she did not invite it in. But doesn't her partial responsibility for its being there itself give it a right to the use of her body?[6] If so, then her aborting it would be more like the boy's taking away the chocolates, and less like your unplugging yourself from the violinist—doing so would be depriving it of what it does have a right to, and thus would be doing it an injustice.

And then, too, it might be asked whether or not she can kill it even to save her own life: If she voluntarily called it into existence, how can she now kill it, even in self-defense?

The first thing to be said about this is that it is something new. Opponents of abortion have been so concerned to make out the independence of the fetus, in order to establish that it has a right to life, just as its mother does, that they have tended to overlook the possible support they might gain from making out that the fetus is *dependent* on the mother, in order to establish that she has a special kind of responsibility for it, a responsibility that gives it rights against her which are not possessed by any independent person—such as an ailing violinist who is a stranger to her.

On the other hand, this argument would give the unborn person a right to its mother's body only if her pregnancy resulted from a voluntary act, undertaken in full knowledge of the chance a pregnancy might result from it. It would leave out entirely the unborn person whose existence is due to rape. Pending the availability of some further argument, then, we would be left

with the conclusion that unborn persons whose existence is due to rape have no right to the use of their mothers' bodies, and thus that aborting them is not depriving them of anything they have a right to and hence is not unjust killing.

And we should also notice that it is not at all plain that this argument really does go even as far as it purports to. For there are cases and cases, and the details make a difference. If the room is stuffy, and I therefore open a window to air it, and a burglar climbs in, it would be absurd to say, "Ah, now he can stay, she's given him a right to the use of her house—for she is partially responsible for his presence there, having voluntarily done what enabled him to get in, in full knowledge that there are such things as burglars, and that burglars burgle." It would be still more absurd to say this if I had had bars installed outside my windows, precisely to prevent burglars from getting in, and a burglar got in only because of a defect in the bars. It remains equally absurd if we imagine it is not a burglar who climbs in, but an innocent person who blunders or falls in. Again, suppose it were like this: people-seeds drift about in the air like pollen, and if you open your windows, one may drift in and take root in your carpets or upholstery. You don't want children, so you fix up your windows with fine mesh screens, the very best you can buy. As can happen, however, and on very, very rare occasions does happen, one of the screens is defective; and a seed drifts in and takes root. Does the person-plant who now develops have a right to the use of your house? Surely not—despite the fact that you voluntarily opened your windows, you knowingly kept carpets and upholstered furniture, and you knew that screens were sometimes defective. Someone may argue that you are responsible for its rooting, that it does have a right to your house, because after all you *could* have lived out your life with bare floors and furniture, or with sealed windows and doors. But this won't do—for by the same token anyone can avoid a pregnancy due to rape by having a hysterectomy, or anyway by never leaving home without a (reliable!) army.

It seems to me that the argument we are looking at can establish at most that there are *some* cases in which the unborn person has a right

---

[6]The need for a discussion of this argument was brought home to me by members of the Society for Ethical and Legal Philosophy, to whom this paper was originally presented.

to the use of its mother's body, and therefore *some* cases in which abortion is unjust killing. There is room for much discussion and argument as to precisely which, if any. But I think we should sidestep this issue and leave it open, for at any rate the argument certainly does not establish that all abortion is unjust killing.

5. There is room for yet another argument here, however. We surely must all grant that there may be cases in which it would be morally indecent to detach a person from your body at the cost of his life. Suppose you learn that what the violinist needs is not nine years of your life, but only one hour: all you need do to save his life is to spend one hour in that bed with him. Suppose also that letting him use your kidneys for that one hour would not affect your health in the slightest. Admittedly you were kidnapped. Admittedly you did not give anyone permission to plug him into you. Nevertheless it seems to me plain you *ought* to allow him to use your kidneys for that hour—it would be indecent to refuse.

Again, suppose pregnancy lasted only an hour, and constituted no threat to life or health. And suppose that a woman becomes pregnant as a result of rape. Admittedly she did not voluntarily do anything to bring about the existence of a child. Admittedly she did nothing at all which would give the unborn person a right to the use of her body. All the same it might well be said, as in the newly emended violinist story, that she *ought* to allow it to remain for that hour—that it would be indecent in her to refuse.

Now some people are inclined to use the term "right" in such a way that it follows from the fact that you ought to allow a person to use your body for the hour he needs, that he has a right to use your body for the hour he needs, even though he has not been given that right by any person or act. They may say that it follows also that if you refuse, you act unjustly toward him. This use of the term is perhaps so common that it cannot be called wrong; nevertheless it seems to me to be an unfortunate loosening of what we would do better to keep a tight rein on. Suppose that box of chocolates I mentioned earlier had not been given to both boys jointly, but was given only to the older boy. There he sits, stolidly eating his way

through the box, his small brother watching enviously. Here we are likely to say "You ought not to be so mean. You ought to give your brother some of those chocolates." My own view is that it just does not follow from the truth of this that the brother has any right to any of the chocolates. If the boy refuses to give his brother any, he is greedy, stingy, callous—but not unjust. I suppose that the people I have in mind will say it does follow that the brother has a right to some of the chocolates, and thus that the boy does act unjustly if he refuses to give his brother any. But the effect of saying this is to obscure what we should keep distinct, namely the difference between the boy's refusal in this case and the boy's refusal in the earlier case, in which the box was given to both boys jointly, and in which the small brother thus had what was from any point of view clear title to half.

A further objection to so using the term "right" that from the fact that A ought to do a thing for B, it follows that B has a right against A that A do it for him, is that it is going to make the question of whether or not a man has a right to a thing turn on how easy it is to provide him with it; and this seems not merely unfortunate, but morally unacceptable. Take the case of Henry Fonda again. I said earlier that I had no right to the touch of his cool hand on my fevered brow, even though I needed it to save my life. I said it would be frightfully nice of him to fly in from the West Coast to provide me with it, but that I had no right against him that he should do so. But suppose he isn't on the West Coast. Suppose he has only to walk across the room, place a hand briefly on my brow—and lo, my life is saved. Then surely he ought to do it, it would be indecent to refuse. Is it to be said "Ah, well, it follows that in this case she has a right to the touch of his hand on her brow, and so it would be an injustice in him to refuse"? So that I have a right to it when it is easy for him to provide it, though no right when it's hard? It's rather a shocking idea that anyone's rights should fade away and disappear as it gets harder and harder to accord them to him.

So my own view is that even though you ought to let the violinist use your kidneys for the one hour he needs, we should not conclude that he has a right to do so—we should say that if you refuse, you are, like the boy who owns all the chocolates and will give none away, self-centered and callous, indecent in fact, but not unjust. And similarly, that even supposing a case in which a woman pregnant due to rape ought to allow the unborn person to use her body for the hour he needs, we should not conclude that he has a right to do so; we should conclude that she is self-centered, callous, indecent, but not unjust, if she refuses. The complaints are no less grave; they are just different. However, there is no need to insist on this point. If anyone does wish to deduce "he has a right" from "you ought," then all the same he must surely grant that there are cases in which it is not morally required of you that you allow that violinist to use your kidneys, and in which he does not have a right to use them, and in which you do not do him an injustice if you refuse. And so also for mother and unborn child. Except in such cases as the unborn person has a right to demand it—and we were leaving open the possibility that there may be such cases—nobody is morally *required* to make large sacrifices, of health, of all other interests and concerns, of all other duties and commitments, for nine years, or even for nine months, in order to keep another person alive. . . .

6. My argument will be found unsatisfactory on two counts by many of those who want to regard abortion as morally permissible. First, while I do argue that abortion is not impermissible, I do not argue that it is always permissible. There may well be cases in which carrying the child to term requires only Minimally Decent Samaritanism of the mother, and this is a standard we must not fall below. I am inclined to think it a merit of my account precisely that it does *not* give a general yes or a general no. It allows for and supports our sense that, for example, a sick and desperately frightened fourteen-year-old schoolgirl, pregnant due to rape, may *of course* choose abortion, and that any law which rules this out is an insane law. And it also allows for and supports our sense that in other cases resort to abortion is even

positively indecent. It would be indecent in the woman to request an abortion, and indecent in a doctor to perform it, if she is in her seventh month, and wants the abortion just to avoid the nuisance of postponing a trip abroad. The very fact that the arguments I have been drawing attention to treat all cases of abortion, or even all cases of abortion in which the mother's life is not at stake, as morally on a par ought to have made them suspect at the outset.

Secondly, while I am arguing for the permissibility of abortion in some cases, I am not arguing for the right to secure the death of the unborn child. It is easy to confuse these two things in that up to a certain point in the life of the fetus it is not able to survive outside the mother's body; hence removing it from her body guarantees its death. But they are importantly different. I have argued that you are not morally required to spend nine months in bed, sustaining the life of that violinist; but to say this is by no means to say that if, when you unplug yourself, there is a miracle and he survives, you then have a right to turn round and slit his throat. You may detach yourself even if this costs him his life; you have no right to be guaranteed his death, by some other means, if unplugging yourself does not kill him. There are some people who will feel dissatisfied by this feature of my argument. A woman may be utterly devastated by the thought of a child, a bit of herself, put out for adoption and never seen or heard of again. She may therefore want not merely that the child be detached from her, but more, that it die. Some opponents of abortion are inclined to regard this as beneath contempt—thereby showing insensitivity to what is surely a powerful source of despair. All the same, I agree that the desire for the child's death is not one which anybody may gratify, should it turn out to be possible to detach the child alive.

At this place, however, it should be remembered that we have only been pretending throughout that the fetus is a human being from the moment of conception. A very early abortion is surely not the killing of a person, and so is not dealt with by anything I have said here.

⚜ REVIEW QUESTIONS

1. What are "slippery slope arguments," and why does Thomson reject them?
2. Explain the example about the famous violinist.
3. What is the "extreme view," and what argument is used to defend it? How does Thomson attack this argument?
4. What is the point of the example about the tiny house and the growing child?
5. Why do women say, "This body is *my* body"? Do they say this?
6. Explain the example about "Henry Fonda's cool hand on my fevered brow."
7. What is the point of the example about people-seeds taking root in the carpet?
8. What are Thomson's conclusions? When is abortion justified and when is it not justified?

⚜ DISCUSSION QUESTIONS

1. Is the case of the famous violinist really analogous to a case of pregnancy caused by rape?
2. What are the limits to the right to self-defense? Do these limits apply to abortion in cases of rape?
3. What obligations do we have to people who have a right to life? Do we have an obligation, for example, to take care of them and feed them?
4. Does a woman who is accidentally pregnant have a right to get an abortion?

On the Moral and Legal Status of Abortion

MARY ANNE WARREN

Mary Anne Warren is professor emeritus of philosophy at San Francisco State University. Her books include *The Nature of Woman* (1980), *Gendercide* (1985), and *Moral Status* (2000).

In the first part of her article, Warren argues that Thomson's argument about the famous violinist proves that abortion is justified in cases of rape but fails to demonstrate that abortion is permissible when pregnancy is not due to rape and is not life-threatening. Warren thinks that more argument is needed to show the permissibility of abortion in those cases.

In the second part, Warren begins by distinguishing between two senses of the term *human being*, a genetic sense and a moral sense. She criticizes Noonan for not providing an argument for saying that whatever is genetically human is also morally human. Thereafter she suggests six criteria for personhood: sentience, emotionality, reason, the capacity to communicate, self-awareness, and moral agency. She claims that the fetus has none of these characteristics of a person in the early stages of development, and thus it is not a person with moral rights in those stages. The fact that a late-term fetus resembles a person is taken seriously by Warren, and she recommends that women wanting an abortion get one before the third trimester. Still, she is not impressed by an appeal to the fetus's potential for becoming a person because she thinks that the rights of an actual person—namely, the mother—will always outweigh the rights of a merely potential person when they conflict. Warren concludes with a reply to the objection that her view justifies infanticide. She argues that there are several reasons why infanticide is more difficult to justify than abortion.

Source: Mary Anne Warren, "On the Moral and Legal Status of Abortion," from *Ethics in Practice*, ed. Hugh LaFollette, pp. 79–90. Copyright © 1997 Blackwell Publishers. Reprinted with permission.

For our purposes, abortion may be defined as the act a woman performs in deliberately terminating her pregnancy before it comes to term, or in allowing another person to terminate it. Abortion usually entails the death of a fetus.[1] Nevertheless, I will argue that it is morally permissible, and should be neither legally prohibited nor made needlessly difficult to obtain, e.g., by obstructive legal regulations.[2]

Some philosophers have argued that the moral status of abortion cannot be resolved by rational means.[3] If this is so then liberty should prevail; for it is not a proper function of the law to enforce prohibitions upon personal behavior that cannot clearly be shown to be morally objectionable, and seriously so. But the advocates of prohibition believe that their position is objectively correct, and not merely a result of religious beliefs or personal prejudices. They argue that the humanity of the fetus is a matter of scientific fact, and that abortion is therefore the moral equivalent of murder, and must be prohibited in all or most cases. (Some would make an exception when the woman's life is in danger, or when the pregnancy is due to rape or incest; others would prohibit abortion even in these cases.)

In response, advocates of a right to choose abortion point to the terrible consequences of prohibiting it, especially while contraception is still unreliable, and is financially beyond the reach of much of the world's population. Worldwide, hundreds of thousands of women die each year from illegal abortions, and many more suffer from complications that may leave them injured or infertile. Women who are poor, under-age, disabled, or otherwise vulnerable, suffer most

from the absence of safe and legal abortion. Advocates of choice also argue that to deny a woman access to abortion is to deprive her of the right to control her own body—a right so fundamental that without it other rights are often all but meaningless.

These arguments do not convince abortion opponents. The tragic consequences of prohibition leave them unmoved, because they regard the deliberate killing of fetuses as even more tragic. Nor do appeals to the right to control one's own body impress them, since they deny that this right includes the right to destroy a fetus. We cannot hope to persuade those who equate abortion with murder that they are mistaken, unless we can refute the standard antiabortion argument: that because fetuses are human beings, they have a right to life equal to that of any other human being. Unfortunately, confusion has prevailed with respect to the two important questions which that argument raises: (1) Is a human fetus really a human being at all stages of prenatal development? and (2) If so, what (if anything) follows about the moral and legal status of abortion?

John Noonan says that "the fundamental question in the long history of abortion is: How do you determine the humanity of a being?"[4] His antiabortion argument is essentially that of the Roman Catholic Church. In his words,

. . . it is wrong to kill humans, however poor, weak, defenseless, and lacking in opportunity to develop their potential they may be. It is therefore morally wrong to kill Biafrans. Similarly, it is morally wrong to kill embryos.[5]

Noonan bases his claim that fetuses are human beings from the time of conception upon what he calls the theologians' criterion of humanity: that whoever is conceived of human beings is a human being. But although he argues at length for the appropriateness of this criterion of humanity, he does not question the assumption that if a fetus

[1]Strictly speaking, a human conceptus does not become a fetus until the primary organ systems have formed, at about six to eight weeks gestational age. However, for simplicity I shall refer to the conceptus as a fetus at every stage of its prenatal development.
[2]The views defended in this article are set forth in greater depth in my book *Moral Status* (Oxford University Press, 2000).
[3]For example, Roger Wertheimer argues, in "Understanding the Abortion Argument," *Philosophy and Public Affairs*, 1 (Fall, 1971), that the moral status of abortion is not a question of fact, but only of how one responds to the facts.

[4]John Noonan, "Abortion and the Catholic Church: A Summary History," *Natural Law Forum*, 12 (1967), p. 125.
[5]John Noonan, "Deciding Who Is Human," *Natural Law Forum*, 13 (1968), p. 134.

is a human being then abortion is almost always immoral.[6]

Judith Thomson has questioned this assumption. She argues that, even if we grant the antiabortionist the claim that a fetus is a human being with the same right to life as any other human being, we can still demonstrate that women are not morally obliged to complete every unwanted pregnancy.[7] Her argument is worth examining, because if it is sound it may enable us to establish the moral permissibility of abortion without having to decide just what makes an entity a human being, or what entitles it to full moral rights. This would represent a considerable gain in the power and simplicity of the pro-choice position.

Even if Thomson's argument does not hold up, her essential insight—that it requires *argument* to show that if fetuses are human beings then abortion is murder—is a valuable one. The assumption that she attacks is invidious, for it requires that in our deliberations about the ethics of abortion we must ignore almost entirely the needs of the pregnant woman and other persons for whom she is responsible. This will not do; determining what moral rights a fetus has is only one step in determining the moral status of abortion. The next step is finding a just solution to conflicts between whatever rights the fetus has, and the rights and responsibilities of the woman who is unwillingly pregnant.

My own inquiry will also have two stages. In Section I, I consider whether abortion can be shown to be morally permissible even on the assumption that a fetus is a human being with a strong right to life. I argue that this cannot be established, except in special cases. Consequently, we cannot avoid facing the question of whether or not a fetus has the same right to life as any human being.

In Section II, I propose an answer to this question, namely, that a fetus is not a member of the moral community—the set of beings with full and equal moral rights. The reason that a fetus is not a member of the moral community is that it is not yet a person, nor is it enough like a person in the morally relevant respects to be regarded the equal of those human beings who are persons. I argue that it is personhood, and not genetic humanity, which is the fundamental basis for membership in the moral community. A fetus, especially in the early stages of its development, satisfies none of the criteria of personhood. Consequently, it makes no sense to grant it moral rights strong enough to override the woman's moral rights to liberty, bodily integrity, and sometimes life itself. Unlike an infant who has already been born, a fetus cannot be granted full and equal moral rights without severely threatening the rights and well-being of women. Nor, as we will see, is a fetus's *potential* personhood a threat to the moral permissibility of abortion, since merely potential persons do not have a moral right to become actual—or none that is strong enough to override the fundamental moral rights of actual persons.

I

Judith Thomson argues that, even if a fetus has a right to life, abortion is often morally permissible. Her argument is based upon an imaginative analogy. She asks you to picture yourself waking up one day, in bed with a famous violinist, who is a stranger to you. Imagine that you have been kidnapped, and your bloodstream connected to that of the violinist, who has an ailment that will kill him unless he is permitted to share your kidneys for nine months. No one else can save him, since you alone have the right type of blood. Consequently, the Society of Music Lovers has arranged for you to be kidnapped and hooked up. If you unhook yourself, he will die. But if you remain in bed with him, then after nine months he will be cured and able to survive without further assistance from you.

Now, Thomson asks, what are your obligations in this situation? To be consistent, the

---

[6]Noonan deviates from the current position of the Roman Catholic Church in that he thinks that abortion is morally permissible when it is the only way of saving the woman's life. See "An Almost Absolute Value in History," in *Contemporary Issues in Bioethics*, edited by Tom L. Beauchamp and LeRoy Walters (Belmont, California: Wadsworth, 1994), p. 283.
[7]Judith Jarvis Thomson, "A Defense of Abortion," *Philosophy and Public Affairs*, 1:1 (Fall, 1971), pp. 173–8.

antiabortionist must say that you are obliged to stay in bed with the violinist: for violinists are human beings, and all human beings have a right to life.[8] But this is outrageous; thus, there must be something very wrong with the same argument when it is applied to abortion. It would be extremely generous of you to agree to stay in bed with the violinist; but it is absurd to suggest that your refusal to do so would be the moral equivalent of murder. The violinist's right to life does not oblige you to do whatever is required to keep him alive; still less does it justify anyone else in forcing you to do so. A law which required you to stay in bed with the violinist would be an unjust law, since unwilling persons ought not to be required to be Extremely Good Samaritans, i.e., to make enormous personal sacrifices for the sake of other individuals towards whom they have no special prior obligation.

Thomson concludes that we can grant the antiabortionist his claim that a fetus is a human being with a right to life, and still hold that a pregnant woman is morally entitled to refuse to be an Extremely Good Samaritan toward the fetus. For there is a great gap between the claim that a human being has a right to life, and the claim that other human beings are morally obligated to do whatever is necessary to keep him alive. One has no duty to keep another human being alive *at great personal cost*, unless one has somehow contracted a special obligation toward that individual; and a woman who is pregnant may have done nothing that morally obliges her to make the burdensome personal sacrifices necessary to preserve the life of the fetus.

This argument is plausible, and in the case of pregnancy due to rape it is probably conclusive. Difficulties arise, however, when we attempt to specify the larger range of cases in which abortion can be justified on the basis of this argument. Thomson considers it a virtue of her argument that it does not imply that abortion is *always* morally permissible. It would, she says, be indecent for a woman in her seventh month of pregnancy to have an abortion in order to

embark on a trip to Europe. On the other hand, the violinist analogy shows that, "a sick and desperately frightened fourteen-year-old schoolgirl, pregnant due to rape, may *of course* choose abortion, and that any law which rules this out is an insane law."[9] So far, so good; but what are we to say about the woman who becomes pregnant not through rape but because she and her partner did not use available forms of contraception, or because their attempts at contraception failed? What about a woman who becomes pregnant intentionally, but then re-evaluates the wisdom of having a child? In such cases, the violinist analogy is considerably less useful to advocates of the right to choose abortion.

It is perhaps only when a woman's pregnancy is due to rape, or some other form of coercion, that the situation is sufficiently analogous to the violinist case for our moral intuitions to transfer convincingly from the one case to the other. One difference between a pregnancy caused by rape and most unwanted pregnancies is that only in the former case is it perfectly clear that the woman is in no way responsible for her predicament. In the other cases, she *might* have been able to avoid becoming pregnant, e.g., by taking birth control pills (more faithfully), or insisting upon the use of high-quality condoms, or even avoiding heterosexual intercourse altogether throughout her fertile years. In contrast, if you are suddenly kidnapped by strange music lovers and hooked up to a sick violinist, then you are in no way responsible for your situation, which you could not have foreseen or prevented. And responsibility does seem to matter here. If a person behaves in a way which she could have avoided, and which she knows might bring into existence a human being who will depend upon her for survival, then it is not entirely clear that if and when that happens she may rightly refuse to do what she must in order to keep that human being alive.

This argument shows that the violinist analogy provides a persuasive defense of a woman's right to choose abortion only in cases where she is in no way morally responsible for her own

---

[8]Ibid., p. 174.

[9]Ibid., p. 187.

pregnancy. In all other cases, the assumption that a fetus has a strong right to life makes it necessary to look carefully at the particular circumstances in order to determine the extent of the woman's responsibility, and hence the extent of her obligation. This outcome is unsatisfactory to advocates of the right to choose abortion, because it suggests that the decision should not be left in the woman's own hands, but should be supervised by other persons, who will inquire into the most intimate aspects of her personal life in order to determine whether or not she is entitled to choose abortion.

A supporter of the violinist analogy might reply that it is absurd to suggest that forgetting her pill one day might be sufficient to morally oblige a woman to complete an unwanted pregnancy. And indeed it is absurd to suggest this. As we will see, a woman's moral right to choose abortion does not depend upon the extent to which she might be thought to be morally responsible for her own pregnancy. But once we allow the assumption that a fetus has a strong right to life, we cannot avoid taking this absurd suggestion seriously. On this assumption, it is a vexing question whether and when abortion is morally justifiable. The violinist analogy can at best show that aborting a pregnancy is a deeply tragic act, though one that is sometimes morally justified.

My conviction is that an abortion is not always this deeply tragic, because a fetus is not yet a person, and therefore does not yet have a strong moral right to life. Although the truth of this conviction may not be self-evident, it does, I believe, follow from some highly plausible claims about the appropriate grounds for ascribing moral rights. It is worth examining these grounds, since this has not been adequately done before.

II

The question we must answer in order to determine the moral status of abortion is: How are we to define the moral community, the set of beings with full and equal moral rights? What sort of entity has the inalienable moral rights to life, liberty, and the pursuit of happiness? Thomas Jefferson attributed these rights to all *men*, and

he may have intended to attribute them *only* to men. Perhaps he ought to have attributed them to all human beings. If so, then we arrive, first, at Noonan's problem of defining what makes an entity a human being, and second, at the question which Noonan does not consider: What reason is there for identifying the moral community with the set of all human beings, in whatever way we have chosen to define that term?

On the Definition of "Human"

The term "human being" has two distinct, but not often distinguished, senses. This results in a slide of meaning, which serves to conceal the fallacy in the traditional argument that, since (1) it is wrong to kill innocent human beings, and (2) fetuses are innocent human beings, therefore (3) it is wrong to kill fetuses. For if "human being" is used in the same sense in both (1) and (2), then whichever of the two senses is meant, one of these premises is question-begging. And if it is used in different senses then the conclusion does not follow.

Thus, (1) is a generally accepted moral truth,[10] and one that does not beg the question about abortion, only if "human being" is used to mean something like "a full-fledged member of the moral community, who is also a member of the human species." I will call this the *moral* sense of "human being." It is not to be confused with what I will call the *genetic* sense, i.e., the sense in which any individual entity that belongs to the human species is a human being, regardless of whether or not it is rightly considered to be an equal member of the moral community. Premise (1) avoids begging the question only if the moral sense is intended; while premise (2) avoids it only if what is intended is the genetic sense.

Noonan argues for the classification of fetuses with human beings by pointing, first, to the presence of the human genome in the cell nuclei of the human conceptus from conception onwards;

---

[10]The principle that it is always wrong to kill innocent human beings may be in need of other modifications, e.g., that it may be permissible to kill innocent human beings in order to save a larger number of equally innocent human beings; but we may ignore these complications here.

and secondly, to the potential capacity for rational thought.[11] But what he needs to show, in order to support his version of the traditional antiabortion argument, is that fetuses are human beings in the moral sense—the sense in which all human beings have full and equal moral rights. In the absence of any argument showing that whatever is genetically human is also morally human—and he gives none—nothing more than genetic humanity can be demonstrated by the presence of human chromosomes in the fetus's cell nuclei. And, as we will see, the strictly potential capacity for rational thought can at most show that the fetus may later *become* human in the moral sense.

Defining the Moral Community

Is genetic humanity sufficient for moral humanity? There are good reasons for not defining the moral community in this way. I would suggest that the moral community consists, in the first instance, of all *persons*, rather than all genetically human entities.[12] It is persons who invent moral rights, and who are (sometimes) capable of respecting them. It does not follow from this that only persons can have moral rights. However, persons are wise not to ascribe to entities that clearly are not persons moral rights that cannot in practice be respected without severely undercutting the fundamental moral rights of those who clearly are.

What characteristics entitle an entity to be considered a person? This is not the place to attempt a complete analysis of the concept of personhood; but we do not need such an analysis to explain why a fetus is not a person. All we need is an approximate list of the most basic criteria of personhood. In searching for these criteria, it is useful to look beyond the set of people with whom we are acquainted, all of whom are human. Imagine, then, a space traveler who lands on a new planet, and encounters organisms unlike any she has ever seen or heard of. If she wants to behave morally toward these organisms, she has somehow to determine whether they are people and thus have full moral rights, or whether they are things that she need not feel guilty about treating, for instance, as a source of food.

How should she go about making this determination? If she has some anthropological background, she might look for signs of religion, art, and the manufacturing of tools, weapons, or shelters, since these cultural traits have frequently been used to distinguish our human ancestors from prehuman beings, in what seems to be closer to the moral than the genetic sense of "human being." She would be right to take the presence of such traits as evidence that the extraterrestrials were persons. It would, however, be anthropocentric of her to take the absence of these traits as proof that they were not, since they could be people who have progressed beyond, or who have never needed, these particular cultural traits.

I suggest that among the characteristics which are central to the concept of personhood are the following:

1. *Sentience*—the capacity to have conscious experiences, usually including the capacity to experience pain and pleasure;
2. *Emotionality*—the capacity to feel happy, sad, angry, loving, etc.;
3. *Reason*—the capacity to solve new and relatively complex problems;
4. *The capacity to communicate*, by whatever means, messages of an indefinite variety of types; that is, not just with an indefinite number of possible contents, but on indefinitely many possible topics;
5. *Self-awareness*—having a concept of oneself, as an individual and/or as a member of a social group; and finally
6. *Moral agency*—the capacity to regulate one's own actions through moral principles or ideals.

It is difficult to produce precise definitions of these traits, let alone to specify universally valid behavioral indications that these traits are present. But let us assume that our explorer knows approximately what these six characteristics mean,

---

[11]Noonan, "Deciding Who Is Human," p. 135.
[12]From here on, I will use "human" to mean "genetically human," since the moral sense of the term seems closely connected to, and perhaps derived from, the assumption that genetic humanity is both necessary and sufficient for membership in the moral community.

and that she is able to observe whether or not the extraterrestrials possess these mental and behavioral capacities. How should she use her findings to decide whether or not they are persons?

An entity need not have *all* of these attributes to be a person. And perhaps none of them is absolutely necessary. For instance, the absence of emotion would not disqualify a being that was personlike in all other ways. Think, for instance, of two of the *Star Trek* characters, Mr. Spock (who is half human and half alien), and Data (who is an android). Both are depicted as lacking the capacity to feel emotion; yet both are sentient, reasoning, communicative, self-aware moral agents, and unquestionably persons. Some people are unemotional; some cannot communicate well; some lack self-awareness; and some are not moral agents. It should not surprise us that many people do not meet all of the criteria of personhood. Criteria for the applicability of complex concepts are often like this: none may be logically necessary, but the more criteria that are satisfied, the more confident we are that the concept is applicable. Conversely, the fewer criteria are satisfied, the less plausible it is to hold that the concept applies. And if none of the relevant criteria are met, then we may be confident that it does not.

Thus, to demonstrate that a fetus is not a person, all I need to claim is that an entity that has *none* of these six characteristics is not a person. Sentience is the most basic mental capacity, and the one that may have the best claim to being a necessary (though not sufficient) condition for personhood. Sentience can establish a claim to moral considerability, since sentient beings can be harmed in ways that matter to them; for instance, they can be caused to feel pain, or deprived of the continuation of a life that is pleasant to them. It is unlikely that an entirely insentient organism could develop the other mental and behavioral capacities that are characteristic of persons. Consequently, it is odd to claim that an entity that is not sentient, and that has never been sentient, is nevertheless a person. Persons who have permanently and irreparably lost all capacity for sentience, but who remain biologically alive, arguably still have strong moral rights by virtue of what they have been in the past. But small fetuses, which have not yet begun to have experiences, are not persons yet and do not have the rights that persons do.

The presumption that all persons have full and equal basic moral rights may be part of the very concept of a person. If this is so, then the concept of a person is in part a moral one; once we have admitted that X is a person, we have implicitly committed ourselves to recognizing X's right to be treated as a member of the moral community.[13] The claim that X is a *human being* may also be voiced as an appeal to treat X decently; but this is usually either because "human being" is used in the moral sense, or because of a confusion between genetic and moral humanity.

If 1–6 are the primary criteria of personhood, then genetic humanity is neither necessary nor sufficient for personhood. Some genetically human entities are not persons, and there may be persons who belong to other species. A man or woman whose consciousness has been permanently obliterated but who remains biologically alive is a human entity who may no longer be a person; and some unfortunate humans, who have never had any sensory or cognitive capacities at all, may not be people either. Similarly, an early fetus is a human entity which is not yet a person. It is not even minimally sentient, let alone capable of emotion, reason, sophisticated communication, self-awareness, or moral agency.[14] Thus, while it may be greatly valued as a future child, it does not yet have the claim to moral consideration that it may come to have later.

Moral agency matters to moral status, because it is moral agents who invent moral rights, and who can be obliged to respect them. Human beings have become moral agents from social necessity. Most social animals exist well enough, with no evident notion of a moral right. But

---

[13]Alan Gewirth defends a similar claim, in *Reason and Morality* (University of Chicago Press, 1978).
[14]Fetal sentience is impossible prior to the development of neurological connections between the sense organs and the brain, and between the various parts of the brain involved in the processing of conscious experience. This stage of neurological development is currently thought to occur at some point in the late second or early third trimester.

human beings need moral rights, because we are not only highly social, but also sufficiently clever and self-interested to be capable of undermining our societies through violence and duplicity. For human persons, moral rights are essential for peaceful and mutually beneficial social life. So long as some moral agents are denied basic rights, peaceful existence is difficult, since moral agents justly resent being treated as something less. If animals of some terrestrial species are found to be persons, or if alien persons come from other worlds, or if human beings someday invent machines whose mental and behavioral capacities make them persons, then we will be morally obliged to respect the moral rights of these non-human persons—at least to the extent that they are willing and able to respect ours in turn.

Although only those persons who are moral agents can participate directly in the shaping and enforcement of moral rights, they need not and usually do not ascribe moral rights only to themselves and other moral agents. Human beings are social creatures who naturally care for small children, and other members of the social community who are not currently capable of moral agency. Moreover, we are all vulnerable to the temporary or permanent loss of the mental capacities necessary for moral agency. Thus, we have self-interested as well as altruistic reasons for extending basic moral rights to infants and other sentient human beings who have already been born, but who currently lack some of these other mental capacities. These human beings, despite their current disabilities, are persons and members of the moral community.

But in extending moral rights to beings (human or otherwise) that have few or none of the morally significant characteristics of persons, we need to be careful not to burden human moral agents with obligations that they cannot possibly fulfill, except at unacceptably great cost to their own well-being and that of those they care about. Women often cannot complete unwanted pregnancies, except at intolerable mental, physical, and economic cost to themselves and their families. And heterosexual intercourse is too important a part of the social lives of most men and women to be reserved for times when pregnancy

is an acceptable outcome. Furthermore, the world cannot afford the continued rapid population growth which is the inevitable consequence of prohibiting abortion, so long as contraception is neither very reliable nor available to everyone. If fetuses were persons, then they would have rights that must be respected, even at great social or personal cost. But given that early fetuses, at least, are unlike persons in the morally relevant respects, it is unreasonable to insist that they be accorded exactly the same moral and legal status.

Fetal Development and the Right to Life

Two questions arise regarding the application of these suggestions to the moral status of the fetus. First, if indeed fetuses are not yet persons, then might they nevertheless have strong moral rights based upon the degree to which they *resemble* persons? Secondly, to what extent, if any, does a fetus's potential to *become* a person imply that we ought to accord to it some of the same moral rights? Each of these questions requires comment.

It is reasonable to suggest that the more like a person something is—the more it appears to meet at least some of the criteria of personhood—the stronger is the case for according it a right to life, and perhaps the stronger its right to life is. That being the case, perhaps the fetus gradually gains a stronger right to life as it develops. We should take seriously the suggestion that, just as "the human individual develops biologically in a continuous fashion . . . the rights of a human person . . . develop in the same way."[15]

A seven-month fetus can apparently feel pain, and can respond to such stimuli as light and sound. Thus, it may have a rudimentary form of consciousness. Nevertheless, it is probably not as conscious, or as capable of emotion, as even a very young infant is; and it has as yet little or no capacity for reason, sophisticated intentional communication, or self-awareness. In these respects,

---

[15]Thomas L. Hayes, "A Biological View," *Commonweal*, 85 (March 17, 1967), pp. 677–8; cited by Daniel Callahan, in *Abortion: Law, Choice, and Morality* (London: Macmillan, 1970).

even a late-term fetus is arguably less like a person than are many nonhuman animals. Many animals (e.g., large-brained mammals such as elephants, cetaceans, or apes) are not only sentient, but clearly possessed of a degree of reason, and perhaps even of self-awareness. Thus, on the basis of its resemblance to a person, even a late-term fetus can have no more right to life than do these animals.

Animals may, indeed, plausibly be held to have some moral rights, and perhaps rather strong ones.[16] But it is impossible in practice to accord full and equal moral rights to all animals. When an animal poses a serious threat to the life or well-being of a person, we do not, as a rule, greatly blame the person for killing it; and there are good reasons for this species-based discrimination. Animals, however intelligent in their own domains, are generally not beings with whom we can reason; we cannot persuade mice not to invade our dwellings or consume our food. That is why their rights are necessarily weaker than those of a being who can understand and respect the rights of other beings.

But the probable sentience of late-term fetuses is not the only argument in favor of treating late abortion as a morally more serious matter than early abortion. Many—perhaps most—people are repulsed by the thought of needlessly aborting a late-term fetus. The late-term fetus has features which cause it to arouse in us almost the same powerful protective instinct as does a small infant.

This response needs to be taken seriously. If it were impossible to perform abortions early in pregnancy, then we might have to tolerate the mental and physical trauma that would be occasioned by the routine resort to late abortion. But where early abortion is safe, legal, and readily available to all women, it is not unreasonable to expect most women who wish to end a pregnancy to do so prior to the third trimester. Most women strongly prefer early to late abortion, because it is far less physically painful and

emotionally traumatic. Other things being equal, it is better for all concerned that pregnancies that are not to be completed should be ended as early as possible. Few women would consider ending a pregnancy in the seventh month in order to take a trip to Europe. If, however, a woman's own life or health is at stake, or if the fetus has been found to be so severely abnormal as to be unlikely to survive or to have a life worth living, then late abortion may be the morally best choice. For even a late-term fetus is not a person yet, and its rights must yield to those of the woman whenever it is impossible for both to be respected.

Potential Personhood and the Right to Life

We have seen that a presentient fetus does not yet resemble a person in ways which support the claim that it has strong moral rights. But what about its *potential*, the fact that if nurtured and allowed to develop it may eventually become a person? Doesn't that potential give it at least some right to life? The fact that something is a potential person may be a reason for not destroying it; but we need not conclude from this that potential people have a strong right to life. It may be that the feeling that it is better not to destroy a potential person is largely due to the fact that potential people are felt to be an invaluable resource, not to be lightly squandered. If every speck of dust were a potential person, we would be less apt to suppose that all potential persons have a right to become actual.

We do not need to insist that a potential person has no right to life whatever. There may be something immoral, and not just imprudent, about wantonly destroying potential people, when doing so isn't necessary. But even if a potential person does have some right to life, that right could not outweigh the right of a woman to obtain an abortion; for the basic moral rights of an actual person outweigh the rights of a merely potential person, whenever the two conflict. Since this may not be immediately obvious in the case of a human fetus, let us look at another case.

Suppose that our space explorer falls into the hands of an extraterrestrial civilization, whose scientists decide to create a few thousand new

---

[16]See, for instance, Tom Regan, *The Case for Animal Rights* (Berkeley: University of California Press, 1983).

human beings by killing her and using some of her cells to create clones. We may imagine that each of these newly created women will have all of the original woman's abilities, skills, knowledge, and so on, and will also have an individual self-concept; in short, that each of them will be a bona fide (though not genetically unique) person. Imagine, further, that our explorer knows all of this, and knows that these people will be treated kindly and fairly. I maintain that in such a situation she would have the right to escape if she could, thus depriving all of these potential people of their potential lives. For her right to life outweighs all of theirs put together, even though they are all genetically human, and have a high probability of becoming people, if only she refrains from acting.

Indeed, I think that our space traveler would have a right to escape even if it were not her life which the aliens planned to take, but only a year of her freedom, or only a day. She would not be obliged to stay, even if she had been captured because of her own lack of caution—or even if she had done so deliberately, knowing the possible consequences. Regardless of why she was captured, she is not obliged to remain in captivity for *any* period of time in order to permit merely potential people to become actual people. By the same token, a woman's rights to liberty and the control of her own body outweigh whatever right to life a fetus may have merely by virtue of its potential personhood.

THE OBJECTION FROM INFANTICIDE

One objection to my argument is that it appears to justify not only abortion, but also infanticide. A newborn infant is not much more personlike than a nine-month fetus, and thus it might appear that if late-term abortion is sometimes justified, then infanticide must also sometimes be justified. Yet most people believe that infanticide is a form of murder, and virtually never justified.

This objection is less telling than it may seem. There are many reasons why infanticide is more difficult to justify than abortion, even though neither fetuses nor newborn infants are clearly persons. In this period of history, the deliberate killing of newborns is virtually never justified. This is in part because newborns are so close to being persons that to kill them requires a very strong moral justification—as does the killing of dolphins, chimpanzees, and other highly personlike creatures. It is certainly wrong to kill such beings for the sake of convenience, or financial profit, or "sport." Only the most vital human needs, such as the need to defend one's own life and physical integrity, can provide a plausible justification for killing such beings.

In the case of an infant, there is no such vital need, since in the contemporary world there are usually other people who are eager to provide a good home for an infant whose own parents are unable or unwilling to care for it. Many people wait years for the opportunity to adopt a child, and some are unable to do so, even though there is every reason to believe that they would be good parents. The needless destruction of a viable infant not only deprives a sentient human being of life, but also deprives other persons of a source of great satisfaction, perhaps severely impoverishing *their* lives.

Even if an infant is unadoptable (e.g., because of some severe physical disability), it is still wrong to kill it. For most of us value the lives of infants, and would greatly prefer to pay taxes to support foster care and state institutions for disabled children, rather than to allow them to be killed or abandoned. So long as most people feel this way, and so long as it is possible to provide care for infants who are unwanted, or who have special needs that their parents cannot meet without assistance, it is wrong to let any infant die who has a chance of living a reasonably good life.

If these arguments show that infanticide is wrong, at least in today's world, then why don't they also show that late-term abortion is always wrong? After all, third-trimester fetuses are almost as personlike as infants, and many people value them and would prefer that they be preserved. As a potential source of pleasure to some family, a fetus is just as valuable as an infant. But there is an important difference between these two cases: once the infant is born, its continued life cannot pose any serious threat to the woman's life or health, since she is free to put it up for adoption or to place it in foster care. While she might, in rare cases, prefer that the child die rather than being raised by others, such a preference would not establish a right on her part.

In contrast, a pregnant woman's right to protect her own life and health outweighs other people's desire that the fetus be preserved—just as, when a person's life or health is threatened by an animal, and when the threat cannot be removed without killing the animal, that person's right to self-defense outweighs the desires of those who would prefer that the animal not be killed. Thus, while the moment of birth may mark no sharp discontinuity in the degree to which an infant resembles a person, it does mark the end of the mother's right to determine its fate. Indeed, if a late abortion can be safely performed without harming the fetus, she has in most cases no right to insist upon its death, for the same reason that she has no right to insist that a viable infant be killed or allowed to die.

It remains true that, on my view, neither abortion nor the killing of newborns is obviously a form of murder. Perhaps our legal system is correct in its classification of infanticide as murder, since no other legal category adequately expresses the force of our disapproval of this action. But some moral distinction remains, and it has important consequences. When a society cannot possibly care for all of the children who are born, without endangering the survival of adults and older children, allowing some infants to die may be the best of a bad set of options. Throughout history, most societies—from those that lived by gathering and hunting to the highly civilized Chinese, Japanese, Greeks, and Romans—have permitted infanticide under such unfortunate circumstances,

regarding it as a necessary evil. It shows a lack of understanding to condemn these societies as morally benighted for this reason alone, since in the absence of safe and effective means of contraception and abortion, parents must sometimes have had no morally better options.

CONCLUSION

I have argued that fetuses are neither persons nor members of the moral community. Furthermore, neither a fetus's resemblance to a person, nor its potential for becoming a person, provides an adequate basis for the claim that it has a full and equal right to life. At the same time, there are medical as well as moral reasons for preferring early to late abortion when the pregnancy is unwanted.

Women, unlike fetuses, are undeniably persons and members of the human moral community. If unwanted or medically dangerous pregnancies never occurred, then it might be possible to respect women's basic moral rights, while at the same time extending the same basic rights to fetuses. But in the real world such pregnancies do occur—often despite the woman's best efforts to prevent them. Even if the perfect contraceptive were universally available, the continued occurrence of rape and incest would make access to abortion a vital human need. Because women are persons, and fetuses are not, women's rights to life, liberty, and physical integrity morally override whatever right to life it may be appropriate to ascribe to a fetus. Consequently, laws that deny women the right to obtain abortions, or that make safe early abortions difficult or impossible for some women to obtain, are an unjustified violation of basic moral and constitutional rights.

⚖ REVIEW QUESTIONS

1. According to Warren, what is the standard anti-abortion argument, and what is the standard pro-choice response?
2. What objection does Warren make to Thomson's argument about the famous violinist?
3. Warren distinguishes between two senses of the term *human being*. What are these two senses?
4. What are the characteristics of a person, according to Warren? Why isn't the fetus a person?

5. Besides saying that the fetus is not a person, what other reasons does Warren give for allowing abortions?
6. Warren grants that there are two problems with her account of the moral status of the fetus. What are these two problems, and how does she respond to them?

⚜ DISCUSSION QUESTIONS

1. What is the moral status of a brain-dead human who is biologically alive but permanently unconscious? What is Warren's view? What do you think?

2. Explain Warren's position on the moral status of nonhuman animals. Do you agree with her? Why or why not?

3. Warren believes that there can be nonhuman persons—for example, alien beings, androids, and even robots—who think and act like humans. Are these beings persons with moral rights? Explain your position.

4. Do the rights of an actual person always outweigh the rights of a merely potential person? Can you think of any counterexamples?

An Argument That Abortion Is Wrong

DON MARQUIS

Don Marquis is professor of philosophy at the University of Kansas. His published articles deal with problems in medical ethics.

   Marquis wants to show why abortion is seriously wrong, but he begins by granting some exceptions, including cases of rape, of abortion during the first fourteen days after conception, of threat to the woman's life, and an anencephalic fetus. After showing why the standard arguments fail to resolve the debate about abortion, he proceeds to his own argument: that abortion is wrong for the same reason that killing us is wrong. It is wrong because it deprives the fetus of a "future like ours," a future containing valuable experiences, activities, projects, and enjoyments.

The purpose of this essay is to set out an argument for the claim that abortion, except perhaps in rare instances, is seriously wrong.[1] One reason for these exceptions is to eliminate from consideration cases whose ethical analysis should be controversial and detailed for clear-headed opponents of abortion. Such cases include abortion after rape and abortion during the first fourteen days after conception when there is an argument that the fetus is not definitely an individual. Another reason for making these exceptions is to allow for those cases in which the permissibility of abortion is compatible with the argument of this essay. Such cases include abortion when continuation of a pregnancy endangers a woman's life and abortion when the fetus is anencephalic. When I speak of the wrongness of abortion in this essay, a reader should presume the above qualifications. I mean by an abortion an action intended to bring about the death of a fetus for the sake of the woman who carries it. (Thus, as is standard on the literature on this subject, I eliminate spontaneous abortions from consideration.) I mean by a fetus a developing human being from the time of conception to the time of birth. (Thus, as is standard, I call embryos and zygotes, fetuses.)

---

[1]This essay is an updated version of a view that first appeared in the *Journal of Philosophy* (1989). This essay incorporates attempts to deal with the objections of McInerney (1990), Norcross (1990), Shirley (1995), Steinbock (1992), and Paske (1994) to the original version of the view.

The argument of this essay will establish that abortion is wrong for the same reason as killing a reader of this essay is wrong. I shall just assume, rather than establish, that killing you is seriously wrong. I shall make no attempt to offer a complete ethics of killing. Finally, I shall make no attempt to resolve some very fundamental and difficult general philosophical issues into which this analysis of the ethics of abortion might lead.

WHY THE DEBATE OVER ABORTION SEEMS INTRACTABLE

Symmetries that emerge from the analysis of the major arguments on either side of the abortion debate may explain why the abortion debate seems intractable. Consider the following standard anti-abortion argument: Fetuses are both human and alive. Humans have the right to life. Therefore, fetuses have the right to life. Of course, women have the right to control their own bodies, but the right to life overrides the right of a woman to control her own body. Therefore, abortion is wrong.

Thomson's View

Judith Thomson (1971) has argued that even if one grants (for the sake of argument only) that fetuses have the right to life, this argument fails. Thomson invites you to imagine that you have been connected while sleeping, bloodstream to bloodstream, to a famous violinist. The violinist, who suffers from a rare blood disease, will die if disconnected. Thomson argues that you surely have the right to disconnect yourself. She appeals to our intuition that having to be in bed with a violinist for an indefinite period is too much for morality to demand. She supports this claim by noting that the body being used is *your* body, not the violinist's body. She distinguishes the right to life, which the violinist clearly has, from the right to use someone else's body when necessary to preserve one's life, which it is not at all obvious the violinist has. Because the case of pregnancy is like the case of the violinist, one is no more morally obligated to remain attached to a fetus than to remain attached to the violinist.

It is widely conceded that one can generate from Thomson's vivid case the conclusion that abortion is morally permissible when a pregnancy is due to rape (Warren, 1973, p. 49; and Steinbock, 1992, p. 79). But this is hardly a general right to abortion. Do Thomson's more general theses generate a more general right to an abortion? Thomson draws our attention to the fact that in a pregnancy, although a fetus uses a woman's body as a life-support system, a pregnant woman does not use a fetus's body as a life-support system. However, an opponent of abortion might draw our attention to the fact that in an abortion the life that is lost is the fetus's, not the woman's. This symmetry seems to leave us with a stand-off.

Thomson points out that a fetus's right to life does not entail its right to use someone else's body to preserve its life. However, an opponent of abortion might point out that a woman's right to use her own body does not entail her right to end someone else's life in order to do what she wants with her body. In reply, one might argue that a pregnant woman's right to control her own body doesn't come to much if it is wrong for her to take any action that ends the life of the fetus within her. However, an opponent of abortion can argue that the fetus's right to life doesn't come to much if a pregnant woman can end it when she chooses. The consequence of all of these symmetries seems to be a stand-off. But if we have the stand-off, then one might argue that we are left with a conflict of rights: a fetal right to life versus the right of a woman to control her own body. One might then argue that the right to life seems to be a stronger right than the right to control one's own body in the case of abortion because the loss of one's life is a greater loss than the loss of the right to control one's own body in one respect for nine months. Therefore, the right to life overrides the right to control one's own body and abortion is wrong. Considerations like these have suggested to both opponents of abortion and supporters of choice that a Thomsonian strategy for defending a general right to abortion will not succeed (Tooley, 1972; Warren, 1973; and Steinbock, 1992). In fairness, one must note that Thomson did not intend her strategy to generate a general moral permissibility of abortion.

Do Fetuses Have the Right to Life?

The above considerations suggest that whether abortion is morally permissible boils down to the question of whether fetuses have the right to life. An argument that fetuses either have or lack the right to life must be based upon some general criterion for having or lacking the right to life. Opponents of abortion, on the one hand, look around for the broadest possible plausible criterion, so that fetuses will fall under it. This explains why classic arguments against abortion appeal to the criterion of being human (Noonan, 1970; Beckwith, 1993). This criterion appears plausible: The claim that all humans, whatever their race, gender, religion or *age*, have the right to life seems evident enough. In addition, because the fetuses we are concerned with do not, after all, belong to another species, they are clearly human. Thus, the syllogism that generates the conclusion that fetuses have the right to life is apparently sound.

On the other hand, those who believe abortion is morally permissible wish to find a narrow, but plausible, criterion for possession of the right to life so that fetuses will fall outside of it. This explains, in part, why the standard prochoice arguments in the philosophical literature appeal to the criterion of being a person (Feinberg, 1986; Tooley, 1972; Warren, 1973; Benn, 1973; Engelhardt, 1986). This criterion appears plausible: The claim that only persons have the right to life seems evident enough. Furthermore, because fetuses neither are rational nor possess the capacity to communicate in complex ways nor possess a concept of self that continues through time, no fetus is a person. Thus, the syllogism needed to generate the conclusion that no fetus possesses the right to life is apparently sound. Given that no fetus possesses the right to life, a woman's right to control her own body easily generates the general right to abortion. The existence of two apparently defensible syllogisms which support contrary conclusions helps to explain why partisans on both sides of the abortion dispute often regard their opponents as either morally depraved or mentally deficient.

Which syllogism should we reject? The anti-abortion syllogism is usually attacked by attacking its major premise: the claim that whatever is biologically human has the right to life. This premise is subject to scope problems because the class of the biologically human includes too much: Human cancer-cell cultures are biologically human, but they do not have the right to life. Moreover, this premise also is subject to moral-relevance problems: The connection of the biological and the moral is merely assumed. It is hard to think of a good *argument* for such a connection. If one wishes to consider the category of "human" a moral category, as some people find it plausible to do in other contexts, then one is left with no way of showing that the fetus is fully human without begging the question. Thus, the classic anti-abortion argument appears subject to fatal difficulties.

These difficulties with the classic anti-abortion argument are well known and thought by many to be conclusive. The symmetrical difficulties with the classic pro-choice syllogism are not as well recognized. The pro-choice syllogism can be attacked by attacking its major premise: Only persons have the right to life. This premise is subject to scope problems because the class of persons includes too little: Infants, the severely retarded, and some of the mentally ill seem to fall outside the class of persons as the supporter of choice understands the concept. The premise is also subject to moral-relevance problems: Being a person is understood by the pro-choicer as having certain psychological attributes. If the pro-choicer questions the connection between the biological and the moral, the opponent of abortion can question the connection between the psychological and the moral. If one wishes to consider "person" a moral category, as is often done, then one is left with no way of showing that the fetus is not a person without begging the question.

Pro-choicers appear to have resources for dealing with their difficulties that opponents of abortion lack. Consider their moral-relevance problem. A pro-choicer might argue that morality rests on contractual foundations and that only those who have the psychological attributes of persons are capable of entering into the moral contract and, as a consequence, being a member of the moral community. [This is essentially Engelhardt's (1986) view.] The great advantage of this contractarian approach to morality is that it seems far more plausible than any approach the anti-abortionist can provide. The great disadvantage of this contractarian approach to morality is that it adds to our earlier scope problems by leaving it unclear how we can have the duty not to inflict pain and suffering on animals.

Contractarians have tried to deal with their scope problems by arguing that duties to some individuals who are not persons can be justified even though those individuals are not contracting members of the moral community. For example, Kant argued that, although we do not have direct duties to animals, we "must practice kindness towards animals, for he who is cruel to animals becomes hard also in his dealings with men" (Kant, 1963, p. 240). Feinberg argues that infanticide is wrong, not because infants have the right to life, but because our society's protection of infants has social utility. If we do not treat infants with tenderness and consideration, then when they are persons they will be worse off and we will be worse off also (Feinberg, 1986, p. 271).

These moves only stave off the difficulties with the pro-choice view; they do not resolve them. Consider Kant's account of our obligations to animals. Kantians certainly know the difference between persons and animals. Therefore, no true Kantian would treat persons as she would treat animals. Thus, Kant's defense of our duties to animals fails to show that Kantians have a duty not to be cruel to animals. Consider Feinberg's attempt to show that infanticide is wrong even though no infant is a person. All Feinberg really shows is that it is a good idea to treat with care and consideration the infants we intend to keep. That is quite compatible with killing the infants we intend to discard. This point can be supported by an analogy with which any pro-choicer will agree. There are plainly good reasons to treat with care and consideration the fetuses we intend to keep. This is quite compatible with aborting those fetuses we intend to discard. Thus, Feinberg's account of the wrongness of infanticide is inadequate.

Accordingly, we can see that a contractarian defense of the pro-choice personhood syllogism fails. The problem arises because the contractarian cannot account for our duties to individuals who are not persons, whether these individuals are animals or infants. Because the pro-choicer wishes to adopt a narrow criterion for the right to life so that fetuses will not be included, the scope of her major premise is too narrow. Her problem is the opposite of the problem the classic opponent of abortion faces.

The argument of this section has attempted to establish, albeit briefly, that the classic anti-abortion argument and the pro-choice argument favored by most philosophers both face problems that are mirror images of one another. A standoff results. The abortion debate requires a different strategy.

THE "FUTURE LIKE OURS" ACCOUNT OF THE WRONGNESS OF KILLING

Why do the standard arguments in the abortion debate fail to resolve the issue? The general principles to which partisans in the debate appeal are either truisms most persons would affirm in the absence of much reflection, or very general moral theories. All are subject to major problems. A different approach is needed.

Opponents of abortion claim that abortion is wrong because abortion involves killing someone like us, a human being who just happens to be very young. Supporters of choice claim that ending the life of a fetus is not in the same moral category as ending the life of an adult human being. Surely this controversy cannot be resolved in the absence of an account of what it is about killing us that makes killing us wrong. On the one hand, if we know what property we possess that makes killing us wrong, then we can ask whether fetuses have the same property. On the other hand, suppose that we do not know what it is about us that makes killing us wrong. If this is so, we do not understand even easy cases in which killing is wrong. Surely, we will not understand the ethics of killing fetuses, for if we do not understand easy cases, then we will not understand hard cases. Both pro-choicer and anti-abortionist agree that it is obvious that it is wrong to kill us. Thus, a discussion of what it is about us that makes killing us not only wrong, but seriously wrong, seems to be the right place to begin a discussion of the abortion issue.

Who is primarily wronged by a killing? The wrong of killing is not primarily explained in terms of the loss to the family and friends of the victim. Perhaps the victim is a hermit. Perhaps one's friends find it easy to make new friends. The wrong of killing is not primarily explained in terms of the brutalization of the killer. The great wrong to the victim explains the brutalization, not the other way around. The wrongness of killing us is understood in terms of what killing does to us. Killing us imposes on us the misfortune of premature death. That misfortune underlies the wrongness.

Premature death is a misfortune because when one is dead, one has been deprived of life. This misfortune can be more precisely specified. Premature death cannot deprive me of my past life. That part of my life is already gone. If I die tomorrow or if I live thirty more years my past life will be no different. It has occurred on either alternative. Rather than my past, my death deprives me of my future, of the life that I would have lived if I had lived out my natural life span.

The loss of a future biological life does not explain the misfortune of death. Compare two scenarios: In the former I now fall into a coma from which I do not recover until my death in thirty years. In the latter I die now. The latter scenario does not seem to describe a greater misfortune than the former.

The loss of our future conscious life is what underlies the misfortune of premature death. Not any future conscious life qualifies, however. Suppose that I am terminally ill with cancer. Suppose also that pain and suffering would dominate my future conscious life. If so, then death would not be a misfortune for me.

Thus, the misfortune of premature death consists of the loss to us of the future goods of consciousness. What are these goods? Much can be said about this issue, but a simple answer will do for the purposes of this essay. The goods of life are whatever we get out of life. The goods of life are those items toward which we take a "pro"

attitude. They are completed projects of which we are proud, the pursuit of our goals, aesthetic enjoyments, friendships, intellectual pursuits, and physical pleasures of various sorts. The goods of life are what make life worth living. In general, what makes life worth living for one person will not be the same as what makes life worth living for another. Nevertheless, the list of goods in each of our lives will overlap. The lists are usually different in different stages of our lives.

What makes the goods of my future good for me? One possible, but wrong, answer is my desire for those goods now. This answer does not account for those aspects of my future life that I now believe I will later value, but about which I am wrong. Neither does it account for those aspects of my future that I will come to value, but which I don't value now. What is valuable to the young may not be valuable to the middle-aged. What is valuable to the middle-aged may not be valuable to the old. Some of life's values for the elderly are best appreciated by the elderly. Thus it is wrong to say that the value of my future to me is just what I value now. What makes my future valuable to me are those aspects of my future that I will (or would) value when I will (or would) experience them, whether I value them now or not.

It follows that a person can believe that she will have a valuable future and be wrong. Furthermore, a person can believe that he will not have a valuable future and also be wrong. This is confirmed by our attitude toward many of the suicidal. We attempt to save the lives of the suicidal and to convince them that they have made an error in judgment. This does not mean that the future of an individual obtains value from the value that others confer on it. It means that, in some cases, others can make a clearer judgment of the value of a person's future to *that person* than the person herself. This often happens when one's judgment concerning the value of one's own future is clouded by personal tragedy. (Compare the views of McInerney, 1990, and Shirley, 1995.)

Thus, what is sufficient to make killing us wrong, in general, is that it causes premature death. Premature death is a misfortune. Premature death is a misfortune, in general, because it deprives an individual of a future of value. An individual's future will be valuable to that individual if that individual will come, or would come, to value it. We know that killing us is wrong. What makes killing us wrong, in general, is that it deprives us of a future of value. Thus, killing someone is wrong, in general, when it deprives her of a future like ours. I shall call this "an FLO."

Arguments in Favor of the FLO Theory

At least four arguments support this FLO account of the wrongness of killing.

The Considered Judgment Argument

The FLO account of the wrongness of killing is correct because it fits with our considered judgment concerning the nature of the misfortune of death. The analysis of the previous section is an exposition of the nature of this considered judgment. This judgment can be confirmed. If one were to ask individuals with AIDS or with incurable cancer about the nature of their misfortune, I believe that they would say or imply that their impending loss of an FLO makes their premature death a misfortune. If they would not, then the FLO account would plainly be wrong.

The Worst of Crimes Argument

The FLO account of the wrongness of killing is correct because it explains why we believe that killing is one of the worst of crimes. My being killed deprives me of more than does my being robbed or beaten or harmed in some other way because my being killed deprives me of all of the value of my future, not merely part of it. This explains why we make the penalty for murder greater than the penalty for other crimes.

As a corollary[,] the FLO account of the wrongness of killing also explains why killing an adult human being is justified only in the most extreme circumstances, only in circumstances in which the loss of life to an individual is outweighed by a worse outcome if that life is not taken. Thus, we are willing to justify killing in self-defense, killing in order to save one's own life, because one's loss if one does not kill in that situation is so very great. We justify killing in a just war for similar reasons. We believe that capital punishment would be justified if, by having such

an institution, fewer premature deaths would occur. The FLO account of the wrongness of killing does not entail that killing is always wrong. Nevertheless, the FLO account explains both why killing is one of the worst of crimes and, as a corollary, why the exceptions to the wrongness of killing are so very rare. A correct theory of the wrongness of killing should have these features.

The Appeal to Cases Argument

The FLO account of the wrongness of killing is correct because it yields the correct answers in many life-and-death cases that arise in medicine and have interested philosophers.

Consider medicine first. Most people believe that it is not wrong deliberately to end the life of a person who is permanently unconscious. Thus we believe that it is not wrong to remove a feeding tube or a ventilator from a permanently comatose patient, knowing that such a removal will cause death. The FLO account of the wrongness of killing explains why this is so. A patient who is permanently unconscious cannot have a future that she would come to value, whatever her values. Therefore, according to the FLO theory of the wrongness of killing, death could not, *ceteris paribus*, be a misfortune to her. Therefore, removing the feeding tube or ventilator does not wrong her.

By contrast, almost all people believe that it is wrong, *ceteris paribus*, to withdraw medical treatment from patients who are temporarily unconscious. The FLO account of the wrongness of killing also explains why this is so. Furthermore, these two unconsciousness cases explain why the FLO account of the wrongness of killing does not include present consciousness as a necessary condition for the wrongness of killing.

Consider now the issue of the morality of legalizing active euthanasia. Proponents of active euthanasia argue that if a patient faces a future of intractable pain and wants to die, then, *ceteris paribus*, it would not be wrong for a physician to give him medicine that she knows would result in his death. This view is so universally accepted that even the strongest *opponents* of active euthanasia hold it. The official Vatican view (Sacred Congregation, 1980) is that it is permissible for a physician to administer to a patient morphine sufficient (although no more than sufficient) to control his pain even if she foresees that the morphine will result in his death. Notice how nicely the FLO account of the wrongness of killing explains this unanimity of opinion. A patient known to be in severe intractable pain is presumed to have a future without positive value. Accordingly, death would not be a misfortune for him and an action that would (foreseeably) end his life would not be wrong.

Contrast this with the standard emergency medical treatment of the suicidal. Even though the suicidal have indicated that they want to die, medical personnel will act to save their lives. This supports the view that it is not the mere *desire* to enjoy an FLO which is crucial to our understanding of the wrongness of killing. *Having* an FLO is what is crucial to the account, although one would, of course, want to make an exception in the case of fully autonomous people who refuse life-saving medical treatment. Opponents of abortion can, of course, be willing to make an exception for fully autonomous fetuses who refuse life support.

The FLO theory of the wrongness of killing also deals correctly with issues that have concerned philosophers. It implies that it would be wrong to kill (peaceful) persons from outer space who come to visit our planet even though they are biologically utterly unlike us. Presumably, if they are persons, then they will have futures that are sufficiently like ours so that it would be wrong to kill them. The FLO account of the wrongness of killing shares this feature with the personhood views of the supporters of choice. Classical opponents of abortion who locate the wrongness of abortion somehow in the biological humanity of a fetus cannot explain this.

The FLO account does not entail that there is another species of animals whose members ought not to be killed. Neither does it entail that it is permissible to kill any non-human animal. On the one hand, a supporter of animals' rights might argue that since some non-human animals have a future of value, it is wrong to kill them also, or at least it is wrong to kill them without a far better reason than we usually have for killing

non-human animals. On the other hand, one might argue that the futures of non-human animals are not sufficiently like ours for the FLO account to entail that it is wrong to kill them. Since the FLO account does not specify which properties a future of another individual must possess so that killing that individual is wrong, the FLO account is indeterminate with respect to this issue. The fact that the FLO account of the wrongness of killing does not give a determinate answer to this question is not a flaw in the theory. A sound ethical account should yield the right answers in the obvious cases; it should not be required to resolve every disputed question.

A major respect in which the FLO account is superior to accounts that appeal to the concept of person is the explanation the FLO account provides of the wrongness of killing infants. There was a class of infants who had futures that included a class of events that were identical to the futures of the readers of this essay. Thus, reader, the FLO account explains why it was as wrong to kill you when you were an infant as it is to kill you now. This account can be generalized to almost all infants. Notice that the wrongness of killing infants can be explained in the absence of an account of what makes the future of an individual sufficiently valuable so that it is wrong to kill that individual. The absence of such an account explains why the FLO account is indeterminate with respect to the wrongness of killing non-human animals.

If the FLO account is the correct theory of the wrongness of killing, then because abortion involves killing fetuses and fetuses have FLOs for exactly the same reasons that infants have FLOs, abortion is presumptively seriously immoral. This inference lays the necessary groundwork for a fourth argument in favor of the FLO account that shows that abortion is wrong.

The Analogy with Animals Argument

Why do we believe it is wrong to cause animals suffering? We believe that, in our own case and in the case of other adults and children, suffering is a misfortune. It would be as morally arbitrary to refuse to acknowledge that animal suffering is wrong as it would be to refuse to acknowledge that the suffering of persons of another race is wrong. It is, on reflection, suffering that is a misfortune, not the suffering of white males or the suffering of humans. Therefore, infliction of suffering is presumptively wrong no matter on whom it is inflicted and whether it is inflicted on persons or nonpersons. Arbitrary restrictions on the wrongness of suffering count as racism or speciesism. Not only is this argument convincing on its own, but it is the only way of justifying the wrongness of animal cruelty. Cruelty toward animals is clearly wrong. (This famous argument is due to Singer, 1979.)

The FLO account of the wrongness of abortion is analogous. We believe that, in our own case and the cases of other adults and children, the loss of a future of value is a misfortune. It would be as morally arbitrary to refuse to acknowledge that the loss of a future of value to a fetus is wrong as to refuse to acknowledge that the loss of a future of value to Jews (to take a relevant twentieth-century example) is wrong. It is, on reflection, the loss of a future of value that is a misfortune; not the loss of a future of value to adults or loss of a future of value to non-Jews. To deprive someone of a future of value is wrong no matter on whom the deprivation is inflicted and no matter whether the deprivation is inflicted on persons or nonpersons. Arbitrary restrictions on the wrongness of this deprivation count as racism, genocide or ageism. Therefore, abortion is wrong. This argument that abortion is wrong should be convincing because it has the same form as the argument for the claim that causing pain and suffering to non-human animals is wrong. Since the latter argument is convincing, the former argument should be also. Thus, an analogy with animals supports the thesis that abortion is wrong.

REPLIES TO OBJECTIONS

The four arguments in the previous section establish that abortion is, except in rare cases, seriously immoral. Not surprisingly, there are objections to this view. There are replies to the four most important objections to the FLO argument for the immorality of abortion.

The Potentiality Objection

The FLO account of the wrongness of abortion is a potentiality argument. To claim that a fetus *has* an FLO is to claim that a fetus now has the potential to be in a state of a certain kind in the future. It is not to claim that all ordinary fetuses *will* have FLOs. Fetuses who are aborted, of course, will not. To say that a standard fetus has an FLO is to say that a standard fetus either will have or would have a life it will or would value. To say that a standard fetus would have a life it would value is to say that it will have a life it will value if it does not die prematurely. The truth of this conditional is based upon the nature of fetuses (including the fact that they naturally age) and this nature concerns their potential.

Some appeals to potentiality in the abortion debate rest on unsound inferences. For example, one may try to generate an argument against abortion by arguing that because persons have the right to life, potential persons also have the right to life. Such an argument is plainly invalid as it stands. The premise one needs to add to make it valid would have to be something like: "If Xs have the right to Y, then potential Xs have the right to Y." This premise is plainly false. Potential presidents don't have the rights of the presidency; potential voters don't have the right to vote.

In the FLO argument potentiality is not used in order to bridge the gap between adults and fetuses as is done in the argument in the above paragraph. The FLO theory of the wrongness of killing adults is based upon the adult's potentiality to have a future of value. Potentiality is in the argument from the very beginning. Thus, the plainly false premise is not required. Accordingly, the use of potentiality in the FLO theory is not a sign of an illegitimate inference.

The Argument from Interests

A second objection to the FLO account of the immorality of abortion involves arguing that even though fetuses have FLOs, nonsentient fetuses do not meet the minimum conditions for having any moral standing at all because they lack interests. Steinbock (1992, p. 5) has presented this argument clearly:

> Beings that have moral status must be capable of caring about what is done to them. They must be capable of being made, if only in a rudimentary sense, happy or miserable, comfortable or distressed. Whatever reasons we may have for preserving or protecting nonsentient beings, these reasons do not refer to their own interests. For without conscious awareness, beings cannot have interests. Without interests, they cannot have a welfare of their own. Without a welfare of their own, nothing can be done for their sake. Hence, they lack moral standing or status.

Medical researchers have argued that fetuses do not become sentient until after 22 weeks of gestation (Steinbock, 1992, p. 50). If they are correct, and if Steinbock's argument is sound, then we have both an objection to the FLO account of the wrongness of abortion and a basis for a view on abortion minimally acceptable to most supporters of choice.

Steinbock's conclusion conflicts with our settled moral beliefs. Temporarily unconscious human beings are nonsentient, yet no one believes that they lack either interests or moral standing. Accordingly, neither conscious awareness nor the capacity for conscious awareness is a necessary condition for having interests.

The counter-example of the temporarily unconscious human being shows that there is something internally wrong with Steinbock's argument. The difficulty stems from an ambiguity. One cannot *take* an interest in something without being capable of caring about what is done to it. However, something can be *in* someone's interest without that individual being capable of caring about it, or about anything. Thus, life support can be in the interests of a temporarily unconscious patient even though the temporarily unconscious patient is incapable of *taking* an interest in that life support. If this can be so for the temporarily unconscious patient, then it is hard to see why it cannot be so for the temporarily unconscious (that is, nonsentient) fetus who requires placental life support. Thus the objection based on interests fails.

The Problem of Equality

The FLO account of the wrongness of killing seems to imply that the degree of wrongness associated with each killing varies inversely with the victim's age. Thus, the FLO account of the wrongness of killing seems to suggest that it is far worse to kill a five-year-old than an 89-year-old because the former is deprived of far more than the latter. However, we believe that all persons have an equal right to life. Thus, it appears that the FLO account of the wrongness of killing entails an obviously false view (Paske, 1994).

However, the FLO account of the wrongness of killing does not, strictly speaking, imply that it is worse to kill younger people than older people. The FLO account provides an explanation of the wrongness of killing that is sufficient to account for the serious presumptive wrongness of killing. It does not follow that killings cannot be wrong in other ways. For example, one might hold, as does Feldman (1992, p. 184), that in addition to the wrongness of killing that has its basis in the future life of which the victim is deprived, killing an individual is also made wrong by the admirability of an individual's past behavior. Now the amount of admirability will presumably vary directly with age, whereas the amount of deprivation will vary inversely with age. This tends to equalize the wrongness of murder.

However, even if, *ceteris paribus*, it is worse to kill younger persons than older persons, there are good reasons for adopting a doctrine of the legal equality of murder. Suppose that we tried to estimate the seriousness of a crime of murder by appraising the value of the FLO of which the victim had been deprived. How would one go about doing this? In the first place, one would be confronted by the old problem of interpersonal comparisons of utility. In the second place, estimation of the value of a future would involve putting oneself, not into the shoes of the victim at the time she was killed, but rather into the shoes the victim would have worn had the victim survived, and then estimating from that perspective the worth of that person's future. This task seems difficult, if not impossible. Accordingly, there are reasons to adopt a convention that murders are equally wrong.

Furthermore, the FLO theory, in a way, explains why we do adopt the doctrine of the legal equality of murder. The FLO theory explains why we regard murder as one of the worst of crimes, since depriving someone of a future like ours deprives her of more than depriving her of anything else. This gives us a reason for making the punishment for murder very harsh, as harsh as is compatible with civilized society. One should not make the punishment for younger victims harsher than that. Thus, the doctrine of the equal legal right to life does not seem to be incompatible with the FLO theory.

The Contraception Objection

The strongest objection to the FLO argument for the immorality of abortion is based on the claim that, because contraception results in one less FLO, the FLO argument entails that contraception, indeed, abstention from sex when conception is possible, is immoral. Because neither contraception nor abstention from sex when conception is possible is immoral, the FLO account is flawed.

There is a cogent reply to this objection. If the argument of the early part of this essay is correct, then the central issue concerning the morality of abortion is the problem of whether fetuses are individuals who are members of the class of individuals whom it is seriously presumptively wrong to kill. The properties of being human and alive, of being a person, and of having an FLO are criteria that participants in the abortion debate have offered to mark off the relevant class of individuals. The central claim of this essay is that having an FLO marks off the relevant class of individuals. A defender of the FLO view could, therefore, reply that since, at the time of contraception, there is no individual to have an FLO, the FLO account does not entail that contraception is wrong. The wrong of killing is primarily a wrong to the individual who is killed; at the time of contraception there is no individual to be wronged.

However, someone who presses the contraception objection might have an answer to this reply. She might say that the sperm and egg are the individuals deprived of an FLO at the time of contraception. Thus, there are individuals whom contraception deprives of an FLO and if depriving an individual of an FLO is what makes killing wrong, then the FLO theory entails that contraception is wrong.

There is also a reply to this move. In the case of abortion, an objectively determinate individual is the subject of harm caused by the loss of an FLO. This individual is a fetus. In the case of contraception, there are far more candidates (see Norcross, 1990). Let us consider some possible candidates in order of the increasing number of individuals harmed: (1) The single harmed individual might be the combination of the particular sperm and the particular egg that would have united to form a zygote if contraception had not been used. (2) The two harmed individuals might be the particular sperm itself, and, in addition, the ovum itself that would have physically combined to form the zygote. (This is modeled on the double homicide of two persons who would otherwise in a short time fuse. (1) is modeled on harm to a single entity some of whose parts are not physically contiguous, such as a university.) (3) The many harmed individuals might be the millions of *combinations* of sperm and the released ovum whose (small) chances of having an FLO were reduced by the successful contraception. (4) The even larger class of harmed individuals (larger by one) might be the class consisting of all of the individual sperm in an ejaculate and, in addition, the individual ovum released at the time of the successful contraception. (1) through (4) are all candidates for being the subject(s) of harm in the case of successful contraception or abstinence from sex. Which should be chosen? Should we hold a lottery? There seems to be no non-arbitrarily determinate subject of harm in the case of successful contraception. But if there is no such subject of harm, then no determinate thing was harmed. If no determinate thing was harmed, then (in the case of contraception) no wrong has been done. Thus, the FLO account of the wrongness of abortion does not entail that contraception is wrong.

CONCLUSION

This essay contains an argument for the view that, except in unusual circumstances, abortion is seriously wrong. Deprivation of an FLO explains why killing adults and children is wrong. Abortion deprives fetuses of FLOs. Therefore, abortion is wrong. This argument is based on an account of the wrongness of killing that is a result of our considered judgment of the nature of the misfortune of premature death. It accounts for why we regard killing as one of the worst of crimes. It is superior to alternative accounts of the wrongness of killing that are intended to provide insight into the ethics of abortion. This account of the wrongness of killing is supported by the way it handles cases in which our moral judgments are settled. This account has an analogue in the most plausible account of the wrongness of causing animals to suffer. This account makes no appeal to religion. Therefore, the FLO account shows that abortion, except in rare instances, is seriously wrong.

REFERENCES

Beckwith, F. J., *Politically Correct Death: Answering Arguments for Abortion Rights* (Grand Rapids, Michigan: Baker Books, 1993).

Benn, S. I., "Abortion, infanticide, and respect for persons," *The Problem of Abortion*, ed. J. Feinberg (Belmont, California: Wadsworth, 1973), pp. 92–104.

Engelhardt, Jr., H. T., *The Foundations of Bioethics* (New York: Oxford University Press, 1986).

Feinberg, J., "Abortion," *Matters of Life and Death: New Introductory Essays in Moral Philosophy*, ed. T. Regan (New York: Random House, 1986).

Feldman, F., *Confrontations with the Reaper: A Philosophical Study of the Nature and Value of Death* (New York: Oxford University Press, 1992).

Kant, I., *Lectures on Ethics*, tr. L. Infeld (New York: Harper, 1963).

Marquis, D. B., "A future like ours and the concept of person: A reply to McInerney and Paske," *The Abortion Controversy: A Reader*, ed. L. P. Pojman and F. J. Beckwith (Boston: Jones and Bartlett, 1994), pp. 354–68.

———, "Fetuses, futures and values: A reply to Shirley," *Southwest Philosophy Review*, 11 (1995): 263–5.

———, "Why abortion is immoral," *Journal of Philosophy*, 86 (1989): 183–202.

McInerney, P., "Does a fetus already have a future like ours?," *Journal of Philosophy*, 87 (1990): 264–8.

Noonan, J., "An almost absolute value in history," in *The Morality of Abortion*, ed. J. Noonan (Cambridge, Massachusetts: Harvard University Press).

Norcross, A., "Killing, abortion, and contraception: A reply to Marquis," *Journal of Philosophy*, 87 (1990): 268–77.

Paske, G., "Abortion and the neo-natal right to life: A critique of Marquis's futurist argument," *The Abortion Controversy: A Reader*, ed. L. P. Pojman and F. J. Beckwith (Boston: Jones and Bartlett, 1994), pp. 343–53.

Sacred Congregation for the Propagation of the Faith, *Declaration on Euthanasia* (Vatican City, 1980).

Shirley, E. S., "Marquis' argument against abortion: A critique," *Southwest Philosophy Review*, 11 (1995): 79–89.

Singer, P., "Not for humans only: The place of nonhumans in environmental issues," *Ethics and Problems of the 21st Century*, ed. K. E. Goodpaster and K. M. Sayre (South Bend: Notre Dame University Press, 1979).

Steinbock, B., *Life Before Birth: The Moral and Legal Status of Embryos and Fetuses* (New York: Oxford University Press, 1992).

Thomson, J. J., "A defense of abortion," *Philosophy and Public Affairs*, 1 (1971): 47–66.

Tooley, M., "Abortion and infanticide," *Philosophy and Public Affairs*, 2 (1972): 37–65.

Warren, M. A., "On the moral and legal status of abortion," *Monist*, 57 (1973): 43–61.

♛ REVIEW QUESTIONS

1. What exceptions does Marquis allow to his claim that abortion is seriously wrong? Why does he make these exceptions?
2. What "symmetries" does Marquis find in the abortion debate? Why do these make the debate seem intractable?
3. Why is killing a person wrong, according to Marquis?
4. State and explain the four arguments Marquis uses to support his account of the wrongness of killing.
5. What is the potentiality objection, and how does Marquis respond to it?
6. State and explain Steinbock's argument from interests. How does Marquis reply?
7. What is the problem of equality? How does Marquis deal with it?
8. Explain the contraception objection and Marquis's reply.

♛ DISCUSSION QUESTIONS

1. There seem to be a number of cases in which the fetus does not have a "future like ours" besides the case of the anencephalic fetus that Marquis mentions. For example, the fetus can be deformed in other ways or have a genetic disease. Or perhaps the child will have abusive parents and a life full of suffering. Does Marquis have to grant that abortion is not wrong in all these cases where the fetus does not have a "future like ours"? Explain your answer.
2. Is the wrongness of killing a matter of degree, such that killing a person at the end of her life is not as wrong as killing a young person? Or is killing the old and the young equally wrong? What is Marquis's position on this? What do you think?
3. Is it wrong to kill nonhuman animals? Why doesn't Marquis take a position on this? What is your view?
4. In his reply to the contraception objection, Marquis assumes that the fetus is one individual. But when the zygote divides into twins there are two individuals, not one. Does twinning pose a problem for Marquis? Why or why not?

The Egg and I: Conception, Identity, and Abortion

EUGENE MILLS

Eugene Mills is associate professor of philosophy at Virginia Commonwealth University. He has published articles on a wide variety of topics, including analytic philosophy, the liar's paradox, personal identity, mental causation, and justification.

Mills challenges the pro-life assumption, made by Noonan and others, that a human being comes into existence at conception. He argues that humans begin either before or after conception, but not *at* conception. (Although his argument is formulated in the first person, he intends it to apply to all human beings.) His argument for this conclusion takes the form of a dilemma. An adult human being is either identical with the zygote in the mother's womb (so that the adult and the zygote are different stages of development of the same ongoing thing) or else the adult is not identical with the zygote but developed out of it. If the adult is not identical with the zygote, but came into existence later (when the fetus is conscious, which is one

Source: "The Egg and I: Conception, Identity, and Abortion Problem Cases" by Eugene Mills from *Philosophical Review*, Vol 117, No 3.
*Editor's Note: The footnotes have been deleted.

standard view), then the adult was never a zygote and did not begin at conception. If the adult is identical with the zygote, then the adult existed earlier than the zygote as an unfertilized egg (an oocyte), which became a zygote when it was fertilized by the sperm. Again, the adult's existence did not begin at conception. So, whether or not the adult was once a zygote, the adult did not originate at conception.

Mills goes on to argue that this metaphysical conclusion about origination raises problems for Marquis and Noonan. Marquis argues that no determinate being is harmed by contraception or abstinence. Mills claims that Marquis is simply mistaken. There is a single determinate subject of harm in cases of contraception or abstinence: namely, the oocyte that would or could have been fertilized. If contraception or abstinence is not seriously wrong, as Marquis maintains, then he should agree that an early abortion is not seriously wrong either. As for Noonan, Mills rejects Noonan's claim that a new being comes into existence at conception. The unfertilized egg is already on the scene. Furthermore, Noonan gives no reason for holding that at conception the zygote becomes a member of the genus *Homo*, as distinguished from being human in the sense in which a liver cell is human.

I. THE METAPHYSICS AND MORALITY OF ORIGINATION

When did I come into existence, and why should you care? Take the second question first. You should care because what goes for me goes for all human persons: we aren't all the same age, but we all came into existence at the same stage of biological development. This fact bears on the morality of abortion. I assume—without argument but for its sake—that you care about *this*.

The answer to the first question may hinge partly on the answer to a different question: what kind of thing am I? I'll suppose for the sake of argument, except where explicitly stated otherwise, that the true, relevant, and known answer is that I'm a "human being" in the sense of a human *animal*, a member of the genus *Homo*. Given this supposition, I'll argue first and foremost that I originated not at the moment of my biological conception, but either before or after. This metaphysical point carries moral freight. I'll argue secondarily that if any familiar "pro-life" moral principle raises moral qualms about the permissibility of zygotic abortion, these qualms apply equally (or at least almost equally) to the permissibility of contraception and abstinence.

Although I think my primary, metaphysical argument is strong, a related but weaker argument will serve for most of my moral purposes. I hope that even if I don't convince you that I originated either before or after conception, I'll at least convince you that it's at least reasonably doubtful that I originated at conception. And if you're convinced of even this much, I'll argue, my primary moral arguments should convince you as well.

Regardless of your moral attitude toward abortion, you probably hold that human biological conception—the fertilization of the egg—creates a new being. You probably hold that this being is at least a candidate for being or becoming a living human being. If you lean one way on abortion's moral status, you probably deny that this being is a person or a "human being" in a moral sense while allowing that it may eventually become one. You may deny that it has moral standing, while allowing that it may eventually gain it. Still, you probably affirm that conception results in *a new being* (even if you think this being a constituent part of the pregnant woman). If you lean the other way on abortion, you're more likely to insist that this new being has moral standing; you may, though you needn't, hold that it's a person right from the start. Whichever way you lean, you probably hold that from conception on, but not before, a being exists that probably will, absent abortion or mishap, become a normal adult human being.

From the retrospective first-person perspective, this shared assumption amounts to the view that I—the human animal that I'm assuming is me—originated with the fertilization of an egg. I'll argue that this assumption is mistaken. "Conception" has an ontological sense on which it's analytic that conception is origination. It's not analytic, though, that *biological* conception is origination. I'll argue that it's not even true; biological conception creates no new being.

I'll then draw out some consequences for abortion. Pro-life arguments typically involve two main premises. The first assigns to the human organism *in utero* some salient metaphysical status. Candidates for this status include: person, potential person, being with the potential for a valuable future, sentient being, and living human being. The second premise is a moral principle to the effect that (at least generally, at least presumptively) it's wrong to kill beings with the metaphysical status in question. I focus here on the metaphysical rather than the moral premise and mainly on the question *at what stage of development* is the salient metaphysical status attained? I argue that there's no good reason to think, for any standard candidate, that biological conception—hereafter, just "conception"—is the point of attainment.

I don't debate whether any sound principle leads from the metaphysical status of beings who could survive to normal adulthood to the presumptive wrongness of abortion. I argue that any such principle of familiar stripe, if true, either renders contraception and sexual abstinence presumptively wrong, or else does *not* rule presumptively wrong zygotic abortion.

"Morning-after pills" destroy zygotes. Though my argument renders no categorical verdict on the permissibility of such destruction, it does show that no familiar basis for condemning morning-after pills while condoning contraception and abstinence can succeed. Given the current public debate over the moral status of morning-after pills, my argument thus has a practical upshot of contemporary relevance.

Here's a sketch of the coming argument. Common sense holds, and I assume for convenience, that an organism existing at one time may be numerically identical to an organism existing at another time, though it grows and otherwise changes in the interim. When I say truly that "I existed ten years ago," I say that I (now) am identical with an organism that existed ten years ago. I argue in section 2 that, given this view, I didn't come into existence at conception. I consider objections in section 3. In sections 5 and 6, I trace some consequences of my metaphysical argument for the morality of abortion.

II. THE EGG AND I

Suppose, again, that I'm a human animal—a member of the genus *Homo*. When did I originate?

I'm intimately related to a zygote that inhabited my mother's womb when she was pregnant with me. Either the intimate relation connecting me with the zygote is identity, or it isn't. If it's identity, then I (now) and the zygote (then) are the same being at different stages of development. If it isn't identity, then our intimate relation consists in my having "developed out of" the zygote in a distinctive way. In either case, I'll argue, I didn't originate at conception.

Suppose I'm not identical with the zygote from which I developed. Now, temporally gappy existence may be possible. (Dismantle a car, scatter its parts, and then recover and reassemble them. Perhaps the car has gappy existence.) Whether or not existence *can* be gappy, though, my actual existence clearly isn't. So if I was never a zygote, then I didn't exist before or during the existence of the zygote to which I'm intimately related. Conception occurred either before or during the existence of that zygote. Hence if I was never a zygote, then I existed neither before conception nor for some time after. Thus I originated some time after conception. So if I was never a zygote, I didn't originate at conception.

Suppose on the other hand that I once was a zygote. A zygote is a fertilized egg. A fertilized egg doesn't pop into existence upon fertilization; it exists, unfertilized, before its encounter with the fertilizing sperm. So if I was once a fertilized egg, then I was once an unfertilized egg. The fertilization of the egg is (biological) conception. Hence if I was once an unfertilized egg, then I existed before conception. So if I was once a fertilized egg—a zygote—then I did not originate at conception.

In sum: whether or not I was once a zygote, I did not originate at conception.

III. SOME OBJECTIONS CONSIDERED

I expect that the first horn of my dilemma—that if I was never a zygote, then my conception wasn't my origination—will raise no eyebrows. I expect that the crucial claim of the second horn—that if I was once a zygote, then I was once an unfertilized egg—will inspire incredulity. I now consider some objections to it.

One objection to my argument for the second horn is as follows. A fertilized egg is not, contrary to my suggestion, an egg—just as a crowned prince is not a prince, a victorious candidate not a candidate. So I wrongly claim that a zygote is an egg that was once unfertilized and then became fertilized.

I note that despite my forthcoming concession of this point for argument's sake, it's utterly implausible. You can buy fertilized hen's eggs in grocery stores. I see no license in common sense, biology, ontology or agribusiness for the claim that they aren't really eggs.

The main point, though, is that my argument doesn't require that a fertilized human egg be an *egg*; it's enough that it's an organism (or, in fact, a *thing*). It would indeed be a mistake to say that a crowned prince is a prince who was once uncrowned and then became crowned. It would be no mistake, though, to say that a crowned prince is a thing that was once uncrowned and then became crowned. What matters is that the crowned prince is identical with—the very same being as—the uncrowned prince, not that this being is a prince at both times under consideration. Similarly, it suffices for my argument that a fertilized egg—a zygote—is a thing that existed before fertilization and then became fertilized.

Let me reinforce this claim. If I was once a fertilized egg but never an unfertilized one, then the organism that's the fertilized egg didn't exist before its union with a sperm. More accurately, it didn't exist before its predecessor's union with

a sperm: the organism that is the fertilized egg never joined with a sperm, on the suggestion I now consider, since on that suggestion the joining precedes the existence of that organism. If this is true, then eggs can't survive fertilization. Eggs never *become fertilized;* nothing is at one time an unfertilized egg and later a zygote. Fertilization annihilates one organism and creates another.

The problem with this suggestion is that it seems plainly false, notwithstanding its wide uncritical acceptance. Review some sex education materials; watch, via microscope, the fertilization of an egg. You see an unfertilized oocyte—the one-celled human egg. A sperm approaches and, after traversing the corona radiata and zona pellucida, contacts the egg's cell wall. The sperm breaches that wall, enters, and dissolves, discharging its contents. The breach in the cell wall is immediately sealed. The most natural description of these events is that you've watched one egg *become fertilized*, not the annihilation of one organism and the creation of another.

To repeat: the sperm breaches the egg's cell wall, enters, and *dissolves*. Its dissolution is its death. The sperm "lives on" as we live on in our children, our works, and the compost our bodies eventually become: that is, figuratively. The sperm doesn't literally exist after conception. The oocyte does. Life is unfair.

You might just insist that fertilization is different from all other processes involving the absorption of extracellular material or the internal rearrangement of parts. One way or another, fertilization *must* mark the beginning of a new being.

This insistence is as ad hoc and unjustified as it is common and unquestioned. Its wide acceptance gives it no support but does call for diagnostic explanation, and I offer one speculative but plausible such explanation. (Whether it's the correct explanation is an empirical matter that exceeds my expertise.) Long before the biology of human reproduction was understood, the clear sign that a new being had been brought into being was a baby. Sex was the salient recognizable link in the causal chain leading to babies: abstinence prevents them, indulgence produces them. (I ignore in-vitro fertilization and the like because these technologies can't be responsible for the common attitudes that predate their existence.) Given their background knowledge, our ancestors had no reason to think that any human beings existed except those that either had been born or were growing inside pregnant women. So it's easy to understand why our ancestors would believe that sex initiated a causal process that resulted in the creation of a new being, and it's easy to understand how such a belief might become entrenched. Biological conception was later found to be the salient concomitant of sex: babies result only when conception occurs, and conception, when it occurs, is an effect of sex. (Again, I ignore alternatives only recently rendered medically possible.) These simple facts are enough to account for the prevailing belief that conception marks the beginning of existence: that belief would result from combining two independently reasonable beliefs. That the resulting conjunctive belief contradicts another, far more reasonable, belief concerning identity over time is something easily and understandably overlooked. The relevant beliefs of biologists need no diagnostic explanation, for biologists don't *have* the false belief in question. (They don't have it, at least, when wearing their biologist-hats. They can change headgear as well as anyone else.) You'll look in vain in the embryology literature for any hint that conception is anything other than an important event punctuating—not originating—the life of a single being.

V. ORIGINATION AND THE MORALITY OF ABORTION

I didn't originate, then, at conception. This fact makes trouble of various kinds for some standard pro-life positions. The trouble may be surmountable, but it must be and hasn't been surmounted.

Perhaps the most philosophically prominent pro-life position is that of Don Marquis. Marquis argues that it's seriously wrong to deprive any being of the potential for certain kinds of valuable future experiences—of a "future like ours" (FLO). (By "seriously wrong," Marquis means "seriously presumptively wrong." I'll follow his lead.) Since abortion typically deprives the fetus of an FLO, Marquis says, it is typically seriously wrong.

Marquis considers the objection that on his account, contraception and abstinence are seriously wrong because they deprive a being of an FLO. To take this as an *objection* is to presuppose, as Marquis seems to do, that contraception and abstinence aren't seriously wrong. It's worth noting that even if contraception and abstinence *do* deprive a being of an FLO, they needn't be equally wrong even by Marquis's lights. If you plump for a morally relevant distinction between acts and omissions, you might well see abstinence as less wrong than contraception and both, perhaps, as less wrong than abortion. For abstinence looks like a (mere?) failure to rescue—though the rescue is in most cases an easy and pleasant one—whereas contraception looks like a more odious active interference with a rescue. You might even think that active interference with a rescue is not, unlike abortion, a matter of active killing, and so you might think it less odious than abortion. I don't endorse this hypothetical parsing of moral gravity, but if you do, no matter. What I'm concerned with is the question whether, given Marquis's assumptions, there's something seriously wrong with abstinence or contraception, not with whether they must be equally wrong or *as* wrong as abortion. If actively depriving something of an FLO is seriously wrong, then surely failing to prevent such deprivation, when prevention is easy, is at least very significantly wrong.

You might pin your hopes on the gap, if there is one, between very significant wrongs and serious ones. You might say, that is, that while actively killing a being with an FLO is seriously wrong, failure to perform an easy rescue of such a being isn't. This surely isn't Marquis's view; if it were, he would have said so in response to the objection at issue. In any case, the view looks desperate and ad hoc on its face. (This isn't to deny, of course, that some serious wrongs are worse than others.) I'll take for granted that if abstinence and contraception deprive a being of an FLO, then they are seriously wrong by Marquis's lights. If you want to insist that they are only very significantly but not seriously wrong, go right ahead.

The question for Marquis is this: which being is deprived of an FLO by contraception or abstinence? Marquis surveys the candidates in order of the increasing number of individuals harmed: (1) The single harmed individual might be the combination of the particular sperm and the particular egg that would have united to form a zygote if contraception had not been used. (2) The two harmed individuals might be the particular sperm itself, and, in addition, the ovum itself that would have physically combined to form the zygote. . . . (3) The many harmed individuals might be the millions of *combinations* of sperm and the released ovum whose (small) chances of having an FLO were reduced by the successful contraception. (4) The even larger class of harmed individuals (larger by one) might be the class consisting of all of the individual sperm in an ejaculate and, in addition, the individual ovum released at the time of the successful contraception. (1) through (4) are all candidates for being the subject(s) of harm in the case of successful contraception or abstinence from sex. Which should be chosen? Should we hold a lottery? There seems to be no non-arbitrarily determinate subject of harm in the case of successful contraception. But if there is no such subject of harm, then no determinate thing was harmed.

Marquis is mistaken. There is a single, nonarbitrarily determinate subject of harm in a case of contraception or abstinence: the unique oocyte that would (or could) otherwise have been fertilized. When a woman ovulates, only one oocyte is (typically) ripe for fertilization. If it's fertilized, *it* survives to become a zygote, and nothing else does. Deprive it of fertilization, and you deprive it of an FLO—if, that is, the zygote is identical with the fetus that it becomes. If I was once a zygote, then, Marquis has no adequate defense against the objection that abstinence and contraception are (by his lights) seriously wrong.

Marquis might allow, in light of this point, that I was never a zygote. Suppose I wasn't. Then the zygote from which I developed didn't survive to fetushood, and its failure to survive is a matter of at least nomological necessity. So that zygote lacked the potential for an FLO. It was hardly unique in this respect: if I was never a zygote,

then no human zygote has the potential for an FLO. So killing a zygote doesn't deprive it of an FLO. Hence Marquis's argument, even if otherwise sound, does nothing to show the serious wrongness of killing a zygote.

This point might not ruffle Marquis. He allows that "during the first fourteen days after conception . . . there is an argument that the fetus is not definitely an individual," and so he allows that perhaps abortion isn't seriously wrong during those two weeks. (Marquis uses "fetus" to encompass zygote, embryo, and fetus proper.) I don't know what argument Marquis has in mind, but this allowance is confused on its face since if there's anything that is *the fetus*, then that thing is ipso facto an individual. The view that Marquis might more plausibly mean to countenance is that during the first two weeks, there's nothing that would be identical with the later fetus were the pregnancy to progress normally. Hence there's no individual during the first fourteen days that abortion would deprive of an FLO.

It may seem, then, that my argument should resolve Marquis's apparent indecision about whether his argument applies from the moment of conception. He ought, by his own lights and absent some other argument, to view early abortion as no worse than contraception and abstinence, and he seems to view these as not seriously (or even significantly) wrong.

If all of this is right, it's a substantial result. For Marquis leaves it open whether his argument applies to zygotes, whereas the foregoing considerations clinch the case that it doesn't, at least if contraception and abstinence aren't seriously wrong.

VI. ACQUIRING HUMANITY AND THE MORALITY OF ABORTION

Consider next the claim that what matters is *being a living human being*.

It may seem platitudinous that every living biological organism belongs to some species or other. It's nevertheless false if "belonging" is a matter of *membership*. Some living organisms are members of no species. Consider a particular living cell that's now a constituent of my liver—call it 'Liv'. A living cell is paradigmatically a living organism, and Liv is a living cell. Yet Liv is not a member of the genus *Homo*; Liv is not a "human being" on the usual meaning of that term. Liv isn't a *member* of any genus at all.

Liv is, however, a *human* liver cell, distinct in biological kind from (say) a canine liver cell. Since Liv is a being, and Liv is human, there's a sense in which Liv is a "human being."

We can, then, distinguish two purely biological senses of "human being," in addition to the sense that includes psychological personhood. Let's say that something is a "human-being-1" if and only if it's a *member* of the genus *Homo*. (This is, I think, the normal biological sense of "human being.") Let's say that something is "human-being-2" if and only if it's an organism that is a (not necessarily proper) part of a human-being-1. Liv is a human-being-2 but not a human-being-1.

The unfertilized egg is, it seems, a human-being-2, but not a human-being-1. A baby is a human-being-1. The suggestion I'm now considering is that biological conception marks the acquisition of the property of *being a human-being-1*.

John Noonan Jr. argues that conception marks the point at which there is a new "human being," and he seems to mean that it is the point at which something *becomes* a human-being-1. In some respects his argument echoes, and shares the fate of, Marquis's defense against the contraception-objection that I've already discussed. Noonan also says something new.

The positive argument for conception as the decisive moment of humanization is that at conception the new being receives the genetic code. It is this genetic information which determines his characteristics, which is the biological carrier of the possibility of human wisdom, which makes him a self-evolving being.

Unfortunately, this argument collapses under scrutiny. Leave aside for a moment the bald claim that at conception a *new being* receives a genetic code. It's false that the genetic information encoded in a (male) fertilized egg determines "his characteristics" if this means that it determines *all* the traits he'll have at maturity. (I suppose

temporarily for argument's sake, as Noonan supposes in fact, that the fertilized egg is identical with the human adult into which it develops.) A zygote's genetic endowment determines some of the adult's traits (ceteris paribus) and not others; some are determined by later genetic alteration, parenting, education, nutrition, and so on. The same goes for the genetic endowment of the unfertilized oocyte: it determines some adult traits (ceteris paribus) and not others. The only truth in the neighborhood is an impotent truism: the diploid genetic information bestowed by conception determines some of a being's characteristics—namely those determined by that diploid genetic information. These aren't all of the being's characteristics, though, and it's an equally impotent truism that the haploid genetic information contained in the unfertilized oocyte determines some of a being's characteristics—namely those determined by that haploid genetic information.

Noonan suggests that a zygote's having a distinctively human diploid genetic endowment is a biologically necessary condition for the eventual development of human wisdom. Suppose this is right. It's equally true that an unfertilized egg's having a distinctively human haploid genetic endowment is a biologically necessary condition for the eventual development of human wisdom. In both cases, we have a biologically necessary condition for the possibility of human wisdom. In neither case do we have a sufficient one. Again, there's no basis here for the view that conception marks the acquisition of being a human-being-1.

What lies behind Noonan's fallacious argument concerning the acquisition of "humanness" seems pretty clearly to be the explicit, unargued, and untenable assumption that biological conception is in fact *ontological* conception. It may not be silly to think—though it's also far from obvious—that whenever a new being appears that will someday be an uncontroversial human-being-1, it's a human-being-1 from the beginning. You argue in a tight, vicious circle, however, if you invoke the thesis that conception confers genus-membership to support the conception-as-origination thesis, and then offer that very thesis as the sole reason for thinking that conception confers genus-membership. As I've shown, there's no good reason to think that a new being appears at conception. It doesn't follow that conception *doesn't* mark the first moment of something's being a human-being-1. I claim merely that no plausible reason for thinking that it *does* has been articulated.

⚜ REVIEW QUESTIONS

1. According to Mills, pro-life arguments typically involve two premises. What are these premises? Which one is the focus of Mills attention?
2. What are the implications of Mills's argument for contraception, sexual abstinence, the morning-after pill, and zygotic abortion?
3. State and explain Mills's argument for the conclusion that he did not begin at conception.
4. How does Mills reply to the objection that a fertilized egg is not an egg?
5. What is Mills's explanation for the common and unquestioned belief that conception marks the beginning of a new being?
6. How does Mills attack Marquis's FLO argument?
7. Explain Mills's criticism of Noonan.

⚜ DISCUSSION QUESTIONS

1. Mills claims that no biologist wearing a "biologist-hat" believes that conception creates a new being. Is this true?
2. If an early abortion is wrong, then is contraception or sexual abstinence wrong too? Why or why not?
3. Does Mills convince you that a human being does not begin at conception? Why or why not?
4. How would Marquis and Noonan reply to Mills's objections?

PROBLEM CASES

1. The Women's Health and Human Life Protection Act

The South Dakota State Legislature passed this law in 2006. It outlawed abortion in almost every circumstance, including cases of rape or incest. The only exception was "a medical procedure designed or intended to prevent the death of the pregnant mother." According to the act, pregnancy begins at conception and not when the embryo becomes implanted in the wall of the uterus. This means that the law banned emergency contraception and some forms of hormonal contraception.

The law was repealed by a voter referendum in November 2006. In early 2007, South Dakota lawmakers submitted a revised act, which allows abortion in cases of rape and incest. In addition, the proposed law allows abortion to prevent the death of the mother and to prevent "a devastating and irreversible injury to the mother's health, which is likely to cause a very significant impairment of the functioning of a major bodily organ or system, and which is likely to cause a very significant impairment of the quality of the mother's life."

The members of the South Dakota legislature as well as South Dakota Governor Mike Rounds acknowledge that the goal of the proposed law is to get the U.S. Supreme Court to overturn the *Roe* decision. Should *Roe* be overturned or not?

Some doctors define pregnancy as beginning at implantation rather than conception. Is this definition acceptable? Why or why not?

Should abortion be allowed in cases of rape or incest? Explain your view.

Should abortion be allowed in cases of threat to the woman's health? If so, how would you define the threat? Is the language of the proposed South Dakota law acceptable or not?

2. Human Embryonic Stem Cell Research and Cloning

(For information on stem cell research and cloning, see The National Institutes of Health website, www .nih.gov.) Human embryonic stem cells are extracted from human embryos at a very early stage of development, when the embryos are as tiny as the tip of a sewing needle. These tiny clusters of about 200 cells are called *blastocysts*. Self-sustaining colonies of stem cells, called *lines*, are derived from the blastocysts, which are destroyed in the process.

Stem cells are unique in that they can theoretically grow into any of the body's more than 200 cell types. For example, they might grow into the nerve cells that secrete dopamine and be used to treat a person who has Parkinson's disease. Scientists are eager to do research with stem cells because they believe stem cells will prove to be the building blocks for a new era of regenerative medicine. The cells may enable the body to heal itself from spinal cord injuries and various diseases such as Parkinson's disease, Alzheimer's disease, type 1 diabetes, and heart disease.

Where do researchers get the stem cells for their research? Currently they come from fertility clinics that have a surplus of blastocysts left over from in vitro fertilization. If not used, these blastocysts are usually discarded. The problem with stem cells from these surplus blastocysts is that they may be rejected by the patient receiving them.

A more promising approach is to use stem cells that are genetically matched to the patient. Advanced Cell Technology, a biotechnology company, is planning to do this using cloning techniques. The company wants to remove the nucleus from a female donor's egg, insert a cell from the skin of another donor or patient, and then stimulate the egg to reprogram the genes of the skin cell to start growing into a blastocyst. Then stem cells would be derived from the blastocyst.

What is the objection to stem cell research? The most common one is that harvesting stem cells from a blastocyst kills it, and this is seen as the equivalent of killing a human being. This is the position taken by Pope John Paul II, the U.S. Conference of Catholic Bishops, and abortion opponents. Others find it hard to believe that a tiny clump of cells in a petri dish is a human being with a right to life or that destroying it is the same as murdering a person.

More objections are raised in The President's Council on Bioethics statement on Human Cloning and Human Dignity (www.bioethics.gov). The cloned embryos could be used to produce children and this is unethical because it crosses a line from sexual to asexual reproduction. The women who are egg donors undergo an unpleasant and risky procedure; they are being exploited for the sake of the research. The cloned embryo is a potential child that is not treated with proper respect; in research it is treated as a means to an end. Cloning of human embryos for research is a slippery slope that will lead to harvesting cloned children for their organs or tissues. (Michael Tooley defends the cloning of children for medical purposes in "The Moral Status of the Cloning of Humans," in *Biomedical Ethics Reviews: Human Cloning*, ed. James Humber and Robert Almeder, Humana Press, 1998, pp. 65–101).

There are a number of questions about this research to cure disease. Are early-stage embryos or blastocysts human lives or human beings with a right to life? Is destroying them murder? Should fertility clinics stop discarding unused blastocysts? If so, what should be done with them? What do you think of cloning embryos for research on disease? Is that morally objectionable? What about cloning human children?

3. The Partial-Birth Abortion Ban Act of 2003

This bill was signed into law by President Bush on November 5, 2003. (The full text of the new law can be found at www.theorator.com.) The law defines "partial-birth abortion" as "deliberately and intentionally vaginally delivering a living fetus" whose head or trunk past

the navel is "outside the body of the mother" and then killing it. The law does not prohibit the procedure if it is deemed necessary to save the life of the mother. The woman receiving the abortion may not be prosecuted under the law, but the doctor who performs it (if not to save the life or health of the mother) may be fined and imprisoned for not more than two years, or both.

The language of the law criminalizes any abortion procedure in which the head or trunk of a living fetus is outside the woman's body. The law does not use exact medical terminology, and for that reason it is subject to interpretation. Defenders of the law say it prohibits a cruel and unnecessary procedure that kills an unborn baby, and use graphic pictures to illustrate what happens. Doctors who perform abortions claim that the law prohibits a procedure that the American College of Obstetrics and Gynecology calls intact dilation and evacuation. This procedure is usually done between twenty and twenty-four weeks of pregnancy, when the fetus has grown too large to fit through the woman's cervix easily. The procedure is used in about 2,000 abortions each year.

What exactly takes place in the procedure? A doctor who has performed 200 such abortions describes it as follows: Twenty-four hours before the abortion, the woman's cervix is dilated through the use of laminaria, which are sterilized sticks of seaweed. The next day, the patient is given a local anesthetic and a sedative. Both the mother and the fetus are asleep during the procedure. The fetus is partly pulled out in a breech position, that is, with the feet first and the head remaining in the womb (thus the phrase "partial birth"). Then the skull of the fetus has to be crushed or perforated with forceps to get it out.

Doctors who perform the intact dilation and evacuation procedure claim that it is safer for the woman than a classic dilation and curettage (D & C), in which the fetus is scraped out with a serrated forceps, dismembering and killing it in the process. The woman's uterus can be perforated by the forceps or by fragments of bone as the fetus disintegrates. It is much safer to manually pull out the fetus intact, the doctors say.

Many abortion providers say that the new law also prohibits D & C because the fetus may start to pass through the cervix while still alive. In that case, D & C seems to fit the law's description of a partial-birth abortion.

No reliable statistics exist on the use of the intact dilation and extraction procedure. Groups opposing the ban originally claimed there were between 450 and 500 a year, but the Catholic bishops estimate that there are between 800 and 2,000 a year.

No reliable statistics are available for abortions performed after viability as defined by *Roe*. Federal statistics define a *late abortion* as one performed between twenty and twenty-four weeks. About 86 percent of these so-called late abortions are done by some kind of dilation and evacuation procedure. About 15,000 late abortions are performed a year, about 1 percent of the 1.3 million abortions that occur in the United States each year.

Doctors who perform late abortions say that they are most often used on poor, young women choosing to end an unwanted pregnancy. But in some cases, they are done for medical reasons—for example, because the fetus is severely abnormal or the woman faces grave health risks.

In June 2004, a federal judge in San Francisco, Phillis J. Hamilton, ruled that the Partial Birth Abortion Ban Act is unconstitutional. First, she argued that the law places an undue burden on women seeking abortions because common abortion methods could violate the law. In *Planned Parenthood* (1992), the Supreme Court ruled that states cannot impose an undue burden on women seeking abortions. Second, she said that the language of the law is unconstitutionally vague. In particular, she objected to the terms "partial-birth abortion" and "overt act." Third, she ruled that the law is unconstitutional because it has no exception for abortions necessary to preserve the woman's health. Citing the testimony of medical experts, she said that the procedure in question is sometimes required to protect the woman's health.

In April 2007, the U.S. Supreme Court decided that the ban on partial-birth abortion is constitutional. The vote in the case (*Gonzales v. Carhart*) was 5-to-4, with Justices Kennedy, Roberts, Scalia, Thomas, and Alito in the majority. The dissenting Justices were Ginsburg, Stevens, Souter, and Breyer. Writing for the majority, Justice Kennedy held that the law is not vague, does not impose an undue burden on the woman, and does not need an exception for the woman's health. In her dissenting opinion, Justice Ruth Bader Ginsburg complained that the decision does not take previous abortion decisions seriously and "tolerates, indeed applauds, federal intervention to ban nationwide a procedure found necessary and proper in certain cases by the American College of Obstetricians and Gynecologists."

When President Clinton vetoed the partial-birth abortion ban in 1996, he surrounded himself with five women who had obtained partial-birth abortions for medical reasons. Do you agree with President Clinton that partial-birth abortions should not be banned? Or do you agree with President Bush that the procedure should be outlawed? Explain your position.

4. *Legalized Abortion in Mexico City*

(See James E. McKinley Jr., "Bill to Legalize Abortion Set to Pass in Mexico City," THE *New York Times*, March 31, 2007.) Mexico City, which has 8 million residents, is ready to pass a bill making it legal to have an abortion for any reason in the first trimester of pregnancy. The procedure will be free at city health facilities. Private hospitals will be required to provide abortions to women who ask for them, but doctors who object will not be required to perform the procedure.

Most countries in Latin America allow abortion only to save the life of the mother, as in the case of a tubal pregnancy, or in cases of rape or incest. Chile, Nicaragua, and El Salvador ban abortion completely, allowing no exceptions. Cuba, Puerto Rico, and Guyana allow abortions for any reason during the first trimester.

Defenders of the new law argue that women throughout Latin America have illegal abortions and risk infection, sterility, or death. They estimate that 110,000 women a year seek an illegal abortion in Mexico. The Health Ministry in Mexico reports that at least eighty-eight women died in 2006 from botched abortions. Also, they point out that many women have no information about or access to contraception, or they are not able to negotiate the use of contraceptives with their partner.

Conservatives respond that abortion is murder and cannot be tolerated. Furthermore, they claim that women will continue to have illegal abortions because of the stigma attached to the procedure.

Should women be allowed to have a free abortion for any reason during the first trimester of pregnancy? Why or why not?

5. *Plan B*

(See Gina Kolata, "A Contraceptive Clears a Hurdle to Wider Access," THE *New York Times*, December 17, 2003). If plan A—contraception—fails or is not used, then women who do not want to be pregnant can use Plan B, an emergency contraceptive that prevents unintended pregnancy. Plan B consists of two high-dose birth control pills; it is meant to be used within 72 hours after unprotected sexual intercourse. If used according to the directions, it can prevent nearly 90 percent of unintended pregnancies.

Although the so-called morning-after pill has been available by prescription only since the late 1990s, it has been largely unavailable and unused. (See the next Problem Case.) In December 2003, however, two expert advisory committees to the Food and Drug Administration (FDA) recommended that Plan B be sold over the counter.

The drug is being marketed by Barr Laboratories. The company says that extensive studies show that Plan B is safe. Side effects such as nausea and vomiting are limited and minor. There have been no deaths resulting from use of the drug, and there are no contraindications except in the rare case of allergies to the pills' ingredients. The company says it will provide detailed information to women on what the pills do and on how to use them. It wants to sell the drug in stories with pharmacies. The prescription drug now sells for $25 to $35.

Dr. James Trussell, an advisory committee member from Princeton University, who voted for the motion to make the drug available over the counter, said that Plan B would have an enormous impact in preventing unwanted pregnancies, second only to the introduction of birth control pills. It is estimated that the drug could prevent as many as half of the 3 million unintended pregnancies in the United States each year.

Opponents of the morning-after pill claim that over-the-counter sales will encourage irresponsible sexual behavior. Furthermore, they argue that women may not understand how the pill works. Although it usually acts by preventing ovulation, it also may prevent the fertilized egg from implanting in the uterus. If pregnancy begins with fertilization, as conservatives believe, then the pills could induce an early abortion. "The pill acts to prevent pregnancy by aborting a child," said Judie Brown, president of the American Life League, an antiabortion group.

In May 2004, the acting director of the FDA's Center for Drug Evaluation and Research, Steven Galson, rejected the application for Plan B on the ground that access to emergency contraception might harm young teenagers. He claimed that the proponents of Plan B failed to supply data about the drug's impact on "the younger age group from 11 to 14, where we know there's a substantial amount of sexual activity." But, according to a report issued by the Centers for Disease Control and Prevention (www.cdc.gov), just 4 percent of girls have sexual intercourse before the age of 13. Furthermore, according to the Alan Guttmacher Institute (www.agi-usa.org), seven out of ten girls who have sex before the age of thirteen do so involuntarily.

Should Plan B be sold over the counter? Should it be available without a prescription to girls under the age of thirteen? Would you be willing to have it sold to adult women? Explain your position.

6. The Morning-After Pill

(Discussed in "The Morning-After Pill," by Jan Hoffman, in THE *New York Times Magazine*, January 10, 1993.) Depending on when a woman takes it, the morning-after pill prevents either fertilization (occurring up to eighteen hours after intercourse) or implantation of the fertilized egg in the lining of the uterus (occurring about a week or two after conception). Because pregnancy tests do not register positive until a day or two after implantation, a woman who takes the pill after intercourse will not know if she has prevented conception or implantation.

The drug most often used as a morning-after pill is Ovral. It is also used as a birth control pill, and it was approved as such by the federal Food and Drug Administration (FDA) in 1968. Other lower-dose pills that can be used as morning-after pills are Lo/Ovral, Nordette, Levlen, Triphasil, and Tri Levlen. All these pills combine estrogen and progestin. They affect a woman's hormones in such a way that the egg cannot be fertilized; or if it is, it cannot become implanted in the lining of the uterus. Instead, the egg is sloughed off during menstruation.

The morning-after pill can be effectively taken up to 72 hours after intercourse, and it reduces the likelihood of pregnancy to below 8 percent. (On her most fertile day, a woman's chance of becoming pregnant is at most about 25 percent.) Although it certainly reduces the chances of becoming pregnant, it is not completely effective because it does not prevent tubal pregnancies. The side effects of the morning-after pill include temporary nausea and breast tenderness, and it is not recommended for women who should not take oral contraceptives.

According to the *Times* article, the morning-after pill has been part of standard care for rape victims for more than a decade. Planned Parenthood affiliates have been offering it for about three years. Use of birth control pills as morning-after pills has not received the approval of the FDA, largely because no drug company has sought approval, and without FDA approval the pills cannot be dispensed in federally supported Title X clinics that serve poor women.

Doctors estimate that by making the morning-after pill widely available, the number of unwanted pregnancies could be reduced by 1.7 million annually and the number of abortions could be reduced by 800,000 annually. Currently, there are about 3.5 million unwanted pregnancies per year in the United States and about 1.4 million abortions.

The morning-after pill raises several interesting questions:

Is preventing implantation an abortion, contraception, interception, or what?
Is the zygote or fertilized egg a person with rights before it becomes implanted?

Intrauterine devices (IUDs) also prevent fertilization or implantation. Does using an IUD amount to getting an abortion?

In the one or two weeks before implantation, many fertilized eggs are naturally sloughed off, and women don't usually think of this as miscarriage. So why should a woman think of preventing implantation as an abortion?

7. Mrs. Sherri Finkbine and Thalidomide

In 1962, Mrs. Sherri Finkbine, the mother of four normal children, became pregnant again. During the pregnancy, Mrs. Finkbine had trouble sleeping, so without consulting her physician, she took some tranquilizers that her husband had brought back from a trip to Europe. These tranquilizers contained the drug thalidomide, which was widely used in Europe.

Later Mrs. Finkbine read that a number of severely deformed children had been born in Europe. These children's limbs failed to develop or developed in malformed ways; some were born blind and deaf or had seriously defective internal organs. The birth defects were traced to the use during pregnancy of a widely used tranquilizer whose active ingredient was thalidomide, the very tranquilizer that she had taken.

Mrs. Finkbine went to her physician, and he confirmed her fears. The tranquilizer did contain thalidomide, and she had a very good chance of delivering a seriously deformed baby. The physician recommended an abortion. Mrs. Finkbine then presented her case to the three-member medical board of Phoenix, and they granted approval for the abortion.

In her concern for other women who might have taken thalidomide, Mrs. Finkbine told her story to a local newspaper. The story made the front page, and it wasn't long before reporters discovered and published Mrs. Finkbine's identity. She became the object of an intense antiabortion campaign, and she was condemned as a murderer by the Vatican newspaper.

As a result of the controversy, the medical board decided that its approval for an abortion would not survive a court test, because the Arizona statute at that time allowed abortion only to save the mother's life. Therefore, the board withdrew its approval.

Eventually Mrs. Finkbine found it necessary to get an abortion in Sweden. After the abortion, Mrs. Finkbine asked if the fetus had been a boy or a girl. The doctor could not say because the fetus had been too badly deformed.

Do you think that Mrs. Finkbine acted wrongly in having an abortion? Explain your answer.

Do you think that the government has a right to prohibit abortions in such cases? Why or why not?

☙ SUGGESTED READINGS

The Alan Guttmacher Institute (www.guttmacher .org/) is a good source for statistics on all aspects of abortion and pregnancy. The Centers for Disease Control and Prevention (www.cdc.gov) provides national data, but focuses on the safety of abortion. The National Right to Life organization (www.nrlc.org) advocates the pro-life view. Another pro-life organization is the Pro-Life Action League (www.prolifeaction.org). The prochoice view is defended on Naral Pro-Choice America (www.prochoiceamerica.org). For advocacy of women's rights, see the Feminist Majority (www.feminist.org).

Sidney Callahan, "Abortion and the Sexual Agenda: A Case for Prolife Feminism," *Commonweal* (April 25, 1986): 232–238, attacks the arguments of pro-choice feminists and defends a pro-life feminist position. She argues that a woman's right to control her body does not apply to abortion.

Elizabeth Harman, "Creation Ethics," *Philosophy and Public Affairs*, 28, 4 (Autumn 1999): 310–324, defends the view that an early abortion requires no moral justification at all because the fetus has no actual future as a person.

Elizabeth Harman, "The Potentiality Problem," *Philosophical Studies*, 114, (May 2003, nos. 1–2):

173–198, argues that the potentiality of the embryo does not give it moral status; but consciousness does give it some moral standing.

William J. Fitzpatrick, "Totipotency and the Moral Status of Embryos: New Problems for an Old Argument," *Journal of Social Philosophy*, 35 (Spring 2004, no. 1): 108–122, critically examines the pro-life argument that appeals to totipotency, that is, the potential to develop into a living organism when placed in a suitable environment. The sperm and egg do not have this property, but the zygote does.

Rosalind Hursthouse, "Virtue Theory and Abortion," *Philosophy and Public Affairs* 20 (1991, no. 3): 223–246, applies virtue theory to the problem of abortion, and concludes that some abortions exhibit vices such as selfishness or callousness, but others display virtues such as modesty or humility.

Sally Markowitz, "Abortion and Feminism," *Social Theory and Practice*, 16 (Spring 1990): 1–17, presents a feminist argument for abortion rights. Basically, her argument is that women should not have to endure an unwanted pregnancy in a sexist society where they are oppressed.

Michael Tooley, "Abortion and Infanticide," *Philosophy and Public Affairs*, 2 (Fall 1972): 47–66, presents a classic defense of the pro-choice view that neither a fetus nor a newborn infant has a serious right to continued existence and that both abortion and infanticide are morally acceptable. Tooley also has a book titled *Abortion and Infanticide* (Oxford, UK: Oxford University Press, 1974), in which he develops his position.

Celia Wolf-Devine, "Abortion and the Feminine Voice," *Public Affairs Quarterly*, 3 (July 1989): 81–97, contends that the feminine voice in morality—the voice that cares for particular others—says that abortion is to be avoided.

Gary M. Atkinson, "The Morality of Abortion," *International Philosophy Quarterly*, 14 (Spring 1974): 347–362, argues, like Tooley, that abortion and infanticide are morally equivalent, but he takes the argument a step further by claiming that each is equivalent to involuntary euthanasia. But because involuntary euthanasia is wrong, on Atkinson's view, it follows that abortion and infanticide are wrong, too.

Jane English, "Abortion and the Concept of a Person," *Canadian Journal of Philosophy*, 5 (October 1975, no. 2): 233–243, argues that the question about whether the fetus is a person or not cannot be conclusively settled because the concept of person cannot be defined in terms of necessary and sufficient conditions. English goes on to argue that even if the fetus is a person, the mother's right to self-defense is strong enough to justify abortions to avoid death or serious harm.

L. W. Sumner, "Abortion," in *Health Care Ethics*, ed. Donald VanDeVeer and Tom Regan (Philadelphia: Temple University Press, 1987), pp. 162–81, proposes a moderate view about the moral standing of the fetus: It acquires moral standing when it becomes sentient—that is, capable of feeling pleasure and pain. Before this dividing line in the development of the fetus (which occurs sometime in the second trimester), abortion is the moral equivalent of contraception, and after this line abortion is the moral equivalent of infanticide.

Susan Sherwin, "Abortion through a Feminist Ethics Lens," *Dialogue*, 30 (1991): 327–342, presents a standard feminist view that freedom to choose abortion is essential for sexual and reproductive freedom, and without it, women will continue to be oppressed by men.

Feminist Philosophies, ed. Janet A. Kourany, James P. Sterba, and Rosemarie Tong (Englewood Cliffs, NJ: Prentice Hall, 1992), has four feminist articles on abortion and reproduction, including "Abortion: Is a Woman a Person?" by Ellen Willis. Willis claims that pro-lifers view the woman as a mere womb and not as a person with rights.

Angela Davis, *Women, Race, and Class* (New York: Random House, 1981), ch. 12, discusses the abortion rights movement in the context of race, class, and the women's liberation movement.

Ronald Dworkin, "A Critical Review of Feminist Analyses of Abortion," *The New York Review of Books* (June 10, 1993), attacks Catharine MacKinnon, Robin West, Carol Gilligan, and other feminists who emphasize the unique relationship between the pregnant woman and the fetus.

Jim Stone, "Why Potentiality Matters," *Canadian Journal of Philosophy*, 17 (December 1987): 815–830, argues that the fetus has a right to life because it is potentially an adult human being.

The Abortion Controversy, eds. Louis P. Pojman and Francis J. Beckwith (Belmont, CA: Wadsworth, 1988), is a comprehensive anthology that includes articles on the *Roe* decision, Thomson's appeal to the woman's right to her body, numerous articles about the personhood of the fetus, and feminist articles.

Alan Zaitchik, "Viability and the Morality of Abortion," *Philosophy and Public Affairs,* 10 (1981, no. 1): 18–24, defends the view that viability is a morally significant dividing line.

Tristram H. Engelhardt, Jr., "The Ontology of Abortion," *Ethics,* 84 (April 1974): 217–234, maintains that the fetus is not a person until the later stages of pregnancy, but after viability it can be treated as if it were a person.

Peter Singer, *Practical Ethics,* 2nd ed. (Cambridge, UK: Cambridge University Press, 1993), Chapter 6, presents a utilitarian view of abortion. The version of utilitarianism that Singer accepts is called preference utilitarianism.

Sissela Bok, "Ethical Problems of Abortion," *Hastings Center Studies,* 2 (January 1974): 33–52, rejects attempts to define humanity and suggests that various reasons for not getting an abortion become stronger as the fetus develops.

Daniel Callahan, *Abortion: Law, Choice and Morality* (New York: Macmillan, 1970), defends the moderate view that the fetus has what he calls a partial moral status.

Joel Feinberg and Barbara Baum Levenbook, "Abortion," in *Matters of Life and Death,* 3rd ed., ed. Tom Regan (New York: Random House, 1993), provide a sophisticated discussion of various issues connected to abortion and end up with a moderate position. In a postscript, though, they decide that a legal ban on abortion may be justified even if abortion is not generally morally wrong.

R. M. Hare, "Abortion and the Golden Rule," *Philosophy and Public Affairs,* 4 (Spring 1975): 201–222, attacks those, such as Judith Jarvis Thomson, who appeal to moral intuition. Hare uses the golden rule as a basic ethical principle to defend a moderate view of abortion.

Susan Nicholson, *Abortion and the Roman Catholic Church* (Knoxsville, TN: Religious Ethics, 1974), explains the position of the Catholic Church on abortion.

CHAPTER THREE

Euthanasia and the Duty to Die

INTRODUCTION

Factual Background

Euthanasia is killing someone for the sake of mercy to relieve great suffering. But when a doctor helps an injured or ill person commit suicide, as Dr. Jack Kevorkian has done in at least 130 cases, it seems that there is little difference between doctor-assisted suicide and euthanasia.

Statistics on euthanasia and physician-assisted suicide are difficult to obtain in the United States. Other than Dr. Kevorkian, few doctors come forward to talk about something that is illegal in every state except Oregon. In one study, 36 percent of the doctors who responded said they would write lethal prescriptions if it were legal, and 24 percent said they would administer lethal injections. Another study, reported in the *Journal of the American Medical Association* (August 12, 1998), found in telephone interviews of 355 oncologists that almost 16 percent had participated in euthanasia or physician-assisted suicide. A national survey found that nearly one in five doctors who care for very ill and dying people said that they had been asked for help in dying, either by delivering a lethal injection or by writing a prescription for lethal drugs, but only 5 percent admitted to administering a lethal injection, and only 3 percent said they had ever written such a prescription.

Euthanasia and physician-assisted suicide have been socially accepted and openly practiced in the Netherlands for about twenty years. Until recently, euthanasia in the Netherlands was technically illegal, but in 2002, the Netherlands became the first country in the world to pass a law decriminalizing voluntary euthanasia. The legislation states that doctors must be convinced that the patient's request is voluntary and well-considered and that the patient is facing unremitting and unbearable suffering. Doctors must have advised the patient of the medical situation and believe there is no reasonable alternative to euthanasia. They must consult with at least one other independent physician. The law allows minors aged twelve to sixteen to request euthanasia with the consent of their parents. The strict conditions established under the law require a commission that includes a doctor, a medical ethics expert, and a lawyer to review each euthanasia case. Only legal residents of the Netherlands are eligible for the procedure. Studies of Dutch euthanasia report that there have been about 2,700 deaths each year by euthanasia or assisted suicide, but this figure does not include deaths caused by an intentional overdose of morphine, which is the most common method of mercy killing.

Oregon was the first state in the United States to make assisted suicide legal for the terminally ill. The state law, known officially as the Death with Dignity Act, took effect in November 1997. The law applies only to adults of sound mind who have, in the opinion of at least two doctors, less than six months to live. Doctors may prescribe but not administer the lethal dose. Those requesting death must fill out and sign a single-page form titled "Request for Medication to End My Life in a Humane and Dignified Manner" and wait fifteen days before receiving the medication. According to the Oregon state website (www.oregon.gov), 401 patients have died under the terms of the law since 1997. In 2008, sixty patients killed themselves and eighty-eight received prescriptions for lethal medications. As in previous years, the most frequently cited reasons for wanting physician-assisted suicide were loss of autonomy (95 percent), decreasing ability to engage in enjoyable activities (92 percent), and loss of dignity (92 percent).

Besides Oregon, physician-assisted suicide is legal in the states of Washington and Montana. In 2008, Washington state voters approved Washington's Death with Dignity Act (Initiative 1000), which made it legal for doctors to prescribe a lethal dose of medication for patients who have less than six months to live. The measure passed by a margin of 59 percent to 41 percent. In Montana, the Supreme Court ruled in the case of *Baxter v. State of Montana* that physician-assisted suicide is not "against pubic policy" in Montana. The Court also ruled that state law protects doctors from prosecution for helping terminally ill patients die.

Currently, forty-four states have laws making physician-assisted suicide illegal. In 1998, Michigan voters overwhelmingly rejected Proposal B, a ballot initiative that would have permitted doctors to administer lethal doses of medication to terminally ill patients. Previously, the state had outlawed assisted suicide for fifteen months in response to the practices of Dr. Kevorkian. In November 1998, CBS's *60 Minutes* aired a videotape showing Dr. Kevorkian giving a lethal injection to Thomas Youk, age fifty-two, who was suffering from Lou Gehrig's disease. Three days later, Michigan charged Dr. Kevorkian with first-degree murder. He was convicted of second-degree murder on April 13, 1999, and sentenced to ten to twenty-five years in prison. He became eligible for parole in 2005, and he was paroled on June 1, 2007. Since being released from prison, Dr. Kevorkian has appeared on television and given popular public lectures defending assisted suicide. In 2008, he ran for Congress as an independent, and received more than 2 percent of the vote.

In June 1997, the U.S. Supreme Court ruled (in *Washington v. Gluksberg*) that laws in New York and Washington making doctor-assisted suicide a crime were not unconstitutional. But the 9-to-0 decision was tentative, and some of the justices seemed to grant that some terminally ill people in intractable pain might be able to claim a constitutional right to a doctor's assistance in hastening their deaths. Justice Sandra Day O'Connor, for example, said that it was still an open question whether "a mentally competent person who is experiencing great suffering" that cannot otherwise be controlled has a constitutionally based "interest in controlling the circumstances of his or her imminent death."

The Readings

Discussions of euthanasia often distinguish between different types of euthanasia. *Voluntary euthanasia* is mercy killing with the consent of the terminally ill or suffering person. Many writers include physician-assisted suicide as a type of voluntary euthanasia. *Nonvoluntary euthanasia,* by contrast, is mercy killing without the consent of the person killed, although the consent of others, such as parents or relatives, may be obtained. Writers who discuss nonvoluntary euthanasia usually have in mind the killing of those who are unable to give consent—for example, a comatose person such as Karen Quinlan or an infant with severe birth defects. Obviously, such a person cannot commit suicide. There is another possibility, however, and that is the mercy killing of a person who is able to give consent but is not asked and does not give it. This can be called *involuntary euthanasia*. This form of euthanasia is not discussed in the readings, but it is safe to assume that all the authors in this book would condemn it.

In the first reading, James Rachels critically examines a further distinction between active and passive euthanasia, or between killing and letting a patient die for the sake of mercy. Just how this distinction should be drawn and whether the distinction should be made at all is controversial. As Rachels explains it, *active euthanasia* is taking a direct action designed to kill the patient, such as giving a lethal injection of morphine. *Passive euthanasia,* by contrast, is allowing the patient to die by withholding treatment—not performing lifesaving surgery on an infant with serious birth defects, for example. Rachels argues that the distinction has no moral significance and that using it leads to pointless suffering and confused moral thinking.

Bonnie Steinbock replies to Rachels. She argues that the AMA statement quoted by Rachels does not assume a distinction between active and passive euthanasia, but makes a different distinction between ordinary and extraordinary means of prolonging life. An example of ordinary means is the use of a respirator to sustain a patient through a bout with a respiratory disease. Use of a respirator to sustain the life of a severely brain-damaged person is an example of extraordinary means. According to Steinbock, patients have the right to refuse extraordinary means of treatment, such as painful surgery or chemotherapy, but this is not the same as passive euthanasia.

Philippa Foot (see the Suggested Readings) does not agree with Rachels. She argues that the distinction between killing and letting die does have moral significance in many important cases. For example, she thinks there is a clear difference between a person sending starving people poisoned food, thereby killing them through an action, and letting them die by not sending food. The difference is that in the first case the person is an agent of harm and in the second case the person is not an agent of harm. Foot goes on to discuss other interesting cases in which our moral intuitions seem to say that we should not kill one person to rescue five people, but it is allowable to let one person die in order to save five. But she admits that sometimes it might not be wrong to kill one person to save five, as in the much-discussed case of the runaway trolley, where there is a choice between killing one person or five standing on the track.

John Harris (see the Suggested Readings) raises more problems for the distinction between killing and letting die in his discussion of the survival lottery. Suppose that we can save two dying patients, Y and Z, by killing an innocent person, A. We take A's heart and give it to Y, who needs a new heart to survive, and we take A's lungs and give them to Z, who needs new lungs. No doubt we are guilty of killing an innocent person, but if we let Y and Z die by failing to perform the transplants, then are we still guilty—guilty of killing two innocent persons instead of one?

In the third reading, Dan W. Brock defends voluntary active euthanasia and replies to objections. He thinks the central argument for allowing it is based on the right of patients to make decisions about their lives according to their conception of the good life. If patients have the right to refuse life-sustaining treatment, then why can't they decide to actively end their lives? Another consideration is that in some cases euthanasia is the only way to relieve severe pain and suffering. Brock says this is the strongest argument for euthanasia. He agrees with Rachels that in the relevant medical cases there is no moral difference between killing and allowing to die or between acts and omissions resulting in death. He gives a detailed discussion of the potential good and bad consequences of allowing euthanasia. He concludes that the good consequences of relief from prolonged suffering and respecting the wishes of dying people and others who want euthanasia as an option outweigh the possible bad effects, which are speculative and difficult to assess.

In the last reading for the chapter, John Hardwig explains and defends a duty to die for the old or ill. He does not think that the distinction between killing and letting die matters when it comes to this duty, which includes not just refusing life-prolonging medical treatment but also suicide. In his view, the basis for this duty to die is the burden the old or ill place on their families. When the burden is too great, the old or ill person has a duty to die. To convince you of this, he presents a case of an eighty-seven-year-old woman dying of congestive heart failure who has only six months to life. Even if the woman wants to live, and wants aggressive life-prolonging treatment, she has a duty to die. Why? Because in this case prolonging her life will impose too great a burden on her fifty-five-year-old daughter, the only remaining family member, who will lose all her savings, her home, her job, and her career in caring for her mother.

Felicia Ackerman (see the Suggested Readings) objects to Hardwig's failure to distinguish between killing and letting die. She agrees that the old or ill have a duty not to burden their families or society by demanding and receiving aggressive life-prolonging medical treatment. She notes that this view is widely accepted. But it is entirely another matter to claim that the old or ill have a duty to kill themselves to avoid imposing a burden on their families. She thinks this view is problematic, if only for the practical reason that it applies to a great many people.

Philosophical Issues

One basic issue is whether or not voluntary euthanasia and physician-assisted suicide are wrong. The standard view, presented by the AMA statement, is that both are wrong. The AMA statement quoted by Rachels says, "The intentional termination of the life of one human being by another—mercy killing—is contrary to that for which the medical profession stands." Steinbock defends the AMA statement against Rachel's attack. She says that the AMA statement does not rest on any distinction between active and passive euthanasia, as Rachels says. Both are wrong if they involve the intentional termination of one human being's life by another human being. The AMA statement does rest on an important distinction between ordinary and extraordinary means of treatment, but this is based on the patient's right to refuse treatment and does not assume any right to die.

Some doctors object to making voluntary active euthanasia legal. For example, Stephen G. Potts (see the Suggested Readings) argues that the legalized practice of voluntary active euthanasia would have a number of bad effects, including the abandonment of hope, increased fear of hospitals and doctors, increased pressure on patients to die, and a slippery slope leading to nonvoluntary euthanasia and even involuntary euthanasia when undesirable people are killed without their consent. These potential bad effects mean that the burden of proof is on those who want to make euthanasia legal.

Brock argues that the potential bad effects of legalizing euthanasia are merely speculative and hard to assess. However, he admits that the slippery-slope objection is serious—indeed, the most serious objection to permitting euthanasia. He replies that abuses of a legal policy permitting euthanasia can be avoided by putting in place various safeguards, such as making sure that the patient's request is fully informed and stable, that all reasonable alternatives have been explored for relieving pain and suffering, and that the patient is not depressed.

Susan M. Wolf (see the Suggested Readings) attacks euthanasia and physician-assisted suicide from a feminist point of view. Women in our sexist society have been socialized to be self-sacrificing, and this means that women will be more inclined to request death than men. If euthanasia and physician-assisted suicide are made legal, more women than men will die. She supports her view by pointing out that the first eight patients killed by Dr. Kevorkian were women.

Rachels focuses on the reduction of pain and suffering. He argues that in some cases active euthanasia is preferable to passive euthanasia because it reduces the amount of time spent in pain and suffering. If there is a choice between a quick and painless death and prolonged suffering, and no other alternative, then Rachels thinks that a quick and painless death is the right choice.

Brock agrees that avoiding prolonged suffering is a good reason for allowing euthanasia for those who want it. He also emphasizes the patient's right of autonomy, the right to make personal decisions about one's life according to one's beliefs about what makes life worth living.

Another important issue, as we have seen, is whether there is a morally significant difference between killing and letting a patient die, or between active and passive euthanasia, or between intentionally causing death and merely permitting death. Both Rachels and Brock reject such distinctions, but Foot defends them. It seems obvious that most doctors make these distinctions: The statistics show that withholding or withdrawing lifesaving treatment is much more common than active euthanasia or physician-assisted suicide.

Another matter of controversy is the distinction between ordinary and extraordinary means of prolonging life. This distinction is found in the AMA statement, which allows cessation of the employment of extraordinary means to prolong the life of the body. Rachels thinks that the cessation of extraordinary means of treatment amounts to passive euthanasia because it is the intentional termination of life. But Steinbock suggests a response to this. She says that the reason for discontinuing extraordinary treatment is not to bring about the patient's death, but to avoid treatment that will cause more suffering than the disease and offers little hope of benefiting the patient. By contrast, cessation of ordinary means of treatment can be seen as neglect or even the intentional infliction of harm.

Although she does not explicitly discuss it, Steinbock seems to accept a traditional view about intentions called the *doctrine of double effect*. (See the article by Philippa Foot cited in the Suggested Readings.) According to this doctrine, as long as the intended consequence of an act is good, a bad foreseen consequence (such as death) can be morally allowed, provided it is not intended and prevents a greater evil (such as great suffering). A common medical practice can be used to illustrate this. Suppose that a doctor gives a terminal cancer patient an overdose of morphine, that is, an amount sufficient to kill the patient. If the doctor intends only to reduce or eliminate the patient's pain and not to kill the patient, and if the death of the patient is not as bad as the patient's suffering, then according to the doctrine of double effect the doctor's action is not wrong, even though the doctor foresees that the patient will die from the overdose.

This kind of reasoning seems fairly common among doctors. It seems to be suggested, for example, when the AMA statement says that it is intentional termination of life that is forbidden. Doesn't this allow for unintentional but foreseen death? In his legal defenses, Dr. Kevorkian repeatedly said that his only intention was to reduce or eliminate great suffering and not to cause death.

Critics of the doctrine of double effect complain that no clear distinction can be made between the two effects, the intended one and the unintended but foreseen one. If Dr. Kevorkian intends to reduce the patient's suffering but also knows that the patient is getting a lethal dose of drugs when she turns the switch on the suicide machine, does it make sense to say that Dr. Kevorkian does not also intend to kill the patient with his machine?

Another important issue is whether or not old and/or ill people have a duty to die to avoid burdening their families. Hardwig thinks so, but Felicia Ackerman disagrees. Ackerman argues that family members have a strong obligation to care for each other. Consider again Hardwig's case of the eighty-seven-year-old woman dying of congestive heart failure. In Ackerman's view, much depends on the mother's relationship with her fifty-five-year-old daughter. Suppose the mother made sacrifices for her daughter. She paid for the daughter's education so that the daughter could have a career. She gave her daughter money so that the daughter could buy a home. She cared for the daughter as a baby and child. All of these considerations suggest that the daughter has a duty to care for her ill mother. Furthermore, in this case the care is supposed to last for only six months. Why couldn't the daughter find another job?

Hardwig does not distinguish between cases of parents and children and cases involving married people. Ackerman, however, thinks they are different. Children have a strong duty to care for their parents because the parents usually put in a long period of caring for their children. Married people do not usually begin with a long period of one-sided caregiving, and unlike children, they freely enter into the arrangement. This gives married people the opportunity to agree upon caregiving duties.

Finally, there is the basic issue of how to make life-or-death decisions. One standard answer, given by Rachels, is to appeal to the quality of a person's life. If a person will have a bad life, then she should be allowed to end it; but if she will have a good life, then it is wrong to end it. But how do we distinguish between good and bad lives? That is a classical problem that resists easy solution. Hedonists would say that a life full of pleasure is good and a life filled with suffering is bad. But Kant and many others would reject this view. It is not represented in the readings, but it is worth mentioning that the Christian view is that all life is sacred and all life is valuable, no matter how much suffering it contains.

Active and Passive Euthanasia

JAMES RACHELS

For biographical information on James Rachels, see the reading in Chapter 1.

Here Rachels attacks the distinction between active and passive euthanasia, and the doctrine apparently accepted by the American Medical Association that taking direct action to kill a patient (active euthanasia) is wrong, but withholding treatment and allowing a patient to die (passive euthanasia) is allowable. Rachels makes three criticisms of this doctrine. First, it results in unnecessary suffering for patients who die slowly and painfully rather than quickly and painlessly. Second, the doctrine leads to moral decisions based on irrelevant considerations. Third, the distinction between killing and letting die assumed by the doctrine is of no moral significance.

The distinction between active and passive euthanasia is thought to be crucial for medical ethics. The idea is that it is permissible, at least in some cases, to withhold treatment and allow a patient to die, but it is never permissible to take any direct action designed to kill the patient. This doctrine seems to be accepted by most doctors, and it is endorsed in a statement adopted by the House of Delegates of the American Medical Association on December 4, 1973:

> The intentional termination of the life of one human being by another—mercy killing—is contrary to that for which the medical profession stands and is contrary to the policy of the American Medical Association. The cessation of the employment of extraordinary means to prolong the life of the body when there is irrefutable evidence that biological

death is imminent is the decision of the patient and/or his immediate family. The advice and judgment of the physician should be freely available to the patient and/or his immediate family.

However, a strong case can be made against this doctrine. In what follows I will set out some of the relevant arguments, and urge doctors to reconsider their views on this matter.

To begin with a familiar type of situation, a patient who is dying of incurable cancer of the throat is in terrible pain, which can no longer be satisfactorily alleviated. He is certain to die within a few days, even if present treatment is continued, but he does not want to go on living for those days since the pain is unbearable. So he asks the doctor for an end to it, and his family joins in the request.

Source: James Rachels, "Active and Passive Euthanasia," from *The Elements of Moral Philosophy* (1986), pp. 90–103. Reprinted with the permission of The McGraw-Hill Companies.

Suppose the doctor agrees to withhold treatment, as the conventional doctrine says he may. The justification for his doing so is that the patient is in terrible agony, and since he is going to die anyway, it would be wrong to prolong his suffering needlessly. But now notice this. If one simply withholds treatment, it may take the patient longer to die, and so he may suffer more than he would if more direct action were taken and a lethal injection given. This fact provides strong reason for thinking that, once the initial decision not to prolong his agony has been made, active euthanasia is actually preferable to passive euthanasia, rather than the reverse. To say otherwise is to endorse the option that leads to more suffering rather than less, and is contrary to the humanitarian impulse that prompts the decision not to prolong his life in the first place.

Part of my point is that the process of being "allowed to die" can be relatively slow and painful, whereas being given a lethal injection is relatively quick and painless. Let me give a different sort of example. In the United States about one in 600 babies is born with Down's syndrome. Most of these babies are otherwise healthy—that is, with only the usual pediatric care, they will proceed to an otherwise normal infancy. Some, however, are born with congenital defects such as intestinal obstructions that require operations if they are to live. Sometimes, the parents and the doctor will decide not to operate, and let the infant die. Anthony Shaw describes what happens then:

> . . . When surgery is denied [the doctor] must try to keep the infant from suffering while natural forces sap the baby's life away. As a surgeon whose natural inclination is to use the scalpel to fight off death, standing by and watching a salvageable baby die is the most emotionally exhausting experience I know. It is easy at a conference, in a theoretical discussion, to decide that such infants should be allowed to die. It is altogether different to stand by in the nursery and watch as dehydration and infection wither a tiny being over hours and days. This is a terrible ordeal for me and the hospital staff—much more so than for the parents who never set foot in the nursery.[1]

[1]A. Shaw: "Doctor, Do We Have a Choice?" *THE New York Times Magazine,* January 30, 1972, p. 54.

I can understand why some people are opposed to all euthanasia, and insist that such infants must be allowed to live. I think I can also understand why other people favor destroying these babies quickly and painlessly. But why should anyone favor letting "dehydration and infection wither a tiny being over hours and days"? The doctrine that says that a baby may be allowed to dehydrate and wither, but may not be given an injection that would end its life without suffering, seems so patently cruel as to require no further refutation. The strong language is not intended to offend, but only to put the point in the clearest possible way.

My second argument is that the conventional doctrine leads to decisions concerning life and death made on irrelevant grounds.

Consider again the case of the infants with Down's syndrome who need operations for congenital defects unrelated to the syndrome to live. Sometimes, there is no operation, and the baby dies, but when there is no such defect, the baby lives on. Now, an operation such as that to remove an intestinal obstruction is not prohibitively difficult. The reason why such operations are not performed in these cases is, clearly, that the child has Down's syndrome and the parents and doctor judge that because of that fact it is better for the child to die.

But notice that this situation is absurd, no matter what view one takes of the lives and potentials of such babies. If the life of such an infant is worth preserving, what does it matter if it needs a simple operation? Or, if one thinks it better that such a baby should not live on, what difference does it make that it happens to have an unobstructed intestinal tract? In either case, the matter of life and death is being decided on irrelevant grounds. It is the Down's syndrome, and not the intestines, that is the issue. The matter should be decided, if at all, on that basis, and not be allowed to depend on the essentially irrelevant question of whether the intestinal tract is blocked.

What makes this situation possible, of course, is the idea that when there is an intestinal blockage, one can "let the baby die," but when there is no such defect there is nothing that can be done, for one must not "kill" it. The fact that this idea leads to such results as deciding life or death on irrelevant grounds is another good reason why the doctrine should be rejected.

One reason why so many people think that there is an important moral difference between active and passive euthanasia is that they think killing someone is morally worse than letting someone die. But is it? Is killing, in itself, worse than letting die? To investigate this issue, two cases may be considered that are exactly alike except that one involves killing whereas the other involves letting someone die. Then, it can be asked whether this difference makes any difference to the moral assessments. It is important that the cases be exactly alike, except for this one difference, since otherwise one cannot be confident that it is this difference and not some other that accounts for any variation in the assessments of the two cases. So, let us consider this pair of cases:

In the first, Smith stands to gain a large inheritance if anything should happen to his six-year-old cousin. One evening while the child is taking his bath, Smith sneaks into the bathroom and drowns the child, and then arranges things so that it will look like an accident.

In the second, Jones also stands to gain if anything should happen to his six-year-old cousin. Like Smith, Jones sneaks in planning to drown the child in his bath. However, just as he enters the bathroom Jones sees the child slip and hit his head and fall face down in the water. Jones is delighted; he stands by, ready to push the child's head back under if it is necessary, but it is not necessary. With only a little thrashing about the child drowns all by himself, "accidentally," as Jones watches and does nothing.

Now Smith killed the child, whereas Jones "merely" let the child die. That is the only difference between them. Did either man behave better, from a moral point of view? If the difference between killing and letting die were in itself a morally important matter, one should say that Jones's behavior was less reprehensible than Smith's. But does one really want to say that? I think not. In the first place, both men acted from the same motive, personal gain, and both had exactly the same end in view when they acted. It may be inferred from Smith's conduct that he is a bad man, although that judgment may be withdrawn or modified if certain further facts are learned about him—for example, that he is mentally deranged. But would not the very same thing be inferred about Jones from his conduct? And would not the same further considerations also be relevant to any modification of this judgment? Moreover, suppose Jones pleaded, in his own defense, "After all, I didn't do anything except just stand there and watch the child drown. I didn't kill him; I only let him die." Again, if letting die were in itself less bad than killing, this defense should have at least some weight. But it does not. Such a "defense" can only be regarded as a grotesque perversion of moral reasoning. Morally speaking, it is no defense at all.

Now, it may be pointed out, quite properly, that the cases of euthanasia with which doctors are concerned are not like this at all. They do not involve personal gain or the destruction of normally healthy children. Doctors are concerned only with cases in which the patient's life is of no further use to him, or in which the patient's life has become or will soon become a terrible burden. However, the point is the same in these cases: the bare difference between killing and letting die does not, in itself, make a moral difference. If a doctor lets a patient die, for humane reasons, he is in the same moral position as if he had given the patient a lethal injection for humane reasons. If his decision was wrong—if, for example, the patient's illness was in fact curable—the decision would be equally regrettable no matter which method was used to carry it out. And if the doctor's decision was the right one, the method used is not in itself important.

The AMA policy statement isolates the crucial issue very well; the crucial issue is "the intentional termination of the life of one human being by another." But after identifying this issue, and forbidding "mercy killing," the statement goes on to deny that the cessation of treatment is the intentional termination of a life. This is where the mistake comes in, for what is the cessation of treatment, in these circumstances, if it is not "the intentional termination of the life of one human being by another"? Of course it is exactly that, and if it were not, there would be no point to it.

Many people will find this judgment hard to accept. One reason, I think, is that it is very easy to conflate the question of whether killing is, in itself, worse than letting die, with the very different question of whether most actual cases of killing are more reprehensible than most actual cases of letting die. Most actual cases of killing are clearly terrible (think, for example, of all the murders reported in the newspapers), and one hears of such cases every day. On the other hand, one hardly ever hears of a case of letting die, except for the actions of doctors who are motivated by humanitarian reasons. So one learns to think of killing in a much worse light than of letting die. But this does not mean that there is something about killing that makes it in itself worse than letting die, for it is not the bare difference between killing and letting die that makes the difference in these cases. Rather, the other factors—the murderer's motive of personal gain, for example, contrasted with the doctor's humanitarian motivation—account for different reactions to the different cases.

I have argued that killing is not in itself any worse than letting die; if my contention is right, it follows that active euthanasia is not any worse than passive euthanasia. What arguments can be given on the other side? The most common, I believe, is the following:

> The important difference between active and passive euthanasia is that, in passive euthanasia, the doctor does not do anything to bring about the patient's death. The doctor does nothing, and the patient dies of whatever ills already afflict him. In active euthanasia, however, the doctor does something to bring about the patient's death: he kills him. The doctor who gives the patient with cancer a lethal injection has himself caused his patient's death; whereas if he merely ceases treatment, the cancer is the cause of the death.

A number of points need to be made here. The first is that it is not exactly correct to say that in passive euthanasia the doctor does nothing, for he does do one thing that is very important: he lets the patient die. "Letting someone die" is certainly different, in some respects, from other types of action—mainly in that it is a kind of action that one may perform by way of not performing certain other actions. For example, one may let a patient die by way of not giving medication, just as one may insult someone by way of not shaking his hand. But for any purpose of moral assessment, it is a type of action nonetheless. The decision to let a patient die is subject to moral appraisal in the same way that a decision to kill him would be subject to moral appraisal: it may be assessed as wise or unwise, compassionate or sadistic, right or wrong. If a doctor deliberately let a patient die who was suffering from a routinely curable illness, the doctor would certainly be to blame for what he had done, just as he would be to blame if he had needlessly killed the patient. Charges against him would then be appropriate. If so, it would be no defense at all for him to insist that he didn't "do anything." He would have done something very serious indeed, for he let his patient die.

Fixing the cause of death may be very important from a legal point of view, for it may determine whether criminal charges are brought against the doctor. But I do not think that this notion can be used to show a moral difference between active and passive euthanasia. The reason why it is considered bad to be the cause of someone's death is that death is regarded as a great evil—and so it is. However, if it has been decided that euthanasia—even passive euthanasia—is desirable in a given case, it has also been decided that in this instance death is no greater an evil than the patient's continued existence. And if this is true, the usual reason for not wanting to be the cause of someone's death simply does not apply.

Finally, doctors may think that all of this is only of academic interest—the sort of thing that philosophers may worry about but that has no practical bearing on their own work. After all, doctors must be concerned about the legal consequences of what they do, and active euthanasia is clearly forbidden by the law. But even so, doctors should also be concerned with the fact that the law is forcing upon them a moral doctrine that may well be indefensible, and has a considerable effect on their practices. Of course, most doctors are not now in the position of being coerced in this matter, for they do not regard themselves as merely going along with what the law requires.

Rather[,] in statements such as the AMA policy statement that I have quoted, they are endorsing this doctrine as a central point of medical ethics. In that statement, active euthanasia is condemned not merely as illegal but as "contrary to that for which the medical profession stands," whereas passive euthanasia is approved. However, the preceding considerations suggest that there is really no moral difference between the two, considered in themselves (there may be important moral differences in some cases in their *consequences*, but, as I pointed out, these differences may make active euthanasia, and not passive euthanasia, the morally preferable option). So, whereas doctors may have to discriminate between active and passive euthanasia to satisfy the law, they should not do any more than that. In particular, they should not give the distinction any added authority and weight by writing it into official statements of medical ethics.

☙ REVIEW QUESTIONS

1. According to Rachels, what is the distinction between active and passive euthanasia?
2. Why does Rachels think that being allowed to die is worse in some cases than a lethal injection?
3. What is Rachels's second argument against the conventional doctrine?
4. According to Rachels, why isn't killing worse than letting die?

☙ DISCUSSION QUESTIONS

1. The AMA statement quoted by Rachels does not use the terminology of active and passive euthanasia. Furthermore, so-called passive euthanasia could be the intentional termination of life rejected by the AMA. Does the AMA really accept this distinction? Why or why not?
2. Is the distinction between killing and letting die morally relevant? What do you think?
3. Should the law be changed to allow active euthanasia or not? Defend your view.

The Intentional Termination of Life

BONNIE STEINBOCK

Bonnie Steinbock is chair and professor of philosophy at the State University of New York (SUNY) at Albany. She is the author of *Life Before Birth* (1992), the editor of *Legal and Ethical Issues in Human Reproduction* (2002), and coeditor of *Ethical Issues in Modern Medicine* (2002).

Steinbock defends the AMA statement on euthanasia from the attack made by Rachels. She argues that the AMA statement does not make the distinction between active and passive euthanasia that Rachels attacks. According to Steinbock, the AMA statement rejects both active and passive euthanasia, but does permit the cessation of extraordinary means of treatment to prolong life. This is not the same as passive euthanasia. Cessation of extraordinary means can be done to respect the patient's right to refuse treatment or because continued treatment is

Source: Bonnie Steinbock, "The Intentional Termination of Life," *Social Science & Medicine*, Vol. 6, No. 1, 1979, pp. 59–64. Used by permission.

painful. Neither reason is the same as letting the patient die. She grants, however, that in some cases the cessation of extraordinary means does amount to letting the patient die and that in some cases a quick and painless death may be preferable to letting a patient die slowly.

According to James Rachels,[2] a common mistake in medical ethics is the belief that there is a moral difference between active and passive euthanasia. This is a mistake, [he] argues, because the rationale underlying the distinction between active and passive euthanasia is the idea that there is a significant moral difference between intentionally killing and letting die. . . . Whether the belief that there is a significant moral difference (between intentionally killing and intentionally letting die) is mistaken is not my concern here. For it is far from clear that this distinction *is* the basis of the doctrine of the American Medical Association which Rachels attacks. And if the killing/ letting die distinction is not the basis of the AMA doctrine, then arguments showing that the distinction has no moral force do not, in themselves, reveal in the doctrine's adherents either "confused thinking" or "a moral point of view unrelated to the interests of individuals." Indeed, as we examine the AMA doctrine, I think it will become clear that it appeals to and makes use of a number of overlapping distinctions, which may have moral significance in particular cases, such as the distinction between intending and foreseeing, or between ordinary and extraordinary care. Let us then turn to the statement, from the House of Delegates of the American Medical Association, which Rachels cites:

> The intentional termination of the life of one human being by another—mercy-killing—is contrary to that for which the medical profession stands and is contrary to the policy of the American Medical Association. The cessation of the employment of extraordinary means to prolong the life of the body when there is irrefutable evidence that biological death is imminent is the decision of the patient and/or his immediate family. The advice and judgment of the physician should be freely available to the patient and/or his immediate family.[3]

Rachels attacks this statement because he believes that it contains a moral distinction between active and passive euthanasia. . . .

I intend to show that the AMA statement does not imply support of the active/passive euthanasia distinction. In forbidding the intentional termination of life, the statement rejects both active and passive euthanasia. It does allow for ". . . the cessation of the employment of extraordinary means . . ." to prolong life. The mistake Rachels makes is in identifying the cessation of life-prolonging treatment with passive euthanasia, or intentionally letting die. If it were right to equate the two, then the AMA statement would be self-contradictory, for it would begin by condemning, and end by allowing, the intentional termination of life. But if the cessation of life-prolonging treatment is not always or necessarily passive euthanasia, then there is no confusion and no contradiction.

Why does Rachels think that the cessation of life-prolonging treatment is the intentional termination of life? He says:

> The AMA policy statement isolates the crucial issue very well: the crucial issue is "the intentional termination of the life of one human being by another." But after identifying this issue, and forbidding "mercy-killing," the statement goes on to deny that the cessation of treatment is the intentional termination of a life. That is where the mistake comes in, for what is the cessation of treatment, in these circumstances, if it is not "the intentional termination of the life of one human being by another"? Of course it is exactly that, and if it were not, there would be no point to it.[4]

However, there *can* be a point (to the cessation of life-prolonging treatment) other than an endeavor to bring about the patient's death,

[2]James Rachels. Active and passive euthanasia. *New Engl. J. Med.*, 292, 78–80, 1975.
[3]Rachels, p. 78.

[4]Rachels, pp. 79–80.

and so the blanket identification of cessation of treatment with the intentional termination of a life is inaccurate. There are at least two situations in which the termination of life-prolonging treatment cannot be identified with the intentional termination of the life of one human being by another.

The first situation concerns the patient's right to refuse treatment. Rachels gives the example of a patient dying of an incurable disease, accompanied by unrelievable pain, who wants to end the treatment which cannot cure him but can only prolong his miserable existence. Why, they ask, may a doctor accede to the patient's request to stop treatment, but not provide a patient in a similar situation with the lethal dose? The answer lies in the patient's right to refuse treatment. In general, a competent adult has the right to refuse treatment, even where such treatment is necessary to prolong life. Indeed, the right to refuse treatment has been upheld even when the patient's reason for refusing treatment is generally agreed to be inadequate.[5] This right can be overridden (if, for example, the patient has dependent children) but, in general, no one may legally compel you to undergo treatment to which you have not consented. "Historically, surgical intrusion has always been considered a technical battery upon the person and one to be excused or justified by consent of the patient or justified by necessity created by the circumstances of the moment. . . ."[6]

At this point, it might be objected that if one has the right to refuse life-prolonging treatment, then consistency demands that one have the right to decide to end his life, and to obtain help in doing so. The idea is that the right to refuse treatment somehow implies a right to voluntary euthanasia, and we need to see why someone might think this. The right to refuse treatment has been considered by legal writers as an example of the right to privacy or, better, the right to bodily self-determination. You have the

right to decide what happens to your own body, and the right to refuse treatment is an instance of that more general right. But if you have the right to determine what happens to your body, then should you not have the right to choose to end your life, and even a right to get help in doing so?

However, it is important to see that the right to refuse treatment is not the same as, nor does it entail, a right to voluntary euthanasia, even if both can be derived from the right to bodily self-determination. The right to refuse treatment is not itself a "right to die"; that one may choose to exercise this right even at the risk of death, or even *in order to die*, is irrelevant. The purpose of the right to refuse medical treatment is not to give persons a right to decide whether to live or die, but to protect them from the unwanted interferences of others. Perhaps we ought to interpret the right to bodily self-determination more broadly so as to include a right to die: but this would be a substantial extension of our present understanding of the right to bodily self-determination, and not a consequence of it. Should we recognize a right to voluntary euthanasia, we would have to agree that people have the right not merely to be left alone, but also the right to be killed. I leave to one side that substantive moral issue. My claim is simply that there can be a reason for terminating life-prolonging treatment other than "to bring about the patient's death."

The second case in which termination of treatment cannot be identified with intentional termination of life is where continued treatment has little chance of improving the patient's condition and brings greater discomfort than relief.

The question here is what treatment is appropriate to the particular case. A cancer specialist describes it in this way:

> My general rule is to administer therapy as long as a patient responds well and has the potential for a reasonably good quality of life. But when all feasible therapies have been administered and a patient shows signs of rapid deterioration, the continuation of therapy can cause more discomfort than the cancer. From that time I recommend surgery, radiotherapy, or chemotherapy only as a means of relieving pain. But if a patient's condition should once again stabilize after the withdrawal of active

---

[5]For example, *In re Yetter*, 62 Pa. D. & C. 2d 619, C.P., Northampton County Ct., 1974.
[6]David W. Meyers, Legal aspects of voluntary euthanasia, *Dilemmas of Euthanasia* (edited by John Behnke and Sissela Bok), p. 56. Anchor Books, New York, 1975.

therapy and if it should appear that he could still gain some good time, I would immediately reinstitute active therapy. The decision to cease anticancer treatment is never irrevocable, and often the desire to live will push a patient to try for another remission, or even a few more days of life.[7]

The decision here to cease anticancer treatment cannot be construed as a decision that the patient die, or as the intentional termination of life. It is a decision to provide the most appropriate treatment for that patient at that time. Rachels suggests that the point of the cessation of treatment is the intentional termination of life. But here the point of discontinuing treatment is not to bring about the patient's death, but to avoid treatment that will cause more discomfort than the cancer and has little hope of benefiting the patient. Treatment that meets this description is often called "extraordinary."[8] The concept is flexible, and what might be considered "extraordinary" in one situation might be ordinary in another. The use of a respirator to sustain a patient through a severe bout with a respiratory disease would be considered ordinary; its use to sustain the life of a severely brain damaged person in an irreversible coma would be considered extraordinary.

Contrasted with extraordinary treatment is ordinary treatment, the care a doctor would normally be expected to provide. Failure to provide ordinary care constitutes neglect, and can even be construed as the intentional infliction of harm, where there is a legal obligation to provide care. The importance of [the] ordinary/extraordinary care distinction lies partly in its connection to the doctor's intention. The withholding of extraordinary care should be seen as a decision not to inflict painful treatment on a patient without reasonable hope of success. The withholding of ordinary care, by contrast, must be seen as neglect. Thus, one doctor says, "We have to draw a distinction between ordinary and extraordinary means. We never withdraw what's needed to make a baby comfortable, we would never withdraw the care a parent would provide. We never kill a baby. . . . But we may decide certain heroic intervention is not worthwhile."[9]

We should keep in mind the ordinary/extraordinary care distinction when considering an example given by Rachels to show the irrationality of the active/passive distinction with regard to infanticide. The example is this: a child is born with Down's syndrome and also has an intestinal obstruction which requires corrective surgery. If the surgery is not performed, the infant will starve to death, since it cannot take food orally. This may take days or even weeks, as dehydration and infection set in. Commenting on this situation, Rachels says:

> I can understand why some people are opposed to all euthanasia, and insist that such infants must be allowed to live. I think I can also understand why other people favor destroying these babies quickly and painlessly. But why should anyone favor letting "dehydration and infection wither a tiny being over hours and days"? The doctrine that says that a baby may be allowed to dehydrate and wither, but may not be given an injection that would end its life without suffering, seems so patently cruel as to require no further refutation.[10]

Such a doctrine perhaps does not need further refutation; but this is not the AMA doctrine. For the AMA statement criticized by Rachels allows only for the cessation of extraordinary means to prolong life when death is imminent. Neither of these conditions is satisfied in this example. Death is not imminent in this situation, any more than it would be if a normal child had an attack of appendicitis. Neither the corrective surgery to remove the intestinal obstruction, nor the intravenous feeding required to keep the infant alive until such surgery is performed, can be regarded as extraordinary means, for neither is particularly expensive, nor does either place an overwhelming

[7]Ernest H. Rosenbaum, Md., *Living with Cancer*, p. 27. Praeger, New York, 1975.

[8]Cf. H. Tristram Engelhardt, Jr., Ethical issues in aiding the death of young children, in *Beneficent Euthanasia* (edited by Marvin Kohl), Prometheus Books, Buffalo, N.Y., 1975.

[9]B. D. Colen, *Karen Ann Quinlan: Living and Dying in the Age of Eternal Life*, p. 115. Nash, 1976.

[10]Rachels, p. 79.

burden on the patient or others. (The continued existence of the child might be thought to place an overwhelming burden on its parents, but that has nothing to do with the characterization of the means to prolong its life as extraordinary. If it had, then *feeding* a severely defective child who required a great deal of care could be regarded as extraordinary.) The chances of success if the operation is undertaken are quite good, though there is always a risk in operating on infants. Though the Down's syndrome will not be alleviated, the child will proceed to an otherwise normal infancy.

It cannot be argued that the treatment is withheld for the infant's sake, unless one is prepared to argue that all mentally retarded babies are better off dead. This is particularly implausible in the case of Down's syndrome babies who generally do not suffer and are capable of giving and receiving love, of learning and playing, to varying degrees.

In a film on this subject entitled, "Who Should Survive?", a doctor defended a decision not to operate, saying that since the parents did not consent to the operation, the doctors' hands were tied. As we have seen, surgical intrusion requires consent, and in the case of infants, consent would normally come from the parents. But, as their legal guardians, parents are required to provide medical care for their children, and failure to do so can constitute criminal neglect or even homicide. In general, courts have been understandably reluctant to recognize a parental right to terminate life-prolonging treatment.[11] Although prosecution is unlikely, physicians who comply with invalid instructions from the parents and permit the infant's death could be liable for aiding and abetting, failure to report child neglect, or even homicide. So it is not true that, in this situation, doctors are legally bound to do as the parents wish.

To sum up, I think that Rachels is right to regard the decision not to operate in the Down's

syndrome example as the intentional termination of life. But there is no reason to believe that either the law or the AMA would regard it otherwise. Certainly the decision to withhold treatment is not justified by the AMA statement. That such infants have been allowed to die cannot be denied; but this, I think, is the result of doctors misunderstanding the law and the AMA position.

Withholding treatment in this case is the intentional termination of life because the infant is deliberately allowed to die; that is the point of not operating. But there are other cases in which that is not the point. If the point is to avoid inflicting painful treatment on a patient with little or no reasonable hope of success, this is not the intentional termination of life. The permissibility of such withholding of treatment, then, would have no implications for the permissibility of euthanasia, active or passive.

The decision whether or not to operate, or to institute vigorous treatment, is particularly agonizing in the case of children born with spina bifida, an opening in the base of the spine usually accompanied by hydrocephalus and mental retardation. If left unoperated, these children usually die of meningitis or kidney failure within the first few years of life. Even if they survive, all affected children face a lifetime of illness, operations and varying degrees of disability. The policy used to be to save as many as possible, but the trend now is toward selective treatment, based on the physician's estimate of the chances of success. If operating is not likely to improve significantly the child's condition, parents and doctors may agree not to operate. This is not the intentional termination of life, for again the purpose is not the termination of the child's life but the avoidance of painful and pointless treatment. Thus, the fact that withholding treatment is justified does not imply that killing the child would be equally justified.

Throughout the discussion, I have claimed that intentionally ceasing life-prolonging treatment is not the intentional termination of life unless the doctor has, as his or her purpose in stopping treatment, the patient's death.

It may be objected that I have incorrectly characterized the conditions for the intentional

---

[11]Cf. Norman L. Cantor, Law and the termination of an incompetent patient's life-preserving care. *Dilemmas of Euthanasia op. cit.*, pp. 69–105.

termination of life. Perhaps it is enough that the doctor intentionally ceases treatment, foreseeing that the patient will die; perhaps the reason for ceasing treatment is irrelevant to its characterization as the intentional termination of life. I find this suggestion implausible, but am willing to consider arguments for it. Rachels has provided no such arguments: indeed, he apparently shares my view about the intentional termination of life. For when he claims that the cessation of life-prolonging treatment is the intentional termination of life, his reason for making the claim is that "if it were not, there would be no point to it." Rachels believes that the point of ceasing treatment, "in these cases," is to bring about the patient's death. If that were not the point, he suggests, why would the doctor cease treatment? I have shown, however, that there can be a point to ceasing treatment which is not the death of the patient. In showing this, I have refuted Rachels'[s] reason for identifying the cessation of life-prolonging treatment with the intentional termination of life, and thus his argument against the AMA doctrine.

Here someone might say: Even if the withholding of treatment is not the intentional termination of life, does that make a difference, morally speaking? If the life-prolonging treatment may be withheld, for the sake of the child, may not an easy death be provided, for the sake of the child, as well? The unoperated child with spina bifida may take months or even years to die. Distressed by the spectacle of children "lying around waiting to die," one doctor has written, "It is time that society and medicine stopped perpetuating the fiction that withholding treatment is ethically different from terminating a life. It is time that society began to discuss mechanisms by which we can alleviate the pain and suffering for those individuals whom we cannot help."[12]

I do not deny that there may be cases in which death is in the best interests of the patient. In such cases, a quick and painless death may be the best thing. However, I do not think that, once active or vigorous treatment is stopped, a quick death is always preferable to a lingering one. We must be cautious about attributing to defective children *our* distress at seeing them linger. Waiting for them to die may be tough on parents, doctors and nurses—it isn't necessarily tough on the child. The decision not to operate need not mean a decision to neglect, and it may be possible to make the remaining months of the child's life comfortable, pleasant and filled with love. If this alternative is possible, surely it is more decent and humane than killing the child. In such a situation, withholding treatment, foreseeing the child's death, is not ethically equivalent to killing the child, and we cannot move from the permissibility of the former to that of the latter. I am worried that there will be a tendency to do precisely that if active euthanasia is regarded as morally equivalent to the withholding of life-prolonging treatment.

CONCLUSION

The AMA statement does not make the distinction Rachels wishes to attack, i.e., that between active and passive euthanasia. Instead, the statement draws a distinction between the intentional termination of life, on the one hand, and the cessation of the employment of extraordinary means to prolong life, on the other. Nothing said by Rachels shows that this distinction is confused. It may be that doctors have misinterpreted the AMA statement, and that this had led, for example, to decisions to allow defective infants slowly to starve to death. I quite agree with Rachels that the decisions to which they allude were cruel and made on irrelevant grounds. Certainly it is worth pointing out that allowing someone to die can be the intentional termination of life, and that it can be just as bad as, or worse than, killing someone. However, the withholding of life-prolonging treatment is not necessarily the intentional termination of life, so that if it is permissible to withhold life-prolonging treatment, it does not follow that, other things being equal, it is permissible to kill. Furthermore, most of the time, other things are not equal. In many of the cases in which it would be right to cease treatment, I do not think that it would also be right to kill.

---

[12]John Freeman, Is there a right to die—quickly?, *J. Pediat.* 80. p. 905.

⚜ REVIEW QUESTIONS

1. According to Steinbock, what mistake does Rachels make in his interpretation of the AMA statement?
2. How does Steinbock understand the right to refuse treatment?
3. How does Steinbock distinguish between extraordinary and ordinary treatment?
4. What is Steinbock's view of the case of the child with Down syndrome, and how does her view differ from that of Rachels?
5. What is Steinbock's view of the treatment of children with spina bifida?
6. Why does Steinbock think that she has refuted Rachels's attack against the AMA statement?
7. Explain Steinbock's conclusion.

⚜ DISCUSSION QUESTIONS

1. In what cases can the right to refuse medical treatment be overridden and why?
2. Steinbock grants that in some cases "a quick and painless death may be the best thing." Can you think of any such cases? Why is death "the best thing" in such cases?

Voluntary Active Euthanasia

DAN W. BROCK

Dan W. Brock is the Frances Glessner Lee Professor of Medical Ethics in the Department of Social Medicine at Harvard University, the Director of the Division of Medical Ethics at the Harvard Medical School, and the Director of the Harvard University Program in Ethics and Health. He is the author (with Allen E. Buchanan) of *Deciding for Others: The Ethics of Surrogate Decisionmaking* (1989), *Life and Death: Philosophical Essays in Biomedical Ethics* (1993), and (with Allen E. Buchanan, Norman Daniels, and Daniel Wikler) *From Chance to Choice: Genes and Social Justice* (2000). In addition, he is the author of more than 150 articles in bioethics and in moral and political philosophy.

Brock focuses on voluntary active euthanasia, as distinguished from involuntary and nonvoluntary euthanasia. The main argument for permitting voluntary euthanasia appeals to the patient's autonomy and well-being. Patients have a right to make decisions about their lives according to their conception of a good life. Brock grants that voluntary euthanasia, whether active or passive, is the deliberate killing of an innocent person. He argues that this is not always morally wrong, because people can waive their right not to be killed, and that actively killing a patient who wants to die is not morally different from allowing a patient to die, which is widely accepted as morally permitted. Turning to the consequences of permitting euthanasia, Brock's view is that, all things considered, the potential good consequences outweigh the potential bad consequences. As for the role of physicians, Brock holds that only they should be permitted to practice euthanasia, with the qualification that they should not be forced to do so if it violates their personal or professional values.

Source: "Voluntary Active Euthanasia" by Dan W. Brock from *Hastings Center Report*, Vol 22, No 2, 1992.
*Editor's Note: The footnotes have been deleted.

Since the case of Karen Quinlan first seized public attention fifteen years ago, no issue in biomedical ethics has been more prominent than the debate about forgoing life-sustaining treatment. Controversy continues regarding some aspects of that debate, such as forgoing life-sustaining nutrition and hydration, and relevant law varies some from state to state. Nevertheless, I believe it is possible to identify an emerging consensus that competent patients, or the surrogates of incompetent patients, should be permitted to weigh the benefits and burdens of alternative treatments, including the alternative of no treatment, according to the patient's values, and either to refuse any treatment or to select from among available alternative treatments. This consensus is reflected in bioethics scholarship, in reports of prestigious bodies such as the President's Commission for the Study of Ethical Problems in Medicine, the Hastings Center, and the American Medical Association, in a large body of judicial decisions in courts around the country, and finally in the beliefs and practices of health care professionals who care for dying patients.

More recently, significant public and professional attention has shifted from life-sustaining treatment to euthanasia—more specifically, voluntary active euthanasia—and to physician-assisted suicide. Several factors have contributed to the increased interest in euthanasia. In the Netherlands, it has been openly practiced by physicians for several years with the acceptance of the country's highest court. In 1988 there was an unsuccessful attempt to get the question of whether it should be made legally permissible on the ballot in California. In November 1991 voters in the state of Washington defeated a widely publicized referendum proposal to legalize both voluntary active euthanasia and physician-assisted suicide. Finally, some cases of this kind, such as "It's Over, Debbie," described in the *Journal of the American Medical Association*, the "suicide machine" of Dr Kevorkian, and the cancer patient "Diane" of Dr. Timothy Quill, have captured wide public and professional attention. . . .

My concern here will be with voluntary euthanasia only—that is, with the case in which a clearly competent patient makes a fully voluntary and persistent request for aid in dying. Involuntary euthanasia in which a competent patient explicitly refuses or opposes receiving euthanasia and nonvoluntary euthanasia, in which a patient is incompetent and unable to express his or her wishes about euthanasia, will be considered here only as potential unwanted side-effects of permitting voluntary euthanasia. I emphasize as well that I am concerned with active euthanasia, not withholding or withdrawing life-sustaining treatment, which some commentators characterize as "passive euthanasia." Finally, I will be concerned with euthanasia where the motive of those who perform it is to respect the wishes of the patient and to provide the patient with a "good death," though one important issue is whether a change in legal policy could restrict the performance of euthanasia to only those cases.

A last introductory point is that I will be examining only secular arguments about euthanasia, though of course many people's attitudes to it are inextricable from their religious views. The policy issue is only whether euthanasia should be permissible, and no one who has religious objections to it should be required to take any part in it, though of course this would not fully satisfy some opponents.

THE CENTRAL ETHICAL ARGUMENT FOR VOLUNTARY ACTIVE EUTHANASIA

The central ethical argument for euthanasia is familiar. It is that the very same two fundamental ethical values supporting the consensus on patient's rights to decide about life-sustaining treatment also support the ethical permissibility of euthanasia. These values are individual self-determination or autonomy and individual well-being. By self-determination as it bears on euthanasia, I mean people's interest in making important decisions about their lives for themselves according to their own values or conceptions of a good life, and in being left free to act on those decisions. Self-determination is valuable because it permits people to form and live in accordance with their own conception of a good life, at least within the bounds of justice and consistent with others doing so as well. In exercising self-determination people take responsibility for their lives and for the kinds of persons they become. A central aspect of human dignity lies in people's capacity to direct their lives in this way. The value of exercising self-determination presupposes some minimum of decision making capacities or competence, which thus limits the scope of euthanasia supported by self-determination; it cannot justifiably be administered, for example, in cases of serious dementia or treatable clinical depression.

Does the value of individual self-determination extend to the time and manner of one's death? Most people are very concerned about the nature of the last stage of their lives. This reflects not just a fear of experiencing substantial suffering when dying, but also a desire to retain dignity and control during this last period of life. Death is today increasingly preceded by a long period of significant physical and mental decline, due in part to the technological interventions of modern medicine. Many people adjust to these disabilities and find meaning and value in new activities and ways. Others find the impairments and burdens in the last stage of their lives at some point sufficiently great to make life no longer worth living. For many patients near death, maintaining the quality of one's life, avoiding great suffering, maintaining one's dignity, and insuring that others remember us as we wish them to become of paramount importance and outweigh merely extending one's life. But there is no single, objectively correct answer for everyone as to when, if at all, one's life becomes all things considered a burden and unwanted. If self-determination is a fundamental value, then the great variability among people on this question makes it especially important that individuals control the manner, circumstances, and timing of their dying and death.

The other main value that supports euthanasia is individual well-being. It might seem that individual well-being conflicts with a person's self-determination when the person requests euthanasia. Life itself is commonly taken to be a central good for persons, often valued for its own sake, as well as necessary for pursuit of all other goods within a life. But when a competent patient decides to forgo all further life-sustaining treatment then the patient, either explicitly or implicitly, commonly decides that the best life possible for him or her with treatment is of sufficiently poor quality that it is worse than no further life at all. Life is no longer considered a benefit by the patient, but has now become a burden. The same judgment underlies a request for euthanasia: continued life is seen by the patient as no longer a benefit, but now a burden. Especially in the often severely compromised and debilitated states of many critically ill or dying patients, there is no objective standard, but only the competent patient's judgment of whether continued life is no longer a benefit.

Of course, sometimes there are conditions, such as clinical depression, that call into question whether the patient has made a competent choice, either to forgo life-sustaining treatment or to seek euthanasia, and then the patient's choice need not be evidence that continued life is no longer a benefit for him or her. Just as with decisions about treatment, a determination of incompetence can warrant not honoring the patient's choice; in the case of treatment, we then transfer decisional authority to a surrogate, though in the case of voluntary active euthanasia a determination that the patient is incompetent means that choice is not possible.

The value or right of self-determination does not entitle patients to compel physicians to act contrary to their own moral or professional values. Physicians are moral and professional agents whose own self-determination or integrity should be respected as well. If performing euthanasia became legally permissible, but conflicted with a particular physician's reasonable understanding of his or her moral or professional responsibilities, the care of a patient who requested euthanasia should be transferred to another.

Most opponents do not deny that there are some cases in which the values of patient self-determination and well-being support euthanasia. Instead, they commonly offer two kinds of arguments against it that on their view outweigh or override this support. The first kind of argument is that in any individual case where considerations of the patient's self-determination and well-being do support euthanasia, it is nevertheless always ethically wrong or impermissible. The second kind of argument grants that in some individual cases euthanasia may not be ethically wrong, but maintains nonetheless that public and legal policy should never permit it. The first kind of argument focuses on features of any individual case of euthanasia, while the second kind focuses on social or legal policy. In the next section I consider the first kind of argument.

EUTHANASIA IS THE DELIBERATE KILLING OF AN INNOCENT PERSON

The claim that any individual instance of euthanasia is a case of deliberate killing of an innocent person is, with only minor qualifications, correct. Unlike forgoing life-sustaining treatment, commonly understood as allowing to die, euthanasia is clearly killing, defined as depriving of life or causing the death of a living being. While providing morphine for pain relief at doses where the risk of respiratory depression and an earlier death may be a foreseen but unintended side effect of treating the patient's pain, in a case of euthanasia the patient's death is deliberate or intended even if in both the physician's ultimate end may be respecting the patient's wishes. If the deliberate killing of an innocent person is wrong, euthanasia would be nearly always impermissible.

In the context of medicine, the ethical prohibition against deliberately killing the innocent derives some of its plausibility from the belief that nothing in the currently accepted practice of medicine is deliberate killing. Thus, in commenting on the "It's Over, Debbie" case, four prominent physicians and bioethicists could entitle their paper "Doctors Must Not Kill." The belief that doctors do not in fact kill requires the corollary belief that forgoing life-sustaining treatment, whether by not starting or by stopping treatment, is allowing to die, not killing. Common though this view is, I shall argue that it is confused and mistaken.

Why is the common view mistaken? Consider the case of a patient terminally ill with ALS disease. She is completely respirator dependent with no hope of ever being weaned. She is unquestionably competent but finds her condition intolerable and persistently requests to be removed from the respirator and allowed to die. Most people and physicians would agree that the patient's physician should respect the patient's wishes and remove her from the respirator, though this will certainly cause the patient's death. The common understanding is that the physician thereby allows the patient to die. But is that correct?

Suppose the patient has a greedy and hostile son who mistakenly believes that his mother will never decide to stop her life-sustaining treatment and that even if she did her physician would not remove her from the respirator. Afraid that his inheritance will be dissipated by a long and expensive hospitalization, he enters his mother's room while she is sedated, extubates her, and she dies. Shortly thereafter the medical staff discovers what he has done and confronts the son. He replies, "I didn't kill her, I merely allowed her to die. It was her ALS disease that caused her death." I think this would rightly be dismissed as transparent sophistry—the son went into his mother's room and deliberately killed her. But, of course, the son performed just the same physical actions, did just the same thing, that the physician would have done. If that is so, then doesn't the physician also kill the patient when he extubates her?

I underline immediately that there are important ethical differences between what the physician and the greedy son do. First, the physician acts with the patient's consent whereas the son does not. Second, the physician acts with a good motive—to respect the patient's wishes and self-determination—whereas the son acts with a bad motive—to protect his own inheritance. Third, the physician acts in a social role through which he is legally authorized to carry out the patient's wishes regarding treatment whereas the son has no such authorization. These and perhaps other ethically important differences show that what the physician did was morally justified whereas what the son did was morally wrong. What they do not show, however, is that the son killed while the physician allowed to die. One can either kill or allow to die with or without consent, with a good or bad motive, within or outside of a social role that authorizes one to do so.

The difference between killing and allowing to die that I have been implicitly appealing to here is roughly that between acts and omissions resulting in death. Both the physician and the greedy son act in a manner intended to cause death, do cause death, and so both kill. One reason this conclusion is resisted is that on a different understanding of the distinction between killing and allowing to die, what the physician does is allow to die. In this account, the mother's ALS is a lethal disease whose normal progression is being held back or blocked by the life-sustaining respirator treatment. Removing this artificial intervention is then viewed as standing aside and allowing the patient to die of her underlying disease. I have argued elsewhere that this alternative account is deeply problematic, in part because it commits us to accepting that what the greedy son does is to allow to die, not kill. Here, I want to note two other reasons why the conclusion that stopping life support is killing is resisted.

The first reason is that killing is often understood, especially within medicine, as unjustified causing of death; in medicine it is thought to be done only accidentally or negligently. It is also increasingly widely accepted that a physician is ethically justified in stopping life support in a case like that of the ALS patient. But if these two beliefs are correct, then what the physician does cannot be killing, and so must be allowing to die. Killing patients is not, to put it flippantly, understood to be part of physicians' job description. What is mistaken in this line of reasoning is the assumption that all killings are unjustified causings of death. Instead, some killings are ethically justified, including many instances of stopping life support.

Another reason for resisting the conclusion that stopping life support is often killing is that it is psychologically uncomfortable. Suppose the physician had stopped the ALS patient's respirator and had made the son's claim, "I didn't kill her, I merely allowed her to die. It was her ALS disease that caused her death." The clue to the psychological role here is how naturally the "merely" modifies "allowed her to die." The

characterization as allowing to die is meant to shift felt responsibility away from the agent—the physician—and to the lethal disease process. Other language common in death and dying contexts plays a similar role; "letting nature take its course" or "stopping prolonging the dying process" both seem to shift responsibility from the physician who stops life support to the fatal disease process. However psychologically helpful these conceptualizations may be in making the difficult responsibility of a physician's role the patient's death bearable, they nevertheless are confusions. Both physicians and family members can instead be helped to understand that it is the patient's decision and consent to stopping treatment that limits their responsibility for the patient's death and that shifts that responsibility to the patient.

Many who accept the difference between killing and allowing to die as the distinction between acts and omissions resulting in death have gone on to argue that killing is not in itself morally different from allowing to die. In this account, very roughly, one kills when one performs an action that causes the death of a person (we are in a boat, you cannot swim, I push you overboard, and you drown), and one allows to die when one has the ability and opportunity to prevent the death of another, knows this, and omits doing so, with the result that the person dies (we are in a boat, you cannot swim, you fall overboard, I don't throw you an available life ring, and you drown). Those who see no moral difference between killing and allowing to die typically employ the strategy of comparing cases that differ in these and no other potentially morally important respects. This will allow people to consider whether the mere difference that one is a case of killing and the other of allowing to die matters morally, or whether instead it is other features that make most cases of killing worse than most instances of allowing to die. Here is such a pair of cases:

Case 1. A very gravely ill patient is brought to a hospital emergency room and sent up to the ICU. The patient begins to develop respiratory failure that is likely to require intubation very soon. At that point the patient's family members and long-standing physician arrive at the ICU and inform the ICU staff that there had been extensive discussion about future care with the patient when he was unquestionably competent. Given his grave and terminal illness, as well as his state of debilitation, the patient had firmly rejected being placed on a respirator under any circumstances, and the family and physician produce the patient's advance directive to that effect. The ICU staff do not intubate the patient, who dies of respiratory failure.

Case 2. The same as Case 1 except that the family and physician are slightly delayed in traffic and arrive shortly after the patient has been intubated and placed on the respirator. The ICU staff extubate the patient, who dies of respiratory failure.

In Case 1 the patient is allowed to die, in Case 2 he is killed, but it is hard to see why what is done in Case 2 is significantly different morally than what is done in Case 1. It must be other factors that make most killings worse than most allowings to die, and if so, euthanasia cannot be wrong simply because it is killing instead of allowing to die.

Suppose both my arguments are mistaken. Suppose that killing is worse than allowing to die and that withdrawing life support is not killing, although euthanasia is. Euthanasia still need not for that reason be morally wrong. To see this, we need to determine the basic principle for the moral evaluation of killing persons. What is it that makes paradigm cases of wrongful killing wrongful? One very plausible answer is that killing denies the victim something that he or she values greatly—continued life or a future. Moreover, since continued life is necessary for pursuing any of a person's plans and purposes, killing brings the frustration of all of these plans and desires as well. In a nutshell, wrongful killing deprives a person of a valued future, and of all the person wanted and planned to do in that future.

A natural expression of this account of the wrongness of killing is that people have a moral right not to be killed. But in this account of the wrongness of killing, the right not to be killed, like other rights, should be waivable when the person makes a competent decision that continued life is no longer wanted or a good, but is instead worse than no further life at all. In this view, euthanasia is properly understood as a case of a person having waived his or her right not to be killed.

This rights view of the wrongness of killing is not, of course, universally shared. Many people's moral views about killing have their origins in religious views that human life comes from God and cannot be justifiably destroyed or taken away, either by the person whose life it is or by another. But in a pluralistic society like our own with a strong commitment to freedom of religion, public policy should not be grounded in religious beliefs which many in that society reject. I turn now to the general evaluation of public policy on euthanasia.

WOULD THE BAD CONSEQUENCES OF EUTHANASIA OUTWEIGH THE GOOD?

The argument against euthanasia at the policy level is stronger than at the level of individual cases, though even here I believe the case is ultimately unpersuasive, or at best indecisive. The policy level is the place where the main issues lie, however, and where moral considerations that might override arguments in favor of euthanasia will be found, if they are found anywhere. It is important to note two kinds of disagreement about the consequences for public policy of permitting euthanasia. First, there is empirical or factual disagreement about what the consequences would be. This disagreement is greatly exacerbated by the lack of firm data on the issue. Second, since on any reasonable assessment there would be both good and bad consequences, there are moral disagreements about the relative importance of different effects. In addition to these two sources of disagreement, there is also no single, well-specified policy proposal for legalizing euthanasia on which policy assessments can focus. But without such specification, and especially without explicit procedures for protecting against well-intentioned misuse and ill-intentioned abuse, the consequences for policy are largely speculative. Despite these difficulties, a preliminary account of the main likely good and bad consequences is possible. This should help clarify where better data or more moral analysis and argument are needed, as well as where policy safeguards must be developed.

Potential Good Consequences of Permitting *Euthanasia*

What are the likely good consequences? First, if euthanasia were permitted it would be possible to respect the self-determination of competent patients who want it, but now cannot get it because of its illegality. We simply do not know how many such patients and people there are. In the Netherlands, with a population of about 14.5 million (in 1987), estimates in a recent study were that about 1,900 cases of voluntary active euthanasia or physician-assisted suicide occur annually. No straightforward extrapolation to the United States is possible for many reasons, among them, that we do not know how many people here who want euthanasia now get it, despite its illegality. Even with better data on the number of persons who want euthanasia but cannot get it, significant moral disagreement would remain about how much weight should be given to any instance of failure to respect a person's self-determination in this way.

One important factor substantially affecting the number of persons who would seek euthanasia is the extent to which an alternative is available. The widespread acceptance in the law, social policy, and medical practice of the right of a competent patient to forgo life-sustaining treatment suggests that the number of competent persons in the United States who would want euthanasia if it were permitted is probably relatively small.

A second good consequence of making euthanasia legally permissible benefits a much larger group. Polls have shown that a majority of the American public believes that people should have a right to obtain euthanasia if they want it. No doubt the vast majority of those who support this right to euthanasia will never in fact come to want euthanasia for themselves. Nevertheless, making it legally permissible would reassure many people that if they ever do want euthanasia they would be able to obtain it. This reassurance would supplement the broader control over the process of dying given by the right to decide about life-sustaining treatment. Having fire insurance on one's house benefits all who have it, not just those whose houses actually burn down, by reassuring them that in the unlikely event of their house burning down, they will receive the money needed to rebuild it. Likewise, the legalization of euthanasia can be thought of as a kind of insurance policy against being forced to endure a protracted dying process that one has come to find burdensome and unwanted, especially when there is no life-sustaining treatment to forgo. The strong concern about losing control of their care expressed by many people who face serious illness likely to end in death suggests that they give substantial importance to the legalization of euthanasia as a means of maintaining this control.

A third good consequence of the legalization of euthanasia concerns patients whose dying is filled with severe and unrelievable pain or suffering. When there is a life-sustaining treatment that, if forgone, will lead relatively quickly to death, then doing so can bring an end to these patients' suffering without recourse to euthanasia. For patients receiving no such treatment, however, euthanasia may be the only release from their otherwise prolonged suffering and agony. This argument from mercy has always been the strongest argument for euthanasia in those cases to which it applies.

The importance of relieving pain and suffering is less controversial than is the frequency with which patients are forced to undergo untreatable agony that only euthanasia could relieve. If we focus first on suffering caused by physical pain, it is crucial to distinguish pain that could be adequately relieved with modern methods of pain control, though it in fact is not, from pain that is relievable only by death. For a variety of reasons, including some physicians' fear of hastening the patient's death, as well as the lack of a publicly accessible means for assessing the amount of the patient's pain, many patients suffer pain that could be, but is not, relieved.

Specialists in pain control, as for example the pain of terminally ill cancer patients, argue that there are very few patients whose pain could not be adequately controlled, though sometimes at the cost of so sedating them that they are effectively unable to interact with other people or their environment. Thus, the argument from mercy in cases of physical pain can probably be met in a large majority of cases by providing adequate measures of pain relief. This should be a high priority, whatever our legal policy on euthanasia—the relief of pain and suffering has long been, quite properly, one of the central goals of medicine. Those cases in which pain could be effectively relieved, but in fact is not, should only count significantly in favor of legalizing euthanasia if all reasonable efforts to change pain management techniques have been tried and have failed.

Dying patients often undergo substantial psychological suffering that is not fully or even principally the result of physical pain. The knowledge about how to relieve this suffering is much more limited than in the case of relieving pain, and efforts to do so are probably more often unsuccessful. If the argument from mercy is extended to patients experiencing great and unrelievable psychological suffering, the numbers of patients to which it applies are much greater.

One last good consequence of legalizing euthanasia is that once death has been accepted, it is often more humane to end life quickly and peacefully, when that is what the patient wants. Such a death will often be seen as better than a more prolonged one. People who suffer a sudden and unexpected death, for example by dying quickly or in their sleep from a heart attack or stroke, are often considered lucky to have died in this way. We care about how we die in part because we care about how others remember us, and we hope they will remember us as we were in "good times" with them and not as we might be when disease has robbed us of our dignity as human beings. As with much in the treatment and care of the dying, people's concerns differ in this respect, but for at least some people, euthanasia will be a more humane death than what they have often experienced with other loved ones and might otherwise expect for themselves.

Some opponents of euthanasia challenge how much importance should be given to any of these good consequences of permitting it, or even whether some would be good consequences

at all. But more frequently, opponents cite a number of bad consequences that permitting euthanasia would or could produce, and it is to their assessment that I now turn.

Potential Bad Consequences of Permitting *Euthanasia*

Some of the arguments against permitting euthanasia are aimed specifically against physicians, while others are aimed against anyone being permitted to perform it. I shall first consider one argument of the former sort. Permitting physicians to perform euthanasia, it is said, would be incompatible with their fundamental moral and professional commitment as healers to care for patients and to protect life. Moreover, if euthanasia by physicians became common, patients would come to fear that a medication was intended not to treat or care, but instead to kill, and would thus lose trust in their physicians. This position was forcefully stated in a paper by Willard Gaylin and his colleagues:

> The very soul of medicine is on trial. . . . This issue touches medicine at its moral center; if this moral center collapses, if physicians become killers or are even licensed to kill, the profession—and, therewith, each physician—will never again be worthy of trust and respect as healer and comforter and protector of life in all its frailty.

These authors go on to make clear that, while they oppose permitting anyone to perform euthanasia, their special concern is with physicians doing so:

We call on fellow physicians to say that they will not deliberately kill. We must also say to each of our fellow physicians that we will not tolerate killing of patients and that we shall take disciplinary action against doctors who kill. And we must say to the broader community that if it insists on tolerating or legalizing active euthanasia, it will have to find nonphysicians to do its killing.

If permitting physicians to kill would undermine the very "moral center" of medicine, then almost certainly physicians should not be permitted to perform euthanasia. But how persuasive is this claim? Patients should not fear, as a consequence of permitting voluntary active euthanasia, that their physicians will substitute a lethal injection for what patients want and believe is part of their care. If active euthanasia is restricted to cases in which it is truly voluntary, then no patient should fear getting it unless she or he has voluntarily requested it. (The fear that we might in time also come to accept nonvoluntary, or even involuntary, active euthanasia is a slippery slope worry I address below.) Patients' trust of their physicians could be increased, not eroded, by knowledge that physicians will provide aid in dying when patients seek it.

Might Gaylin and his colleagues nevertheless be correct in their claim that the moral center of medicine would collapse if physicians were to become killers? This question raises what at the deepest level should be the guiding aims of medicine, a question that obviously cannot be fully explored here. But I do want to say enough to indicate the direction that I believe an appropriate response to this challenge should take. In spelling out above what I called the positive argument for voluntary active euthanasia, I suggested that two principal values—respecting patients' self-determination and promoting their well-being—underlie the consensus that competent patients, or the surrogates of incompetent patients, are entitled to refuse any life-sustaining treatment and to choose from among available alternative treatments. It is the commitment to these two values in guiding physicians' actions as healers, comforters, and protectors of their patients' lives that should be at the "moral center" of medicine, and these two values support physicians' administering euthanasia when their patients make competent requests for it.

What should not be at that moral center is a commitment to preserving patients' lives as such, without regard to whether those patients want their lives preserved or judge their preservation a benefit to them. Vitalism has been rejected by most physicians, and despite some statements that suggest it, is almost certainly not what Gaylin and colleagues intended. One of them, Leon Kass, has elaborated elsewhere the view that medicine is a moral profession whose proper aim is "the naturally given end of health," understood as the wholeness and well-working of the human being; "for the physician, at least, human life in living bodies commands respect and reverence—by its very nature." Kass continues, "the deepest ethical principle restraining the physician's power is not the autonomy or freedom of the patient; neither is it his own compassion or good intention. Rather, it is the dignity and mysterious power of human life itself." I believe Kass is in the end mistaken about the proper account of the aims of medicine and the limits on physicians' power, but this difficult issue will certainly be one of the central themes in the continuing debate about euthanasia.

A second bad consequence that some foresee is that permitting euthanasia would weaken society's commitment to provide optimal care for dying patients. We live at a time in which the control of health care costs has become, and is likely to continue to be, the dominant focus of health care policy. If euthanasia is seen as a cheaper alternative to adequate care and treatment, then we might become less scrupulous about providing sometimes costly support and other services to dying patients. Particularly if our society comes to embrace deeper and more explicit rationing of health care, frail, elderly, and dying patients will need to be strong and effective advocates for their own health care and other needs, although they are hardly in a position to do this. We should do nothing to weaken their ability to obtain adequate care and services.

This second worry is difficult to assess because there is little firm evidence about the likelihood of the feared erosion in the care of dying patients. There are at least two reasons, however, for skepticism about this argument. The first is that the same worry could have been directed at recognizing patients' or surrogates' rights to forgo life-sustaining treatment, yet there is no persuasive evidence that recognizing the right to refuse treatment has caused a serious erosion in the quality of care of dying patients. The second reason for skepticism about this worry is that only a very small proportion of deaths would occur from euthanasia if it were permitted. In the Netherlands, where euthanasia under specified circumstances is permitted by the courts, though not authorized by statute, the best estimate of the proportion of overall deaths that result from it is about 2 percent. Thus, the vast majority of critically ill and dying patients will not request it, and so will still have to be cared for by physicians, families, and others. Permitting euthanasia should not diminish people's commitment and concern to maintain and improve the care of these patients.

A third possible bad consequence of permitting euthanasia (or even a public discourse in which strong support for euthanasia is evident) is to threaten the progress made in securing the rights of patients or their surrogates to decide about and to refuse life-sustaining treatment. This progress has been made against the backdrop of a clear and firm legal prohibition of euthanasia, which has provided a relatively bright line limiting the dominion of others over patients' lives. It has therefore been an important reassurance to concerns about how the authority to take steps ending life might be misused, abused, or wrongly extended.

Many supporters of the right of patients or their surrogates to refuse treatment strongly oppose euthanasia, and if forced to choose might well withdraw their support of the right to refuse treatment rather than accept euthanasia. Public policy in the last fifteen years has generally let life-sustaining treatment decisions be made in health care settings between physicians and patients or their surrogates, and without the involvement of the courts. However, if euthanasia is made legally permissible greater involvement of the courts is likely, which could in turn extend to a greater court involvement in life-sustaining treatment decisions. Most agree, however, that increased involvement of the courts in these decisions would be undesirable, as it would make sound decision-making more cumbersome and difficult without sufficient compensating benefits.

As with the second potential bad consequence of permitting euthanasia, this third consideration too is speculative and difficult to assess. The feared erosion of patients' or surrogates' rights to decide about life-sustaining treatment, together with greater court involvement in those decisions, are both possible. However, I believe there is reason to discount this general worry. The legal rights of competent patients

and, to a lesser degree, surrogates of incompetent patients to decide about treatment are very firmly embedded in a long line of informed consent and life-sustaining treatment cases, and are not likely to be eroded by a debate over, or even acceptance of, euthanasia. It will not be accepted without safeguards that reassure the public about abuse, and if that debate shows the need for similar safeguards for some life-sustaining treatment decisions they should be adopted there as well. In neither case are the only possible safeguards greater court involvement, as the recent growth of institutional ethics committees shows.

The fourth potential bad consequence of permitting euthanasia has been developed by David Velleman and turns on the subtle point that making a new option or choice available to people can sometimes make them worse off, even if once they have the choice they go on to choose what is best for them. Ordinarily, people's continued existence is viewed by them as given, a fixed condition with which they must cope. Making euthanasia available to people as an option denies them the alternative of staying alive by default. If people are offered the option of euthanasia, their continued existence is now a choice for which they can be held responsible and which they can be asked by others to justify. We care, and are right to care, about being able to justify ourselves to others. To the extent that our society is unsympathetic to justifying a severely dependent or impaired existence, a heavy psychological burden of proof may be placed on patients who think their terminal illness or chronic infirmity is not a sufficient reason for dying. Even if they otherwise view their life as worth living, the opinion of others around them that it is not can threaten their reason for living and make euthanasia a rational choice. Thus the existence of the option becomes a subtle pressure to request it.

This argument correctly identifies the reason why offering some patients the option of euthanasia would not benefit them. Velleman takes it not as a reason for opposing all euthanasia, but for restricting it to circumstances where there are "unmistakable and overpowering reasons for persons to want the option of euthanasia," and for denying the option in all other cases. But there are at least three reasons why such restriction may not be warranted. First, polls and other evidence support that most Americans believe euthanasia should be permitted (though the recent defeat of the referendum to permit it in the state of Washington raises some doubt about this support). Thus, many more people seem to want the choice than would be made worse off by getting it. Second, if giving people the option of ending their life really makes them worse off, then we should not only prohibit euthanasia, but also take back from people the right they now have to decide about life-sustaining treatment. The feared harmful effect should already have occurred from securing people's right to refuse life-sustaining treatment, yet there is no evidence of any such widespread harm or any broad public desire to rescind that right. Third, since there is a wide range of conditions in which reasonable people can and do disagree about whether they would want continued life, it is not possible to restrict the permissibility of euthanasia as narrowly as Velleman suggests without thereby denying it to most persons who would want it; to permit it only in cases in which virtually everyone would want it would be to deny it to most who would want it.

A fifth potential bad consequence of making euthanasia legally permissible is that it might weaken the general legal prohibition of homicide. This prohibition is so fundamental to civilized society, it is argued, that we should do nothing that erodes it. If most cases of stopping life support are killing, as I have already argued, then the court cases permitting such killing have already in effect weakened this prohibition. However, neither the courts nor most people have seen these cases as killing and so as challenging the prohibition of homicide. The courts have usually grounded patients' or their surrogates' rights to refuse life-sustaining treatment in rights to privacy, liberty, self-determination, or bodily integrity, not in exceptions to homicide laws.

Legal permission for physicians or others to perform euthanasia could not be grounded in patients' rights to decide about medical treatment. Permitting euthanasia would require qualifying, at least in effect, the legal prohibition against homicide, a prohibition that in general does not allow the consent of the victim to justify or excuse the act. Nevertheless, the very same fundamental basis of the right to decide about life-sustaining treatment—respecting a person's self-determination—does support euthanasia as well. Individual self-determination has long been a well-entrenched and fundamental value in the law, and so extending it to euthanasia would not require appeal to novel legal values or principles. That suicide or attempted suicide is no longer a criminal offense in virtually all states indicates an acceptance of individual self-determination in the taking of one's own life analogous to that required for voluntary active euthanasia. The legal prohibition (in most states) of assisting in suicide and the refusal in the law to accept the consent of the victim as a possible justification of homicide are both arguably a result of difficulties in the legal process of establishing the consent of the victim after the fact. If procedures can be designed that clearly establish the voluntariness of the person's request for euthanasia it would under those procedures represent a carefully circumscribed qualification on the legal prohibition of homicide. Nevertheless, some remaining worries about this weakening can be captured in the final potential bad consequence, to which I will now turn.

This final potential bad consequence is the central concern of many opponents of euthanasia and, I believe, is the most serious objection to a legal policy permitting it. According to this "slippery slope" worry, although active euthanasia may be morally permissible in cases in which it is unequivocally *voluntary* and the patient finds his or her condition unbearable, a legal policy permitting euthanasia would inevitably lead to active euthanasia being performed in many other cases in which it would be morally wrong. To prevent those other wrongful cases of euthanasia we should not permit even morally justified performance of it.

Slippery slope arguments of this form are problematic and difficult to evaluate. From one perspective, they are the last refuge of conservative defenders of the status quo. When all the opponent's objections to the wrongness of euthanasia itself have been met, the opponent then shifts ground and acknowledges both that it is not in itself wrong and that a legal policy which resulted only in its being performed would not be bad. Nevertheless, the opponent maintains, it should still not be permitted because doing so would result in its being performed in other cases in which it is not voluntary and would be wrong. In this argument's most extreme form, permitting euthanasia is the first and fateful step down the slippery slope to Nazism. Once on the slope we will be unable to get off.

Now it cannot be denied that it is possible that permitting euthanasia could have these fateful consequences, but that cannot be enough to warrant prohibiting it if it is otherwise justified. A similar possible slippery slope worry could have been raised to securing competent patients' rights to decide about life support, but recent history shows such a worry would have been unfounded. It must be relevant how likely it is that we will end with horrendous consequences and an unjustified practice of euthanasia. How likely and widespread would the abuses and unwarranted extensions of permitting it be? By abuses, I mean the performance of euthanasia that fails to satisfy the conditions required for voluntary active euthanasia, for example, if the patient has been subtly pressured to accept it. By unwarranted extensions of policy, I mean later changes in legal policy to permit not just voluntary euthanasia, but also euthanasia in cases in which, for example, it need not be fully voluntary. Opponents of *voluntary euthanasia* on slippery slope grounds have not provided the data or evidence necessary to turn their speculative concerns into well-grounded likelihoods.

It is at least clear, however, that both the character and likelihood of abuses of a legal policy permitting euthanasia depend in significant part on the procedures put in place to protect against them. I will not try to detail fully what such procedures might be, but will just give some examples of what they might include:

1. The patient should be provided with all relevant information about his or her medical condition, current prognosis, available alternative treatments, and the prognosis of each.
2. Procedures should ensure that the patient's request for euthanasia is stable or enduring (a brief waiting period could be required) and fully voluntary (an advocate for the patient might be appointed to ensure this).
3. All reasonable alternatives must have been explored for improving the patient's quality of life and relieving any pain or suffering.
4. A psychiatric evaluation should ensure that the patient's request is not the result of a treatable psychological impairment such as depression.

These examples of procedural safeguards are all designed to ensure that the patient's choice is fully informed, voluntary, and competent, and so a true exercise of self-determination. Other proposals for euthanasia would restrict its permissibility further—for example, to the terminally ill—a restriction that cannot be supported by self-determination. Such additional restrictions might, however, be justified by concern for limiting potential harms from abuse. At the same time, it is important not to impose procedural or substantive safeguards so restrictive as to make euthanasia impermissible or practically infeasible in a wide range of justified cases.

These examples of procedural safeguards make clear that it is possible to substantially reduce, though not to eliminate, the potential for abuse of a policy permitting voluntary active euthanasia. Any legalization of the practice should be accompanied by a well-considered set of procedural safeguards together with an ongoing evaluation of its use. Introducing euthanasia into only a few states could be a form of carefully limited and controlled social experiment that would give us evidence about the benefits and harms of the practice. Even then firm and uncontroversial data may remain elusive, as the continuing controversy over what has taken place in the Netherlands in recent years indicates.

The Slip into Nonvoluntary Active Euthanasia

While I believe slippery slope worries can largely be limited by making necessary distinctions both in principle and in practice, one slippery slope concern is legitimate. There is reason to expect that legalization of voluntary active euthanasia might soon be followed by strong pressure to legalize some nonvoluntary euthanasia of incompetent patients unable to express their own wishes. Respecting a person's self-determination and recognizing that continued life is not always of value to a person can support not only voluntary active euthanasia, but some nonvoluntary euthanasia as well. These are the same values that ground competent patients' right to refuse life-sustaining treatment. Recent history here is instructive. In the medical ethics literature, in the courts since *Quinlan*, and in norms of medical practice, that right has been extended to incompetent patients and exercised by a surrogate who is to decide as the patient would have decided in the circumstances if competent. It has been held unreasonable to continue life-sustaining treatment that the patient would not have wanted just because the patient now lacks the capacity to tell us that. Life-sustaining treatment for incompetent patients is today frequently forgone on the basis of a surrogate's decision, or less frequently on the basis of an advance directive executed by the patient while still competent. The very same logic that has extended the right to refuse life-sustaining treatment from a competent patient to the surrogate of an incompetent patient (acting with or without a formal advance directive from the patient) may well extend the scope of active euthanasia. The argument will be, Why continue to force unwanted life on patients just because they have now lost the capacity to request euthanasia from us?

A related phenomenon may reinforce this slippery slope concern. In the Netherlands, what the courts have sanctioned has been clearly restricted to voluntary euthanasia. In itself, this serves as some evidence that permitting it need not lead to permitting the nonvoluntary variety. There is some indication, however, that for many Dutch physicians euthanasia is no longer viewed as a special action, set apart from their usual practice and restricted only to competent persons. Instead, it is seen as one end of a spectrum of caring for dying patients. When viewed in this way it will be difficult to deny euthanasia to a patient for whom it is seen as the best or most appropriate form of care simply because

that patient is now incompetent and cannot request it.

Even if voluntary active euthanasia should slip into nonvoluntary active euthanasia, with surrogates acting for incompetent patients, the ethical evaluation is more complex than many opponents of euthanasia allow. Just as in the case of surrogates' decisions to forgo life-sustaining treatment for incompetent patients, so also surrogates' decisions to request euthanasia for incompetent persons would often accurately reflect what the incompetent person would have wanted and would deny the person nothing that he or she would have considered worth having. Making nonvoluntary active euthanasia legally permissible, however, would greatly enlarge the number of patients on whom it might be performed and substantially enlarge the potential for misuse and abuse. As noted above, frail and debilitated elderly people, often demented or otherwise incompetent and thereby unable to defend and assert their own interests, may be especially vulnerable to unwanted euthanasia.

For some people, this risk is more than sufficient reason to oppose the legalization of voluntary euthanasia. But while we should in general be cautious about inferring much from the experience in the Netherlands to what our own experience in the United States might be, there may be one important lesson that we can learn from them. One commentator has noted that in the Netherlands families of incompetent patients have less authority than do families in the United States to act as surrogates for incompetent patients in making decisions to forgo life-sustaining treatment. From the Dutch perspective, it may be we in the United States who are already on the slippery slope in having given surrogates broad authority to forgo life-sustaining treatment for incompetent persons. In this view, the more important moral divide, and the more important with regard to potential for abuse, is not between forgoing life-sustaining treatment and euthanasia, but instead between voluntary and nonvoluntary performance of either. If this is correct, then the more important issue is ensuring the appropriate principles and procedural safeguards for the exercise of decisionmaking authority by surrogates for incompetent persons in all decisions at the end of life. This may be the correct response to slippery slope worries about euthanasia.

I have cited both good and bad consequences that have been thought likely from a policy change permitting voluntary active euthanasia, and have tried to evaluate their likelihood and relative importance. Nevertheless, as I noted earlier, reasonable disagreement remains both about the consequences of permitting euthanasia and about which of these consequences are more important. The depth and strength of public and professional debate about whether, all things considered, permitting euthanasia would be desirable or undesirable reflects these disagreements. While my own view is that the balance of considerations supports permitting the practice, my principal purpose here has been to clarify the main issues.

THE ROLE OF PHYSICIANS

If euthanasia is made legally permissible, should physicians take part in it? Should only physicians be permitted to perform it, as is the case in the Netherlands? In discussing whether euthanasia is incompatible with medicine's commitment to curing, caring for, and comforting patients, I argued that it is not at odds with a proper understanding of the aims of medicine, and so need not undermine patients' trust in their physicians. If that argument is correct, then physicians probably should not be prohibited, either by law or by professional norms, from taking part in a legally permissible practice of euthanasia (nor, of course, should they be compelled to do so if their personal or professional scruples forbid it). Most physicians in the Netherlands appear not

to understand euthanasia to be incompatible with their professional commitments.

Sometimes patients who would be able to end their lives on their own nevertheless seek the assistance of physicians. Physician involvement in such cases may have important benefits to patients and others beyond simply assuring the use of effective means. Historically, in the United States suicide has carried a strong negative stigma that many today believe unwarranted. Seeking a physician's assistance, or what can almost seem a physician's blessing, may be a way of trying to remove that stigma and show others that the decision for suicide was made with due seriousness and was justified under the circumstances. The physician's involvement provides a kind of social approval, or more accurately helps counter what would otherwise be unwarranted social disapproval.

There are also at least two reasons for restricting the practice of euthanasia to physicians only. First, physicians would inevitably be involved in some of the important procedural safeguards necessary to a defensible practice, such as seeing to it that the patient is well-informed about his or her condition, prognosis, and possible treatments, and ensuring that all reasonable means have been taken to improve the quality of the patient's life. Second, and probably more important, one necessary protection against abuse of the practice is to limit the persons given authority to perform it, so that they can be held accountable for their exercise of that authority. Physicians, whose training and professional norms give some assurance that they would perform euthanasia responsibly, are an appropriate group of persons to whom the practice may be restricted.

⚜ REVIEW QUESTIONS

1. How does Brock distinguish between voluntary, involuntary, and nonvoluntary euthanasia?
2. According to Brock, what is the central argument for voluntary euthanasia?
3. Should doctors be forced to practice euthanasia? What is Brock's view?
4. How does Brock reply to the argument that euthanasia is wrong because it is the deliberate killing of an innocent person?
5. According to Brock, what are the potentially good consequences of legalizing euthanasia?
6. What is the strongest argument for voluntary euthanasia in Brock's view?

7. What are the potentially bad consequences of permitting voluntary euthanasia, according to Brock?
8. How does Brock reply to the objection that legalizing euthanasia will lead to morally unjustified killing?

9. What role should physicians play in euthanasia, according to Brock?

⚜ DISCUSSION QUESTIONS

1. Does a person's right to autonomy morally permit her to commit suicide with the assistance of a doctor or be voluntarily killed? If so, should there be any restrictions on this right?
2. Is allowing a patient to die, either by not starting or by stopping treatment, morally the same as killing the patient? What is Brock's view? What do you think?

3. Brock claims that the right not to be killed can be waived by a competent adult. Do you agree? Why or why not?
4. Does the argument from mercy convince you that euthanasia is justified in cases of substantial physical and mental suffering? Why or why not?

Is There a Duty to Die?

JOHN HARDWIG

John Hardwig is professor of philosophy and head of the department at the University of Tennessee, Knoxville. He is the author of *Is There a Duty to Die? and Other Essays in Bioethics* (1999), which primarily collects previously published articles.

Hardwig argues that there is a duty to die that goes beyond refusing life-prolonging treatment. In some cases this duty may require one to end one's life, even in the absence of any terminal illness, and even if one would prefer to live. These are cases in which the burdens of providing care become too great, such that they outweigh the obligation to provide care. In reply to objections, Hardwig denies that there are higher duties, such as a duty to God; that the duty to die is inconsistent with human dignity; and that the sacrifice of life is always greater than the burden of caring. He does not specify exactly who has this duty to die, but he lists a number of considerations such as age, illness, lifestyle, and having had a rich and full life. He does not believe that the incompetent have any such duty, and he notes that social policies such as providing long-term care would dramatically reduce the incidence of the duty. Finally, he argues that the duty to die gives meaning to death because it affirms moral agency and family connections.

When Richard Lamm made the statement that old people have a duty to die, it was generally shouted down or ridiculed. The whole idea is just too preposterous to entertain. Or too threatening. In fact, a fairly common argument against legalizing physician-assisted suicide is that if it were legal, some people might somehow get the idea that they have a duty to die. These people

Source: John Hardwig, "Is There a Duty to Die?" *Hastings Center Report* 27, no. 2 (1997): 34–42. Reprinted by permission of the publisher.

could only be the victims of twisted moral reasoning or vicious social pressure. It goes without saying that there is no duty to die.

But for me the question is real and very important. I feel strongly that I may very well some day have a duty to die. I do not believe that I am idiosyncratic, morbid, mentally ill, or morally perverse in thinking this. I think many of us will eventually face precisely this duty. But I am first of all concerned with my own duty. I write partly to clarify my own convictions and to prepare myself. Ending my life might be a very difficult thing for me to do.

This notion of a duty to die raises all sorts of interesting theoretical and metaethical questions. I intend to try to avoid most of them because I hope my argument will be persuasive to those holding a wide variety of ethical views. Also, although the claim that there is a duty to die would ultimately require theoretical underpinning, the discussion needs to begin on the normative level. As is appropriate to my attempt to steer clear of theoretical commitments, I will use "duty," "obligation," and "responsibility" interchangeably, in a pretheoretical or pre-analytic sense.[1]

CIRCUMSTANCES AND A DUTY TO DIE

Do many of us really believe that no one ever has a duty to die? I suspect not. I think most of us probably believe that there is such a duty, but it is very uncommon. Consider Captain Oates, a member of Admiral Scott's expedition to the South Pole. Oates became too ill to continue. If the rest of the team stayed with him, they would all perish. After this had become clear, Oates left his tent one night, walked out into a raging blizzard, and

was never seen again.[2] That may have been a heroic thing to do, but we might be able to agree that it was also no more than his duty. It would have been wrong for him to urge—or even to allow—the rest to stay and care for him.

This is a very unusual circumstance—a "lifeboat case"—and lifeboat cases make for bad ethics. But I expect that most of us would also agree that there have been cultures in which what we would call a duty to die has been fairly common. These are relatively poor, technologically simple, and especially nomadic cultures. In such societies, everyone knows that if you manage to live long enough, you will eventually become old and debilitated. Then you will need to take steps to end your life. The old people in these societies regularly did precisely that. Their cultures prepared and supported them in doing so.

Those cultures could be dismissed as irrelevant to contemporary bioethics; their circumstances are so different from ours. But if that is our response, it is instructive. It suggests that we assume a duty to die is irrelevant to us because our wealth and technological sophistication have purchased exemption for us . . . except under very unusual circumstances like Captain Oates's.

But have wealth and technology really exempted us? Or are they, on the contrary, about to make a duty to die common again? We like to think of modern medicine as all triumph with no dark side. Our medicine saves many lives and enables most of us to live longer. That is wonderful, indeed. We are all glad to have access to this medicine. But our medicine also delivers most of us over to chronic illnesses and it enables many of us to survive longer than we can take care of ourselves, longer than we know what to do with ourselves, longer than we even are ourselves.

The costs—and these are not merely monetary—of prolonging our lives when we are no longer able to care for ourselves are often staggering. If further medical advances wipe out

---

[1]Given the importance of relationships in my thinking, "responsibility"—rooted as it is in "respond"—would perhaps be the most appropriate word. Nevertheless, I often use "duty" despite its legalistic overtones, because Lamm's famous statement has given the expression "duty to die" a certain familiarity. But I intend no implication that there is a law that grounds this duty, nor that someone has a right corresponding to it.

[2]For a discussion of the Oates case, see Tom L. Beauchamp, "What Is Suicide?" in *Ethical Issues in Death and Dying,* ed. Tom L. Beauchamp and Seymour Perlin (Englewood Cliffs, N.J.: Prentice-Hall, 1978).

many of today's "killer diseases"—cancers, heart attacks, strokes, ALS, AIDS, and the rest—then one day most of us will survive long enough to become demented or debilitated. These developments could generate a fairly widespread duty to die. A fairly common duty to die might turn out to be only the dark side of our life-prolonging medicine and the uses we choose to make of it.

Let me be clear. I certainly believe that there is a duty to refuse life-prolonging medical treatment and also a duty to complete advance directives refusing life-prolonging treatment. But a duty to die can go well beyond that. There can be a duty to die before one's illnesses would cause death, even if treated only with palliative measures. In fact, there may be a fairly common responsibility to end one's life in the absence of any terminal illness at all. Finally, there can be a duty to die when one would prefer to live. Granted, many of the conditions that can generate a duty to die also seriously undermine the quality of life. Some prefer not to live under such conditions. But even those who want to live can face a duty to die. These will clearly be the most controversial and troubling cases; I will, accordingly, focus my reflections on them.

THE INDIVIDUALISTIC FANTASY

Because a duty to die seems such a real possibility to me, I wonder why contemporary bioethics has dismissed it without serious consideration. I believe that most bioethics still shares in one of our deeply embedded American dreams: the individualistic fantasy. This fantasy leads us to imagine that lives are separate and unconnected, or that they could be so if we chose. If lives were unconnected, things that happened in my life would not or need not affect others. And if others were not (much) affected by my life, I would have no duty to consider the impact of my decisions on others. I would then be free morally to live my life however I please, choosing whatever life and death I prefer for myself. The way I live would be nobody's business but my own. I certainly would have no duty to die if I preferred to live.

Within a health care context, the individualistic fantasy leads us to assume that the patient is the only one affected by decisions about her medical treatment. If only the patient were affected, the relevant questions when making treatment decisions would be precisely those we ask: What will benefit the patient? Who can best decide that? The pivotal issue would always be simply whether the patient wants to live like this and whether she would consider herself better off dead.[3] "Whose life is it, anyway?" we ask rhetorically.

But this is morally obtuse. We are not a race of hermits. Illness and death do not come only to those who are all alone. Nor is it much better to think in terms of the bald dichotomy between "the interests of the patient" and "the interests of society" (or a third-party payer), as if we were isolated individuals connected only to "society" in the abstract or to the other, faceless members of our health maintenance organization.

Most of us are affiliated with particular others and most deeply, with family and loved ones. Families and loved ones are bound together by ties of care and affection, by legal relations and obligations, by inhabiting shared spaces and living units, by interlocking finances and economic prospects, by common projects and also commitments to support the different life projects of other family members, by shared histories, by ties of loyalty. This life together of family and loved ones is what defines and sustains us; it is what gives meaning to most of our lives. We would not have it any other way. We would not want to be all alone, especially when we are seriously ill, as we age, and when we are dying.

But the fact of deeply interwoven lives debars us from making exclusively self-regarding decisions, as the decisions of one member of a family may dramatically affect the lives of all the rest. The impact of my decisions upon my family and

---

[3]Most bioethicists advocate a "patient-centered ethics"—an ethics which claims only the patient's interests should be considered in making medical treatment decisions. Most health care professionals have been trained to accept this ethic and to see themselves as patient advocates. For arguments that a patient-centered ethics should be replaced by a family-centered ethics, see John Hardwig, "What About the Family?" *Hastings Center Report* 20, no. 2 (1990): 5–10; Hilde L. Nelson and James L. Nelson, *The Patient in the Family* (New York: Routledge,1995).

loved ones is the source of many of my strongest obligations and also the most plausible and likeliest basis of a duty to die. "Society," after all, is only very marginally affected by how I live, or by whether I live or die.

A BURDEN TO MY LOVED ONES

Many older people report that their one remaining goal in life is not to be a burden to their loved ones. Young people feel this, too: when I ask my undergraduate students to think about whether their death could come too late, one of their very first responses always is, "Yes, when I become a burden to my family or loved ones." Tragically, there are situations in which my loved ones would be much better off—all things considered, the loss of a loved one notwithstanding—if I were dead.

The lives of our loved ones can be seriously compromised by caring for us. The burdens of providing care or even just supervision twenty-four hours a day, seven days a week are often overwhelming.[4] When this kind of caregiving goes on for years, it leaves the caregiver exhausted, with no time for herself or life of her own. Ultimately, even her health is often destroyed. But it can also be emotionally devastating simply to live with a spouse who is increasingly distant, uncommunicative, unresponsive, foreign, and unreachable. Other family members' needs often go unmet as the caring capacity of the family is exceeded. Social life and friendships evaporate, as there is no opportunity to go out to see friends and the home is no longer a place suitable for having friends in.

We must also acknowledge that the lives of our loved ones can be devastated just by having to pay for health care for us. One part of the recent SUPPORT study documented the financial aspects of caring for a dying member of a family. Only those who had illnesses severe enough to

give them less than a 50 percent chance to live six more months were included in this study. When these patients survived their initial hospitalization and were discharged[,] about one-third required considerable caregiving from their families; in 20 percent of cases a family member had to quit work or make some other major lifestyle change; almost one-third of these families lost all of their savings; and just under 30 percent lost a major source of income.[5]

If talking about money sounds venal or trivial, remember that much more than money is normally at stake here. When someone has to quit work, she may well lose her career. Savings decimated late in life cannot be recouped in the few remaining years of employability, so the loss compromises the quality of the rest of the caregiver's life. For a young person, the chance to go to college may be lost to the attempt to pay debts due to an illness in the family, and this decisively shapes an entire life.

A serious illness in a family is a misfortune. It is usually nobody's fault; no one is responsible for it. But we face choices about how we will respond to this misfortune. That's where the responsibility comes in and fault can arise. Those of us with families and loved ones always have a duty not to make selfish or self-centered decisions about our lives. We have a responsibility to try to protect the lives of loved ones from serious threats or greatly impoverished quality, certainly an obligation not to make choices that will jeopardize or seriously compromise their futures. Often, it would be wrong to do just what we want or just what is best for ourselves; we should choose in light of what is best for all concerned. That is our duty in sickness as well as in health. It is out of these responsibilities that a duty to die can develop.

I am not advocating a crass, quasi-economic conception of burdens and benefits, nor a shallow, hedonistic view of life. Given a suitably rich understanding of benefits, family members sometimes do benefit from suffering through the long illness of a loved one. Caring for the sick or aged

---

[4]A good account of the burdens of caregiving can be found in Elaine Brody, *Women in the Middle: Their Parent-Care Years* (New York: Springer Publishing Co., 1990). Perhaps the best article-length account of these burdens is Daniel Callahan, "Families as Caregivers; the Limits of Morality" in *Aging and Ethics: Philosophical Problems in Gerontology*, ed. Nancy Jecker (Totowa, N.J.: Humana Press, 1991).

[5]Kenneth E. Covinsky et al., "The Impact of Serious Illness on Patients' Families," *JAMA* 272 (1994): 1839–44.

can foster growth, even as it makes daily life immeasurably harder and the prospects for the future much bleaker. Chronic illness or a drawn-out death can also pull a family together, making the care for each other stronger and more evident. If my loved ones are truly benefiting from coping with my illness or debility, I have no duty to die based on burdens to them.

But it would be irresponsible to blithely assume that this always happens, that it will happen in my family, or that it will be the fault of my family if they cannot manage to turn my illness into a positive experience. Perhaps the opposite is more common: A hospital chaplain once told me that he could not think of a single case in which a family was strengthened or brought together by what happened at the hospital.

Our families and loved ones also have obligations, of course—they have the responsibility to stand by us and to support us through debilitating illness and death. They must be prepared to make significant sacrifices to respond to an illness in the family. I am far from denying that. Most of us are aware of this responsibility and most families meet it rather well. In fact, families deliver more than 80 percent of the long-term care in this country, almost always at great personal cost. Most of us who are a part of a family can expect to be sustained in our time of need by family members and those who love us.

But most discussions of an illness in the family sound as if responsibility were a one-way street. It is not, of course. When we become seriously ill or debilitated, we too may have to make sacrifices. To think that my loved ones must bear whatever burdens my illness, debility, or dying process might impose upon them is to reduce them to means to my well-being. And that would be immoral. Family solidarity, altruism, bearing the burden of a loved one's misfortune, and loyalty are all important virtues of families, as well. But they are all also two-way streets.

OBJECTIONS TO A DUTY TO DIE

To my mind, the most serious objections to the idea of a duty to die lie in the effects on my loved ones of ending my life. But to most others, the important objections have little or nothing to do with family and loved ones. Perhaps the most common objections are: (1) there is a higher duty that always takes precedence over a duty to die; (2) a duty to end one's own life would be incompatible with a recognition of human dignity or the intrinsic value of a person; and (3) seriously ill, debilitated, or dying people are already bearing the harshest burdens and so it would be wrong to ask them to bear the additional burden of ending their own lives.

These are all important objections; all deserve a thorough discussion. Here I will only be able to suggest some moral counterweights—ideas that might provide the basis for an argument that these objections do not always preclude a duty to die.

An example of the first line of argument would be the claim that a duty to God, the giver of life, forbids that anyone take her own life. It could be argued that this duty always supersedes whatever obligations we might have to our families. But what convinces us that we always have such a religious duty in the first place? And what guarantees that it always supersedes our obligations to try to protect our loved ones?

Certainly, the view that death is the ultimate evil cannot be squared with Christian theology. It does not reflect the actions of Jesus or those of his early followers. Nor is it clear that the belief that life is sacred requires that we never take it. There are other theological possibilities.[6] In any case, most of us—bioethicists, physicians, and patients alike—do not subscribe to the view that we have an obligation to preserve human life as long as possible. But if not, surely we ought to agree that I may legitimately end my life for other-regarding reasons, not just for self-regarding reasons.

---

[6]Larry Churchill, for example, believes that Christian ethics takes us far beyond my present position: "Christian doctrines of stewardship prohibit the extension of one's own life at a great cost to the neighbor. . . . And such a gesture should not appear to us a sacrifice, but as the ordinary virtue entailed by a just, social conscience." Larry Churchill, *Rationing Health Care in America* (South Bend, Ind.: Notre Dame University Press, 1988), p. 112.

Secondly, religious considerations aside, the claim could be made that an obligation to end one's own life would be incompatible with human dignity or would embody a failure to recognize the intrinsic value of a person. But I do not see that in thinking I had a duty to die I would necessarily be failing to respect myself or to appreciate my dignity or worth. Nor would I necessarily be failing to respect you in thinking that you had a similar duty. There is surely also a sense in which we fail to respect ourselves if in the face of illness or death, we stoop to choosing just what is best for ourselves. Indeed, Kant held that the very core of human dignity is the ability to act on a self-imposed moral law, regardless of whether it is in our interest to do so.[7] We shall return to the notion of human dignity.

A third objection appeals to the relative weight of burdens and thus, ultimately, to considerations of fairness or justice. The burdens that an illness creates for the family could not possibly be great enough to justify an obligation to end one's life—the sacrifice of life itself would be a far greater burden than any involved in caring for a chronically ill family member.

But is this true? Consider the following case:

An 87-year-old woman was dying of congestive heart failure. Her APACHE score predicted that she had less than a 50 percent chance to live for another six months. She was lucid, assertive, and terrified of death. She very much wanted to live and kept opting for rehospitalization and the most aggressive life-prolonging treatment possible. That treatment successfully prolonged her life (though with increasing debility) for nearly two years. Her 55-year-old daughter was her only remaining family, her caregiver, and the main source of her financial support. The daughter duly cared for her mother. But before her mother died, her illness had cost the daughter all of her savings, her home, her job, and her career.

This is by no means an uncommon sort of case. Thousands of similar cases occur each year. Now, ask yourself which is the greater burden:

a. To lose a 50 percent chance of six more months of life at age 87?
b. To lose all your savings, your home, and your career at age 55?

Which burden would you prefer to bear? Do we really believe the former is the greater burden? Would even the dying mother say that (a) is the greater burden? Or has she been encouraged to believe that the burdens of (b) are somehow morally irrelevant to her choices?

I think most of us would quickly agree that (b) is a greater burden. That is the evil we would more hope to avoid in our lives. If we are tempted to say that the mother's disease and impending death are the greater evil, I believe it is because we are taking a "slice of time" perspective rather than a "lifetime perspective."[8] But surely the lifetime perspective is the appropriate perspective when weighing burdens. If (b) is the greater burden, then we must admit that we have been promulgating an ethics that advocates imposing greater burdens on some people in order to provide smaller benefits for others just because they are ill and thus gain our professional attention and advocacy.

A whole range of cases like this one could easily be generated. In some, the answer about which burden is greater will not be clear. But in many it is. Death—or ending your own life—is simply not the greatest evil or the greatest burden.

This point does not depend on a utilitarian calculus. Even if death were the greatest burden (thus disposing of any simple utilitarian argument), serious questions would remain about the moral justifiability of choosing to impose crushing burdens on loved ones in order to avoid having to bear this burden oneself. The fact that I

---

[7]Kant, as is well known, was opposed to suicide. But he was arguing against taking your life out of self-interested motives. It is not clear that Kant would or we should consider taking your life out of a sense of duty to be wrong. See Hilde L. Nelson, "Death with Kantian Dignity," *Journal of Clinical Ethics* 7 (1996): 215–21.

[8]Obviously, I owe this distinction to Norman Daniels. Norman Daniels, *Am I My Parents' Keeper? An Essay on Justice Between the Young and the Old* (New York: Oxford University Press, 1988). Just as obviously, Daniels is not committed to my use of it here.

suffer greater burdens than others in my family does not license me simply to choose what I want for myself, nor does it necessarily release me from a responsibility to try to protect the quality of their lives.

I can readily imagine that, through cowardice, rationalization, or failure of resolve, I will fail in this obligation to protect my loved ones. If so, I think I would need to be excused or forgiven for what I did. But I cannot imagine it would be morally permissible for me to ruin the rest of my partner's life to sustain mine or to cut off my sons' careers, impoverish them, or compromise the quality of their children's lives simply because I wish to live a little longer. This is what leads me to believe in a duty to die.

WHO HAS A DUTY TO DIE?

Suppose, then, that there can be a duty to die. Who has a duty to die? And when? To my mind, these are the right questions, the questions we should be asking. Many of us may one day badly need answers to just these questions.

But I cannot supply answers here, for two reasons. In the first place, answers will have to be very particular and contextual. Our concrete duties are often situated, defined in part by the myriad details of our circumstances, histories, and relationships. Though there may be principles that apply to a wide range of cases and some cases that yield pretty straightforward answers, there will also be many situations in which it is very difficult to discern whether one has a duty to die. If nothing else, it will often be very difficult to predict how one's family will bear up under the weight of the burdens that a protracted illness would impose on them. Momentous decisions will often have to be made under conditions of great uncertainty.

Second and perhaps even more importantly, I believe that those of us with family and loved ones should not define our duties unilaterally, especially not a decision about a duty to die. It would be isolating and distancing for me to decide without consulting them what is too much of a burden for my loved ones to bear. That way of deciding about my moral duties is not only

atomistic, it also treats my family and loved ones paternalistically. They must be allowed to speak for themselves about the burdens my life imposes on them and how they feel about bearing those burdens.

Some may object that it would be wrong to put a loved one in a position of having to say, in effect, "You should end your life because caring for you is too hard on me and the rest of the family." Not only will it be almost impossible to say something like that to someone you love, it will carry with it a heavy load of guilt. On this view, you should decide by yourself whether you have a duty to die and approach your loved ones only after you have made up your mind to say good-bye to them. Your family could then try to change your mind, but the tremendous weight of moral decision would be lifted from their shoulders.

Perhaps so. But I believe in family decisions. Important decisions for those whose lives are interwoven should be made together, in a family discussion. Granted, a conversation about whether I have a duty to die would be a tremendously difficult conversation. The temptations to be dishonest could be enormous. Nevertheless, if I am contemplating a duty to die, my family and I should, if possible, have just such an agonizing discussion. It will act as a check on the information, perceptions, and reasoning of all of us. But even more importantly, it affirms our connectedness at a critical juncture in our lives and our life together. Honest talk about difficult matters almost always strengthens relationships.

However, many families seem unable to talk about death at all, much less a duty to die. Certainly most families could not have this discussion all at once, in one sitting. It might well take a number of discussions to be able to approach this topic. But even if talking about death is impossible, there are always behavioral clues—about your caregiver's tiredness, physical condition, health, prevailing mood, anxiety, financial concerns, outlook, overall well-being, and so on. And families unable to talk about death can often talk about how the caregiver is feeling, about finances, about tensions within the family resulting from the illness, about concerns for the future.

Deciding whether you have a duty to die based on these behavioral clues and conversation about them honors your relationships better than deciding on your own about how burdensome you and your care must be.

I cannot say when someone has a duty to die. Still, I can suggest a few features of one's illness, history, and circumstances that make it more likely that one has a duty to die. I present them here without much elaboration or explanation.

1. A duty to die is more likely when continuing to live will impose significant burdens—emotional burdens, extensive caregiving, destruction of life plans, and, yes, financial hardship—on your family and loved ones. This is the fundamental insight underlying a duty to die.

2. A duty to die becomes greater as you grow older. As we age, we will be giving up less by giving up our lives, if only because we will sacrifice fewer remaining years of life and a smaller portion of our life plans. After all, it's not as if we would be immortal and live forever if we could just manage to avoid a duty to die. To have reached the age of, say, seventy-five or eighty years without being ready to die is itself a moral failing, the sign of a life out of touch with life's basic realities.[9]

3. A duty to die is more likely when you have already lived a full and rich life. You have already had a full share of the good things life offers.

4. There is greater duty to die if your loved ones' lives have already been difficult or impoverished, if they have had only a small share of the good things that life has to offer (especially if through no fault of their own).

5. A duty to die is more likely when your loved ones have already made great contributions—perhaps even sacrifices—to make your life a good one. [This is especially [so] if you have not made similar sacrifices for their well-being or for the well-being of other members of your family.

6. To the extent that you can make a good adjustment to your illness or handicapping condition, there is less likely to be a duty to die. A good adjustment means that smaller sacrifices will be required of loved ones and there is more compensating interaction for them. Still, we must also recognize that some diseases—Alzheimer or Huntington chorea—will eventually take their toll on your loved ones no matter how courageously, resolutely, even cheerfully you manage to face that illness.

7. There is less likely to be a duty to die if you can still make significant contributions to the lives of others, especially your family. The burdens to family members are not only or even primarily financial, neither are the contributions to them. However, the old and those who have terminal illnesses must also bear in mind that the loss their family members will feel when they die cannot be avoided, only postponed.

8. A duty to die is more likely when the part of you that is loved will soon be gone or seriously compromised. Or when you soon will no longer be capable of giving love. Part of the horror of dementing disease is that it destroys the capacity to nurture and sustain relationships, taking away a person's agency and the emotions that bind her to others.

9. There is a greater duty to die to the extent that you have lived a relatively lavish lifestyle instead of saving for illness or old age. Like most upper middle-class Americans, I could easily have saved more. It is a greater wrong to come to your family for assistance if your need is the result of having chosen leisure or a spendthrift lifestyle. I may eventually have to face the moral consequences of decisions I am now making.

These, then, are some of the considerations that give shape and definition to the duty to die. If we can agree that these considerations are all relevant, we can see that the correct course of action will often be difficult to discern. A decision about when I should end my life will sometimes prove to be every bit as difficult as the decision about whether I want treatment for myself.

CAN THE INCOMPETENT HAVE A DUTY TO DIE?

Severe mental deterioration springs readily to mind as one of the situations in which I believe I could have a duty to die. But can incompetent

---

[9]Daniel Callahan, *The Troubled Dream of Life* (New York: Simon & Schuster, 1993).

people have duties at all? We can have moral duties we do not recognize or acknowledge, including duties that we never recognized. But can we have duties we are unable to recognize? Duties when we are unable to understand the concept of morality at all? If so, do others have a moral obligation to help us carry out this duty? These are extremely difficult theoretical questions. The reach of moral agency is severely strained by mental incompetence.

I am tempted to simply bypass the entire question by saying that I am talking only about competent persons. But the idea of a duty to die clearly raises the specter of one person claiming that another—who cannot speak for herself—has such a duty. So I need to say that I can make no sense of the claim that someone has a duty to die if the person has never been able to understand moral obligation at all. To my mind, only those who were formerly capable of making moral decisions could have such a duty.

But the case of formerly competent persons is almost as troubling. Perhaps we should simply stipulate that no incompetent person can have a duty to die, not even if she affirmed belief in such a duty in an advance directive. If we take the view that formerly competent people may have such a duty, we should surely exercise extreme caution when claiming a formerly competent person would have acknowledged a duty to die or that any formerly competent person has an unacknowledged duty to die. Moral dangers loom regardless of which way we decide to resolve such issues.

But for me personally, very urgent practical matters turn on their resolution. If a formerly competent person can no longer have a duty to die (or if other people are not likely to help her carry out this duty), I believe that my obligation may be to die while I am still competent, before I become unable to make and carry out that decision for myself. Surely it would be irresponsible to evade my moral duties by temporizing until I escape into incompetence. And so I must die sooner than I otherwise would have to. On the other hand, if I could count on others to end my life after I become incompetent, I might be able to fulfill my responsibilities while also living

out all my competent or semi-competent days. Given our society's reluctance to permit physicians, let alone family members, to perform aid-in-dying, I believe I may well have a duty to end my life when I can see mental incapacity on the horizon.

There is also the very real problem of sudden incompetence—due to a serious stroke or automobile accident, for example. For me, that is the real nightmare. If I suddenly become incompetent, I will fall into the hands of a medical-legal system that will conscientiously disregard my moral beliefs and do what is best for me, regardless of the consequences for my loved ones. And that is not at all what I would have wanted!

SOCIAL POLICIES AND A DUTY TO DIE

The claim that there is a duty to die will seem to some a misplaced response to social negligence. If our society were providing for the debilitated, the chronically ill, and the elderly as it should be, there would be only very rare cases of a duty to die. On this view, I am asking the sick and debilitated to step in and accept responsibility because society is derelict in its responsibility to provide for the incapacitated.

This much is surely true: There are a number of social policies we could pursue that would dramatically reduce the incidence of such a duty. Most obviously, we could decide to pay for facilities that provided excellent long-term care (not just health care!) for all chronically ill, debilitated, mentally ill, or demented people in this country. We probably could still afford to do this. If we did, sick, debilitated, and dying people might still be morally required to make sacrifices for their families. I might, for example, have a duty to forgo personal care by a family member who knows me and really does care for me. But these sacrifices would only rarely include the sacrifice of life itself. The duty to die would then be virtually eliminated.

I cannot claim to know whether in some abstract sense a society like ours should provide care for all who are chronically ill or debilitated. But the fact is that we Americans seem to be unwilling to pay for this kind of long-term care, except for ourselves and our own. In fact, we are moving in precisely the opposite direction—we are trying to shift the burdens of caring for the seriously and chronically ill onto families in order to save costs for our health care system. As we shift the burdens of care onto families, we also dramatically increase the number of Americans who will have a duty to die.

I must not, then, live my life and make my plans on the assumption that social institutions will protect my family from my infirmity and debility. To do so would be irresponsible. More likely, it will be up to me to protect my loved ones.

A DUTY TO DIE AND THE MEANING OF LIFE

A duty to die seems very harsh, and often it would be. It is one of the tragedies of our lives that someone who wants very much to live can nevertheless have a duty to die. It is both tragic and ironic that it is precisely the very real good of family and loved ones that gives rise to this duty. Indeed, the genuine love, closeness, and supportiveness of family members is a major source of this duty: we could not be such a burden if they did not care for us. Finally, there is deep irony in the fact that the very successes of our life-prolonging medicine help to create a widespread duty to die. We do not live in such a happy world that we can avoid such tragedies and ironies. We ought not to close our eyes to this reality or pretend that it just doesn't exist. We ought not to minimize the tragedy in any way.

And yet, a duty to die will not always be as harsh as we might assume. If I love my family, I will want to protect them and their lives. I will want not to make choices that compromise their futures. Indeed, I can easily imagine that I might want to avoid compromising their lives more than I would want anything else. I must also admit that I am not necessarily giving up so much in giving up my life: the conditions that give rise to a duty to die would usually already have compromised the quality of the life I am required to end. In

any case, I personally must confess that at age fifty-six, I have already lived a very good life, albeit not yet nearly as long a life as I would like to have.

We fear death too much. Our fear of death has led to a massive assault on it. We still crave after virtually any life-prolonging technology that we might conceivably be able to produce. We still too often feel morally impelled to prolong life—virtually any form of life—as long as possible. As if the best death is the one that can be put off longest.

We do not even ask about meaning in death, so busy are we with trying to postpone it. But we will not conquer death by one day developing a technology so magnificent that no one will have to die. Nor can we conquer death by postponing it ever longer. We can conquer death only by finding meaning in it.

Although the existence of a duty to die does not hinge on this, recognizing such a duty would go some way toward recovering meaning in death. Paradoxically, it would restore dignity to those who are seriously ill or dying. It would also reaffirm the connections required to give life (and death) meaning. I close now with a few words about both of these points.

First, recognizing a duty to die affirms my agency and also my moral agency. I can still do things that make an important difference in the lives of my loved ones. Moreover, the fact that I still have responsibilities keeps me within the community of moral agents. My illness or debility has not reduced me to a mere moral patient (to use the language of the philosophers). Though it may not be the whole story, surely Kant was onto something important when he claimed that human dignity rests on the capacity for moral agency within a community of those who respect the demands of morality.

By contrast, surely there is something deeply insulting in a medicine and an ethic that would ask only what I want (or would have wanted) when I become ill. To treat me as if I had no moral responsibilities when I am ill or debilitated implies that my condition has rendered me morally incompetent. Only small children, the demented or insane, and those totally lacking in the capacity to act are free from moral duties. There is dignity, then, and a kind of meaning in moral agency, even as it forces extremely difficult decisions upon us.

Second, recovering meaning in death requires an affirmation of connections. If I end my life to spare the futures of my loved ones, I testify in my death that I am connected to them. It is because I love and care for precisely these people (and I know they care for me) that I wish not to be such a burden to them. By contrast, a life in which I am free to choose whatever I want for myself is a life unconnected to others. A bioethics that would treat me as if I had no serious moral responsibilities does what it can to marginalize, weaken, or even destroy my connections with others.

But life without connection is meaningless. The individualistic fantasy, though occasionally liberating, is deeply destructive. When life is good and vitality seems unending, life itself and life lived for yourself may seem quite sufficient. But if not life, certainly death without connection is meaningless. If you are only for yourself, all you have to care about as your life draws to a close is yourself and your life. Everything you care about will then perish in your death. And that—the end of everything you care about—is precisely the total collapse of meaning. We can, then, find meaning in death only through a sense of connection with something that will survive our death.

This need not be connections with other people. Some people are deeply tied to land (for example, the family farm), to nature, or to a transcendent reality. But for most of us, the connections that sustain us are to other people. In the full bloom of life, we are connected to others in many ways—through work, profession, neighborhood, country, shared faith and worship, common leisure pursuits, friendship. Even the guru meditating in isolation on his mountain top is connected to a long tradition of people united by the same religious quest.

But as we age or when we become chronically ill, connections with other people usually become much more restricted. Often, only ties with family and close friends remain and remain important to us. Moreover, for many of us, other connections just don't go deep enough. As Paul Tsongas has reminded us, "When it comes time to die, no one says, 'I wish I had spent more time at the office.'"

If I am correct, death is so difficult for us partly because our sense of community is so weak. Death seems to wipe out everything when we can't fit it into the lives of those who live on. A death motivated by the desire to spare the futures of my loved ones might well be a better death for me than the one I would get as a result of opting to continue my life as long as there is any pleasure in it for me. Pleasure is nice, but it is meaning that matters.

* * *

I don't know about others, but these reflections have helped me. I am now more at peace about facing a duty to die. Ending my life if my duty required might still be difficult. But for me, a far greater horror would be dying all alone or stealing the futures of my loved ones in order to buy a little more time for myself. I hope that if the time comes when I have a duty to die, I will recognize it, encourage my loved ones to recognize it too, and carry it out bravely.

ACKNOWLEDGMENTS

I wish to thank Mary English, Hilde Nelson, Jim Bennett, Tom Townsend, the members of the Philosophy Department at East Tennessee State University, and anonymous reviewers of the *Report* for many helpful comments on earlier versions of this paper. In this paper, I draw on material in John Hardwig, "Dying at the Right Time; Reflections on (Un) Assisted Suicide" in *Practical Ethics*, ed. H. LaFollette (London: Blackwell, 1996), with permission.

⚜ REVIEW QUESTIONS

1. Hardwig begins with the case of Captain Oates. What is this case supposed to prove?
2. What are the requirements of the duty to die, in Hardwig's view?
3. What is the "individualistic fantasy," as Hardwig calls it? What is wrong with this fantasy?
4. What is Hardwig's position on the burdens of providing care to the ill?
5. According to Hardwig, what is the most serious objection to the idea of a duty to die?
6. What are the most common objections? How does Hardwig reply to these objections?
7. Hardwig lists nine considerations relevant to the duty to die. What are they?
8. What is Hardwig's view of the incompetent? Do they have any duty to die?
9. According to Hardwig, what social policies would dramatically reduce the incidence of the duty to die?

⚜ DISCUSSION QUESTIONS

1. Is there any duty to die? If so, does it require one to actively end one's life? Why or why not?
2. How much of a burden would you accept to care for a family member? Would you be willing to provide full-time care? Would you give up a career?
3. Does Hardwig have a good reply to the objection that there is a higher duty to God? Explain your view.
4. Do you agree with Hardwig that excellent long-term care should be provided for all chronically ill, debilitated, mentally ill, or demented people in this country? If so, how should this be financed?
5. Does the duty to die give meaning to death, as Hardwig says? Why or why not?

PROBLEM CASES

1. Terminal Sedation

(See Anemona Hartocollis, "Hard Choice for a Comfortable Death: Sedation," *The New York Times*, December 27, 2009.) It is estimated that as many as 50 percent of the terminally ill patients in hospice care are given drugs that sedate them and cause an early death. Some doctors call the practice "terminal sedation" or "slow euthanasia" because it causes death to occur more quickly than it would without the drugs. Other doctors prefer to label it "palliative sedation" because it reduces pain and suffering even though an early death is foreseen.

For sedation, drugs such as lorazepam, midazolam, and phenobarbital are used. For pain, opioid drugs such as morphine and methadone are used. Another drug used for sedation is ketamine, which is an anesthetic and sedative popular at rave parties. Another anesthetic is propofol. This is the drug that, along with lorazepam, caused Michael Jackson's death.

In some cases, the patient is rendered unconscious until death. Consider the case of Leo Olzik, an eighty-eight-year-old man with dementia, congestive heart failure, and kidney disease. When he was brought to the hospital by his wife and son, he was agitated and ripping off his clothes. He was given lorazepam and morphine, a combination that slows breathing and heart rate, making it difficult or impossible to eat or drink. The effect of the drugs is to hasten death. After sleeping soundly for eight days with his mouth open, he died without waking.

Defenders of terminal sedation appeal to the doctrine of double effect. If the doctor's intention is to reduce pain, and not cause death, then the practice is not wrong, even though death is foreseen as a consequence. Critics insist that the doctors are killing the patients. This violates the principle of doing no harm to patients. Terminal sedation is simply a convenient way of causing death to occur in a relatively short time rather than keeping the patient alive as long as possible.

Is terminal sedation morally acceptable? Explain your position.

2. The Trolley Problem

(See Philippa Foot, "Killing and Letting Die," in the Suggested Readings.) Suppose a runaway trolley is headed toward a track on which five people are standing, unaware that the trolley is fast approaching. A railway engineer can quickly switch the tracks, thereby diverting the trolley onto another track on which only one person is standing. If the railway man does this, then only one person will be killed. But if he does nothing, and lets the trolley continue on its course, it will hit and kill five people.

What should the railway engineer do? If he switches the track, he will be guilty of actively killing one person, and thus violating that person's right not to be killed. If he does not switch the tracks, then he will be responsible for letting five people die, people he could have saved if only he had switched the tracks. But he doesn't kill them by acting, he only lets them die by an omission, by not acting.

3. Terri Schiavo

(For more information see the Terri Schiavo Foundation, www.terrisfight.org.) Terri Schiavo, age forty, has been in a persistent vegetative state since 1990, when her heart stopped temporarily and she suffered brain damage. The cause was diagnosed by doctors as potassium deficiency. She was twenty-six at the time and had not signed a living will. Since then she has been kept alive with a feeding tube that supplies nutrition and hydration.

According to the National Institute for Neurological Disorders and Stroke (www.ninds.nin.gov), people in a persistent vegetative state (PVS) have lost their thinking abilities and awareness of surroundings. They retain noncognitive function, normal sleep patterns, breathing, and circulation. They may be able to cry or laugh, and may appear somewhat normal. But they do not speak or respond to commands.

Ms. Schiavo has been in this state for thirteen years. It is generally agreed that the prognosis is poor for PVS patients who do not become responsive within six months after injury. Also, Ms. Schiavo suffered severe brain damage because oxygen was cut off to her brain for fourteen minutes when her heart stopped. This makes a full recovery unlikely.

Michael Schiavo, the husband and legal guardian of Ms. Schiavo, has sought to have the feeding tube

removed since 1998, testifying that his wife told him that she would never want to be kept alive artificially. Her parents, Robert and Mary Schindler, have fought Mr. Schiavo every step of the way. They have made videos of their daughter smiling, grunting, and moaning in response to her mother's voice, and following a balloon with her eyes. They believe their daughter may recover some day.

On October 21, 2003, the Florida legislature passed a bill, known as "Terri's bill," which allowed Jeb Bush, Florida's governor, to issue an executive order that Ms. Schiavo be kept alive with a feeding tube. Mr. Bush, the brother of former President George W. Bush, is a Roman Catholic who believes passionately in the sanctity of life. The hastily passed law overrode years of court rulings and came six days after Ms. Schiavo's feeding tube was removed.

Mr. Schiavo immediately sued, arguing that the law was unconstitutional. On May 6, 2004, Judge Douglas Baird of the Sixth Circuit Court struck down "Terri's law" as unconstitutional. He wrote that the law authorizes the governor to summarily deprive Florida citizens of their constitutional right to privacy. The ruling voided the law and allowed Ms. Schiavo's feeding tube to be disconnected. But lawyers for both sides said that the tube would remain in place while Mr. Bush appealed.

Should Ms. Schiavo be kept alive with a feeding tube or not? Why or why not?

Who has the right to make a life-or-death decision in this case? Does Governor Bush have this right? Does the husband and legal guardian have the right to decide? What about the parents? Should they get to decide?

Suppose Ms. Schiavo had signed a living will specifically saying that she did not want to be kept alive with a feeding tube. Should her instructions be followed? Why or why not?

4. *Tracy Lynn Latimer*

Tracy suffered from a severe form of cerebral palsy, but she was not terminally ill. At the age of twelve, she was quadriplegic and bedridden most of the time, although she was able to get about in a wheelchair. Her condition was permanent, having been caused by neurological damage at the time of her birth. She was said to have the mental capacity of a four-month-old baby, and could communicate only by means of facial expressions such as laughing or crying. According to Laura Latimer, her mother, Tracy enjoyed music, bonfires, and being with her family and the circus. She liked to play music on the radio attached to her wheelchair, which she could control with a special button. She was completely dependent on others for her care. She had five to six seizures daily, despite taking anti-epileptic medication. Like many quadriplegic children with cerebral palsy, Tracy developed scoliosis, an abnormal curvature and rotation in the back. She underwent numerous surgeries in her short life, including operations to implant metal rods that supported her back. Tracy was thought to be in a great deal of pain, and the pain could not be reduced by medication because the pain medication conflicted with her anti-seizure medication, and she had difficulty swallowing. Before her death she developed further problems in her right hip, which had become dislocated and caused considerable pain.

Tracy's doctors anticipated that she would have to undergo repeated surgeries. She could have been fed with a feeding tube into her stomach. This treatment would have improved her nutrition and health, and might have allowed more effective pain medication to be administered. This option was rejected by the parents as being intrusive and as representing the first step on a path of preserving Tracy's life artificially.

Tracy was scheduled to undergo further surgery to correct the dislocated hip on November 19, 1993. The procedure involved removing her upper thigh bone, which would leave her lower leg loose without any connecting bone. It would be held in place by muscle and tissue. The expected recovery time for this surgery was one year. The Latimers were told that this operation would be very painful, and the doctors said that further surgery would be required to relieve pain in various joints in Tracy's body. According to Laura Latimer, these further surgeries were perceived as mutilations. Robert Latimer, the father, decided that Tracy's life was not worth living, and decided to take her life.

On October 24, 1993, while his wife and Tracy's siblings were at church, Robert carried Tracy to his pickup truck parked in a shed. He put her in the cab of the truck and inserted a hose from the truck's exhaust pipe into the cab. Tracy died from carbon monoxide poisoning.

Robert was initially charged with first-degree murder and convicted by a jury of second-degree murder. The Court of Appeal for Saskatchewan upheld this conviction and a life sentence with no eligibility for parole for ten years. The case was appealed, and in a second trial, Robert was again convicted of second-degree murder. A third appeal was made and rejected by the court on June 13, 2001.

There is no doubt that Robert killed Tracy. He confessed to the crime and re-enacted his actions on videotape. But how should he be punished? The community where the Latimers lived, in North Battleford, Saskatchewan, reacted to the crime with sympathy rather than anger. By all accounts, Robert was a caring and involved parent who was well-liked by the community. Some jury members who found him guilty were upset by the life sentence. Did he deserve this sentence? In his defense, Robert said the killing was an act of mercy to save his daughter from long-term pain and suffering. Do you agree? If so, was his act morally wrong or not? Why or why not?

5. *Cruzan v. Director, Missouri Department of Health*

(U.S. Supreme Court. 110 S. Ct. 2841 [1990])

In this case, the U.S. Supreme Court ruled on a petition to terminate the artificial nutrition and hydration of Nancy Cruzan, a twenty-five-year-old woman existing in a persistent vegetative state following an automobile accident.

On the night of January 11, 1983, Cruzan rolled her car over while driving down Elm Road in Jasper County, Missouri. She was found lying in a ditch. She was not breathing, and her heart was not beating. Paramedics were able to restore her breathing and heartbeat, but she remained unconscious. She remained in a coma for about three weeks. To keep her alive, surgeons implanted a gastrostomy feeding and hydration tube; she remained in a persistent vegetative state—a condition in which a person exhibits motor reflexes but no sign of consciousness or cognitive function.

After it became clear that Cruzan had practically no chance of recovery, her parents asked the doctors to terminate the artificial feeding and hydration. The doctors and the parents agreed that this would cause Cruzan's death. The doctors refused to do this without a court order. The parents petitioned a court and received authorization to terminate treatment. But the Supreme Court of Missouri reversed the decision of the trial court and ruled that treatment could not be terminated without "clear and convincing evidence" that termination is what Cruzan would have wanted.

The case went to the U.S. Supreme Court, which upheld the judgment of the Missouri Supreme Court that termination of treatment was unconstitutional in this case. The decision was 5-to-4, and the majority opinion was written by Justice William H. Rehnquist. In his opinion, Rehnquist granted that a competent person has a right to refuse lifesaving nutrition and hydration. But he ruled that in the case of an incompetent person such as Nancy Cruzan, it is constitutional for Missouri to require that feeding and hydration be terminated only if there is clear and convincing evidence that this is what Cruzan would have wanted. Because such evidence was not provided, the decision to deny the request for termination was upheld.

In later developments, the parents presented new evidence to show that Cruzan would have chosen termination of treatment, and the feeding and hydration were stopped. Nancy Cruzan finally died in December of 1990, seven years after the accident.

This case raises several troubling questions:

1. What would be the AMA position in this case? Are artificial feeding and hydration ordinary or extraordinary means of prolonging life? If they are ordinary means, then is cessation of treatment not allowed? If they are extraordinary means, then is cessation of treatment allowed? Is the AMA position defensible in this case?

2. Is termination of treatment in this case active or passive euthanasia? Is it an act that causes Cruzan's death, or does it just allow her to die from natural causes? Does it cause death or permit death?

3. Suppose that there were no "clear and convincing evidence" that termination of treatment is what Cruzan would have wanted. Does this mean that termination is wrong in this case? On the other hand, suppose that there were such evidence. Does this mean that termination is not wrong?

6. *The Case of Baby Jane Doe*

In October 1983, Baby Jane Doe (as the infant was called by the court to protect her anonymity) was born with spina bifida and a host of other congenital defects. According to the doctors consulted by the parents, the child would be severely mentally retarded, be bedridden, and suffer considerable pain. After consultations with doctors and religious counselors, Mr. and Mrs. A (as the parents were called in the court documents) decided not to consent to lifesaving surgery.

At this point, a right-to-life activist lawyer tried to legally force lifesaving surgery for Baby Doe, but two New York appeals courts and a state children's agency decided not to override the parents' right to make a decision in the case. Then the U.S. Justice Department intervened in the case. It sued to obtain records from the University Hospital in Stony Brook, New York, to determine if the hospital had violated a federal law that forbids discrimination against the handicapped. Dr. C. Everett Koop, the U.S. surgeon general, appeared on television to express the view that the government has the moral obligation to intercede on behalf of such infants in order to protect their right to life.

Two weeks later, Federal District Judge Leonard Wexler threw out the Justice Department's unusual suit. Wexler found no discrimination. The hospital had been willing to do the surgery but had failed to do so because the parents refused to consent to the surgery. Wexler found the parents' decision to be a reasonable one in view of the circumstances.

The day after the ruling, the Justice Department appealed. On January 9, 1984, federal regulations were issued preventing federally funded hospitals from withholding treatment in such cases.

Do parents have a right to make life-or-death decisions for their defective children? Why or why not?

Do you agree with Dr. Koop that the government has a moral obligation to save the lives of such infants, even when their parents do not wish it? Explain your position.

If the government forces us to save the lives of defective infants like Baby Doe, then should it assume the responsibility for the cost of surgery, intensive care, and so on? If so, then how much money should be spent on this program? If not, then who is going to pay the bills?

7. Carolyn Heibrun

(Reported by Katha Pollitt in *The New York Times Magazine*, December 28, 2003. Also see Heibrun's book, *The Last Gift of Time* (1997).) Heibrun was a famous professor of modern British literature at Columbia University. She was the first woman to be given tenure at Columbia. She taught there for thirty-three years, resigning in 1992 to protest the fact that her male colleagues refused to promote a woman.

She committed suicide at the age of seventy-seven by overdosing with pills, and putting a plastic bag over her head so that she would be found without muss or fuss by a friend. She had long intended to kill herself at age seventy. In her book, *The Last Gift of Time*, she said, "Quit while you're ahead was, and is, my motto." "Having supposed the sixties would be downhill all the way, I had long held a determination to commit suicide

at seventy." When she killed herself (in 2003), she was not sick and her son said that she was not depressed. She had turned in an essay on Henry James the week before she died, and the December 2003 issue of *The Women's Review of Books* ran her essay on Patricia Highsmith.

In her review of Heibrun's life in *THE New York Times Magazine*, Katha Pollitt characterizes Heibrun's suicide as rational: that is, it was done to avoid something worse. Committing suicide to avoid execution or humiliation was practiced in Rome—consider Brutus, Cleopatra, or Seneca; it was also traditional in medieval Japan. But is it rational to commit suicide to avoid the difficulties of old age? Does concern about being a burden to your family justify suicide in old age, even if you are still in good health? What is your view?

8. Dr. Anna M. Pou

Dr. Pou, a respected medical professor, and two nurses, Lori L. Budo and Cheri A. Landry, have been accused of murdering four patients at Memorial Medical Center in New Orleans after Hurricane Katrina. The accusations were made by Charles C. Foti, Jr., the attorney general of Louisiana. He arrested Dr. Pou and the

two nurses on July 17, 2006. Each was booked on four counts of "principal to second-degree murder" and released on $100,000 bond.

Dr. Pou and the nurses were responsible for the care of seriously ill patients. It is claimed that they injected the four patients, ages sixty-two, sixty-six, eighty-nine, and ninety, with a lethal cocktail of morphine and midazolam hydrochloride. Both drugs are central nervous system depressants, and taken together, they can cause death. Three witnesses say that Dr. Pou told them she was going to inject a lethal dose into patients who were unlikely to survive.

After Hurricane Katrina hit, the Memorial Medical Center was a storm refuge for up to 2,000 people. After four days, the hospital was surrounded by floodwater. There was no electrical power, no water, and an almost complete lack of sanitation. The lifesaving medical equipment did not work. Food was running low. The heat was over 100 degrees. No relief was in sight. People were dying; later, a total of forty-five patients were found dead and decomposed. The hospital was not fully evacuated for nearly a week.

On September 24, 2006, Dr. Pou was interviewed by Morley Safer on *60 Minutes* about the allegations against her and the two nurses. She said:

You have to understand that there were very sick people in the hospital. You had this intense heat. We had the lack of all the tools that we normally used. And so people were dying from the horrible conditions. . . . I do not believe in euthanasia. . . . What I do believe in is comfort care and that means that we ensure that they do not suffer pain.

Dr. Pou does not deny administering the drugs. Her defense seems to be that her intention was to provide "comfort care" even if this caused death and that this is not the same as euthanasia. Is this an acceptable defense or not? Explain your answer.

It is standard medical practice to give patients morphine to reduce their pain, and it is not uncommon for terminally ill patients to die after receiving a high dose of morphine. Is this practice morally wrong? Does it amount to euthanasia? What is your view?

☙ SUGGESTED READINGS

For more information on euthanasia and suicide, see the International Task Force on Euthanasia and Assisted Suicide website (http://www.iaetf.org). For a website opposing euthanasia, see Euthanasia.com (http://www.euthanasia.com). A website sympathetic to euthanasia, having the slogan "Good Life, Good Death," is that of the Euthanasia World Directory (http://www.finalexit.org).

Stephen G. Potts, "Looking for the Exit Door: Killing and Caring in Modern Medicine," *Houston Law Review* 25 (1988): 504–511, is a physician who argues that the legalized practice of voluntary euthanasia will have many bad effects. Also, he denies that patients have any right to be killed.

Susan M. Wolf, "Gender, Feminism, and Death: Physician-Assisted Suicide," in Susan M. Wolf, ed., *Feminism and Bioethics: Beyond Reproduction* (Oxford: Oxford University Press, 1996), argues that if physician-assisted suicide and euthanasia are legalized in the United States, more women than men will die.

John Hardwig, *Is There a Duty to Die?* (London: Routledge, 2000), has several essays by Hardwig; critical commentaries by Nat Hentoff, Daniel Callahan, and others; and a response by Hardwig on dying responsibly.

Philippa Foot, "Killing and Letting Die," in Joy L. Garfield and Patricia Hennessy, eds., *Abortion: Moral and Legal Perspectives* (Amherst: The University of Massachusetts Press, 1984): 177–185, defends the controversial distinction between killing and letting die. She illustrates the distinction by comparing two cases. In Rescue 1, we can save five and let one die; and in Rescue 2, we can kill one in order to save five. She thinks it would be wrong to kill one to save five, but not wrong to let one die to save five. But the runaway trolley example, explained in the Problem Cases, presents a problem for her view.

John Harris, "The Survival Lottery," *Philosophy* 50 (1975): 87–95, tests our moral intuitions about killing and letting die with a thought experiment about a survival lottery where two or more patients can be saved by organ transplants from healthy innocent persons.

David J. Velleman, "A Right to Self-Termination," *Ethics* 109, no. 3 (April 1999): 606–628, holds that people have a value independent of their interests or choices, and that giving people a right to self-termination conflicts with this value.

T. M. Scanlon, "The Illusory Appeal of Double Effect," in T. M. Scanlon, *Moral Dimensions*

(Cambridge, MA: Belknap Press of Harvard University Press, 2008): 8–36, criticizes the doctrine of double effect. In some cases the doctrine is irrelevant, and in other cases it confuses the permissibility of an action with criticism of the agent's deliberation.

Felicia Ackerman, "'For Now Have I My Death': The 'Duty to Die' versus the Duty to Help the Ill Stay Alive," *Midwest Studies in Philosophy* 24 (2000): 172–185, replies to Hardwig.

James M. Humber and Robert F. Almeder, eds., *Is There a Duty to Die?* (Totowa, NJ: Humana Press, 2000), is a collection of articles by twelve philosophers critically responding to John Hardwig on the duty to die.

John D. Moreno, ed., *Arguing Euthanasia: The Controversy Over Mercy Killing, Assisted Suicide, and the "Right to Die"* (New York: Simon & Schuster, 1995), is a collection of articles on the Death with Dignity movement, including papers by Ronald Dworkin, Sidney Hook, and Daniel Callahan.

Gerald Dworkin, R. G. Frey, and Sissela Bok, *Euthanasia and Physician-Assisted Suicide: For and Against* (Cambridge, UK: Cambridge University Press, 1998). Dworkin and Frey argue that physician-assisted suicide is morally permissible and ought to be legal, while Bok is against legalizing physician-assisted suicide and active voluntary euthanasia.

Margaret P. Battin, Rosamond Rhoades, and Anita Silvers, eds., *Physician Assisted Suicide: Expanding the Debate* (London: Routledge, 1998), is a collection of essays on the legalization of physician-assisted suicide, with some for it and others against it.

Daniel Callahan, "Killing and Allowing to Die," *Hastings Center Report* 19 (January/February 1989): 5–6, defends the distinction between killing and allowing to die attacked by Rachels.

Derek Humphry's *Final Exit* (Hemlock Society, 1991) is a controversial book that tells you how to commit suicide or get assistance from a doctor. Critics of the book charge that there has been a 31 percent increase in plastic-bag suicides, the method recommended in the book.

St. Thomas Aquinas, *Summa Theologica* 2 (New York: Benziger Brothers, 1925), part 2, question 64, argues that suicide is unnatural and immoral.

Richard B. Brandt, "On the Morality and Rationality of Suicide," in *A Handbook for the Study of Suicide,* ed. Seymour Perlin (Oxford, UK: Oxford University Press, 1975), 61–76, maintains that it is not wrong, blameworthy, or irrational for a person suffering from a painful terminal illness to commit suicide. Brandt argues that it is morally right to actively terminate defective newborns in "Defective Newborns and the Morality of Termination," in *Infanticide and the Value of Life*, ed. Marvin Kohl (Amherst, NY: Prometheus Books, 1978), 46–57.

Arthur J. Dyck, "An Alternative to the Ethic of Euthanasia," in *To Live and to Let Die,* ed. R. H. Williams (New York: Springer-Verlag 1973), 98–112, attacks the ethic of euthanasia and defends an ethic of benemortasia, which forbids suicide but allows a person to refuse medical interventions that prolong dying.

J. Gay-Williams, "The Wrongfulness of Euthanasia," in *Intervention and Reflection: Basic Issues in Medical Ethics,* 5th ed., ed. Ronald Munson (Belmont, CA: Wadsworth, 1996), 168–171, argues that euthanasia is inherently wrong because it is unnatural, is contrary to self-interest, and has bad effects.

Philippa Foot, "The Problem of Abortion and the Doctrine of Double Effect," *Oxford Review* 5 (1967): 5–15, presents a classic discussion of the doctrine of double effect. She discusses euthanasia in "Euthanasia," *Philosophy and Public Affairs* 6 (Winter 1977): 85–112.

Jonathan Glover, *Causing Death and Saving Lives* (Harmondsworth, UK: Penguin, 1977), applies utilitarianism to the problem of euthanasia and to other problems of killing, such as abortion and capital punishment.

Infanticide and the Value of Life, ed. Marvin Kohl (New York: Prometheus Books, 1978), is an anthology that concentrates on the morality of euthanasia for severely defective newborns.

Killing and Letting Die, ed. Bonnie Steinbock (Englewood Cliffs, NJ: Prentice Hall, 1980), is a collection of readings that focus on the controversial distinction between killing and letting die.

Tom L. Beauchamp, "A Reply to Rachels on Active and Passive Euthanasia," in *Ethical Issues in Death and Dying*, ed. Tom L. Beauchamp and Seymour Perlin (Englewood Cliffs, NJ: Prentice Hall, 1978), 246–258, defends the moral significance of the distinction between active and passive euthanasia.

Thomas D. Sullivan, "Active and Passive Euthanasia: An Impertinent Distinction?" *Human Life Review* 3 (Summer 1977): 40–46, argues that Rachels's distinction between active and passive euthanasia is impertinent and irrelevant. Rachels's reply to Sullivan is titled "More Impertinent Distinctions," in *Biomedical Ethics,* ed. T. A. Mappes and J. S. Zembaty (New York: McGraw-Hill, 1981), 355–359.

John Ladd, "Positive and Negative Euthanasia," in *Ethical Issues Relating to Life and Death,* ed. John Ladd (Oxford, UK: Oxford University Press, 1979), 164–186, argues that no clear distinction can be made between killing and letting die but that they are not morally equivalent, either. His own position is that the distinction always depends on the context.

James Rachels, "Euthanasia," in *Matters of Life and Death,* 3rd ed., ed. Tom Regan (New York: Random House, 1993), 30–68, relates the history of euthanasia, discusses the arguments for and against active euthanasia, and concludes with a proposal for how to legalize active euthanasia.

James Rachels, *The End of Life: Euthanasia and Morality* (Oxford, UK: Oxford University Press, 1986), develops his view of euthanasia and defends it from criticism.

Robert Young, "Voluntary and Nonvoluntary Euthanasia," *The Monist* 59 (April 1976): 264–282, reviews a number of arguments used to show that voluntary active euthanasia is not justified and concludes that none of them is successful.

John A. Robertson, "Involuntary Euthanasia of Defective Newborns," *Stanford Law Review 27* (January 1975): 213–261, argues that the utilitarian defense of euthanasia for defective newborns does not succeed in showing that it is justified.

Robert F. Weir, *Selective Nontreatment of Handicapped Newborns: Moral Dilemmas in Neonatal Medicine* (Oxford, UK: Oxford University Press, 1984), discusses moral issues relating to the care and treatment of defective or handicapped newborns.

"Cruzan: Clear and Convincing?" *Hastings Center Report* 20 (September/October 1990): 5–11, has six articles discussing the *Cruzan* case.

Peter Senger, "Justifying Voluntary Euthanasia" *Practical Ethics*, 2nd ed. (Cambridge, UK: Cambridge University Press, 1993), 176–200, argues that voluntary euthanasia and assisted suicide are morally justified in cases of incurable disease or very distressing condition.

Capital Punishment

- **Introduction**
  - Factual Background
  - The Readings
  - Philosophical Issues

Lessons from Death Row inmates (David R. Dow Dow

1) Death Row the final 24 hrs

INTRODUCTION

Factual Background

Since 1976 (including 2009), there have been 1,188 executions in the United States. There were only eleven executions in the years 1976 to 1983. After that, the number of executions increased to a high of ninety-eight in 1998. Since then, the number dropped to fifty-two executions in 2009.

In 2005, 2,148 people were executed worldwide. More than 90 percent of the executions occurred in China, Iran, Saudi Arabia, and the United States. There were ninety-four in Iran, eighty-six in Saudi Arabia, and sixty in the United States.

In the United States, only eleven women have been executed since 1976. The case of one of them, a thirty-eight-year-old born-again Christian named Karla Faye Tucker, received worldwide attention. (See the Problem Cases.) As for minorities, an almost equal number of whites and blacks have been executed since 1930, even though blacks constituted only about a tenth of the U.S. population during this period. A recent statistical study in Philadelphia found that for similar crimes, blacks received the death penalty at a 38 percent higher rate than all others.

As of July 1, 2009, there were a total of 3,279 prisoners on death row waiting to be executed. This number includes those being held by the U.S. government and the U.S. military. Of these, 1,364 were black, 379 were Hispanic, 1,457 were white, and 77 were classified as "other." There were fifty-two women, including one who used to be a man.

In 2009, thirty-six states had the death penalty. In March 2009, New Mexico voted to abolish the death penalty. New York's death penalty law was declared unconstitutional in 2004 and has not been replaced. The death penalty is also used by the U.S. government and by the U.S. military.

Since 1973, more than 120 innocent people have been sentenced to death, and a number of inmates now on death row claim that they are innocent. Seventeen inmates on death row have been proven innocent and exonerated by DNA testing. Since 1973, more than 100 prisoners have been released from death row after presentation of evidence of their innocence. On average, these innocent inmates spent about nine years in prison before release. In 2003, Governor George Ryan of Illinois commuted all of Illinois's death sentences. As one of his reasons for eliminating death sentences, he cited the fact that seventeen men had been wrongly convicted, including one who was unjustly imprisoned for fifteen years. (See the Problem Cases.)

The most common method of execution is lethal injection. All thirty-six states that have the death penalty use this method or allow it to be used as an alternative to other methods. Electrocution is used in nine states, and the gas chamber in eleven states. Hanging is used in three states, and the firing squad in two states.

Execution by lethal injection is not always quick or painless. Usually two intravenous lines are inserted, one in each arm. The procedure can be botched if a suitable vein cannot be found. The procedure involves injecting three different drugs in sequence: a barbiturate causing unconsciousness, a muscle relaxant producing paralysis, and potassium chloride to stop the heart. There can be a violent reaction to these drugs. Also, the dosage may not be strong enough to cause death. It took thirty-four minutes to kill Angel Diaz by lethal injection; as a result, Florida Governor Jeb Bush suspended all executions.

In the case of *Baze v. Rees* (2008), the U.S. Supreme Court ruled by a vote of 7-to-2 that lethal injection as it is done in most states is constitutional. The Court rejected a challenge to the three-drug procedure used in Kentucky, a procedure identical to the method used in most states.

The death penalty is expensive. It costs states millions of dollars to win a death penalty verdict, which requires a second expensive trial, new witnesses, and long voir dire sessions for jury selection. Death rows require extra security and hence incur high maintenance costs. California spends $114 million per year beyond the cost of life imprisonment for death-row convicts. The state has executed thirteen people since 1976. Counting all the costs involved, the total for each execution is $250 million. Florida spends an extra $51 million a year keeping inmates on death row, money that could be saved if the state abolished the death penalty. The state spends $24 million for each execution; this figure is based on the forty-four executions in Florida since 1976. Maryland has spent about $186 million for five executions between 1978 and 1999. In Texas, the cost per case is $2.3 million, but that is still three times the cost of keeping a criminal in maximum security for forty years. In North Carolina, the cost is $2.16 million per execution over the cost of life in prison without parole. In 2003, the state of Kansas issued a report saying that capital cases are 70 percent more expensive than comparable noncapital cases, including incarceration. Various studies in North Carolina, Texas, Florida, and other states show that the total costs of the death penalty exceeded the costs of life without parole sentences by about 38 percent.

The Eighth Amendment to the Constitution of the United States prohibits cruel and unusual punishment. For example, the medieval punishment of cutting off the hands of thieves seems to be cruel and unusual punishment. Is the death penalty another example of cruel and unusual punishment, and thus unconstitutional? The U.S. Supreme Court has given contradictory answers, saying it is unconstitutional in the cases of *Furman* (1972) and *Woodson* (1976), and then reversing itself and affirming that it is constitutional in *Gregg v. Georgia* (1976).

To be more specific, in the case of *Furman v. Georgia* (1972), the U.S. Supreme Court ruled (by a mere 5-to-4 majority) that the death penalty was unconstitutional because it was being administered in an arbitrary and capricious manner. Juries were allowed to impose the death sentence without any explicit guidelines or standards, and the result was that blacks were much more likely to receive the death penalty than whites.

After the *Furman* decision, states wishing to retain the death penalty reacted in two ways. One was to correct the arbitrary discretion of juries by making the death penalty mandatory for certain crimes. But in *Woodson v. North Carolina* (1976), the Court ruled (again by a 5-to-4 majority) that mandatory death sentences were unconstitutional.

The second attempt to counter the objection raised in *Furman* was to provide standards for juries. Georgia specified in its law ten statutory aggravating circumstances, one of which the jury had to find beyond reasonable doubt in order to render a death sentence. This second approach proved to be successful, for in *Gregg v. Georgia* (1976) the majority ruled, with Justices Marshall and Brennan dissenting, that the death penalty is not unconstitutional for the crime of murder, provided there are safeguards against any arbitrary or capricious imposition by juries.

In the case of *Atkins v. Virginia* (2002), the Supreme Court ruled that the execution of those with mental retardation is cruel and unusual punishment prohibited by the Eighth Amendment. Prior to the decision, eighteen states and the federal government prohibited such executions.

The Readings

The first reading is taken from *Gregg v. Georgia* (1976), the landmark decision legalizing the death penalty. In their majority opinion, Justices Stewart, Powell, and Stevens try to explain why the death penalty is not cruel and unusual, and thus not in violation of the Eighth Amendment. They begin with an explanation of the concept of cruel and unusual. In their view, a punishment is cruel and unusual if it either fails to accord with evolving standards of decency or fails to accord with the dignity of humans that is the basic concept underlying the Eighth Amendment. This second stipulation rules out excessive punishment that involves unnecessary pain or is disproportionate to the crime. They argue that the death penalty does not satisfy either of these stipulations. It is acceptable to the majority of people. (A Gallup poll in 2006 found that 65 percent supported the death penalty and 32 percent opposed it.) In 1976, thirty-five states had the death penalty, and in 2007 there were thirty-eight capital-punishment states. Furthermore, the Justices argue, the death penalty is not excessive because it achieves two important social purposes, retribution and deterrence.

To fully understand the appeal to retribution, it is necessary to examine the theory on which it is based, namely, retributivism. The classical formulation of this theory is given by Immanuel Kant in the readings. According to Kant, the only justification for punishing a person is guilt. If a person is guilty of a crime, then justice requires that he or she be punished; if a person is not guilty, then no punishment is justified. In other words, guilt is both a necessary and a sufficient condition for justified punishment. Furthermore, Kant's view is that the punishment must fit the crime (or be proportionate to the crime) according to the biblical principle of retaliation (*lex talionis*) that says "eye for eye, tooth for tooth, life for life." Now, what punishment fits the crime of murder, using this principle? Kant insists that death, and only death, is the proper punishment for murder; no other punishment will satisfy the requirements of legal justice.

The other purpose of punishment that the Justices appeal to in the majority opinion in *Gregg* is deterrence. The Justices admit that the statistical evidence for deterrence seems inconclusive. Nevertheless, the Justices still believe that the death penalty is a deterrent to carefully contemplated murders, such as murder for hire and murder by a person already in prison.

Critics present various objections to capital punishment. It is intentionally killing a person, and as such it is wrong unless proven otherwise. Thus, the burden of proof is on those who want to defend it. It results in the execution of innocent people, and this injustice cannot be corrected. It is unfairly applied to minorities and the poor. Contrary to what the Supreme Court Justices say, critics claim there is substantial evidence that capital punishment is not a better deterrent than life imprisonment, and in fact there is evidence that it acts as a counterdeterrent—that is, that it motivates suicidal people to commit murder. The 2002 FBI *Uniform Crime Report* says that the South accounts for more than 80 percent of executions but also has the highest murder rate. By contrast, the Northeast, which carries out less than 1 percent of all executions in the country, has the lowest murder rate.

Ernest van den Haag replies to some of the objections raised by critics. The fact that the death penalty is applied in a discriminatory or capricious fashion is irrelevant to its justice or morality, according to van den Haag. All that matters is whether the person to be executed deserves the punishment. If it is morally justified, then its distribution is irrelevant. Furthermore, the application of capital punishment is no more or less unjust than any other punishment. As for the fact that innocent people are executed, van den Haag points out that many human activities (such as trucking) cost the lives of innocent bystanders, and we do not give up these activities just because innocent people die. He agrees with the Supreme Court Justices that there is no conclusive statistical evidence that the death penalty is a better deterrent than alternative punishments. But, also like the Justices, he believes that death is feared more than imprisonment, and for this reason it deters some murderers who are not deterred by imprisonment. He adds, using a version of the best-bet argument (as I shall call it), that it is better to save the lives of a few prospective victims by deterring their murderers than to preserve the lives of convicted murderers because of the possibility that executing them will not deter others. The victim's lives are valuable and the lives of murderers are not. Instead of risking innocent lives by not executing, we should end the worthless lives of murderers, and bet that this will save some innocent lives. Van den Haag goes on to assert that the costs of the death penalty are not as important as doing justice, and that the penalty is not inhuman or degrading or inconsistent with human dignity. It is the only fitting retribution for heinous crimes like murder.

Jeffrey Reiman is against the death penalty. He agrees with Kant that the law of retaliation, *lex talionis*, is an undeniable element of justice, and that it justifies executing some murderers. However, he does not agree that murderers *must* die. Instead, we can and should use a lesser punishment such as imprisonment, which is not so horrible. To help us see that a lesser punishment satisfies justice, he remarks that we do not rape rapists. Rapists are not raped but put in prison. He agrees with van den Haag that the death penalty would be justified if needed to deter future murders. But statistical studies give no evidence that capital punishment deters murder more effectively than prison sentences. In fact, some evidence seems to show that the death penalty has no deterrent effect. Reiman also rejects the commonsense argument that people will be more deterred by death than by imprisonment. Again, the evidence seems to show that a life sentence can do all the deterring that can be done. Reiman argues that a civilized society should refrain from using the death penalty in principle because it is cruel and horrible. In his view, it is in the same category as torture, something that a civilized people will not do even to give evil people what they deserve. Like torture, execution is horrible because the victim is completely subject to another's power and because of the intense pain, either physical or psychological or both. Furthermore, Reiman thinks that the death penalty is bad in practice because it is imposed in arbitrary and discriminatory ways; for example, it is applied to the poor more than the rich.

Philosophical Issues

How do we justify punishment? This is the basic issue at the heart of the debate about capital punishment. There seem to be two main theories about this, utilitarianism and retributivism.

Utilitarians justify punishment by appealing to good consequences, such as rehabilitation, protection of society, and deterrence of crime. Of course, capital punishment does not rehabilitate the person killed, and imprisonment would do the job of protecting society from criminals. Capital punishment is not necessary for protection of society. It seems, then, that deterrence of crime is the only possible justification of the death penalty for utilitarians, and indeed there has been much debate about the deterrence value of the death penalty.

Three main arguments have been used to demonstrate that execution deters criminals. First, there is the appeal to statistics. Even though the Supreme Court Justices in the *Gregg* decision and van den Haag think that the statistics are inconclusive, critics do not agree. They argue that there is evidence refuting the claim that capital punishment is a better deterrent than life imprisonment. According to a survey of the former and present presidents of the country's top academic criminological societies, 84 percent of these experts rejected the claim that the death penalty acts as a deterrent to murder.

Second, there are intuitive or commonsense arguments used by both the Supreme Court Justices and van den Haag. The Justices think that those who calculate their crimes will be deterred, and van den Haag believes that those who fear death will be motivated to avoid it. Against this, critics claim that instead of being deterred, suicidal people will be motivated to commit capital crimes. As we have seen, Reiman thinks the argument is based on unwarranted assumptions.

Third, there is van den Haag's best-bet argument, the argument that given uncertainties about whether execution deters, the best bet is to execute, for this involves gambling with guilty lives rather than innocent ones. The bet, of course, is that the executions will deter and thus save innocent lives. Critics deny the uncertainty; they claim that we have substantial evidence that execution does not deter better than life imprisonment. Reiman accepts the brutalization hypothesis that murders increase following executions rather than decrease. So, if we want to save innocent lives, the best bet is to not execute murderers.

The other theory that is the focus of debate is retributivism. There are at least two different retributive principles, *lex talionis* and the principle of proportionality. The principle of proportionality says that the punishment should fit the crime or be proportional to the crime; therefore, a serious crime should receive a harsh punishment. No doubt murder is a serious crime, but is death the only punishment that fits this crime, as Kant says? Why isn't life imprisonment without parole a punishment that fits this crime, too? The trouble with the principle of proportionality is that it does not tell us which punishments fit which crimes. Not only is this a problem for the crime of murder, it is also a problem for crimes such as rape and torture and treason. Perhaps these crimes should be punished by execution, too. Or maybe death is not harsh enough; perhaps those crimes should be punished by solitary confinement or castration or even torture.

The biblical principle of *lex talionis* requires us to do to the criminal what he or she has done, "an eye for an eye." This principle is attacked by critics. They claim that this principle does not justify capital punishment because of the simple fact that most murderers are sent to prison, not executed. Clearly, we think that many crimes of murder do not deserve the death penalty; for example, we do not have the death sentence for homicides that are unpremeditated or accidental. Another objection is that we do have the death sentence for nonhomicidal crimes such as treason. This shows that the death sentence can be justified for crimes other than murder.

Gregg v. Georgia (1976)

THE U.S. SUPREME COURT

Potter Stewart (1915–1985) and Lewis F. Powell, Jr. (1908–1998) served as associate Justices of the U.S. Supreme Court. John Paul Stevens retired from the Court in June 2010. Thurgood Marshall (1908–1993) retired from the Court in 1991; he was the first black ever to be appointed.

The main issue before the Court in the case of *Gregg v. Georgia* (1976) was whether the death penalty violates the Eighth Amendment prohibition of cruel and unusual punishment. The majority of the Court, with Justice Marshall and Justice Brennan dissenting, held that the death penalty does not violate the Eighth Amendment because it is in accord with contemporary standards of decency. It serves both a deterrent and a retributive purpose, and in the case of the Georgia law being reviewed it is no longer arbitrarily applied.

In his dissenting opinion, Justice Marshall objects that the death sentence is excessive because a less severe penalty—life imprisonment—would accomplish the legitimate purposes of punishment. In reply to the claim that the death sentence is necessary for deterrence, Marshall asserts that the available evidence shows that this is not the case. As for the appeal to retribution, Marshall argues that the justification for the death penalty is not consistent with human dignity.

Source: U.S. Supreme Court, *Gregg v. Georgia*, 428 U.S. 153 (1976).

The issue in this case is whether the imposition of the sentence of death for the crime of murder under the law of Georgia violates the Eighth and Fourteenth Amendments.

I

The petitioner, Troy Gregg, was charged with committing armed robbery and murder. In accordance with Georgia procedure in capital cases, the trial was in two stages, a guilt stage and a sentencing stage. . . .

. . . The jury found the petitioner guilty of two counts . . . of murder.

At the penalty stage, which took place before the same jury . . . the trial judge instructed the jury that it could recommend either a death sentence or a life prison sentence on each count. . . . The jury returned verdicts of death on each count.

The Supreme Court of Georgia affirmed the convictions and the imposition of the death sentences for murder. . . . The death sentences imposed for armed robbery, however, were vacated on the grounds that the death penalty had rarely been imposed in Georgia for that offense. . . .

II

. . . The Georgia statute, as amended after our decision in *Furman v. Georgia* (1972), retains the death penalty for six categories of crime: murder, kidnapping for ransom or where the victim is harmed, armed robbery, rape, treason, and aircraft hijacking. . . .

III

We address initially the basic contention that the punishment of death for the crime of murder is, under all circumstances, "cruel and unusual" in violation of the Eighth and Fourteenth Amendments of the Constitution. In Part IV of this opinion, we will consider the sentence of death imposed under the Georgia statutes at issue in this case.

The Court on a number of occasions has both assumed and asserted the constitutionality of capital punishment. In several cases that assumption provided a necessary foundation for the decision, as the Court was asked to decide whether a particular method of carrying out a capital sentence would be allowed to stand under the Eighth Amendment. But until *Furman v. Georgia* (1972), the Court never confronted squarely the fundamental claim that the punishment of death always, regardless of the enormity of the offense or the procedure followed in imposing the sentence, is cruel and unusual punishment in violation of the Constitution. Although this issue was presented and addressed in *Furman*, it was not resolved by the Court. Four Justices would have held that capital punishment is not unconstitutional *per se*; two Justices would have reached the opposite conclusion; and three Justices, while agreeing that the statutes then before the Court were invalid as applied, left open the question whether such punishment may ever be imposed. We now hold that the punishment of death does not invariably violate the Constitution.

A

The history of the prohibition of "cruel and unusual" punishment already has been reviewed at length. The phrase first appeared in the English Bill of Rights of 1689, which was drafted by Parliament at the accession of William and Mary. The English version appears to have been directed against punishments unauthorized by statute and beyond the jurisdiction of the sentencing court, as well as those disproportionate to the offense involved. The American draftsmen, who adopted the English phrasing in drafting the Eighth Amendment, were primarily concerned, however, with proscribing "tortures" and other "barbarous" methods of punishment.

In the earliest cases raising Eighth Amendment claims, the Court focused on particular methods of execution to determine whether they were too cruel to pass constitutional muster. The constitutionality of the sentence of death itself was not at issue, and the criterion used to evaluate the mode of execution was its similarity to "torture" and other "barbarous" methods. . . .

But the Court has not confined the prohibition embodied in the Eighth Amendment to "barbarous" methods that were generally outlawed in the 18th century. Instead, the Amendment has been interpreted in a flexible and dynamic manner. The Court early recognized that "a principle to be vital must be capable of wider application than the mischief which gave it birth." Thus the clause forbidding "cruel and unusual" punishments "is not fastened to the obsolete but may acquire meaning as public opinion becomes enlightened by a humane justice." . . .

It is clear from the foregoing precedents that the Eighth Amendment has not been regarded as a static concept. As Mr. Chief Justice Warren said, in an oft quoted phrase, "[t]he Amendment must draw its meaning from the evolving standards of decency that mark the progress of a maturing society." Thus, an assessment of contemporary values concerning the infliction of a challenged sanction is relevant to the application of the Eighth Amendment. As we develop below more fully, this assessment does not call for a subjective judgment. It requires, rather, that we look to objective indicia that reflect the public attitude toward a given sanction.

But our cases also make clear that public perceptions of standards of decency with respect to criminal sanctions are not conclusive. A penalty also must accord with "the dignity of man," which is the "basic concept underlying the Eighth Amendment." This means, at least, that the punishment not be "excessive." When a form of punishment in the abstract (in this case, whether capital punishment may ever be imposed as a sanction for murder) rather than in the particular (the propriety of death as a penalty to be applied to a specific defendant for a specific crime) is under consideration, the inquiry into "excessiveness" has two aspects. First, the punishment must not involve the unnecessary and wanton infliction of pain. Second, the punishment must not be grossly out of proportion to the severity of the crime.

B

Of course, the requirements of the Eighth Amendment must be applied with an awareness of the limited role to be played by the courts.

This does not mean that judges have no role to play, for the Eighth Amendment is a restraint upon the exercise of legislative power. . . .

But, while we have an obligation to ensure that constitutional bounds are not over-reached, we may not act as judges as we might as legislators. . . .

Therefore, in assessing a punishment selected by a democratically elected legislature against the constitutional measure, we presume its validity. We may not require the legislature to select the least severe penalty possible so long as the penalty selected is not cruelly inhumane or disproportionate to the crime involved. And a heavy burden rests on those who would attack the judgment of the representatives of the people.

This is true in part because the constitutional test is intertwined with an assessment of contemporary standards and the legislative judgment weighs heavily in ascertaining such standards. "[I]n a democratic society legislatures, not courts, are constituted to respond to the will and consequently the moral values of the people."

The deference we owe to the decisions of the state legislatures under our federal system is enhanced where the specification of punishments is concerned, for "these are peculiarly questions of legislative policy." Caution is necessary lest this Court become, "under the aegis of the Cruel and Unusual Punishment Clause, the ultimate arbiter of the standards of criminal responsibility . . . throughout the country." A decision that a given punishment is impermissible under the Eighth Amendment cannot be reversed short of a constitutional amendment. The ability of the people to express their preference through the normal democratic processes, as well as through ballot referenda, is shut off. Revisions cannot be made in the light of further experience.

C

In the discussion to this point we have sought to identify the principles and considerations that guide a court in addressing an Eighth Amendment claim. We now consider specifically whether the sentence of death for the crime of murder is a *per se* violation of the Eighth and Fourteenth

Amendments to the Constitution. We note first that history and precedent strongly support a negative answer to this question.

The imposition of the death penalty for the crime of murder has a long history of acceptance both in the United States and in England. . . .

It is apparent from the text of the Constitution itself that the existence of capital punishment was accepted by the Framers. At the time the Eighth Amendment was ratified, capital punishment was a common sanction in every State. Indeed, the First Congress of the United States enacted legislation providing death as the penalty for specified crimes. . . .

For nearly two centuries, this Court, repeatedly and often expressly, has recognized that capital punishment is not invalid *per se*. . . .

Four years ago, the petitioners in *Furman* and its companion cases predicated their argument primarily upon the asserted proposition that standards of decency had evolved to the point where capital punishment no longer could be tolerated. The petitioners in those cases said, in effect, that the evolutionary process had come to an end, and that standards of decency required that the Eighth Amendment be construed finally as prohibiting capital punishment for any crime regardless of its depravity and impact on society. This view was accepted by two Justices. Three other Justices were unwilling to go so far; focusing on the procedures by which convicted defendants were selected for the death penalty rather than on the actual punishment inflicted, they joined in the conclusion that the statutes before the Court were constitutionally invalid.

The petitioners in the capital cases before the Court today renew the "standards of decency" argument, but developments during the four years since *Furman* have undercut substantially the assumptions upon which their argument rested. Despite the continuing debate, dating back to the nineteenth century, over the morality and utility of capital punishment, it is now evident that a large proportion of American society continues to regard it as an appropriate and necessary criminal sanction.

The most marked indication of society's endorsement of the death penalty for murder is the legislative response to *Furman*. The legislatures of at least thirty-five States have enacted new statutes that provide for the death penalty for at least some crimes that result in the death of another person. And the Congress of the United States, in 1974, enacted a statute providing the death penalty for aircraft piracy that results in death. These recently adopted statutes have attempted to address the concerns expressed by the Court in *Furman* primarily (i) by specifying the factors to be weighed and the procedures to be followed in deciding when to impose a capital sentence, or (ii) by making the death penalty mandatory for specified crimes. But all of the post-*Furman* statutes make clear that capital punishment itself has not been rejected by the elected representatives of the people. . . .

The jury also is a significant and reliable objective index of contemporary values because it is so directly involved. The Court has said that "one of the most important functions any jury can perform in making . . . a selection [between life imprisonment and death for a defendant convicted in a capital case] is to maintain a link between contemporary community values and the penal system." It may be true that evolving standards have influenced juries in recent decades to be more discriminating in imposing the sentence of death. But the relative infrequency of jury verdicts imposing death sentence does not indicate rejection of capital punishment *per se*. Rather, the reluctance of juries in many cases to impose the sentence may well reflect the humane feeling that this most irrevocable of sanctions should be reserved for a small number of extreme cases. Indeed, the actions of juries in many states since *Furman* are fully compatible with the legislative judgments, reflected in the new statutes, as to the continued utility and necessity of capital punishment in appropriate cases. At the close of 1974 at least 254 persons had been sentenced to death since *Furman*, and by the end of March 1976, more than 460 persons were subject to death sentences.

As we have seen, however, the Eighth Amendment demands more than that a challenged punishment be acceptable to contemporary society. The Court also must ask whether it comports with the basic concept of human dignity at the core of the amendment. Although we cannot "invalidate a category of penalties because we deem less severe penalties adequate to serve the ends of penology," the sanction imposed cannot be so totally without penological justification that it results in the gratuitous infliction of suffering.

The death penalty is said to serve two principal social purposes: retribution and deterrence of capital crimes by prospective offenders.[1]

In part, capital punishment is an expression of society's moral outrage at particularly offensive conduct. This function may be unappealing to many, but it is essential in an ordered society that asks its citizens to rely on legal processes rather than self-help to vindicate their wrongs.

The instinct for retribution is part of the nature of man, and channeling that instinct in the administration of criminal justice serves an important purpose in promoting the stability of a society governed by law. When people begin to believe that organized society is unwilling or unable to impose upon criminal offenders the punishment they "deserve," then there are sown the seeds of anarchy—of self-help, vigilante justice, and lynch law. *Furman v. Georgia* (Stewart, J., concurring).

Retribution is no longer the dominant objective of the criminal law, but neither is it a forbidden objective nor one inconsistent with our respect for the dignity of men. Indeed, the decision that capital punishment may be the appropriate sanction in extreme cases is an expression of the community's belief that certain crimes are themselves so grievous an affront to humanity that the only adequate response may be the penalty of death.

Statistical attempts to evaluate the worth of the death penalty as a deterrent to crimes of potential offenders have occasioned a great deal of debate. The results simply have been inconclusive. . . .

Although some of the studies suggest that the death penalty may not function as a significantly greater deterrent than lesser penalties, there is no convincing empirical evidence either supporting or refuting this view. We may nevertheless assume safely that there are murderers, such as those who act in passion, for whom the threat of death has little or no deterrent effect. But for many others, the death penalty undoubtedly is a significant deterrent. There are carefully contemplated murders, such as murder for hire, where the possible penalty of death may well enter into the cold calculus that precedes the decision to act. And there are some categories of murder, such as murder by a life prisoner, where other sanctions may not be adequate.

The value of capital punishment as a deterrent of crime is a complex factual issue the resolution of which properly rests with the legislatures, which can evaluate the results of statistical studies in terms of their own local conditions and with a flexibility of approach that is not available to the courts. Indeed, many of the post-*Furman* statutes reflect just such a responsible effort to define those crimes and those criminals for which capital punishment is most probably an effective deterrent.

In sum, we cannot say that the judgment of the Georgia Legislature that capital punishment may be necessary in some cases is clearly wrong. Considerations of federalism, as well as respect for the ability of a legislature to evaluate, in terms of its particular State, the moral consensus concerning the death penalty and its social utility as a sanction, require us to conclude, in the absence of more convincing evidence, that the infliction of death as a punishment for murder is not without justification and thus is not constitutionally severe.

Finally, we must consider whether the punishment of death is disproportionate in relation to the crime for which it is imposed. There is no question that death as a punishment is unique in its severity and irrevocability. When a defendant's life is at stake, the Court has been particularly sensitive to insure that every safeguard is observed. But we are concerned here only with the imposition of capital punishment for the crime of murder, and when a life has been taken deliberately

---

[1]Another purpose that has been discussed is the incapacitation of dangerous criminals and the consequent prevention of crimes that they may otherwise commit in the future.

by the offender,[2] we cannot say that the punishment is invariably disproportionate to the crime. It is an extreme sanction, suitable to the most extreme of crimes.

We hold that the death penalty is not a form of punishment that may never be imposed, regardless of the circumstances of the offense, regardless of the character of the offender, and regardless of the procedure followed in reaching the decision to impose it.

IV

We now consider whether Georgia may impose the death penalty on the petitioner in this case.

A

While *Furman* did not hold that the infliction of the death penalty *per se* violates the Constitution's ban on cruel and unusual punishments, it did recognize that the penalty of death is different in kind from any other punishment imposed under our system of criminal justice. Because of the uniqueness of the death penalty, *Furman* held that it could not be imposed under sentencing procedures that created a substantial risk that it would be inflicted in an arbitrary and capricious manner. . . .

Furman mandates that where discretion is afforded a sentencing body on a matter so grave as the determination of whether a human life should be taken or spared, that discretion must be suitably directed and limited so as to minimize the risk of wholly arbitrary and capricious action.

It is certainly not a novel proposition that discretion in the area of sentencing be exercised in an informed manner. We have long recognized that "[f]or the determination of sentences, justice generally requires . . . that there be taken into account the circumstances of the offense together with the character and propensities of the offender." . . .

Jury sentencing has been considered desirable in capital cases in order "to maintain a link between contemporary community values and the penal system—a link without which the determination of punishment could hardly reflect 'the evolving standards of decency that mark the progress of a maturing society.'" But it creates special problems. Much of the information that is relevant to the sentencing decision may have no relevance to the question of guilt, or may even be extremely prejudicial to a fair determination of that question. This problem, however, is scarcely insurmountable. Those who have studied the question suggest that a bifurcated procedure—one in which the question of sentence is not considered until the determination of guilt has been made—is the best answer. . . . When a human life is at stake and when the jury must have information prejudicial to the question of guilt but relevant to the question of penalty in order to impose a rational sentence, a bifurcated system is more likely to ensure elimination of the constitutional deficiencies identified in *Furman*.

But the provision of relevant information under fair procedural rules is not alone sufficient to guarantee that the information will be properly used in the imposition of punishment, especially if sentencing is performed by a jury. Since the members of a jury will have had little, if any, previous experience in sentencing, they are unlikely to be skilled in dealing with the information they are given. To the extent that this problem is inherent in jury sentencing, it may not be totally correctable. It seems clear, however, that the problem will be alleviated if the jury is given guidance regarding the factors about the crime and the defendant that the State, representing organized society, deems particularly relevant to the sentencing decision. . . .

While some have suggested that standards to guide a capital jury's sentencing deliberations are impossible to formulate, the fact is that such standards have been developed. When the drafters of the Model Penal Code faced this problem, they concluded "that it is within the realm of possibility to point to the main circumstances of aggravation and of mitigation that should be weighed *and weighed against each other* when they are presented

---

[2]We do not address here the question whether the taking of the criminal's life is a proportionate sanction where no victim has been deprived of life—for example, when capital punishment is imposed for rape, kidnapping, or armed robbery that does not result in the death of any human being.

in a concrete case."[3] While such standards are by necessity somewhat general, they do provide guidance to the sentencing authority and thereby reduce the likelihood that it will impose a sentence that fairly can be called capricious or arbitrary. Where the sentencing authority is required to specify the factors it relied upon in reaching its decision, the further safeguard of meaningful appellate review is available to ensure that death sentences are not imposed capriciously or in a freakish manner.

---

[3]The Model Penal Code proposes the following standards:
(3) Aggravating Circumstances.
(a) The murder was committed by a convict under sentence of imprisonment.
(b) The defendant was previously convicted of another murder or of a felony involving the use or threat of violence to the person.
(c) At the time the murder was committed the defendant also committed another murder.
(d) The defendant knowingly created a great risk of death to many persons.
(e) The murder was committed while the defendant was engaged or was an accomplice in the commission of, or an attempt to commit, or flight after committing or attempting to commit robbery, rape or deviate sexual intercourse by force or threat of force, arson, burglary or kidnapping.
(f) The murder was committed for the purpose of avoiding or preventing a lawful arrest or effecting an escape from lawful custody.
(g) The murder was committed for pecuniary gain.
(h) The murder was especially heinous, atrocious or cruel, manifesting exceptional depravity.
(4) Mitigating Circumstances.
(a) The defendant has no significant history of prior criminal activity.
(b) The murder was committed while the defendant was under the influence of extreme mental or emotional disturbance.
(c) The victim was a participant in the defendant's homicide conduct or consented to the homicidal act.
(d) The murder was committed under circumstances which the defendant believed to provide a moral justification or extenuation for his conduct.
(e) The defendant was an accomplice in a murder committed by another person and his participation in the homicide act was relatively minor.
(f) The defendant acted under duress or under the domination of another person.
(g) At the time of the murder, the capacity of the defendant to appreciate the criminality (wrongfulness) of his conduct or to conform his conduct to the requirements of law was impaired as a result of mental disease or defect or intoxication.
(h) The youth of the defendant at the time of the crime. (ALI Model Penal Code §210.6, Proposed Official Draft 1962).

In summary, the concerns expressed in *Furman* that the penalty of death not be imposed in an arbitrary or capricious manner can be met by a carefully drafted statute that ensures that the sentencing authority is given adequate information and guidance. As a general proposition these concerns are best met by a system that provides for a bifurcated proceeding at which the sentencing authority is apprised of the information relevant to the imposition of sentence and provided with standards to guide its use of the information.

We do not intend to suggest that only the above-described procedures would be permissible under *Furman* or that any sentencing system constructed along these general lines would inevitably satisfy the concerns of *Furman*, for each distinct system must be examined on an individual basis. Rather, we have embarked upon this general exposition to make clear that it is possible to construct capital-sentencing systems capable of meeting *Furman*'s constitutional concerns.

B

We now turn to consideration of the constitutionality of Georgia's capital-sentencing procedures. In the wake of *Furman*, Georgia amended its capital punishment statute, but chose not to narrow the scope of its murder provisions. Thus, now as before *Furman*, in Georgia "[a] person commits murder when he unlawfully and with malice aforethought, either express or implied, causes the death of another human being." All persons convicted of murder "shall be punished by death or by imprisonment for life."

Georgia did act, however, to narrow the class of murderers subject to capital punishment by specifying ten statutory aggravating circumstances, one of which must be found by the jury to exist beyond a reasonable doubt before a death sentence can ever be imposed. In addition, the jury is authorized to consider any other appropriate aggravating or mitigating circumstances. The jury is not required to find any mitigating circumstance in order to make a recommendation of mercy that is binding on the trial court, but it must find a *statutory* aggravating circumstance before recommending a sentence of death.

These procedures require the jury to consider the circumstances of the crime and the criminal before it recommends sentence. No longer can a Georgia jury do as *Furman*'s jury did: reach a finding of the defendant's guilt and then, without guidance or direction, decide whether he should live or die. Instead, the jury's attention is directed to the specific circumstances of the crime: Was it committed in the course of another capital felony? Was it committed for money? Was it committed on a peace officer or judicial officer? Was it committed in a particularly heinous way or in a manner that endangered the lives of many persons? In addition, the jury's attention is focused on the characteristics of the person who committed the crime: Does he have a record of prior convictions for capital offenses? Are there any special facts about this defendant that mitigate against imposing capital punishment (e.g., his youth, the extent of his cooperation with the police, his emotional state at the time of the crime)? As a result, while some jury discretion still exists, "the discretion to be exercised is controlled by clear and objective standards so as to produce nondiscriminatory application."

As an important additional safeguard against arbitrariness and caprice, the Georgia statutory scheme provides for automatic appeal of all death sentences to the State's Supreme Court. That court is required by statute to review each sentence of death and determine whether it was imposed under the influence of passion or prejudice, whether the evidence supports the jury's finding of statutory aggravating circumstance, and whether the sentence is disproportionate compared to those sentences imposed in similar cases.

In short, Georgia's new sentencing procedures require[,] as a prerequisite to the imposition of the death penalty, specific jury findings as to the circumstances of the crime or the character of the defendant. Moreover, to guard further against a situation comparable to that presented in *Furman*, the Supreme Court of Georgia compares each death sentence with the sentences imposed on similarly situated defendants to ensure that the sentence of death in a particular case is not disproportionate. On their face these procedures seem to satisfy the concerns of *Furman*. No

longer should there be "no meaningful basis for distinguishing the few cases in which [the death penalty] is imposed from the many cases in which it is not." . . .

V

The basic concern of *Furman* centered on those defendants who were being condemned to death capriciously and arbitrarily. Under the procedures before the Court in that case, sentencing authorities were not directed to give attention to the nature or circumstances of the crime committed or to the character or record of the defendant. Left unguided, juries imposed the death sentence in a way that could only be called freakish. The new Georgia sentencing procedures, by contrast, focus the jury's attention on the particularized nature of the crime and the particularized characteristics of the individual defendant. While the jury is permitted to consider any aggravating or mitigating circumstances, it must find and identify at least one statutory aggravating factor before it may impose a penalty of death. In this way the jury's discretion is channeled. No longer can a jury wantonly and freakishly impose the death sentence; it is always circumscribed by the legislative guidelines. In addition, the review function of the Supreme Court of Georgia affords additional assurance that the concerns that prompted our decision in *Furman* are not present to any significant degree in the Georgia procedure applied here.

For the reasons expressed in this opinion, we hold that the statutory system under which Gregg was sentenced to death does not violate the Constitution. Accordingly, the judgment of the Georgia Supreme Court is affirmed.

DISSENTING OPINION

In *Furman v. Georgia* (1972) (concurring opinion), I set forth at some length my views on the basic issue presented to the Court in [this case]. The death penalty, I concluded, is a cruel and unusual punishment prohibited by the Eighth and Fourteenth Amendments. That continues to be my view.

I have no intention of retracing the "long and tedious journey" that led to my conclusion in *Furman*. My sole purposes here are to consider the suggestion that my conclusion in *Furman* has been undercut by developments since then, and briefly to evaluate the basis for my Brethren's holding that the extinction of life is a permissible form of punishment under the Cruel and Unusual Punishments Clause.

In *Furman*, I concluded that the death penalty is constitutionally invalid for two reasons. First, the death penalty is excessive. And second, the American people, fully informed as to the purposes of the death penalty and its liabilities, would in my view reject it as morally unacceptable.

Since the decision in *Furman*, the legislatures of thirty-five States have enacted new statutes authorizing the imposition of the death sentence for certain crimes, and Congress has enacted a law providing the death penalty for air piracy resulting in death. I would be less than candid if I did not acknowledge that these developments have a significant bearing on a realistic assessment of the moral acceptability of the death penalty to the American people. But if the constitutionality of the death penalty turns, as I have urged, on the opinion of an *informed* citizenry, then even the enactment of new death statutes cannot be viewed as conclusive. In *Furman*, I observed that the American people are largely unaware of the information critical to a judgment on the morality of the death penalty, and concluded that if they were better informed they would consider it shocking, unjust, and unacceptable. A recent study, conducted after the enactment of the post-*Furman* statutes, has confirmed that the American people know little about the death penalty, and that the opinions of an informed public would differ significantly from those of a public unaware of the consequences and effects of the death penalty.

Even assuming, however, that the post-*Furman* enactment of statutes authorizing the death penalty renders the prediction of the views of an informed citizenry an uncertain basis for a constitutional decision, the enactment of those statutes has no bearing whatsoever

on the conclusion that the death penalty is unconstitutional because it is excessive. An excessive penalty is invalid under the Cruel and Unusual Punishments Clause "even though popular sentiment may favor" it. The inquiry here, then, is simply whether the death penalty is necessary to accomplish the legitimate legislative purposes in punishment, or whether a less severe penalty—life imprisonment—would do as well.

The two purposes that sustain the death penalty as nonexcessive in the Court's view are general deterrence and retribution. In *Furman*, I canvassed the relevant data on the deterrent effect of capital punishment. The state of knowledge at that point, after literally centuries of debate, was summarized as follows by a United Nations Committee:

> It is generally agreed between the retentionists and abolitionists, whatever their opinions about the validity of comparative studies of deterrence, that the data which now exist show no correlation between the existence of capital punishment and lower rates of capital crime.

The available evidence, I concluded in *Furman*, was convincing that "capital punishment is not necessary as a deterrent to crime in our society." . . .

The evidence I reviewed in *Furman* remains convincing, in my view, that "capital punishment is not necessary as a deterrent to crime in our society." The justification for the death penalty must be found elsewhere.

The other principal purpose said to be served by the death penalty is retribution. The notion that retribution can serve as a moral justification for the sanction of death finds credence in the opinion of my Brothers Stewart, Powell, and Stevens. . . . It is this notion that I find to be the most disturbing aspect of today's unfortunate [decision].

The concept of retribution is a multifaceted one, and any discussion of its role in the criminal law must be undertaken with caution. On one level, it can be said that the notion of retribution or reprobation is the basis of our insistence that only those who have broken the law be punished, and in this sense the notion is quite obviously central to a just system of criminal sanctions. But our recognition that retribution plays a crucial role in determining who may be punished by no means requires approval of retribution as a general justification for punishment. It is the question whether retribution can provide a moral justification for punishment—in particular, capital punishment—that we must consider.

My Brothers Stewart, Powell, and Stevens offer the following explanation of the retributive justification for capital punishments:

> The instinct for retribution is part of the nature of man, and channeling that instinct in the administration of criminal justice serves an important purpose in promoting the stability of a society governed by law. When people begin to believe that organized society is unwilling or unable to impose upon criminal offenders the punishment they "deserve," then there are sown the seeds of anarchy—of self-help, vigilante justice, and lynch law.

This statement is wholly inadequate to justify the death penalty. As my Brother Brennan stated in *Furman*, "[t]here is no evidence whatever that utilization of imprisonment rather than death encourages private blood feuds and other disorders." It simply defies belief to suggest that the death penalty is necessary to prevent the American people from taking the law into their own hands.

In a related vein, it may be suggested that the expression of moral outrage through the imposition of the death penalty serves to reinforce basic moral values—that it marks some crimes as particularly offensive and therefore to be avoided. The argument is akin to a deterrence argument, but differs in that it contemplates the individual's shrinking from antisocial conduct, not because he fears punishment, but because he has been told in the strongest possible way that the conduct is wrong. This contention, like the previous one, provides no support for the death penalty. It is inconceivable that any individual concerned about conforming his conduct to what society says is "right" would fail to realize that murder is "wrong" if the penalty were simply life imprisonment.

The foregoing contentions—that society's expression of moral outrage through the imposition of the death penalty preempts the citizenry from taking the law into its own hands and reinforces moral values—are not retributive in the purest sense. They are essentially utilitarian in that they portray the death penalty as valuable because of its beneficial results. These justifications for the death penalty are inadequate because the penalty is, quite clearly I think, not necessary to the accomplishment of those results.

There remains for consideration, however, what might be termed the purely retributive justification for the death penalty—that the death penalty is appropriate, not because of its beneficial effect on society, but because the taking of the murderer's life is itself morally good. Some of the language of the opinion of my Brothers Stewart, Powell, and Stevens . . . appears positively to embrace this notion of retribution for its own sake as a justification for capital punishment. They state:

> [T]he decision that capital punishment may be the appropriate sanction in extreme cases is an expression of the community's belief that certain crimes are themselves so grievous an affront to humanity that the only adequate response may be the penalty of death.

They then quote with approval from Lord Justice Denning's remarks before the British Commission on Capital Punishment:

> The truth is that some crimes are so outrageous that society insists on adequate punishment, because the wrong-doer deserves it, irrespective of whether it is a deterrent or not.

Of course, it may be that these statements are intended as no more than observations as to the popular demands that it is thought must be responded to in order to prevent anarchy. But the implication of the statements appears to me to be quite different—namely, that society's judgment that the murderer "deserves" death must be respected not simply because the preservation of order requires it, but because it is appropriate that society make the judgment and carry it out. It is the latter notion, in particular, that I consider to be fundamentally at odds with the Eighth Amendment. The mere fact that the community demands the murderer's life in return for the evil he has done cannot sustain the death penalty, for as Justices Stewart, Powell, and Stevens remind us, "the Eighth Amendment demands more than that a challenged punishment be acceptable to contemporary society." To be sustained under the Eighth Amendment, the death penalty must "compor[t] with the basic concept of human dignity at the core of the Amendment"; the objective in imposing it must be "[consistent] with our respect for the dignity of [other] men." Under these standards, the taking of life "because the wrongdoer deserves it" surely must fail, for such a punishment has as its very basis the total denial of the wrongdoer's dignity and worth.

The death penalty, unnecessary to promote the goal of deterrence or to further any legitimate notion of retribution, is an excessive penalty forbidden by the Eighth and Fourteenth Amendments. I respectfully dissent from the Court's judgment upholding the [sentence] of death imposed upon the [petitioner in this case].

⚜ REVIEW QUESTIONS

1. How did the Justices rule in *Furman v. Georgia* (1972), and by contrast, how do they rule in this case?
2. According to the Justices, what is the basic concept underlying the Eighth Amendment?
3. According to the Justices, in what two ways may a punishment be excessive?
4. According to the Justices, why doesn't the death penalty violate contemporary standards of decency?
5. The Justices say that the death penalty serves two principal social purposes. What are they, and how are they supposed to work?
6. What safeguards against the arbitrary and capricious application of the death sentence are suggested by the Justices?
7. Explain Justice Marshall's objections and his criticisms of the majority opinion.

⚜ DISCUSSION QUESTIONS

1. The Georgia statute retains the death penalty for six crimes, including rape, armed robbery, and treason. Do you agree that persons guilty of these crimes should receive the death sentence? Explain your view.
2. Try to give a precise definition of the phrase "cruel and unusual." Can you do it?
3. How could it be conclusively proven that the death penalty deters potential criminals better than life imprisonment?
4. Should the instinct for retribution be satisfied? Defend your answer.

The Retributive Theory of Punishment

IMMANUEL KANT

For biographical information on Kant, see his reading in Chapter 1.

In Kant's retributive theory of punishment, punishment is justified not by any good results but simply by the criminal's guilt. Criminals must pay for their crimes; otherwise an injustice has occurred. Furthermore, the punishment must fit the crime. Kant asserts that the only punishment that is appropriate for the crime of murder is the death of the murderer. As he puts it, "Whoever has committed a murder must *die*."

Source: Immanuel Kant, "The Retributive Theory of Punishment," from *The Philosophy of Law*, Part II, trans. W. Hastie (1887).

Judicial or juridical punishment (*poena forensis*) is to be distinguished from natural punishment (*poena naturalis*), in which crime as vice punishes itself, and does not as such come within the cognizance of the legislator. Juridical punishment can never be administered merely as a means for promoting another good, either with regard to the criminal himself or to civil society, but must in all cases be imposed only because the individual on whom it is inflicted *has committed a crime*. For one man ought never to be dealt with merely as a means subservient to the purpose of another, nor be mixed up with the subjects of real right. Against such treatment his inborn personality has a right to protect him, even although he may be condemned to lose his civil personality. He must first be found guilty and *punishable*, before there can be any thought of drawing from his punishment any benefit for himself or his fellow-citizens. The penal law is a categorical imperative; and woe to him who creeps through the serpent-windings of utilitarianism to discover some advantage that may discharge him from the justice of punishment, or even from the due measure of it, according to the pharisaic maxim: "It is better that *one* man should die than that the whole people should perish." For if justice and righteousness perish, human life would no longer have any value in the world. What, then, is to be said of such a proposal as to keep a criminal alive who has been condemned to death, on his being given to understand that if he agreed to certain dangerous experiments being performed upon him, he would be allowed to survive if he came happily through them? It is argued that physicians might thus obtain new information that would be of value to the commonweal. But a court of justice would repudiate with scorn any proposal of this kind if made to it by the medical faculty; for justice would cease to be justice, if it were bartered away for any consideration whatever.

But what is the mode and measure of punishment which public justice takes as its principle and standard? It is just the principle of equality, by which the pointer of the scale of justice is made to incline no more to the one side than the other. It may be rendered by saying that the undeserved evil which any one commits on another, is to be regarded as perpetrated on himself. Hence it may be said: "If you slander another, you slander yourself; if you steal from another, you steal from yourself; if you strike another, you strike yourself; if you kill another, you kill yourself." This is the right of retaliation (*jus talionis*); and properly understood, it is the only principle which in regulating a public court, as distinguished from mere private judgment, can definitely assign both the quality and the quantity of a just penalty. All other standards are wavering and uncertain; and on account of other considerations involved in them, they contain no principle conformable to the sentence of pure and strict justice. It may appear, however, that difference of social status would not admit the application of the principle of retaliation, which is that of "like with like." But although the application may not in all cases be possible according to the letter, yet as regards the effect it may always be attained in practice, by due regard being given to the disposition and sentiment of the parties in the higher social sphere. Thus a pecuniary penalty on account of a verbal injury, may have no direct proportion to the injustice of slander; for one who is wealthy may be able to indulge himself in this offense for his own gratification. Yet the attack committed on the honor of the party aggrieved may have its equivalent in the pain inflicted upon the pride of the aggressor, especially if he is condemned by the judgment of the court, not only to retract and apologize, but to submit to some meaner ordeal, as kissing the hand of the injured person. In like manner, if a man of the highest rank has violently assaulted an innocent citizen of the lower orders, he may be condemned not only to apologize but to undergo a solitary and painful imprisonment, whereby, in addition to the discomfort endured, the vanity of the offender would be painfully affected, and the very shame of his position would constitute an adequate retaliation after the principle of like with like. But how then would we render the statement: "If you *steal* from another, you steal from yourself"? In this way, that whoever steals anything makes the property of all insecure; he therefore robs himself of all security in property, according to the right of retaliation. Such a one has nothing, and can acquire nothing, but he has the will to live; and this is only possible by others supporting him. But as the state should not do this gratuitously, he must for this purpose yield his powers to the state to be used in penal labour; and thus he falls for a time, or it may be for life, into a condition of slavery. But whoever has committed murder, must *die*. There is, in this case, no juridical substitute or surrogate, that can be given or taken for the satisfaction of justice. There is no *likeness* or proportion between life, however painful, and death; and therefore there is no equality between the crime of murder and the retaliation of it but what is judicially accomplished by the execution of the criminal. His death, however, must be kept free from all maltreatment that would make the humanity suffering in his person loathsome or abominable. Even if a civil society resolved to dissolve itself with the consent of all its members—as might be supposed in the case of a people inhabiting an island resolving to separate and scatter themselves throughout the whole world—the last murderer lying in the prison ought to be executed before the resolution was carried out. This ought to be done in order that everyone may realize the desert of his deeds, and that bloodguiltiness may not remain upon the people; for otherwise they might all be regarded as participators in the murder as a public violation of justice.

The equalization of punishment with crime, is therefore only possible by the cognition of the judge extending even to the penalty of death, according to the right of retaliation.

REVIEW QUESTIONS

1. According to Kant, who deserves judicial punishment?
2. Why does Kant reject the maxim "It is better that *one* man should die than that the whole people should perish"?
3. How does Kant explain the principle of retaliation?

DISCUSSION QUESTIONS

1. Does Kant have any good reason to reject the "serpent-windings of utilitarianism"?
2. Is death always a just punishment for murder? Can you think of any exceptions?

The Ultimate Punishment

ERNEST VAN DEN HAAG

Ernest van den Haag (1915–2002) was John M. Olin Professor of Jurisprudence and Public Policy at Fordham University. For many years he had a private practice in psychoanalytical counseling, and for forty-five years he was a consultant and contributor to the *National Review*. His books include *The Fabric of Society* (1957), *Political Violence and Civil Disobedience* (1973), and *Punishing Criminals: Concerning a Very Old and Painful Question* (1975).

Van den Haag replies to various objections to capital punishment. The fact that capital punishment is applied in a discriminatory manner is irrelevant to its morality. Nor does it matter if innocents die, because many activities, such as trucking and construction, cost the

Source: Reprinted by permission of the Harvard Law Review Association and William S. Hein Company from *The Harvard Law Review*, Vol. 99, pp. 1662–1669.

lives of innocent bystanders. The cost is not as important as doing justice. It is not excessive punishment for heinous crimes, and it is not inconsistent with human dignity. Van den Haag agrees that there is no conclusive evidence showing that the death penalty is a more effective deterrent than other punishments. But he thinks that deterrence is not decisive for either those opposed or those in favor of the death penalty. Still, he believes that the death penalty is feared more than imprisonment, and for that reason deters some potential murderers. He goes on to use a subtle argument, sometimes called the "best-bet argument," to conclude that we should still use the death penalty because it might save innocents whose lives are more valuable than guilty murderers who are executed. In effect, the death penalty is a better bet than other punishments because it involves gambling with guilty lives rather than innocent lives.

In an average year about 20,000 homicides occur in the United States. Fewer than 300 convicted murderers are sentenced to death. But because no more than 30 murderers have been executed in any recent year, most convicts sentenced to death are likely to die of old age.[1] Nonetheless, the death penalty looms large in discussions: It raises important moral questions independent of the number of executions.[2]

The death penalty is our harshest punishment.[3] It is irrevocable: it ends the existence of those punished, instead of temporarily imprisoning them. Further, although not intended to cause physical pain, execution is the only corporal punishment still applied to adults.[4] These singular characteristics contribute to the perennial, impassioned controversy about capital punishment.

I. DISTRIBUTION

Consideration of the justice, morality, or usefulness of capital punishment is often conflated with objections to its alleged discriminatory or capricious distribution among the guilty. Wrongly so. If capital punishment is immoral *in se*, no distribution cannot affect the quality of what is distributed, be it punishments or rewards. Discriminatory or capricious distribution thus could not justify abolition of the death penalty. Further, maldistribution inheres no more in capital punishment than in any other punishment.

Maldistribution between the guilty and the innocent is, by definition, unjust. But the injustice does not lie in the nature of the punishment. Because of the finality of the death penalty, the most grievous maldistribution occurs when it is imposed on the innocent. However, the frequent allegations of discrimination and capriciousness refer to maldistribution among the guilty and not to the punishment of the innocent.[5]

Maldistribution of any punishment among those who deserve it is irrelevant to its justice or morality. Even if poor or black convicts guilty of capital offenses suffer capital punishment, and other convicts equally guilty of the same crimes do not, a more equal distribution, however desirable, would merely be more equal. It would not be more just to the convicts under sentence of death.

Punishments are imposed on persons, not on racial or economic groups. Guilt is personal. The only relevant question is, does the person to be executed deserve the punishment? Whether or not others who deserved the same punishment,

---

[1]Death row as a semipermanent residence is cruel, because convicts are denied the normal amenities of prison life. Thus, unless death row residents are integrated into the prison population, the continuing accumulation of convicts on death row should lead us to accelerate either the rate of executions or the rate of commutations. I find little objection to integration.

[2]The debate about the insanity defense is important for analogous reasons.

[3]Some writers, for example, Cesare Bonesana, Marchese di Beccaria, have thought that life imprisonment is more severe. *See* C. Beccaria, *Dei Delitti e Delle Pene* (1764) pp. 62–70. More recently, Jacques Barzun has expressed this view. *See* Barzun, *In Favor of Capital Punishment*, in *The Death Penalty in America*, ed. H. Bedau (1964), p. 154. However, the overwhelming majority of both abolitionists and of convicts under death sentence prefer life imprisonment to execution.

[4]For a discussion of the sources of opposition to corporal punishment, see E. van den Haag, *Punishing Criminals* (1975) pp. 196–206.

[5]See *infra* pp. 1664–65.

whatever their economic or racial group, have avoided execution is irrelevant. If they have, the guilt if the executed convicts would not be diminished, nor would their punishment be less deserved. To put the issue starkly, if the death penalty were imposed on guilty blacks, but not on guilty whites, or, if it were imposed by a lottery among the guilty, this irrationally discriminatory or capricious distribution would neither make the penalty unjust, nor cause anyone to be unjustly punished, despite the undue impunity bestowed on others.[6]

Equality, in short, seems morally less important than justice. And justice is independent of distributional inequalities. The ideal of equal justice demands that justice be equally distributed, not that it be replaced by equality. Justice requires that as many of the guilty as possible be punished, regardless of whether others have avoided punishment. To let these others escape the deserved punishment does not do justice to them, or to society. But it is not unjust to those who could not escape.

These moral considerations are not meant to deny that irrational discrimination, or capriciousness, would be inconsistent with constitutional requirements. But I am satisfied that the Supreme Court has in fact provided for adherence to the constitutional requirement of equality as much as is possible. Some inequality is indeed unavoidable as a practical matter in any system.[7] But, *ultra*

posse nemo obligatur (nobody is bound beyond ability).[8]

Recent data reveal little direct racial discrimination in the sentencing of those arrested and convicted of murder.[9] The abrogation of the death penalty for rape has eliminated a major source of racial discrimination. Concededly, some discrimination based on the race of murder victims may exist; yet, this discrimination affects criminal murder victimizers in an unexpected way. Murderers of whites are thought more likely to be executed than murderers of blacks. Black victims, then, are less fully vindicated than white ones. However, because most black murderers kill blacks, black murderers are spared the death penalty more often than are white murderers. They fare better than most white murderers.[10] The motivation behind unequal distribution of the death penalty may well have been to discriminate against blacks, but the result has favored them. Maldistribution is thus a straw man for empirical as well as analytical reasons.

II. MISCARRIAGES OF JUSTICE

In a recent survey Professors Hugo Adam Bedau and Michael Radelet found that 7,000 persons were executed in the United States between 1900 and 1985 and that 35 were innocent of capital crimes.[11] Among the innocents they list Sacco and Vanzetti as well as Ethel and Julius Rosenberg. Although their data may be questionable, I do not doubt that, over a long enough period,

---

[6]Justice Douglas, concurring in *Furman v. Georgia*, 408 U.S. 238 (1972), wrote that "a law which . . . reaches that [discriminatory] result in practice has no more sanctity that a law which in terms provides the same." *Id.* at 256 (Douglas, J., concurring). Indeed, a law legislating this result "in terms" would be inconsistent with the "equal protection of the laws" provided the result could be changed by changing the distributional practice. Thus, Justice Douglas notwithstanding, a discriminatory result does not make the death penalty unconstitutional, unless the penalty ineluctably must produce that result to an unconstitutional degree.

[7]The ideal of equality, unlike the ideal retributive justice (which can be approximated separately in each instance), is clearly unattainable unless all guilty persons are apprehended, and thereafter tried, convicted, and sentenced by the same court, at the same time. Unequal justice is the best we can do; it is still better than the injustice, equal or unequal, that occurs if, for the sake of equality, we deliberately allow some who could be punished to escape.

[8]Equality, even without justice, may remain a strong psychological, and therefore political, demand. Yet Charles Black, by proving the *inevitability* of "caprice" (inequality), undermines his own constitutional argument, because it seems unlikely that the Constitution's fifth and fourteenth amendments were meant to authorize the death penalty only under unattainable conditions. See Black, *Capital Punishment: The Inevitability of Caprice and Mistake* (1974).

[9]See Bureau of Justice Statistics, U.S. Dept of Justice, Bulletin No. NCJ-98,399, Capital Punishment, 1984, at 9 (1985); Johnson, *The Executioner's Bias*, Nat'l Rev. (Nov. 15, 1985) 44.

[10]It barely need be said that any discrimination *against* (for example, black murderers of whites) must also be discrimination *for* (for example, black murderers of blacks).

[11]Bedau and Radelet, *Miscarriages of Justice in Potentially Capital Cases* (1st draft, Oct. 1985) (on file at Harvard Law School Library).

miscarriages of justice will occur even in capital cases.

Despite precautions, nearly all human activities, such as trucking, lighting, or construction, cost the lives of some innocent bystanders. We do not give up these activities, because the advantages, moral or material, outweigh the unintended losses.[12] Analogously, for those who think the death penalty just, miscarriages of justice are offset by the moral benefits and the usefulness of doing justice. For those who think the death penalty unjust even when it does not miscarry, miscarriages can hardly be decisive.

III. DETERRENCE

Despite much recent work, there has been no conclusive statistical demonstration that the death penalty is a better deterrent than are alternative punishments.[13] However, deterrence is less than decisive for either side. Most abolitionists acknowledge that they would continue to favor abolition even if the death penalty were shown to deter more murders than alternatives could deter.[14] Abolitionists appear to value the life of a convicted murderer or, at least, his nonexecution, more highly than they value the lives of the innocent victims who might be spared by deterring prospective murderers.

Deterrence is not altogether decisive for me either. I would favor retention of the death penalty as retribution even if it were shown that the threat of execution could not deter prospective murderers not already deterred by the threat of imprisonment.[15] Still, I believe the death penalty, because of its finality, is more feared than imprisonment, and deters some prospective murderers not deterred by the thought of imprisonment. Sparing the lives of even a few prospective victims by deterring their murderers is more important than preserving the lives of convicted murderers because of the possibility, or even the probability, that executing them would not deter others. Whereas the lives of the victims who might be saved are valuable, that of the murderer has only negative value, because of his crime. Surely the criminal law is meant to protect the lives of potential victims in preference to those of actual murderers.

Murder rates are determined by many factors; neither the severity nor the probability of the threatened sanction is always decisive. However, for the long run, I share the view of Sir James Fitzjames Stephen: "Some men, probably, abstain from murder because they fear that if they committed murder they would be hanged. Hundreds of thousands abstain from it because they regard it with horror. One great reason why they regard it with horror is that murderers are hanged."[16] Penal sanctions are useful in the long run for the formation of the internal restraints so necessary to control crime. The severity and finality of the death penalty is

---

[12]An excessive number of trucking accidents or of miscarriages of justice could offset the benefits gained by trucking or the practice of doing justice. We are, however, far from this situation.

[13]For a sample of conflicting views on the subject, see Baldus and Cole, "A Comparison of the Work of Thorsten Sellin and Isaac Ehrlich on the Deterrent Effect of Capital Punishment," 85 *Yale L.J.* 170 (1975); Bowers and Pierce, "Deterrence or Brutalization: What Is the Effect of Executions?" 26 *Crime & Delinq.* 453 (1980); Bowers and Pierce, "The Illusion of Deterrence in Isaac Ehrlich's Research on Capital Punishment," 85 *Yale L.J.* 187 (1975); Ehrlich, "Fear of Deterrence: A Critical Evaluation of the 'Report of the Panel on Research on Deterrent and Incapacitate Effects'," 6 *J. Legal Stud.* 293 (1977); Ehrlich, "The Deterrent Effect of Capital Punishment: A Question of Life and Death," 65 *Am. Econ. Rev.* 397 (1975): 415–16; Ehrlich and Gibbons, "On the Measurement of the Deterrent Effect of Capital Punishment and the Theory of Deterrence," 6 *J. Legal Stud.* 35 (1977).

[14]For most abolitionists, the discrimination argument, *see supra* pp. 1662–64, is similarly nondecisive: they would favor abolition even if there could be no racial discrimination.

[15]If executions were shown to increase the murder rate in the long run, I would favor abolition. Sparing the innocent victims who would be spared, *ex hypothesi*, by the nonexecution of murderers would be more important to me than the execution, however just, of murderers. But although there is a lively discussion of the subject, no serious evidence exists to support the hypothesis that executions produce a higher murder rate. *Cf.* Phillips, "*The Deterrent Effect of Capital Punishment: New Evidence on an Old Controversy,*" 86 *Am. J. Soc.* 139 (1980) (arguing that murder rates drop immediately after executions of criminals).

[16]H. Gross, *A Theory of Criminal Justice* 489 (1979) (attributing this passage to Sir James Fitzjames Stephen).

appropriate to the seriousness and the finality of murder.[17]

IV. INCIDENTAL ISSUES: COST, RELATIVE SUFFERING, BRUTALIZATION

Many nondecisive issues are associated with capital punishment. Some believe that the monetary cost of appealing a capital sentence is excessive.[18] Yet most comparisons of the cost of life imprisonment with the cost of execution, apart from their dubious relevance, are flawed at least by the implied assumption that life prisoners will generate no judicial costs during their imprisonment. At any rate, the actual monetary costs are trumped by the importance of doing justice.

Others insist that a person sentenced to death suffers more than his victim suffered, and that this (excess) suffering is undue according to the *lex talionis* (rule of retaliation).[19] We cannot know whether the murderer on death row suffers more than his victim suffered; however, unlike the murderer, the victim deserved none of the suffering inflicted. Further, the limitations of the *lex talionis* were meant to restrain private vengeance, not the social retribution that has taken its place. Punishment—regardless of the motivation—is not intended to revenge, offset, or compensate for the victim's suffering, or to be measured by it. Punishment is to vindicate the law and the social order undermined by the crime. This is why a kidnapper's penal confinement is not limited to the period for which he imprisoned his victim; nor is a burglar's confinement meant merely to offset the suffering or the harm he caused his victim; nor is it meant only to offset the advantage he gained.[20]

Another argument heard at least since Beccaria[21] is that, by killing a murderer, we encourage, endorse, or legitimize unlawful killing Yet, although all punishments are meant to be unpleasant, it is seldom argued that they legitimize the unlawful imposition of identical unpleasantness. Imprisonment is not thought to legitimize kidnapping; neither are fines thought to legitimize robbery. The difference between murder and execution, or between kidnapping and imprisonment, is that the first is unlawful and undeserved, the second a lawful and deserved punishment for an unlawful act. The physical similarities of the punishment to the crime are irrelevant. The relevant difference is not physical, but social.[22]

V. JUSTICE, EXCESS, DEGRADATION

We threaten punishments in order to deter crime. We impose them not only to make the threats credible but also as retribution (justice) for the crimes that were not deterred. Threats and punishments are necessary to deter and deterrence is a sufficient practical justification for them.

---

[17] *Weems v. United States*, 217 U.S. 349 (1910) suggests that penalties be proportionate to the seriousness of the crime—a common theme in criminal law. Murder, therefore, demands more than life imprisonment. In modern times, our sensibility requires that the range of punishments be narrower than the range of crime—but not so narrow as to exclude the death penalty.

[18] *Cf.* Kaplan, "Administering Capital Punishment," 36 *U. Fla. L. Rev.* 177, 178 (1984): 190–91 (noting the high cost of appealing a capital sentence).

[19] For an example of this view, see A. Camus, *Reflections on the Guillotine* (1959), pp. 24–30. On the limitations allegedly imposed by the *lex talionis*, see Reiman, "*Justice, Civilization and the Death Penalty: Answering van den Haag*," 14 *Phil. & Pub. Aff.* 115, (1985), 119–34.

[20] Thus restitution (a civil liability) cannot satisfy the punitive purpose of penal sanctions, whether the purpose be retributive or deterrent.

[21] *See supra* note 3.

[22] Some abolitionists challenge: If the death penalty is just and serves as a deterrent, why not televise executions? The answer is simple. The death, even of a murderer, however well-deserved, should not serve as public entertainment. It so served in earlier centuries. But in this respect our sensibility has changed for the better, I believe. Further, television unavoidably would trivialize executions, wedged in, as they would be, between game shows, situation comedies, and the like. Finally, because televised executions would focus on the physical aspects of the punishment, rather than the nature of the crime and the suffering of the victim, a televised execution would present the executed as the victim of the state. Far from communicating the moral significance of the execution, television would shift that focus to the pitiable fear of the murderer. We no longer place in cages those sentenced to imprisonment to expose them to public view. Why should we so expose those sentenced to execution?

Retribution is an independent moral justification.[23] Although penalties can be unwise, repulsive, or inappropriate, and those punished can be pitiable, in a sense the infliction of legal punishment on a guilty person cannot be unjust. By committing the crime, the criminal volunteered to assume the risk of receiving a legal punishment that he could have avoided by not committing the crime. The punishment he suffers is the punishment he voluntarily risked suffering and, therefore, it is no more unjust to him than any other event for which one knowingly volunteers to assume the risk. Thus, the death penalty cannot be unjust to the guilty criminal.[24]

There remain, however, two moral objections. The penalty may be regarded as always excessive as retribution and always morally degrading. To regard the death penalty as always excessive, one must believe that no crime—no matter how heinous—could possibly justify capital punishment. Such a belief can be neither corroborated nor refuted; it is an article of faith.

Alternatively, or concurrently, one may believe that everybody, the murderer no less than the victim, has an imprescriptible (natural?) right to life. The law therefore should not deprive anyone of life. I share Jeremy Bentham's view that

any such "natural and imprescriptible rights" are "nonsense upon stilts."[25]

Justice Brennan has insisted that the death penalty is "uncivilized," "inhuman," inconsistent with "human dignity" and with "the sanctity of life,"[26] that it "treats members of the human race as nonhumans, as objects to be toyed with and discarded,"[27] that it is "uniquely degrading to human dignity"[28] and "by its very nature, [involves] a denial of the executed person's humanity."[29] Justice Brennan does not say why he thinks execution "uncivilized." Hitherto most civilizations have had the death penalty, although it has been discarded in Western Europe, where it is currently unfashionable probably because of its abuse by totalitarian regimes.

By "degrading," Justice Brennan seems to mean that execution degrades the executed convicts. Yet philosophers, such as Immanuel Kant and G.F.W. Hegel, have insisted that, when deserved, execution, far from degrading the executed convict, affirms his humanity by affirming his rationality and his responsibility for his actions. They thought that execution, when deserved, is required for the sake of the convict's dignity. (Does not life imprisonment violate human dignity more than execution, by keeping alive a prisoner deprived of all autonomy?[30])

Common sense indicates that it cannot be death—our common fate—that is inhuman. Therefore, Justice Brennan must mean that death degrades when it comes not as a natural or accidental event, but as a deliberate social imposition. The murderer learns through his

---

[23]See van den Haag, *"Punishment as a Device for Controlling the Crime Rate,"* 33 *Rutgers L. Rev.* (1981), 706, 719 (explaining why the desire for retribution, although independent, would have to be satisfied even if deterrence were the only purpose of punishment).

[24]An explicit threat of punitive action is necessary to the justification of any legal punishment: *nulla poena sine lege* (no punishment without [preexisting] law). To be sufficiently justified, the threat must in turn have a rational and legitimate purpose. "Your money or your life" does not qualify; nor does the threat of an unjust law; nor, finally, does a threat that is altogether disproportionate to the importance of its purpose. In short, preannouncement legitimizes the threatened punishment only if the threat is warranted. But this leaves a very wide range of justified threats. Furthermore, the punished person is aware of the penalty for his actions and thus volunteers to take the risk even of an unjust punishment. His victim, however, doesn't act illegally and thus doesn't volunteer to risk anything. The question whether any self-inflicted injury—such as legal punishment—ever can be unjust to a person who knowingly risked it is a matter that requires more analysis than possible here.

[25]*The Works of Jeremy Bentham*, ed. J. Bowring (1973), p. 105. However, I would be more polite about prescriptible natural rights, which Bentham described as "simple nonsense." *Id.* (It does not matter whether natural rights are called "moral" or "human" rights as they currently are by most writers.)

[26]*The Death Penalty in America*, 3rd ed., ed. H. Bedau (1982), pp. 256–63 (quoting *Furman v. Georgia*, 408 U.S. 238, 286, 305 (1972) (Brennan, J., concurring).

[27]*Id.* at 272–73; *see also Gregg v. Georgia*, 428 U.S. 153, 230 (1976) (Brennan, J., dissenting).

[28]*Furman v. Georgia*, 408 U.S. 238, 291 (1972) (Brennan, J., concurring).

[29]*Id.* at 290.

[30]*See* Barzun, *supra* note 3, *passim*.

punishment that his fellow men have found him unworthy of living; that because he has murdered, he is being expelled from the community of the living. This degradation is self-inflicted. By murdering, the murderer has so dehumanized himself that he cannot remain among the living. The social recognition of his self-degradation is the punitive essence of execution. To believe, as Justice Brennan appears to, that the degradation is inflicted by the execution reverses the direction of causality.

Execution of those who have committed heinous murders may deter only one murder per year. If it does, it seems quite warranted. It is also the only fitting retribution for murder I can think of.

⚜ REVIEW QUESTIONS

1. How does van den Haag reply to the objection that capital punishment is discriminatory?
2. What is his response to the claim that innocent people are mistakenly executed?
3. According to van den Haag, why does the possibility or probability of deterrence support the use of the death penalty?
4. How does he reply to the objections about cost, excessive suffering, legitimizing killing, the right to life, and human dignity?

⚜ DISCUSSION QUESTIONS

1. Do you agree that the death penalty is the harshest punishment? Can you think of worse punishments?
2. Are you willing to accept the execution of innocent people as van den Haag does? Why or why not?
3. Are you convinced by van den Haag's arguments about deterrence? (You may want to read Reiman's objections in the next reading.)

Against the Death Penalty

JEFFREY H. REIMAN

Jeffrey Reiman is William Fraser McDowell Professor of Philosophy at The American University in Washington, D.C. He is the author of *In Defense of Political Philosophy* (1972), *Critical Moral Liberation* (1997), *The Rich Get Richer and the Poor Get Prison* (8th ed., 2006), *Abortion and the Ways We Value Life* (1999), and co-editor (with Paul Leighton) of *Criminal Justice Ethics* (2001). He has published more than fifty articles in philosophy and criminal justice journals and anthologies.

Reiman is against the death penalty, both in principle and in practice. Avoiding the death principle is good in principle because it reduces our toleration of cruelty. In his view the death penalty is like torture, it is a "torture until death," and as such it is too horrible to be used by a civilized society. The death penalty is unjust in practice because it is applied in arbitrary and discriminatory ways. In reply to Kant and others who appeal to *lex talionis*, the law of retaliation, Reiman grants that the death penalty is a just punishment for some murderers, but he

Source: "Against the Death Penalty" by Jeffrey Reiman from *Living Well* by S. Luper. Copyright © 1998. NY: Houghton Mifflin Harcourt.

thinks that justice does not *require* the death penalty for murderers. The alternative punishment of life imprisonment satisfies the requirements of justice. He notes that we do not torture torturers or rape rapists. As for the argument of van den Haag and others that the death penalty has a deterrent effect, Reiman argues that there is no reason to believe it is necessary to deter future murders. The evidence shows that the death penalty is no better than life imprisonment as a deterrent, and may not deter at all.

My position about the death penalty as punishment for murder can be summed up in the following four propositions:

1. though the death penalty is a just punishment for some murderers, it is not unjust to punish murderers less harshly (down to a certain limit);
2. though the death penalty would be justified if needed to deter future murders, we have no good reason to believe that it is needed to deter future murders; and
3. in refraining from imposing the death penalty, the state, by its vivid and impressive example, contributes to reducing our tolerance for cruelty and thereby fosters the advance of human civilization as we understand it.

Taken together, these three propositions imply that we do no injustice to actual or potential murder victims, and we do some considerable good, in refraining from executing murderers. This conclusion will be reinforced by another argument, this one for the proposition:

4. though the death penalty is *in principle* a just penalty for murder, it is unjust *in practice* in America because it is applied in arbitrary and discriminatory ways, and this is likely to continue into the foreseeable future.

This fourth proposition conjoined with the prior three imply the overall conclusion *that it is good in principle to avoid the death penalty and bad in practice to impose it*. In what follows, I shall state briefly the arguments for each of these propositions.[1] For ease of identification, I shall number the first paragraph in which the argument for each proposition begins.

1. Before showing that the death penalty is just punishment for some murders, it is useful to dispose of a number of popular but weak arguments against the death penalty. One such popular argument contends that, if murder is wrong, then the death penalty is wrong as well. But this argument proves too much! It would work against *all* punishments since all are wrong if done by a regular citizen under normal circumstances. (If I imprison you in a little jail in my basement, I am guilty of kidnaping; if I am caught and convicted, the state will lock me up in jail and will not have committed the same wrong that I did.) The point here is that what is wrong about murder is not merely that it is killing per se, but the killing of a legally innocent person by a nonauthorized individual—and this doesn't apply to executions that are the outcome of conviction and sentencing at a fair trial.

Another argument that some people think is decisive against capital punishment points to the irrevocability of the punishment. The idea here is that innocents are sometimes wrongly convicted and if they receive the death penalty there is no way to correct the wrong done to them. While there is some force to this claim, its force is at best a relative matter. To be sure, if someone is executed and later found to have been innocent, there is no way to give him back the life that has been taken. But, if someone is sentenced to life in prison and is found to have been innocent, she can be set free and perhaps given money to make up for the years spent in prison—but those years cannot be given back. On the other hand, the innocent person who has been executed can at least be compensated in the form of money to his family and he can have his named cleared. So, it's not that the death penalty is irrevocable and other punishments are revocable; rather, all punishments are irrevocable though the death penalty is, so to speak, relatively more irrevocable than the rest. In any event, this only makes a difference in cases of mistaken conviction of the innocent, and the evidence is that such mistakes—particularly in capital cases—are quite rare.[2] And, further, since we accept the death of innocents elsewhere, on the highways, as a cost of progress, as a necessary accompaniment of military operations, and so on, it is not plausible to think that the execution of a small number of innocent persons is so terrible as to outweigh all other considerations, especially when every effort is made to make sure that it does not occur.

Finally, it is sometimes argued that if we use the death penalty as a means to deter future murderers, we kill someone to protect others (from different people than the one we have executed), and thus we violate the Kantian prohibition against using individuals as means to the welfare of others. But the Kantian prohibition is not against using others as means, it is against using others as *mere* means (that is, in total disregard of their own desires and goals). Though you use the busdriver as a means to your getting home, you don't use him as a mere means because the job pays him a living and thus promotes his desires and goals as it does yours. Now, if what deters criminals is the existence of an effective system of deterrence, then criminals punished as part of that system are not used as mere means since their desires and goals are also served, inasmuch as they have also benefited from deterrence of other criminals. Even criminals don't want to be crime victims. Further, if there is a right to threaten punishment in self-defense, then a society has the right to threaten punishment to defend its members, and there is no more violation of the Kantian maxim in imposing such punishment than there is in carrying out any threat to defend oneself against unjust attack.[3]

One way to see that the death penalty is a just punishment for at least some murders (the cold-blooded, premeditated ones) is to reflect on the *lex talionis*, an eye for an eye, a tooth for a tooth, and all that. Some regard this as a primitive rule, but it has I think an undeniable element of justice. And many who think that the death penalty is just punishment for murder are responding to this element. To see what the element is consider how similar the *lex talionis* is to the Golden

Rule. The Golden Rule tells us to do unto others what we would have others do unto us, and the *lex talionis* counsels that we do to others what they have done to us. Both of these reflect a belief in the equality of all human beings. Treating others as you *would* have them treat you means treating others as equal to you, because it implies that you count their suffering to be as great a calamity as your own suffering, that you count your right to impose suffering on them as no greater than their right to impose suffering on you, and so on. The Golden Rule would not make sense if it were applied to two people, one of whom was thought to be inherently more valuable than the other. Imposing a harm on the more valuable one would be worse than imposing the same harm on the less valuable one—and neither could judge her actions by what she would have the other do to her. Since *lex talionis* says that you are rightly paid back for the harm you have caused another with a similar harm, it implies that the value of what of you have done to another is the same as the value of having it done to you—which, again, would not be the case, if one of you were thought inherently more valuable than the other. Consequently, treating people according to the *lex talionis* (like treating them according to the Golden Rule) affirms the equality of all concerned—and this supports the idea that punishing according to *lex talionis* is just.

Furthermore, on the Kantian assumption that a rational individual implicitly endorses the universal form of the intention that guides his action, a rational individual who kills another implicitly endorses the idea that he may be killed, and thus, he authorizes his own execution thereby absolving his executioner of injustice. What's more, much as above we saw that acting on *lex talionis* affirms the equality of criminal and victim, this Kantian-inspired argument suggests that acting on *lex talionis* affirms the rationality of criminal and victim. The victim's rationality is affirmed because the criminal only authorizes his own killing if he has intended to kill another rational being like himself—then, he implicitly endorses the universal version of that intention, thereby authorizing his own killing. A person who intentionally kills an animal does not implicitly endorse his own being killed; only someone who kills someone like himself authorizes his own killing. In this way, the Kantian argument also invokes the equality of criminal and victim.

On the basis of arguments like this, I maintain that the idea that people deserve having done to them roughly what they have done (or attempted to do) to others affirms both the equality and rationality of human beings and for that reason is just. Kant has said: "no one has ever heard of anyone condemned to death on account of murder who complained that he was getting too much [punishment] and therefore was being treated unjustly; everyone would laugh in his face if he were to make such a statement."[4] If Kant is right, then even murderers recognize the inherent justice of the death penalty.

However, while the justice of the *lex talionis* implies the justice of executing some murderers, it does not imply that punishing less harshly is automatically unjust. We can see this by noting that the justice of the *lex talionis* implies also the justice of torturing torturers and raping rapists. I am certain and I assume my reader is as well that we need not impose these latter punishments to do justice (even if there were no other way of equaling the harm done or attempted by the criminal). Otherwise the price of doing justice would be matching the cruelty of the worst criminals, and that would effectively price justice out of the moral market. It follows that justice can be served with lesser punishments. Now, I think that there are two ways that punishing less harshly than the *lex talionis* could be unjust: it could be unjust to the actual victim of murder or to the future victims of potential murderers. It would be unjust to the actual victim if the punishment we mete out instead of execution were so slight that it trivialized the harm that the murderer did. This would make a sham out of [the] implicit affirmation of equality that underlies the justice of the *lex talionis*. However, life imprisonment, or even a lengthy prison sentence—say, twenty years or more without parole—is a very grave punishment and not one that trivializes the harm done by the murderer. Punishment would be unjust to future victims if it is so mild that it fails to be a reasonable

deterrent to potential murderers. Thus, refraining from executing murderers could be wrong if executions were needed to deter future murderers. In the following section, I shall say why there is no reason to think that this is so.

2. I grant that, if the death penalty were needed to deter future murderers, that would be a strong reason in favor of using the death penalty, since otherwise we would be sacrificing the future victims of potential murderers whom we could have deterred. And I think that this is a real injustice to those future victims, since the we in question is the state. Because the state claims a monopoly on the use of force, it owes its citizens protection, and thus does them injustice when it fails to provide the level of protection it reasonably could provide. However, there is no reason to believe that we need the death penalty to deter future murderers. The evidence we have strongly supports the idea that we get the same level of deterrence from life imprisonment, and even from substantial prison terms, such as twenty years without parole.

Before 1975, the most important work on the comparative deterrent impact of the capital punishment versus life in prison was that of Thorsten Sellin. He compared the homicide rates in states with the death penalty to the rates in similar states without the death penalty, and found no greater incidence of homicide in states without the death penalty than in similar states with it. In 1975, Isaac Ehrlich, a University of Chicago econometrician, reported the results of a statistical study which he claimed proved that, in the period from 1933 to 1969, each execution deterred as many as eight murders. This finding was, however, widely challenged. Ehrlich found a deterrent impact of executions in the period from 1933 to 1969, which includes the period of 1963 to 1969, a time when hardly any executions were carried out and crime rates rose for reasons that are arguably independent of the existence or nonexistence of capital punishment. When the 1963–9 period is excluded, no significant deterrent effect shows. This is a very serious problem since the period from 1933 through to the end of the 1930s was one in which executions were carried out at the highest rate in American history—before or after.

That no deterrent effect turns up when the study is limited to 1933 to 1962 almost seems evidence *against* the deterrent effect of the death penalty!

Consequently, in 1978, *after Ehrlich's study,* the editors of a National Academy of Sciences' study of the impact of punishment wrote: "In summary, the flaws in the earlier analyses (i.e., Sellin's and others) and the sensitivity of the more recent analyses to minor variation in model specification and the serious temporal instability of the results lead the panel to conclude that the available studies provide no useful evidence on the deterrent effect of capital punishment."[5] Note that, while the deterrence research commented upon here generally compares the deterrent impact of capital punishment with that of life imprisonment, the failure to prove that capital punishment deters murder more than does incarceration goes beyond life in prison. A substantial proportion of people serving life sentences are released on parole before the end of their sentences. Since this is public knowledge, we should conclude from these studies that we have no evidence that capital punishment deters murder more effectively than prison sentences that are less than life, though still substantial, such as twenty years.

Another version of the argument for the greater deterrence impact of capital punishment compared to lesser punishments is called *the argument from common sense.* It holds that, whatever the social science studies do or don't show, it is only common sense that people will be more deterred by what they fear more, and since people fear death more than life in prison, they will be deterred more by execution than by a life sentence. This argument for the death penalty, however, assumes without argument or evidence that deterrence increases continuously and endlessly with the fearfulness of threatened punishment rather than leveling out at some threshold beyond which increases in fearfulness produce no additional increment of deterrence. That being tortured for a year is worse than being tortured for six months doesn't imply that a year's torture will deter you from actions that a half-year's torture would not deter—since a half-year's torture may be bad enough to deter you from all the actions that you can be deterred from doing. Likewise,

though the death penalty may be worse than life in prison, that doesn't imply that the death penalty will deter acts that a life sentence won't because a life sentence may be bad enough to do all the deterring that can be done—and that is precisely what the social science studies seem to show. And, as I suggested above, what applies here to life sentences applies as well to substantial prison sentences.

I take it then that there is no reason to believe that we save more innocent lives with the death penalty than with less harsh penalties such as life in prison or some lengthy sentence, such as twenty years without parole. But then we do no injustice to the future victims of potential murderers by refraining from the death penalty. And, in conjunction with the argument of the previous section, it follows that we do no injustice to actual or potential murder victims if we refrain from executing murderers and sentence them instead to life in prison or to some substantial sentence, say, twenty or more years in prison without parole. But it remains to be seen what good will be served by doing the latter instead of executing.

3. Here I want to suggest that, in refraining from imposing the death penalty, the state, by its vivid and impressive example, contributes to reducing our tolerance for cruelty and thereby fosters the advance of human civilization as we understand it. To see this, note first that it has long been acknowledged that the state, and particularly the criminal justice system, plays an educational role in society as a model of morally accepted conduct and an indicator of the line between morally permissible and impermissible actions. Now, consider the general repugnance that is attached to the use of torture—even as punishment for criminals who have tortured their victims. It seems to me that, by refraining from torturing even those who deserve it, our state plays a role in promoting that repugnance. That we will not torture even those who have earned it by their crimes conveys a message about the awfulness of torture, namely, that it is something that civilized people will not do even to give evil people their just deserts. Thus it seems to me that in this case the state advances the cause of human civilization by contributing to a

reduction in people's tolerance for cruelty. I think that the modern state is uniquely positioned to do this sort of thing because of its size (representing millions, even hundreds of millions of citizens) and its visibility (starting with the printing press that accompanied the birth of modern nations, increasing with radio, television and the other media of instantaneous communication). And because the state can do this, it should. Consequently, I contend that if the state were to put execution in the same category as torture, it would contribute yet further to reducing our tolerance for cruelty and to advancing the cause of human civilization. And because it can do this, it should.

To make this argument plausible, however, I must show that execution is horrible enough to warrant its inclusion alongside torture. I think that execution is horrible in a way similar to (though not identical with) the way in which torture is horrible. Torture is horrible because of two of its features, which also characterize execution: intense pain and the spectacle of one person being completely subject to the power of another.[6] This latter is separate from the issue of pain, since it is something that offends people about unpainful things, such as slavery (even voluntarily entered) and prostitution (even voluntarily chosen as an occupation). Execution shares this separate feature. It enacts the total subjugation of one person to his fellows, whether the individual to be executed is strapped into an electric chair or bound like a laboratory animal on a hospital gurney awaiting lethal injection.

Moreover, execution, even by physically painless means, is characterized by a special and intense psychological pain that distinguishes it from the loss of life that awaits us all. This is because execution involves the most psychologically painful features of death. We normally regard death from human causes as worse than death from natural causes, since a humanly caused shortening of life lacks the consolation of unavoidability. And we normally regard death whose coming is foreseen by its victim as worse than sudden death because a foreseen death adds to the loss of life the terrible consciousness of that impending loss. An execution combines the worst of both: Its coming is foreseen, in that its date is normally already set, and it lacks the consolation of unavoidability, in that it depends on the will of one's fellow human beings, not on natural forces beyond human control. It was on just such grounds that Albert Camus regarded the death penalty as itself a kind of torture: "As a general rule, a man is undone by waiting for capital punishment well before he dies. Two deaths are inflicted on him, the first being worse than the second, whereas he killed but once. Compared to such torture, the penalty of retaliation [the *lex talionis*] seems like a civilized law."[7]

Consequently, if a civilizing message is conveyed about torture when the state refrains from torturing, I believe we can and should try to convey a similar message about killing by having the state refrain from killing even those who have earned killing by their evil deeds. Moreover, if I am right about this, then it implies further that refraining from executing murderers will have the effect of deterring murder in the long run and thereby make our society safer. This much then shows that it would be good in principle to refrain from imposing capital punishment. I want now to show why it would be good in practice as well.

4. However just in principle the death penalty may be, it is applied unjustly in practice in America and is likely to be so for the foreseeable future. The evidence for this conclusion comes from various sources. Numerous studies show that killers of whites are more likely to get the death penalty than killers of blacks, and that black killers of whites are far more likely to be sentenced to death than white killers of blacks. Moreover, just about everyone recognizes that poor people are more likely to be sentenced to death and to have those sentences carried out than well-off people. And these injustices persist even after all death penalty statutes were declared unconstitutional in 1972[8] and only those death penalty statutes with provisions for reducing arbitrariness in sentencing were admitted as constitutional in 1976.[9] In short, injustice in the application of the death penalty persists even after legal reform, and this strongly suggests that it is so deep that it will not be corrected in the foreseeable future.

It might be objected that discrimination is also found in the handing out of prison sentences and thus that this argument would prove that we should abolish prison as well as the death penalty. But I accept that we need some system of punishment to deter crime and mete out justice to criminals, and for that reason even a discriminatory punishment system is better than none. Then, the objection based on discrimination works only against those elements of the punishment system that are not needed either to deter crime or to do justice, and I have shown above that this is true of the death penalty. Needless to say we should also strive to eliminate discrimination in the parts of the criminal justice that we cannot do without.

Other, more subtle, kinds of discrimination also affect the way the death penalty is actually carried out. There are many ways in which the actions of well-off people lead to death which are not counted as murder. For example, many more people die as a result of preventable occupational diseases (due to toxic chemicals, coal and textile dust, and the like, in the workplace) or preventable environmental pollution than die as a result of what is treated legally as homicide.[10] So, in addition to all the legal advantages that money can buy a wealthy person accused of murder, the law also helps the wealthy by not defining as murder many of the ways in which the wealthy are responsible for the deaths of fellow human beings. Add to this that many of the killings that we do treat as murders, the ones done by the poor in our society, are the predictable outcome of remediable social injustice—the discrimination and exploitation that, for example, have helped to keep African Americans at the bottom of the economic ladder for centuries. Those who benefit from injustice and who could remedy it bear some of the responsibility for the crimes that are the predictable outcome of injustice—and that implies that plenty of well-off people share responsibility with many of our poor murderers. But since these more fortunate folks are not likely to be held responsible for murder, it is unfair to hold only the poor victims of injustice responsible—and wholly responsible to boot!

Finally, we already saw that the French existentialist, Albert Camus, asserted famously that life on death row is a kind of torture. Recently, Robert Johnson has studied the psychological effects on condemned men on death row and confirmed Camus' claim. In his book *Condemned to Die*, Johnson recounts the painful psychological deterioration suffered by a substantial majority of the death row prisoners he studied.[11] Since the death row inmate faces execution, he is viewed as having nothing to lose and thus is treated as the most dangerous of criminals. As a result, his confinement and isolation are nearly total. Since he has no future for which to be rehabilitated, he receives the least and the worst of the prison's facilities. Since his guards know they are essentially warehousing him until his death, they treat him as something less than human—and so he is brutalized, taunted, powerless and constantly reminded of it. The effect of this on the death row inmate, as Johnson reports it, is quite literally the breaking down of the structures of the ego—a process not unlike that caused by brainwashing. Since we do not reserve the term "torture" only for processes resulting in physical pain, but recognize processes that result in extreme psychological suffering as torture as well (consider sleep deprivation or the so-called Chinese water torture), Johnson's and Camus' application of this term to the conditions of death row confinement seems reasonable.

It might be objected that some of the responsibility for the torturous life of death row inmates is the inmates' own fault, since in pressing their legal appeals, they delay their executions and thus prolong their time on death row. Capital murder convictions and sentences, however, are reversed on appeal with great frequency, nearly ten times the rate of reversals in noncapital cases. This strongly supports the idea that such appeals are necessary to test the legality of murder convictions and death penalty sentences. To hold the inmate somehow responsible for the delays that result from his appeals, and thus for the (increased) torment he suffers as a consequence, is effectively to confront him with the choice of accepting execution before its legality is fully tested or suffering torture until it is. Since no just society should expect (or even want) a person to accept a sentence until its legal validity has been established, it is unjust to torture him until it has and perverse to assert that he has brought the torture on himself by his insistence that the legality of his sentence be fully tested before it is carried out.

The worst features of death row might be ameliorated, but it is unlikely that its torturous nature will be eliminated, or even that it is possible to eliminate it. This is, in part, because it is linked to an understandable psychological strategy used by the guards in order to protect themselves against natural, painful, and ambivalent feelings of sympathy for a person awaiting a humanly inflicted death. Johnson writes: "I think it can also be argued . . . that humane death rows will not be achieved in practice because the purpose of death row confinement is to facilitate executions by de-humanizing both the prisoners and (to a lesser degree) their executioners and thus make it easier for both to conform to the etiquette of ritual killing."[12]

If conditions on death row are and are likely to continue to be a real form of psychological torture, if Camus and Johnson are correct, then it must be admitted that the death penalty is in practice not merely a penalty of death—it is a penalty of torture until death. Then the sentence of death is more than the *lex talionis* allows as a just penalty for murder—and thus it is unjust in practice.

I think that I have proven that it would be good in principle to refrain from imposing the death penalty and bad in practice to continue using it. And, I have proven this while accepting the two strongest claims made by defenders of capital punishment, namely, that death is just punishment for at least some murderers, and that, if the death penalty were a superior deterrent to murder than imprisonment that would justify using the death penalty.

NOTES

1. The full argument for these propositions, along with supporting data, references, and replies to objections, is in Louis Pojman and Jeffrey Reiman, *The Death Penalty: For and Against* (Lanham, MD: Rowman & Littlefield Publishers, Inc., 1998), pp. 67–132, 151–63. That essay in turn is based upon and substantially revises my "Justice,

Civilization, and the Death Penalty: Answering van den Haag," *Philosophy and Public Affairs* 14, no. 2 (Spring 1985): 115–48, and my "The Justice of the Death Penalty in an Unjust World," in *Challenging Capital Punishment: Legal and Social Science Approaches*, ed. K. Haas J. Inciardi (Beverly Hills, CA: Sage, 1988), pp. 29–48.

2. Some recent developments, most notably the use of DNA testing to exonerate a number of death row inmates, suggest that this claim may be overly optimistic. In that case, the risk of condemning the innocent would become a stronger argument against capital punishment and, in fact, has recently led to calls for a moratorium on executions. In January 2000, Illinois Governor George Ryan, "a Republican who supports capital punishment, cited the exoneration of 13 death row inmates since Illinois re-adopted the death penalty in 1977 and said he would permit no more executions until a study was completed of a system he described as 'fraught with error'" (Sara Rimer, "U.S. Cities Call for Death Penalty Moratorium," *International Herald Tribune*, November 1, 2000, p. 7). Philadelphia, Atlanta, Baltimore, San Francisco and Charlotte, North Carolina, are among two dozen cities that have recently passed non-legally binding moratorium resolutions, and polls show that support for the death penalty among Americans is at its lowest in 20 years—down to two-thirds from a high of 75 percent in 1994.

3. Elsewhere I have argued at length that punishment needed to deter reasonable people is deserved by criminals. See Pojman and Reiman, *The Death Penalty*, pp. 79–85.

4. Immanuel Kant, "The Metaphysical Elements of Justice," pt. 1 of *The Metaphysics of Morals*, trans. J. Ladd (Indianapolis, IN: Bobbs-Merrill, 1965; originally published 1797), p. 104, see also p. 133.

5. Alfred Blumstein, Jacqueline Cohen, and Daniel Nagin, eds., *Deterrence and Incapacitation: Estimating the Effects of Criminal Sanctions on Crime Rates* (Washington, DC: National Academy of Sciences, 1978), p. 9.

6. Hugo Bedau has developed this latter consideration at length with respect to the death penalty. See Hugo A. Bedau, "Thinking about the Death Penalty as a Cruel and Unusual Punishment," *U.C. Davis Law Review* 18 (Summer 1985): 917ff. This article is reprinted in Hugo A. Bedau, *Death Is Different: Studies in the Morality, Law, and Politics of Capital Punishment* (Boston: Northeastern

University Press, 1987); and Hugo A. Bedau, ed., *The Death Penalty in America: Current Controversies* (New York: Oxford University Press, 1997).

7. Albert Camus, "Reflections on the Guillotine," in Albert Camus, *Resistance, Rebellion, and Death* (New York: Knopf, 1961), p. 205.

8. *Furman* v *Georgia*, 408 U.S. 238 (1972).

9. *Gregg* v *Georgia*, 428 U.S. 153 (1976).

10. Jeffrey Reiman, *The Rich Get Richer and the Poor Get Prison: Ideology, Class, and Criminal Justice*, 6th ed. (Needham Heights, MA: Allyn Bacon, 2001), pp. 79–85, 88–94.

11. Robert Johnson, *Condemned to Die: Life under Sentence of Death* (New York: Elsevier, 1981), pp. 129ff.

12. Robert Johnson, personal correspondence to author.

PROBLEM CASES

1. Gary Graham

(This case was widely reported in the media, including coverage in Europe where opposition to the death penalty is unanimous.) Gary Graham, a black man also known as Shaka Shankofa, was convicted in 1981 of killing Bobby Lambert (age fifty-three) during a robbery attempt at a Houston supermarket. Mr. Lambert was shot to death at night in the parking lot of a Safeway supermarket. There was no physical evidence linking Graham to the crime. Mr. Graham was arrested with a .22 caliber pistol a week after the murder, but the police firearms examiner determined that Mr. Graham's weapon could not have fired the fatal bullet. Mr. Graham claimed that he was miles away from the Safeway when the crime occurred. Four witnesses who passed polygraph tests stated that Mr. Graham was with them the night of the murder.

The jury convicted Mr. Graham based on the testimony of one witness, Bernadine Skillern, who insisted that she saw him through the windshield of her car that night. She testified that she saw the assailant's face for two or three seconds, from a distance of thirty to forty feet. She said, "I saw that young man walk up and shoot that man." Mr. Graham was seventeen at the time, a minor.

There were other eyewitnesses in the store. One of them was standing next to the killer in the supermarket checkout line. She had the best look at the killer, and she emphatically said that Mr. Graham was the wrong man. At the trial she was not asked if Mr. Graham was the suspect. Of the six living crime scene witnesses other than Ms. Skillern, all described the assailant as shorter than Mr. Lambert, who was five feet six inches tall. Mr. Graham was five feet nine inches tall.

Mr. Graham had a court-appointed lawyer, Ron Mock, who failed to investigate the case. Mr. Mock later admitted that he believed Graham was guilty and therefore he did nothing to find proof of innocence. None of the other witnesses were called to testify at the trial, and no investigation was done about the lack of physical evidence.

Mr. Graham received the death sentence, but his execution was delayed five times on appeal. The appeal for a new trial was denied, based on a Texas rule that bars court review on any evidence of innocence brought forward more than thirty days after the trial conviction.

Mr. Graham was executed in June 2000 after the Texas Board of Pardons and Paroles denied a final clemency petition, and Texas Governor George W. Bush refused to grant a stay of execution. During Bush's five years as governor, the state of Texas carried out 134 executions, the most in the nation.

In general, should juveniles (under the age of eighteen at the time of the crime) be executed? (Nineteen states plus the federal government have an age minimum of at least eighteen for capital punishment.)

Based on the evidence given, did Gary Graham deserve to die? Suppose, for the sake of discussion, that Mr. Mock was right and Mr. Graham was indeed guilty as charged. Should he still have been executed?

In 2004, Texas had 458 inmates on death row, more than any state except California, which had 634. Should they all be promptly executed with no more appeals? Why or why not?

2. Napoleon Beazley

(Reported by Jim Yardley in *The New York Times*, August 10, 2001.) On April 19, 1994, Napoleon Beazley and two friends ambushed John Luttig on his driveway in Tyler, Texas. It was supposed to be a carjacking, but in a panic Mr. Beazley shot Mr. Luttig twice in the head, killing him as his wife crawled under the car.

When he committed this crime, Mr. Beazley was seventeen years old. Only six countries in the world execute juvenile offenders, and only thirteen of the thirty-eight states having the death penalty provide the death penalty for juveniles. Texas is one of those states. Mr. Beazley was found guilty and received the death sentence after the two codefendants agreed to a plea bargain, and testified against him. The two codefendants escaped capital prosecution.

Mr. Beazley was black, and Mr. Luttig was white. Mr. Luttig also happened to be the father of a very prominent federal judge, Michael Luttig of the Court of Appeals for the Fourth Circuit in Virginia. Judge Luttig closely observed and participated in the case against Mr. Beazley. As a result, the prosecution was able to dismiss a prospective black juror and seat an all-white jury, including Maxine Herbst, who was president of the local branch of the Daughters of the Confederacy and displayed the Confederate flag from her home.

On August 13, 2001, the U.S. Supreme Court turned down a request for a stay of execution for Mr. Beazley. Three Justices—Antonin Scalia, David Souter, and Clarence Thomas—disqualified themselves because of their close ties to Judge Luttig. Because a majority is needed for a stay of execution, the Court's 3–3 decision was a defeat for Mr. Beazley.

This case raises some important questions. Is it fair to have an all-white jury for a black defendant? How can we provide a fair trial when the rich and powerful are involved?

3. Karla Faye Tucker

(Reported by Daniel Pedersen in *Newsweek*, February 2, 1998.) On June 13, 1983, a few hours before dawn, Tucker used a pickax to kill two people who had annoyed her. The male victim, Jerry Lynn Dean, had once dripped motor oil on her living-room carpet and had cut up some photographs of Tucker's mother. The female victim, Deborah Thorton, just happened to be asleep beside Dean in his Houston apartment; Tucker didn't even know her. Tucker and her boyfriend hacked away at both victims until they were dead and then left a two-foot blade imbedded seven inches into Thorton's chest. On a tape played at her trial, Tucker boasted that she had felt a surge of sexual pleasure with every swing of the pickax.

Tucker was found guilty and was sentenced to death by lethal injection. But fourteen years later, shortly before she was to be executed, Tucker launched an impressive last-minute campaign to have her sentence commuted to life imprisonment. Her appeal attracted worldwide media attention. One reason for all the publicity was Tucker's gender. Texas has carried out more executions than any other state, and the death penalty is popular in Texas, but a woman had not been executed there since the middle of the Civil War.

Tucker's appeal was not based on her gender, however. She claimed that when she committed the crime, she was a drug-addicted prostitute, but now she was a born-again Christian who was sincerely repentant and reformed. She was married to a prison minister. She was an active evangelist, writing essays and making antidrug videotapes. She appeared on Pat Robertson's Christian cable TV show, *The 700 Club.* She managed to muster the support of a wide variety of character witnesses and sympathizers, including Pope John Paul II, Bianca Jagger, the European Parliament, prison guards, former prosecutors, the detective who arrested her, one of the jurors in her case, and even the brother of the woman she murdered.

Tucker's appeal was unsuccessful. The Texas parole board voted 16 to 0 against commuting her sentence. Texas Governor George W. Bush refused to grant a thirty-day reprieve, and the Supreme Court rejected Tucker's final appeal less than an hour before she was put to death.

At 6:45 PM on February 3, 1998, Tucker was pronounced dead, eight minutes after the injection of lethal drugs. In Europe, opinion writers called it a "barbaric act." In the United States, some feminists voiced approval that women had achieved equal rights in capital litigation; not like Russia, where the death penalty is used for men but not women.

Was the execution of Tucker justified or not? Why or why not?

If there is a death penalty, should it be applied equally to men and women? What is your view?

4. The Sacco-Vanzetti Case

On April 15, 1920, a paymaster for a shoe company in South Braintree, Massachusetts, and his guard were shot and killed by two men who escaped with more than $15,000. Witnesses thought the two men were Italians, and Nicola Sacco and Bartolomeo Vanzetti were arrested. Both men were anarchists and had evaded the army draft. Upon their arrest, they made false statements. Both carried firearms; but neither had a criminal record, nor was there any evidence that they had the money. In July 1921, they were found guilty and sentenced to death. The conduct of the trial by Judge Webster Thayer was criticized, and indeed much of the evidence against them was

later discredited. The court denied their appeal for a new trial, and Governor Alvan T. Fuller, after postponing the execution, allowed them to be executed on August 22, 1927. Many regarded the two as innocent, prompting worldwide sympathy demonstrations. The case has been the subject of many books, most of which agree that Vanzetti was innocent but that Sacco may have been guilty. The gun found on Sacco was tested with modern ballistics equipment in 1961, and these tests seem to show that the gun had been used to kill the guard.

Was it morally right to execute these two men? Why or why not?

5. Governor George Ryan of Illinois

(See George Ryan, "I Must Act," in Hugo Bedau and Paul Cassell, eds., *Debating the Death Penalty* (Oxford, UK: University Press, 2004), pp. 218–34). George Ryan was the thirty-ninth governor of Illinois. On January 11, 2003, he announced the commutation of all of Illinois's death sentences. In a speech delivered at Northwestern University College of Law, Governor Ryan explained his reasons for ending the death sentence in Illinois. To begin with, seventeen men had been wrongly convicted. One of these men, Aaron Patterson, was unjustly imprisoned for fifteen years. Another one of the condemned, LeRoy Orange, lost seventeen of the best years of his life on death row. Most of the major allies of the United States—Europe, Canada, Mexico, and most of South and Central American—do not have the death penalty. Even Russia has called a moratorium on the punishment. The death penalty has been abolished in twelve states and in none of these states has the homicide rate increased. In Illinois one is five times more likely to get the death sentence for first-degree murder in rural areas than in

Cook County. Nearly half of the three hundred or so capital cases in Illinois had been reversed for a new trial or resentencing. Thirty-three of the death row inmates were represented at trial by an attorney who had later been disbarred or suspended from practicing law. Thirty-five of the black defendants had been convicted or condemned by all-white juries. More than two-thirds of the inmates on death row were black. Forty-six inmates were convicted on the basis of testimony from jailhouse informants. Illinois had the dubious distinction of having exonerated more men than it had executed: thirteen men found innocent, twelve executed. The overwhelming majority of those executed were psychotic, alcoholic, drug-addicted, or mentally ill. They were poor; few people with money or prestige are convicted of capital crimes, and even fewer are executed. All these considerations led Governor Ryan to conclude that the Illinois death penalty system is arbitrary and capricious, and therefore immoral.

Do you agree with Governor Ryan? Why or why not?

6. *Lethal Injection*

Lethal injection is used in thirty-six states having the death penalty. It has been adopted by these states in response to the objection that other methods of execution, such as gassing or electrocution, are extremely painful and thus violate the Eighth Amendment ban on cruel and unusual punishment.

Three drugs are used in the standard lethal injection procedure. The first is a barbiturate that is supposed to render the prisoner unconscious. The second is pancuronium bromide, a relative of curare. If administered by itself, it paralyzes the body while leaving the subject conscious but unable to cry out. The third is potassium chloride, which stops the heart and can cause severe pain as it goes through the veins.

Critics say that the paralytic chemical serves no purpose and may mask excruciating pain. Also, they claim that the procedure is often done by untrained personnel, with the result that the inmate dies painfully.

A recent example of a painful execution is the botched killing of Angel Diaz in Florida in 2007.

Mr. Diaz took thirty-four minutes to die, gasping and grimacing with pain as the procedure stalled. A preliminary medical examiner's report found that the intravenous needles had not been properly placed in Mr. Diaz's arms. An autopsy revealed large chemical burns on his right and left arms.

Jeb Bush, the governor of Florida, halted executions shortly after the execution of Mr. Diaz and appointed a panel to study lethal injection protocols.

One problem is that doctors refuse to assist in the lethal injection procedure because it violates their professional code of conduct. As a result, the procedure is often done by people without medical qualifications. Should doctors be required to do the procedure? Why or why not?

If doctors cannot be found to assist in the execution, then who should do it? Perhaps special executioners should be trained. Is this a good idea or not?

As currently practiced, does lethal injection violate the Eighth Amendment or not? Explain your view.

SUGGESTED READINGS

For facts about the death penalty, see the Death Penalty Information Center (http://www.deathpenalty.org). For current information, see the American Civil Liberties Union (http://www.aclu.org). The death penalty is defended on Pro-Death Penalty.Com (http://www.prodeathpenalty.com). For objections to the death penalty, see the Campaign to End the Death Penalty (http://www.nodeath-penalty.ort/index.html). Death Penalty Focus (http://www.deathpenalty.org) and the National Coalition to Abolish the Death Penalty (http://www.ncadp.org) provide more information online about the death penalty.

Hugo Adam Bedau, "The Case Against the Death Penalty," in the ACLU online archives (http://archive.aclu.org/library/case against death.html), presents eight objections to the death penalty. The ACLU is opposed to the death penalty.

Hugo Bedau and Paul Cassell, eds., *Debating the Death Penalty* (Oxford, UK: Oxford University Press, 2004), contains essays for and against the death penalty. Bedau presents a history of the death penalty in the United States; Louis P. Pojman and Paul Cassell defend it.

Louis P. Pojman and Jeffrey Reiman, *The Death Penalty: For and Against* (Lanham, MD: Rowman & Littlefield, 1988). Pojman defends the utilitarian argument that capital punishment is justified because it deters potential murderers, and Reiman replies with objections.

Jonathan Glover, *Causing Death and Saving Lives* (Harmondsworth, UK: Pelican Books, 1977), pp. 228–245, attacks Kant's retributive theory and argues for the abolition of the death penalty from a utilitarian point of view.

Hugo Adam Bedau, "How to Argue About the Death Penalty," *Israel Law Review* 25, 2–4 (Summer/Autumn 1991): 466–480, argues that a preponderance of reasons favors abolition of the death penalty.

Hugo Adam Bedau, "Capital Punishment," in *Matters of Life and Death*, 3rd ed., ed. Tom Regan (New York: Random House, 1993), pp. 160–194, argues that neither the appeal to retribution nor the appeal to deterrence justifies the death penalty as opposed to the alternative punishment of life imprisonment.

Hugo Adam Bedau, ed., *The Death Penalty in America*, 3rd ed. (Oxford, UK: Oxford University Press, 1982), provides a number of useful articles on factual data relevant to the death penalty, and articles both for and against it.

Mark Costanzo, *Just Revenge: Costs and Consequences of the Death Penalty* (New York: St. Martin's Press, 1997), covers various aspects of the death penalty and concludes that it should be abolished.

Robert M. Baird and Stuart E. Rosenbaum, eds., *Punishment and the Death Penalty: The Current Debate* (Amherst, NY: Prometheus Books, 1995), is an anthology with readings on the justification of punishment and the death penalty.

Tom Sorell, *Moral Theory and Capital Punishment* (Oxford, UK: Blackwell, 1988) defends the death penalty.

Tom Sorell, "Aggravated Murder and Capital Punishment," *Journal of Applied Philosophy*, 10 (1993): 201–213, argues in favor of the death penalty for the most serious murders.

Charles L. Black, Jr., *Capital Punishment: The Inevitability of Caprice and Mistake* (New York: W.W. Norton, 1981), maintains that mistakes cannot be eliminated from the imposition of the death penalty, and for that reason it ought to be abolished.

Walter Berns, *For Capital Punishment* (New York: Basic Books, 1979), defends a retributivist justification of capital punishment.

Robert S. Gerstein, "Capital Punishment—'Cruel and Unusual?' A Retributivist Response," *Ethics* 85 (January 1975): 75–79, defends retributivism against the complaint that it is mere vengeance.

Steven Goldberg, "On Capital Punishment," *Ethics* 85 (October 1974): 67–74, examines the factual issue of whether the death penalty is a uniquely effective deterrent. A revised version, titled "Does Capital Punishment Deter?," appears in *Today's Moral Problems*, 2nd ed., ed. Richard A. Wasserstrom (New York: Macmillan, 1979), pp. 538–551.

Sidney Hook, "The Death Sentence," in *The Death Penalty in America*, ed. Hugo Adam Bedau (Garden City, NY: Doubleday, 1967), supports the retention of the death penalty in two cases: (1) defendants convicted of murder who choose death rather than life imprisonment, and (2) those who have been sentenced to prison for murder and then murder again while in prison.

Bruce N. Waller, "From Hemlock to Lethal Injection: The Case for Self-Execution," *International Journal of Applied Philosophy* 4 (Fall 1989): 53–58, argues that prisoners condemned to death should be offered the chance to kill themselves.

Robert Johnson, "This Man Has Expired. Witness to an Execution," *Commonweal* (January 13, 1989): 9–13, gives a detailed and graphic description of an electric-chair execution.

Stephen Nathanson, *An Eye for an Eye? The Morality of Punishing Death* (Lanham, MD: Rowman & Littlefield, 1987), discusses issues surrounding the death penalty and develops a case for abolishing it.

Welsh S. White, *The Death Penalty in the Nineties* (Ann Arbor: University of Michigan Press, 1991), examines the way the death penalty has been administered in the 1990s.

Same-Sex Marriage

- **Introduction**
  - Factual Background
  - The Readings
  - Philosophical Issues

JEFF JORDAN **Is It Wrong to Discriminate on the Basis of Homosexuality?**

DAVID BOONIN **Same-Sex Marriage and the Argument from Public Disagreement**

JONATHAN RAUCH **Who Needs Marriage?**

MAGGIE GALLAGER **What Marriage Is For**

PROBLEM CASES

SUGGESTED READINGS

INTRODUCTION

Factual Background

Same-sex marriage is a legal contract or socially recognized union between two persons of the same biological sex or gender. UCLA researchers estimate that there are more than 32,000 legally married same-sex couples in the United States, and an additional 150,000 couples that refer to one another as husband or wife. The same-sex couples had an average age of 52 and household incomes of more than $90,000 a year. More than 30 percent of the same-sex couples are raising children, as compared to 40 percent of the married heterosexual couples who are raising children.

Marriage gives the married persons important obligations, rights, and privileges. There is usually a promise to love and care for each other. There is a right to the dead spouse's Social Security pension and veteran's benefits. While married, there is a right to benefits such as Supplemental Security income, disability payments, Medicaid, and income-tax deductions. After divorce, there are custodial rights to children, shared property, child support, and alimony. According to the U.S. Government Accountability Office, there are more than a thousand laws giving married persons various benefits, rights, and privileges.

Same-sex marriages or unions are not a new phenomenon. Historians claim that they occurred in ancient Rome and Greece, medieval Japan and China, in Native American tribes, and in some tribes in Africa. According to historian Allan A. Tulchin, same-sex marriage was recognized more than 600 years ago in medieval

France. The term *affrerement* (roughly, brotherment) was used to refer to a legal contract where two men pledged to love and live together. They shared property and became each other's legal heir.

Worldwide, five countries sanction same-sex marriage: The Netherlands, Belgium, Canada, Spain, Norway, and Sweden. Denmark, Finland, Hungary, and Iceland allow registered partnerships, which are almost equal to marriage.

Same-sex marriage is controversial in the United States. The controversy became intense when the Supreme Court of Hawaii ruled in 1993 that the denial of marriage licenses to three gay couples was unconstitutional sexual discrimination. In 1994, the Hawaii legislature responded by passing a bill defining marriage as a "man-woman unity" capable of procreation. In 1998, Hawaii voters rejected the legalization of same-sex marriage.

In view of the prospect of states legalizing same-sex marriage, the United States Congress in 1996 approved the Defense of Marriage Act, which defines marriage as a legal union exclusively between one man and one woman. The bill denies federal benefits to same-sex married couples and allows states to ignore same-sex marriages performed in other states. President Bill Clinton signed the bill into law.

Despite this setback, the activists eventually succeeded in getting Massachusetts to legalize same-sex marriage. In 2004, the Supreme Court in Massachusetts ruled that same-sex marriage was required under the equal protection of rights clause in the state's constitution. The court recognized the right to marriage as a basic right that could not be denied on the basis of sex. By 2009, four more states had legalized same-sex marriage: Vermont, New Hampshire, Connecticut, and Iowa. It should be noted that these states legalized same-sex marriage by legislation or court ruling, not by popular vote. In thirty-one states where the issue has been put to a popular vote, there have been constitutional amendments banning same-sex marriage.

At the time of this writing, Maine and California remain battlegrounds. In Maine, a state law that would have allowed same-sex couples to wed was repealed by a popular referendum. In California, the Supreme Court ruled in 2008 that a state law banning same-sex marriage constituted illegal sexual discrimination and that domestic partnerships were not an adequate substitute. The court held that marriage must be granted to all couples meeting the marriage requirements no matter what sex or gender. Opponents of same-sex marriage launched Proposition 8, a measure prohibiting same-sex marriage. The measure passed in November 2008, with 52 percent of the vote in favor. The California Supreme Court upheld the voter-approved ban, but decided that the 18,000 same-sex marriages that had taken place before the ban were still legal.

The Readings

Jeff Jordan defends a ban on same-sex marriage. He argues that even though this ban discriminates against homosexuals, this legal discrimination is morally permissible in the case of same-sex marriage. His first argument for this discrimination, the argument from conflicting claims, assumes that the only acceptable way to resolve the public dilemma about same-sex marriage is for the state to refuse to sanction same-sex marriage but to tolerate private homosexual acts. To do otherwise is to fail to respect the religious condemnation of homosexuality. His second argument, the no-exit argument, assumes that same-sex marriage will force citizens to support a practice that they find morally or religiously objectionable.

David Boonin replies to Jordan and defends same-sex marriage. Jordan's first argument fails because the public dilemma is not resolved by Jordan's accommodation proposal. If the state tolerates private homosexual acts, then those who feel strongly that these acts are immoral are not satisfied. If the state bans same-sex marriage, then those who strongly desire it are frustrated. There is no resolution because one group always ends up unsatisfied. Also, if the state bans same-sex marriage, then it ought to ban mixed-race marriage because there are those who oppose it. Boonin thinks this would be intolerable. Finally, the right to marry the person of choice is a basic right that should not be denied. If so, then same-sex marriage should be allowed in a society that recognizes basic rights.

Jonathan Rauch also defends same-sex marriage. He grants that modern marriage is based on religious traditions, but he rejects the idea that secular marriage must give any consideration to religious doctrine or respect the Christian nation crowd. This can be viewed as a reply to Jordan's second argument, the no-exit argument. As Rauch puts the point, "Religious doctrine has no special standing in the world of secular law and policy." He denies that allowing gays to marry will have bad effects in our society; allowing a few percent of the population to marry will have little or no effect on society. Even if there are some bad effects, allowing gay marriage is still the right thing to do. Besides, he thinks there will be good effects, such as civilizing young males and providing married people with a caregiver.

Maggie Gallagher attacks same-sex marriage or gay marriage, but her objections do not appeal to religious teachings about the immorality of homosexuality. Instead, she argues that gay marriage challenges the fundamental purpose of marriage, which in her view is not about love and commitment but procreation and caring for children. She assumes that only mothers and fathers can raise children satisfactorily; gay men, lesbians, single parents, or grandparents cannot do this. Prohibiting gay marriage does not constitute discrimination against gay men or lesbians because they can marry and have children with members of the opposite sex. Erotic attachment is irrelevant; what matters is sexual fidelity, mutual caregiving, and shared parenting.

Philosophical Issues

Who has rights, and what are they? These are fundamental questions raised by the readings. Rauch defends the position that gay men and lesbians have the same rights as other minorities such as blacks. These rights include the right to marry and the right to have children or adopt and care for them. Boonin agrees that most people have a right to marry whomever they wish and have this marriage publicly recognized. This is a very commonly recognized right, and failing to respect it for Jews and by implication gays is simply outrageous. Jordan and Gallagher want to deny gay men and lesbians the right to marry. Jordan admits that this is discrimination, but he thinks it is morally permissible. Gallagher claims that she is not discriminating against gay men and lesbians, but it is clear that she wants to deny them the right to marry the one they love and are committed to if this is a person of the same sex. This is certainly a restriction on their right to marry.

Is homosexual conduct morally wrong? This is another basic issue that comes up in the readings. Jordan says that the theistic tradition of Judaism, Christianity, and Islam clearly says that homosexual behavior is sinful and morally wrong. This may settle the issue for religious people, but not for Rauch, Boonin, and other nonreligious people. The Vatican "Declaration on Sexual Ethics" (see the Suggested Readings) argues that homosexual behavior is seriously disordered and morally wrong because it opposes the natural end of sex, which is procreation. Masturbation is morally wrong for the same reason. Critics of this view such as Alan Goldman (see the Suggested Readings) argue that sex has other purposes besides reproduction; for example, it is an expression of love and affection or just fun. Another objection is that homosexual behavior is somehow unnatural. The meaning of the word *unnatural*, however, is subject to debate. For example, flying in an airplane may be unnatural, but it is not morally wrong. David Bradshaw (see the Suggested Readings) argues that homosexual acts are morally wrong because they involve a misuse of the body, a violation of the body's "moral space." The idea is that heterosexual sex somehow "fits" the body's moral space, whereas homosexual sex does not do this. Gays and lesbians can reply that there is more than one sexual fit, and using one's body to express love is not a misuse of the body, but morally right.

What would be the consequences of allowing secular same-sex marriage? This is a practical issue that is addressed in the readings. Martha C. Nussbaum (see the Suggested Readings) contends that it is desirable for gay men and lesbians to live together and provide emotional and material support, love, intimacy, companionship, and the other goods of marriage. As for having and raising children, she says there is no evidence that same-sex parents are worse parents than heterosexual parents. Rauch argues that allowing a small percentage of the population to marry will not make much difference, or not as much difference as other social changes such as legalizing contraception. One good result is that gays and lesbians will have reliable caregivers. Jordan and Gallagher do not agree. Jordan appeals to the fact that many religious people think homosexual behavior is morally wrong. If gay marriage becomes legal, they will be offended and forced to support practices they find objectionable. Gallagher argues that allowing gay marriage would change our legal, public, and social conception of what marriage is, and this would threaten the core purpose of marriage, which is procreation and childrearing. In sharp contrast, Nussbaum suggests that changing the institution of heterosexual marriage would be desirable because heterosexual marriage has grave moral problems, including child abuse, marital rape, and domestic violence.

Is It Wrong to Discriminate on the Basis of Homosexuality?

JEFF JORDAN

Jeff Jordan is professor of philosophy at the University of Delaware. He is the author of *Gambling on God* (2002) and *Pascal's Wager* (2006).

Jordan deploys two arguments to justify discrimination against homosexuals in marriage and other areas of controversy. The argument from conflicting claims resolves the public dilemma about same-sex marriage by an accommodation that prohibits state-sanctioned

Source: "Is It Wrong to Discriminate on the Basis of Homosexuality?" by Jeff Jordan, from *Journal of Social Philosophy*, 1995. Reprinted by permission of Blackwell Publishing, Ltd.

same-sex marriage but tolerates private homosexual acts. The no-exit argument appeals to the basic principle that citizens should not be forced to violate their religious beliefs.

Much like the issue of abortion in the early 1970s, the issue of homosexuality has exploded to the forefront of social discussion. Is homosexual sex on a moral par with heterosexual sex? Or is homosexuality in some way morally inferior? Is it wrong to discriminate against homosexuals—to treat homosexuals in less favorable ways than one does heterosexuals? Or is some discrimination against homosexuals morally justified? These questions are the focus of this essay.

In what follows, I argue that there are situations in which it is morally permissible to discriminate against homosexuals because of their homosexuality. That is, there are some morally relevant differences between heterosexuality and homosexuality which, in some instances, permit a difference in treatment. The issue of marriage provides a good example. While it is clear that heterosexual unions merit the state recognition known as marriage, along with all the attendant advantages—spousal insurance coverage, inheritance rights, ready eligibility of adoption—it is far from clear that homosexual couples ought to be accorded that state recognition.

The argument of this essay makes no claim about the moral status of homosexuality per se. Briefly put, it is the argument of this essay that the moral impasse generated by conflicting views concerning homosexuality, and the public policy ramifications of those conflicting views justify the claim that it is morally permissible, in certain circumstances, to discriminate against homosexuals.[1]

1. THE ISSUE

The relevant issue is this: Does homosexuality have the same moral status as heterosexuality? Put differently, since there are no occasions in which it is morally permissible to treat heterosexuals unfavorably, whether because they are heterosexual or because of heterosexual acts, are there occasions in which it is morally permissible to treat homosexuals unfavorably, whether because they are homosexuals or because of homosexual acts?

A negative answer to the above can be termed the "parity thesis." The parity thesis contends that *homosexuality has the same moral status as heterosexuality.* If the parity thesis is correct, then it would be immoral to discriminate against homosexuals because of their homosexuality. An affirmative answer can be termed the "difference thesis" and contends that there are morally relevant differences between heterosexuality and homosexuality which justify a difference in moral status and treatment between homosexuals and heterosexuals. The difference thesis entails that *there are situations in which it is normally permissible to discriminate against homosexuals.*

It is perhaps needless to point out that the difference thesis follows as long as there is at least one occasion in which it is morally permissible to discriminate against homosexuals. If the parity thesis were true, then on no occasion would a difference in treatment between heterosexuals and homosexuals ever be justified. The difference thesis does not, even if true, justify discriminatory actions on every occasion. Nonetheless, even though the scope of the difference thesis is relatively modest, it is, if true, a significant principle which has not only theoretical import but import practical consequences as well.[2]

A word should be said about the notion of discrimination. To discriminate against X means treating X in an unfavorable way. The word "discrimination" is not a synonym for "morally unjustifiable treatment." Some discrimination is morally unjustifiable; some is not. For example, we discriminate against convicted felons in that they are disenfranchised. This legal discrimination is morally permissible even though it involves treating one person unfavorably different from how other persons are treated.

The difference thesis entails that there are circumstances in which it is morally permissible to discriminate against homosexuals.

2. AN ARGUMENT FOR THE PARITY THESIS

One might suppose that an appeal to a moral right, the right to privacy, perhaps, or the right to liberty, would provide the strongest grounds for the parity thesis. Rights talk, though sometimes helpful, is not very helpful here. If there is reason to think that the right to privacy or the right to liberty encompasses sexuality (which seems plausible enough), it would do so only with regard to private acts and not public acts. Sexual acts performed in public (whether heterosexual or homosexual) are properly suppressible. It does not take too much imagination to see that the right to be free from offense would soon be offered as a counter consideration by those who find homosexuality morally problematic. Furthermore, how one adjudicates between the competing rights claims is far from clear. Hence, the bald appeal to a right will not, in this case anyway, take one very far.

Perhaps the strongest reason to hold that the parity thesis is true is something like the following:

(1) Homosexual acts between consenting adults harm no one. And,
(2) respecting persons' privacy and choices in harmless sexual matters maximizes individual freedom. And,
(3) individual freedom should be maximized. But,
(4) discrimination against homosexuals, because of their homosexuality, diminishes individual freedom since it ignores personal choice and privacy. So,
(5) the toleration of homosexuality rather than discriminating against homosexuals is the preferable option since it would maximize individual freedom. Therefore,
(6) the parity thesis is more plausible than the difference thesis.

Premise (2) is unimpeachable: if an act is harmless and if there are persons who want to do it

and who choose to do it, then it seems clear that respecting the choices of those people would tend to maximize their freedom.[3] Step (3) is also beyond reproach: since freedom is arguably a great good and since there does not appear to be any ceiling on the amount of individual freedom—no "too much of a good thing"—(3) appears to be true.

At first glance, premise (1) seems true enough as long as we recognize that if there is any harm involved in the homosexual acts of consenting adults, it would be harm absorbed by the freely consenting participants. This is true, however, only if the acts in question are done in private. Public acts may involve more than just the willing participants. Persons who have no desire to participate, even if only as spectators, may have no choice if the acts are done in public. A real probability of there being unwilling participants is indicative of the public realm and not the private. However, where one draws the line between private acts and public acts is not always easy to discern, it is clear that different moral standards apply to public acts than to private acts.[4]

If premise (1) is understood to apply only to acts done in private, then it would appear to be true. The same goes for (4): discrimination against homosexuals for acts done in private would result in a diminishing of freedom. So (1)–(4) would lend support to (5) only if we understand (1)–(4) to refer to acts done in private. Hence, (5) must be understood as referring to private acts; and, as a consequence, (6) also must be read as referring only to acts done in private.

With regard to acts which involve only willing adult participants, there may be no morally relevant difference between homosexuality and heterosexuality. In other words, acts done in private. However, acts done in public add a new ingredient to the mix; an ingredient which has moral consequence. Consequently, the argument (1)–(6) fails in supporting the parity thesis. The argument (1)–(6) may show that there are some circumstances in which the moral status of homosexuality and heterosexuality are the same, but it gives us no reason for thinking that this result holds for all circumstances.[5]

3. MORAL IMPASSES AND PUBLIC DILEMMAS

Suppose one person believes that X is morally wrong, while another believes that X is morally permissible. The two people, let's stipulate, are not involved in a semantical quibble; they hold genuinely conflicting beliefs regarding the moral status of X. If the first person is correct, then the second person is wrong; and, of course, if the second person is right, then the first must be wrong. This situation of conflicting claims is what we will call an "impasse." Impasses arise out of moral disputes. Since the conflicting parties in an impasse take contrary views, the conflicting views cannot all be true, nor can they all be false.[6] Moral impasses may concern matters only of a personal nature, but moral impasses can involve public policy. An impasse is likely to have public policy ramifications if large numbers of people hold the conflicting views, and the conflict involves matters which are fundamental to a person's moral identity (and, hence, from a practical point of view, are probably irresolvable) and it involves acts done in public. Since not every impasse has public policy ramifications, one can mark off "public dilemma" as a special case of moral impasses: those moral impasses that have public policy consequences. Public dilemmas, then, are impasses located in the public square. Since they have public policy ramifications and since they arise from impasses, one side or another of the dispute will have its views implemented as public policy. Because of the public policy ramifications, and also because social order is sometimes threatened by the volatile parties involved in the impasse, the state has a role to play in resolving a public dilemma.

A public dilemma can be actively resolved in two ways.[7] The first is when the government allies itself with one side of the impasse and, by state coercion and sanction, declares that side of the impasse the correct side. The American Civil War was an example of this: the federal government forcibly ended slavery by aligning itself with the Abolitionist side of the impasse.[8] Prohibition is another example. The 18th Amendment and the Volstead Act allied the state with the Temperance side of the impasse. State mandated affirmative action programs provide a modern example of this. This kind of resolution of a public dilemma we can call a "resolution by declaration." The first of the examples cited above indicates that declarations can be morally proper, the right thing to do. The second example, however, indicates that declarations are not always morally proper. The state does not always take the side of the morally correct; nor is it always clear which side is the correct one.

The second way of actively resolving a public dilemma is that of accommodation. An accommodation in this context means resolving the public dilemma in a way that gives as much as possible to all sides of the impasse. A resolution by accommodation involves staking out some middle ground in a dispute and placing public policy in that location. The middle ground location of a resolution via accommodation is a virtue since it entails that there are no absolute victors and no absolute losers. The middle ground is reached in order to resolve the public dilemma in a way which respects the relevant views of the conflicting parties and which maintains social order. The Federal Fair Housing Act and, perhaps, the current status of abortion (legal but with restrictions) provide examples of actual resolutions via accommodation.[9]

In general, governments should be, at least as far as possible, neutral with regard to the disputing parties in a public dilemma. Unless there is some overriding reason why the state should take sides in a public dilemma—the protection of innocent life, or abolishing slavery, for instance—the state should be neutral, because no matter which side of the public dilemma the state takes, the other side will be the recipient of unequal treatment by the state. A state which is partial and takes sides in moral disputes via declaration, when there is no overriding reason why it should, is tyrannical. Overriding reasons involve, typically, the protection of generally recognized rights.[10] In the case of slavery, the right to liberty; in the case of protecting innocent life, the right involved is the negative right to life. If a public dilemma must be actively resolved, the state should do so (in the absence of an overriding reason) via accommodation and not declaration since the latter entails that a sizable number of people would be forced to live under a government which "legitimizes" and does not just tolerate activities which they find immoral. Resolution via declaration is appropriate only if there is an overriding reason for the state to throw its weight behind one side in a public dilemma.

Is moral rightness an overriding reason for a resolution via declaration? What better reason might there be for a resolution by declaration than that it is the right thing to do? Unless one is prepared to endorse a view that is called "legal moralism"—that immorality alone is a sufficient reason for the state to curtail individual liberty—then one had best hold that moral rightness alone is not an overriding reason. Since some immoral acts neither harm nor offend nor violate another's rights, it seems clear enough that too much liberty would be lost if legal moralism were adopted as public policy.[11]

Though we do not have a definite rule for determining *a priori* which moral impasses genuinely constitute public dilemmas, we can proceed via a case by case method. For example, many people hold that cigarette smoking is harmful and, on that basis, is properly suppressible. Others disagree. Is this a public dilemma? Probably not. Whether someone engages in an imprudent action is, as long as it involves no unwilling participants, a private matter and does not, on that account, constitute a public dilemma. What about abortion? Is abortion a public dilemma? Unlike cigarette smoking, abortion is a public dilemma. This is clear from the adamant and even violent contrary positions involved in the impasse. Abortion is an issue which forces itself into the public square. So, it is clear that, even though we lack a rule which filters through moral impasses designating some as public dilemmas, not every impasse constitute a public dilemma.

4. CONFLICTING CLAIMS ON HOMOSEXUALITY

The theistic tradition, Judaism and Christianity and Islam, has a clear and deeply entrenched position on homosexual acts: they are prohibited. Now it seems clear enough that if one is

going to take seriously the authoritative texts of the respective religions, then one will have to adopt the views of those texts, unless one wishes to engage in a demythologizing of them with the result that one ends up being only a nominal adherent of that tradition.[12] As a consequence, many contemporary theistic adherents of the theistic tradition, in no small part because they can read, hold that homosexual behavior is sinful. Though God loves the homosexual, these folk say, God hates the sinful behavior. To say that act X is a sin entails that X is morally wrong, not necessarily because it is harmful or offensive, but because X violates God's will. So, the claim that homosexuality is sinful entails the claims that it is also morally wrong. And, it is clear, many people adopt the difference thesis just because of their religious views: because the Bible or the Koran holds that homosexuality is wrong, they too hold that view.

Well, what should we make of these observations? We do not, for one thing, have to base our moral conclusions on those views, if for no other reason than not every one is a theist. If one does not adopt the religion-based moral view, one must still respect those who do: they cannot just be dismissed out of hand.[13] And, significantly, this situation yields a reason for thinking that the difference thesis is probably true. Because many religious people sincerely believe homosexual acts to be morally wrong and many others believe that homosexual acts are not morally wrong, there results a public dilemma.[14]

The existence of this public dilemma gives us reason for thinking that the difference thesis is true. It is only via the difference thesis and not the parity thesis, that an accommodation can be reached. Here again, the private/public distinction will come into play.

To see this, take as an example the issue of homosexual marriages. A same-sex marriage would be a public matter. For the government to sanction same-sex marriages—to grant the recognition and reciprocal benefits which attach to marriage—would ally the government with one side of the public dilemma and against the adherents of religion-based moralities. This is especially true given that, historically, no government has sanctioned same-sex marriages. The status quo has been no same-sex marriages. If the state were to change its practice now, it would be clear that the state has taken sides in the impasse. Given the history, for a state to sanction a same-sex marriage now would not be a neutral act.

Of course, some would respond here that by not sanctioning same-sex marriages, the state is, and historically has been, taking sides to the detriment of homosexuals. There is some truth in this claim. But one must be careful here. The respective resolutions of this issue—whether the state should recognize and sanction same-sex marriages—do not have symmetrical implications. The asymmetry of this issue is a function of the private/public distinction and the fact that marriage is a public matter. If the state sanctions same-sex marriages, then there is no accommodation available. In that event, the religion-based, morality proponents are faced with a public, state-sanctioned matter which they find seriously immoral. This would be an example of a resolution via declaration. On the other hand, if the state does not sanction same-sex marriages, there is an accommodation available: in the public realm the state sides with the religion-based moral view, but the state can tolerate private homosexual acts. That is, since homosexual acts are not essentially public acts, they can be, and historically have been, performed in private. The state, by not sanctioning same-sex marriages is acting in the public realm, but it can leave the private realm to personal choice.[15]

5. THE ARGUMENT FROM CONFLICTING CLAIMS

It was suggested in the previous section that the public dilemma concerning homosexuality, and in particular whether states should sanction same-sex marriages, generates an argument in support of the difference thesis. The argument, again using same-sex marriages as the particular case, is as follows:

(7) There are conflicting claims regarding whether the state should sanction same-sex marriages. And,

(8) this controversy constitutes a public dilemma. And,

(9) there is an accommodation possible if the state does not recognize same-sex marriages. And,

(10) there is no accommodation possible if the state does sanction same-sex marriages. And,

(11) there is no overriding reason for a resolution via declaration. Hence,

(12) the state ought not sanction same-sex marriages. And,

(13) the state ought to sanction heterosexual marriages. So,

(14) there is at least one morally relevant case in which discrimination against homosexuals, because of their homosexuality, is morally permissible. Therefore,

(15) the difference thesis is true.

Since proposition (14) is logically equivalent to the difference thesis, then, if (7)–(14) are sound, proposition (15) certainly follows.

Premises (7) and (8) are uncontroversial. Premises (9) and (10) are based on the asymmetry that results from the public nature of marriage. Proposition (11) is based on our earlier analysis of the argument (1)–(6). Since the strongest argument in support of the parity thesis fails, we have reason to think that there is no overriding reason why the state ought to resolve the public dilemma via declaration in favor of same-sex marriages. We have reason, in other words, to think that (11) is true.

Proposition (12) is based on the conjunction of (7)–(11) and the principle that, in the absence of an overriding reason for state intervention via declaration, resolution by accommodation is the preferable route. Proposition (13) is just trivially true. So, given the moral difference mentioned in (12) and (13), proposition (14) logically follows.

6. TWO OBJECTIONS CONSIDERED

The first objection to the argument from conflicting claims would contend that it is unsound because a similar sort of argument would permit discrimination against some practice which, though perhaps controversial at some earlier time, is now widely thought to be morally permissible. Take mixed-race marriages, for example. The opponent of the argument from conflicting claims could argue that a similar argument would warrant prohibition against mixed-race marriages. If it does, we would have good reason to reject (7)–(14) as unsound.

There are three responses to this objection. The first response denies that the issue of mixed-race marriages is in fact a public dilemma. It may have been so at one time, but it does not seem to generate much, if any, controversy today. Hence, the objection is based upon a faulty analogy.

The second response grants for the sake of the argument that the issue of mixed-race marriages generates a public dilemma. But the second response points out that there is a relevant difference between mixed-race marriages and same-sex marriages that allows for a resolution by declaration in the case but not the other. As evident from the earlier analysis of the argument in support of (1)–(6), there is reason to think that there is no overriding reason for a resolution by declaration in support of the parity thesis. On the other hand, it is a settled matter that state protection from racial discrimination is a reason sufficient for a resolution via declaration. Hence, the two cases are only apparently similar, and, in reality, they are crucially different. They are quite different because, clearly enough, if mixed-race marriages do generate a public dilemma, the state should use resolution by declaration in support of such marriages. The same cannot be said for same-sex marriages.

One should note that the second response to the objection does not beg the question against the proponent of the parity thesis. Though the second response denies that race and sexuality are strict analogues, it does so for a defensible and independent reason: it is a settled matter that race is not a sufficient reason for disparate treatment; but, as we have seen from the analysis of (1)–(6), there is no overriding reason to think the same about sexuality.[16]

The third response to the first objection is that the grounds of objection differ in the respective cases: one concerns racial identity; the other concerns behavior thought to be morally problematic. A same-sex marriage would involve behavior which many people find morally objectionable; a mixed-race marriage is objectionable to some, not because of the participants' behavior, but because of the racial identity of the participants. It is the race of the marriage partners which some find of primary complaint concerning mixed-race marriages. With same-sex marriages, however, it is the behavior which is primarily objectionable. To see this latter point, one should note that, though promiscuously Puritan in tone, the kind of sexual acts that are likely involved in a same-sex marriage are objectionable to some, regardless of whether done by homosexuals or heterosexuals.[17] So again, there is reason to reject the analogy between same-sex marriages and mixed-race marriages. Racial identity is an immutable trait and a complaint about mixed-race marriages necessarily involves, then, a complaint about an immutable trait. Sexual behavior is not an immutable trait and it is possible to object to same-sex marriages based on the behavior which would be involved in such marriages. Put succinctly, the third response could be formulated as follows: objections to mixed-race marriages necessarily involve objections over status, while objections to same-sex marriages could involve objections over behavior. Therefore, the two cases are not analogues since there is a significant modal difference in the ground of the objection.

The second objection to the argument from conflicting claims can be stated so: if homosexuality is biologically based—if it is inborn[18]—then how can discrimination ever be justified? If it is not a matter of choice, homosexuality is an immutable trait which is, as a consequence, morally permissible. Just as it would be absurd to hold someone morally culpable for being of a certain race, likewise it would be absurd to hold someone morally culpable for being a homosexual.

Consequently, according to this objection, the argument from conflicting claims "legitimizes" unjustifiable discrimination.

But this second objection is not cogent, primarily because it ignores an important distinction. No one could plausibly hold that homosexuals act by some sort of biological compulsion. If there is a biological component involved in sexual identity, it would incline but it would not compel. Just because one naturally (without any choice) has certain dispositions, is not in itself a morally cogent reason for acting upon that disposition. Most people are naturally selfish but it clearly does not follow that selfishness is in any way permissible on that account. Even if it is true that one has a predisposition to do X as a matter of biology and not as a matter of choice, it does not follow that doing X is morally permissible. For example, suppose that pyromania is an inborn predisposition. Just because one has an inborn and, in that sense, natural desire to set fires, one still has to decide whether or not to act on that desire.[19] The reason that the appeal to biology is specious is that it ignores the important distinction between being a homosexual and homosexual acts. One is status; the other is behavior. Even if one has the status naturally, it does not follow that the behavior is morally permissible, nor that others have a duty to tolerate the behavior.

But, while moral permissibility does not necessarily follow if homosexuality should turn out to be biologically based, what does follow is this: in the absence of a good reason to discriminate between homosexuals and heterosexuals, then, assuming that homosexuality is inborn, one ought not discriminate between them. If a certain phenomenon X is natural in the sense of being involuntary and nonpathological, and if there is no good reason to hold that X is morally problematic, then that is reason enough to think that X is morally permissible. In the absence of a good reason to repress X, one should tolerate it since, as per supposition, it is largely nonvoluntary. The argument from conflicting claims, however, provides a good reason which overrides this presumption.

7. A SECOND ARGUMENT FOR THE DIFFERENCE THESIS

A second argument for the difference thesis, similar to the argument from conflicting claims, is what might be called the "no-exit argument." This argument is based on the principle that:

> A. no just government can coerce a citizen into violating a deeply held moral belief or religious belief.

Is (A) plausible? It seems to be since the prospect of a citizen being coerced by the state into a practice which she finds profoundly immoral appears to be a clear example of an injustice. Principle (A), conjoined with there being a public dilemma arising over the issue of same-sex marriages, leads to the observation that if the state were to sanction same-sex marriages, then persons who have profound religious or moral objections to such unions would be legally mandated to violate their beliefs since there does not appear to be any feasible "exit right" possible with regard to state sanctioned marriage. An exit right is an exemption from some legally mandated practice, granted to a person or group, the purpose of which is to protect the religious or moral integrity of that person or group. Prominent examples of exit rights include conscientious objection and military service, home-schooling of the young because of some religious concern, and property used for religious purposes being free from taxation.

It is important to note that marriage is a public matter in the sense that, for instance, if one is an employer who provides health care benefits to the spouses of employees, one must provide those benefits to any employee who is married. Since there is no exit right possible in this case, one would be coerced, by force of law, into subsidizing a practice one finds morally or religiously objectionable.[20]

In the absence of an exit right, and if (A) is plausible, then the state cannot morally force persons to violate deeply held beliefs that are moral or religious in nature. In particular, the state morally could not sanction same-sex marriages since this would result in coercing some into violating a deeply held religious conviction.

8. A CONCLUSION

It is important to note that neither the argument from conflicting claims nor the no-exit argument licenses wholesale discrimination against homosexuals. What they do show is that some discrimination against homosexuals, in this case refusal to sanction same-sex marriages, is not only legally permissible but also morally permissible. The discrimination is a way of resolving a public policy dilemma that accommodates, to an extent, each side of the impasse and, further, protects the religious and moral integrity of a good number of people. In short, the arguments show us that there are occasions in which it is morally permissible to discriminate on the basis of homosexuality.[21]

NOTES

1. The terms "homosexuality" and "heterosexuality" are defined as follows: The former is defined as sexual feelings or behavior directed toward individuals of the same sex; the latter, naturally enough, is defined as sexual feelings or behavior directed toward individuals of the opposite sex.

   Sometimes the term "gay" is offered as an alternative to "homosexual." Ordinary use of "gay" has it as a synonym of a male homosexual (hence, the common expression, "gays and lesbians"). Given this ordinary usage, the substitution would lead to a confusing equivocation. Since there are female homosexuals, it is best to use "homosexual" to refer to both male and female homosexuals, and reserve "gay" to signify male homosexuals, and "lesbian" for female homosexuals in order to avoid the equivocation.

2. Perhaps we should distinguish the weak difference thesis (permissible discrimination on *some* occasions) from the strong difference thesis (given the relevant moral differences, discrimination on *any* occasion is permissible).

3. This would be true even if the act in question is immoral.

4. The standard answer is, of course, that the line between public and private is based on the notion of harm. Acts which carry a real probability of harming third parties are public acts.

5. For other arguments supporting the moral parity of homosexuality and heterosexuality, see Richard Mohr, *Gays/Justice: A Study of Ethics, Society and Law* (NY: Columbia, 1988); and see Michael Ruse, "The Morality of Homosexuality," in *Philosophy and Sex*, eds. R. Baker & F. Elliston (Buffalo, NY. Prometheus Books, 1984), pp. 370–390.

6. Perhaps it would be better to term the disputing positions "contradictory" views rather than "contrary" views.

7. Resolutions can also be passive in the sense of the state doing nothing. If the state does nothing to resolve the public dilemma, it stands pat with the status quo, and the public dilemma is resolved gradually by sociological changes (changes in mores and in beliefs).

8. Assuming, plausibly enough, that the disputes over the sovereignty of the Union and concerning states' rights were at bottom disputes about slavery.

9. The Federal Fair Housing Act prohibits discrimination in housing on the basis of race, religion, and sex. But it does not apply to the rental of rooms in single-family houses, or to a building of five units or less if the owner lives in one of the units. See 42 U.S.C. Section 3603.

10. Note that overriding reasons involve *generally recognized rights*. If a right is not widely recognized and the state nonetheless uses coercion to enforce it, there is a considerable risk that the state will be seen by many or even most people as tyrannical.

11. This claim is, perhaps, controversial. For a contrary view see Richard George, *Making Men Moral* (Oxford: Clarendon Press, 1993).

12. See, for example, Leviticus 18:22, 21:3; and Romans 1:22–32; and Koran IV:13.

13. For an argument that religiously-based moral views should not be dismissed out of hand, see Stephen Carter, *The Culture of Disbelief: How American Law and Politics Trivialize Religious Devotion* (NY: Basic Books, 1993).

14. Two assumptions are these: that the prohibitions against homosexuality activity are part of the religious doctrine and not just an extraneous addition; second, that if X is part of one's religious belief or religious doctrine, then it is morally permissible to hold X. Though this latter principle is vague, it is, I think, clear enough for our purposes here (I ignore here any points concerning the rationality of religious belief in general, or in particular cases).

15. This point has implications for the moral legitimacy of sodomy laws. One implication would be this: the private acts of consenting adults should not be criminalized.

16. An *ad hominem* point: If this response begs the question against the proponent of the parity thesis, it does not beg the question any more than the original objection does by presupposing that sexuality is analogous with race.

17. Think of the sodomy laws found in some states which criminalize certain sexual acts, whether performed by heterosexuals or homosexuals.

18. There is some interesting recent research which, though still tentative, strongly suggests that homosexuality is, at least in part, biologically based. See Simon LeVay, *The Sexual Brain* (Cambridge, MA: MIT Press, 1993), pp. 120–122; and J.M. Bailey & R.C. Pillard, "A Genetic Study of Male Sexual Orientation," *Archives of General Psychiatry* 48 (1991): 1089–1096; and C. Burr, "Homosexuality and Biology," *The Atlantic* 271/3 (March, 1993): 64; and D. Hamer, S. Hu, V. Magnuson, N. Hu, A. Pattatucci, "A Linkage Between DNA Markers on the X Chromosome and Male Sexual Orientation," *Science* 261 (16 July 1993): 321–327; and see the summary of this article by Robert Pool, "Evidence for Homosexuality Gene," *Science* 261 (16 July 1993): 291–292.

19. I do not mean to suggest that homosexuality is morally equivalent or even comparable to pyromania.

20. Is the use of subsidy here inappropriate? It does not seem so since providing health care to spouses, in a society where this is not legally mandatory, seems to be more than part of a salary and is a case of providing supporting funds for a certain end.

21. I thank David Haslett, Kate Rogers, Louis Pojman, and Jim Fieser for helpful and critical comments.

⚜ REVIEW QUESTIONS

1. Distinguish between Jordan's "parity thesis" and his "difference thesis." Which one does Jordan defend?
2. How does Jordan explain the concept of discrimination?
3. Why does the argument for the parity thesis fail, according to Jordan?
4. How does Jordan explain public dilemmas? How can they be resolved?
5. According to Jordan, what is the religious view of homosexuality?
6. Explain the argument from conflicting claims. How does Jordan respond to the two objections?
7. Explain Jordan's no-exit argument.

⚜ DISCUSSION QUESTIONS

1. Do Jordan's arguments justify discrimination against homosexuals in employment, education, and the military? Do they justify legally prohibiting same-sex marriage? Why or why not?
2. The accommodation that Jordan recommends assumes a distinction between the public discrimination and tolerance of private acts, but is this distinction clear? Is this accommodation acceptable or not?
3. Should our laws respect religious teachings about homosexuality? Why or why not?

Same-Sex Marriage and the Argument from Public Disagreement

DAVID BOONIN

David Boonin is associate professor of philosophy and Chair of the philosophy department at the University of Colorado, Boulder. He is the author of *The Problem of Punishment* (2008), *What's Wrong: Applied Ethics and Their Critics* (with Graham Oddie, 2004), *A Defense of Abortion* (2002), and *Thomas Hobbes and the Science of Moral Virtue* (1994).

    Boonin replies to Jordan's argument for the state's refusal to sanction same-sex marriage. He presents three objections. First, the argument is unsound. The public dilemma about same-sex marriage (Premise 2) is ambiguous; it can be about homosexual acts or about same-sex marriage. If it is about same-sex marriage, then the state's refusal to sanction it is no accommodation at all for those who want it. In contrast, if the dilemma is about homosexual acts, and the state allows these acts in private, then this is no accommodation for those who think homosexual acts are immoral. Either way, the dilemma is not resolved by accommodation; one side or other remains unsatisfied. (Premise 3 is false.) Second, the argument is vulnerable to a *reductio ad absurdum*: if the state refuses to sanction same-sex marriage because of the public dilemma, then it should also refuse to sanction mixed-race marriage for the same reason, and this is intolerable. Boonin discusses and replies to three possible responses from Jordan. Finally, the most basic objection is simply the fact that it is widely agreed that consenting adults have a right to marry whomever they wish. If it is outrageous to deny this right to heterosexual Jews, then it is just as objectionable to deny it to homosexuals and lesbians.

Most arguments against same-sex marriage rest at least in part on claims about the moral status of homosexuality: claims to the effect that homosexual behavior is morally objectionable in itself, or that homosexuals as a class are predisposed to commit acts (such as infidelity or child molestation) that are morally objectionable on independent grounds. In "Is It Wrong to Discriminate on the Basis of Homosexuality?" Jeff Jordan claims to produce an argument against same-sex marriage that makes no such assumptions.[1] Rather than relying on claims about the morality of homosexuality per se, Jordan attempts to show that it is morally permissible for the state to refuse to sanction same-sex marriages by appealing to the fact that marriage is a public rather than private institution, and that there *is* widespread public disagreement about the moral status of homosexuality. I will begin by presenting a brief summary of Jordan's principal argument for this claim and will

then argue that it should be rejected for three distinct reasons: the argument itself is unsound, it is subject to a *reductio ad absurdum* that Jordan fails to overcome, and, contrary to Jordan's claim, it does in fact depend on claims about the morality of homosexuality, claims that stand in need of support and that Jordan has not defended.

I

Jordan begins by defining an "impasse" over the moral status of *x* as a situation in which people hold "genuinely conflicting beliefs regarding the moral status of *x*, and a "public dilemma" as an impasse that has "public policy consequences" (73). In cases of genuine public dilemmas, the state will have to act in a way that has some implications with respect to *x*, and as a result will not be able to fully satisfy the interests of everyone on both sides of the impasse. When it does so

Source: Same-Sex Marriage and the Argument from Public Disagreement by David Boonin from *Journal of Social Philosophy*, Vol. 30, No. 2, 1999, pp. 251–259. Oxford, UK: Wiley-Blackwell.

by putting its power and authority squarely on one side of the impasse, as in the case of the federal government's forcibly ending slavery, it in effect "declares that side of the impasse the correct side," and Jordan refers to this as "resolution by declaration" (75, 76). When it finds a way to stake out some kind of middle ground "in a way that gives as much as possible to all sides of the impasse," it ensures that "there are no absolute victors and no absolute losers" in the impasse and that the views of all sides are respected. Jordan refers to this as "resolution by accommodation" (76), and cites abortion as a possible example (pornography might be another): the government permits its use, but restricts its availability. Jordan then argues, quite plausibly, that whenever a public dilemma must be actively resolved, the state should institute a resolution by accommodation rather than by declaration, unless there is an "overriding reason" that it should take sides, where such reasons typically involve "the protection of generally recognized rights" (76).

With this general framework in place, Jordan then makes the following claims about same-sex marriage in particular (77–78): First, there is a moral impasse over the question of whether or not homosexual acts are morally permissible. Many people think that they are and many think that they are not. Second, whereas engaging in homosexual conduct in itself is essentially a private matter, entering into a relationship of marriage is essentially a public one. Marriage involves a public recognition of a personal relationship between two people and people who are married become eligible for various sorts of public benefits that are unavailable to unmarried couples. As a result, the debate over same-sex marriage represents not merely a moral impasse, but a public dilemma. Third, for the government to sanction same-sex marriage is for it to resolve this public dilemma by declaration in favor of one side of the dispute, in a way that leaves no room for accommodation. If it does this, then members of one segment of the population "are faced with a public, state sanctioned matter which they find seriously immoral" (78). But, fourth, if the state instead refuses to sanction same-sex marriage, this counts as a resolution by accommodation, provided that the state permits private homosexual acts between

consenting adults. If it does this, then each side of the impasse gets some but not all of what it wants and thus neither side is an absolute victor or loser. Fifth, and finally, there is no overriding reason for the state to take sides in this dispute. What is at stake is not comparable to what is at stake in those cases, such as the abolition of slavery, where there is plainly reason for the state to resolve the issue by declaration.

If these five claims are correct, and if Jordan's general framework is defensible, the result is that the state should refuse to sanction same-sex marriages. We can represent the argument as follows:

P1 If (a) there is a public dilemma about *x*, *and* (b) resolution of the dilemma by accommodation is possible, *and* (c) there is no overriding reason to prefer resolution of the dilemma by declaration, *then* (d) the state should resolve the public dilemma about *x* by accommodation.

P2 There is a public dilemma about same-sex marriage.

P3 It is possible for the state to resolve the dilemma by accommodation if it refuses to sanction same-sex marriage (provided that it permits private homosexual acts between consenting adults).

P4 It is not possible for the state to resolve the dilemma by accommodation if it sanctions same-sex marriage (since that amounts to resolving the dilemma by declaration and leaves no room for accommodation).

P5 There is no overriding reason for the state to resolve the dilemma by declaration.

C The state should refuse to sanction same-sex marriage (provided that it permits private homosexual acts between consenting adults).

At the end of his paper, Jordan characterizes the thesis this argument is meant to defend as one on which it is "morally permissible" for the state to refuse to sanction same-sex marriages (82), but this puts things far too modestly. If Jordan's argument is successful, it shows not merely that it would be *permissible* for the state to do this, but that this is what the state in fact *ought* to do. Indeed, if the argument is successful, it is difficult to see how one could avoid the conclusion that it would be positively *wrong* for the state to sanction same-sex marriages, because it would be wrong for it, in general, to fully favor one side of a moral dispute over another without a compelling reason for doing so. So a good deal is at stake if Jordan's argument is successful.

But I want now to show that Jordan's argument is not successful. In section II, I will argue that one of the argument's premises is importantly ambiguous, and that either way of resolving the ambiguity renders two of the other premises false. In section III, I will argue that the argument is undermined by a *reductio ad absurdum* objection that Jordan tries, but fails, to overcome. And in section IV, I will argue that, contrary to Jordan's characterization of the argument, it does, in fact, presuppose a particular and contentious claim about the moral status of homosexuality.

II

Let me begin by raising a question about P2: the claim that there is a public dilemma about same-sex marriage. On the face of it, this might seem to be the clearest and least problematic of all of the premises in Jordan's argument. If anything at all about same-sex marriage is uncontroversial it is the fact that it is controversial. But what, exactly, does the claim made by P2 mean? Jordan, remember, defines a public dilemma as a special case of a moral impasse, and a moral impasse as a situation in which people "hold genuinely conflicting beliefs regarding the moral status of *x*." The question is: in the case of the public dilemma about same-sex marriage, what does the *x* stand for?

There are two possibilities: it can stand for acts of homosexual behavior, or it can stand for acts of participating in a same-sex marriage. Jordan at one point speaks of "*the* public dilemma concerning homosexuality, and in particular whether states should sanction same-sex marriages" (78, emphasis added), as if there is a single subject of dispute here, but these are in fact two distinct subjects of disagreement. The former concerns the moral permissibility of certain forms of sexual behavior, regardless of whether the people who engage in them are generally heterosexual or homosexual in their orientation. The latter concerns the moral

permissibility of granting certain forms of social recognition and public benefits to same-sex couples, regardless of whether or not they engage in such (or any) sexual behavior.[2]

Suppose that the genuinely conflicting beliefs that generate the dilemma referred to in P2 are beliefs regarding the moral status of acts of participating in a same-sex marriage. This seems to be the most natural interpretation, since the dilemma itself is about same-sex marriage and since a dilemma is simply a special case of an impasse, which is itself a case of conflicting beliefs about something. If this is what is meant by P2, then P3 and P4 are false. P3 says that if the state refuses to sanction same-sex marriages, then it resolves the public dilemma by accommodation (provided that it permits private homosexual acts between consenting adults). If we conflate the two distinct questions about private acts and public benefits into one issue, and think of it as "the" dispute over homosexuality, then this seems plausible enough. Each side gets some of what it wants, and neither side gets all of what it wants. But if the conflict is over the permissibility of same-sex *marriage* in particular, as opposed to about the complex cluster of issues relating to homosexuality taken as a whole, then this is no accommodation at all. It is simply a declaration that one side of the debate is entirely correct (those who oppose same-sex marriages) and the other side entirely incorrect (those who support them). It is as if one were to join together the distinct but related debates about whether or not the government should fund the arts and whether or not it should ban violent pornography, announce that the government will permit violent pornography but will not subsidize it, and declare that "the" debate in question had been settled in a way that accommodates both sides. This would not be a resolution by accommodation of one dilemma, but rather a resolution by declaration of two distinct but related dilemmas.

On this understanding of P2, P4 is also false, for similar but distinct reasons. P4 says that if the state sanctions same-sex marriage, then it resolves the public dilemma by declaration and leaves no room for accommodation. But if the dilemma is over same-sex marriage rather than over same-sex

sex, this too is incorrect. If accommodation is reached in controversies such as that over pornography or abortion by permitting but discouraging the controversial practice, then the same would hold here as well. The state could sanction same-sex marriage, but make it more difficult to obtain a same-sex marriage license than to obtain an opposite-sex marriage license. For example, it could require proof that a homosexual couple had been engaged for two years before obtaining a same-sex marriage license, but not require such proof from heterosexual couples, or require extensive premarital counseling, or charge a greater licensing fee. And it could discourage homosexuals from marrying in other ways, such as by taxing married homosexuals at a higher rate (higher than married heterosexuals and/or higher than unmarried homosexuals), or making it more difficult for them to obtain divorces or to adopt children than it is for heterosexual couples.

None of these suggestions will be fully satisfactory to defenders of same-sex marriage, of course. What they demand is marriage for homosexuals that is on an equal footing with marriage for heterosexuals. Nor will any of these proposals be fully satisfactory to opponents of same-sex marriage. What they demand is that there be no such thing as same-sex marriage. But that is precisely the point. If Jordan is correct that dilemmas of this sort should be resolved by accommodation, and if the dilemma is understood to be one over marriage and not over sex, then following a proposal that is fully satisfactory to neither side is exactly what his argument demands that we do. As in other such cases, the state should find a way to allow those who wish to engage in the disputed behavior to engage in it while at the same time expressing society's disapproval or at least lack of approval of the behavior in question.

Suppose, on the other hand, that the genuinely conflicting beliefs that generate the dilemma referred to in P2 are beliefs regarding the moral status of acts of homosexual behavior. This seems to be what Jordan typically has in mind when he introduces his argument. When he supports the contention that there exists a public dilemma that needs some sort of resolution, for example, he cites the fact that "[t]he theistic tradition, Judaism

and Christianity and Islam, has a clear and deeply entrenched position on homosexual *acts:* they are prohibited" (77, emphasis added). And he concludes his argument for the claim by saying that "[b]ecause many religious people sincerely believe homosexual *acts* to be morally wrong and many others believe that homosexual *acts* are not morally wrong, there results a public dilemma" (77, emphasis added).

But if the genuinely conflicting beliefs that generate the dilemma referred to in P2 are beliefs regarding the moral status of acts of homosexual behavior, then P3 and P4 are again false, for different but parallel reasons. If the state sanctions same-sex marriage, it does not resolve the conflicting beliefs about the moral permissibility of acts of homosexual behavior in a way that leaves no room for accommodation. For example, the state could recognize both same-sex and opposite-sex marriage and make it illegal to have homosexual intercourse outside of such a relation while legal to have heterosexual intercourse outside of such a relation. This would have the effect of permitting but restricting the form of behavior whose moral status is the subject of genuinely conflicting beliefs. So if the conflicting beliefs referred to in P2 concern the permissibility of acts of homosexual behavior, then P4 is false. Similarly, if the state refuses to sanction same-sex marriage and permits private homosexual acts between consenting adults, it does not resolve the conflicting beliefs about the moral permissibility of acts of homosexual behavior by accommodation. Rather, it simply declares that one side of the conflict is the correct side, namely, the side that believes that such acts are permissible. Doing so thus renders P3 false as well. So either way that we specify the meaning of the claim made in P2, the argument as a whole proves to be unsound.

III

A second objection to Jordan's argument takes the form of a *reductio ad absurdum*: if the state should refuse to sanction same-sex marriage because it is the subject of a moral impasse, then it should also refuse to sanction mixed-race marriage on the same ground. But the claim that the state should refuse to sanction mixed-race marriage is surely intolerable. So, therefore, is Jordan's argument. Jordan provides three responses to this objection, but none of them are satisfactory.

His first response is that unlike the issue of same-sex marriage, the issue of mixed-race marriages "does not seem to generate much, if any, controversy today" (79). On this account, there is no such public dilemma in the first place, and so it does not matter that Jordan's position would justify forbidding mixed-race marriage if there were. This response is unsuccessful for two reasons. First, it is not at all clear that there is no such dilemma about mixed-race marriage. In many communities in the South, at least, there remains substantial opposition to interracial *dating*, let alone interracial marriage. And although such opposition is traditionally associated with white racists, there is a more recent and hardly less heated controversy within the black community in all parts of the country about whether or not black men, in particular, have an obligation to marry black women.[3] Second, and more importantly, even if Jordan is right that there is no longer a moral impasse on this issue, this response makes the impermissibility of laws forbidding mixed-race marriage contingent on this fact. And surely such laws were impermissible even when many racists supported them.

Jordan's second response to the mixed-race objection is to say that even if it does represent a public dilemma, it is one in which there is an overriding reason in favor of resolution by declaration. The reason is that "it is a settled matter that state protection from racial discrimination is a reason sufficient for a resolution via declaration" while the same is not true of protection from discrimination according to sexual orientation (80). This response fails for the simple reason that a law banning mixed-race marriages does not discriminate against people on racial grounds. It says that *every* person, regardless of race, is free to marry anyone else of his or her race, and that *every* person, regardless of race, is prohibited from marrying anyone else of some other race. A white person who falls in love with a black person is adversely affected in just the same way as is a black person

who falls in love with a white person. And since every black-white couple consists of one black person and one white person, the total number of blacks and whites who are adversely affected in this way is the same. As a result, a law recognizing mixed-race marriage does not protect anyone from racial discrimination that would occur without such a law.

A law forbidding same-sex marriage, it is worth noting, is fundamentally different in this respect. It says that a heterosexual man can marry any member of the sex he is attracted to while a homosexual man can marry any member of the sex he is *not* attracted to, and that a heterosexual man is forbidden to marry any member of the sex that he is not attracted to while a homosexual man is forbidden to marry any member of the sex that he *is* attracted to. This law does discriminate by sexual orientation, since all of the people who are adversely affected by it (at least directly) are homosexuals. And thus a law recognizing same-sex marriage does protect people from discrimination on the basis of sexual orientation that would otherwise occur without such a law. In short, laws banning mixed-race marriage treat people of all races equally while laws banning same-sex marriage do not treat people of all sexual orientations equally. So Jordan has failed to show that there is an overriding reason for the state to resolve the mixed-race marriage issue by declaration that does not also apply to the case of same-sex marriages. Indeed, if anything, he has pointed to an overriding reason to resolve the same-sex marriage issue by declaration that does not apply to the mixed-race marriage issue.

Jordan's final response to the mixed-race marriage objection turns on his attempt to identify a second disanalogy between the two cases: "A same-sex marriage would involve behavior which many people find morally objectionable; a mixed-race marriage is objectionable to some, not because of the participants' behavior, but because of the racial identity of the participants" (80). And since objections based on a person's identity are different from objections based on a person's behavior, it does not follow from the fact that the objection to mixed-race marriage should be overruled by a resolution by declaration that the objection to same-sex marriage should also be overruled in this manner.

This response must be rejected because it rests on a misdescription of the view held by those who object to mixed-race marriage. It is not that they object to the *identity* of the individuals involved. White racists need not have anything against blacks marrying other blacks, and black separatists surely have nothing against white people marrying other whites. It is not the identity of the individuals that they object to, but the act they perform: the act of weakening the purity of the race, or of violating the obligation to put one's own community first. In this sense, they are no different from the antihomosexual people Jordan describes: they say they object not to what homosexuals are, but to what they do.

IV

I have argued that Jordan's argument is unsound, and I have argued that it is subject to an important objection by *reductio ad absurdum*. In doing this, I have accepted Jordan's claim that if his argument succeeds, it does so without depending on any claims about the moral status of homosexuality. I want to conclude by questioning this claim.

I do so by raising a question about the one premise about same-sex marriage that I have to this point set aside. This is the claim made by P5 that there is no overriding reason for the state to resolve the public dilemma about same-sex marriage by declaration. Jordan does not provide specific criteria for distinguishing overriding reasons from less weighty ones, but his comment that they typically involve "the protection of generally recognized rights" seems to me sufficient for my purposes. The claim that a right is a generally recognized one can be taken in two distinct ways. In the case of the United States prior to the Civil War, for example, there is one sense in which the right not to be enslaved was a generally recognized one. If you tried to enslave a white person during this period, it would have been generally recognized that you were

violating his rights. But there is another sense in which the right not to be enslaved was not generally recognized, since it was not generally recognized that it was enjoyed by all people regardless of race.

Now if a right must be generally recognized in this second sense in order for there to be an overriding reason for the state to take sides in a public dilemma, then Jordan will be unable to account for the fact that the morally right thing for the state to do was to abolish slavery. Indeed, if this is what is needed in order for there to be an overriding reason for the state to so act, then P5 will be vacuous: if a right is generally recognized in this sense, there will for that very reason be no public dilemma about it. So the argument can only succeed if the rights that suffice to underwrite an overriding reason in P5 are ones that are widely agreed to be held by most people, even if many people refrain from attributing them to all people. And this is what creates the final problem with Jordan's argument. For surely it is widely agreed that most people have a right to marry whomever they wish, and to have their marriage publicly recognized. Suppose that the government announced that, starting tomorrow, the state would no longer sanction marriages between heterosexual Jews. For purposes of taxes, child custody, property ownership, next-of-kin visitation rights, and so on, there would no longer be a distinction between married heterosexual Jewish couples and pairs of Jewish people of opposite sexes who happen to live in the same dwelling. Most people would regard this as outrageous. And although I am sympathetic toward those who complain that the language of rights is too often stretched beyond reason, I suspect that most people would object to the edict by saying that it violated a very commonly recognized right, the right of consenting adults to marry whomever they please and to have their marriages publicly recognized. But if it is generally recognized that this is a right that most people have, even if it is not generally recognized that this is a right that all people have, then this is sufficient to establish that there is an overriding reason to resolve the dilemma by declaration in favor of same-sex marriage. It is not sufficient only if there is some morally relevant difference between homosexuals and heterosexuals, just as it would not be sufficient if there were some morally relevant difference between Jews and non-Jews.

Now I do not mean to suggest that this argument provides anything like a conclusive resolution of the debate about same-sex marriage. It is simply the first step that then leaves open any number of responses that might be given to undermine the claim that if heterosexuals have the right to marry whomever they please then so do homosexuals. My point here is simply that it is very difficult to see how any such response could succeed in vindicating P5 without at some point depending at least in part on the claim that there is a morally relevant difference between homosexuals and heterosexuals or between homosexual and heterosexual relationships. This is precisely the sort of argument that Jordan's argument was meant to avoid. And this suggests that even if his argument were not subject to the objections I have presented in the previous two sections, it would still prove incapable of accomplishing the task it set out to accomplish.

NOTES

1. *Journal of Social Philosophy*, 25, no. 1 (Spring 1995), reprinted in Robert M. Baird and Stuart E. Rosenbaum, eds., *Same-Sex Marriage: The Moral and Legal Debate* (Amherst, NY: Prometheus Books, 1997), 72–83. References in the text are to the page numbers in the Baird and Rosenbaum volume.

2. It is also worth noting that from the mere claim that a certain kind of behavior is morally impermissible, it does not follow that the state should not sanction marriages between people who engage in such behavior. There are genuinely conflicting moral beliefs about the permissibility of abortion, contraception, pornography, sexual promiscuity, and the use of animals in medical research, to name but a few, but there is no parallel conflict over whether or not the state should sanction marriages between pornographers, animal researchers, people who use contraception or perform abortion, or who have long and varied sexual histories.

3. That this debate cannot be easily dismissed is shown by Charles W. Mills, "Do Black Men Have a Moral Duty to Marry Black Women?" *Journal of Social Philosophy*, 25th Anniversary Special Issue (1994), 131–53.

⚜ REVIEW QUESTIONS

1. If successful, what does Jordan's argument show, according to Boonin?
2. Why does Boonin think that Jordan's argument is unsound?
3. What is Boonin's *reductio ad absurdum* objection and how might Jordan reply? How does Boonin respond to the three possible objections?
4. What is Boonin's final objection to Jordan's argument?

⚜ DISCUSSION QUESTIONS

1. Do you agree that most people have a right to marry whomever they wish? Why or why not? Who doesn't have this right, in your view?
2. If the state sanctions same-sex marriage, then it should also sanction plural marriage. Do you agree? Why or why not?
3. Boonin suggests that accommodation in controversies such as pornography and abortion is reached by discouraging the controversial practice. Why couldn't this be done for the same-sex marriage controversy? What is your view?
4. Does Jordan have a good reply to Boonin? If so, what is it?

Who Needs Marriage?

JONATHAN RAUCH

Jonathan Rauch writes a biweekly column for *National Journal* and is writer in residence at the Brookings Institution in Washington, D.C. He is the author of *Kindly Inquisitors* (1993), *Demosclerosis* (1994), and *Government's End: Why Washington Stopped Working* (1999).

Rauch replies to the Hayekian argument (as he calls it) that reforming marriage by allowing gays to marry will produce chaos in our society or destroy the institution of marriage. He doubts that extending marriage to a mere 3 to 5 percent of the population will have as much an effect on marriage as other changes, such as no-fault divorce. (He is in favor of strengthening the institution of marriage by making divorce harder to get.) Furthermore, even if a social change (like allowing contraception) has bad effects, it may still be right. And social changes can have good effects, too. As for the purpose of marriage, Rauch denies that love is essential for marriage. He grants that having and raising children is one of the main purposes of marriage, but it is not the only purpose. He suggests that marriage has two other social purposes: it tames and civilizes young males and it provides the married person with a reliable caregiver. He argues that gay marriage accomplishes these two additional social purposes, and so it should be allowed and even encouraged for gay people.

Whatever else marriage may or may not be, it is certainly falling apart. Half of today's new marriages will end in divorce, and far more costly still (from a social point of view) are the marriages that never happen at all, leaving mothers poor, children fatherless, and neighborhoods chaotic. With a sense of timing worthy of Neville Chamberlain, at just this moment, homosexuals are pressing to be able to marry, and Hawaii's courts are moving toward letting them do so. I'll believe in gay marriage in America when I see it, but if it gets as far as being even temporarily legalized in Hawaii, then the uproar about this final insult to a besieged institution will be deafening.

Whether gay marriage makes sense—and, for that matter, whether straight marriage makes sense—depends on what marriage is actually for. Oddly enough, at the moment, secular thinking on this question is shockingly sketchy. Gay activists say: marriage is for love, and we love each other, therefore we should be able to marry. Traditionalists say: marriage is for children, and homosexuals do not (or should not) have children,

therefore you should not be able to marry. That, unfortunately, pretty well covers the spectrum. I say "unfortunately" because both views are wrong. They misunderstand and impoverish the social meaning of marriage.

I admit to being an interested party: I am a homosexual, and I want the right to marry. In fact, I want more than the right; I want the actual marriage (when Mr. Wonderful comes along, God willing). Nevertheless, I do not want to destroy the most basic of all social institutions, backbone of the family, and bedrock of civilization. It is not enough for gay marriage to make sense for gay people; if they ask society to recognize and bless it, it should also make sense from society's broader point of view.

So what is marriage for?

AGAINST LOVE

In its religious dress, marriage has a straightforward justification. It is as it is because that is how God wants it. Depending on the religion, God

Source: "Who Needs Marriage" from *Beyond Queer: Challenging Gay Left Orthodoxy*, edited by Bruce Bawer (Free Press, 1996), pp. 296–313. Reprinted by permission.

has various things to say about who may marry and what should go on within a marriage. Modern marriage is, of course, based upon traditions that religion helped to codify and enforce. But religious doctrine has no special standing in the world of secular law and policy, with all due apologies to the "Christian nation" crowd. If we want to know what and whom marriage is for in modern America, we need a sensible secular doctrine.

At one point, marriage in secular society was largely a matter of business: cementing family ties, providing social status for men and economic support for women, conferring dowries, and so on. Marriages were typically arranged, and "love" in the modern sense was no prerequisite. In Japan today, there are remnants of this system, and it works surprisingly well. Couples stay together because they view their marriage as a partnership: an investment in social stability for themselves and their children. Because Japanese couples don't expect as much emotional fulfillment as Americans do, they are less inclined to break up. They also take a somewhat more relaxed attitude toward adultery. What's a little extracurricular love, provided that each partner is fulfilling his or her many other marital duties?

In the West, of course, love is a defining element. The notion of lifelong love is charming, if ambitious, and certainly love is a desirable element of marriage. It cannot, however, be the defining element in society's eyes. You may or may not love your husband, but the two of you are just as married either way. You may love your mistress, but that certainly does not make her your spouse. Love helps make sense of marriage from an emotional point of view, but it is not terribly important, I think, in making sense of marriage from the point of view of social policy.

If blessing love does not define the purpose of secular marriage, what does? Neither the law nor secular thinking provides a very clear answer to this question. Today, marriage is almost entirely a voluntary arrangement whose contents are up to the people making the deal. There are few if any behaviors that automatically end a marriage. If a man beats his wife—which is about the worst thing he can do to her—he may be convicted of assault, but his marriage is not automatically

dissolved. Couples can be adulterous (or "open") yet still be married, so long as that is what they choose to be. They can be celibate, too; consummation is not required. All in all, it is an impressive and also rather astonishing victory for modern individualism that so important an institution should be so bereft of formal social instruction as to what should go on inside of it.

Secular society tells us only a few things about marriage. Among them are the following. First, marriage happens only with the consent of the parties. Second, the parties are not children. Third, a number of parties is two. Fourth, one is a man and the other is a woman. Within those rules, a marriage is whatever anyone says it is. So the standard rules say almost nothing about what marriage is for.

AGAINST TRADITION

Perhaps it doesn't matter what marriage is for. Perhaps it is enough simply to say that marriage is as it is and should not be tampered with. This sounds like a crudely reactionary position. In fact, however, of all the arguments against reforming marriage, it is probably the most powerful.

I'll call it a Hayekian argument, after the great libertarian economist F. A. Hayek, who developed this line of thinking in his book *The Fatal Conceit*. In a market system, the prices generated by impersonal forces may not make sense from any one person's point of view, but they encode far more information than even the cleverest person could ever gather. In a similar fashion, human societies evolve rich and complicated webs of nonlegal rules in the forms of customs, traditions, and institutions. Like prices, the customs generated by societies may often seem irrational or arbitrary. But the very fact that they are the customs that have evolved implies that there is a kind of practical logic embedded in them that may not be apparent from even a sophisticated analysis. And the web of custom cannot be torn apart and reordered at will, because once its internal logic is violated, it falls apart. Intellectuals, like Marxists or feminists, who seek to deconstruct and rationally rebuild social traditions will produce not better order, but merely chaos. Thus hallowed social tradition should not be tampered with except in the very last extremity.

For secular intellectuals who are unhappy with the evolved framework for marriage and who are excluded from it—in other words, for people like me—this Hayekian argument is very troubling. It is also very powerful. Age-old stigmas on illegitimacy and out-of-wedlock pregnancy were crude and unfair to women and children. On the male side, shotgun marriages were, in an informal way, coercive and intrusive. But when modern societies began playing around with the age-old stigmas on illegitimacy and divorce and all the rest, whole portions of the social structure just caved in.

So the Hayekian view argues strongly against gay marriage. It says that the current rules for marriage may not be the best ones, and they may even be unfair. But they are all we have, and once you say that marriage need not be male-female, soon marriage will stop being anything at all. You can't mess with the formula without causing unforeseen consequences, possibly including the implosion of the institution of marriage itself.

But I demur. There are problems with the Hayekian position. The biggest is that it is untenable in its extreme form and unhelpful in its milder version. In its extreme form, it implies that no social reforms should ever be undertaken. Indeed, no social laws should be passed, because they will interfere with the natural evolution of social mores. One would thus have to say that because in the past slavery was customary in almost all human societies, it should not have been forcibly abolished. Obviously, neither Hayek nor his sympathizers would actually say this. They would point out that slavery violated fundamental moral principles and was scaldingly inhumane. But in doing so, they do what must be done if we are to be human: they establish a moral platform from which to judge social rules. They thus acknowledge that abstracting social debate from moral concerns is not possible.

If the ban on gay marriage were only mildly unfair and if the social costs of changing it were certain to be enormous, then the ban could stand on Hayekian grounds. However, if there is any social policy today that has a fair claim to being

scaldingly inhumane, it is the ban on gay marriage. As conservatives tirelessly and rightly point out, marriage is the most fundamental institution of society. To bar any class of people from marrying as they choose is an extraordinary deprivation. When, not so long ago, it was illegal in parts of America for blacks to marry whites, no one could claim this was a trivial disenfranchisement. Granted, gay marriage raises issues that interracial marriage does not; but no one can argue that the deprivation itself is a minor one.

To outweigh such a serious claim and rule out homosexual marriage purely on Hayekian grounds, saying that bad things might happen is not enough. Bad things might always happen. Bad things happened as a result of legalizing contraception, but that did not make it the wrong thing to do, and in any case, good things happened also. It is not at all clear, on the merits, that heterosexual marriage would be eroded by legalizing homosexual marriage. On the contrary, marriage might be strengthened if it were held out as the norm for everybody, including homosexuals.

Besides, it seems doubtful that extending marriage to, say, another 3 or 5 percent of the population would have anything like the effects that no-fault divorce has had, to say nothing of contraception and the sexual revolution. By now, the "traditional" understanding of marriage has been tampered with by practically everybody in all kinds of ways. It is hard to think of a bigger affront to tradition, for instance, than allowing married women to own property independently of their husbands or allowing them to charge their husbands with rape. Surely it is a bit unfair to say that marriage may be reformed for the sake of anyone and everyone except homosexuals, who must respect the dictates of tradition.

Faced with these problems, the milder version of the Hayekian argument says, not that social traditions shouldn't be tampered with at all, but that they shouldn't be tampered with lightly. Fine, and thank you. In this case, no one is talking about casual messing around or about some lobby's desire to score political points; the issue is about allowing people to live as grown-ups and full citizens. One could write pages on this point, but I won't. I'll set human rights claims to one side and in return ask the Hayekians to recognize that appeals to blind tradition and to the risks inherent in social change do not, a priori, settle anything in this instance. They merely warn against frivolous change. If the issue at hand is whether gay marriage is good or bad for society as well as for gay people, there is no avoiding a discussion about the *purpose* of marriage.

AGAINST CHILDREN

So we turn to what has become the standard view of marriage's purpose. Its proponents would probably like to call it a child-centered view, but a more accurate description would call it an antigay view, as will become clear. Whatever you call it, it is certainly the view that is heard most often, and in the context of the debate over gay marriage, it is heard almost exclusively. In its most straightforward form, it goes as follows (I quote from James Q. Wilson's fine book *The Moral Sense*):

> A family is not an association of independent people; it is a human commitment designed to make possible the rearing of moral and healthy children. Governments care—or ought to care—about families for this reason, and scarcely for any other.

Wilson speaks about "family" rather than "marriage" as such, but one may, I think, read him as speaking of marriage without doing any injustice to his meaning. The resulting proposition—government ought to care about marriage almost entirely because of children and scarcely for any other reason—seems reasonable. It certainly accords with our commonsense feeling that marriage and children go together. But there are problems. The first, obviously, is that gay couples may have children, either through adoption or (for lesbians) by using artificial insemination. I will leave for some other essay the contentious issue of gay adoption. For now, the obvious point is that if the mere presence of children is the test, then homosexual relationships can certainly pass it.

You might note, correctly, that heterosexual marriages are more likely to wind up with children in the mix than homosexual ones. When granting marriage licenses to heterosexuals, however, we do not ask how likely the couple is to have children. We assume that they are entitled to get married whether they end up with children or not. Understanding this, conservatives often then make an interesting further move. In seeking to justify the state's interest in marriage, they shift from the actual presence of children to the anatomical possibility of making them. Hadley Arkes, a law professor and prominent opponent of homosexual marriage, makes the case this way:

> The traditional understanding of marriage is grounded in the "natural teleology of the body"—in the inescapable fact that only a man and a woman, and only two people, not three, can generate a child. Once marriage is detached from that natural teleology of the body, what ground of principle would thereafter confine marriage to two people rather than some larger grouping? That is, on what ground of principle would the law reject the claim of a gay couple that their love is not confined to a coupling of two, but that they are woven into a larger ensemble with yet another person or two?

What he seems to be saying is that where the possibility of natural children is nil, the meaning of marriage is nil. If marriage is allowed between members of the same sex, then the concept of marriage has been emptied of content except to ask whether the parties love each other. Then anything goes, including polygamy. This reasoning presumably is what antigay activists have in mind when they claim that once gay marriage is legal, marriage to pets will follow close behind.

Arkes and his sympathizers have here made two mistakes, both of them instructive. To see them, break down the Arkes-type claim into two components:

1. Two-person marriage derives its special status from the anatomical possibility that the partners can create natural children.
2. Apart from 1, two-person marriage has no purpose sufficiently strong to justify its special status. That is, absent justification 1, anything goes.

The first proposition is peculiar, because it is wholly at odds with the way society actually views marriage. Leave aside the insistence that natural, as opposed to adoptive, children define the importance of marriage. The deeper problem, apparent right away, is the issue of sterile heterosexual couples. Here the "anatomical possibility" crowd has a problem, for a homosexual union is, anatomically speaking, nothing but one variety of sterile union and no different even in principle: a woman without a uterus has no more potential for giving birth than a man without a vagina.

It may sound like carping to stress the case of barren heterosexual marriage; the vast majority of newlywed heterosexual couples, after all, can have children and probably will. But the point here is fundamental. There are far more sterile heterosexual unions in America than homosexual ones. The "anatomical possibility" crowd cannot have it both ways. If the possibility of children is what gives meaning to marriage, then a postmenopausal woman who tries to take out a marriage license should be turned away at the courthouse door. What's more, she should be hooted at and condemned for stretching the meaning of marriage beyond its natural basis and so reducing the institution to frivolity. People at the Family Research Council or Concerned Women for America should point at her and say, "If she can marry, why not polygamy? Why not marriage to pets?"

Obviously, the "anatomical" conservatives do not say this, because they are sane. They instead flail around, saying that sterile men and women were at least born with the right-shaped parts for making children, and so on. As they struggle to include sterile heterosexual marriages while excluding homosexual ones, their position is soon revealed to be a nonposition. It says that the "natural children" rationale defines marriage when homosexuals are involved but not when heterosexuals are involved. When the parties to union are sterile heterosexuals, the justification for marriage must be something else. But what?

Now arises the oddest part of the "anatomical" argument. Look at proposition 2 above. It says that, absent the anatomical justification for marriage, anything goes. In other words, it

dismisses the idea that there might be some other compelling reasons for society to sanctify marriage above other kinds of relationships. Why would anybody want to make this move? I'll just hazard a guess: to exclude homosexuals. Any rationale that justifies sterile heterosexual marriages can also apply to homosexual ones. For instance, marriage makes women more financially secure. Very nice, say the conservatives. But that rationale could be applied to lesbians, so it's definitely out.

The end result of this stratagem is perverse to the point of being funny. The attempt to ground marriage in children (or the anatomical possibility thereof) falls flat. But having lost that reason for marriage, the antigay people can offer no other. In their fixation on excluding homosexuals, they leave themselves no consistent justification for the privileged status of *heterosexual* marriage. They thus tear away any coherent foundation that secular marriage might have, which is precisely the opposite of what they claim they want to do. If they have to undercut marriage to save it from homosexuals, so be it!

If you feel my argument here has a slightly Thomist ring, the reason, of course, is that the "child-centered" people themselves do not really believe that natural children are the only, or even the overriding, reason society blesses marriage. In the real world, it's obvious that sterile people have every right to get married and that society benefits by allowing and, indeed, encouraging them to do so. No one seriously imagines that denying marriage to a sterile heterosexual couple would strengthen the institution of marriage, or that barring sterile marriages would even be a decent thing to do. The "natural children" people know this perfectly well, and they admit it implicitly when they cheerfully bless sterile unions. In truth, their real posture has nothing at all to do with children, or even with the "anatomical possibility" of children. It is merely antigay. All it really says is this: the defining purpose of marriage is to exclude homosexuals.

This is not an answer to the question of what marriage is for. Rather, it makes of marriage, as Richard Mohr aptly puts it, "nothing but an empty space, delimited only by what it excludes—gay couples." By putting a nonrationale at the center of modern marriage, these conservatives leave the institution worse off than if they had never opened their mouths. This is not at all helpful.

If one is to set hypocrisy aside, one must admit that there are compelling reasons for marriage other than children—reasons that may or may not apply to homosexual unions. What might those reasons be?

ROGUE MALES AND AILING MATES

For the record, I would be the last to deny that children are one central reason for the privileged status of marriage. Rather, I gladly proclaim it. When men and women get together, children are a likely outcome; and, as we are learning in ever more unpleasant ways, when children appear without two parents, all kinds of trouble ensues. Without belaboring the point, I hope I won't be accused of saying that children are a trivial reason for marriage. They just cannot be the only reason.

And what are the others? I can think of several possibilities, such as the point cited above about economic security for women (or men). There is a lot of intellectual work to be done trying to sort out which are the essential reasons and which incidental. It seems to me that the two strongest candidates are these: settling males and providing reliable caregivers. Both purposes are critical to the functioning of a humane and stable society, and both are much better served by marriage— that is, by one-to-one lifelong commitment— than by any other institution.

Wilson writes, in *The Moral Sense*, of the human male's need to hunt, defend, and attack. "Much of the history of civilization can be thought of as an effort to adapt these male dispositions to contemporary needs by restricting aggression or channeling it into appropriate channels," he says. I think it is probably fair to say that civilizing young males is one of any society's two or three biggest problems. Wherever unattached males gather in packs, you see no end of trouble: wildings in Central Park, gangs in

Los Angeles, football hooligans in Britain, skinheads in Germany, fraternity hazings in universities, grope lines in the military, and (in a different but ultimately no less tragic way) the bathhouses and wanton sex of gay San Francisco or New York in the 1970s.

For taming males, marriage is unmatched. "Of all the institutions through which men may pass—schools, factories, the military—marriage has the largest effect," Wilson writes. A token of the casualness of current thinking about marriage is that the man who wrote those words could, later in the very same book, say that government should care about fostering families for "scarcely any other" reason than children. If marriage— that is, the binding of men into couples—did nothing else, its power to settle men, to keep them at home and out of trouble, would be ample justification for its special status.

Of course, women and older men don't generally travel in marauding or orgiastic packs. But in their case, the second rationale comes strongly into play. A second enormous problem for society is what to do when someone is beset by some sort of burdensome contingency. It could be cancer, a broken back, unemployment, or depression; it could be exhaustion from work or stress under pressure. If marriage has any meaning at all, it is that when you collapse from a stroke, there will be at least one other person whose "job" is to drop everything and come to your aid; or that when you come home after being fired by the postal service, there will be someone to persuade you not to commit a massacre.

All by itself, marriage is society's first and, often, second and third line of support for the troubled individual. Absent a spouse, the burdens of contingency fall immediately and sometimes crushingly upon people who have more immediate problems of their own (relatives, friends, neighbors), then upon charities and welfare programs that are expensive and often not very good. From the broader society's point of view, the unattached person is an accident waiting to happen. Married people are happier, healthier, and live longer; married men have lower rates of homicide, suicide, accidents, and mental illness. In large part, the reason is simply that married people have someone to look after them, and know it.

Obviously, both of these rationales—the need to settle males, the need to have people looked after—apply to sterile people as well as to fertile ones, and apply to childless couples as well as to ones with children. The first explains why everybody feels relieved when the town delinquent gets married, and the second explains why everybody feels happy when an aging widow takes a second husband. From a social point of view, it seems to me, both rationales are far more compelling as justification of marriage's special status than, say, love. And both of them apply to homosexuals as well as to heterosexuals.

Take the matter of settling men. It is probably true that women and children, more than just the fact of marriage, help civilize men. But that hardly means that the settling effect of marriage on homosexual men is negligible. To the contrary, being tied into a committed relationship plainly helps stabilize gay men. Even without marriage, coupled gay men have steady sex partners and relationships that they value, so they tend to be less wanton. Add marriage, and you bring to bear a further array of stabilizing influences. One of the main benefits of publicly recognized marriage is that it binds couples together not only in their own eyes, but also in the eyes of society at large. Around the partners is weaved a web of expectations that they will spend nights together, go to parties together, take out mortgages together, buy furniture at Ikea together, and so on—all of which helps tie them together and keep them off the streets and at home. ("It's 1:00 A.M.; do you know where your husband is?" Chances are you do.) Surely that is a very good thing, especially as compared to the closet-gay culture of furtive sex with innumerable partners in parks and bathhouses.

The other benefit of marriage—caretaking— clearly applies to homosexuals, with no reservations at all. One of the first things many people worry about when coming to terms with their homosexuality is, "Who will take care of me when I'm old?" Society needs to care about this, too, as the AIDS crisis has made horribly clear. If that crisis showed anything, it is that homosexuals can

and will take care of each other, sometimes with breathtaking devotion—and that no institution can begin to match the care of a devoted partner. Legally speaking, marriage creates kin. Surely, society's interest in kin creation is strongest of all for people who are unlikely to be supported by children in old age and who may well be rejected by their own parents in youth.

Gay marriage, then, is far from being a mere exercise in political point making or rights mongering. On the contrary, it serves two of the three social purposes that make marriage so indispensable and irreplaceable for heterosexuals. Two out of three may not be the whole ball of wax, but it is more than enough to give society a compelling interest in marrying off homosexuals.

Moreover, marriage is the *only* institution that adequately serves these purposes. People who are uncomfortable with gay marriage—including some gay people—argue that the benefits can just as well be had through private legal arrangements and domestic-partnership laws. But only the fiduciary and statutory benefits of marriage can be arranged that way, and therein lies a world of difference. The promise of one-to-one lifetime commitment is very hard to keep. The magic of marriage is that it wraps a dense ribbon of social approval around each partnership, then reinforces commitment with a hundred informal mechanisms from everyday greetings ("How's the wife?") to gossipy sneers ("Why does she put up with that cheating bastard Bill?"). The power of marriage is not just legal, but social. It seals its promise with the smiles and tears of family, friends, and neighbors. It shrewdly exploits ceremony (big, public weddings) and money (expensive gifts, dowries) to deter casual commitment and to make bailing out embarrassing. Stag parties and bridal showers signal that what is beginning is not just a legal arrangement, but a whole new stage of life. "Domestic-partner" laws do none of these things. Me, I can't quite imagine my mother sobbing with relief as she says, "Thank heaven, Jonathan has finally found a domestic partner."

I'll go further: far from being a substitute for the real thing, "lite" marriage more likely undermines it. Marriage is a deal between a couple and society, not just between two people: society recognizes the sanctity and autonomy of the pair-bond, and in exchange, each spouse commits to being the other's caregiver, social worker, and police officer of first resort. Each marriage is its own little society within society. Any step that weakens this deal by granting the legal benefits of marriage without also requiring the public commitment is begging for trouble.

From gay couples' point of view, pseudomarriage is second best to the real thing; but from society's point of view, it may be the worst policy of all. From both points of view, gay marriage—real social recognition, real personal commitment, real social pressure to shore up personal commitment—makes the most sense. That is why government should be wary of offering "alternatives" to marriage. And, one might add, that is also why the full social benefits of gay marriage will come only when churches as well as governments customarily bless it: when women marry women in big church weddings as mothers weep and priests, solemnly smiling, intone the vows.

AGAINST GAY DIVORCE

So gay marriage makes sense for several of the same reasons that straight marriage makes sense; fine. That would seem a natural place to stop. But the logic of the argument compels one to go a twist further. If I am right, then there are implications for heterosexuals and homosexuals alike—not entirely comfortable ones.

If society has a strong interest in seeing people married off, then it must also have some interest in seeing them stay together. For many years, that interest was assumed and embodied in laws and informal stigmas that made divorce a painful experience. My guess is that this was often bad for adults but quite good for children, though you could argue that point all day. In any event, things have radically changed. Today, more and more people believe that a divorce should be at least a bit harder to get.

I'm not going to wade into the debate about toughening the divorce laws. Anyway, in a liberal society, there is not much you can do to keep people together without trampling their rights.

The point that's relevant here is that, if I'm right, the standard way of thinking about this issue is incomplete, even misleading. The usual argument is that divorce is bad for children, which is why we should worry about it. I wouldn't deny this for a moment. Some people advocate special counseling or cooling-off periods for divorcing couples with children. That may well be a good idea. But it should not be assumed that society has no interest in helping childless couples stay together, also—for just the reason I've outlined.

Childless couples, of course, include gay couples. In my opinion, if one wants to shore up the institution of marriage, then one had better complicate divorce (if that's what you're going to do) for all couples, including gay ones and childless heterosexual ones. Otherwise, you send the message that marriage can be a casual affair if you don't happen to have children. Gay spouses should understand that once they are together, they are *really* together. The upshot is that gay divorce should be every bit as hard to get as straight divorce—and both should probably be harder to get than is now the case.

Another implication follows, too. If it is good for society to have people attached, then it is not enough just to make marriage available. Marriage should also be *expected*. This, too, is just as true for homosexuals as for heterosexuals. So if homosexuals are justified in expecting access to marriage, society is equally justified in expecting them to use it. I'm not saying that out-of-wedlock sex should be scandalous or that people should be coerced into marriage or anything like that. The mechanisms of expectation are more subtle. When Grandma cluck-clucks over a still-unmarried young man, or when Mom says she wishes her little girl would settle down, she is expressing a strong and well-justified preference—one that is quietly echoed in a thousand ways throughout society and that produces subtle but important pressure to form and sustain unions. This is a good and necessary thing, and it will be as necessary for homosexuals as for heterosexuals. If gay marriage is recognized, single gay people over a certain age should not be surprised when they are subtly disapproved of or pitied. That is a vital part of what makes marriage work.

Moreover, if marriage is to work, it cannot be merely a "lifestyle option." It must be privileged. That is, it must be understood to be better, on average, than other ways of living. Not mandatory, not good where everything else is bad, but better: a general norm, rather than a personal taste. The biggest worry about gay marriage, I think, is that homosexuals might get it but then mostly not use it. Unlike a conservative friend of mine, I don't think that gay neglect of marriage would greatly erode what remains of the bonding power of heterosexual marriage (remember, homosexuals are only a tiny fraction of the population). But it would certainly not help, and in any case, it would denude the benefits and cheapen the meaning of homosexual marriage. And heterosexual society would rightly feel betrayed if, after legalization, homosexuals treated marriage as a minority taste rather than as a core institution of life. It is not enough, I think, for gay people to say we want the right to marry. If we do not use it, shame on us.

⚜ REVIEW QUESTIONS

1. Why does Rauch reject a religious account of marriage?
2. Why isn't love the defining element of marriage, according to Rauch?
3. What is the Hayekian argument? Why doesn't Rauch accept it?
4. What is the antigay view of marriage, as Rauch calls it? Why does Rauch reject this view?
5. What are the main social purposes of marriage, in Rauch's view?
6. Why is Rauch in favor of making divorce harder to get?

⚜ DISCUSSION QUESTIONS

1. What do you think is the primary purpose of marriage? Defend your answer.
2. Do you agree that divorce should be harder to get? Explain your answer.
3. Has Rauch given a satisfactory reply to Schulman? Why or why not?

What Marriage Is For

MAGGIE GALLAGHER

Maggie Gallagher is president of the Institute for Marriage and Public Policy (www.IMAPP.org), a nationally syndicated columnist, and the author (with Linda Waite) of *The Case for Marriage* (2001), *The Age of Unwed Mothers* (1999), *and Enemies of Eros* (1989).

Gallagher is opposed to same-sex marriage. She rejects the view that marriage is the public endorsement of the love and commitment of a couple. In her view, the purpose of marriage is to have and raise children and not just to show love and commitment. She thinks that childrearing is best done by loving and committed mothers and fathers and not by people of the same sex or by single parents. To endorse same-sex marriage would "gut marriage of its central presumption about family in order to accommodate a few adults' desires." Married couples that remain childless do not challenge the core meaning of marriage because they are discouraged from having children outside marriage. Denying marriage to same-sex couples does not amount to discrimination, she argues, because they can always marry members of the opposite sex.

Source: "What Marriage Is For" by Maggie Gallagher from *The Weekly Standard*, 2003. Reprinted by permission of Maggie Gallagher.

Gay marriage is no longer a theoretical issue. Canada has it. Massachusetts is expected to get it any day. The *Goodridge* decision there could set off a legal, political, and cultural battle in the courts of 50 states and in the U.S. Congress. Every politician, every judge, every citizen has to decide: Does same-sex marriage matter? If so, how and why?

The timing could not be worse. Marriage is in crisis, as everyone knows: High rates of divorce and illegitimacy have eroded marriage norms and created millions of fatherless children, whole neighborhoods where lifelong marriage is no longer customary, driving up poverty, crime, teen pregnancy, welfare dependency, drug abuse, and mental and physical health problems. And yet, amid the broader negative trends, recent signs point to a modest but significant recovery.

Divorce rates appear to have declined a little from historic highs; illegitimacy rates, after doubling every decade from 1960 to 1990, appear to have leveled off, albeit at a high level (33 percent of American births are to unmarried women); teen pregnancy and sexual activity are down; the proportion of homemaking mothers is up; marital fertility appears to be on the rise. Research suggests that married adults are more committed to marital permanence than they were twenty years ago. A new generation of children of divorce appears on the brink of making a commitment to lifelong marriage. In 1977, 55 percent of American teenagers thought a divorce should be harder to get; in 2001, 75 percent did.

A new marriage movement—a distinctively American phenomenon—has been born. The scholarly consensus on the importance of marriage has broadened and deepened; it is now the conventional wisdom among child welfare organizations. As a Child Trends research brief summed up: "Research clearly demonstrates that family structure matters for children, and the family structure that helps children the most is a family headed by two biological parents in a low-conflict marriage. Children in single-parent families, children born to unmarried mothers, and children in stepfamilies or cohabiting relationships face higher risks of poor outcomes. . . . There is thus

value for children in promoting strong, stable marriages between biological parents."

What will court-imposed gay marriage do to this incipient recovery of marriage? For, even as support for marriage in general has been rising, the gay marriage debate has proceeded on a separate track. Now the time has come to decide: Will unisex marriage help or hurt marriage as a social institution?

Why should it do either, some may ask? How can Bill and Bob's marriage hurt Mary and Joe? In an exchange with me in the just-released book "Marriage and Same Sex Unions: A Debate," Evan Wolfson, chief legal strategist for same-sex marriage in the Hawaii case, *Baer v. Lewin,* argues there is "enough marriage to share." What counts, he says, "is not family structure, but the quality of dedication, commitment, self-sacrifice, and love in the household."

Family structure does not count. Then what is marriage for? Why have laws about it? Why care whether people get married or stay married? Do children need mothers and fathers, or will any sort of family do? When the sexual desires of adults clash with the interests of children, which carries more weight, socially and legally?

These are the questions that same-sex marriage raises. Our answers will affect not only gay and lesbian families, but marriage as a whole.

In Ordering Gay Marriage on June 10, 2003, the highest court in Ontario, Canada, explicitly endorsed a brand new vision of marriage along the lines Wolfson suggests: "Marriage is, without dispute, one of the most significant forms of personal relationships. . . . Through the institution of marriage, individuals can publicly express their love and commitment to each other. Through this institution, society publicly recognizes expressions of love and commitment between individuals, granting them respect and legitimacy as a couple."

The Ontario court views marriage as a kind of Good Housekeeping Seal of Approval that government stamps on certain registered intimacies because, well, for no particular reason the court can articulate except that society likes to recognize expressions of love and commitment. In this view, endorsement of gay marriage is a no-brainer, for nothing really important rides on whether anyone gets married or stays married. Marriage is merely individual expressive conduct, and there is no obvious reason why some individuals' expression of gay love should hurt other individuals' expressions of non-gay love.

There is, however, a different view—indeed, a view that is radically opposed to this: Marriage is the fundamental, cross-cultural institution for bridging the male-female divide so that children have loving, committed mothers and fathers. Marriage is inherently normative: It is about holding out a certain kind of relationship as a social ideal, especially when there are children involved. Marriage is not simply an artifact of law; neither is it a mere delivery mechanism for a set of legal benefits that might as well be shared more broadly. The laws of marriage do not create marriage, but in societies ruled by law they help trace the boundaries and sustain the public meanings of marriage.

In other words, while individuals freely choose to enter marriage, society upholds the marriage option, formalizes its definition, and surrounds it with norms and reinforcements, so we can raise boys and girls who aspire to become the kind of men and women who can make successful marriages. Without this shared, public aspect, perpetuated generation after generation, marriage becomes what its critics say it is: a mere contract, a vessel with no particular content, one of a menu of sexual lifestyles, of no fundamental importance to anyone outside a given relationship.

The marriage idea is that children need mothers and fathers, that societies need babies, and that adults have an obligation to shape their sexual behavior so as to give their children stable families in which to grow up.

Which view of marriage is true? We have seen what has happened in our communities where marriage norms have failed. What has happened is not a flowering of libertarian freedom, but a breakdown of social and civic order that can reach frightening proportions. When law and culture retreat from sustaining the marriage idea, individuals cannot create marriage on their own.

In a complex society governed by positive law, social institutions require both social and legal support. To use an analogy, the government does not create private property. But to make a market system a reality requires the assistance of law as well as culture. People have to be raised to respect the property of others, and to value the traits of entrepreneurship, and to be law-abiding generally. The law cannot allow individuals to define for themselves what private property (or law-abiding conduct) means. The boundaries of certain institutions (such as the corporation) also need to be defined legally, and the definitions become socially shared knowledge. We need a shared system of meaning, publicly enforced, if market-based economies are to do their magic and individuals are to maximize their opportunities.

Successful social institutions generally function without people's having to think very much about how they work. But when a social institution is contested—as marriage is today—it becomes critically important to think and speak clearly about its public meanings.

Again, what is marriage for? Marriage is a virtually universal human institution. In all the wildly rich and various cultures flung throughout the ecosphere, in society after society, whether tribal or complex, and however bizarre, human beings have created systems of publicly approved sexual union between men and women that entail well-defined responsibilities of mothers and fathers. Not all these marriage systems look like our own, which is rooted in a fusion of Greek, Roman, Jewish, and Christian culture. Yet everywhere, in isolated mountain valleys, parched deserts, jungle thickets, and broad plains, people have come up with some version of this thing called marriage. Why?

Because sex between men and women makes babies, that's why. Even today, in our technologically advanced contraceptive culture, half of all pregnancies are unintended: Sex between men and women *still* makes babies. Most men and women are powerfully drawn to perform a sexual act that can and does generate life. Marriage is our attempt to reconcile and harmonize the erotic, social, sexual, and financial needs of men and women with the needs of their partner and their children.

How to reconcile the needs of children with the sexual desires of adults? Every society has to face that question, and some resolve it in ways that inflict horrendous cruelty on children born outside marriage. Some cultures decide these children don't matter: Men can have all the sex they want, and any children they create outside of marriage will be throwaway kids; marriage is for citizens—slaves and peasants need not apply. You can see a version of this elitist vision of marriage emerging in America under cover of acceptance of family diversity. Marriage will continue to exist as the social advantage of elite communities. The poor and the working class? Who cares whether their kids have dads? We can always import people from abroad to fill our need for disciplined, educated workers.

Our better tradition, and the only one consistent with democratic principles, is to hold up a single ideal for all parents, which is ultimately based on our deep cultural commitment to the equal dignity and social worth of all children. All kids need and deserve a married mom and dad. All parents are supposed to at least try to behave in ways that will give their own children this important protection. Privately, religiously, emotionally, individually, marriage may have many meanings. But this is the core of its public, shared meaning: Marriage is the place where having children is not only tolerated but welcomed and encouraged, because it gives children mothers and fathers.

Of course, many couples fail to live up to this ideal. Many of the things men and women have to do to sustain their own marriages, and a culture of marriage, are *hard*. Few people will do them consistently if the larger culture does not affirm the critical importance of marriage as a social institution. Why stick out a frustrating relationship, turn down a tempting new love, abstain from sex outside marriage, or even take pains not to conceive children out of wedlock if family structure does not matter? If marriage is not a shared norm, and if successful marriage is not socially valued, do not expect it to survive as the

generally accepted context for raising children. If marriage is just a way of publicly celebrating private love, then there is no need to encourage couples to stick it out for the sake of the children. If family structure does not matter, why have marriage laws at all? Do adults, or do they not have a basic obligation to control their desires so that children can have mothers and fathers?

The problem with endorsing gay marriage is not that it would allow a handful of people to choose alternative family forms, but that it would require society at large to gut marriage of its central presumptions about family in order to accommodate a few adults' desires.

The debate over same-sex marriage, then, is not some sideline discussion. It *is* the marriage debate. Either we win—or we lose the central meaning of marriage. The great threat unisex marriage poses to marriage as a social institution is not some distant or nearby slippery slope, it is an abyss at our feet. If we cannot explain why unisex marriage is, in itself, a disaster, we have already lost the marriage ideal.

Same-sex marriage would enshrine in law a public judgment that the desire of adults for families of choice outweighs the need of children for mothers and fathers. It would give sanction and approval to the creation of a motherless or fatherless family as a deliberately chosen "good." It would mean the law was neutral as to whether children had mothers and fathers. Motherless and fatherless families would be deemed just fine.

Same-sex marriage advocates are startlingly clear on this point. Marriage law, they repeatedly claim, has nothing to do with babies or procreation or getting mothers and fathers for children. In forcing the state legislature to create civil unions for gay couples, the high court of Vermont explicitly ruled that marriage in the state of Vermont has nothing to do with procreation. Evan Wolfson made the same point in "Marriage and Same Sex Unions": "[I]sn't having the law pretend that there is only one family model that works (let alone exists) a lie?" He goes on to say that in law, "marriage is not just about procreation—indeed is not necessarily about procreation at all."

Wolfson is right that in the course of the sexual revolution the Supreme Court struck down many legal features designed to reinforce the connection of marriage to babies. The animus of elites (including legal elites) against the marriage idea is not brand new. It stretches back at least thirty years. That is part of the problem we face, part of the reason 40 percent of our children are growing up without their fathers.

It is also true, as gay-marriage advocates note, that we impose no fertility tests for marriage: Infertile and older couples marry, and not every fertile couple chooses procreation. But every marriage between a man and a woman is capable of giving any child they create or adopt a mother and father. Every marriage between a man and a woman discourages either from creating fatherless children outside the marriage vow. In this sense, neither older married couples nor childless husbands and wives publicly challenge or dilute the core meaning of marriage. Even when a man marries an older woman and they do not adopt, his marriage helps protect children. How? His marriage means, if he keeps his vows, that he will not produce out-of-wedlock children.

Does marriage discriminate against gays and lesbians? Formally speaking, no. There are no sexual-orientation tests for marriage; many gays and lesbians do choose to marry members of the opposite sex, and some of these unions succeed. Our laws do not require a person to marry the individual to whom he or she is most erotically attracted, so long as he or she is willing to promise sexual fidelity, mutual caretaking, and shared parenting of any children of the marriage.

But marriage is unsuited to the wants and desires of many gays and lesbians, precisely because it is designed to bridge the male-female divide and sustain the idea that children need mothers and fathers. To make a marriage, what you need is a husband and a wife. Redefining marriage so that it suits gays and lesbians would require fundamentally changing our legal, public, and social conception of what marriage is in ways that threaten its core public purposes.

Some who criticize the refusal to embrace gay marriage liken it to the outlawing of interracial marriage, but the analogy is woefully false. The Supreme Court overturned anti-miscegenation laws because they frustrated the core purpose of marriage in order to sustain a racist legal order. Marriage laws, by contrast, were not invented to express animus toward homosexuals or anyone else. Their purpose is not negative, but positive: They uphold an institution that developed, over thousands of years, in thousands of cultures, to help direct the erotic desires of men and women into a relatively narrow but indispensably fruitful channel. We need men and women to marry and make babies for our society to survive. We have no similar public stake in any other family form—in the union of same-sex couples or the singleness of single moms.

Meanwhile, *cui bono?* To meet the desires of whom would we put our most basic social institution at risk? No good research on the marriage intentions of homosexual people exists. For what it's worth, the Census Bureau reports that 0.5 percent of households now consist of same-sex partners. To get a proxy for how many gay couples would avail themselves of the health insurance benefits marriage can provide, I asked the top 10 companies listed on the Human Rights Campaign's website as providing same-sex insurance benefits how many of their employees use this option. Only one company, General Motors, released its data. Out of 1.3 million employees, 166 claimed benefits for a same-sex partner, *one one-hundredth of one percent.*

People who argue for creating gay marriage do so in the name of high ideals: justice, compassion, fairness. Their sincerity is not in question. Nevertheless, to take the already troubled institution most responsible for the protection of children and throw out its most basic presumption in order to further adult interests in sexual freedom would not be high-minded. It would be morally callous and socially irresponsible.

If we cannot stand and defend this ground, then face it: The marriage debate is over. Dan Quayle was wrong. We lost.

✿ REVIEW QUESTIONS

1. What is the view of marriage held by the Canadian court, according to Gallagher? Why doesn't she accept it?
2. Explain Gallagher's view of marriage.
3. What is the problem with endorsing gay marriage, in Gallagher's view?
4. According to Gallagher, why don't childless married couples present a problem for her view about marriage?
5. Why doesn't the denial of same-sex marriage amount to discrimination or animus, according to Gallagher?

✿ DISCUSSION QUESTIONS

1. Is marriage essentially about procreation and raising children and not about love, commitment, emotional and financial support, and caregiving? Does marriage have only one purpose?
2. Do lesbian couples that have and raise children fulfill the purpose of marriage? Can gay couples that adopt and raise children satisfy this purpose?
3. Nussbaum finds it "flatly inconsistent" to deny marriage rights to lesbian and gay couples and yet grant them to postmenopausal women, sterile individuals, and those who do not want children and will not have them. Do you agree? Why or why not?
4. Is denying marriage to same-sex couples discrimination against them? Is it analogous to denying marriage to mixed-race couples?

PROBLEM CASES

1. Ellen DeGeneres and Portia de Rossi

Ellen DeGeneres is a stand-up comic, talk-show hostess (*The Ellen DeGeneres Show*) and actress. She is also a judge on *American Idol*. As an actress, she starred in *Mr. Wrong* and provided the voice of Dory in *Finding Nemo*. In 1997, she came out as a lesbian on *The Oprah Winfrey Show*.

Portia de Rossi is an Australian actress. She acted in the television show *Ally McBeal* (as the lawyer Nelle Porter) and played the role of Lindsay Bluth Fanke in the sitcom *Arrested Development*. Currently she is Veronica Palmer in the sitcom *Better Off Ted*. She was married to Mel Metcalfe (a male) from 1996 to 1999, but now she is openly lesbian.

DeGeneres and de Rossi began dating in 2004, and in 2008 DeGeneres announced on her show that she and de Rossi were engaged. DeGeneres sealed the engagement with the gift of a three-carat pink diamond ring. They were married on August 16, 2008, at their California home, with nineteen guests (including their mothers) attending. At that time, same-sex marriage

was legal in California. The passage of Proposition 8 made the legal status of the marriage questionable, but as noted in the Introduction, the California Supreme Court ruled that marriages performed before Proposition 8 was passed were still valid. Hence, DeGeneres and de Rossi are still legally married.

According to *People Magazine* (March 16, 2009), the couple is very happy, but they are not quite ready to have children. At age 36, de Rossi could become pregnant by in vitro fertilization. She discounts numerous rumors about her plans to start a family, but she doesn't rule it out. She said, "Maybe one day I'll want to have kids, but it's not something we've talked about recently."

Suppose de Rossi does become pregnant and has a baby girl. She and DeGeneres want to raise the girl. Do you have any objections to their raising a family? If so, what are they?

This marriage is legal, but is it morally acceptable? Why or why not?

2. *Goodridge v. Department of Public Health* (2003)

(For the text of the decision, see www.FindLaw.com.) In this case, the Massachusetts Supreme Court ruled (4 to 3) that a state law banning same-sex marriage violated the Massachusetts constitution, and ordered a stay of entry of the judgment for 180 days to "permit the Legislature to take such action as it may deem appropriate in light of this opinion."

In the majority opinion, Chief Justice Margaret H. Marshall said that marriage is a vital social institution that brings stability to society and provides love and mutual support to those who are married. It provides many legal, financial, and social benefits. The question before the court was "whether, consistent with the Massachusetts Constitution, the Commonwealth could deny those protections, benefits, and obligations to two individuals of the same sex who wish to marry." In ruling that the Commonwealth could not do so, the majority opinion said that the Massachusetts Constitution "affirms the dignity and equality of all individuals" and "forbids the creation of second-class citizens."

Furthermore, the court argued that the marriage ban for same-sex couples "works a deep and scarring hardship" on same-sex families "for no rational reason." It prevents children of same-sex couples from enjoying the advantages that flow from a "stable family structure in which children will be reared, educated, and socialized." "It cannot be rational under our laws," the court held, "to penalize children by depriving them of State benefits" because of their parents' sexual orientation.

The court denied that the primary purpose of marriage is procreation. Rather, the purpose of marriage was said to be "the exclusive and permanent commitment of marriage partners to one another, not the begetting of children, that is the sine qua non of marriage."

The majority opinion changed the common-law definition of civil marriage to mean "the voluntary union of two persons as spouses, to the exclusion of all others." The court noted that civil marriage was a civil right, and concluded that "the right to marry means little if it does not include the right to marry the person of one's choice."

There were three dissenting opinions. Justice Cordy argued that the marriage statute defining marriage as the union of one man and one woman did not violate the Massachusetts Constitution because "it furthers the legitimate State purpose of ensuring, promoting, and supporting an optimal social structure for the bearing and raising of children."

Justice Spina stated that what was at stake in the case was not the unequal treatment of individuals, but rather "the power of the Legislature to effectuate social change without interference from the courts." He said that the "power to regulate marriage lies with the Legislature, not with the judiciary."

Justice Sosman held that the issue was whether changing the definition of marriage "can be made at this time without damaging the institution of marriage." She asserted that "it is rational for the Legislature to postpone any redefinition of marriage that would include same-sex couples until such time as it is certain that redefinition will not have unintended and undesirable social consequences."

Do you agree with the majority opinion, or with one or more of the dissenting opinions? Explain your position.

In May 2004, the state of Massachusetts issued thousands of marriage licenses to same-sex couples. Did this produce any harm to heterosexual marriages or to the institution of marriage? If so, explain the nature of this harm.

3. *Stephan Davis and Jeffrey Busch*

(Reported in *The New York Times*, December 6, 2009.) Mr. Davis (age fifty-eight) and Mr. Busch (age forty-six) were married in Westport, Connecticut, on November 29, 2009. Previously they were in a group of same-sex couples that sued Connecticut

for the right to marry. The group won the case in October 2008.

Mr. Busch is a judge for the New York City Department of Finance. Mr. Davis is a librarian at Columbia University. They have a seven-year-old son,

Elijah Davis Busch. Iris Busch (age seventy-two), Mr. Busch's mother, also lives with the family. She helps take care of Elijah.

The couple does not know which of them is the biological father of Elijah. They each donated sperm to eggs provided by donors. A surrogate mother gave birth to the child.

The couple did not want a civil union. Mr. Busch said, "Nobody says, 'Oh, I want to civil union you.'" He added, "Steven loves me in the marrying kind of way."

This couple is satisfying a traditional purpose of marriage, which is procreation and raising children. They also love each other. Their marriage is legal. Is it morally acceptable? Why or why not?

4. Dan Conlin and Bob Elsen

Dan Conlin and Bob Elsen are gay partners living in San Francisco, California. Conlin is forty-two, and Elsen is forty-one. Conlin is a physician with a prosperous gastroenterology practice. Elsen is also a doctor. They met during their residences at New England Deaconess Hospital in Boston. They have a magnificent home in family-friendly Ashbury Heights and a stable, loving relationship. They both come from big, supportive families.

There are very few gay men with adopted children in the Bay Area. The norm for same-sex parents is lesbian couples whose children have been fathered by sperm donors. Yet Conlin and Elsen were highly motivated to adopt and raise children. After advertising, they found a pregnant woman in Florida who did not want her child. They witnessed the birth of the child, Michael, and became his legal guardians. (Same-sex couples cannot legally adopt children in Florida, but they can in California.) The formal legal adoption of Michael by Conlin and Elsen occurred in California.

They also adopted another newborn boy, Matthew, who was born in Reno, Nevada. Again the legal adoption was performed in California.

Both adoptions are open; that is, Colin and Elsen know the identity and location of the biological mothers, and vice versa. But the relationships between the children and mothers is distant. The men give the mothers birthday pictures, and Michael's mother calls occasionally, but other than that there is no contact.

Michael refers to his adoptive parents as "Daddy Dan" and "Daddy Bob" and does not seem to miss his mother. The children do not lack contact with women. They have a full-time female nanny, Coco; and regularly interact with nurses at the doctor's office, and various women in the family's circle of friends. Other children seem to have no problem with the fact that the children have two dads and no mom around.

Is there any reason why gay men such as Conlin and Elsen should or should not be allowed to adopt children? If so, what is it? Or if not, why not?

5. Polygamy

(For more information, see www.polygamy.com.) *Polygamy* is usually defined as the practice of a man having more than one wife at the same time, where we are talking about consenting adults and not children or those who do not agree to such an arrangement. Also, we are not concerned with serial polygamy, that is, when a man marries one woman, divorces her, then marries another woman, and so on, so that he has more than one wife over time.

Consensual polygamy is not quite the same as bigamy. Legally, *bigamy* is defined as legally marrying one

person while already legally married to another, usually keeping the second marriage a secret. All fifty states have statutes making bigamy a crime. In most states, bigamy is a felony.

It is estimated that there are more than 100,000 consensual polygamists in the United States. They avoid prosecution for bigamy by not registering their plural marriages with the state. Then they are guilty of cohabitation or fornication or adultery, but even though these are crimes in many states, they are not usually prosecuted.

Defenders of polygamy appeal to religious texts that condone it or command it. The Old Testament has several such passages. Exodus 21:10 says, "If he take him another wife; her food, her raiment, and her duty of marriage, shall he not diminish." Deuteronomy 25:7–10 says that if a man dies without children, then his brother is obliged to marry the widow. Deuteronomy 21:15–17 addresses the inheritance rights of children of two different wives. David had at least seven wives, apart from Bathsheba. King Solomon had many wives and concubines as well. Jacob limited himself to four wives.

Islam specifically recommends polygamy, but limits the number of wives to four. The Koran 4:3 says, "Marry women of your choice, two or three or four; but if you fear that you shall not be able to deal justly with them, then only one or one that your right hands possess. That will be more suitable, to prevent you from doing injustice." The Prophet Muhammad argued that if wars cause the number of women to greatly exceed the number of men, then men should marry the extra women to care for them.

In the United States, the majority of those practicing polygamy are Mormon Fundamentalists who believe they are following God's law as set forth in Section 132 of The Doctrine and Covenants. The revered prophet Joseph Smith describes plural marriage as part of "the most holy and important doctrine ever revealed to man on earth" and he taught that a man needs at least three wives to attain the fullness of exaltation in the afterlife (quoted by Jon Krakauer in *Under the Banner of Heaven* [Doubleday, 2003], p. 6.) According to Krakauer, there are more than 30,000 Mormon Fundamentalist polygamists living in Canada, Mexico, and throughout the American West.

Polygamy seems to be a practice that is at the heart of Islam and Mormon Fundamentalism. Does religious tolerance require us to allow polygamy when it is practiced for religious reasons? Why or why not?

⚜ SUGGESTED READINGS

For facts, laws, and news about same-sex marriage, see The Public Agenda website (www.publicagenda .org). Another useful source is the information center at www.loveandpride.com. For new stories and opinion polls about gay marriage, see www .speakout.com. An attack on same-sex marriage is found on The Family Research Council website (www.frx.org). A lesbian view of marriage is given at www.lesbianlife.about.com.

David Blankenhorn, *The Future of Marriage* (New York: Encounter Books, 2009), is against gay marriage because it cannot perform the social function of uniting biological parents and children. Also, it will lead to polygamy and bisexual people marrying one male and one female.

Jonathan Rauch, *Gay Marriage* (New York: Holt Paperbacks, 2004), argues that gay marriage will strengthen the traditional institution of marriage, and that a substitute marriage (marriage "lite") will not do the job.

Martha Nussbaum, *Sex and Social Justice* (New York: Oxford University Press America, 2000). In Chapter 7, "A Defense of Lesbian and Gay Rights," Nussbaum argues that the rights of gays to marry and to raise and/or adopt children are important and defensible.

Daniel R. Pinello, *America's Struggle for Same-Sex Marriage* (Cambridge: Cambridge University Press, 2006), covers the struggle to make same-sex marriage legal in the United States.

Claudia Card, "Against Marriage and Motherhood," *Hypatia* 11, 3 (Summer 1996): 1–23, attacks marriage and motherhood as currently practiced. Gay and lesbian partners should work to eliminate or just ignore state sanctions of marriage and motherhood. Children should have many caregivers and not just one mother.

Cheshire Calhoun, "Family Outlaws," *Philosophical Studies* 85, 2–3 (March 1997): 181–193, argues that feminist critiques of motherhood neglect the historical constructions of gay men and lesbians as outlaws unfit for marriage and parenting.

Rhonda E. Howard-Hassman, "Gay Rights and the Right to a Family," *Human Rights Quarterly* 23, 1 (2001): 73–95, analyzes the debate in Canada about gay rights and the right of gays to form a family. (In 2005, Canada legalized same-sex marriage nationwide.)

Andrew Sullivan, ed., *Same Sex Marriage* (New York: Vintage Books, 2004), is a comprehensive anthology of readings about same-sex marriage, both pro and con. Included is a chapter on the slippery-slope argument that permitting same-sex marriage will force acceptance of polygamy.

Robert M. Baird and Stuart E. Rosenbaum, eds., *Same Sex Marriage* (Buffalo, NY: Prometheus Books, 2004), presents a diverse collection of readings, from religious conservatives to lesbian feminists.

Kathleen E. Hull, *Same-Sex Marriage* (Cambridge: Cambridge University Press, 2007), interviewed more than seventy people in same-sex relationships and reports on their commitment and practices.

Sam Schulman, "Gay Marriage—and Marriage," *Commentary* (November 2003): 1–10, rejects the civil rights argument for gay marriage and argues that the essence of marriage is to sanction the connection of opposites that creates new human life.

Morris B. Kaplan, "Intimacy and Equality," *Philosophical Forum* 25 (Summer 1994): 333–360, argues that gays and lesbians should be granted the same rights as heterosexuals to marry.

The Vatican, "Declaration on Sexual Ethics," Sacred Congregation for the Doctrine of the Faith (issued December 29, 1975), defends the Christian doctrine that "every genital act must be within the framework of marriage." Homosexuality and masturbation are specifically condemned as serious disorders that frustrate the natural end of sex, which is procreation.

Alan Goldman, "Plain Sex," *Philosophy and Public Affairs* 6 (Spring 1977): 267–287, attacks the means–end analysis of sex that requires sex as a means to some end such as reproduction. Plain sex is sex that fulfills sexual desire without being used to satisfy some other goal, and as such, it is not intrinsically immoral.

Michael Ruse, *Homosexuality* (Oxford: Basil Blackwell, 1990), gives a careful and detailed discussion of various issues related to homosexuality. He argues that it is not unnatural, not immoral, and not a sexual perversion.

Robert Baird and Katherine Baird, eds., *Homosexuality* (Buffalo, NY: Prometheus Books, 1995), is an anthology dealing with the morality of homosexuality.

Michael Levin, "Why Homosexuality Is Abnormal," *The Monist* 67, 2 (1984): 260–276, argues that homosexuality is inherently abnormal and immoral because it is a misuse of body parts.

John Corvino, "Why Shouldn't Tommy and Jim Have Sex?" in *Same Sex*, ed. John Corvino (Lanham, MD: Rowman & Littlefield, 1997), pp. 3–16, argues that homosexuality is not unnatural and that biblical injunctions against it no longer apply.

David Bradshaw, "A Reply to Corvino," in *Same Sex*, ed. John Corvino (Lanham, MD: Rowman & Littlefield, 1997), 17–30, argues that homosexual practice is morally wrong because it violates the body's "moral space."

Animal Liberation and Vegetarianism

INTRODUCTION

Factual Background

Humans cause a great deal of animal suffering. According to Peter Singer, the use and abuse of animals raised for food in factory farms far exceeds, in numbers, any other kind of mistreatment. In his book *Animal Liberation*, first published in 1975, Singer said that hundreds of millions of cattle, pigs, and sheep were raised and killed in the United States each year. But now Singer says that more than 10 *billion* birds and mammals are raised and killed for food in the United States annually, with tens of millions of animals used in animal experiments. Most of these factory-farmed animals spend their lives confined indoors with no fresh air, sun, or grass until they are slaughtered. But do they suffer? Consider the way they are killed. Gail Eisnitz's book *Slaughterhouse* (see the Suggested Readings) gives graphic descriptions of the way these animals are treated in major American slaughterhouses. There are shocking accounts of animals being skinned and dismembered while still alive and conscious. Or consider the treatment of veal calves. To make their flesh pale and tender, these calves are given special treatment. They are put in narrow stalls and tethered with a chain so that they cannot turn around, lie down comfortably, or groom themselves. They are fed a totally liquid diet to promote rapid weight gain. This diet is deficient in iron; as a result, the calves lick the sides of the stall, which are impregnated with urine containing iron. They are given no water because thirsty animals eat more than ones that drink water. This system of keeping calves has been illegal in Britain for many years, and became illegal throughout the European Union by 2007. Even Spain, which is criticized for having bullfighting, has better treatment of its animals raised for food. For example, by 2012, Spain and other European egg producers will be required to give their hens access to a perch and a nesting box to lay their eggs in, and to allow at least 120 square inches per bird. These changes will improve the living situation of more than 200 million birds. By contrast, United States egg producers give their nesting hens only 48 square inches per bird, about half the size of a sheet of letter paper.

Another cause of animal suffering is experimentation. The military conducts experiments on animals in secret, but we know from published accounts that a lot of research is being done. According to a Department of Defense report, more than 330,000 dogs, cats, guinea pigs, hamsters, rabbits, monkeys, dolphins, and other animals were subjected to military experiments in 2001. This figure does not include experiments contracted out to nongovernmental laboratories.

In one experiment, monkeys were given near-lethal doses of radiation over twenty-one days; then some of the monkeys were given a drug to relieve symptoms, while the control group suffered from radiation sickness. In another experiment conducted at the Lovelace Foundation in New Mexico, experimenters forced sixty-four beagles to inhale radioactive strontium 90. Twenty-five of the dogs died; initially, most of them were feverish and anemic, suffering from hemorrhages and bloody diarrhea. One of the deaths occurred during an epileptic seizure, and another resulted from a brain hemorrhage.

At Lackland Air Force Base, pigs had their throats cut, and after forty-five minutes of bleeding, researchers tried to resuscitate them. Pigs that survived the initial experiment were killed to study the effects of the shock on their organs and blood. Other military experiments include subjecting animals to decompression sickness, exposure to jet fuel, inhalation of high concentrations of carbon monoxide, and exposure to biological and chemical warfare agents.

Another source of animal suffering is genetic alteration. To produce bigger pigs, chickens, and cows, factory farmers are raising genetically altered animals. These animals gain weight rapidly but are susceptible to disease and suffer from arthritis and other problems. Some of them cannot walk. A famous example is the Beltsville Pig, a genetic disaster for a company called GM. The researchers inserted a human cancer gene into a pig embryo. The idea was to create a faster-growing animal, and the pig did grow faster than a normal pig. Unfortunately, the cancer gene also caused the pig's organs to swell, and it developed severe arthritis in its joints so that it could not walk or move. It lived in anguish until its death.

Commercial product testing is still another major source of animal suffering. Every year millions of animals are poisoned and killed in tests designed to evaluate the toxicity of consumer products such as cosmetics and household products. To determine the toxicity of a product or chemical, the substance is given to animals in high doses by force-feeding or forced inhalation. The animals in high-dose groups may suffer abdominal pain, diarrhea, convulsions, seizures, paralysis, and bleeding before they die.

The most common test is the lethal dose 50 percent test (LD50); this test measures the amount of a toxic substance that will kill, in a single dose, 50 percent of the animals in a test group. The test is used each year on about 5 million dogs, rabbits, rats, monkeys, and other animals in the United States. It is mainly used to test cosmetics and household products such as weed killers, oven cleaners, insecticides, and food additives, to satisfy the Food and Drug Administration (FDA) requirement that a product be "adequately substantiated for safety." But the LD50 test is not actually required by the FDA. In the administration of the test, no painkillers are used. The experimental substance is forced into the animal's throat or pumped into its stomach by a tube, sometimes causing death by stomach rupture or from the sheer bulk of the chemical dose. Substances are also injected under the skin, into a vein, or into the lining of the stomach. The chemicals are often applied to the eyes, rectum, and vagina or are forcibly inhaled through a gas mask.

The Readings

Immanuel Kant gives a classic statement of the view that animals should be treated differently than humans. Kant assumes that humans are self-conscious and rational, whereas animals are not. In Kant's view, this factual difference implies that we have no direct duties to animals themselves; we have direct duties only to humans who are self-conscious and rational. Our duties to animals insofar as they exist are merely indirect duties to humans. In other words, the moral treatment of animals—for example, not being excessively cruel—is merely a means of cultivating moral treatment of humans. We should not mistreat animals because this produces mistreatment of humans.

Kant's view seems to be an example of what Peter Singer calls speciesism in the next reading. As Singer defines it, *speciesism* is "a prejudice or attitude of bias toward the interests of members of one's own species and against those of members of other species." Singer argues that speciesism is analogous to racism and sexism. It is unjust to discriminate against blacks because of their skin color or against women because of their gender. Their interests (for example, their interest in voting) should be considered equally with those of whites and men. Racism and sexism violate a fundamental principle of justice, namely the principle of the equal consideration of interests. Similarly, it is unjust to discriminate against animals because of their species. They have interests too, not an interest in voting of course, but an interest in not suffering, and the principle of equal consideration of interests requires us to consider this interest. The practical consequence of Singer's argument is that we should stop unnecessary and painful animal experimentation and eliminate factory farming of animals for food.

Bonnie Steinbock responds to Singer. She agrees that we should not be cruel to animals. But she thinks Singer's principle of the equal consideration of interests has counterintuitive results. It implies, for example, that it is unfair to feed starving children before feeding starving dogs. It is obvious to Steinbock that the interests of humans are more important than those of animals. Why is this? According to Steinbock, humans have a higher moral status than animals because humans have certain morally relevant capacities that animals do not have: for example, the capacities to be morally responsible for actions, to have altruistic or moral reasons, and to desire self-respect.

Alastair Norcross defends vegetarianism and also replies to Steinbock and others who maintain that humans have a higher moral status than nonhumans. He begins with an imaginative story about Fred, a man who tortures puppies in order to harvest a substance called cocoamone, which allows him to enjoy chocolate. Norcross assumes that we would be horrified by Fred's behavior. But if so, then why aren't we equally horrified by the suffering of chickens and pigs in factory farms? Norcross claims that there is no morally relevant difference between the puppies and the pigs. The fact that puppies are cute and pigs are not, for example, is irrelevant. Norcross goes on to critically examine the view that humans have an ethical status superior to that of animals. According to Norcross, this view has two serious problems. First, there is the problem of marginal cases, that is, cases of humans who do not have the morally relevant capacities picked out by Steinbock. Severely mentally disabled persons or the irreversibly comatose, for example, do not have the capacity to be morally responsible or have moral reasons. Does that mean they have the same moral status as animals? The second problem is that even if animals cannot be moral *agents*, they can still be moral *patients*, and that is all that is required to give them a full moral status worth considering.

James Rachels (see the Suggested Readings) also defends vegetarianism. Rachels gives two arguments for vegetarianism, one that appeals to our duty to not waste food when people are starving, and another that appeals to our moral duty to not cause suffering unless there is a good reason. He goes on to give a defense of animals' right to life. Given the facts about animals—that they live in communities, communicate with one another, have social relationships, and are capable of suffering and happiness—the burden of proof is on those who claim that they do not have a right to life. He compares animals to severely retarded humans and asks, "What could be the rational basis for saying that a severely retarded human, who is inferior in every important respect to an intelligent animal, has a right to life but the animal doesn't?"

Philosophical Issues

What is the criterion of moral standing? Who deserves moral consideration? These are basic issues raised by the readings. Kant holds that self-consciousness gives a person moral standing; to use Kant's terminology, a self-conscious being is an end in itself and not just a means. On this criterion, normal human beings have moral standing as ends, but animals do not; they are mere means to fulfilling human purposes. Or so Kant believed. To be consistent, Kant would have to agree that nonhumans that are self-conscious (for example, angels or aliens or apes) have moral standing, and humans who are not self-conscious (for example, infants and the comatose) do not have any moral standing.

Roger Scruton (see the Suggested Readings) defends a position very much like Kant's. Humans have rights and duties because they are moral beings endowed with rationality and self-consciousness, and animals do not have rights and duties because they do not have these features. Scruton avoids the problem of animals that are rational and self-conscious by simply stipulating that animals by definition lack self-consciousness and rationality. He complicates his position by adding a principle of the sanctity of human life in order to give mentally impaired humans a moral status, and a potentiality principle to give rights to infants.

What exactly is the moral standing of a severely retarded infant or someone in a state of advanced senility? This is an important issue that comes up in the reading. Singer suggests that the life of a chimpanzee, dog, or pig having a high degree of self-awareness might be more valuable than the life of a retarded infant or senile adult. Steinbock does not agree. At the end of her paper, she hints at two reasons for valuing the life of the retarded or senile over that of an animal. First, there is the thought

"That could be me." Second, she mentions that we feel a special obligation to care for members of our own species. Rachels says that there is no rational basis for saying that the severely retarded human being has a right to life but an animal does not. So it would appear that in his view the human and the animal have an equal right to life.

The utilitarian criterion of moral standing accepted by Singer is sentience or consciousness. Animals are conscious; they are capable of feeling pain or pleasure, so they have moral standing. But living but permanently comatose or brain-dead persons are not conscious or even capable of consciousness, so they would have no moral standing at all in Singer's view. Steinbock would grant such persons a moral standing based on the fact that they are human. Environmentalists attack Singer's view as still another kind of bias, namely sentientism, the belief that only conscious or sentient beings deserve moral consideration. In their view the animal liberation movement has escaped one prejudice, speciesism, only to embrace another one, sentientism.

A practical issue raised by the readings is whether eating meat is morally wrong. Singer's utilitarian view is that meat-eating is wrong because it causes pain and suffering for factory-farmed animals. Following this view would greatly reduce meat-eating but not completely eliminate it, for it seems to morally allow the raising and eating of animals that do not suffer and are killed painlessly. Indeed, this seems to be morally right in the utilitarian view, as it would increase the total amount of happiness in the world. (See the problem case about happy chickens.) Another argument for not eating meat, given by Rachels, is that it wastes food and resources. If we used the grain that we feed animals to feed people instead, we would be able to solve or greatly reduce hunger and malnutrition in the world. Scruton does not defend factory farming, but he argues that there is nothing wrong with eating animals that have a satisfactory life and an easy death. Besides, he points out, most of these animals exist only because they are eaten. If everyone became a vegetarian, then what would become of all the animals raised for food?

Our Duties to Animals

IMMANUEL KANT

For biographical information on Kant, see his reading in Chapter 1.

Kant maintains that we have no direct duties to animals because they are not self-conscious. Our duties to animals are merely indirect duties to human beings; that is, the duty to animals is a means of cultivating a corresponding duty to humans. For example, we should not be cruel to animals because this tends to produce cruelty to humans.

Source: Immanuel Kant, "Our Duties to Animals" from *Lectures on Ethics*, trans. Louis Infield, pp. 239–241. Reprinted with permission of the Taylor & Francis Group.

Baumgarten speaks of duties towards beings which are beneath us and beings which are above us. But so far as animals are concerned, we have no direct duties. Animals are not self-conscious and are there merely as a means to an end. That end is man. We can ask, 'Why do animals exist?' But to ask, 'Why does man exist?' is a meaningless question. Our duties towards animals are merely indirect duties towards humanity. Animal nature has analogies to human nature, and by doing our duties to animals in respect of manifestations which correspond to manifestations of human nature, we indirectly do our duty towards humanity. Thus, if a dog has served his master long and faithfully, his service, on the analogy of human service, deserves reward, and when the dog has grown too old to serve, his master ought to keep him until he dies. Such action helps to support us in our duties towards human beings, where they are bounden duties. If then any acts of animals are analogous to human acts and spring from the same principles, we have duties towards the animals because thus we cultivate the corresponding duties towards human beings. If a man shoots his dog because the animal is no longer capable of service, he does not fail in his duty to the dog, for the dog cannot judge, but his act is inhuman and damages in himself that humanity which it is his duty to show towards mankind. If he is not to stifle his human feelings, he must practise kindness towards animals, for he who is cruel to animals becomes hard also in his dealings with men. We can judge the heart of a man by his treatment of animals. Hogarth[1] depicts

this in his engravings. He shows how cruelty grows and develops. He shows the child's cruelty to animals, pinching the tail of a dog or a cat; he then depicts the grown man in his cart running over a child; and lastly, the culmination of cruelty in murder. He thus brings home to us in a terrible fashion the rewards of cruelty, and this should be an impressive lesson to children. The more we come in contact with animals and observe their behaviour, the more we love them, for we see how great is their care for their young. It is then difficult for us to be cruel in thought even to a wolf. Leibnitz used a tiny worm for purposes of observation, and then carefully replaced it with its leaf on the tree so that it should not come to harm through any act of his. He would have been sorry—a natural feeling for a humane man—to destroy such a creature for no reason. Tender feelings towards dumb animals develop humane feelings towards mankind. In England butchers and doctors do not sit on a jury because they are accustomed to the sight of death and hardened. Vivisectionists who use living animals for their experiments, certainly act cruelly, although their aim is praiseworthy, and they can justify their cruelty, since animals must be regarded as man's instruments; but any such cruelty for sport cannot be justified. A master who turns out his ass or his dog because the animal can no longer earn its keep manifests a small mind. The Greeks' ideas in this respect were high-minded, as can be seen from the fable of the ass and the bell of ingratitude. Our duties towards animals, then, are indirect duties towards mankind.

---

[1]Hogarth's four engravings, 'The Stages of Cruelty', 1751.

♛ REVIEW QUESTIONS

1. According to Kant, why don't we have direct duties to animals? What is the difference between animals and humans, in Kant's view?

2. What does Kant mean when he says that our duty to animals is only an indirect duty to humans?

♛ DISCUSSION QUESTIONS

1. Comatose people and newborn infants do not seem to be self-conscious. Does this mean we have no direct duties to them? What would Kant say? What is your view?

2. People who hunt and kill deer do not usually do the same to humans. Is this a problem for Kant's view? Why or why not?

All Animals Are Equal

PETER SINGER

Peter Singer is the Ira W. DeCamp Professor of Bioethics at the University Center for Human Values, Princeton University, and Laureate Professor, Centre for Applied Philosophy and Public Ethics, University of Melbourne. He has authored, coauthored, and edited forty books, and published more than a hundred articles in professional journals. A recent book is *The Life You Can Save: Acting Now to End World Poverty* (2009).

Singer defines *speciesism* as a prejudice toward the interests of members of one's own species and against those of members of other species. He argues that speciesism is analogous to racism and sexism. If it is unjust to discriminate against women and blacks by not considering their interests, it is also unfair to ignore the interests of animals, particularly their interest in not suffering.

"Animal liberation" may sound more like a parody of other liberation movements than a serious objective. The idea of "The Rights of Animals" actually was once used to parody the case for women's rights. When Mary Wollstonecraft, a forerunner of today's feminists, published her *Vindication of the Rights of Women* in 1792, her views were widely regarded as absurd, and before long an anonymous publication appeared entitled *A Vindication of the Rights of Brutes*. The author of this satirical work (now known to have been Thomas Taylor, a distinguished Cambridge philosopher) tried to refute Mary Wollstonecraft's arguments by showing that they could be carried one stage further. If the argument for equality was sound when applied to women, why should it not be applied to dogs, cats, and horses? The reasoning seemed to hold for these "brutes" too, yet to hold that brutes had rights was manifestly absurd; therefore the reasoning by which this conclusion had been reached must be unsound, and if unsound when applied to brutes, it must also be unsound when applied to women, since the very same arguments had been used in each case.

In order to explain the basis of the case for the equality of animals, it will be helpful to start with an examination of the case for the equality of women. Let us assume that we wish to defend the case for women's rights against the attack by Thomas Taylor. How should we reply?

One way in which we might reply is by saying that the case for equality between men and women cannot validly be extended to nonhuman animals. Women have a right to vote, for instance, because they are just as capable of making rational decisions about the future as men are; dogs, on the other hand, are incapable of understanding the significance of voting, so they cannot have the right to vote. There are many other obvious ways in which men and women resemble each other closely, while humans and animals differ greatly. So, it might be said, men and women are similar beings and should have similar rights, while humans and nonhumans are different and should not have equal rights.

The reasoning behind this reply to Taylor's analogy is correct up to a point, but it does not go far enough. There *are* important differences between humans and other animals, and these differences must give rise to *some* differences in the rights that each have. Recognizing this obvious fact, however, is no barrier to the case for extending the basic principle of equality to

Source: Peter Singer, "All Animals Are Equal" from *Animal Liberation* (New York: New York Review of Books, 1975), pp. 1–22. Used by permission of the author.

nonhuman animals. The differences that exist between men and women are equally undeniable, and the supporters of Women's Liberation are aware that these differences may give rise to different rights. Many feminists hold that women have the right to an abortion on request. It does not follow that since these same feminists are campaigning for equality between men and women they must support the right of men to have abortions too. Since a man cannot have an abortion, it is meaningless to talk of his right to have one. Since a dog can't vote, it is meaningless to talk of its right to vote. There is no reason why either Women's Liberation or Animal Liberation should get involved in such nonsense. The extension of the basic principle of equality from one group to another does not imply that we must treat both groups in exactly the same way, or grant exactly the same rights to both groups. Whether we should do so will depend on the nature of the members of the two groups. The basic principle of equality does not require equal or identical *treatment*; it requires equal *consideration*. Equal consideration for different beings may lead to different treatment and different rights.

So there is a different way of replying to Taylor's attempt to parody the case for women's rights, a way that does not deny the obvious differences between humans and nonhumans but goes more deeply into the question of equality and concludes by finding nothing absurd in the idea that the basic principle of equality applies to so-called brutes. At this point such a conclusion may appear odd; but if we examine more deeply the basis on which our opposition to discrimination on grounds of race or sex ultimately rests, we will see that we would be on shaky ground if we were to demand equality for blacks, women, and other groups of oppressed humans while denying equal consideration to nonhumans. To make this clear we need to see first, exactly why racism and sexism are wrong.

When we say that all human beings, whatever their race, creed, or sex, are equal, what is it that we are asserting? Those who wish to defend hierarchical, inegalitarian societies have often pointed out that by whatever test we choose it simply is not true that all humans are equal. Like it or not we must face the fact that humans come in different shapes and sizes; they come with different moral capacities, different intellectual abilities, different amounts of benevolent feeling and sensitivity to the needs of others, different abilities to communicate effectively, and different capacities to experience pleasure and pain. In short, if the demand for equality were based on the actual equality of all human beings, we would have to stop demanding equality.

Still, one might cling to the view that the demand for equality among human beings is based on the actual equality of the different races and sexes. Although, it may be said, humans differ as individuals there are no differences between the races and sexes *as such*. From the mere fact that a person is black or a woman we cannot infer anything about that person's intellectual or moral capacities. This, it may be said, is why racism and sexism are wrong. The white racist claims that whites are superior to blacks, but this is false—although there are differences among individuals, some blacks are superior to some whites in all of the capacities and abilities that could conceivably be relevant. The opponent of sexism would say the same: a person's sex is no guide to his or her abilities, and this is why it is unjustifiable to discriminate on the basis of sex.

The existence of individual variations that cut across the lines of race or sex, however, provides us with no defense at all against a more sophisticated opponent of equality, one who proposes that, say, the interests of all those with IQ scores below 100 be given less consideration than the interests of those with ratings over 100. Perhaps those scoring below the mark, would, in this society, be made the slaves of those scoring higher. Would a hierarchical society of this sort really be so much better than one based on race or sex? I think not. But if we tie the moral principle of equality to the factual equality of the different races or sexes, taken as a whole, our opposition to racism and sexism does not provide us with any basis for objecting to this kind of inegalitarianism.

There is a second important reason why we ought not to base our opposition to racism and sexism on any kind of actual equality, even the limited kind that asserts that variations in capacities and abilities are spread evenly between the different races and sexes: we can have no absolute guarantee that these capacities and abilities really are distributed evenly, without regard to race or sex, among human beings. So far as actual abilities are concerned there do seem to be certain measurable differences between both races and sexes. These differences do not, of course, appear in each case, but only when averages are taken. More important still, we do not yet know how much of these differences is really due to the different genetic endowments of the different races and sexes, and how much is due to poor schools, poor housing, and other factors that are the result of past and continuing discrimination. Perhaps all of the important differences will eventually prove to be environmental rather than genetic. Anyone opposed to racism and sexism will certainly hope that this will be so, for it will make the task of ending discrimination a lot easier; nevertheless it would be dangerous to rest the case against racism and sexism on the belief that all significant differences are environmental in origin. The opponent of, say, racism who takes this line will be unable to avoid conceding that *if* differences in ability do after all prove to have some genetic connection with race, racism would in some way be defensible.

Fortunately there is no need to pin the case for equality to one particular outcome of a scientific investigation. The appropriate response to those who claim to have found evidence of genetically based differences in ability between the races or sexes is not to stick to the belief that the genetic explanation must be wrong, whatever evidence to the contrary may turn up: instead we should make it quite clear that the claim to equality does not depend on intelligence, moral capacity, physical strength, or similar matters of fact. Equality is a moral idea, not an assertion of fact. There is no logically compelling reason for assuming that a factual difference in ability between two people justifies any difference in the amount of consideration we give to their needs and interests. *The principle of the equality of human beings is not a description of an alleged actual equality among humans; it is a prescription of how we should treat humans.*

Jeremy Bentham, the founder of the reforming utilitarian school of moral philosophy, incorporated the essential basis of moral equality into his system of ethics by means of the formula: "Each to count for one and none for more than one." In other words, the interests of every being affected by an action are to be taken into account and given the same weight as the like interests of any other being. A later utilitarian, Henry Sidgwick, put the point in this way: "The good of any one individual is of no more importance, from the point of view (if I may say so) of the Universe, than the good of any other." More recently the leading figures in contemporary moral philosophy have shown a great deal of agreement in specifying as a fundamental presupposition of their moral theories some similar requirement that operates so as to give everyone's interests equal consideration—although these writers generally cannot agree on how this requirement is best formulated.[1]

It is an implication of this principle of equality that our concern for others and our readiness to consider their interests ought not to depend on what they are like or on what abilities they may possess. Precisely what this concern or consideration requires us to do may vary according to the characteristics of those affected by what we do: concern for the well-being of a child growing up in America would require that we teach him to read; concern for the well-being of a pig may require no more than that we leave him alone with other pigs in a place where there is adequate food and room to run freely. But the basic element— the taking into account of the interests of the being, whatever those interests may be—must,

---

[1] For Bentham's moral philosophy, see his *Introduction to the Principles of Morals and Legislation*, and for Sidgwick's see *The Methods of Ethics* (the passage quoted is from the seventh edition, pp. 382). As examples of leading contemporary moral philosophers who incorporate a requirement of equal consideration of interests, see R. M. Hare, *Freedom and Reason* (New York, Oxford University Press, 1963) and John Rawls, *A Theory of Justice* (Cambridge: Harvard University Press, Belknap Press, 1972). For a brief account of the essential agreement on this issue between these and other positions, see R. M. Hare, "Rules of War and Moral Reasoning," *Philosophy and Public Affairs* 1 (1972).

according to the principle of equality, be extended to all beings, black or white, masculine or feminine, human or nonhuman.

Thomas Jefferson, who was responsible for writing the principle of the equality of men into the American Declaration of Independence, saw this point. It led him to oppose slavery even though he was unable to free himself fully from his slaveholding background. He wrote in a letter to the author of a book that emphasized the notable intellectual achievements of Negroes in order to refute the then common view that they had limited intellectual capacities:

> Be assured that no person living wishes more sincerely than I do, to see a complete refutation of the doubts I have myself entertained and expressed on the grade of understanding allotted to them by nature, and to find that they are on a par with ourselves . . . but whatever be their degree of talent it is no measure of their rights. Because Sir Isaac Newton was superior to others in understanding, he was not therefore lord of the property or person of others.[2]

Similarly when in the 1850s the call for women's rights was raised in the United States a remarkable black feminist named Sojourner Truth made the same point in more robust terms at a feminist convention:

> . . . they talk about this thing in the head; what do they call it? ["Intellect," whispered someone near by.] That's it. What's that got to do with women's rights or Negroes' rights? If my cup won't hold but a pint and yours holds a quart, wouldn't you be mean not to let me have my little half-measure full?[3]

It is on this basis that the case against racism and the case against sexism must both ultimately rest; and it is in accordance with this principle that the attitude that we may call "speciesism," by analogy with racism, must also be condemned. Speciesism—the word is not an attractive one, but I can think of no better term—is a prejudice or attitude of bias toward the interests of members of one's own species and against those members of other species. It should be obvious that the fundamental objections to racism and sexism made by Thomas Jefferson and Sojourner Truth apply equally to speciesism. If possessing a higher degree of intelligence does not entitle one human to use another for his own ends, how can it entitle humans to exploit nonhumans for the same purpose?[4]

Many philosophers and other writers have proposed the principle of equal consideration of interests, in some form or other, as a basic moral principle, but not many of them have recognized that this principle applies to members of other species as well as to our own. Jeremy Bentham was one of the few who did realize this. In a forward-looking passage written at a time when black slaves had been freed by the French but the British dominions were still being treated in the way we now treat animals, Bentham wrote:

> The day may come when the rest of the animal creation may acquire those rights which never could have been withholden from them but by the hand of tyranny. The French have already discovered that the blackness of the skin is no reason why a human being should be abandoned without redress to the caprice of a tormentor. It may one day come to be recognized that the number of the legs, the villosity of the skin, or the termination of the *os sacrum* are reasons equally insufficient for abandoning a sensitive being to the same fate. What else is it that should trace the insuperable line? Is it the faculty of reason, or perhaps the faculty of discourse? But a full-grown horse or dog is beyond comparison a more rational, as well as a more conversable animal, than an infant of a day or a week or even a month old. But suppose they were otherwise, what would it avail? The question is not, Can they reason? nor Can they talk? but, Can they suffer?[5]

In this passage Bentham points to the capacity for suffering as the vital characteristic that gives a being the right to equal consideration. The capacity for suffering—or more strictly, for suffering and/or enjoyment or happiness—is not

---

[2]Letter to Henri Gregoire, February 25, 1809.
[3]Reminiscences by Francis D. Gage, from Susan B. Anthony, *The History of Woman Suffrage*, vol. 1; the passage is to be found in the extract in Leslie Tanner, ed., *Voices from Women's Liberation* (New York: Signet, 1970).

[4]I owe the term "speciesism" to Richard Ryder.
[5]*Introduction to the Principles of Morals and Legislation*, chapter 17.

just another characteristic like the capacity for language or higher mathematics. Bentham is not saying that those who try to mark "the insuperable line" that determines whether the interests of a being should be considered happen to have chosen the wrong characteristic. By saying that we must consider the interests of all beings with the capacity for suffering or enjoyment Bentham does not arbitrarily exclude from consideration any interests at all—as those who draw the line with reference to the possession of reason or language do. The capacity for suffering and enjoyment is a *prerequisite for having interests at all*, a condition that must be satisfied before we can speak of interests in a meaningful way. It would be nonsense to say that it was not in the interests of a stone to be kicked along the road by a schoolboy. A stone does not have interests because it cannot suffer. Nothing that we can do to it could possibly make any difference to its welfare. A mouse, on the other hand, does have an interest in not being kicked along the road, because it will suffer if it is.

If a being suffers there can be no moral justification for refusing to take that suffering into consideration. No matter what the nature of the being, the principle of equality requires that its suffering be counted equally with the like suffering—in so far as rough comparisons can be made—of any other being. If a being is not capable of suffering, or of experiencing enjoyment or happiness, there is nothing to be taken into account. So the limit of sentience (using the term as a convenient if not strictly accurate shorthand for the capacity to suffer and/or experience enjoyment) is the only defensible boundary of concern for the interests of others. To mark this boundary by some other characteristic like intelligence or rationality would be to mark it in an arbitrary manner. Why not choose some other characteristic, like skin color?

The racist violates the principle of equality by giving greater weight to the interests of members of his own race when there is a clash between their interests and the interests of those of another race. The sexist violates the principle of equality by favoring the interests of his own sex. Similarly the speciesist allows the interests of his own species to override the greater interests of members of other species. The pattern is identical in each case.

Most human beings are speciesists. Ordinary human beings—not a few exceptionally cruel or heartless humans, but the overwhelming majority of humans—take an active part in, acquiesce in, and allow their taxes to pay for practices that require the sacrifice of the most important interests of members of other species in order to promote the most trivial interests of our own species. . . .

Animals can feel pain. As we saw earlier, there can be no moral justification for regarding the pain (or pleasure) that animals feel as less important than the same amount of pain (or pleasure) felt by humans. But what exactly does this mean, in practical terms? To prevent misunderstanding I shall spell out what I mean a little more fully.

If I give a horse a hard slap across its rump with my open hand, the horse may start, but it presumably feels little pain. Its skin is thick enough to protect it against a mere slap. If I slap a baby in the same way, however, the baby will cry and presumably does feel pain, for its skin is more sensitive. So it is worse to slap a baby than a horse, if both slaps are administered with equal force. But there must be some kind of blow—I don't know exactly what it would be, but perhaps a blow with a heavy stick—that would cause the horse as much pain as we cause a baby by slapping it with our hand. That is what I mean by "the same amount of pain" and if we consider it wrong to inflict that much pain on a baby for no good reason then we must, unless we are speciesists, consider it equally wrong to inflict the same amount of pain on a horse for no good reason.

There are other differences between humans and animals that cause other complications. Normal adult human beings have mental capacities which will, in certain circumstances, lead them to suffer more than animals would in the same circumstances. If, for instance, we decided to perform extremely painful or lethal scientific experiments on normal adult humans, kidnapped at random from public parks for this purpose, every adult who entered a park would become fearful that he would be kidnapped. The resultant terror would be a form of suffering additional to the pain of the experiment. The same experiments performed on nonhuman animals would cause less suffering since the animals would not have the anticipatory dread of being kidnapped and experimented upon. This does not mean, of course, that it would be right to perform the experiment on animals, but only that there is a reason, which is *not* speciesist, for preferring to use animals rather than normal adult humans, if the experiment is to be done at all. It should be noted, however, that this same argument gives us a reason for preferring to use human infants—orphans perhaps—or retarded humans for experiments, rather than adults, since infants and retarded humans would also have no idea of what was going to happen to them. So far as this argument is concerned nonhuman animals and infants and retarded humans are in the same category; and if we use this argument to justify experiments on nonhuman animals we have to ask ourselves whether we are also prepared to allow experiments on humans, on what basis can we do it, other than a barefaced—and morally indefensible—preference for members of our own species?

There are many areas in which the superior mental powers of normal adult humans make a difference: anticipation, more detailed memory, greater knowledge of what is happening, and so on. Yet these differences do not all point to greater suffering on the part of the normal human being. Sometimes an animal may suffer more because of his more limited understanding. If, for instance, we are taking prisoners in wartime we can explain to them that while they must submit to capture, search, and confinement they will not otherwise be harmed and will be set free at the conclusion of hostilities. If we capture a wild animal, however, we cannot explain that we are not threatening its life. A wild animal cannot distinguish an attempt to overpower and confine from an attempt to kill; the one causes as much terror as the other.

It may be objected that comparisons of the sufferings of different species are impossible to make, and that for this reason when the interests of animals and humans clash the principle of equality gives no guidance. It is probably true that comparisons of suffering between members

of different species cannot be made precisely, but precision is not essential. Even if we were to prevent the infliction of suffering on animals only when it is quite certain that the interests of humans will not be affected to anything like the extent that animals are affected, we would be forced to make radical changes in our treatment of animals that would involve our diet, the farming methods we use, experimental procedures in many fields of science, our approach to wildlife and to hunting, trapping and the wearing of furs, and areas of entertainment like circuses, rodeos, and zoos. As a result, a vast amount of suffering would be avoided.

So far I have said a lot about the infliction of suffering on animals, but nothing about killing them. This omission has been deliberate. The application of the principle of equality to the infliction of suffering is, in theory at least, fairly straightforward. Pain and suffering are bad and should be prevented or minimized, irrespective of the race, sex, or species of the being that suffers. How bad a pain is depends on how intense it is and how long it lasts, but pains of the same intensity and duration are equally bad, whether felt by humans or animals.

The wrongness of killing a being is more complicated. I have kept, and shall continue to keep, the question of killing in the background because in the present state of human tyranny over other species the more simple, straightforward principle of equal consideration of pain or pleasure is a sufficient basis for identifying and protesting against all the major abuses of animals that humans practice. Nevertheless, it is necessary to say something about killing.

Just as most humans are speciesists in their readiness to cause pain to animals when they would not cause a similar pain to humans for the same reason, so most humans are speciesists in their readiness to kill other animals when they would not kill humans. We need to proceed more cautiously here, however, because people hold widely differing views about when it is legitimate to kill humans, as the continuing debates over abortion and euthanasia attest. Nor have moral philosophers been able to agree on exactly what it is that makes it wrong to kill humans, and under what circumstances killing a human being may be justifiable.

Let us consider first the view that it is always wrong to take an innocent human life. We may call this the "sanctity of life" view. People who take this view oppose abortion and euthanasia. They do not usually, however, oppose the killing of nonhumans—so perhaps it would be more accurate to describe this view as the "sanctity of *human* life" view.

The belief that human life, and only human life, is sacrosanct is a form of speciesism. To see this, consider the following example.

Assume that, as sometimes happens, an infant has been born with massive and irreparable brain damage. The damage is so severe that the infant can never be any more than a "human vegetable," unable to talk, recognize other people, act independently of others, or develop a sense of self-awareness. The parents of the infant, realizing that they cannot hope for any improvement in their child's condition and being in any case unwilling to spend, or ask the state to spend, the thousands of dollars that would be needed annually for proper care of the infant, ask the doctor to kill the infant painlessly.

Should the doctor do what the parents ask? Legally, he should not, and in this respect the law reflects the sanctity of life view. The life of every human being is sacred. Yet people who would say this about the infant do not object to the killing of nonhuman animals. How can they justify their different judgments? Adult chimpanzees, dogs, pigs, and many other species far surpass the brain-damaged infant in their ability to relate to others, act independently, be self-aware, and any other capacity that could reasonably be said to give value to life. With the most intensive care possible, there are retarded infants who can never achieve the intelligence level of a dog. Nor can we appeal to the concern of the infant's parents, since they themselves, in this imaginary example (and in some actual cases) do not want the infant kept alive.

The only thing that distinguishes the infant from the animal, in the eyes of those who claim it has a "right to life," is that it is, biologically, a member of the species *Homo sapiens*, whereas chimpanzees, dogs, and pigs are not. But to use *this* difference as the basis for granting a right to life to the infant and not to the other animals is, of course, pure speciesism.[6] It is exactly the kind of arbitrary difference that the most crude and overt kind of racist uses in attempting to justify racial discrimination.

This does not mean that to avoid speciesism we must hold that it is as wrong to kill a dog as it is to kill a normal human being. The only position that is irredeemably speciesist is the one that tries to make the boundary of the right to life run exactly parallel to the boundary of our own species. Those who hold the sanctity of life view do this because while distinguishing sharply between humans and other animals they allow no distinctions to be made within our own species, objecting to the killing of the severely retarded and the hopelessly senile as strongly as they object to the killing of normal adults.

To avoid speciesism we must allow that beings which are similar in all relevant respects have a similar right to life—and mere membership in our own biological species cannot be a morally relevant criterion for this right. Within these limits we could still hold that, for instance, it is worse to kill a normal adult human, with a capacity for self-awareness, and the ability to plan for the future and have meaningful relations with others, than it is to kill a mouse, which presumably does not share all of these characteristics; or we might appeal to the close family and other personal ties which humans have but mice do not have to the same degree; or we might think that it is the consequences for other humans, who will be put in fear of their own lives, that makes the crucial difference; or we might think it is some combination of these factors, or other factors altogether.

---

[6] I am here putting aside religious views, for example the doctrine that all and only humans have immortal souls, or are made in the image of God. Historically these views have been very important, and no doubt are partly responsible for the idea that human life has a special sanctity. Logically, however, these religious views are unsatisfactory, since a reasoned explanation of why it should be that all humans and no non-humans have immortal souls is not offered. This belief too, therefore, comes under suspicion as a form of speciesism. In any case, defenders of the "sanctity of life" view are generally reluctant to base their position on purely religious doctrines, since these doctrines are no longer as widely accepted as they once were.

Whatever criteria we choose, however, we will have to admit that they do not follow precisely the boundary of our own species. We may legitimately hold that there are some features of certain beings which make their lives more valuable than those of other beings; but there will surely be some nonhuman animals whose lives, by any standards, are more valuable than the lives of some humans. A chimpanzee, dog, or pig, for instance, will have a higher degree of self-awareness and a greater capacity for meaningful relations with others than a severely retarded infant or someone in a state of advanced senility. So if we base the right to life on these characteristics we must grant these animals a right to life as good as, or better than, such retarded or senile humans.

Now this argument cuts both ways. It could be taken as showing that chimpanzees, dogs, and pigs, along with some other species, have a right to life and we commit a grave moral offense whenever we kill them, even when they are old and suffering and our intention is to put them out of their misery. Alternatively one could take the argument as showing that the severely retarded and hopelessly senile have no right to life and may be killed for quite trivial reasons, as we now kill animals.

Since the focus here is on ethical questions concerning animals and not on the morality of euthanasia I shall not attempt to settle this issue finally. I think it is reasonably clear, though, that while both of the positions just described avoid speciesism, neither is entirely satisfactory. What we need is some middle position that would avoid speciesism but would not make the lives of the retarded and senile as cheap as the lives of pigs and dogs now are, nor make the lives of pigs and dogs so sacrosanct that we think it wrong to put them out of hopeless misery. What we must do is bring nonhuman animals within our sphere of moral concern and cease to treat their lives as expendable for whatever trivial purposes we may have. At the same time, once we realize that the fact that a being is a member of our own species is not in itself enough to make it always wrong to kill that being, we may come to reconsider our policy of preserving human lives at all costs, even when there is no prospect of a meaningful life or of existence without terrible pain.

I conclude, then, that a rejection of speciesism does not imply that all lives are of equal worth. While self-awareness, intelligence, the capacity for meaningful relations with others, and so on are not relevant to the question of inflicting pain—since pain is pain, whatever other capacities, beyond the capacity to feel pain, the being may have—these capacities may be relevant to the question of taking life. It is not arbitrary to hold that the life of a self-aware being, capable of abstract thought, of planning for the future, of complex acts of communication, and so on, is more valuable than the life of a being without these capacities. To see the difference between the issues of inflicting pain and taking life, consider how we would choose within our own species. If we had to choose to save the life of a normal human or a mentally defective human, we would probably choose to save the life of the normal human; but if we had to choose between preventing pain in the normal human or the mental defective—imagine that both have received painful but superficial injuries, and we only have enough painkiller for one of them—it is not nearly so clear how we ought to choose. The same is true when we consider other species. The evil of pain is, in itself, unaffected by the other characteristics of the being that feels the pain; the value of life is affected by these other characteristics.

Normally this will mean that if we have to choose between the life of a human being and the life of another animal we would choose to save the life of the human, but there may be special cases in which the reverse holds true, because the human being in question does not have the capacities of a normal human being. So this view is not speciesist, although it may appear to be at first glance. The preference, in normal cases, for saving a human life over the life of an animal when a choice *has* to be made is a preference based on the characteristics that normal humans have, and not on the mere fact that they are members of our own species. This is why when we consider members of our own species who lack the characteristics of normal humans we can no longer say that their lives are always to be preferred to those of other animals.

In general, the question of when it is wrong to kill (painlessly) an animal is one to which we need give no precise answer. As long as we remember that we should give the same respect to the lives of animals as we give to the lives of those humans at a similar mental level, we shall not go far wrong.

In any case, the conclusions that are argued for here flow from the principle of minimizing suffering alone. The idea that it is also wrong to kill animals painlessly gives some of these conclusions additional support which is welcome, but strictly unnecessary. Interestingly enough, this is true even of the conclusion that we ought to become vegetarians, a conclusion that in the popular mind is generally based on some kind of absolute prohibition on killing.

☙ REVIEW QUESTIONS

1. Explain the principle of equality that Singer adopts.
2. How does Singer define *speciesism*?

3. What is the sanctity of life view? Why does Singer reject this view?

☙ DISCUSSION QUESTIONS

1. Is speciesism analogous to racism and sexism? Why or why not?
2. Is there anything wrong with killing animals painlessly? Defend your view.

3. Do human interests outweigh animal interests? Explain your position.

Speciesism and the Idea of Equality

BONNIE STEINBOCK

For biographical information on Steinbock, see her reading in Chapter 3.

Steinbock presents a defense of speciesism, the practice of weighing human interests more heavily than those of nonhuman animals. While she agrees with Singer that nonhuman pain and suffering deserve some moral consideration, she denies that this consideration should be equal to that given to humans. She claims that humans have morally relevant capacities that nonhuman animals do not have, and this entitles humans to greater moral consideration. These capacities include the ability to be morally responsible, to reciprocate in ways that animals cannot, and to desire self-respect.

Most of us believe that we are entitled to treat members of other species in ways which would be considered wrong if inflicted on members of our own species. We kill them for food, keep them confined, use them in painful experiments. The moral philosopher has to ask what relevant difference justifies this difference in treatment. A look at this question will lead us to re-examine the distinctions which we have assumed make a moral difference.

It has been suggested by Peter Singer[1] that our current attitudes are "speciesist," a word

---

Source: Speciesism and the Idea of Equality by Bonnie Steinbock from *Philosophy*, Vol. 53, No. 24, 1978, pp. 247–256. NY: Cambridge University Press.

intended to make one think of "racist" or "sexist." The idea is that membership in a species is in itself not relevant to moral treatment, and that much of our behavior and attitudes towards nonhuman animals is based simply on this irrelevant fact.

There is, however, an important difference between racism or sexism and "speciesism." We do not subject animals to different moral treatment simply because they have fur and feathers, but because they are in fact different from human beings in ways that could be morally relevant. It is false that women are incapable of being benefited by education, and therefore that claim cannot serve to justify preventing them from attending school. But this is not false of cows and dogs, even chimpanzees. Intelligence is thought to be a morally relevant capacity because of its relation to the capacity for moral responsibility.

What is Singer's response? He agrees that nonhuman animals lack certain capacities that human animals possess, and that this may justify different treatment. But it does not justify giving less consideration to their needs and interests. According to Singer, the moral mistake which the racist or sexist makes is not essentially the factual error of thinking that blacks or women are inferior to white men. For even if there were no factual error, even if it were true that blacks and women are less intelligent and responsible than whites and men, this would not justify giving less consideration to their needs and interests. It is important to note that the term "speciesism" is in one way like, and in another way unlike, the terms "racism" and "sexism." What the term "speciesism" has in common with these terms is the reference to focusing on a characteristic which is, in itself, irrelevant to moral treatment. And it is worth reminding us of this. But Singer's real aim is to bring us to a new understanding of the idea of equality. The question is, on what do claims to equality rest? The demand for human equality is a demand that the interests of all human beings be considered equally, unless there is a moral justification for not doing so. But why should the interests of all human beings be considered equally? In order to answer this question, we have to give some sense to the phrase, "All men (human beings) are created equal." Human beings are manifestly not equal, differing greatly in intelligence, virtue and capacities. In virtue of what can the claim to equality be made?

It is Singer's contention that claims to equality do not rest on factual equality. Not only do human beings differ in their capacities, but it might even turn out that intelligence, the capacity for virtue, etc., are not distributed evenly among the races and sexes:

> The appropriate response to those who claim to have found evidence of genetically based differences in ability between the races or sexes is not to stick to the belief that the genetic explanation must be wrong, whatever evidence to the contrary may turn up; instead we should make it quite clear that the claim to equality does not depend on intelligence, moral capacity, physical strength, or similar matters of fact. Equality is a moral ideal, not a simple assertion of fact. There is no logically compelling reason for assuming that a factual difference in ability between two people justifies any difference in the amount of consideration we give to satisfying their needs and interests. The principle of equality of human beings is not a description of an alleged actual equality among humans: it is a prescription of how we should treat humans.[2]

Insofar as the subject is human equality, Singer's view is supported by other philosophers. Bernard Williams, for example, is concerned to show that demands for equality cannot rest on factual equality among people, for no such equality exists.[3] The only respect in which all men are equal, according to Williams, is that they are all equally men. This seems to be a platitude, but Williams denies that it is trivial. Membership in the species *Homo sapiens* in itself has no special moral significance, but rather the fact that all men are human serves as a reminder that being human involves the possession of characteristics that are morally relevant. But on what characteristics does Williams focus? Aside from the desire for self-respect (which I will discuss later), Williams is not concerned with uniquely human capacities. Rather, he focuses on the capacity to feel pain and the capacity to feel affection. It is in virtue of these capacities, it seems, that he idea of equality is to be justified.

Apparently Richard Wasserstrom has the same idea as he sets out the racist's "logical and moral mistakes" in "Rights, Human Rights and Racial Discrimination."[4] The racist fails to acknowledge that the black person is as capable of suffering as the white person. According to Wasserstrom, the reason why a person is said to have a right not to be made to suffer acute physical pain is that we all do in fact value freedom from such pain. Therefore, if anyone has a right to be free from suffering acute physical pain everyone has this right, for there is no possible basis of discrimination. Wasserstrom says, "For, if all persons do have equal capacities of these sorts and if the existence of these capacities is the reason for ascribing these rights to anyone, then all persons ought to have the right to claim equality of treatment in respect to the possession and exercise of these rights."[5] The basis of equality, for Wasserstrom as for Williams, lies not in some uniquely human capacity, but rather in the fact that all human beings are alike in their capacity to suffer. Writers on equality have focused on this capacity, I think, because it functions as some sort of lowest common denominator, so that whatever the other capacities of a human being, he is entitled to equal consideration because, like everyone else, he is capable of suffering.

If the capacity to suffer is the reason for ascribing a right to freedom from acute pain, or a right to well-being, then it certainly looks as though these rights must be extended to animals as well. This is the conclusion Singer arrives at. The demand for human equality rests on the equal capacity of all human beings to suffer and to enjoy well-being. But if this is the basis of the demand for equality, then this demand must include all beings which have an equal capacity to suffer and enjoy well-being. That is why Singer places at the basis of the demand for equality, not intelligence or reason, but sentience. And equality will mean, not equality of treatment, but "equal consideration of interests." The equal consideration of interests will often mean quite different treatment, depending on the nature of the entity being considered. (It would be as absurd to talk of a dog's right to vote, Singer says, as to talk of a man's right to have an abortion.)

It might be thought that the issue of equality depends on a discussion of rights. According to this line of thought, animals do not merit equal consideration of interests because, unlike human beings they do not, or cannot, have rights. But I am not going to discuss rights, important as the issue is. The fact that an entity does not have rights does not necessarily imply that its interests are going to count for less than the interests of entities which are right-bearers. According to the view of rights held by H. L. A. Hart and S. I. Benn, infants do not have rights, nor do the mentally defective, nor do the insane, in so far as they all lack certain minimal conceptual capabilities for having rights.[6] Yet it certainly does not seem that either Hart or Benn would agree that therefore their interests are to be counted for less, or that it is morally permissible to treat them in ways in which it would not be permissible to treat right-bearers. It seems to mean only that we must give different sorts of reasons for our obligations to take into consideration the interests of those who do not have rights.

We have reasons concerning the treatment of other people which are clearly independent of the notion of rights. We would say that it is wrong to punch someone because doing that infringes his rights. But we could also say that it is wrong because doing that hurts him, and that is, ordinarily, enough of a reason not to do it. Now this particular reason extends not only to human beings, but to all sentient creatures. One has a prima facie reason not to pull the cat's tail (whether or not the cat has rights) because it hurts the cat. And this is the only thing, normally, which is relevant in this case. The fact that the cat is not a "rational being," that it is not capable of moral responsibility, that it cannot make free choices or shape its life—all of these differences from us have nothing to do with the justifiability of pulling its tail. Does this show that rationality and the rest of it are irrelevant to moral treatment?

I hope to show that this is not the case. But first I want to point out that the issue is not one of cruelty to animals. We all agree that cruelty is wrong, whether perpetrated on a moral or nonmoral, rational or nonrational agent. Cruelty is defined as the infliction of unnecessary pain or suffering. What is to count as necessary or unnecessary is determined, in part, by the nature of the end pursued. Torturing an animal is cruel, because although the pain is logically necessary for the action to be torture, the end (deriving enjoyment from seeing the animal suffer) is monstrous. Allowing animals to suffer from neglect or for the sake of large profits may also be thought to be unnecessary and therefore cruel. But there may be some ends, which are very good (such as the advancement of medical knowledge), which can be accomplished by subjecting animals to pain in experiments. Although most people would agree that the pain inflicted on animals used in medical research ought to be kept to a minimum, they would consider pain that cannot be eliminated "necessary" and therefore not cruel. It would probably not be so regarded if the subjects were nonvoluntary human beings. Necessity, then, is defined in terms of human benefit, but this is just what is being called into question. The topic of cruelty to animals, while important from a practical viewpoint, because much of our present treatment of animals involves the infliction of suffering for no good reason, is not very interesting philosophically. What is philosophically interesting is whether we are justified in having different standards of necessity for human suffering and for animal suffering. Singer says, quite rightly I think, "If a being suffers, there can be no moral justification for refusing to take that suffering into consideration."[7] But he thinks that the principle of equality requires that, no matter what the nature of the being, its suffering be counted equally with the like suffering of any other being. In other words sentience does not simply provide us with reasons for acting; it is the only relevant consideration for equal consideration of interests. It is this view that I wish to challenge.

I want to challenge it partly because it has such counter-intuitive results. It means, for example, that feeding starving children before feeding starving dogs is just like a Catholic charity's feeding hungry Catholics before feeding hungry non-Catholics. It is simply a matter of taking care of one's own, something which is usually morally permissible. But whereas we would admire the Catholic agency which did not discriminate, but

fed all children, first come, first served, we would feel quite differently about someone who has this policy for dogs and children. Nor is this, it seems to me, simply a matter of sentimental preference for our own species. I might feel much more love for my dog than for a strange child—and yet I might feel morally obliged to feed the child before I fed my dog. If I gave in to the feelings of love and fed my dog and let the child go hungry, I would probably feel guilty. This is not to say that we can simply rely on such feelings. Huck Finn felt guilty at helping Jim escape, which he viewed as stealing from a woman who had never done him any harm. But while the existence of such feelings does not settle the morality of an issue, it is not clear to me that they can be explained away. In any event, their existence can serve as a motivation for trying to find a rational justification for considering human interests above nonhuman ones.

However, it does seem to me that this requires a justification. Until now, common sense (and academic philosophy) have seen no such need. Benn says, "No one claims equal consideration for all mammals—human beings count, mice do not, though it would not be easy to say why not. . . . Although we hesitate to inflict unnecessary pain on sentient creatures, such as mice or dogs, we are quite sure that we do not need to show good reasons for putting human interests before theirs."[8]

I think we do have to justify counting our interests more heavily than those of animals. But how? Singer is right, I think, to point out that it will not do to refer vaguely to the greater value of human life, to human worth and dignity:

Faced with a situation in which they see a need for some basis for the moral gulf that is commonly thought to separate humans and animals, but can find no concrete difference that will do this without undermining the equality of humans, philosophers tend to waffle. They resort to high-sounding phrases like 'the intrinsic dignity of the human individual.' They talk of 'the intrinsic worth of all men' as if men had some worth that other beings do not have or they say that human beings, and only human beings, are 'ends in themselves,' while 'everything other than a person can only have value for a person.' . . .

Why should we not attribute 'intrinsic dignity' or 'intrinsic worth' to ourselves? Why should we not say that we are the only things in the universe that have intrinsic value? Our fellow human beings are unlikely to reject the accolades we so generously bestow upon them, and those to whom we deny the honor are unable to object.[9]

Singer is right to be skeptical of terms like "intrinsic dignity" and "intrinsic worth." These phrases are no substitute for a moral argument. But they may point to one. In trying to understand what is meant by these phrases, we may find a difference or differences between human beings and nonhuman animals that will justify different treatment while not undermining claims for human equality. While we are not compelled to discriminate among people because of different capacities, if we can find a significant difference in capacities between human and nonhuman animals, this could serve to justify regarding human interests as primary. It is not arbitrary or smug, I think, to maintain that human beings have a different moral status from members of other species because of certain capacities which are characteristic of being human. We may not all be equal in these capacities but all human beings possess them to some measure and nonhuman animals do not. For example, human beings are normally held to be responsible for what they do. In recognizing that someone is responsible for his or her actions, you accord that person a respect which is reserved for those possessed of moral autonomy, or capable of achieving such autonomy. Secondly, human beings can be expected to reciprocate in a way that nonhuman animals cannot. Nonhuman animals cannot be motivated by altruistic or moral reasons; they cannot treat you fairly or unfairly. This does not rule out the possibility of an animal being motivated by sympathy or pity. It does rule out altruistic motivation in the sense of motivation due to the recognition that the needs and interests of others provide one with certain reasons for acting.[10] Human beings are capable of altruistic motivation in this sense. We are sometimes motivated simply by the recognition that someone else is in pain, and that pain is a bad thing, no matter who suffers it. It is this sort of reason that I claim cannot motivate an animal or

any entity not possessed of fairly abstract concepts. (If some nonhuman animals do possess the requisite concepts—perhaps chimpanzees who have learned a language—they might well be capable of altruistic motivation.) This means that our moral dealings with animals are necessarily much more limited than our dealings with other human beings. If rats invade our houses, carrying disease and biting our children, we cannot reason with them, hoping to persuade them of the injustice they do us. We can only attempt to get rid of them. And it is this that makes it reasonable for us to accord them a separate and not equal moral status, even though their capacity to suffer provides us with some reason to kill them painlessly, if this can be done without too much sacrifice of human interests. Thirdly, as Williams points out, there is the "desire for self-respect": "a certain human desire to be identified with what one is doing, to be able to realize purposes of one's own, and not to be the instrument of another's will unless one has willingly accepted such a role."[11] Some animals may have some form of this desire, and to the extent that they do, we ought to consider their interest in freedom and self-determination. (Such considerations might affect our attitudes toward zoos and circuses.) But the desire for self-respect per se requires the intellectual capacities of human beings, and this desire provides us with special reasons not to treat human beings in certain ways. It is an affront to the dignity of a human being to be a slave (even if a well-treated one); this cannot be true for a horse or a cow. To point this out is of course only to say that the justification for the treatment of an entity will depend on the sort of entity in question. In our treatment of other entities, we must consider the desire for autonomy, dignity and respect, but only where such a desire exists. Recognition of different desires and interests will often require different treatment, a point Singer himself makes.

But is the issue simply one of different desires and interests justifying and requiring different treatment? I would like to make a stronger claim, namely, that certain capacities, which seem to be unique to human beings, entitle their possessors to a privileged position in the moral community. Both rats and human beings dislike pain, and so we have a prima facie reason not to inflict pain on either. But if we can free human beings from crippling diseases, pain and death through experimentation which involves making animals suffer, and if this is the only way to achieve such results, then I think that such experimentation is justified because human lives are more valuable than animals' lives. And this is because of certain capacities and abilities that normal human beings have which animals apparently do not, and which human beings cannot exercise if they are devastated by pain or disease.

My point is not that the lack of the sorts of capacities I have been discussing gives us a justification for treating animals just as we like, but rather that it is these differences between human beings and nonhuman animals which provide a rational basis for different moral treatment and consideration. Singer focuses on sentience alone as the basis of equality, but we can justify the belief that human beings have a moral worth that nonhuman animals do not, in virtue of specific capacities, and without resorting to "high-sounding phrases."

Singer thinks that intelligence, the capacity for moral responsibility, for virtue, etc., are irrelevant to equality, because we would not accept a hierarchy based on intelligence any more than one based on race. We do not think that those with greater capacities ought to have their interests weighed more heavily than those with lesser capacities, and this, he thinks, shows that differences in such capacities are irrelevant to equality. But it does not show this at all. Kevin Donaghy argues (rightly, I think) that what entitles us human beings to a privileged position in the moral community is a certain minimal level of intelligence, which is a prerequisite for morally relevant capacities.[12] The fact that we would reject a hierarchical society based on degree of intelligence does not show that a minimal level of intelligence cannot be used as a cut-off point, justifying giving greater consideration to the interests of those entities which meet this standard.

Interestingly enough, Singer concedes the rationality of valuing the lives of normal human beings over the lives of nonhuman animals.[13] We are not required to value equally the life of a normal human being and the life of an animal, he thinks,

but only their suffering. But I doubt that the value of an entity's life can be separated from the value of its suffering in this way. If we value the lives of human beings more than the lives of animals, this is because we value certain capacities that human beings have and animals do not. But freedom from suffering is, in general, a minimal condition for exercising these capacities, for living a fully human life. So, valuing human life more involves regarding human interests as counting for more. That is why we regard human suffering as more deplorable than comparable animal suffering.

But there is one point of Singer's which I have not yet met. Some human beings (if only a very few) are less intelligent than some nonhuman animals. Some have less capacity for moral choice and responsibility What status in the moral community are these members of our species to occupy? Are their interests to be considered equally with ours? Is experimenting on them permissible where such experiments are painful or injurious, but somehow necessary for human well-being? If it is certain of our capacities which entitle us to a privileged position, it looks as if those lacking those capacities are not entitled to a privileged position. To think it is justifiable to experiment on an adult chimpanzee but not on a severely mentally incapacitated human being seems to be focusing on membership in a species where that has no moral relevance. (It is being "speciesist" in a perfectly reasonable use of the word.) How are we to meet this challenge?

Donaghy is untroubled by this objection. He says that it is fully in accord with his intuitions, that he regards the killing of a normally intelligent human being as far more serious than the killing of a person so severely limited that he lacked the intellectual capacities of an adult pig. But this parry really misses the point. The question is whether Donaghy thinks that the killing of a human being so severely limited that he lacked the intellectual capacities of an adult pig would be less serious than the killing of that pig. If superior intelligence is what justifies privileged status in the moral community, then the pig who is smarter than a human being ought to have superior moral status. And I doubt that this is fully in accord with Donaghy's intuitions.

I doubt that anyone will be able to come up with a concrete and morally relevant difference that would justify, say, using a chimpanzee in an experiment rather than a human being with less capacity for reasoning, moral responsibility, etc. Should we then experiment on the severely retarded? Utilitarian considerations aside (the difficulty of comparing intelligence between species, for example), we feel a special obligation to care for the handicapped members of our own species, who cannot survive in this world without such care. Nonhuman animals manage very well, despite their "lower intelligence" and lesser capacities; most of them do not require special care from us. This does not, of course, justify experimenting on them. However, to subject to experimentation those people who depend on us seems even worse than subjecting members of other species to it. In addition, when we consider the severely retarded, we think, "That could be me." It makes sense to think that one might have been born retarded, but not to think that one might have been born a monkey. And so, although one can imagine oneself in the monkey's place, one feels a closer identification with the severely retarded human being. Here we are getting away from such things as "morally relevant differences" and are talking about something much more difficult to articulate, namely, the role of feelings and sentiment in moral thinking. We would be horrified by the use of the retarded in medical research. But what are we to make of this horror? Has it moral significance or is it "mere" sentiment, of no more import than the sentiment of whites against blacks? It is terribly difficult to know how to evaluate such feelings.[14] I am not going to say more about this, because I think that the treatment of severely incapacitated human beings does not pose an insurmountable objection to the privileged status principle. I am willing to admit that my horror at the thought of experiments being performed on severely mentally incapacitated human beings in cases in which I would find it justifiable and preferable to perform the same experiments on nonhuman animals (capable of similar suffering) may not be a moral emotion. But it is certainly not wrong of us to extend special care to members of our own species, motivated by feelings of sympathy, protectiveness, etc. If this is speciesism, it is stripped of its tone of moral condemnation. It is not racist to provide special care to members of your own race; it is racist to fall below your moral obligation to a person because of his or her race. I have been arguing that we are morally obliged to consider the interests of all sentient creatures, but not to consider those interests equally with human interests. Nevertheless, even this recognition will mean some radical changes in our attitude toward and treatment of other species.[15]

NOTES

1. Peter Singer, *Animal Liberation* (A New York Review Book, 1975).
2. Singer, 5.
3. Bernard Williams, "The Idea of Equality," *Philosophy, Politics and Society* (Second Series), Laslett and Runciman (Eds.) (Blackwell, 1962), 110–131, reprinted in *Moral Concepts*, Feinberg (Ed.) (Oxford, 1970), 15S 171.
4. Richard Wasserstrom, "Rights, Human Rights, and Racial Discrimination," *Journal of Philosophy 61*, No. 20 (1964), reprinted in *Human Rights*, A. 1. Melden (Ed.) (Wadsworth, 1970), 96–110.
5. Ibid., 106.
6. H. L. A. Hart, "Are There Any Natural Rights?," *Philosophical Review 64* (1955), and S. I. Benn, "Abortion, Infanticide, and Respect for Persons," *The Problem of Abortion*, Feinberg (Ed.) (Wadsworth, 1973), 92–104.
7. Singer, 9.
8. Benn, "Equality, Moral and Social," *The Encyclopedia of Philosophy* 3, 40.
9. Singer, 266–267.
10. This conception of altruistic motivation comes from Thomas Nagel's *The Possibility of Altruism* (Oxford, 1970).
11. Williams, op. cit., 157.
12. Kevin Donaghy, "Singer on Speciesism," *Philosophic Exchange* (Summer 1974).
13. Singer, 22.
14. We run into the same problem when discussing abortion. Of what significance are our feelings toward the unborn when discussing its status? Is it relevant or irrelevant that it looks like a human being?
15. I would like to acknowledge the help of, and offer thanks to, Professor Richard Arneson of the University.

⚜ REVIEW QUESTIONS

1. According to Steinbock, what is the important difference between racism or sexism and speciesism?
2. What is the basis for equality, according to Singer, Williams, Wasserstrom, and Steinbock?
3. Steinbock claims that Singer's view has counterintuitive results. What are they?
4. According to Steinbock, why are we justified in counting human interests more heavily than those of animals?

⚜ DISCUSSION QUESTIONS

1. Steinbock maintains that we should give greater moral consideration to severely mentally incapacitated humans than to animals that may have a greater mental capacity. Does she give a good reason for this? How would Singer reply?
2. Suppose alien beings invade the earth. They are superior to humans in intelligence, moral virtue, the desire for self-respect, and so on. What is their moral status? Are they equal to humans, or do they have a higher moral status than humans, just as humans have a higher moral status than animals? If they have a higher moral status than humans, are they morally permitted to perform experiments on humans and eat them? What would Steinbock say? What do you think?

Puppies, Pigs, and People: Eating Meat and Marginal Cases

ALASTAIR NORCROSS

Alastair Norcross is associate professor of philosophy at the University of Colorado, Boulder. He is the editor (with Bonnie Steinbock) of *Killing and Letting Die* (1994) and more than thirty articles in ethics.

Norcross defends a version of vegetarianism that morally requires us to refrain from eating the meat of factory-farmed animals. He argues that the behavior of Americans who eat this meat is analogous to Fred enjoying the taste of chocolate that he can only get by torturing puppies. He defends this analogy by claiming that there is no morally relevant difference between the puppies and the factory-farmed animals, and no relevant difference between Fred, the puppy torturer, and the people who eat factory-farmed animals knowing full well about their suffering. If torturing puppies for the sake of gustatory pleasure is wrong, then so is eating factory-farmed animals because of the way they taste.

Norcross attacks philosophers such as Steinbock who hold that humans have a higher moral status than animals because normal humans have moral and rational capacities that most animals lack. First, he discusses the challenge of marginal cases: cases of humans who lack the relevant capacities, such as the severely senile and the irreversibly comatose. Do these humans have the same moral status as animals? Most people find this unacceptable. Second, even if animals cannot be moral agents, as Steinbock and others maintain, they can still be moral patients, and that is all that is required to give animals a full moral status.

Source: Puppies, Pigs, and People: Eating Meat and Marginal Cases by Alastair Norcross from *Philosophical Perspectives*, Vol. 18, 2004, pp. 229–245. Oxford, UK: Wiley-Blackwell.

1. FRED'S BASEMENT

Consider the story of Fred, who receives a visit from the police one day. They have been summoned by Fred's neighbors, who have been disturbed by strange sounds emanating from Fred's basement. When they enter the basement they are confronted by the following scene: Twenty-six small wire cages, each containing a puppy, some whining, some whimpering, some howling. The puppies range in age from newborn to about six months. Many of them show signs of mutilation. Urine and feces cover the bottoms of the cages and the basement floor. Fred explains that he keeps the puppies for twenty-six weeks, and then butchers them while holding them upside-down. During their lives he performs a series of mutilations on them, such as slicing off their noses and their paws with a hot knife, all without any form of anesthesia. Except for the mutilations, the puppies are never allowed out of the cages, which are barely big enough to hold them at twenty-six weeks. The police are horrified, and promptly charge Fred with animal abuse. As details of the case are publicized, the public is outraged. Newspapers are flooded with letters demanding that Fred be severely punished. There are calls for more severe penalties for animal abuse. Fred is denounced as a vile sadist.

Finally, at his trial, Fred explains his behavior, and argues that he is blameless and therefore deserves no punishment. He is, he explains, a great lover of chocolate. A couple of years ago, he was involved in a car accident, which resulted in some head trauma. Upon his release from hospital, having apparently suffered no lasting ill effects, he visited his favorite restaurant and ordered their famous rich dark chocolate mousse. Imagine his dismay when he discovered that his experience of the mousse was a pale shadow of its former self. The mousse tasted bland, slightly pleasant, but with none of the intense chocolaty flavor he remembered so well. The waiter assured him that the recipe was unchanged from the last time he had tasted it, just the day before his accident. In some consternation, Fred rushed out to buy a bar of his favorite Belgian chocolate. Again, he was dismayed to discover that his

experience of the chocolate was barely even pleasurable. Extensive investigation revealed that his experience of other foods remained unaffected, but chocolate, in all its forms, now tasted bland and insipid. Desperate for a solution to his problem, Fred visited a renowned gustatory neurologist, Dr. T. Bud. Extensive tests revealed that the accident had irreparably damaged the godiva gland, which secretes cocoamone, the hormone responsible for the experience of chocolate. Fred urgently requested hormone replacement therapy. Dr. Bud informed him that, until recently, there had been no known source of cocoamone, other than the human godiva gland, and that it was impossible to collect cocoamone from one person to be used by another. However, a chance discovery had altered the situation. A forensic veterinary surgeon, performing an autopsy on a severely abused puppy, had discovered high concentrations of cocoamone in the puppy's brain. It turned out that puppies, who don't normally produce cocoamone, could be stimulated to do so by extended periods of severe stress and suffering. The research, which led to this discovery, while gaining tenure for its authors, had not been widely publicized, for fear of antagonizing animal welfare groups. Although this research clearly gave Fred the hope of tasting chocolate again, there were no commercially available sources of puppy-derived cocoamone. Lack of demand, combined with fear of bad publicity, had deterred drug companies from getting into the puppy torturing business. Fred appeals to the court to imagine his anguish, on discovering that a solution to his severe deprivation was possible, but not readily available. But he wasn't inclined to sit around bemoaning his cruel fate. He did what any chocolate lover would do. He read the research, and set up his own cocoamone collection lab in his basement. Six months of intense puppy suffering, followed by a brutal death, produced enough cocoamone to last him a week, hence the twenty-six cages. He isn't a sadist or an animal abuser, he explains. If there were a method of collecting cocoamone without torturing puppies, he would gladly employ it. He derives no pleasure from the suffering of the puppies itself. He sympathizes with those who are horrified by the pain and misery of the animals, but the court must realize that human pleasure is at stake. The puppies, while undeniably cute, are mere animals. He admits that he would be just as healthy without chocolate, if not more so. But this isn't a matter of survival or health. His life would be unacceptably impoverished without the experience of chocolate.

End of story. Clearly, we are horrified by Fred's behavior, and unconvinced by his attempted justification. It is, of course, unfortunate for Fred that he can no longer enjoy the taste of chocolate, but that in no way excuses the imposition of severe suffering on the puppies. I expect near universal agreement with this claim (the exceptions being those who are either inhumanly callous or thinking ahead, and wish to avoid the following conclusion, to which such agreement commits them). No decent person would even contemplate torturing puppies merely to enhance a gustatory experience. However, billions of animals endure intense suffering every year for precisely this end. Most of the chicken, veal, beef, and pork consumed in the US comes from intensive confinement facilities, in which the animals live cramped, stress-filled lives and endure unanaesthetized mutilations.[1] The vast majority of people would suffer no ill health from the elimination of meat from their diets. Quite the reverse. The supposed benefits from this system of factory farming, apart from the profits accruing to agribusiness, are increased levels of gustatory pleasure for those who claim that they couldn't enjoy a meat-free diet as much as their current meat-filled diets. If we are prepared to condemn Fred for torturing puppies merely to enhance his gustatory experiences, shouldn't we similarly condemn the millions who purchase and consume factory-raised meat? Are there any morally significant differences between Fred's behavior and their behavior?

2. FRED'S BEHAVIOR COMPARED WITH OUR BEHAVIOR

The first difference that might seem to be relevant is that Fred tortures the puppies himself, whereas most Americans consume meat that comes from animals that have been tortured by others. But is this really relevant? What if Fred had been squeamish and had employed someone else to torture the puppies and extract the cocoamone? Would we have thought any better of Fred? Of course not.

Another difference between Fred and many consumers of factory-raised meat is that many, perhaps most, such consumers are unaware of the treatment of the animals, before they appear in neatly wrapped packages on supermarket shelves. Perhaps I should moderate my challenge, then. If we are prepared to condemn Fred for torturing puppies merely to enhance his gustatory experiences, shouldn't we similarly condemn those who purchase and consume factory-raised meat, in full, or even partial, awareness of the suffering endured by the animals? While many consumers are still blissfully ignorant of the appalling treatment meted out to meat, that number is rapidly dwindling, thanks to vigorous publicity campaigns waged by animal welfare groups. Furthermore, any meat-eating readers of this article are now deprived of the excuse of ignorance.

Perhaps a consumer of factory-raised animals could argue as follows: While I agree that Fred's behavior is abominable, mine is crucially different. If Fred did not consume his chocolate, he would not raise and torture puppies (or pay someone else to do so). Therefore Fred could prevent the suffering of the puppies. However, if I did not buy and consume factory-raised meat, no animals would be spared lives of misery. Agribusiness is much too large to respond to the behavior of one consumer. Therefore I cannot prevent the suffering of any animals. I may well regret the suffering inflicted on animals for the sake of human enjoyment. I may even agree that the human enjoyment doesn't justify the suffering. However, since the animals will suffer no matter what I do, I may as well enjoy the taste of their flesh.

There are at least two lines of response to this attempted defense. First, consider an analogous case. You visit a friend in an exotic location, say Alabama. Your friend takes you out to eat at the finest restaurant in Tuscaloosa. For dessert you select the house specialty, "Chocolate Mousse à la Bama," served with a small cup of coffee, which you are instructed to drink before eating the mousse. The mousse is quite simply the most delicious dessert you have ever tasted. Never before has chocolate tasted so rich and satisfying. Tempted to order a second, you ask your friend what makes this mousse so delicious. He informs you that the mousse itself is ordinary, but the coffee contains a concentrated dose of cocoamone, the newly discovered chocolate-enhancing hormone. Researchers at Auburn University have perfected a technique for extracting cocoamone from the brains of freshly slaughtered puppies, who have been subjected to lives of pain and frustration. Each puppy's brain yields four doses, each of which is effective for about fifteen minutes, just long enough to enjoy one serving of mousse. You are, naturally, horrified and disgusted. You will certainly not order another serving, you tell your friend. In fact, you are shocked that your friend, who had always seemed to be a morally decent person, could have both recommended the dessert to you and eaten one himself, in full awareness of the loathsome process necessary for the experience. He agrees that the suffering of the puppies is outrageous, and that the gain in human pleasure in no way justifies the appalling treatment they have to endure. However, neither he nor you can save any puppies by refraining from consuming cocoamone. Cocoamone production is now Alabama's leading industry, so it is much too large to respond to the behavior of one or two consumers. Since the puppies will suffer no matter what either of you does, you may as well enjoy the mousse.

If it is as obvious as it seems that a morally decent person, who is aware of the details of cocoamone production, couldn't order Chocolate Mousse à la Bama, it should be equally obvious that a morally decent person, who is aware of the details of factory farming, can't purchase and consume factory-raised meat. If the attempted excuse of causal impotence is compelling in the latter case, it should be compelling in the former case. But it isn't.

The second response to the claim of causal impotence is to deny it. Consider the case of chickens, the most cruelly treated of all animals raised for human consumption, with the possible exception of veal calves. In 1998, almost 8 billion chickens were slaughtered in the US,[2] almost all of them raised on factory farms. Suppose that there are 250 million chicken eaters in the US, and that each one consumes, on average, 25 chickens per year (this leaves a fair number of chickens slaughtered for nonhuman consumption, or for export). Clearly, if only one of those chicken eaters gave up eating chicken, the industry would not respond. Equally clearly, if they all gave up eating chicken, billions of chickens (approximately 6.25 billion per year) would not be bred, tortured, and killed. But there must also be some number of consumers, far short of 250 million, whose renunciation of chicken would cause the industry to reduce the number of chickens bred in factory farms. The industry may not be able to respond to each individual's behavior, but it must respond to the behavior of fairly large numbers. Suppose that the industry is sensitive to a reduction in demand for chicken equivalent to 10,000 people becoming vegetarians. (This seems like a reasonable guess, but I have no idea what the actual numbers are, nor is it important.) For each group of 10,000 who give up chicken, a quarter of a million fewer chickens are bred per year. It appears, then, that if you give up eating chicken, you have only a one in ten thousand chance of making any difference to the lives of chickens, unless it is certain that fewer than 10,000 people will ever give up eating chicken, in which case you have no chance. Isn't a one in ten thousand chance small enough to render your continued consumption of chicken blameless? Not at all. While the chance that your behavior is harmful may be small, the harm that is risked is enormous. The larger the numbers needed to make a difference to chicken production, the larger the difference such numbers would make. A one in ten thousand chance of saving 250,000 chickens per year from excruciating lives is morally and mathematically equivalent to the certainty of saving 25 chickens per year. We commonly accept that even small risks of great harms are unacceptable. That is why we disapprove of parents who fail to secure their children in car seats or with seat belts, who leave their small children unattended at home, or who drink or smoke heavily during pregnancy.

Or consider commercial aircraft safety measures. The chances that the oxygen masks, the lifejackets, or the emergency exits on any given plane will be called on to save any lives in a given week, are far smaller than one in ten thousand. And yet we would be outraged to discover that an airline had knowingly allowed a plane to fly for a week with nonfunctioning emergency exits, oxygen masks, and lifejackets. So, even if it is true that your giving up factory-raised chicken has only a tiny chance of preventing suffering, given that the amount of suffering that would be prevented is in inverse proportion to your chance of preventing it, your continued consumption is not thereby excused.

But perhaps it is not even true that your giving up chicken has only a tiny chance of making any difference. Suppose again that the poultry industry only reduces production when a threshold of 10,000 fresh vegetarians is reached. Suppose also, as is almost certainly true, that vegetarianism is growing in popularity in the US (and elsewhere). Then, even if you are not the one, newly converted vegetarian, to reach the next threshold of 10,000, your conversion will reduce the time required before the next threshold is reached. The sooner the threshold is reached, the sooner production, and therefore animal suffering, is reduced. Your behavior, therefore, does make a difference. Furthermore, many people who become vegetarians influence others to become vegetarian, who in turn influence others, and so on. It appears, then, that the claim of causal impotence is mere wishful thinking, on the part of those meat lovers who are morally sensitive enough to realize that human gustatory pleasure does not justify inflicting extreme suffering on animals.

Perhaps there is a further difference between the treatment of Fred's puppies and the treatment of animals on factory farms. The suffering of the puppies is a necessary means to the production of gustatory pleasure, whereas the suffering of animals on factory farms is simply a by-product of the conditions dictated by economic considerations. Therefore, it might be argued, the suffering of the puppies is *intended as a means* to Fred's pleasure, whereas the suffering of factory raised animals is merely *foreseen* as a side-effect of a system

that is a means to the gustatory pleasures of millions. The distinction between what is intended, either as a means or as an end in itself, and what is 'merely' foreseen is central to the Doctrine of Double Effect. Supporters of this doctrine claim that it is sometimes permissible to bring about an effect that is merely foreseen, even though the very same effect could not permissibly be brought about if intended. (Other conditions have to be met in order for the Doctrine of Double Effect to judge an action permissible, most notably that there be an outweighing good effect.) Fred acts impermissibly, according to this line of argument, because he intends the suffering of the puppies as a means to his pleasure. Most meat eaters, on the other hand, even if aware of the suffering of the animals, do not intend the suffering.

In response to this line of argument, I could remind the reader that Samuel Johnson said, or should have said, that the Doctrine of Double Effect is the last refuge of a scoundrel.[3] I won't do that, however, since neither the doctrine itself, nor the alleged moral distinction between intending and foreseeing can justify the consumption of factory-raised meat. The Doctrine of Double Effect requires not merely that a bad effect be foreseen and not intended, but also that there be an outweighing good effect. In the case of the suffering of factory-raised animals, whatever good could plausibly be claimed to come out of the system clearly doesn't outweigh the bad. Furthermore, it would be easy to modify the story of Fred to render the puppies' suffering 'merely' foreseen. For example, suppose that the cocoamone is produced by a chemical reaction that can only occur when large quantities of drain-cleaner are forced down the throat of a conscious, unanaesthetized puppy. The consequent appalling suffering, while not itself a means to the production of cocoamone, is nonetheless an unavoidable side-effect of the means. In this variation of the story, Fred's behavior is no less abominable than in the original.

One last difference between the behavior of Fred and the behavior of the consumers of factory-raised meat is worth discussing, if only because it is so frequently cited in response to the arguments of this paper. Fred's behavior is abominable, according to this line of thinking, because it involves the suffering of *puppies*. The behavior of meat-eaters, on the other hand, 'merely' involves the suffering of chickens, pigs, cows, calves, sheep, and the like. Puppies (and probably dogs and cats in general) are morally different from the other animals. Puppies *count* (morally, that is), whereas the other animals don't, or at least not nearly as much.

So, what gives puppies a higher moral status than the animals we eat? Presumably there is some morally relevant property or properties possessed by puppies but not by farm animals. Perhaps puppies have a greater degree of rationality than farm animals, or a more finely developed moral sense, or at least a sense of loyalty and devotion. The problems with this kind of approach are obvious. It's highly unlikely that any property that has even an outside chance of being ethically relevant[4] is both possessed by puppies and not possessed by any farm animals. For example, it's probably true that most puppies have a greater degree of rationality (whatever that means) than most chickens, but the comparison with pigs is far more dubious. Besides, if Fred were to inform the jury that he had taken pains to acquire particularly stupid, morally obtuse, disloyal and undevoted puppies, would they (or we) have declared his behavior to be morally acceptable? Clearly not. This is, of course, simply the puppy version of the problem of marginal cases (which I will discuss later). The human version is no less relevant. If their lack of certain degrees of rationality, moral sensibility, loyalty, devotion, and the like makes it permissible to torture farm animals for our gustatory pleasure, it should be permissible to do the same to those unfortunate humans who also lack those properties. Since the latter behavior isn't permissible, the lack of such properties doesn't justify the former behavior.

Perhaps, though, there *is* something that separates puppies, even marginal puppies (and marginal humans) from farm animals—our sympathy. Puppies count more than other animals, because we care more about them. We are outraged to hear of puppies abused in scientific experiments, but unconcerned at the treatment of laboratory rats or animals on factory farms. Before the 2002 World Cup, several members of the England team sent a letter to the government of South Korea protesting the treatment of dogs and cats raised for food in that country. The same players have not protested the treatment of animals on factory farms in England. This example, while clearly illustrating the difference in attitudes towards cats and dogs on the one hand, and farm animals on the other, also reveals one of the problems with this approach to the question of moral status. Although the English footballers, and the English (and US) public in general, clearly care far more about the treatment of cats and dogs than of farm animals, the South Koreans, just as clearly, do not. Are we to conclude that Fred's behavior would not be abominable were he living in South Korea, where dogs and cats are routinely abused for the sake of gustatory pleasure? Such relativism is, to put it mildly, hard to swallow. Perhaps, though, we can maintain the view that human feelings determine the moral status of animals, without condoning the treatment of dogs and cats in South Korea (and other countries). Not all human feelings count. Only the feelings of those who have achieved exactly the right degree of moral sensibility. That just so happens to be those in countries like the US and Britain who care deeply for the welfare of dogs and cats, but not particularly for the welfare of cows, chickens, pigs, and other factory-raised animals. Dog and cat eaters in South Korea are insufficiently sensitive, and humane farming advocates in Britain and the US are overly so. But, of course, it won't do simply to insist that this is the right degree of moral sensibility. We need an explanation of why this is the right degree of sensibility. Moral sensibility consists, at least in part, in reacting differently to different features of situations, actions, agents, and patients. If the right degree of moral sensibility requires reacting differently to puppies and to farm animals, there must be a morally relevant difference between puppies and farm animals. Such a difference can't simply consist in the fact that (some) people do react differently to them. The appeal to differential human sympathy illustrates a purely descriptive psychological difference between the behavior of Fred and that of someone who knowingly consumes factory-raised meat. It can do no serious moral work.

I have been unable to discover any morally relevant differences between the behavior of Fred, the puppy torturer, and the behavior of the millions of people who purchase and consume factory-raised meat, at least those who do so in the knowledge that the animals live lives of suffering and deprivation. If morality demands that we not torture puppies merely to enhance our own eating pleasure, morality also demands that we not support factory farming by purchasing factory-raised meat.

3. THE TEXAN'S CHALLENGE

Perhaps what I have said thus far is enough to convince many that the purchase and consumption of factory-raised meat is immoral. It is clear that the attribution of a different (and elevated) moral status to puppies from that attributed to farm animals is unjustified. But, one philosopher's *modus ponens*, as they say, is another Texan's *modus tollens*. Here is the *modus ponens* I have been urging:

(1) If it's wrong to torture puppies for gustatory pleasure, it's wrong to support factory farming.
(2) It is wrong to torture puppies for gustatory pleasure.
(3) Therefore it's wrong to support factory farming.

But some may be so convinced that supporting factory farming is not wrong that they may substitute that conviction for the second premise, and conclude that it is not wrong to torture puppies for gustatory pleasure. Thus we are confronted with the Texan's *modus tollens*:

(T1) If it's wrong to torture puppies for gustatory pleasure, then it's wrong to support factory farming.
(T2) It's not wrong to support factory farming.
(T3) Therefore it's not wrong to torture puppies for gustatory pleasure.

I'm not saying that there is a large risk that many people, even Texans, will start breeding puppies for food (outside of those countries where it is already accepted practice). What they may do (and have done when I have presented them with

this argument) is explain their reluctance to do so as a mere sentimental preference, as opposed to a morally mandated choice. They may claim, in a somewhat Kantian spirit, that someone who can treat puppies like that may be more likely to mistreat humans. They may agree that all animals deserve equal consideration of their interests. They may then justify their different treatment of animals either on the grounds that they are simply giving some animals *more* than they deserve, or that they are attending to their own interests. If the former, they could claim that morality mandates minimal standards of conduct, but that nothing prevents us from choosing to go beyond the requirements of morality when we feel like it. If the latter, they could claim that their sentimental attachment to puppies, kittens, and the like, makes it in their own interests not to raise and kill them for food. Nonetheless, they may insist, in terms of moral status, there is a clear difference between humans and other animals. Humans have a moral status so far above that of other animals that we couldn't even consider raising humans for food (even humanely), or experimenting on them without their consent, even though we routinely do such things to other animals.

4. HUMANS' VERSUS ANIMALS' ETHICAL STATUS—THE RATIONALITY GAMBIT

For the purposes of this discussion, to claim that humans have a superior ethical status to animals is to claim that it is morally right to give the interests of humans greater weight than those of animals in deciding how to behave. Such claims will often be couched in terms of rights, such as the rights to life, liberty or respect, but nothing turns on this terminological matter. One may claim that it is generally wrong to kill humans, but not animals, because humans are rational, and animals are not. Or one may claim that the suffering of animals counts less than the suffering of humans (if at all), because humans are rational, and animals are not. These claims may proceed through the intermediate claim that the rights of humans are more extensive and stronger than those (if any) of animals. Alternatively, one may directly ground the judgment about the moral status of certain types of behavior in claims about the alleged natural properties of the individuals involved. Much of the debate over the moral status of abortion proceeds along these lines. Many opponents of abortion appeal to features that fetuses have in common with adult humans, in order to argue that it is, at least usually, just as seriously wrong to kill them as it is to kill us. For example, John Noonan claims that it is the possession of a full human genetic code that grounds the attribution to fetuses of this exalted ethical status. Such an argument may, but doesn't have to, proceed through the intermediate claim that anything that possesses a full human genetic code has a right to life. Many proponents of the moral permissibility of abortion, on the other hand, claim features such as self-consciousness or linguistic ability as necessary conditions of full moral status, and thus deny such status to fetuses.

What could ground the claim of superior moral status for humans? Just as the defender of a higher moral status for puppies than for farm animals needs to find some property or properties possessed by puppies but not by farm animals, so the defender of a higher moral status for humans need to find some property or properties possessed by humans but not by other animals. The traditional view, dating back at least to Aristotle, is that rationality is what separates humans, both morally and metaphysically, from other animals. With a greater understanding of the cognitive powers of some animals, recent philosophers have often refined the claim to stress the kind and level of rationality required for moral reasoning. Let's start with a representative sample of three. Consider first these claims of Bonnie Steinbock:

> While we are not compelled to discriminate among people because of different capacities, if we can find a significant difference in capacities between human and non-human animals, this could serve to justify regarding human interests as primary. It is not arbitrary or smug, I think, to maintain that human beings have a different moral status

from members of other species because of certain capacities which are characteristic of being human. We may not all be equal in these capacities, but all human beings possess them to some measure, and non-human animals do not. For example, human beings are normally held to be responsible for what they do. . . . Secondly, human beings can be expected to reciprocate in a way that non-human animals cannot. . . . Thirdly, . . . there is the 'desire for self-respect'.[5]

Similarly, Mary Anne Warren argues that "the rights of persons are generally stronger than those of sentient beings which are not persons." Her main premise to support this conclusion is the following:

> [T]here is one difference [between human and non-human nature] which has a clear moral relevance: people are at least sometimes capable of being moved to action or inaction by the force of reasoned argument.[6]

Carl Cohen, one of the most vehement modern defenders of what Peter Singer calls 'speciesism' states his position as follows:

> Between species of animate life, however— between (for example) humans on the one hand and cats or rats on the other—the morally relevant differences are enormous, and almost universally appreciated. Humans engage in moral reflection; humans are morally autonomous; humans are members of moral communities, recognizing just claims against their own interest. Human beings do have rights, theirs is a moral status very different from that of cats or rats.[7]

So, the claim is that human interests and/or rights are stronger or more important than those of animals, because humans possess a kind and level of rationality not possessed by animals. How much of our current behavior towards animals this justifies depends on just how much consideration should be given to animal interests, and on what rights, if any, they possess. Both Steinbock and Warren stress that animal interests need to be taken seriously into account. Warren claims that animals have important rights, but not as important as human rights. Cohen, on the other hand, argues that we should actually *increase* our use of animals.

5. THE CHALLENGE OF MARGINAL CASES

One of the most serious challenges to this defense of the traditional view involves a consideration of what philosophers refer to as 'marginal cases.' Whatever kind and level of rationality is selected as justifying the attribution of superior moral status to humans will either be lacking in some humans or present in some animals. To take one of the most commonly-suggested features, many humans are incapable of engaging in moral reflection. For some, this incapacity is temporary, as is the case with infants, or the temporarily cognitively disabled. Others who once had the capacity may have permanently lost it, as is the case with the severely senile or the irreversibly comatose. Still others never had and never will have the capacity, as is the case with the severely mentally disabled. If we base our claims for the moral superiority of humans over animals on the attribution of such capacities, won't we have to exclude many humans? Won't we then be forced to the claim that there is at least as much moral reason to use cognitively deficient humans in experiments and for food as to use animals? Perhaps we could exclude the only temporarily disabled, on the grounds of potentiality, though that move has its own problems. Nonetheless, the other two categories would be vulnerable to this objection.

I will consider two lines of response to the argument from marginal cases. The first denies that we have to attribute different moral status to marginal humans, but maintains that we are, nonetheless, justified in attributing different moral status to animals who are just as cognitively sophisticated as marginal humans, if not more so. The second admits that, strictly speaking, marginal humans are morally inferior to other humans, but proceeds to claim pragmatic reasons for treating them, at least usually, *as if* they had equal status.

As representatives of the first line of defense, I will consider arguments from three philosophers, Carl Cohen, Alan White, and David Schmidtz. First, Cohen:

> [the argument from marginal cases] fails; it mistakenly treats an essential feature of humanity as

though it were a screen for sorting humans. The capacity for moral judgment that distinguishes humans from animals is not a test to be administered to human beings one by one. Persons who are unable, because of some disability, to perform the full moral functions natural to human beings are certainly not for that reason ejected from the moral community. The issue is one of kind. . . . What humans retain when disabled, animals have never had.[8]

Alan White argues that animals don't have rights, on the grounds that they cannot intelligibly be spoken of in the full language of a right. By this he means that they cannot, for example, claim, demand, assert, insist on, secure, waive, or surrender a right. This is what he has to say in response to the argument from marginal cases:

> Nor does this, as some contend, exclude infants, children, the feeble-minded, the comatose, the dead, or generations yet unborn. Any of these may be for various reasons empirically unable to fulfill the full role of right-holder. But . . . they are logically possible subjects of rights to whom the full language of rights can significantly, however falsely, be used. It is a misfortune, not a tautology, that these persons cannot exercise or enjoy, claim, or waive, their rights or do their duty or fulfil their obligations.[9]

David Schmidtz defends the appeal to typical characteristics of species, such as mice, chimpanzees, and humans, in making decisions on the use of different species in experiments. He also considers the argument from marginal cases:

> Of course, some chimpanzees lack the characteristic features in virtue of which chimpanzees command respect as a species, just as some humans lack the characteristic features in virtue of which humans command respect as a species. It is equally obvious that some chimpanzees have cognitive capacities (for example) that are superior to the cognitive capacities of some humans. But whether every human being is superior to every chimpanzee is beside the point. The point is that we can, we do, and we should make decisions on the basis of our recognition that mice, chimpanzees, and humans are relevantly different *types*. We can have it both ways after all. Or so a speciesist could argue.[10]

There is something deeply troublesome about the line of argument that runs through all three of these responses to the argument from marginal cases. A particular feature, or set of features, is claimed to have so much moral significance that its presence or lack can make the difference [as] to whether a piece of behavior is morally justified or morally outrageous. But then it is claimed that the presence or lack of the feature in any *particular* case is not important. The relevant question is whether the presence or lack of the feature is *normal*. Such an argument would seem perfectly preposterous in most other cases. Suppose, for example, that ten famous people are on trial in the afterlife for crimes against humanity. On the basis of conclusive evidence, five are found guilty and five are found not guilty. Four of the guilty are sentenced to an eternity of torment, and one is granted an eternity of bliss. Four of the innocent are granted an eternity of bliss, and one is sentenced to an eternity of torment. The one innocent who is sentenced to torment asks why he, and not the fifth guilty person, must go to hell. Saint Peter replies, "Isn't it obvious, Mr. Gandhi? You are male. The other four men— Adolph Hitler, Joseph Stalin, George W. Bush, and Richard Nixon—are all guilty. Therefore the normal condition for a male defendant in this trial is guilt. The fact that you happen to be innocent is irrelevant. Likewise, of the five female defendants in this trial, only one was guilty. Therefore the normal condition for female defendants in this trial is innocence. That is why Margaret Thatcher gets to go to heaven instead of you."

As I said, such an argument is preposterous. Is the reply to the argument from marginal cases any better? Perhaps it will be claimed that a biological category such as a species is more 'natural,' whatever that means, than a category like 'all the male (or female) defendants in this trial.' Even setting aside the not inconsiderable worries about the conventionality of biological categories, it is not at all clear why this distinction should be morally relevant. What if it turned out that there were statistically relevant differences in the mental abilities of men and women? Suppose that men were, on average, more skilled at manipulating numbers than women, and that women were, on average, more empathetic than men. Would such differences in what was 'normal' for men and women justify us in preferring an innumerate man to a female math genius for a job as an accountant, or an insensitive woman to an ultra-sympathetic man for a job as a counselor? I take it that the biological distinction between male and female is just as real as that between human and chimpanzee.

A second response to the argument from marginal cases is to concede that cognitively deficient humans really do have an inferior moral status to normal humans. Can we, then, use such humans as we do animals? I know of no-one who takes the further step of advocating the use of marginal humans for food (though R.G. Frey has made some suggestive remarks concerning experimentation). How can we advocate this second response while blocking the further step? Warren suggests that "there are powerful practical and emotional reasons for protecting non-rational human beings, reasons which are absent in the case of most non-human animals."[11] It would clearly outrage common human sensibilities, if we were to raise retarded children for food or medical experiments.[12] Here is Steinbock in a similar vein:

> I doubt that anyone will be able to come up with a concrete and morally relevant difference that would justify, say, using a chimpanzee in an experiment rather than a human being with less capacity for reasoning, moral responsibility, etc. Should we then experiment on the severely retarded? Utilitarian considerations aside, we feel a special obligation to care for the handicapped members of our own species, who cannot survive in this world without such care. . . . In addition, when we consider the severely retarded, we think, 'That could be me.' It makes sense to think that one might have been born retarded, but not to think that one might have been born a monkey. . . . Here we are getting away from such things as 'morally relevant differences' and are talking about something much more difficult to articulate, namely, the role of feeling and sentiment in moral thinking.[13]

This line of response clearly won't satisfy those who think that marginal humans really do deserve equal moral consideration with other humans. It is also a very shaky basis on which to justify our current practices. What outrages human sensibilities is a very fragile thing. Human history is littered with examples of widespread acceptance of the systematic mistreatment of some groups who didn't generate any sympathetic response from others. That we do feel a kind of sympathy for retarded humans that we don't feel for dogs is, if true, a contingent matter. To see just how shaky a basis this is for protecting retarded humans, imagine that a new kind of birth defect (perhaps associated with beef from cows treated with bovine growth hormone) produces severe mental retardation, green skin, and a complete lack of emotional bond between parents and child. Furthermore, suppose that the mental retardation is of the same kind and severity as that caused by other birth defects that don't have the other two effects. It seems likely that denying moral status to such defective humans would not run the same risks of outraging human sensibilities as would the denial of moral status to other, less easily distinguished and more loved defective humans. Would these contingent empirical differences between our reactions to different sources of mental retardation justify us in ascribing different direct moral status to their subjects? The only difference between them is skin color and whether they are loved by others. Any theory that could ascribe moral relevance to differences such as these doesn't deserve to be taken seriously.[14]

Finally, perhaps we could claim that the practice of giving greater weight to the interests of all humans than of animals is justified on evolutionary grounds. Perhaps such differential concern has survival value for the species. Something like this may well be true, but it is hard to see the moral relevance. We can hardly justify the privileging of human interests over animal interests on the grounds that such privileging serves human interests!

6. AGENT AND PATIENT—THE SPECIESIST'S CENTRAL CONFUSION

Although the argument from marginal cases certainly poses a formidable challenge to any proposed criterion of full moral standing that excludes animals, it doesn't, in my view, constitute the most serious flaw in such attempts to justify the status quo. The proposed criteria are all variations on the Aristotelian criterion of rationality. But what is the moral relevance of rationality? Why should we think that the possession of a certain level or kind of rationality renders the possessor's interests of greater moral significance than those of a merely sentient being? In Bentham's famous words "The question is not, Can they reason? nor Can they talk? But, Can they suffer?"[15]

What do defenders of the alleged superiority of human interests say in response to Bentham's challenge? Some, such as Carl Cohen, simply reiterate the differences between humans and animals that they claim to carry moral significance. Animals are not members of moral communities, they don't engage in moral reflection, they can't be moved by moral reasons, *therefore* (?) their interests don't count as much as ours. Others, such as Steinbock and Warren, attempt to go further. Here is Warren on the subject:

> Why is rationality morally relevant? It does not make us "better" than other animals or more "perfect". . . . But it is morally relevant insofar as it provides greater possibilities for cooperation and for the nonviolent resolution of problems.[16]

Warren is certainly correct in claiming that a certain level and kind of rationality is morally relevant. Where she, and others who give similar arguments, go wrong is in specifying what the moral relevance amounts to. If a being is incapable of moral reasoning, at even the most basic level, if it is incapable of being moved by moral reasons, claims, or arguments, then it cannot be a moral agent. It cannot be subject to moral obligations, to moral praise or blame. Punishing a dog for doing something "wrong" is no more than an attempt to alter its future behavior. So long as we are undeceived about the dog's cognitive capacities, we are not, except metaphorically, expressing any moral judgment about the dog's behavior. (We may, of course, be expressing a moral judgment about the behavior of the dog's owner, who didn't train it very well.) All this is well and good, but what is the significance for the question of what weight to give to animal interests? That animals can't be moral *agents* doesn't seem to be relevant to their status as moral *patients*. Many, perhaps most, humans are both moral agents and patients. Most, perhaps all, animals are only moral patients. Why would the lack of moral agency give them diminished status as moral patients? Full status as a moral patient is not some kind of reward for moral agency. I have heard students complain in this regard that it is *unfair* that humans bear the burdens of moral responsibility, and don't get enhanced consideration of their interests in return. This is a very strange claim. Humans are subject to moral obligations, because they are the kind of creatures who *can* be. What grounds moral agency is simply different from what grounds moral standing as a patient. It is no more unfair that humans and not animals are moral agents, than it is unfair that real animals and not stuffed toys are moral patients.

One other attempt to justify the selection of rationality as the criterion of full moral standing is worth considering. Recall the suggestion that rationality is important insofar as it facilitates cooperation. If we view the essence of morality as reciprocity, the significance of rationality is obvious. A certain twisted, but all-too-common, interpretation of the Golden Rule is that we should 'do unto others in order to get them to do unto us.' There's no point, according to this approach, in giving much, if any, consideration to the interests of animals, because they are simply incapable of giving like consideration to our interests. In discussing the morality of eating meat, I have, many times, heard students claim that we are justified in eating meat, because "the animals would eat us, if given half a chance." (That they say this in regard to our practice of eating cows and chickens is depressing testimony to their knowledge of the animals they gobble up with such gusto.) Inasmuch as there is a consistent view being expressed here at all, it concerns self-interest, as opposed to morality. Whether it serves my interests to give the same weight to the interests of animals as to those of humans is an interesting question, but it is not the same question as whether it is *right* to give animals' interests equal weight. The same point, of course, applies to the question of whether to give equal weight to my interests, or those of my family, race, sex, religion, etc. as to those of other people.

Perhaps it will be objected that I am being unfair to the suggestion that the essence of morality is reciprocity. Reciprocity is important, not because it serves *my* interests, but because it serves the interests of all. Reciprocity facilitates cooperation, which in turn produces benefits for all. What we should say about this depends on the scope of 'all.' If it includes all sentient beings, then the significance of animals' inability to reciprocate is in what it tells us about *how* to give their interests equal consideration. It certainly can't tell us that we should give less, or no, consideration to their interests. If, on the other hand, we claim that rationality is important for reciprocity, which is important for cooperation, which is important for benefiting humans, which is the ultimate goal of morality, we have clearly begged the question against giving equal consideration to the interests of animals.

It seems that any attempt to justify the claim that humans have a higher moral status than other animals by appealing to some version of rationality as the morally relevant difference between humans and animals will fail on at least two counts. It will fail to give an adequate answer to the argument from marginal cases, and, more importantly, it will fail to make the case that such a difference is morally relevant to the status of animals as moral patients as opposed to their status as moral agents.

I conclude that our intuitions that Fred's behavior is morally impermissible are accurate. Furthermore, given that the behavior of those who knowingly support factory farming is morally indistinguishable, it follows that their behavior is also morally impermissible.[17]

NOTES

1. For information on factory farms, see, for example, Jim Mason and Peter Singer, *Animal Factories*, 2d ed. (New York: Harmony Books, 1990), Karen Davis, *Prisoned Chickens, Poisoned Eggs: An Inside Look at the Modern Poultry Industry* (Summertown, TN: Book Publishing Co., 1996), John Robbins, *Diet for a New America* (Walpole, NH: Stillpoint, 1987).

2. *Livestock Slaughter 1998 Summary*, NASS, USDA (Washington, D.C.: March 1999), 2; and *Poultry Slaughter*, NASS, USDA (Washington, D.C.: February 2, 1999), 1f.

3. For a fine critique of the Doctrine of Double Effect, see Jonathan Bennett, *The Act Itself* (Oxford 1995), ch. 11.

4. If someone were to assert that 'puppyishness' or simply 'being a puppy' were ethically relevant, I could do no more than favor them with an incredulous stare.

5. Bonnie Steinbock, "Speciesism and the Idea of Equality," *Philosophy* 53, no. 204 (April 1978). Reprinted in *Contemporary Moral Problems*, 5th edition, James E. White (ed.) (West, 1997) 467–468.

6. Mary Anne Warren, "Difficulties with the Strong Animal Rights Position," *Between the Species* 2, no. 4, 1987. Reprinted in *Contemporary Moral Problems*, 5th edition, James E. White (ed.) (West. 1997), 482.

7. Carl Cohen, "The Case for the Use of Animals in Biomedical Research," *The New England Journal of Medicine*, vol. 315, 1986. Reprinted in *Social Ethics*, 4th edition, Thomas A. Mappes and Jane S. Zembaty (eds.) (New York: McGraw-Hill, 1992), 463.

8. Cohen, op. cit. 461.

9. Alan White, *Rights* (OUP 1984). Reprinted in *Animal Rights and Human Obligations*, 2nd edition, Tom Regan and Peter Singer (eds.) (Prentice Hall, 1989), 120.

10. David Schmidtz, "Are all Species Equal?", *Journal of Applied Philosophy*, Vol. 15, no. 1 (1998), 61, my emphasis.

11. Warren, op. cit. 483.

12. For a similar argument, see Peter Carruthers, *The Animals Issue: Moral Theory in Practice* (Cambridge University Press, 1992).

13. Steinbock, op. cit. 469–470.

14. Certain crude versions of the so-called ethics of care do seem to entail that the mere fact of being loved gives a different ethical status.

15. Jeremy Bentham, *Introduction to the Principles of Morals and Legislation*, (Various), chapter 17.

16. Warren, op. cit. 482.

17. This paper, in various forms, has been presented in more places than I can remember, and has benefited from the comments of more people than I can shake a stick at. I particularly wish to thank, for their helpful comments, Doug Ehring, Mylan Engel, Mark Heller, and Steve Sverdlik.

REVIEW QUESTIONS

1. Explain Norcross's story about Fred. Why does Fred torture puppies? How is Fred's behavior supposed to be like Americans who eat meat?

2. How does Norcross reply to those who reject his analogy?

3. What is Norcross's answer to those who appeal to the doctrine of double effect?

4. How does Norcross respond to those who argue that humans have a higher moral status than animals?

DISCUSSION QUESTIONS

1. Is Fred's behavior really analogous to that of Americans who eat meat? Why or why not?

2. Do puppies have a higher moral status than pigs? Defend your answer.

3. Should you give up eating meat even though there is only a small chance that this will reduce animal suffering? What is Norcross's view? What do you think?

4. Do humans have a higher moral status than animals? If so, why? Suppose aliens arrive who are more rational and moral than humans. Do they have a higher moral status than humans? Are they morally permitted to kill and eat humans?

PROBLEM CASES

1. Killing Chickens

Suppose a farmer raises happy chickens on this farm. They are well fed, they have plenty of room, they have a comfortable place to sleep; in short, they are well cared for and happy. Each year the farmer kills the oldest chickens, the ones that will die of disease or old age. He kills them quickly and with little or no pain. Then he thanks the chickens for their bodies; he is a religious man and believes that the chickens have eternal souls that blissfully unite with the Great Spirit after death and that killing them does not harm their eternal souls. In fact, liberating the chicken souls from their mortal bodies is a natural and good thing to do. That done, he carefully prepares the chicken meat and eats it with great relish. He replaces the chickens he kills with new chickens each year so that the chicken population remains stable.

Does this farmer do anything that is morally wrong? Explain your position.

2. The Draize Test

The Draize eye test is used by cosmetic companies such as Revlon and Procter & Gamble to test the eye irritancy of their products—cosmetics, hair shampoos, and so on. The substance to be tested is injected into the eyes of rabbits; more specifically, 0.1 milligram (a large-volume dose) is injected into the conjunctival sac of one eye of each of six rabbits, with the other eye serving as a control. The lids are held together for one second and then the animal is released. The eyes are examined at twenty-four, forty-eight, and seventy-two hours to see if there is corneal damage. Although the test is very painful, as you can imagine, anesthetics are not used. The eyes are not washed. Very large doses are used (often resulting in permanent eye damage) to provide a large margin of safety in extrapolating for human response.

Should companies continue to test their new products in this way? Why or why not?

3. Eating Whales

(Reported by Andrew Pollack in *The New York Times*, May 3, 1993.) Eating whale meat is popular in Japan. At the crowded restaurant of Kiyoo Tanahahi in Tokyo, customers dine on whale steak, whale bacon, fried whale, smoked whale, raw whale, and whale tongue. Of course, to satisfy the Japanese demand for whale meat, many whales must be hunted and killed. But the International Whaling Commission, the thirty-nine-nation group that regulates whaling, has a moratorium on commercial whaling that has been in effect since 1986. The position of Japan and Norway, the two countries that continue to hunt and kill whales, is that the moratorium is no longer necessary to protect whales. It was originally put in place to protect species of whales endangered by decades of excessive whaling; now, according to Japan and Norway, it is no longer needed for certain types of whales. They estimate that there are more than 760,000 minkes (a relatively small whale) in the Southern Hemisphere. Japan claims that killing 2,000 minkes a year has no effect on the total population.

Those opposed think that all whales, including the minkes, should be protected. They point out that whales are majestic creatures with high intelligence, and they argue that it is morally wrong to kill them. Japan replies that the ban on whaling is just a form of discrimination against Japan and the imposition of one nation's morals on another. Why should Western nations be allowed to kill chickens, cows, and pigs, and Japan not be allowed to kill whales?

What do you think? Should there be a ban on whaling? If so, should Western nations stop killing chickens, cows, and pigs?

4. Human Rights for Apes

(Reported by Seth Mydaus in *The New York Times*, August 12, 2001.) Some scientists link the five great apes into one biologically similar group. The five types of apes are chimpanzees, gorillas, orangutans, bonobos, and humans. Humans are just another type of ape. These scientists note that humans and chimpanzees are 99 percent identical genetically, have similar blood groups, and have similar brain structures. Humans and chimpanzees show nearly identical behavior in their first three years of life. All five types of ape have self-awareness and moral awareness, as displayed in their behavior.

One of the rights-for-apes advocates, Richard Wranghan, a chimpanzee expert at Harvard University, describes chimpanzees as follows: "Like humans, they laugh, make up after a quarrel, support each other in times of trouble, medicate themselves with chemical and physical remedies, stop each other from eating poisonous foods, collaborate in the hunt, help each other over physical boundaries, raid neighboring groups, lose their tempers, get excited by dramatic weather, invent ways to show off, have family traditions and group traditions, make tools, devise plans, deceive, play tricks, grieve, and are cruel and are kind."

If chimpanzees and other apes are so like humans, then why not give them basic human rights, such as a right to live and a right not to suffer from cruel treatment, such as in medical experiments?

Moreover, rights-for-apes advocates want to recognize the other four great apes as persons under law rather than property. As such, they would be provided with guardians to safeguard their rights, like young or impaired humans.

In 1999, New Zealand became the first nation to adopt a law giving rights to apes. They are protected from scientific experimentation not in their interest.

Do great apes deserve basic human rights? Should they be treated as persons under the law? What is your view?

5. Hunting Baby Seals

(Reported by Clifford Krauss in *The New York Times*, April 5, 2004.) In the 1970s, animal rights advocates succeeded in shutting down the American and European markets for the fur of baby harp seals. But now the market has revived. Seal products are banned in the United States, but new markets have emerged in Russia, Ukraine, and Poland, with a fashion trend for sealskin hats and accessories. The price for top-grade harp sealskin has more than doubled since 2001, to about $42. Canadian officials say that seal hunting is worth about $30 million annually to the Newfoundland economy, which has suffered from the collapse of cod fishing. There are about 5,000 hunters and 350 workers who process the skins. In 2004, the Canadian government increased the quota of seals killed to 350,000, the largest number hunted in at least half a century. The large increase is possible, officials say, because the seal population was replenished during the long hunting slump. The Canadian harp seal population has tripled in size since 1970, according to the Department of Fisheries and Oceans, to more than 5 million today.

How are the seals hunted? On the ice fields of the Gulf of St. Lawrence, men with clubs roam in snowmobiles looking for the silvery young pups. The seal pups have not been weaned from their mother's milk and do not know how to swim. They cannot escape and are easy to kill. The men club them over the head, crushing the skull, and sometimes leaving the seals in convulsions. Then the men drag the bodies to waiting ships or skin them on the spot.

In the past, hunters skinned the pups while they were still alive, but new regulations were added in 2004 to stop this. Now the hunters are required to examine the skull of the seal or touch the eyes to guarantee that the seal is brain dead before skinning. The government requires novice seal hunters to obtain an assistant's license and to train for two years before getting a professional license. The killing of whitecoats—the youngest pups up to 12 days old—is now banned. The regulations say that only seals that have shed their white coats are "beaters." The beaters are at least three weeks old, and have a black-spotted silvery fur that is valuable.

Animal rights advocates are revving up a campaign against the hunting of baby harp seals. They are calling for a tourism boycott of Canada. They are flying journalists over the ice fields to photograph the slaughter.

The hunters say they are just trying to make a living. Jason Spence, the thirty-two-year-old captain of *Ryan's Pride*, a fishing boat hunting seals in the Gulf of St. Lawrence, argues that hunting seals is no worse than "people taking the heads off chickens, butchering cows, and butchering pigs."

What is your view of hunting seals? Is it just like killing chickens, cows, and pigs? Is it morally objectionable? Why or why not?

6. Fur Coats

According to the Fur Information Council of America (FICA), retail fur sales in the United States are increasing, from $1.53 billion total sales in 2001 to $1.82 billion total sales in 2005. The fur industry employs 32,000 full-time workers and provides part-time employment for more than 155,000 workers. The top consumers of fur are the United States, Italy, Russia, and China. In the United States, New York City has the most people buying fur, followed by Chicago. One in five women in the United States owns a fur coat, and the most popular are mink coats, which account for more than 70 percent of sales. The FICA lists many models and celebrities who wear fur, including Naomi Campbell, Jennifer Lopez, Sharon Stone, Beyoncé Knowles, and many more. Recently, Madonna was seen leaving a restaurant in London wearing a $70,000 chinchilla coat. Hip-hop and bling king Sean P. Diddy Combs has his own line of fur coats. (It turns out that some of his faux-fur coats were really made of dogs from China.) The Lakers star Kobe Bryant has a golden-colored mink coat, and his former teammate Shaquille O'Neal is also said to be a fur fan.

Paul McCartney and other animal rights activists object to fur coats. They claim that the animals killed are badly treated, but the FICA denies this. According to People for the Ethical Treatment of Animals (PETA), mink raised on fur farms are packed into small cages where they pace back and forth and bite their skin, tails, and feet. Then they are killed by anal or genital electrocution or by gassing or poison injection. Some animals are skinned alive.

The FICA website gives no details about the treatment of animals in fur farms. They assert that under anticruelty statutes, "anyone who mistreats an animal faces investigation, prosecution, fines, jail time and even the loss of his animals."

Wild mink are trapped along with other fur-bearing animals such as fox (the second most popular fur), sable, raccoon, beaver, chinchilla, lynx, and others. About 10 million animals are trapped for fur each year. The steel-jaw leg-hold trap is the trap most commonly used by the fur industry. When the animal steps on the spring of the trap, the steel jaws close on the foot or leg. When the animal tries to escape, the trap cuts into the flesh down to the bone, mutilating the foot or leg. Animals caught in the trap can suffer for days before they are killed and skinned. (State laws about trapping vary from state to state; some require trappers to check their traps weekly, but others have no regulations.) Some trapped animals escape by chewing off their feet, but they die later from blood loss, gangrene, or predators. The fur trappers kill the animals by strangling, beating, or stomping on them. Then the animals are skinned, sometimes before they are dead.

The FICA position on the trapping of wild animals is that this is "the most efficient method of controlling overpopulation," and trappers are performing a "vital function." PETA's view is that animal populations can and do regulate their numbers if they are left alone, and that trapping disrupts wildlife populations by killing healthy animals. What do you think? Is trapping necessary to control wildlife population?

The FICA claims that most people buy fur coats for their warmth and not for fashion or vanity. If you are buying a coat for warmth, then why not buy a down jacket or wool coat? If you object to using animal products such as wool, you might consider a faux-fur coat or a Patagonia jacket made from recycled Polartec. If you want to reduce the number of coats going in the landfill, why not look for a warm and fashionable used coat at Savers? Which coat is best, in your opinion? Explain your choice.

7. Bullfighting

Bullfighting is a traditional spectator sport or spectacle practiced mainly in Spain and Portugal. It was glamorized by Ernest Hemingway in his "Death in the Afternoon," a manifesto on bullfighting published in *Esquire* in 1932.

No two bullfights are the same, but there is more or less a standard script. The ritual or ceremony begins with the bullfighter (*matador*) and his assistants parading across the ring. The matador is traditionally male, but there have been a few females. Perhaps the most famous female matador was Cristina Sanchez, who received 316 bull's ears, which are awarded for an especially good show.

Next the angry bull charges into the ring. The fight begins with the matador playing with the bull by teasing him with a red cape. The idea is to get the bull to charge past as close as possible while the matador makes stylish moves. After a few passes the *picadors* (assistants mounted on horses) start spearing the bull at the back of the neck to weaken him.

In the next phase of the fight, the matador's assistants on foot (*banderilleros*) torment the bull by plunging sharp sticks in the bull's neck. After a short intermission, the matador asks permission to kill the bull and dedicate the kill to a lucky spectator. After some more passes, the matador tries to kill the bull with a sword. Doing this requires thrusting the sword between the shoulder blades. This is not so easy to do; often it takes several bloody thrusts before the sword stays in and the bull finally dies.

Throughout the fight, the crowd shouts encouragement (*olé*) or disapproval if the matador shows fear or incompetence. After a good fight, the matador may be awarded the bull's ear and/or tail as a souvenir.

Bullfighting is a venerable part of traditional Spanish culture, but it also seems to be a cruel spectacle that requires torturing and killing a bull for the sake of entertainment. Is it morally acceptable or not? Why or why not?

⚜ SUGGESTED READINGS

People for the Ethical Treatment of Animals (www.peta.org) has fact sheets and current information about the mistreatment of animals around the world. The Humane Society of the United States (www.hsus.org) works to prevent animal cruelty, exploitation, and neglect. Animal Rights (www.animal rights.net) attacks the animal rights movement.

James Rachels, "Vegetarianism and 'the Other Weight Problem,'" in *World Hunger and Moral Obligation*, ed. William Aiken and Hugh LaFollette (Englewood Cliffs, NJ: Prentice Hall, 1977): 180–193, argues that meat-eating wastes food, and for that reason it is morally wrong. Also, factory-farmed animals suffer when they are raised and killed for food, and this suffering is not justified by the enjoyment of eating their flesh.

Jonathan Safran Foer, *Eating Animals* (New York: Little, Brown, 2009), explains his conversion to vegetarianism and vividly describes the brutality of factory farming.

Tom Regan, "The Case for Animal Rights," in Peter Singer, ed., *In Defense of Animals* (Oxford: Blackwell Publishers, 1985), pp. 13–26, defends the view that animals have rights based on their inherent value as experiencing subjects of a life, and attacks other views, including indirect-duty views, the cruelty-kindness view, and Singer's utilitarianism.

Mary Anne Warren, "Difficulties with the Strong Rights Position," *Between the Species* 2, no. 4 (Fall 1987): 433–441, attacks Regan's strong animal rights position. She argues that it rests on an obscure concept of inherent value, and fails to draw a sharp line between living things having inherent value and other living things that don't have this value.

Tibor R. Machan, "Do Animals Have Rights?" *Public Affairs Quarterly* 5, no. 2 (April 1991): 163–173, defends the Kantian view that humans have a higher moral status than animals because humans have a moral life and act as moral agents and make moral decisions.

Gary Steiner, *Animals and the Moral Community* (New York: Columbia University Press, 2008), presents a theory of animal mental life. Animals have perceptual intelligence; this is sufficient to give them a moral status as members of the moral community.

Roger Scruton, *Animal Rights and Wrongs*, 3rd ed. (London: Metro Books, 2000), defends the Kantian position that humans are members of moral communities and animals are not. On his view, animals do not have moral rights or duties.

Paola Cavalieri, *The Animal Question: Why Non-Humans Deserve Human Rights*, trans. Catherine Woolland (Oxford: Oxford University Press, 2004), argues that we should extend basic moral and legal rights to nonhuman animals.

Gail Eisnitz, *Slaughterhouse: The Shocking Story of Greed, Neglect, and Inhuman Treatment Inside the U.S. Meat Industry* (Buffalo, NY: Prometheus Books, 1997), gives a vivid account of dirty conditions and cruel treatment of animals in slaughterhouses.

Eric Schlosser, *Fast Food Nation: The Dark Side of the All-American Meal* (New York: HarperCollins, 2002), is an expose of the fast-food industry revealing how the food is produced and what's really in it.

Leslie Pickering Francis and Richard Norman, "Some Animals Are More Equal Than Others," *Philosophy* 53 (October 1978): 507–527, agree with Singer that it is wrong to cause animal suffering but deny that this requires us to adopt vegetarianism or abandon animal experimentation.

Roger Crisp, "Utilitarianism and Vegetarianism," *International Journal of Applied Philosophy* 4 (1988): 41–49, argues that utilitarianism morally requires us both to abstain from eating the flesh of intensively reared animals and to eat the flesh of certain nonintensively reared animals. He calls this the Compromise Requirement View.

R. G. Frey, *Interests and Rights: The Case against Animals* (Oxford: Clarendon Press, 1980), argues that animals have neither interests nor moral rights.

Joel Feinberg, "The Rights of Animals and Unborn Generations," in *Philosophy and Environmental Crisis*, ed. William T. Blackstone (Athens: University of Georgia Press, 1974), analyzes the concept of a right and contends that humans and animals have rights but rocks and whole species do not. Future generations have rights but only contingent on their coming into existence.

H. J. McCloskey, "Moral Rights and Animals," *Inquiry* 22 (Spring/Summer 1979): 25–54, attacks Feinberg's analysis of the concept of a right and presents his own account. According to McCloskey, a *right* is an entitlement to something and not a claim against someone. In his view, animals do not have rights.

James Rachels, *Created from Animals: The Moral Implications of Darwinism* (Oxford: Oxford University Press, 1990), defends animal rights.

Stephen R. L. Clark, *Animals and Their Moral Standing* (New York: Routledge, 1997). This book collects the major writings of Clark on animals. It includes discussions of the rights of wild animals, the problems with speciesism, and the difficulty of calculating costs and benefits.

Kerry S. Walters and Lisa Pormess, eds., *Ethical Vegetarianism: From Pythagoras to Peter Singer* (Albany: State University of New York Press, 1999). This anthology covers the 2,000-year Western tradition of vegetarianism, beginning with Pythagoras, Seneca, and Plutarch.

Frances Moore Lappé, *Diet for a Small Planet*, 20th anniversary ed. (New York: Ballantine Books, 1992). This is the latest edition of the classic best-selling book that tells you how to be a vegetarian and why you should be one.

Daniel A. Dombrowski, *Babies and Beasts: The Argument from Marginal Cases* (Urbana: University of Illinois Press, 1997), discusses an important argument used to defend animal rights, the argument that there is no morally relevant difference between animals and "marginal humans," such as the severely mentally retarded.

Daniel R. Dombrowski, *The Philosophy of Vegetarianism* (Amherst: University of Massachusetts Press, 1984), presents a history of the arguments for vegetarianism, beginning with Porphyry's *On Abstinence*.

Mary Midgley, *Animals and Why They Matter* (Athens: University of Georgia Press, 1998), explains why we should have moral concern for animals. Unlike many others, she does not rely on utilitarianism.

Josephine Donovan and Carol J. Adams, eds., *Beyond Animal Rights: A Feminist Caring Ethic for the Treatment of Animals* (La Vergne, TN: Continuum Publishers, 1996). This anthology has eight articles that extend the feminist care ethic to the treatment of animals, thus moving beyond the appeal to animal rights.

Tom Regan and Peter Singer, eds., *Animal Rights and Human Obligations* (Upper Saddle River, NJ: Prentice Hall, 1989). This is a collection of articles on animals that includes discussions of animal rights, the treatment of farm animals, and the treatment of animals in science.

Carl Cohen, "The Case for the Use of Animals in Biomedical Research," *New England Journal of Medicine* 315 (October 2, 1986): 865–870, defends speciesism and the use of animals in biomedical research. Cohen attacks both Singer and Regan, arguing that speciesism is not analogous to racism and sexism and that animals have no rights.

Barbara F. Orlans, *In the Name of Science: Issues in Responsible Animal Experimentation* (Oxford: Oxford University Press, 1993), gives a detailed and well-informed discussion of the issues raised by animal experimentation.

Barbara Orlans and Rebecca Dresser, *The Human Use of Animals: Case Studies in Ethical Choice* (Oxford: Oxford University Press, 1997). This book presents various cases of research using animals, including baboon–human liver transplants, cosmetic safety testing, Washoe and other language-using chimpanzees, and monkeys without mothers.

Deborah Blum, *The Monkey Wars* (Oxford: Oxford University Press, 1977), gives detailed information about various animal activists, from the moderate Animal Welfare Institute to the radical Animal Liberation Front (now on the FBI's terrorist list). Among other things, we find out about Washoe and four other chimpanzees who were trained in the use of sign language.

Harlan B. Miller and William H. Williams, eds., *Ethics and Animals* (Totowa, NJ: Humana Press, 1983). This is an anthology dealing with topics such as animal rights, hunting, and animal experimentation.

Bernard E. Rollin, *The Unheeded Cry: Animal Consciousness, Animal Pain and Science* (Oxford: Oxford University Press, 1989), surveys attitudes toward animal consciousness and pain, beginning with George Romanes in the nineteenth century.

World Poverty and Hunger

INTRODUCTION

Factual Background

The statistics on world poverty and hunger are grim. According to the World Bank, about 1.4 billion people in the developing world (one in four) are living in absolute poverty on less than $1.25 a day. This is a level of income below what is necessary to satisfy the most basic needs. These people suffer from lack of adequate shelter, safe water, and health services. They are malnourished. Many die. The World Health Organization (WHO) estimates that 18 million people die each year from causes related to poverty. More than 3 billion people in the world survive on less than $2.50 a day, and at least 80 percent of the world's population lives on less than $10 a day. All of these people can be viewed as poor, at least by the standard of the U.S. Census, which puts the poverty line at an annual income of $10,830 per person or about $30 a day.

There are wide differences in income. The 358 billionaires in the world have assets greater than the combined annual income of 45 percent of the world's people. The poorest 40 percent of the world's population account for only 5 percent of global income, while the richest 20 percent account for three-fourths of the world's income.

One of the main effects of poverty is hunger and malnutrition. There is disagreement about how many people in the world suffer from malnutrition. The statistic often cited comes from the United Nations Food and Agriculture

Organization (FAO). The most recent estimate, given in 2009, is that about a billion people are undernourished. Most of these people are in Africa, Asia, the Pacific, Latin America, and the Caribbean.

The most obvious victims of undernourishment are children. The United Nations Children's Fund (UNICEF) says that 129 million children under the age of five are underweight and chronically malnourished. Most of these children are in either South Asia or Africa. If these children survive at all, they will suffer from lasting effects—stunted growth and brain damage from lack of protein. Poor nutrition plays a role in at least 5 million child deaths each year. Undernourishment and malnutrition makes children vulnerable to every disease including diarrhea, measles, malaria, and pneumonia. Hunger and malnutrition are the number one risk to health worldwide—greater than the risk of AIDS, malaria, and tuberculosis combined.

Is it possible to feed all the hungry people in the world? According to the FAO, world agriculture produces 17 percent more calories per person today than it did 30 years ago, despite a 70 percent increase in population. This is enough to provide everyone in the world with an adequate diet of about 3,000 kilocalories per person per day. Given some international cooperation, everyone could be fed, at least in principle.

Not all the available land is used for food production. According to the World-watch Institute, less than 60 percent of the world's farmland is under cultivation, and in almost every country where there is widespread hunger and environmental destruction, much of the best agricultural land is used to raise export crops or livestock. These countries could produce more food by growing grain instead of raising livestock and growing export crops.

But if enough food is produced to feed everyone, then why are people undernourished? Why do children starve to death? One answer is that the rich nations consume more than their fair share of the food. Specifically, the United States, Russia, European countries, and Japan consume 70 percent more protein than the rest of the world. They do this by consuming grain indirectly via feedstock converted into animal protein rather than directly in the form of bread, noodles, rice, and so on. In other words, the problem is the result of unequal food distribution rather than inadequate food production.

The Readings

Thomas Pogge begins by noting the radical inequalities in per capita income and consumption. The rich countries have an average per capita income nearly 180 times greater than the poor countries, and they consume more than 80 percent of the global produce while having only one-third of the population. Given these facts, Pogge thinks we could eradicate world poverty if we wanted to do so. But we do not do this, and this means we are inflicting ongoing harm on the poor. He rejects the popular assumption that reducing severe poverty is generous but not a moral duty that we owe to the poor. Furthermore, he denies that radical inequality between the rich and the poor can be morally justified by appealing to actual or fictional history or to the global economic order. The rich continue to harm the poor by imposing the lasting effects of historical crimes, by denying them a fair share of resources, and by imposing an unjust global economic order. He rejects explanatory nationalism, the view that poor nations are themselves responsible for their poverty because of incompetence, corruption, and oppression by the rulers. Instead, he thinks that there are global factors that must be considered, such as protectionism, enforcement of intellectual property rights, and the rich states' support of oppressive rulers of resource-rich nations.

John McMillan argues that we cannot eliminate world poverty by simply redistributing the wealth. He tries to demonstrate this with a thought experiment. Suppose we redistribute the wealth of the millionaires in the world. There are 7 million millionaires in the world with assets totaling $25 trillion. There are 2.8 billion people in the world earning less than $2 a day. If we divide the $25 trillion among the 2.8 billion people, they would each get $9,000. This seems like a good deal for the poor people, but McMillan notes that this would be a one-time transfer of money, and even though it would raise the annual income to about $1,500, they would still be relatively poor.

In McMillan's view, the only real and long-term solution to world poverty is economic growth. He gives examples of this, notably Hong Kong, South Korea, Singapore, and Taiwan. But he cautions that severe poverty, inequality, political unrest, unstable institutions, and other factors can prevent growth. Growth is produced by two basic factors: investment and institutions. For growth to occur, there must be investment in factories and machines, education, and ideas and research. There should be stable institutions allowing property rights, contract enforcement, free markets, competition, and the prevention of corruption and fraud.

Peter Singer defends the view rejected by McMillan: namely, that we morally ought to give money to the poor. His argument is straightforward. It is obvious that suffering from lack of food and other necessities of life is bad. We ought to prevent something bad unless we have to sacrifice something morally significant. But luxury items such as jewelry, perfume, and high-fashion clothes are not morally significant. If people in rich countries gave money to the poor instead of wasting their money on these luxuries, the hungry people in the world could all be fed. According to Netaid, just $13 billion a year would satisfy the basic health and food needs of the world's poorest people—and this is about the amount that rich people spend on perfume each year.

In a "Postscript" to his article (see the Suggested Readings), Singer says that there is still an ongoing world food crisis even though there are no major famines (at the time he was writing). He replies to the objection made by Hardin and others that famine relief merely postpones starvation unless something is done about population growth. This is only an objection to the *type* of aid given, and not an objection to giving aid, which can take the form of assistance with agricultural development. He grants that if a country refuses to take steps to control population, aid should not be given.

Garrett Hardin does not agree that we ought to give money to the poor. In his view, welfare-style transfers of money from rich nations to poor ones just make poverty and hunger worse. He compares nations to lifeboats. Just as a lifeboat has a limited carrying capacity, rich nations have a limited ability to feed the poor nations. If aid is given to the poor nation, the result is a vicious cycle of overpopulation, more starvation, more aid, and so on until there is an ecological disaster, a "tragedy of the commons," as Hardin calls it. The implication is that we have no moral obligation to help poor people. We should just let people in poor nations die from hunger and lack of medical care. This is not morally wrong because it amounts to letting people die rather than actively killing them.

Philosophical Issues

Let's assume that it is possible to reduce and even eliminate severe poverty and hunger in the world. Do we have any moral obligation to do this? Do rich countries such as the United States have a moral duty to relieve severe poverty and prevent people from starving to death in poor countries?

Because obligations imply rights, another way of posing the problem is to ask if poor and hungry people have a positive right or entitlement to the basic necessities of life such as food, clothing, shelter, and medical care.

A standard view of the matter uses the familiar distinction between killing and letting die. We have a negative duty to not kill people by our actions, say by shooting them, but we do not have a positive duty to prevent people from dying of starvation by feeding them. They do not have a positive right to food. To be sure, it is a good thing to give to charity to prevent this, but such generosity is supererogatory—it is not required by duty, and lies above and beyond the requirements of morality. It is morally optional.

The standard view takes a similar position about severe poverty. We have a negative duty to not steal from people, but we have no positive duty to give money to the poor. They do not have a positive right to money. Such generosity is admirable, but it is not required by morality. You do nothing wrong if you give nothing to the poor.

This standard view is explained and attacked by James Rachels (see the Suggested Readings). He argues that our duty to not let people die of starvation is just as strong as our duty to not kill them. He defends this "Equivalence Thesis" against various objections, for example, the claim that in letting someone die we do nothing. Letting someone die *is* doing something, in his view.

Both Pogge and Singer also reject the standard view. Pogge holds that we are morally responsible for inflicting ongoing harm on poor and hungry people in the world. Because of the huge death toll, he says we are "guilty of the largest crime against humanity ever committed." He denies that we are morally entitled to our wealth. If so, we have a positive moral obligation to take steps to eradicate severe poverty and hunger in the world. This is not generosity, but something we owe the poor and hungry.

Singer also rejects the view that giving aid to needy people is morally optional charity and not a positive moral duty. He argues that the standard distinction between duty and charity cannot be drawn, or at least not drawn in the traditional way. He thinks that helping poor and starving people in other countries should not be viewed as charity, but as a morally required duty. According to Singer, this duty can be derived from intuitively obvious moral principles.

McMillan seems to support the standard view. He argues that giving money to the poor will not solve the problem of world poverty, and thus it seems to follow that we have no moral obligation to do so. In McMillan's view, the only real solution to world poverty is economic growth, which is generated by investments and institutions such as free markets. Although rich countries can do some things to encourage free markets (for example, lowering trade barriers), the basic responsibility to eliminate poverty falls on the poor themselves. As McMillan puts it, "Successful economic performance reflects the country's own internal policy decisions. Handicaps left over from history aside, countries can affect their own destiny."

Hardin also seems to accept the standard view. He grants that it is unjust for rich people to enjoy their wealth while poor people suffer from hunger, disease, and poverty. However, the rich have no moral obligation to help the poor. In terms of his lifeboat metaphor, the rich people have no duty to give up their place on the comfortable lifeboat. If the rich feel guilty about their good luck, then they should just get out of the boat. Hardin assumes that nobody is going to do this. Or, if they did, that would eliminate conscience from the boat: "The lifeboat, as it were, purifies itself of guilt."

World Poverty and Human Rights

THOMAS POGGE

Thomas Pogge is the Leitner Professor of Philosophy and International Affairs at Yale University. He is the author or editor of more than twenty books and numerous publications on global justice and justice in health care. He also writes on Rawls and Kant. His most recent books are *Politics as Usual: What Lies behind the Pro-Poor Rhetoric* (2010) and *World Poverty and Human Rights: Cosmopolitan Responsibilities and Reforms* (2nd ed., 2008).

Pogge argues that rich, developed countries are actively harming poor countries by producing and supporting severe poverty. This radical inequality in wealth cannot be justified historically because it came about by horrendous crimes. It cannot be justified by an appeal to a fictional history such as that described by John Locke. It cannot be justified by consequences because the global economic order has resulted in massive deprivations. Pogge goes on to distinguish between three ways in which the rich harm the poor. Poor people are worse off because of the effects of historical crimes, they are prevented from a fair use of natural resources, and they are harmed by the imposition of an unjust global institutional order. This unjust order includes protectionism by affluent countries, the enforcement of intellectual property rights, and the support of corrupt rulers of resource-rich countries.

Despite a high and growing global average income, billions of human beings are still condemned to life-long severe poverty, with all its attendant evils of low life expectancy, social exclusion, ill health, illiteracy, dependency, and effective enslavement. The annual death toll from poverty-related causes is around 18 million, or one-third of all human deaths, which adds up to approximately 270 million deaths since the end of the Cold War.[1]

This problem is hardly unsolvable, in spite of its magnitude. Though constituting 44 percent of the world's population, the 2,735 million people the World Bank counts as living below its more generous $2 per day international poverty line consume only 1.3 percent of the global product, and would need just 1 percent more to escape poverty so defined.[2] The high-income countries, with 955 million citizens, by contrast, have about

[1] World Health Organization, *World Health Report 2004* (Geneva: WHO, 2004), Annex Table 2; available at www.who.int/whr/2004.

[2] For detailed income poverty figures, see Shaohua Chen and Martin Ravallion, "How Have the World's Poorest Fared since the Early 1980s?" *World Bank Research Observer* 19, no. 2 (2004), p. 153; also available at wbro.oupjournals.org/cgi/content/abstract/19/2/141 (reporting 2001 data). Ravallion and Chen have managed the World Bank's income poverty assessments for well over a decade. My estimate of the poor's share of the global product is justified in Thomas W. Pogge, "The First UN Millennium Development Goal: A Cause for Celebration?" *Journal of Human Development* 5, no. 3 (2004), p. 387. For a methodological critique of the World Bank's poverty statistics, see "The First UN Millennium Development Goal," pp. 381–85, based on my joint work with Sanjay G. Reddy, "How *Not* to Count the Poor"; available at www.socialanalysis.org.

Source: World Poverty and Human Rights by Thomas Pogge from *Ethics & International Affairs,* Vol. 19, No. 1, 2005. Oxford, UK: Wiley-Blackwell. Reprinted by permission.

81 percent of the global product.[3] With our average per capita income nearly 180 times greater than that of the poor (at market exchange rates), we could eradicate severe poverty worldwide if we chose to try—in fact, we could have eradicated it decades ago.

Citizens of the rich countries are, however, conditioned to downplay the severity and persistence of world poverty and to think of it as an occasion for minor charitable assistance. Thanks in part to the rationalizations dispensed by our economists, most of us believe that severe poverty and its persistence are due exclusively to local causes. Few realize that severe poverty is an ongoing harm we inflict upon the global poor. If more of us understood the true magnitude of the problem of poverty and our causal involvement in it, we might do what is necessary to eradicate it.

That world poverty is an ongoing harm *we* inflict seems completely incredible to most citizens of the affluent countries. We call it tragic that the basic human rights of so many remain unfulfilled, and are willing to admit that we should do more to help. But it is unthinkable to us that we are actively responsible for this catastrophe. If we were, then we, civilized and sophisticated denizens of the developed countries, would be guilty of the largest crime against humanity ever committed, the death toll of which exceeds, every week, that of the recent tsunami and, every three years, that of World War II, the concentration camps and gulags included. What could be more preposterous?

But think about the unthinkable for a moment. Are there steps the affluent countries could take to reduce severe poverty abroad? It seems very likely that there are, given the enormous inequalities in income and wealth already mentioned. The common assumption, however, is that reducing severe poverty abroad at the expense of our own affluence would be generous on our part, not something we owe, and that our failure to do this is thus at most a lack of generosity that does not make us morally responsible for the continued deprivation of the poor.

I deny this popular assumption. I deny that the 955 million citizens of the affluent countries are morally entitled to their 81 percent of the global product in the face of three times as many people mired in severe poverty. Is this denial really so preposterous that one need not consider the arguments in its support? Does not the radical inequality between our wealth and their dire need at least put the burden on us to show why we should be morally entitled to so much while they have so little? In *World Poverty and Human Rights*,[4] I dispute the popular assumption by showing that the usual ways of justifying our great advantage fail. My argument poses three mutually independent challenges.

ACTUAL HISTORY

Many believe that the radical inequality we face can be justified by reference to how it evolved, for example through differences in diligence, culture, and social institutions, soil, climate, or fortune. I challenge this sort of justification by invoking the common and very violent history through which the present radical inequality accumulated. Much of it was built up in the colonial era, when today's affluent countries ruled today's poor regions of the world: trading their people like cattle, destroying their political institutions and cultures, taking their lands and natural resources, and forcing products and customs upon them. I recount these historical facts specifically for readers who believe that even the most radical inequality is morally justifiable if it evolved in a benign way. Such readers disagree about the conditions a historical process must meet for it to justify such vast inequalities in life chances. But I can bypass these disagreements because the actual historical crimes were so horrendous, diverse, and consequential that no historical entitlement conception could credibly support the view that our common history was sufficiently benign to justify today's huge inequality in starting places.

Challenges such as this are often dismissed with the lazy response that we cannot be held

[3]World Bank, *World Development Report 2003* (New York: Oxford University Press, 2003), p. 235 (giving data for 2001).

[4]Thomas W. Pogge, *World Poverty and Human Rights: Cosmopolitan Responsibilities and Reforms* (Cambridge: Polity Press, 2002). All in-text citation references are to this book.

responsible for what others did long ago. This response is true but irrelevant. We indeed cannot inherit responsibility for our forefathers' sins. But how then can we plausibly claim the *fruits* of their sins? How can we have been entitled to the great head start our countries enjoyed going into the postcolonial period, which has allowed us to dominate and shape the world? And how can we be entitled to the huge advantages over the global poor we consequently enjoy from birth? The historical path from which our exceptional affluence arose greatly weakens our moral claim to it—certainly in the face of those whom the same historical process has delivered into conditions of acute deprivation. They, the global poor, have a much stronger moral claim to that 1 percent of the global product they need to meet their basic needs than we affluent have to take 81 rather than 80 percent for ourselves. Thus, I write, "A morally deeply tarnished history must not be allowed to result in *radical* inequality" (p. 203).

FICTIONAL HISTORIES

Since my first challenge addressed adherents of historical entitlement conceptions of justice, it may leave others unmoved. These others may believe that it is permissible to uphold any economic distribution, no matter how skewed, if merely it *could* have come about on a morally acceptable path. They insist that we are entitled to keep and defend what we possess, even at the cost of millions of deaths each year, unless there is conclusive proof that, without the horrors of the European conquests, severe poverty world-wide would be substantially less today.

Now, *any* distribution, however unequal, *could* be the outcome of a sequence of voluntary bets or gambles. Appeal to such a fictional history would "justify" anything and would thus be wholly implausible. John Locke does much better, holding that a fictional history can justify the status quo only if the changes in holdings and social rules it involves are ones that all participants could have rationally agreed to. He also holds that in a state of nature persons would be entitled to a proportional share of the world's natural resources. Whoever deprives others of "enough and as

good"—either through unilateral appropriations or through institutional arrangements, such as a radically inegalitarian property regime—harms them in violation of a *negative* duty. For Locke, the justice of any institutional order thus depends on whether the worst-off under it are at least as well off as people would be in a state of nature with a proportional resource share.[5] This baseline is imprecise, to be sure, but it suffices for my second challenge: however one may want to imagine a state of nature among human beings on this planet, one could not realistically conceive it as involving suffering and early deaths on the scale we are witnessing today. Only a thoroughly organized state of civilization can produce such horrendous misery and sustain an enduring poverty death toll of 18 million annually. The existing distribution is then morally unacceptable on Lockean grounds insofar as, I point out, "the better-off enjoy significant advantages in the use of a single natural resource base from whose benefits the worse-off are largely, and without compensation, excluded" (p. 202).

The attempt to justify today's coercively upheld radical inequality by appeal to some morally acceptable *fictional* historical process that *might* have led to it thus fails as well. On Locke's permissive account, a small elite may appropriate all of the huge cooperative surplus produced by modern social organization. But this elite must not enlarge its share even further by reducing the poor *below* the state-of-nature baseline to capture *more* than the entire cooperative surplus. The citizens and governments of the affluent states are violating this negative duty when we, in collaboration with the ruling cliques of many poor countries, coercively exclude the global poor from a proportional resource share and any equivalent substitute.

PRESENT GLOBAL INSTITUTIONAL ARRANGEMENTS

A third way of thinking about the justice of a radical inequality involves reflection on the institutional rules that give rise to it. Using this

---

[5]For a fuller reading of Locke's argument, see Pogge, *World Poverty and Human Rights*, ch. 5.

approach, one can justify an economic order and the distribution it produces (irrespective of historical considerations) by comparing them to feasible alternative institutional schemes and the distributional profiles they would produce. Many broadly consequentialist and contractualist conceptions of justice exemplify this approach. They differ in how they characterize the relevant affected parties (groups, persons, time slices of persons, and so on), in the metric they employ for measuring how well off such parties are (in terms of social primary goods, capabilities, welfare, and so forth), and in how they aggregate such information about well-being into an overall assessment (for example, by averaging, or in some egalitarian, prioritarian, or sufficientarian way). These conceptions consequently disagree about how economic institutions should be best shaped under modern conditions. But I can bypass such disagreements insofar as these conceptions agree that an economic order is unjust when it—like the systems of serfdom and forced labor prevailing in feudal Russia or France—foreseeably and avoidably gives rise to massive and severe human rights deficits. My third challenge, addressed to adherents of broadly consequentialist and contractualist conceptions of justice, is that we are preserving our great economic advantages by imposing a global economic order that is unjust in view of the massive and avoidable deprivations it foreseeably reproduces: "There is a shared institutional order that is shaped by the better-off and imposed on the worse-off," I contend. "This institutional order is implicated in the reproduction of radical inequality in that there is a feasible institutional alternative under which such severe and extensive poverty would not persist. The radical inequality cannot be traced to extra-social factors (such as genetic handicaps or natural disasters) which, as such, affect different human beings differentially" (p. 199).

THREE NOTIONS OF HARM

These three challenges converge on the conclusion that the global poor have a compelling moral claim to some of our affluence and that we, by denying them what they are morally entitled to and urgently need, are actively contributing to their deprivations. Still, these challenges are addressed to different audiences and thus appeal to diverse and mutually inconsistent moral conceptions.

They also deploy different notions of harm. In most ordinary contexts, the word "harm" is understood in a historical sense, either diachronically or subjunctively: someone is harmed when she is rendered worse off than she was at some earlier time, or than she would have been had some earlier arrangements continued undisturbed. My first two challenges conceive harm in this ordinary way, and then conceive justice, at least partly, in terms of harm: we are behaving unjustly toward the global poor by imposing on them the lasting effects of historical crimes, or by holding them below any credible state-of-nature baseline. But my third challenge does not conceive justice and injustice in terms of an independently specified notion of harm. Rather, it relates the concepts of *harm* and *justice* in the opposite way, conceiving harm in terms of an independently specified conception of social justice: we are *harming* the global poor if and insofar as we collaborate in imposing an *unjust* global institutional order upon them. And this institutional order is definitely unjust if and insofar as it foreseeably perpetuates large-scale human rights deficits that would be reasonably avoidable through feasible institutional modifications.[6]

The third challenge is empirically more demanding than the other two. It requires me to substantiate three claims: Global institutional arrangements are causally implicated in the reproduction of massive severe poverty. Governments of our affluent countries bear primary responsibility for these global institutional arrangements and

---

[6]One might say that the existing global order is not unjust if the only feasible institutional modifications that could substantially reduce the offensive deprivations would be extremely costly in terms of culture, say, or the natural environment. I preempt such objections by inserting the word "reasonably." Broadly consequentialist and contractualist conceptions of justice agree that an institutional order that foreseeably gives rise to massive severe deprivations is unjust if there are feasible institutional modifications that foreseeably would greatly reduce these deprivations without adding other harms of comparable magnitude.

can foresee their detrimental effects. And many citizens of these affluent countries bear responsibility for the global institutional arrangements their governments have negotiated in their names.

TWO MAIN INNOVATIONS

In defending these three claims, my view on these more empirical matters is as oddly perpendicular to the usual empirical debates as my diagnosis of our moral relation to the problem of world poverty is to the usual moral debates.

The usual *moral* debates concern the stringency of our moral duties to help the poor abroad. Most of us believe that these duties are rather feeble, meaning that it isn't very wrong of us to give no help at all. Against this popular view, some (Peter Singer, Henry Shue, Peter Unger) have argued that our positive duties are quite stringent and quite demanding; and others (such as Liam Murphy) have defended an intermediate view according to which our positive duties, insofar as they are quite stringent, are not very demanding. Leaving this whole debate to one side, I focus on what it ignores: our moral duties not to harm. We do, of course, have positive duties to rescue people from life-threatening poverty. But it can be misleading to focus on them when more stringent negative duties are also in play: duties not to expose people to life-threatening poverty and duties to shield them from harms for which we would be actively responsible.

The usual *empirical* debates concern how developing countries should design their economic institutions and policies in order to reduce severe poverty within their borders. The received wisdom (often pointing to Hong Kong and, lately, China) is that they should opt for free and open markets with a minimum in taxes and regulations so as to attract investment and to stimulate growth. But some influential economists call for extensive government investment in education, health care, and infrastructure (as illustrated by the example of the Indian state of Kerala), or for some protectionist measures to "incubate" fledgling niche industries until they become internationally competitive (as illustrated by the example of South Korea). Leaving these

debates to one side, I focus once more on what is typically ignored: the role that the design of the *global* institutional order plays in the persistence of severe poverty.

Thanks to the inattention of our economists, many believe that the existing global institutional order plays no role in the persistence of severe poverty, but rather that national differences are the key factors. Such "explanatory nationalism" (p. 139ff.) appears justified by the dramatic performance differentials among developing countries, with poverty rapidly disappearing in some and increasing in others. Cases of the latter kind usually display plenty of incompetence, corruption, and oppression by ruling elites, which seem to give us all the explanation we need to understand why severe poverty persists there.

But consider this analogy. Suppose there are great performance differentials among the students in a class, with some improving greatly while many others learn little or nothing. And suppose the latter students do not do their readings and skip many classes. This case surely shows that local, student-specific factors play a role in explaining academic success. But it decidedly *fails* to show that global factors (the quality of teaching, textbooks, classroom, and so forth) play no such role. A better teacher might well greatly improve the performance of the class by eliciting stronger student interest in the subject and hence better attendance and preparation.

Once we break free from explanatory nationalism, global factors relevant to the persistence of severe poverty are easy to find. In the WTO negotiations, the affluent countries insisted on continued and asymmetrical protections of their markets through tariffs, quotas, anti-dumping duties, export credits, and huge subsidies to domestic producers. Such protectionism provides a compelling illustration of the hypocrisy of the rich states that insist and command that their own exports be received with open markets (pp. 15–20). And it greatly impairs export opportunities for the very poorest countries and regions. If the rich countries scrapped their protectionist barriers against imports from poor countries, the populations of the latter would benefit greatly: hundreds of millions would escape unemployment, wage levels would rise substantially, and incoming export revenues would be higher by hundreds of billions of dollars each year.

The same rich states also insist that their intellectual property rights—ever-expanding in scope and duration—must be vigorously enforced in the poor countries. Music and software, production processes, words, seeds, biological species, and drugs—for all these, and more, rents must be paid to the corporations of the rich countries as a condition for (still multiply restricted) access to their markets. Millions would be saved from diseases and death if generic producers could freely manufacture and market life-saving drugs in the poor countries.[7]

While charging billions for their intellectual property, the rich countries pay nothing for the externalities they impose through their vastly disproportional contributions to global pollution and resource depletion. The global poor benefit least, if at all, from polluting activities, and also are least able to protect themselves from the impact such pollution has on their health and on their natural environment (such as flooding due to rising sea levels). It is true, of course, that we pay for the vast quantities of natural resources we import. But such payments cannot make up for the price effects of our inordinate consumption, which restrict the consumption possibilities of the global poor as well as the development possibilities of the poorer countries and regions (in comparison to the opportunities our countries could take advantage of at a comparable stage of economic development).

More important, the payments we make for resource imports go to the rulers of the resource-rich countries, with no concern about whether they are democratically elected or at least minimally attentive to the needs of the people they rule. It is on the basis of effective power alone that we recognize any such ruler as entitled to sell us the resources of "his" country and to borrow, undertake treaty commitments, and buy arms in its name. These international resource,

borrowing, treaty, and arms privileges we extend to such rulers are quite advantageous to them, providing them with the money and arms they need to stay in power—often with great brutality and negligible popular support. These privileges are also quite convenient to us, securing our resource imports from poor countries irrespective of who may rule them and how badly. But these privileges have devastating effects on the global poor by enabling corrupt rulers to oppress them, to exclude them from the benefits of their countries' natural resources, and to saddle them with huge debts and onerous treaty obligations. By substantially augmenting the perks of governmental power, these same privileges also greatly strengthen the incentives to attempt to take power by force, thereby fostering coups, civil wars, and interstate wars in the poor countries and regions—especially in Africa, which has many desperately poor but resource-rich countries, where the resource sector constitutes a large part of the gross domestic product.

Reflection on the popular view that severe poverty persists in many poor countries because they govern themselves so poorly shows, then, that it is evidence not for but against explanatory nationalism. The populations of most of the countries in which severe poverty persists or increases do not "govern themselves" poorly, but *are* very poorly governed, and much against their will. They are helplessly exposed to such "government" because the rich states recognize their rulers as entitled to rule on the basis of effective power alone. We pay these rulers for their people's resources, often advancing them large sums against the collateral of future exports, and we eagerly sell them the advanced weaponry on which their continued rule all too often depends. Yes, severe poverty is fueled by local misrule. But such local misrule is fueled, in turn, by global rules that we impose and from which we benefit greatly.

Once this causal nexus between our global institutional order and the persistence of severe poverty is understood, the injustice of that order, and of our imposition of it, becomes visible: "What entitles a small global elite—the citizens of the rich countries *and* the holders of political

---

[7]See Thomas W. Pogge, "Human Rights and Global Health," *Metaphilosophy* 36, nos. 1–2 (2005), pp. 182–209.

and economic power in the resource-rich developing countries—to enforce a global property scheme under which we may claim the world's natural resources for ourselves and can distribute these among ourselves on mutually agreeable terms?" I ask. "How, for instance, can our ever so free and fair agreements with tyrants give us property rights in crude oil, thereby dispossessing the local population and the rest of humankind?" (p. 142).

REVIEW QUESTIONS

1. Why does Pogge think that world poverty is an ongoing harm inflicted on the poor?
2. According to Pogge, how was the radical inequality in wealth historically caused? How does this show that the inequality is not morally justified?
3. How does Locke try to justify unequal economic distribution? Why does Pogge believe the present unequal distribution is morally unacceptable on Lockean grounds?
4. How does Pogge explain the current global economic order?
5. In what three ways are the rich harming the poor, according to Pogge?
6. Why does Pogge object to explanatory nationalism?
7. According to Pogge, what global practices are relevant to the explanation of severe poverty?

DISCUSSION QUESTIONS

1. Do you agree that rich countries are actively harming poor people? If so, is there a negative duty not to harm them?
2. Are we entitled to our wealth while others live in poverty? What is Pogge's view? What do you think?
3. Do rich countries have a positive duty to help poor people?
4. Should rich countries eliminate protectionist barriers against imports from poor countries? Should they abandon intellectual property rights for music, software, drugs, and so on? What is your view?
5. Pogge claims that rich countries support corrupt rulers. Can you give examples of this?

Antipoverty Warriors

JOHN MCMILLAN

John McMillan (1951–2007) was the Jonathan B. Lovelace Professor of Economics in Stanford University's Graduate School of Business. He was the author of *Reinventing the Bazaar: A Natural History of Markets* (2002); *Games, Strategies, and Managers* (1992); *Incentives in Government Contracting* (with R. Preston McAfee, 1988); and *Game Theory in International Economics* (1986). In addition, he was the author or co-author of fifty published articles.

McMillan argues that a redistribution of wealth will not eliminate world poverty. There are too many poor people and the income gaps are too wide. The only real solution to poverty is economic growth—or, at least, economic growth is a necessary condition for the reduction or elimination of poverty. Extreme poverty, inequality, political instability, trade barriers, and unstable institutions can prevent growth. Producing successful economic growth requires

Source: Antipoverty Warriors from *Reinventing the Bazaar* by John McMillan, pp. 211–223. Copyright © 2002. NY: W. W. Norton & Company, Inc.

investment in machinery, education, and research. Markets rather than governments should guide the investment, and the markets must be free, that is, without trade barriers and other interference. Markets by themselves do not bring growth. They have to be supported by secure institutions, property rights, prevention of corruption, functioning laws of contract, and political stability.

China and Russia were both planned communist economies; Russia was a middle-income and industrialized country, and China was much poorer and mostly agricultural. Despite their differences, these . . . countries' responses to reform have some common elements. Designing the market economy entails restructuring the existing firms, creating new firms, and building labor, product, and financial markets—it is difficult in any country.

"Plodding wins the race," as the tortoise said to the hare in Aesop's fable. China's gradualism turned out to be a speedier route to markets than Russia's shock therapy. After eight years of reform, markets were working more effectively in China than in Russia. By 1986, China's agriculture had been marketized, a vast number of new firms were thriving, prices generally were aligned with costs, and per capita income had risen sharply. In each of these respects the China of 1986 was ahead of the Russia of 2000.

The fastest route from a planned economy to functioning markets, it turns out, was not frenetically tearing down the old institutions, starting with a clean slate, and enacting top-down reforms. It entailed letting the new economy grow up around the old one, maintaining some stability to let people create new ways of doing business.

In different circumstances, however, shock therapy could be warranted. In a country like New Zealand where market-supporting institutions already exist—secure property rights, well-defined laws of contract, and active financial markets—the main case against shock therapy loses its force.

Well-functioning markets rely on a judicious mix of formal and informal controls. While the government helps to set the rules for the market, so do the market participants. An economy cannot be designed from above. If it were possible to plan the reforms, it would have been possible to plan the economy.

Human rights activists, labor union members, revolutionaries, religious groups, environmentalists, and animal rights advocates assembled in December 1999 on the streets of Seattle. What brought this incongruent coalition together was their hatred of globalization, symbolized for them by a meeting of the World Trade Organization.

The protesters turned on street theater. Singers and rappers, dancers and jugglers entertained the crowds. Environmentalists dressed up in costumes: there were sea turtles and dolphins, and a "genetically modified" man. Black-clad anarchists, scarves covering their faces, smashed the windows of McDonald's and Niketown, stores they saw as signifying American world dominance. The confrontation turned violent when the police reacted, perhaps overreacted, to the anarchists' provocations, spraying tear gas, firing rubber bullets, and wielding truncheons. The spectacle flashed nightly on the world's television news. After a similar set of protests in Genoa in June 2001, the *Economist* remarked that the protesters had done "what the public relations departments of the WTO, the IMF, the World Bank and the EU have failed to do in half a century: they have made economics exciting."

To the protesters, globalization was to blame for a host of evils: the widening income disparities between rich and poor nations and within rich nations, environmental degradation, the excessive power of the multinational corporations, the homogenization of national cultures. Globalization denoted Bangladeshi children working grindingly long days making soccer balls; Salvadorian women sewing designer jeans in sweatshops; Indonesian workers making athletic shoes in hot, airless factories while breathing toxic glue fumes. Vandana Shiva, an Indian activist, said globalization was "a new kind of corporate colonialism visited upon poor countries and the poor in rich countries."[1]

Globalization arises from the ever-closer linking of the world's markets. Changes in technology helped initiate it. With containerized ships and jumbo jets, the cost of transporting goods plummeted. Networked computers now shift money instantaneously. Changes in policy also played a role, as governments around the world abolished restrictions on trade and barriers to foreign investors. Globalization has even transformed the way its foes organize themselves: the internet links them via sites such as the appositely named www.protest.net.

Let us think about the most fundamental of the antiglobalization protesters' concerns: the impoverishment of the developing world. The protesters made some compelling points. Imposing Western-style intellectual property protections on developing countries, for example, can damage the poor, as the case of the AIDS drugs discussed earlier illustrates. Overall, though, are the world's poor the victims of globalization? Why are poor countries poor?

* * *

Nearly half the world's people, 2.8 billion, live on less than $2 a day. This blunt, shameful fact underlies what angered the Seattle protesters. The child labor, the sweat shops, the environmental problems will not go away until extreme poverty disappears.

The gap between rich and poor countries is vast. In China, the average income is about one-tenth that in the United States. In India it is one-fourteenth. In Tanzania, to take an extreme case, it is one-sixtieth. A typical American spends in less than a week what a Tanzanian must eke out over a whole year. (These comparisons are done in purchasing-power-parity terms, which take account of the cross-country variations in the cost of living; without such an adjustment, the disparities would be still bigger.)[2]

The world's millionaires number seven million, according to the firm Gemini Consulting. Millionaires therefore make up just over one-thousandth of the world's population. Their assets total $25 trillion.[3] Most of those earning less than $2 per day are in Africa and Asia; most of the millionaires are in Western Europe and North America. The total annual income of the poorest 2.8 billion is about $1.5 trillion. If we assume the millionaires' annual consumption amounts to 6 percent of their wealth (probably an underestimate), then their consumption is $1.5 trillion. The richest 0.1 percent of the world consumes about as much as the poorest 45 percent.

Is sharing the wealth an option to ease the misery of the poor? Let us do some hypothetical arithmetic. Imagine that the wealth of the millionaires is confiscated and distributed to everyone earning less than $2 per day. Dividing $25 trillion among 2.8 billion people would give $9,000 to each.

Such a drastic redistribution would require authoritarian methods. It would be infeasible for many reasons, one of which is that taxing income at 100 percent would squash any incentive to earn it. It is not going to happen. But putting aside all the obvious objections, even if this redistribution could be done, it would not eliminate poverty. The sum of $9,000 is a large sum for a Tanzanian or Bangladeshi, but it is a once-only transfer, since in our thought experiment it is wealth that is confiscated. If the recipients invested their windfall and earned ten percent per year from it, in addition to what they already are earning, their annual incomes would be about $1,500; the per capita income of Algeria or Ecuador. While this redistribution would markedly reduce extreme poverty, the poor would still be poor.

Global poverty cannot be eliminated by sharing the wealth. The poor outnumber the rich by too much, and the income gaps are too wide. Even if a massive worldwide redistribution could be implemented, any gains to the poor countries would be limited. The only real solution,

[1] *Economist*, June 23, 2001, p. 13. The Shiva quote is from www.gn.apc.org/resurgence/articles/mander.htm, accessed September 26, 2001.
[2] World Bank purchasing-power-parity data for 1999, www.worldbank.org/data/databytopic/GNPPC.pdf.

[3] The data on millionaires, for 1999, are at www.gemcon.com/fs/wealth 2000.htm. The number of the poor, an estimate for 1998, is reported at www.worldbank.org/poverty/data/trends/income.htm.

therefore, is economic growth, to expand the world's total resources. Growth simply means an increase in a nation's income. That poverty reduction entails growth is almost tautological, but not quite, for the effects on poverty depend on how evenly the growth is distributed.

Growth is effective: it has brought major improvements in living standards. The average American today earns six times more than a century ago. A typical American family in 1900 lived in a house the size of a two-car garage today. Then, people spent most of their money on the necessities of food, clothing and shelter; now much of it is freed for more discretionary uses. (In 1900, the average American spent over a third of his or her income on food; by 2000 this had dropped to just one-seventh.) Ordinary people in the United States and Western Europe today are better off in material terms than everyone bar the very wealthiest who ever lived prior to the twentieth century.

The good news is that the majority of the world's people, not just those in the West, are steadily becoming better off. Most countries, rich and poor, most of the time are growing. India, for example, grew slowly but consistently between 1950 and 1980 (about 1.5 percent real per capita growth), and somewhat faster in the 1980s and 1990s (4 percent or more). As a result, the average person in India in 2000 was more than twice as well off than in 1950.

While most countries have been growing, the growth is uneven. The countries that were relatively rich at the start of the twentieth century have for the most part continued to grow. The countries that started out poor have followed widely differing growth patterns. Some have grown very fast and many have grown steadily, but some of the poorest have grown little or not at all. The current inequality among countries is the consequence of differing rates of growth in the past. Countries are poor because they have been growing slowly or not at all over a long period of time. Shrinking the global inequalities necessitates speeding these countries' growth.

It can be done. Impressive success has been achieved by the Asian tigers—Hong Kong, South Korea, Singapore, and Taiwan—as well

as, notably, Botswana. From 1960 to 1990 these five countries grew at per capita annual rates of 6 percent or more, meaning that people's incomes doubled every twelve years. (You can calculate roughly how many years it takes for income to double by dividing the growth rate into 72.) By 2000, per capita income in Botswana was seven times higher than the average for sub-Saharan Africa. Botswana was lucky, in having diamond mines; but it was not simply luck, for some other mineral-rich countries have failed to grow.

The potency of compound growth is shown by the example of Singapore. In the mid-1960s the average person earned a measly U.S.$500 (equivalent to less than U.S.$3,000 in 2000 dollars). The future looked bleak on both political and economic grounds. Singapore had just been ejected from a federation with Malaysia, and it faced a risk of a communist coup. It had no natural resources and little industry. Overcoming its unpromising beginnings, it grew to genuine affluence. By 2000, with a per capita national income of more than U.S.$30,000, Singapore had caught up with the world's richest countries. Prime Minister Goh Chok Tong boasted, "We have come this far on nothing."

Most of the world's poor countries have become less poor over time, though more gradually than Singapore. In some of the poorest countries, however, such as Guyana, Chad, Mali, and Zambia, per capita incomes have fallen over time.[4]

* * *

Let us look now at the effects of economic growth within a given country. Who gains from growth? Does it benefit the poor or only the rich? This is a question of fact, not ideology. We must look at the data.

Goethe said, "It has been asserted that the world is governed by figures. I do know this: figures tell us whether it is being governed well or badly." Research in economics has become increasingly empirical of late, as advances in computers have put massive amounts of data-crunching

---

[4]Data from Temple (1999) and Pritchett and Summers (1996). The Goh Chok Tong quote is from the *Economist*, August 22, 1992, p. 25.

power on every economist's desk, and new statistical techniques have produced sharper ways of making inferences from the data. Facts about the economy do not come to us in a clean form. Drawing lessons from the data involves judgment as well as technique, and to the extent that judgment is involved, reasonable people can disagree. But one of the main achievements of modern economics has been refinements in statistical techniques that narrow the range of judgment needed.

A better understanding of economic growth is one of the results. Huge data sets covering many countries over many years—showing growth rates, investment levels, school enrollment, fertility rates, indexes of corruption and the rule of law, the incidence of poverty, and so on—have been brought to bear on economic growth. Later we will look at what this research has found about the sources of economic growth. For now, let us see what the data tell us about the effects of growth on the poor.

Distributed evenly, a 5 percent increase in a nation's income would mean everyone in the country has that much extra. But growth need not be spread evenly. To study the effect of growth on individuals, economists use two distinct measures: poverty and inequality. Poverty is an absolute measure: the number of people who earn less than the minimum necessary to purchase basic food and shelter. Inequality is a relative measure: the breadth of the gap between the poor and the rich.

Inequality is calculated in various ways; one simple measure is the fraction of national income going to the poorest 20 percent of the population. Poverty is measured by a somewhat arbitrary line. Studies of global poverty customarily take income of $1 or $2 per day as the cutoff. Rich countries set their own poverty line higher. In the United States in 2000, the Census Bureau defined as poor any family of four with an annual income of less than $17,761. (There are two ways of looking at this number. On the one hand, one-fourth of it exceeds the per capita income of most developing countries. On the other, most Americans cannot conceive how a family of four can get by on less than $20,000.)

To see the distinction between the two concepts, inequality and poverty, suppose the income of tenant farmers in India, who are barely getting by, has risen 12 percent over the past two years. Has this change improved things? By the poverty criterion, the outcome is more fair than before, for the poor can buy more and better food for their families. By the inequality criterion, in contrast, it depends on what happened to the incomes of the affluent. If rich landlords at the same time also become 12 percent richer, the nation is no better off. Perhaps in affluent countries inequality may be salient, but in poor countries, in most economists' view, poverty is the more pressing concern.

Poverty is usually reduced, the data show, by economic growth. The rising tide tends to raise all boats. By the $1-a-day definition of poverty, the fraction of the world's population who are poor fell from 24 percent in 1987 to 20 percent in 1999. Poverty has fallen almost everywhere growth has occurred. It is most persistent in countries that fail to grow. An analysis of data from eighty countries over four decades finds that while the effects of growth vary a lot from country to country, the poor usually share in the fruits of growth. The incomes of the poorest 20 percent of the population, in a typical country, rise one for one with overall economic growth.[5] The poor become better off in lockstep with everyone else.

The degree of inequality within a country, in other words, tends to stay constant over time, so any growth means some reduction in poverty. But this is a statement about averages; how much growth helps the poor varies across countries and over time.

The amount of poverty reduction depends on the degree of inequality. In countries with low inequality, growth has a bigger impact on poverty than in very unequal countries.

In the United States over the second half of the twentieth century, growth brought uneven gains. Inequality widened as the rich got richer, mainly from technological changes that increased the wages of the skilled relative to the unskilled.

---

[5]The cross-country evidence is given by Dollar and Kraay (2000), whose study covers 80 countries over four decades; Timmer (1997) and Easterly (1999) report similar results.

But growth still brought widespread gains. The robust growth of the 1990s reduced the incidence of poverty, mainly by creating jobs. Over a fifth of the people living below the official poverty line in 1992 had been lifted above it by 1999. (The number below the poverty line fell from 15.1 percent of the population to 11.8 percent.) Rebecca Blank, an expert on poverty in the United States, concluded that the "most important lesson for anti-poverty warriors from the 1990s is that sustained economic growth is a wonderful thing."[6]

In China, as we saw, economic growth and poverty reduction on a massive scale followed the restructuring of agriculture. China is not unique. In India also, the productivity of farms rose—not as in China from a radical reform of a deeply inefficient economic system, but from technological advance. The green revolution, with its improved seed varieties, spurred increases in food production. The fruits of the economic growth that followed from India's higher farm productivity have been widely spread.[7] Over a thirty-five-year period, absolute levels of poverty were significantly reduced. Many millions were lifted out of extreme poverty.

* * *

This is not to say that growth alone can eliminate poverty, or that redistribution from rich to poor is necessarily unwarranted. Growth is not the whole of the solution to poverty. But it is an indispensable part of it.

One reason why growth by itself may not solve poverty is that extreme poverty might actually prevent any growth from getting started. While growth usually brings benefits to the poor as well as the rich, the data show that inequality affects the rate of growth—in a direction that runs counter to conventional wisdom. Countries that have a more equal distribution of income grow faster on average than those with wider income gaps. In countries with extreme

inequality, conversely, the inequality in itself can be a hindrance to growth.[8]

Poor countries on the whole are more unequal than rich countries. A measure of inequality is the ratio of the average income in the richest 40 percent of the population to the average income in the lower 60 percent. In the industrialized countries this ratio lies between 2 and 3 (in Germany it is 2.4, in the United Kingdom 2.5, in France 2.7, in the United States 2.9). While in some of the developing countries the degree of inequality is similar (in Pakistan it is 2.2 and in Egypt 2.5), in most it is much higher (in the Philippines it is 4.3, and in Brazil it is as high as 6.4).[9]

Why is inequality an obstacle to growth? One reason is that wide inequality generates unrest and political instability, harming the economy. Another is that in countries that are both poor and unequal, large numbers of people live in extreme poverty. The poor are unable to take advantage of investment opportunities. Potential entrepreneurs cannot borrow or save the capital they would need to start firms. The children of the poor cannot afford an education and so are excluded from skilled employment. Where there is extreme inequality of opportunity, growth is slow simply because much of the nation's talent is wasted.

In Taiwan in the early 1950s, for example, just before the start of its rapid growth spurt, the government enacted a major land reform, redistributing the nation's farming assets toward the poor. The ensuing drop in inequality—Taiwan by then had one of the world's least unequal income distributions—arguably helped to jump-start the economy in its growth to affluence.[10] Other poor countries remain trapped in a vicious cycle of inequality causing low growth, which perpetuates the inequality.

Economic growth is not an end in itself, but a means to the end of higher living standards. More is needed than growth to end the misery of the world's poor. Growth is not a sufficient condition for correcting social wrongs—but it is a necessary condition. Having more resources does not automatically make people's lives better, but it helps.

---

[6]On the United States, see Blank (2000) (the quote is from p. 10) and Haveman and Schwabish (1999). The data on poverty rates are from www.census.gov/hhes/poverty/histpov/hstpov5.html.

[7]Datt and Ravallion (1998); Desai (1999, p. 40).

[8]Aghion, Caroli, and Garcia-Penalosa (1999), Barro (2000), Benabou (1996).

[9]Data from Albanesi (2000).

[10]Fei, Ranis, and Kuo (2000).

Health is one measure of living standards. As a country's income rises, its people become measurably healthier. Measures like calorie intake, protein intake, and hospital beds per capita are significantly higher where income is higher. As a result, life expectancy is longer. Child mortality falls when national income rises. It is not just income that affects health levels, to be sure; public-health programs and new knowledge about diseases are crucial. But richer countries are healthier countries.

Gender inequities also tend to fall as the economy grows. Discrimination is largely cultural, but culture can respond to economic changes. In the poorest countries like Bangladesh and Somalia, girls spend about half as many years in school on average as boys. In lower-middle-income countries like the Philippines and Botswana, girls and boys receive about equal schooling. (In Middle Eastern and North African countries like Tunisia, Algeria, and Iraq, though, girls consistently average about two years less in school than boys.) Women workers also benefit from growth: gender pay differentials tend to be narrower in richer countries. Growth helps shrink the gender gap.[11]

* * *

The consequences of economic growth for human welfare, said Nobel laureate Robert Lucas, "are simply staggering: Once one starts to think about them, it is hard to think of anything else."[12] Understanding how to achieve successful economic performance is urgent. We are far from having all the answers, but we have some.

Investment—broadly defined to include investment in equipment and machinery, in people through education, and in ideas through research and development—is the direct route to growth. Countries that invest more in equipment grow faster, as the statistical studies of growth show. Investment in ever more machines, however, eventually hits diminishing returns. A country that already has a large stock of capital gets a smaller boost from any additional investment, other things

equal, than a country with little capital. This implies that poor countries should be growing faster than rich countries because investments should yield larger returns in poor countries. Countries' income levels should be converging. But they aren't.

The rich countries have been able to avoid diminishing returns to physical investment by means of technological progress. New and better ideas offer an escape from the limits of growth. Further, a country can benefit from the world's stock of ideas only if it educates its people. Education, or investment in human capital, is a major source of growth, in addition to investment in machines and equipment. Countries that spend more on education grow significantly faster. Education spurs growth.[13]

The rapid growth in Singapore, for example, is sometimes described as a miracle, but it actually has a straightforward explanation. Singapore simply mobilized its resources. The primary source of growth was massive investment in physical capital. Singaporeans saved and invested as much as 40 percent of their income. A further source of growth was investment in people. In 1966, more than half the workforce had no formal education; by 1990 two-thirds had completed secondary education.[14] Singapore's growth, far from a miracle, was based on cumulative investment.

Investment in machines, people, and ideas is not enough to ensure growth. The investment must be well directed if it is to be productive. For this, markets are needed.

We can obtain a measure of the scope of markets by calculating the fraction of national income that is spent by the government; the remaining fraction passes through the private sector. Big government, it turns out, is statistically related to its rate of growth, in the way most would expect. Large government expenditure is associated with slow growth. A government that controls too much of the economy's resources slows down the economy.[15]

[11]On health and growth, see Pritchett and Summers (1996), Easterly (1999), and Rains, Stewart, and Ramirez (2000). On gender inequalities, see Forsythe, Korzeneiwicz, and Durrant (2000), Hill and King (2000), and Tzannatos (1999).
[12]Lucas (1988, p. 5).
[13]On ideas as a source of growth, see Romer (1986), and on education, see Krueger and Lindahl (2001).
[14]Krugman (1996, p. 175).
[15]On the statistical link between government expenditure and growth, see Alesina (1997), Barro (1991), Levine and Renelt (1992), and Kneller, Bleaney, and Gemmell (1999).

Two further measures of a country's reliance on markets are its openness to international trade and the degree of development of its financial markets. High trade barriers signify government intervention in the everyday workings of the economy. Prohibiting trade across borders means not letting markets operate fully. Price signals are distorted, so investment goes into unproductive areas, such as capital-intensive projects in a capital-poor country. The absence of competition from overseas means firms can be lazy monopolists, rather than being forced to make themselves lean to survive. Low trade barriers, on the other hand, foster an efficient domestic industry. The statistical growth studies corroborate this: countries that are relatively open to international trade tend to invest more and grow faster.

Financial markets promote growth. Where the financial system is inadequate, it is hard for firms to grow large enough to benefit from economies of scale, as industry tends to be owned and run by a politically favored clique. Financial markets allow the entry and growth of new firms. The statistical growth studies find that countries that have workable banks and stock markets tend to invest more and grow faster. Also, controlling inflation is part of financial health. Inflation makes doing business uncertain, by increasing the risks of borrowing and lending and by making prices unreliable signals of demands and supplies. Low inflation turns out to be correlated with faster growth.[16]

* * *

Markets are needed, then, to generate investment that is both at a sufficient level and directed in the right areas to sustain economic growth. Contrary to the assertions of the more fervent fans of the free market, however, markets are not all that is needed.

If the government is small, then by default much of the economy is left to markets. Small government does not necessarily mean fast growth. Government spending has a negative effect on growth, as noted, but only up to a point. When the government is a large part of the economy, smaller government tends to go with faster growth—but not when it is a very small part.[17] To foster growth, the government must not be absent. Some investment is needed from the government. Growth is faster, the data show, in countries that build workable public infrastructure such as roads, railroads, bridges, ports, and telephone and electricity networks. If a country's infrastructure is sparse, congested, or unreliable, it is hard to do business and growth is impeded. Government can be too small.

Allowing markets to encompass most of the economy is no guarantee of economic success. Some of the poorest countries are predominantly market economies. They fail to grow despite leaving most decisions to markets. In the sub-Saharan African countries, for example, government expenditure accounts for just 26 percent of national income, little more than in the other developing countries. (In East Asia, South Asia, and Latin America this figure is between 20 and 24 percent.) During the 1980s and 1990s the African countries overall had negative economic growth, despite the fact that their governments accounted for only one-fourth of their economies.

Somalia is an extreme case of small government: in Amnesty International's phrase, it is a country without a state. It was devastated in the early 1990s by civil war. As of the year 2000, five years after the United Nations peacekeepers left, admitting failure to stabilize the country, the economy had started to bounce back. By then it was a pure free-market economy. No taxes were collected. Business boomed, with firms competing fiercely for customers. But the economy did not run smoothly. Firms faced high transaction costs. "You have to provide everything for yourself," said Abdi Muhammad Sabria, a Mogadishu businessman. "You have to collect the garbage on your own street."[18] With no police force, firms had to pay armed thugs to protect their property. They generated their own electricity and found their own sources of water. The lack of a working port meant it was hard

---

[16]Levine (1997), Temple (1999), Wacziarg (2001).

[17]That smaller government tends to go with faster growth when the government is a large part of the economy is argued by Barro and Sala-i-Martin (1992). On infrastructure: Temple (1999).

[18]*New York Times,* August 10, 2000, p. A3.

to get imported inputs. Competition among the three telephone companies had driven rates low, but they did not interconnect, so a firm needed three telephone lines. The ubiquity of markets, and the absence of government, did not lead to an efficient economy.

Markets do not automatically bring growth. It is not enough that the government stays out of the economy and just leaves things to markets. The sustained high investment needed for long-term growth requires more than that. The statistical evidence further indicates that a country grows if it has sound institutions. Growth is faster in countries that have secure property rights, workable rules preventing corruption, functioning laws of contract, and political stability.[19]

The links between growth and these institutional variables are easy to see. Political instability both discourages economic activity by raising the risks of doing business and diverts firms' resources away from productive activities into a quest for political favors. Corruption discourages investment. Insecure property rights and unreliable contract enforcement impede markets.

What is cause and what is effect? Do countries grow faster because their officials are honest, or does corruption fall as a consequence of increasing affluence? Are effective laws a cause or a consequence of growth? The causality goes both ways, the evidence indicates: most of these variables both lead and follow economic growth.[20] Growth, as a result, can be self-reinforcing. A country may grow because it educates its people; the growth then means it can afford a higher level of education, which brings still further growth. A country that succeeds in lowering corruption boosts its growth, with the result that it is able to devote still more resources to fighting corruption, and so it grows still more. Growth benefits from virtuous feedbacks. By the same logic in reverse, however, the very poorest countries can become trapped. Their dysfunctional institutions mean they are poor, and their poverty means they

cannot afford to do what it would take to improve their institutions.

The variables that economists have found to be associated with increases in per capita income, to sum up, fall under two headings: *investment* and *institutions*. Economic growth requires not only that markets be extensive but also that they be well designed. A sturdy platform is needed: mechanisms to protect property rights and contracting, accessible financial markets, a competitive environment for firms, bounds on government expenditure, stable politics and low inflation to limit the uncertainties of doing business, and adequate public infrastructure for transportation and communication. Given this platform, markets generate growth.

That some countries are comfortably affluent while others are grindingly poor is explained in large part by the quality of their institutions. The economic and political environment determines the efficiency of market activity: manufacturing, inventing, investing, buying, selling. If the platform for markets is inadequate, the nation's scarce resources are wasted.

* * *

Globalization has turned out to be a sideshow as far as poverty is concerned. It neither impoverishes poor countries nor enriches them. Countries are poor because they fail to grow. Globalization does not prevent them from growing: some developing countries, after all, succeeded in growing fast while globalization proceeded. Neither does it necessarily do much, though, to help them grow. Many countries were growing as slowly in 2000 as in 1970; globalization had passed them by.

Globalization could help the poor countries if it made markets in rich countries accessible to their products. Hypocritically preaching the virtues of the global economy, the United States and Western Europe have been notably reluctant to expose their own firms to competition from third-world producers. Some poor countries have obtained an alternative benefit from globalization. By lowering their own trade barriers, they have both widened the range of consumer goods for their citizens and induced their own firms, now facing foreign competition, to become more

---

[19]See, among others, Alesina (1997), Barro (1991), Hall and Jones (1999), Keefer and Knack (1997), Levine (1997), Mauro (1995), and Temple (1999).

[20]Chong and Calderón (2000), Mauro (1995).

efficient. Countries with lower trade barriers, the data show, do tend to grow faster. Openness to trade is just one of the sources of growth success, however, and not the chief one.

Poverty need not be a trap. Growth can be achieved, and when it is, impressive poverty reduction follows. China's rapid growth of the 1980s and 1990s resulted, according to the World Bank, in more than 200 million people escaping poverty.[21] It is homegrown policies that make the difference between fast growth and no growth. Successful economic performance reflects the country's own internal policy decisions. Handicaps left over from history aside, countries can affect their own destiny.

Fixing an underperforming economy, as Russia shows, is a lengthy and sometimes painful process. There is uncertainty about what policies will work. We still have a lot to learn about what a country must do to achieve economic growth. "There is not some glorious theoretical synthesis of capitalism that you can write down in a book and follow," as Nobel economist Robert Solow said. "You have to grope your way."[22]

While there is no recipe book for economic success, the broad-brush growth studies summarized in this chapter and the more close-up analyses in the earlier chapters yield some lessons. Growth requires getting the institutions right. This means the state must take appropriate actions. It also means letting markets do what they do best. For this, the market system must be well designed, so that market information flows smoothly, trading relationships can develop, contracts are enforced, property rights are assured, harmful externalities are controlled, and competition is fostered.

The deepest justification for the market economy is that where it works, it is the best remedy we have for poverty. The deepest reason for studying market design is that markets can work badly and thus fail to do away with poverty.

---

[21]Nyberg and Rozelle (1999, p. 95).

[22]*New York Times*, September 29, 1991, p. E1.

⚜ REVIEW QUESTIONS

1. Why does McMillan think that giving money to the poor will not eliminate poverty?
2. According to McMillan, what is the only real solution to global poverty?
3. How does McMillan distinguish between inequality and poverty? Why is reduction in poverty different from reduction in equality?
4. According to McMillan, what factors prevent economic growth?
5. How can a country achieve successful economic growth, according to McMillan?

⚜ DISCUSSION QUESTIONS

1. "Global poverty cannot be eliminated by sharing the wealth." Do you agree? Why or why not?
2. McMillan argues that inequality is an obstacle to growth. If so, should we try to reduce or eliminate inequality? Why is this your view?
3. "Financial markets promote growth." Is this true? Explain your answer.

Famine, Affluence, and Morality

PETER SINGER

For biographical information on Singer, see his reading in Chapter 6.

In this reading, Singer begins with two moral principles. The first is that suffering and death from lack of food, shelter, and medical care are bad. He expects us to accept this principle without argument. The second principle is more controversial, and is formulated in a strong and a weak version. The strong version is that if we can prevent something bad from happening "without thereby sacrificing anything of comparable moral importance," then we should do it. The weak version is that we ought to prevent something bad from happening "unless we have to sacrifice something morally significant." It follows from those two moral principles, Singer argues, that it is a moral duty, and not just a matter of charity, for affluent nations to help starving people in countries like East Bengal.

As I write this, in November 1971, people are dying in East Bengal from lack of food, shelter, and medical care. The suffering and death that are occurring there now are not inevitable, not unavoidable in any fatalistic sense of the term. Constant poverty, a cyclone, and a civil war have turned at least nine million people into destitute refugees; nevertheless, it is not beyond the capacity of the richer nations to give enough assistance to reduce any further suffering to very small proportions. The decisions and actions of human beings can prevent this kind of suffering. Unfortunately, human beings have not made the necessary decisions. At the individual level, people have, with very few exceptions, not responded to the situation in any significant way. Generally, speaking, people have not given large sums to relief funds; they have not written to their parliamentary representatives demanding increased government assistance; they have not demonstrated in the streets, held symbolic fasts, or done anything else directed toward providing the refugees with the means to satisfy their essential needs. At the government level, no government has given the sort of massive aid that would enable the refugees to survive for more than a few days. Britain, for instance, has given rather more than most countries. It has, to date, given £14,750,000. For comparative purposes, Britain's share of the nonrecoverable development costs of the Anglo-French Concorde project is already in excess of £275,000,000, and on present estimates will reach £440,000,000. The implication is that the British government values a supersonic transport more than thirty times as highly as it values the lives of the nine million refugees. Australia is another country which, on a per capita basis, is well up in the "aid to Bengal" table. Australia's aid, however, amounts to less than one-twelfth of the cost of Sydney's new opera house. The total amount given, from all sources, now stands at about £65,000,000. The estimated cost of keeping the refugees alive for one year is £464,000,000. Most of the refugees have now been in the camps for more than six months. The World Bank has said that India needs a minimum of £300,000,000 in assistance from other countries before the end of the year. It seems obvious that assistance on this scale will not be forthcoming. India will be forced to choose between letting the refugees starve or diverting funds from her own development program, which will mean that more of her own people will starve in the future.[1]

Source: From Peter Singer, "Famine, Affluence, and Morality," *Philosophy & Public Affairs,* Vol. 1, No 3 (Spring 1972). Copyright © 1972 Princeton University Press. Reprinted with permission of Blackwell Publishing.

These are the essential facts about the present situation in Bengal. So far as it concerns us here, there is nothing unique about this situation except its magnitude. The Bengal emergency is just the latest and most acute of a series of major emergencies in various parts of the world, arising both from natural and from man-made causes. There are also many parts of the world in which people die from malnutrition and lack of food independent of any special emergency. I take Bengal as my example only because it is the present concern, and because the size of the problem has ensured that it has been given adequate publicity. Neither individuals nor governments can claim to be unaware of what is happening there.

What are the moral implications of a situation like this? In what follows, I shall argue that the way people in relatively affluent countries react to a situation like that in Bengal cannot be justified; indeed, the whole way we look at moral issues—our moral conceptual scheme—needs to be altered, and with it, the way of life that has come to be taken for granted in our society.

In arguing for this conclusion I will not, of course, claim to be morally neutral. I shall, however, try to argue for the moral position that I take, so that anyone who accepts certain assumptions, to be made explicit, will, I hope, accept my conclusion.

I begin with the assumption that suffering and death from lack of food, shelter, and medical care are bad. I think most people will agree about this, although one may reach the same view by different routes. I shall not argue for this view. People can hold all sorts of eccentric positions, and perhaps from some of them it would not follow that death by starvation is in itself bad. It is difficult, perhaps impossible, to refute such positions, and so for brevity I will henceforth take this assumption as accepted. Those who disagree need read no further.

My next point is this: if it is in our power to prevent something bad from happening, without thereby sacrificing anything of comparable moral importance, we ought, morally, to do it. By "without sacrificing anything of comparable moral importance" I mean without causing anything else comparably bad to happen, or doing something that is wrong in itself, or failing to promote some moral good, comparable in significance to the bad thing that we can prevent. This principle seems almost as uncontroversial as the last one. It requires us only to prevent what is bad, and not to promote what is good, and it requires this of us only when we can do it without sacrificing anything that is, from the moral point of view, comparably important. I could even, as far as the application of my argument to the Bengal emergency is concerned, qualify the point so as to make it: if it is in our power to prevent something very bad from happening, without thereby sacrificing anything morally significant, we ought, morally, to do it. An application of this principle would be as follows: if I am walking past a shallow pond and see a child drowning in it, I ought to wade in and pull the child out. This will mean getting my clothes muddy, but this is insignificant, while the death of the child would presumably be a very bad thing.

The uncontroversial appearance of the principle just stated is deceptive. If it were acted upon, even in its qualified form, our lives, our society, and our world would be fundamentally changed. For the principle takes, firstly, no account of proximity or distance. It makes no moral difference whether the person I can help is a neighbor's child ten yards from me or a Bengali whose name I shall never know, ten thousand miles away. Secondly, the principle makes no distinction between cases in which I am the only person who could possibly do anything and cases in which I am just one among millions in the same position.

I do not think I need to say much in defense of the refusal to take proximity and distance into account. The fact that a person is physically near to us, so that we have personal contact with him, may make it more likely that we *shall* assist him, but this does not show that we *ought* to help him rather than another who happens to be further away. If we accept any principle of impartiality, universalizability, equality, or whatever, we cannot discriminate against someone merely because he is far away from us (or we are far away from him). Admittedly, it is possible that we are in a better position to judge what needs to be done to help a person near to us than one far away, and perhaps also to provide the assistance we judge to be necessary. If this were the case, it would be a reason for helping those near to us first. This may once have been a justification for being more concerned with the poor in one's own town than with famine victims in India. Unfortunately for those who like to keep their moral responsibilities limited, instant communication and swift transportation have changed the situation. From the moral point of view, the development of the world into a "global village" has made an important, though still unrecognized, difference to our moral situation. Expert observers and supervisors, sent out by famine relief organizations or permanently stationed in famine-prone areas, can direct our aid to a refugee in Bengal almost as effectively as we could get it to someone in our own block. There would seem, therefore, to be no possible justification for discriminating on geographical grounds.

There may be a greater need to defend the second implication of my principle—that the fact that there are millions of other people in the same position, in respect to the Bengali refugees, as I am, does not make the situation significantly different from a situation in which I am the only person who can prevent something very bad from occurring. Again, of course, I admit that there is a psychological difference between the cases; one feels less guilty about doing nothing if one can point to others, similarly placed, who have also done nothing. Yet this can make no real difference to our moral obligations.[2] Should I consider that I am less obliged to pull the drowning child out of the pond if on looking around I see other people, no further away than I am, who have also noticed the child but are doing nothing? One has only to ask this question to see the absurdity of the view that numbers lessen obligation. It is a view that is an ideal excuse for inactivity; unfortunately most of the major evils—poverty, overpopulation, pollution— are problems in which everyone is almost equally involved.

The view that numbers do make a difference can be made plausible if stated in this way: if everyone in circumstances like mine gave £5 to the Bengal Relief Fund, there would be enough to provide food, shelter, and medical care for the refugees; there is no reason why I should give more than anyone else in the same circumstances as

I am; therefore I have no obligation to give more than £5. Each premise in this argument is true, and the argument looks sound. It may convince us, unless we notice that it is based on a hypothetical premise, although the conclusion is not stated hypothetically. The argument would be sound if the conclusion were: if everyone in circumstances like mine were to give £5, I would have no obligation to give more than £5. If the conclusion were so stated, however, it would be obvious that the argument has no bearing on a situation in which it is not the case that everyone else gives £5. This, of course, is the actual situation. It is more or less certain that not everyone in circumstances like mine will give £5. So there will not be enough to provide the needed food, shelter, and medical care. Therefore by giving more than £5 I will prevent more suffering than I would if I gave just £5.

It might be thought that this argument has an absurd consequence. Since the situation appears to be that very few people are likely to give substantial amounts, it follows that I and everyone else in similar circumstances ought to give as much as possible, that is, at least up to the point at which by giving more one would begin to cause serious suffering for oneself and one's dependents—perhaps even beyond this point to the point of marginal utility, at which by giving more one would cause oneself and one's dependents as much suffering as one would prevent in Bengal. If everyone does this, however, there will be more than can be used for the benefit of the refugees, and some of the sacrifice will have been unnecessary. Thus, if everyone does what he ought to do, the result will not be as good as it would be if everyone did a little less than he ought to do, or if only some do all that they ought to do.

The paradox here arises only if we assume that the actions in question—sending money to the relief funds—are performed more or less simultaneously, and are also unexpected. For if it is to be expected that everyone is going to contribute something, then clearly each is not obliged to give as much as he would have been obliged to had others not been giving too. And if everyone is not acting more or less simultaneously, then those giving later will know how much more is needed, and will have no obligation to give more than is necessary to reach this amount. To say this is not to deny the principle that people in the same circumstances have the same obligations, but to point out that the fact that others have given, or may be expected to give, is a relevant circumstance: those giving after it has become known that many others are giving and those giving before are not in the same circumstances. So the seemingly absurd consequence of the principle I have put forward can occur only if people are in error about the actual circumstances—that is, if they think they are giving when others are not, but in fact they are giving when others are. The result of everyone doing what he really ought to do cannot be worse than the result of everyone doing less than he ought to do, although the result of everyone doing what he reasonably believes he ought to do could be.

If my argument so far has been sound, neither our distance from a preventable evil nor the number of other people who, in respect to that evil, are in the same situation as we are, lessens our obligation to mitigate or prevent that evil. I shall therefore take as established the principle I asserted earlier. As I have already said, I need to assert it only in its qualified form: if it is in our power to prevent something very bad from happening, without thereby sacrificing anything else morally significant, we ought, morally, to do it.

The outcome of this argument is that our traditional moral categories are upset. The traditional distinction between duty and charity cannot be drawn, or at least, not in the place we normally draw it. Giving money to the Bengal Relief Fund is regarded as an act of charity in our society. The bodies which collect money are known as "charities." These organizations see themselves in this way—if you send them a check, you will be thanked for your "generosity." Because giving money is regarded as an act of charity, it is not thought that there is anything wrong with not giving. The charitable man may be praised, but the man who is not charitable is not condemned. People do not feel in any way ashamed or guilty about spending money on new clothes or a new car instead of giving it to famine relief. (Indeed, the alternative does not occur

to them.) This way of looking at the matter cannot be justified. When we buy new clothes not to keep ourselves warm but to look "well-dressed" we are not providing for any important need. We would not be sacrificing anything significant if we were to continue to wear our old clothes, and give the money to famine relief. By doing so, we would be preventing another person from starving. It follows from what I have said earlier that we ought to give money away, rather than spend it on clothes which we do not need to keep us warm. To do so is not charitable, or generous. Nor is it the kind of act which philosophers and theologians have called "supererogatory"—an act which it would be good to do, but not wrong not to do. On the contrary, we ought to give the money away, and it is wrong not to do so.

I am not maintaining that there are no acts which are charitable, or that there are no acts which it would be good to do but not wrong not to do. It may be possible to redraw the distinction between duty and charity in some other place. All I am arguing here is that the present way of drawing the distinction, which makes it an act of charity for a man living at the level of affluence which most people in the "developed nations" enjoy to give money to save someone else from starvation, cannot be supported. It is beyond the scope of my argument to consider whether the distinction should be redrawn or abolished altogether. There would be many other possible ways of drawing the distinction—for instance, one might decide that it is good to make other people as happy as possible, but not wrong not to do so.

Despite the limited nature of the revision in our moral conceptual scheme which I am proposing, the revision would, given the extent of both affluence and famine in the world today, have radical implications. These implications may lead to further objections, distinct from those I have already considered. I shall discuss two of these.

One objection to the position I have taken might be simply that it is too drastic a revision of our moral scheme. People do not ordinarily judge in the way I have suggested they should. Most people reserve their moral condemnation for those who violate some moral norm, such as the norm against taking another person's property. They do not condemn those who indulge in luxury instead of giving to famine relief. But given that I did not set out to present a morally neutral description of the way people make moral judgments, the way people do in fact judge has nothing to do with the validity of my conclusion. My conclusion follows from the principle which I advanced earlier, and unless that principle is rejected, or the arguments shown to be unsound, I think the conclusion must stand, however strange it appears.

It might, nevertheless, be interesting to consider why our society, and most other societies, do judge differently from the way I have suggested they should. In a well-known article, J. O. Urmson suggests that the imperatives of duty, which tell us what we must do, as distinct from what it would be good to do but not wrong not to do, function so as to prohibit behavior that is intolerable if men are to live together in society.[3] This may explain the origin and continued existence of the present division between acts of duty and acts of charity. Moral attitudes are shaped by the needs of society, and no doubt society needs people who will observe the rules that make social existence tolerable. From the point of view of a particular society, it is essential to prevent violations of norms against killing, stealing, and so on. It is quite inessential, however, to help people outside one's own society.

If this is an explanation of our common distinction between duty and supererogation, however, it is not a justification of it. The moral point of view requires us to look beyond the interests of our own society. Previously, as I have already mentioned, this may hardly have been feasible, but it is quite feasible now. From the moral point of view, the prevention of the starvation of millions of people outside our society must be considered at least as pressing as the upholding of property norms within our society.

It has been argued by some writers, among them Sidgwick and Urmson, that we need to have a basic moral code which is not too far beyond the capacities of the ordinary man, for otherwise there will be a general breakdown of compliance with the moral code. Crudely stated, this argument suggests that if we tell people that they ought to refrain from murder and give everything they do not really need to famine relief, they will do neither, whereas if we tell them that they ought to refrain from murder and that it is good to give to famine relief but not wrong not to do so, they will at least refrain from murder. The issue here is: Where should we draw the line between conduct that is required and conduct that is good although not required, so as to get the best possible result? This would seem to be an empirical question, although a very difficult one. One objection to the Sidgwick-Urmson line of argument is that it takes insufficient account of the effect that moral standards can have on the decisions we make. Given a society in which a wealthy man who gives five percent of his income to famine relief is regarded as most generous, it is not surprising that a proposal that we all ought to give away half our incomes will be thought to be absurdly unrealistic. In a society which held that no man should have more than enough while others have less than they need, such a proposal might seem narrow-minded. What it is possible for a man to do and what he is likely to do are both, I think, very greatly influenced by what people around him are doing and expecting him to do. In any case, the possibility that by spreading the idea that we ought to be doing very much more than we are to relieve famine we shall bring about a general breakdown of moral behavior seems remote. If the stakes are an end to widespread starvation, it is worth the risk. Finally, it should be emphasized that these considerations are relevant only to the issue of what we should require from others, and not to what we ourselves ought to do.

The second objection to my attack on the present distinction between duty and charity is one which has from time to time been made against utilitarianism. It follows from some forms of utilitarian theory that we all ought, morally, to be working full time to increase the balance of happiness over misery. The position I have taken here would not lead to this conclusion in all circumstances, for if there were no bad occurrences that we could prevent without sacrificing something of comparable moral importance, my argument would have no application. Given the present conditions in many parts of the world, however, it does follow from my argument that we ought, morally, to be working full time to relieve great suffering of the sort that occurs as a result of famine or other disasters. Of course, mitigating circumstances can be adduced—for instance, that if we wear ourselves out through overwork, we shall be less effective than we would otherwise have been. Nevertheless, when all considerations of this sort have been taken into account, the conclusion remains: we ought to be preventing as much suffering as we can without sacrificing something else of comparable moral importance. This conclusion is one which we may be reluctant to face. I cannot see, though, why it should be regarded as a criticism of the position for which I have argued, rather than a criticism of our ordinary standards of behavior. Since most people are self-interested to some degree, very few of us are likely to do everything that we ought to do. It would, however, hardly be honest to take this as evidence that it is not the case that we ought to do it.

It may still be thought that my conclusions are so wildly out of line with what everyone else thinks and has always thought that there must be something wrong with the argument somewhere. In order to show that my conclusions, while certainly contrary to contemporary Western moral standards, would not have seemed so extraordinary at other times and in other places, I would like to quote a passage from a writer not normally thought of as a way-out radical, Thomas Aquinas.

> Now, according to the natural order instituted by divine providence, material goods are provided for the satisfaction of human needs. Therefore the division and appropriation of property, which proceeds from human law, must not hinder the satisfaction of man's necessity from such goods. Equally, whatever a man has in superabundance is owed, of natural right, to the poor for their sustenance. So Ambrosius says, and it is also to be found in the *Decretum Gratiani*: "The bread which you withhold belongs to the hungry; the clothing you shut away, to the naked; and the money you bury in the earth is the redemption and freedom of the penniless."[4]

I now want to consider a number of points, more practical than philosophical, which are relevant to the application of the moral conclusion we have reached. These points challenge not the

idea that we ought to be doing all we can to prevent starvation, but the idea that giving away a great deal of money is the best means to this end.

It is sometimes said that overseas aid should be a government responsibility, and that therefore one ought not to give to privately run charities. Giving privately, it is said, allows the government and the noncontributing members of society to escape their responsibilities.

This argument seems to assume that the more people there are who give to privately organized famine relief funds, the less likely it is that the government will take over full responsibility for such aid. This assumption is unsupported, and does not strike me as at all plausible. The opposite view—that if no one gives voluntarily, a government will assume that its citizens are uninterested in famine relief and would not wish to be forced into giving aid—seems more plausible. In any case, unless there were a definite probability that by refusing to give one would be helping to bring about massive government assistance, people who do refuse to make voluntary contributions are refusing to prevent a certain amount of suffering, without being able to point to any tangible beneficial consequence of their refusal. So the onus of showing how their refusal will bring about government action is on those who refuse to give.

I do not, of course, want to dispute the contention that governments of affluent nations should be giving many times the amount of genuine, no-strings-attached aid that they are giving now. I agree, too, that giving privately is not enough, and that we ought to be campaigning actively for entirely new standards for both public and private contributions to famine relief. Indeed, I would sympathize with someone who thought that campaigning was more important than giving oneself, although I doubt whether preaching what one does not practice would be very effective. Unfortunately, for many people the idea that "it's the government's responsibility" is a reason for not giving which does not appear to entail any political action either.

Another more serious reason for not giving to famine relief funds is that until there is effective population control, relieving famine merely postpones starvation. If we save the Bengal refugees now, others, perhaps the children of these refugees, will face starvation in a few years' time. In support of all this, one may cite the now well-known facts about the population explosion and the relatively limited scope for expanded production.

This point, like the previous one, is an argument against relieving suffering that is happening now, because of a belief about what might happen in the future; it is unlike the previous point in that very good evidence can be adduced in support of this belief about the future. I will not go into the evidence here. I accept that the earth cannot support indefinitely a population rising at the present rate. This certainly poses a problem for anyone who thinks it important to prevent famine. Again, however, one could accept the argument without drawing the conclusion that it absolves one from any obligation to do anything to prevent famine. The conclusion that should be drawn is that the best means of preventing famine, in the long run, is population control. It would then follow from the position reached earlier that one ought to be doing all one can to promote population control (unless one held that all forms of population control were wrong in themselves, or would have significantly bad consequences). Since there are organizations working specifically for population control, one would then support them rather than more orthodox methods of preventing famine.

A third point raised by the conclusion reached earlier relates to the question of just how much we all ought to be giving away. One possibility, which has already been mentioned, is that we ought to give until we reach the level of marginal utility—that is, the level at which, by giving more, I would cause as much suffering to myself or my dependents as I would relieve by my gift. This would mean, of course, that one would reduce oneself to very near the material circumstances of a Bengali refugee. It will be recalled that earlier I put forward both a strong and a moderate version of the principle of preventing bad occurrences. The strong version, which required us to prevent bad things from happening unless in doing so we would be sacrificing something of comparable moral significance, does seem to require reducing ourselves to the level of marginal utility. I should also say that the strong version seems to me to be the correct one. I proposed the more moderate version—that we should prevent bad occurrences unless, to do so, we had to sacrifice something morally significant—only in order to show that even on this surely undeniable principle a great change in our way of life is required. On the more moderate principle, it may not follow that we ought to reduce ourselves to the level of marginal utility, for one might hold that to reduce oneself and one's family to this level is to cause something significantly bad to happen. Whether this is so I shall not discuss, since, as I have said, I can see no good reason for holding the moderate version of the principle rather than the strong version. Even if we accepted the principle only in its moderate form, however, it should be clear that we would have to give away enough to ensure that the consumer society, dependent as it is on people spending on trivia rather than giving to famine relief, would slow down and perhaps disappear entirely. There are several reasons why this would be desirable in itself. The value and necessity of economic growth are now being questioned not only by conservationists, but by economists as well.[5] There is no doubt, too, that the consumer society has had a distorting effect on the goals and purposes of its members. Yet looking at the matter purely from the point of view of overseas aid, there must be a limit to the extent to which we should deliberately slow down our economy; for it might be the case that if we gave away, say, forty percent of our Gross National Product, we would slow down the economy so much that in absolute terms we would be giving less than if we gave twenty-five percent of the much larger GNP that we would have if we limited our contribution to this smaller percentage.

I mention this only as an indication of the sort of factor that one would have to take into account in working out an ideal. Since Western societies generally consider one percent of the GNP an acceptable level for overseas aid, the matter is entirely academic. Nor does it affect the question of how much an individual should give in a society in which very few are giving substantial amounts.

It is sometimes said, though less often now than it used to be, that philosophers have no special role to play in public affairs, since most public issues depend primarily on an assessment of facts. On questions of fact, it is said, philosophers as such have no special expertise, and so it has been possible to engage in philosophy without committing oneself to any position on major public issues. No doubt there are some issues of social policy and foreign policy about which it can truly be said that a really expert assessment of the facts is required before taking sides or acting, but the issue of famine is surely not one of these. The facts about the existence of suffering are beyond dispute. Nor, I think, is it disputed that we can do something about it, either through orthodox methods of famine relief or through population control or both. This is therefore an issue on which philosophers are competent to take a position. The issue is one which faces everyone who has more money than he needs to support himself and his dependents, or who is in a position to take some sort of political action. These categories must include practically every teacher and student of philosophy in the universities of the Western world. If philosophy is to deal with matters that are relevant to both teachers and students, this is an issue that philosophers should discuss.

Discussion, though, is not enough. What is the point of relating philosophy to public (and personal) affairs if we do not take our conclusions seriously? In this instance, taking our conclusion seriously means acting upon it. The philosopher will not find it any easier than anyone else to alter his attitudes and way of life to the extent that, if I am right, is involved in doing everything that we ought to be doing. At the very least, though, one can make a start. The philosopher who does so will have to sacrifice some of the benefits of the consumer society, but he can find compensation in the satisfaction of a way of life in which theory and practice, if not yet in harmony, are at least coming together.

NOTES

1. There was also a third possibility: that India would go to war to enable the refugees to return to their lands. Since I wrote this paper, India has taken this way out. The situation is no longer that described above, but this does not affect my argument, as the next paragraph indicates.

2. In view of the special sense philosophers often give to the term, I should say that I use "obligation" simply as the abstract noun derived from "ought," so that "I have an obligation to" means no more, and no less, than "I ought to." This usage is in accordance with the definition of "ought" given by the *Shorter Oxford English Dictionary*: "the general verb to express duty or obligation." I do not think any issue of substance hangs on the way the term is used; sentences in which I use "obligation" could all be rewritten, although somewhat clumsily, as sentences in which a clause containing "ought" replaces the term "obligation."

3. J. O. Urmson, "Saints and Heroes," in *Essays in Moral Philosophy*, ed., Abraham I. Melden (Seattle and London, 1958), p. 214. For a related but significantly different view see also Henry Sidgwick, *The Methods of Ethics*, 7th edn. (London, 1907), pp. 220–221, 492–493.

4. *Summa Theologica*, II-II, Question 66, Article 7, in *Aquinas, Selected Political Writings*, ed. A. P. d'Entreves, trans. J. G. Dawson (Oxford, 1948), p. 171.

5. See, for instance, John Kenneth Galbraith, *The New Industrial State* (Boston, 1967); and E. J. Mishan, *The Costs of Economic Growth* (London, 1967).

☥ REVIEW QUESTIONS

1. According to Singer, what are the moral implications of the situation that occurred in East Bengal?

2. What is Singer's first moral principle?

3. What is the second principle? Distinguish between the two different versions of this principle.

4. Explain Singer's view of the distinction between duty and charity.

5. What is the Sidgwick–Urmson line of argument? How does Singer respond to it?

6. What is the criticism of utilitarianism? How does Singer reply?

7. What are Singer's conclusions?

<ins>DISCUSSION QUESTIONS</ins>

1. Toward the end of his essay, Singer says that it would be desirable in itself if the consumer society would disappear. Do you agree? Why or why not?
2. What does the phrase "morally significant" in the weak version of the second principle mean? See if you can give a clear definition of this crucial phrase.
3. Singer grants that "until there is effective population control, relieving famine merely postpones starvation." Is this a good reason for not giving aid to countries that refuse to adopt any measures to control population? What is your view?
4. Singer attacks the traditional distinction between duty and charity. Is there any way to save the distinction? How?
5. Is Singer a utilitarian? Why or why not?

Living on a Lifeboat

GARRETT HARDIN

Garrett Hardin (1915–2003) was professor of biology at the University of California at Santa Barbara. He was the author of nine books and more than fifteen articles. His books include *The Limits of Altruism: An Ecologist's View of Survival* (1977); *Living within Limits: Ecology, Economics, and Population Taboos* (1993); and most recently, *The Ostrich Factor: Our Population Myopia* (1999).

Hardin uses the metaphor of a lifeboat to argue that rich nations such as the United States do not have any moral obligation to help poor nations with needy people. He claims that aid to the poor in the form of food just makes matters worse; it results in more population growth, which in turn leads to a tragedy of the commons, that is, a destruction of natural resources caused by overuse.

Susanne Langer (1942) has shown that it is probably impossible to approach an unsolved problem save through the door of metaphor. Later, attempting to meet the demands of rigor, we may achieve some success in cleansing theory of metaphor, though our success is limited if we are unable to avoid using common language, which is shot through and through with fossil metaphors. (I count no less than five in the preceding two sentences.)

Since metaphorical thinking is inescapable it is pointless merely to weep about our human limitations. We must learn to live with them, to understand them, and to control them. "All of us," said George Eliot in *Middlemarch*, "get our thoughts entangled in metaphors, and act fatally on the strength of them." To avoid unconscious suicide we are well advised to pit one metaphor against another. From the interplay of competitive metaphors, thoroughly developed, we may come closer to metaphor-free solutions to our problems.

No generation has viewed the problem of the survival of the human species as seriously as we have. Inevitably, we have entered this world of concern through the door of metaphor. Environmentalists have emphasized the image of the earth as a spaceship—Spaceship Earth. Kenneth Boulding (1966) is the principal architect of this metaphor. It is time, he says, that we replace the wasteful "cowboy economy" of the past with the frugal "spaceship economy" required for

Source: "Living on a Lifeboat" by Garrett Hardin from *Bioscience*, Vol. 24, 1974, pp. 561–568. Washington, DC: American Institute of Biological Sciences.

continued survival in the limited world we now see ours to be. The metaphor is notably useful in justifying pollution control measures.

Unfortunately, the image of a spaceship is also used to promote measures that are suicidal. One of these is a generous immigration policy, which is only a particular instance of a class of policies that are in error because they lead to the tragedy of the commons (Hardin 1968). These suicidal policies are attractive because they mesh with what we unthinkingly take to be the ideals of "the best people." What is missing in the idealistic view is an insistence that rights and responsibilities must go together. The "generous" attitude of all too many people results in asserting inalienable rights while ignoring or denying matching responsibilities.

For the metaphor of a spaceship to be correct, the aggregate of people on board would have to be under unitary sovereign control (Ophuls 1974). A true ship always has a captain. It is conceivable that a ship could be run by a committee. But it could not possibly survive if its course were determined by bickering tribes that claimed rights without responsibilities.

What about Spaceship Earth? It certainly has no captain, and no executive committee. The United Nations is a toothless tiger, because the signatories of its charter wanted it that way. The spaceship metaphor is used only to justify spaceship demands on common resources without acknowledging corresponding spaceship responsibilities.

An understandable fear of decisive action leads people to embrace "incrementalism"— moving toward reform by tiny stages. As we shall see, this strategy is counterproductive in the area discussed here if it means accepting rights before responsibilities. Where human survival is at stake, the acceptance of responsibilities is a precondition to the acceptance of rights, if the two cannot be introduced simultaneously.

LIFEBOAT ETHICS

Before taking up certain substantive issues let us look at an alternative metaphor, that of a lifeboat. In developing some relevant examples the following numerical values are assumed. Approximately two-thirds of the world is desperately poor, and only one-third is comparatively rich. The people in poor countries have an average per capita GNP (Gross National Product) of about $200 per year, the rich, of about $3,000. (For the United States it is nearly $5,000 per year.) Metaphorically, each rich nation amounts to a lifeboat full of comparatively rich people. The poor of the world are in other, much more crowded, lifeboats. Continuously, so to speak, the poor fall out of their lifeboats and swim for a while in the water outside, hoping to be admitted to a rich lifeboat, or in some other way to benefit from the "goodies" on board. What should the passengers on a rich lifeboat do? This is the central problem of "the ethics of a lifeboat."

First we must acknowledge that each lifeboat is effectively limited in capacity. The land of every nation has a limited carrying capacity. The exact limit is a matter for argument, but the energy crunch is convincing more people every day that we have already exceeded the carrying capacity of the land. We have been living on "capital"— stored petroleum and coal—and soon we must live on income alone.

Let us look at only one lifeboat: ours. The ethical problem is the same for all, and is as follows. Here we sit, say 50 people in a lifeboat. To be generous, let us assume our boat has a capacity of 10 more, making 60. (This, however, is to violate the engineering principle of the "safety factor." A new plant disease or a bad change in the weather may decimate our population if we don't preserve some excess capacity as a safety factor.)

The 50 of us in the lifeboat see 100 others swimming in the water outside, asking for admission to the boat, or for handouts. How shall we respond to their calls?

There are several possibilities.

One. We may be tempted to try to live by the Christian ideal of being "our brother's keeper," or by the Marxian ideal (Marx 1875) of "from each according to his abilities, to each according to his needs." Since the needs of all are the same, we take all the needy into our boat, making a total of 150 in a boat with a capacity of 60. The boat is swamped, and everyone drowns. Complete justice, complete catastrophe.

Two. Since the boat has an unused excess capacity of 10, we admit just 10 more to it. This has the disadvantage of getting rid of the safety factor, for which action we will sooner or later pay dearly. Moreover, which 10 do we let in? "First come, first served?" The best 10? The neediest 10? How do we *discriminate*? And what do we say to the 90 who are excluded?

Three. Admit no more to the boat and preserve the small safety factor. Survival of the people in the lifeboat is then possible (though we shall have to be on our guard against boarding parties).

The last solution is abhorrent to many people. It is unjust, they say. Let us grant that it is.

"I feel guilty about my good luck," say some. The reply to this is simple: *Get out and yield your place to others.* Such a selfless action might satisfy the conscience of those who are addicted to guilt but it would not change the ethics of the lifeboat. The needy person to whom a guilt-addict yields his place will not himself feel guilty about his sudden good luck. (If he did he would not climb aboard.) The net result of conscience-stricken people relinquishing their unjustly held positions is the elimination of their kind of conscience from the lifeboat. The lifeboat, as it were, purifies itself of guilt. The ethics of the lifeboat persist, unchanged by such momentary aberrations.

This then is the basic metaphor within which we must work out our solutions. Let us enrich the image step by step with substantive additions from the real world.

REPRODUCTION

The harsh characteristics of lifeboat ethics are heightened by reproduction, particularly by reproductive differences. The people inside the lifeboats of the wealthy nations are doubling in numbers every 87 years; those outside are doubling every 35 years, on the average. And the relative difference in prosperity is becoming greater.

Let us, for a while, think primarily of the U.S. lifeboat. As of 1973, the United States had a population of 210 million people who were increasing by 0.8% per year, that is, doubling in number every 87 years.

Although the citizens of rich nations are outnumbered two to one by the poor, let us imagine an equal number of poor people outside our lifeboat—a mere 210 million poor people reproducing at a quite different rate. If we imagine these to be the combined populations of Colombia, Venezuela, Ecuador, Morocco, Thailand, Pakistan, and the Philippines, the average rate of increase of the people "outside" is a 3.3% per year. The doubling time of this population is 21 years.

Suppose that all these countries, and the United States, agreed to live by the Marxian ideal, "to each according to his needs," the ideal of most Christians as well. Needs, of course, are determined by population size, which is affected by reproduction. Every nation regards its rate of reproduction as a sovereign right. If our lifeboat were big enough in the beginning it might be possible to live *for a while* by Christian-Marxian ideals. *Might.*

Initially, in the model given, the ratio of non-Americans to Americans would be one to one. But consider what the ratio would be 87 years later. By this time Americans would have doubled to a population of 420 million. The other group (doubling every 21 years) would now have swollen to 3,540 million. Each American would have more than eight people to share with. How could the lifeboat possibly keep afloat?

All this involves extrapolation of current trends into the future and is consequently suspect. Trends may change. Granted, but the change will not necessarily be favorable. If,—as seems likely—the rate of population increase falls faster in the ethnic group presently inside the lifeboat than it does among those now outside, the future will turn out to be even worse than mathematics predicts, and sharing will be even more suicidal.

RUIN IN THE COMMONS

The fundamental error of the sharing ethics is that it leads to the tragedy of the commons. Under a system of private property the man (or group of men) who own property recognize their responsibility to care for it, for if they don't they will eventually suffer. A farmer, for instance, if he is intelligent, will allow no more cattle in a pasture than its carrying capacity justifies. If he overloads the pasture, weeds take over, erosion sets in, and the owner loses in the long run.

But if a pasture is run as a commons open to all, the right of each to use it is not matched by an operational responsibility to take care of it. It is no use asking independent herdsmen in a commons to act responsibly, for they dare not. The considerate herdsman who refrains from overloading the commons suffers more than a selfish one who says his needs are greater. (As Leo Durocher says, "Nice guys finish last.") Christian-Marxian idealism is counterproductive. That it *sounds* nice is no excuse. With distribution systems, as with individual morality, good intentions are no substitute for good performance.

A social system is stable only if it is insensitive to errors. To the Christian-Marxian idealist a selfish person is a sort of "error." Prosperity in the system of the commons cannot survive errors. If *everyone* would only restrain himself, all would be well; but it takes *only one less than everyone* to ruin a system of voluntary restraint. In a crowded world of less than perfect human beings—and we will never know any other—mutual ruin is inevitable in the commons. This is the core of the tragedy of the commons.

One of the major tasks of education today is to create such an awareness of the dangers of the commons that people will be able to recognize its many varieties, however disguised. There is pollution of the air and water because these media are treated as commons. Further growth of population and growth in the per capita conversion of natural resources into pollutants require that the system of the commons be modified or abandoned in the disposal of "externalities."

The fish populations of the oceans are exploited as commons, and ruin lies ahead. No technological invention can prevent this fate: in fact, all improvements in the art of fishing merely hasten the day of complete ruin. Only the replacement of the system of the commons with a responsible system can save oceanic fisheries.

The management of western rangelands, though nominally rational, is in fact (under the steady pressure of cattle ranchers) often merely a government-sanctioned system of the commons, drifting toward ultimate ruin for both the rangelands and the residual enterprisers.

WORLD FOOD BANKS

In the international arena we have recently heard a proposal to create a new commons, namely an international depository of food reserves to which nations will contribute according to their abilities, and from which nations may draw according to their needs. Nobel laureate Norman Borlaug has lent the prestige of his name to this proposal.

A world food bank appeals powerfully to our humanitarian impulses. We remember John Donne's celebrated line, "Any man's death diminishes me." But before we rush out to see for whom the bell tolls, let us recognize where the greatest political push for international granaries comes from, lest we be disillusioned later. Our experience with Public Law 480 clearly reveals the answer. This was the law that moved billions of dollars worth of U.S. grain to food-short, population-long countries during the past two decades. When P. L. 480 first came into being, a headline in the business magazine *Forbes* (Paddock and Paddock 1970) revealed the power behind it: "Feeding the World's Hungry Millions: How It Will Mean Billions for U.S. Business."

And indeed it did. In the years 1960 to 1970 a total of $7.9 billion was spent on the "Food for Peace" program, as P. L. 480 was called. During the years 1948 to 1970 an additional $49.9 billion were extracted from American taxpayers to pay for other economic aid programs, some of which went for food and food-producing machinery. (This figure does not include military aid.) That P. L. 480 was a give-away program was concealed. Recipient countries went through the motions of paying for P. L. 480 food—with IOUs. In December 1973 the charade was brought to an end as far as India was concerned when the United States "forgave" India's $3.2 billion debt (Anonymous 1974). Public announcement of the cancellation of the debt was delayed for two months; one wonders why.

"Famine—1974!" (Paddock and Paddock 1970) is one of the few publications that points out the commercial roots of this humanitarian attempt. Though all U.S. taxpayers lost by P. L. 480, special interest groups gained handsomely. Farmers benefited because they were not asked to contribute the grain—it was bought from them by the taxpayers. Besides the direct benefit there was the indirect effect of increasing demand and thus raising prices of farm products generally. The manufacturers of farm machinery, fertilizers, and pesticides benefited by the farmers' extra efforts to grow more food. Grain elevators profited from storing the grain for varying lengths of time. Railroads made money hauling it to port, and shipping lines by carrying it overseas. Moreover, once the machinery for P. L. 480 was established, an immense bureaucracy had a vested interest in its continuance regardless of its merits.

Very little was ever heard of these selfish interests when P. L. 480 was defended in public. The emphasis was always on its humanitarian effects. The combination of multiple and relatively silent selfish interests with highly vocal humanitarian apologists constitutes a powerful lobby for extracting money from taxpayers. Foreign aid has become a habit that can apparently survive in the absence of any known justification. A news commentator in a weekly magazine (Lansner 1974), after exhaustively going over all the conventional arguments for foreign aid—self-interest, social justice, political advantage, and charity—and concluding that none of the known arguments really held water, concluded: "So the search continues for some logically compelling reasons for giving aid. . . ." In other words, Act now, Justify later—if ever. (Apparently a quarter of a century is too short a time to find the justification for expending several billion dollars yearly.)

The search for a rational justification can be short-circuited by interjecting the word "emergency." Borlaug uses this word. We need to look sharply at it. What is an "emergency"? It is surely something like an accident, which is correctly defined as *an event that is certain to happen, though with a low frequency* (Hardin 1972a). A well-run organization prepares for everything that is certain, including accidents and emergencies. It budgets for them. It saves for them. It expects them—and mature decision-makers do not waste time complaining about accidents when they occur.

What happens if some organizations budget for emergencies and other do not? If each organization is solely responsible for its own well-being, poorly managed ones will suffer. But they should be able to learn from experience. They have a chance to mend their ways and learn to budget for infrequent but certain emergencies. The weather, for instance, always varies and periodic crop failures are certain. A wise and competent government saves out of the production of the good years in anticipation of bad years that are sure to come. This is not a new idea. The Bible tells us that Joseph taught this policy to Pharaoh in Egypt more than two thousand years ago. Yet it is literally true that the vast majority of the governments of the world today have no such policy. They lack either the wisdom or the competence, or both. Far more difficult than the transfer of wealth from one country to another is the transfer of wisdom between sovereign powers or between generations.

"But it isn't their fault! How can we blame the poor people who are caught in an emergency? Why must we punish them?" The concepts of blame and punishment are irrelevant. The question is, what are the operational consequences of establishing a world food bank? If it is open to every country every time a need develops, slovenly rulers will not be motivated to take Joseph's advice. Why should they? Others will bail them out whenever they are in trouble.

Some countries will make deposits in the world food bank and others will withdraw from it: There will be almost no overlap. Calling such a depository-transfer unit a "bank" is stretching the metaphor of bank beyond its elastic limits. The proposers, of course, never call attention to the metaphorical nature of the word they use.

THE RATCHET EFFECT

An "international food bank" is really, then, not a true bank but a disguised one-way transfer device for moving wealth from rich countries to poor. In the absence of such a bank, in a world inhabited by individually responsible sovereign nations, the population of each nation would repeatedly go through a cycle of the sort shown in Figure 1. P_2 is greater than P_1, either in absolute numbers or because a deterioration of the food supply has removed the safety factor and produced a dangerously low ratio of resources to population. P_2 may be said to represent a state of overpopulation, which becomes obvious upon the appearance of an "accident," e.g., a crop failure. If the "emergency" is not met by outside help, the population drops back to the "normal" level—the "carrying capacity" of the environment or even below. In the absence of population control by a sovereign, sooner or later the population grows to P_2 again and the cycle repeats. The long-term population curve (Hardin 1966) is an irregularly fluctuating one, equilibrating more or less about the carrying capacity.

A demographic cycle of this sort obviously involves great suffering in the restrictive phase, but such a cycle is normal to any independent country with inadequate population control. The third century theologian Tertullian (Hardin 1969a) expressed what must have been the recognition of many wise men when he wrote: *"The scourges of pestilence, famine, wars, and earthquakes have come to be regarded as a blessing to overcrowded nations, since they serve to prune away the luxuriant growth of the human race."*

Only under a strong and farsighted sovereign—which theoretically could be the people themselves, democratically organized—can a population equilibrate at some set point below the carrying capacity, thus avoiding the pains normally caused by periodic and unavoidable disasters. For this happy state to be achieved it is necessary that those in power be able to contemplate with equanimity the "waste" of surplus food in times of bountiful harvests. It is essential that those in power resist the temptation to convert extra food into extra babies. On the public relations level it is necessary that the phrase "surplus food" be replaced by "safety factor."

But wise sovereigns seem not to exist in the poor world today.

The most anguishing problems are created by poor countries that are governed by rulers insufficiently wise and powerful. If such countries can draw on a world food bank in times of "emergency," the population *cycle* of Figure 1 will be replaced by the population escalator of Figure 2. The input of food from a food bank acts as the pawl of a ratchet, preventing the population from retracing its steps to a lower level. Reproduction pushes the population upward, inputs from the World Food Bank prevent its moving downward. Population size escalates, as does the absolute magnitude of "accidents" and "emergencies." The process is brought to an end only by the total collapse of the whole system, producing a catastrophe of scarcely imaginable proportions.

Such are the implications of the well-meant sharing of food in a world of irresponsible reproduction.

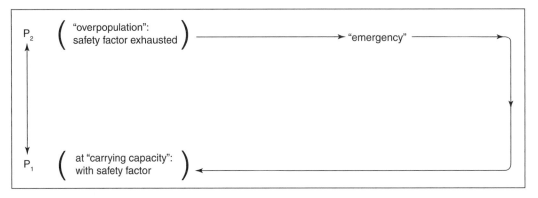

FIGURE 1. The population cycle of a nation that has no effective, conscious population control, and which receives no aid from the outside. P_2 is greater than P_1.

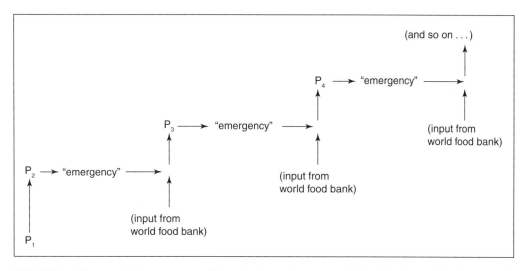

FIGURE 2. The population escalator. Note that input from a world food bank acts like the pawl of a ratchet, preserving the normal population cycle shown in Figure 1 from being completed. P_{n+1} is greater than P_n, and the absolute magnitude of the "emergencies" escalates. Ultimately the entire system crashes. The crash is not shown, and few can imagine it.

I think we need a new word for systems like this. The adjective "melioristic" is applied to systems that produce continual improvement; the English word is derived from the Latin *meliorare*, to become or make better. Parallel with this it would be useful to bring in the word *pejoristic* (from the Latin *pejorare*, to become or make worse). This word can be applied to those systems which, by their very nature, can be relied upon to make matters worse. A world food bank coupled with sovereign state irresponsibility in reproduction is an example of a pejoristic system.

This pejoristic system creates an unacknowledged commons. People have more motivation to draw from than to add to the common store. The license to make such withdrawals diminishes whatever motivation poor countries might otherwise have to control their populations. Under the guidance of this ratchet, wealth can be steadily moved in one direction only, from the slowly-breeding rich to the rapidly-breeding poor, the process finally coming to a halt only when all countries are equally and miserably poor.

All this is terribly obvious once we are acutely aware of the pervasiveness and danger of the commons. But many people still lack this awareness

and the euphoria of the "benign demographic transition" (Hardin 1973) interferes with the realistic appraisal of pejoristic mechanisms. As concerns public policy, the deductions drawn from the benign demographic transition are these:

1. If the per capita GNP rises the birth rate will fall; hence, the rate of population increase will fall, ultimately producing ZPG (Zero Population Growth).

2. The long-term trend all over the world (including the poor countries) is of a rising per capita GNP (for which no limit is seen).

3. Therefore, all political interference in population matters is unnecessary; all we need to do is foster economic "development"—note the metaphor—and population problems will solve themselves.

Those who believe in the benign demographic transition dismiss the pejoristic mechanism of Figure 2 in the belief that each input of food from the world outside fosters development within a poor country thus resulting in a drop in the rate of population increase. Foreign aid has proceeded on this assumption for more than two decades. Unfortunately, it has produced no indubitable instance of the asserted effect. It has, however, produced a library of excuses. The air is filled with plaintive calls for more massive foreign aid appropriations so that the hypothetical melioristic process can get started.

The doctrine of demographic laissez-faire implicit in the hypothesis of the benign demographic transition is immensely attractive. Unfortunately there is more evidence against the melioristic system than there is for it (Davis 1963). On the historical side there are many counterexamples. The rise in per capita GNP in France and Ireland during the past century has been accompanied by a rise in population growth. In the 20 years following the Second World War the same positive correlation was noted almost everywhere in the world. Never in world history before 1950 did the worldwide population growth reach 1% per annum. Now the average population growth is over 2% and shows no signs of slackening.

On the theoretical side, the denial of the pejoristic scheme of Figure 2 probably springs from the hidden acceptance of the "cowboy economy" that Boulding castigated. Those who recognize the limitations of a spaceship, if they are unable to achieve population control at a safe and comfortable level, accept the necessity of the corrective feedback of the population cycle shown in Figure 1. No one who knew in his bones that he was living on a true spaceship would countenance political support of the population escalator shown in Figure 2.

ECO-DESTRUCTION VIA THE GREEN REVOLUTION

The demoralizing effect of charity on the recipient has long been known. "Give a man a fish and he will eat for a day; teach him how to fish and he will eat for the rest of his days." So runs an ancient Chinese proverb. Acting on this advice the Rockefeller and Ford Foundations have financed a multipronged program for improving agriculture in the hungry nations. The result, known as the "Green Revolution," has been quite remarkable. "Miracle wheat" and "miracle rice" are splendid technological achievements in the realm of plant genetics.

Observant critics have shown how much harm we wealthy nations have already done to poor nations through our well-intentioned but misguided attempts to help them.

Whether or not the Green Revolution can increase food production is doubtful (Harris 1972, Paddock 1970, Wilkes 1972), but in any event not particularly important. What is missing in this great and well-meaning humanitarian effort is a firm grasp of fundamentals. Considering the importance of the Rockefeller Foundation in this effort it is ironic that the late Alan Gregg, a much-respected vice-president of the Foundation, strongly expressed his doubts of the wisdom of all attempts to increase food production some two decades ago. (This was before Borlaug's work—supported by Rockefeller—had resulted in the development of "miracle wheat.") Gregg (1955) likened the growth and spreading of humanity over the surface of the earth to the metastasis of cancer in the human body, wryly remarking that "Cancerous growths demand food; but, as far as I know, they have never been cured by getting it."

"Man does not live by bread alone"—the scriptural statement has a rich meaning even in the material realm. Every human being born constitutes a draft on all aspects of the environment—food, air, water, unspoiled scenery, occasional and optional solitude, beaches, contact with wild animals, fishing, hunting—the list is long and incompletely known. Food can, perhaps, be significantly increased: but what about clean beaches, unspoiled forests, and solitude? If we satisfy the need for food in a growing population we necessarily decrease the supply of other goods, and thereby increase the difficulty of equitably allocating scarce goods (Hardin 1969b, 1972b).

The present population of India is 600 million, and it is increasing by 15 million per year. The environmental load of this population is already great. The forests of India are only a small fraction of what they were three centuries ago. Soil erosion, floods, and the psychological costs of crowding are serious. Every one of the net 15 million lives added each year stresses the Indian environment more severely. *Every life saved this year in a poor country diminishes the quality of life for subsequent generations.*

Observant critics have shown how much harm we wealthy nations have already done to poor nations through our well-intentioned but misguided attempts to help them (Paddock and Paddock 1973). Particularly reprehensible is our failure to carry out post-audits of these attempts (Farvar and Milton 1972). Thus have we shielded our tender consciences from knowledge of the harm we have done. Must we Americans continue to fail to monitor the consequences of our external "do-gooding"? If, for instance, we thoughtlessly make it possible for the present 600 million Indians to swell to 1,200 million by the year 2001—as their present growth rate promises—will posterity in India thank us for facilitating an even greater destruction of their Environment? Are good intentions ever a sufficient excuse for bad consequences?

IMMIGRATION CREATES A COMMONS

I come now to the final example of a commons in action, one for which the public is least prepared for rational discussion. The topic is at present enveloped by a great silence which reminds me of a comment made by Sherlock Holmes in A. Conan Doyle's story "Silver Blaze." Inspector Gregory had asked, "Is there any point to which you would wish to draw my attention?" To this Holmes responded:

> "To the curious incident of the dog in the night-time."
> "The dog did nothing in the nighttime," said the Inspector.
> "That was the curious incident," remarked Sherlock Holmes.

By asking himself what would repress the normal barking instinct of a watchdog, Holmes realized that it must be the dog's recognition of his master as the criminal trespasser. In a similar way we should ask ourselves what repression keeps us from discussing something as important as immigration.

It cannot be that immigration is numerically of no consequence. Our government acknowledges a net inflow of 400,000 a year. Hard data are understandably lacking on the extent of illegal entries, but a not implausible figure is

600,000 per year (Buchanan 1973). The natural increase of the resident population is now about 1.7 million per year. This means that the yearly gain from immigration is at least 19%, and may be 37%, of the total increase. It is quite conceivable that educational campaigns like that of Zero Population Growth, Inc., coupled with adverse social and economic factors—inflation, housing shortage, depression, and loss of confidence in national leaders—may lower the fertility of American women to a point at which all of the yearly increase in population would be accounted for by immigration. Should we not at least ask if that is what we want? How curious it is that we so seldom discuss immigration these days!

Curious, but understandable—as one finds out the moment he publicly questions the wisdom of the status quo in immigration. He who does so is promptly charged with *isolationism, bigotry, prejudice, ethnocentrism, chauvinism,* and *selfishness.* These are hard accusations to bear. It is pleasanter to talk about other matters, leaving immigration policy to wallow in the crosscurrents of special interests that take no account of the good of the whole—*or of the interests of posterity.*

We Americans have a bad conscience because of things we said in the past about immigrants. Two generations ago the popular press was rife with references to *Dagos, Wops, Polacks, Japs, Chinks, and Krauts*—all pejorative terms which failed to acknowledge our indebtedness to Goya, Leonardo, Copernicus, Hiroshige, Confucius, and Bach. Because the implied inferiority of foreigners was *then* the justification for keeping them out, it is now thoughtlessly assumed that restrictive policies can only be based on the assumption of immigrant inferiority. *This is not so.*

Existing immigration laws exclude idiots and known criminals; future laws will almost certainly continue this policy. But should we also consider the quality of the average immigrant, as compared with the quality of the average resident? Perhaps we should, perhaps we shouldn't. (What is "quality" anyway?) But the quality issue is not our concern here.

From this point on, it will be assumed that *immigrants and native-born citizens are of exactly equal quality*, however quality may be defined. The focus is only on quantity. The conclusions reached depend on nothing else, so all charges of ethnocentrism are irrelevant.

World food banks move food to the people, thus facilitating the exhaustion of the environment of the poor. By contrast, unrestricted immigration moves people to the food, thus speeding up the destruction of the environment in rich countries. Why poor people should want to make this transfer is no mystery; but why should rich hosts encourage it? This transfer, like the reverse one, is supported by both selfish interests and humanitarian impulses.

The principal selfish interest in unimpeded immigration is easy to identify: It is the interest of the employers of cheap labor, particularly that needed for degrading jobs. We have been deceived about the forces of history by the lines of Emma Lazarus inscribed [inside the entrance to] the Statue of Liberty:

> *Give me your tired, your poor*
> *Your huddled masses yearning to breathe free,*
> *The wretched refuse of your teeming shore,*
> *Send these, the homeless, tempest-tossed, to me:*
> *I lift my lamp beside the golden door.*

The image is one of an infinitely generous earth-mother, passively opening her arms to hordes of immigrants who come here on their own initiative. Such an image may have been adequate for the early days of colonization, but by the time these lines were written (1886) the force for immigration was largely manufactured inside our own borders by factory and mine owners who sought cheap labor not to be found among laborers already here. One group of foreigners after another was thus enticed into the United States to work at wretched jobs for wretched wages.

At present, it is largely the Mexicans who are being so exploited. It is particularly to the advantage of certain employers that there be many illegal immigrants. Illegal immigrant workers dare not complain about their working conditions for fear of being repatriated. Their presence reduces the bargaining power of all Mexican-American laborers. Cesar Chavez has repeatedly pleaded with congressional committees

to close the doors to more Mexicans so that those here can negotiate effectively for higher wages and decent working conditions. Chavez understands the ethics of a lifeboat.

The interests of the employers of cheap labor are well served by the silence of the intelligentsia of the country. WASPS—White Anglo-Saxon Protestants—are particularly reluctant to call for a closing of the doors to immigration for fear of being called ethnocentric bigots. It was, therefore, an occasion of pure delight for this particular WASP to be present at a meeting when the points he would like to have made were made better by a non-WASP, speaking to other non-WASPS. It was in Hawaii, and most of the people in the room were second-level Hawaiian officials of Japanese ancestry. All Hawaiians are keenly aware of the limits of their environment, and the speaker had asked how it might be practically and constitutionally possible to close the doors to more immigrants to the islands. (To Hawaiians, immigrants from the other 49 states are as much of a threat as those from other nations. There is only so much room in the islands, and the islanders know it. Sophistical arguments that imply otherwise do not impress them.)

Yet the Japanese-Americans of Hawaii have active ties with the land of their origin. This point was raised by a Japanese-American member of the audience who asked the Japanese-American speaker: "But how can we shut the doors now? We have many friends and relations in Japan that we'd like to bring to Hawaii some day so that they can enjoy this land."

The speaker smiled sympathetically and responded slowly: "Yes, but we have children now and someday we'll have grandchildren. We can bring more people here from Japan only by giving away some of the land that we hope to pass on to our grandchildren some day. What right do we have to do that?"

To be generous with one's own possessions is one thing; to be generous with posterity's is quite another. This, I think, is the point that must be gotten across to those who would, from a commendable love of distributive justice, institute a ruinous system of the commons, either in the form of a world food bank or that of unrestricted immigration. Since every speaker is a member of some ethnic group it is always possible to charge him with ethnocentrism. But even after purging an argument of ethnocentrism the rejection of the commons is still valid and necessary if we are to save at least some parts of the world from environmental ruin. Is it not desirable that at least some of the grandchildren of people now living should have a decent place in which to live?

THE ASYMMETRY OF DOOR-SHUTTING

We must now answer this telling point: "How can you justify slamming the door once you're inside?" You say that immigrants should be kept out. But aren't we all immigrants, or the descendants of immigrants? Since we refuse to leave, must we not, as a matter of justice and symmetry, admit all others?"

It is literally true that we Americans of non-Indian ancestry are the descendants of thieves. Should we not, then, "give back" the land to the Indians; that is, give it to the now-living Americans of Indian ancestry? As an exercise in pure logic I see no way to reject this proposal. Yet I am unwilling to live by it; and I know no one who is. Our reluctance to embrace pure justice may spring from pure selfishness. On the other hand, it may arise from an unspoken recognition of consequences that have not yet been clearly spelled out.

Suppose, becoming intoxicated with pure justice, we "Anglos" should decide to turn our land over to the Indians. Since all our other wealth has also been derived from the land, we would have to give that to the Indians, too. Then what would we non-Indians do? Where would we go? There is no open land in the world on which men without capital can make their living (and not much unoccupied land on which men with capital can, either). Where would 209 million putatively justice-loving, non-Indian, Americans go? Most of them—in the persons of their ancestors—came from Europe, but they wouldn't be welcomed back there. Anyway, Europeans have no better title to their land than we to ours. They also would have to give up their homes. But to whom?

And where would *they* go?

Clearly, the concept of pure justice produces an infinite regress. The law long ago invented statutes of limitations to justify the rejection of pure justice, in the interest of preventing massive disorder. The law zealously defends property rights—but only *recent* property rights. It is as though the physical principle of exponential decay applies to property rights. Drawing a line in time may be unjust, but any other action is practically worse.

We are all the descendants of thieves, and the world's resources are inequitably distributed, but we must begin the journey to tomorrow from the point where we are today. We cannot remake the past. We cannot, without violent disorder and suffering, give land and resources back to the "original" owners—who are dead anyway.

We cannot safely divide the wealth equitably among all present peoples, so long as people reproduce at different rates, because to do so would guarantee that our grandchildren—everyone's grandchildren—would have only a ruined world to inhabit.

MUST EXCLUSION BE ABSOLUTE?

To show the logical structure of the immigration problem I have ignored many factors that would enter into real decisions made in a real world. No matter how convincing the logic may be it is probable that we would want, from time to time, to admit a few people from the outside to our lifeboat. Political refugees in particular are likely to cause us to make exceptions: We remember the Jewish refugees from Germany after 1933, and the Hungarian refugees after 1956. Moreover, the interests of national defense, broadly conceived, could justify admitting many men and women of unusual talents, whether refugees or not. (This raises the quality issue, which is not the subject of this essay.)

Such exceptions threaten to create runaway population growth inside the lifeboat, i.e., the receiving country. However, the threat can be neutralized by a population policy that includes immigration. An effective policy is one of flexible control.

Suppose, for example, that the nation has achieved a stable condition of ZPG, which (say) permits 1.5 million births yearly. We must suppose that an acceptable system of allocating birthrights to potential parents is in effect. Now suppose that an inhumane regime in some other part of the world creates a horde of refugees, and that there is a widespread desire to admit some to our country. At the same time, we do not want to sabotage our population control system. Clearly, the rational path to pursue is the following: If we decide to admit 100,000 refugees this year we should compensate for this by reducing the allocation of birth rights in the following year by a similar amount,—that is, downward to a total of 1.4 million. In that way we could achieve both humanitarian and population control goals. (And the refugees would have to accept the population controls of the society that admits them. It is not inconceivable that they might be given proportionately fewer rights than the native population.)

In a democracy, the admission of immigrants should properly be voted on. But, by whom? It is not obvious. The usual rule of a democracy is votes for all. But it can be questioned whether a universal franchise is the most just one in a case of this sort. Whatever benefits there are in the admission of immigrants presumably accrue to everyone. But the costs would be seen as falling most heavily on potential parents, some of who would have to postpone or forego having their (next) child because of the influx of immigrants. The double question *Who benefits? Who pays?* suggests that a restriction of the usual democratic franchise would be appropriate and just in this case. Would our particular quasi-democratic form of government be flexible enough to institute such a novelty? If not, the majority might, out of humanitarian motives, impose an unacceptable burden (the foregoing of parenthood) on a minority, thus producing political instability. Plainly many new problems will arise when we consciously face the immigration question and seek rational answers. No workable answers can be found if we ignore population problems. And—if the argument of this essay is correct—so long as there is no true world government to control reproduction everywhere it is impossible to survive in dignity if we are to be guided by spaceship ethics. Without a world government that is sovereign in reproductive matters mankind lives, in fact, on a number of sovereign lifeboats.

For the foreseeable future survival demands that we govern our actions by the ethics of a lifeboat. Posterity will be ill served if we do not.

REFERENCES

Anonymous. 1974. Wall Street Journal, 19 Feb.

Borlaug, N. "Civilization's Future: A Call for International Granaries." *Bull. At. Sci.* 29:7–15, 1973.

Boulding, K. 1966. "The Economics of the Coming Spaceship Earth." In H. Jarrett, ed., *Environmental Quality in a Growing Economy*. Johns Hopkins Press, Baltimore.

Buchanan, W. 1973. "Immigration Statistics." *Equilibrium* 1(3):16–19.

Davis, K. 1963. "Population." *Sci. Amer.* 209(3): 62–71.

Farvar, M. T., and J. P. Milton. 1972. *The Careless Technology*. Natural History Press, Garden City, N.Y.

Gregg, A. 1955. "A Medical Aspect of the Population Problem." *Science* 121:681–682.

Hardin, G. 1966. Chapter 9 in *Biology: Its Principles and Implications*, 2nd ed. Freeman, San Francisco.

———— 1968. "The Tragedy of the Commons," *Science* 162: 1243–1248.

———— 1969a. Page 18 in *Population, Evolution and Birth Control*, 2nd ed. Freeman, San Francisco.

———— 1969b. "The Economics of Wilderness." *Nat. Hist.* 78(6):20–27.

———— 1972a. Pages 81–82 in *Exploring New Ethics for Survival: The Voyage of the Spaceship Beagle*. Viking, N.Y.

———— 1972b. "Preserving Quality on Spaceship Earth." In J. B. Trefethen, ed. *Transactions of the Thirty-Seventh North American Wildlife and Natural Resources Conference*, Wildlife Management Institute, Washington, DC.

_____ 1973. Chapter 23 in *Stalking the Wild Taboo*. Kaufmann, Los Altos, CA.

Harris, M. 1972. "How Green the Revolution?" *Nat. Hist.* 81(3):28-30.

Langer, S. K. 1942. *Philosophy in a New Key*. Harvard University Press, Cambridge.

Lansner, K. 1974. "Should Foreign Aid Begin at Home?" *Newsweek*, 11 Feb., p.32.

Marx, K. 1875. "Critique of the Gotha Program." Page 388 in R. C. Tucker, ed. *The Marx-Engels Reader*. Norton, N.Y., 1972.

Ophuls, W. 1974. "The Scarcity Society." *Harpers* 243(1487):47–52.

Paddock, W. C. 1970. "How Green Is the Green Revolution?" *BioScience* 20:897–902.

Paddock, W., and E. Paddock. 1973. *We Don't Know How*. Iowa State University Press, Ames, Iowa.

Paddock, W., and P. Paddock. 1967. *Famine—1975!* Little, Brown, Boston.

Wilkes, H. G. 1972. "The Green Revolution." *Environment* 14(8):32–39.

REVIEW QUESTIONS

1. What is wrong with the spaceship metaphor, according to Hardin?
2. Explain Hardin's lifeboat metaphor. How does it apply to rich and poor countries?
3. According to Hardin, why can't we live by the Christian or Marxist ideal of helping others and meeting their needs?
4. Explain what Hardin calls the tragedy of the commons. How is this supposed to apply to rich and poor nations?
5. Explain the ratchet effect and a pejoristic system.
6. Why isn't a benign demographic transition possible, according to Hardin?
7. Why does Hardin think that the Green Revolution will not solve the problem of world hunger?
8. Why is Hardin opposed to unrestricted immigration?

DISCUSSION QUESTIONS

1. Is the lifeboat metaphor accurate? Are there any respects in which the United States is not a lifeboat?
2. Is there a solution to the problem of overpopulation in poor countries that does not involve letting people die from hunger and disease? If so, what is it?
3. Is there any way of avoiding the tragedy of the commons that does not involve private ownership? What is your view?
4. Can the ratchet effect be avoided? How?
5. Should the United States allow more people to immigrate from Mexico and other countries? Why or why not?

PROBLEM CASES

1. Food Crisis in West Africa

According to Oxfam, about 10 million people in West Africa were threatened with severe food shortages in 2010 (see www.oxfam.org). About 10 million people across the Sahel region were in danger of malnutrition or starvation. The area affected includes Niger, Chad, Sudan, Ethiopia, and Mali. The worst affected country was Niger, where 8 million people were at risk. About 2 million people were threatened in Chad, as well as a substantial number in Mali. Parts of Nigeria and Burkina Faso were also at risk.

The crisis was caused by infrequent rains in 2009, which led to a poor harvest in 2010. In Niger the harvest was 26 percent lower than the previous year, and some areas had no harvest at all. There was a deficit of at least 1 million tons of cereal. Rains were not expected until June, and prices of cereals such as millet and sorghum rose higher. Oxfam called on donors to respond to Niger's request for international aid. Up to $123 million was requested to fund the national response plan.

This was not the first food crisis in Niger and the Sahel region. In 2005, lack of rain, locust damage, high food prices, and chronic poverty produced a food crisis for more than 3 million people including 800,000 children under the age of five. These children were facing malnutrition or outright starvation. According to UNICEF, about 300,000 children died of malnutrition in the Sahel belt, and another 300,000 died of disease.

The response by the United Nations to the 2005 crisis was slow. Donors gave less than half of the $81 million requested. In June 2005, some 2,000 people marched through the streets of Niamey, the capital of Niger, demanding free food. The government refused their demands, saying this was "foolish," even though 150,000 children were severely malnourished at the time.

Mamadou Biteye, Oxfam's West Africa Regional Director, said that in 2005 thousands of lives were lost because the world failed to act, and that this mistake should not be made again. Some critics, such as Singer and others, argue that you have a moral obligation to give money to Oxfam to help save lives in Niger and other countries facing food shortages. Do you agree? Are you willing to donate money to Oxfam? Why or why not?

2. Global Tax to End Hunger

(See Tor Norretraanders at www.Edge.org.) There are about 6 billion human beings currently alive on the planet. At least 1 billion live with malnutrition, hunger, and polluted drinking water, whereas about 1 billion, including you and me, do not have a problem with hunger or safe drinking water.

If the 1 billion relatively rich people wanted to provide the economic resources to end hunger, how much would they need to pay in the form of private donations to end hunger? The cost of providing 1 billion people with 250 kilograms of grain a year is about $40 billion a year. No doubt this is a large sum, but if 1 billion people were willing to contribute it would not be such a big deal: it would be about $40 a year for each person. Think of it as a small global tax to end hunger. If each person contributed just one dollar a week, which is less than the cost of one Starbucks latte, then everyone could be fed with money left over. A more modest estimate of what it would take to feed the hungry is given by the organization Netaid. They say that just $13 billion a year is all it would take to satisfy the basic health and food needs of the world's poorest people. This is about the sum that the wealthy spend on perfume each year.

The Internet is a simple way of collecting the money. Just send your contribution to organizations such as Netaid, Hungerside, or Oxfam and they will do the rest. Every user of the Internet ought to be able to contribute a dollar a week. If everyone does this, the problem of global hunger will be solved.

Will you contribute? Why or why not?

3. Illegal Immigrants

(See "Illegal Immigration and the American Workforce" at www.hoover.org.) It is estimated that there are more than 12 million illegal immigrants in the United States. About 75 percent of them come from Mexico or Latin America. They come to work and escape poverty in their native lands. They work at low-paying, unpleasant, and physically demanding jobs in agriculture, construction, and service. They do jobs that many Americans seem unwilling to do.

There is debate about the effects illegal immigrants have on the U.S. economy. Some economists argue that immigrants who work for less money and benefits than citizens take jobs away from U.S. citizens. They assert that illegal immigrants cost the federal government $10 billion a year in social services, education, and health care. They maintain that the taxes paid by illegal workers do not cover the cost of the benefits they receive. Also, many of these workers do not pay taxes at all because they are paid in cash.

Other economists argue that the illegal workers contribute at least 4 percent to economic growth, and without them the economy would decline. For example, when authorities cracked down on illegal workers in 2004, farmers in western states suffered at least

$1 billion in losses because they were unable to hire workers to pick the lettuce crops, which were left to rot in the fields. Hoover Fellow Russell Roberts argues that the United States can survive without illegal workers, but the economy would suffer. Work that is now done by illegal workers would be done at higher wages, resulting in higher prices, particularly for food picked by hand such as lettuce and strawberries. Some work would have to be done by machines or not at all.

The federal government has tried and failed to pass immigration reform legislation. The most recent bill, the Comprehensive Immigration Reform Act of 2007, did not come to a vote. The bill gave temporary legal status to illegal immigrants currently residing in the country and provided more funding for border security. Opponents of the bill objected to "guest worker" provisions.

What should be done about the 12 million illegal workers already in the country? It seems impractical if not impossible to deport them all. Should they be given some sort of legal status? Why or why not?

Another approach is to target businesses that employ illegal workers. At least thirty states have passed laws aimed at limiting or stopping the hiring of illegal aliens. For example, Arizona has passed a law requiring businesses to verify the eligibility of all newly hired employees by using the Department of Homeland Security's E-Verify system, which is an Internet-based system that can be used to check the information given by the employee. Businesses that fail to comply risk losing their state and local licenses if they intentionally employ undocumented workers. The result in Arizona was that numerous business owners were forced to lay off many employees. This was not good for business.

Is this a good law? If so, should it become a federal law? Why or why not?

4. Sweatshops in China

(See "Secrets, Lies, and Sweatshops" in *Business Week*, November 27, 2006.) China is the largest single source of goods imported to the United States by Wal-Mart, Target, Nike, and other big corporations. In 2006, China's factories shipped nearly $300 billion worth of goods to the United States to satisfy American consumers' demand for cheap goods.

To keep consumer prices low and generate profits, American companies continually demand lower prices from Chinese suppliers. Wal-Mart, for example, is able to sell clothes, electronics, and other consumer goods at very low prices. To give one example, the local Wal-Mart sells Faded Glory Jeans (made in China) for $9 each. By comparison, made-in-America Carhartt work pants usually cost more than $30.

How does China produce goods at such low prices? According to *Business Week*, Chinese factories cheat on the labor standards promoted by American companies such as Wal-Mart, Target, Nike, and Eddie Bauer. They pay less than the minimum wages set by local or provincial governments, which can be as low as forty-three cents an hour. They force the workers to labor for sixty or seventy hours a week with no extra pay, and for months at a time without a day off. They use workers under the legal working age of sixteen. They hide these practices by keeping two or even three sets of books, and coaching the workers to mislead investigators about their pay and working conditions. They also send some of the production to secret contractors who are not supervised. A 2005 survey commissioned by Nike of 569 factories it uses in China and around the world that employ more than 300,000 workers found labor-code violations in every one.

Almost every product American consumers buy is made in China or another country that exploits its workers. Hewlett-Packard, Dell, and other companies rely on suppliers in China for personal computers, digital cameras, printers, and other electronic goods. Wal-Mart and Target get most of their goods from China and other countries. Nike gets its sneakers and sports apparel made in China, Vietnam, and Indonesia. Black & Decker gets tools from China. Home Depot and Sears have their lamps and tools made in China.

Naomi Klein (see the Suggested Readings) argues that big American companies such as Nike and Wal-Mart have moved most of the jobs to other countries where labor is cheaper than in the United States. They do so to make big profits. In particular, she accuses Nike of having its shoes made in Asian sweatshops for pennies an hour and then selling them at a huge markup: for example, Michael Jordan basketball shoes are made for $5 and sold for $150.

Nike has responded that it tries to enforce labor standards set by China and other countries, and it exposes cheating when it is discovered. The managers in China, however, claim that Nike simply does not pay enough for the goods it wants. Peter Wang, a manager at China's Zhi Qiao Garments Company, complains that it is just impossible to produce clothes at the price Nike wants to pay, and the result is that he has reduced costs by not paying for overtime and making his workers come in to work on Saturdays, Sundays, and holidays.

Nike is the largest sports footwear and apparel company in the world, with sales of more than $19 billion a year. The company spends more than $2 billion annually on marketing. Nike is famous for paying superstars like Michael Jordan huge sums for endorsements. LeBron James has a seven-year, $90 million contract. Roger Federer has a ten-year contract worth more than $100 million. Tiger Woods's contract is believed to be worth about $40 million annually. Andre Agassi's deal with Nike in 1995 was said to be worth more than $100 million, including royalties on sales. If Nike can afford to pay this much for endorsements, they can and should pay their overseas workers a living wage, or at least more than forty-three cents an hour. Do you agree? Why or why not?

Also, consider Nike's executive compensation in 2009, a year when sales were down 20 percent. Mark Parker took home $7,306,690 in basic compensation. Charles Denson received $5,899,550, and CEO Philip Knight got $3,456,450. According to Forbes.com, Knight is number 24 on the Forbes list of the richest Americans, with a net worth of nearly $1 billion. If Nike can pay executives this kind of money, why shouldn't the company pay its poor workers at least two or three dollars an hour? What is your view?

Some activists recommend not buying Nike shoes and other products made in China and other countries that exploit their workers. You should buy shoes and clothes "Made in America." But to do this you need to be sure that what you are buying really is manufactured in America. New Balance claims that its running shoes are "Made in the U.S.," but according to newbalance.com., only 25 percent of NB shoes sold in the United States are actually made or assembled in five New England factories. The other 75 percent are made in foreign countries, including China. Carhartt sells clothing made in other countries, but some of its products, such as the popular Carhartt Double Front Work Dungarees, are advertised as "Union-Made in America."

Are you willing to buy shoes, clothes, and other products manufactured entirely in the United States even if they are more expensive than foreign-made products? Why or why not?

☖ SUGGESTED READINGS

There are many websites dealing with world poverty and hunger. Some useful ones are the World Health Organization (www.who.int/en), the Worldwatch Institute (www.worldwatch.org), the United Nations Food and Agriculture Organization (www.fao.org), the United Nations Children's Fund (www.unicef.org), and Oxfam (www.oxfam.org).

William Aiken and Hugh LaFollette (eds.), *World Hunger and Moral Obligation* (Englewood Cliffs, NJ: Prentice-Hall, 1977), is a useful anthology on the moral obligation to give aid to the hungry. It includes Peter Singer's "Postscript" to "Famine, Affluence and Morality." Another important article in this volume is John Arthur's "Rights and the Duty to Bring Aid." Arthur argues that the rights of the affluent to satisfy their interests can outweigh the rights of those suffering from starvation. Also see James Rachels, "Vegetarianism and 'the Other Weight Problem.'" Rachels argues that meat-eating wastes food and for that reason it is morally wrong. If we stopped eating meat, there would be plenty of food for everyone.

Peter Singer, *The Life You Can Save: Acting Now to End World Poverty* (New York: Random House, 2009), continues to make his case for giving to the poor. Now he suggests that you contribute at least 5 percent of your income to charities such as Oxfam or UNICEF.

Peter Unger, *Living High and Letting Die* (Oxford: Oxford University Press, 1996), argues that a prosperous person who does not contribute to a charity like UNICEF, while knowing that doing this would ensure that fewer children die, is doing something monstrously wrong by commonly accepted moral standards. The mistaken belief that it is not wrong is based on various psychological distractions such as the fact that the victims are far away and the feeling that helping is futile because you cannot save all the children.

Muhammad Yunus, *Creating a World Without Poverty: Social Business and the Future of Capitalism* (Jackson, TN: Publishing, 2009). Unlike Singer and Unger, Yunus advocates a capitalist solution to world poverty. He describes the Grameen Bank, which makes small loans to poor people who use the money to start social businesses that serve the poor. For example, he discusses a business that sells high-nutrition, lost-cost yogurt in Bangladesh.

Naomi Klein, *No Logo* (New York: Picador, 2002), accuses Nike and other corporations of exploiting workers in poor countries in order to generate bigger profits. Nike published a response at nikebiz.com.

Thomas W. Pogge, *World Poverty and Human Rights* (Oxford: Polity Press, 2008), argues that high-income countries continue to impose an unjust global institutional order that perpetuates world poverty and hunger while under the illusion that they are doing nothing wrong. A clear example of this is the way they apply patents for new medicines, which raises the price too high for the world's sick and needy people.

James Rachels, "Killing and Starving to Death," *Philosophy* 54, no. 208 (April 1979): 159–171, argues that our duty to not let people die of starvation is equivalent to our duty to not kill them.

Julian L. Simon, *The Ultimate Resource* (Princeton, NJ: Princeton University Press, 1981), defends a position directly opposed to that of Hardin.

Onora O'Neill, "Lifeboat Earth," *Philosophy and Public Affairs* 4, no. 3 (Spring 1975): 273–292, maintains that people on the lifeboat Earth have a right not to be killed except in cases of unavoidable killing and self-defense, and that there is a corollary duty to not kill others. It follows from this, she argues, that we ought to adopt policies that will prevent others from dying of starvation.

Onora O'Neill, "The Moral Perplexities of Famine and World Hunger," in Tom Regan, ed., *Matters of Life and Death*, 2nd ed. (New York: Random House, 1986): 294–337, compares the utilitarian and the Kantian approaches to famine relief.

Amartya Sen, "Population: Delusion and Reality," *The New York Review of Books*, 41, no. 15 (September 22, 1994): 62–71, argues that Malthus's predictions about the population outgrowing the food supply have been wrong. The global food supply is more plentiful than population demand. But the population has to be controlled either by voluntary collaboration or override, which overrides voluntarism through legal or economic coercion.

Peter Singer, "Rich and Poor," in *Practical Ethics* (Cambridge, UK: Cambridge University Press, 1979): 158–181, develops his argument that rich nations have a moral obligation to help poor nations.

John Arthur, "Famine Relief and the Ideal Moral Code," in Hugh LaFollette, ed., *Ethics in Practice* (Oxford: Blackwell Publishing, 2002): 582–590, attacks Singer. He argues that Singer ignores the important idea of entitlement, that people can justly deserve something and this also has moral significance.

David A. Crocker, "Hunger, Capacity, and Development," in Hugh LaFollette, ed., *Ethics in Practice* (Oxford: Blackwell Publishing, 2002): 591–603, distinguishes between famine relief and chronic malnutrition, which do not always go together. He argues that the best cure for hunger is national and international development rather than emergency food aid.

Amartya Sen, "The Right Not to Be Hungry," in *Contemporary Philosophy: A New Survey*, Vol. II (The Hague: Martinus Nijhoff, 1982): 343–360, explains the right not to be hungry in terms of entitlements. Starvation and famine occur because people are not entitled, in the prevailing system of institutional rights, to an adequate means of survival.

James P. Sterba, "Human Rights: A Social Contract Perspective," *American Catholic Philosophical Association Proceedings*, 55 (1981): 268–275, interprets the right to life as noninterference with a person's attempts to acquire the goods and resources necessary for satisfying the basic needs of food, shelter, and medical care.

Henry Shue, *Basic Rights* (Princeton, NJ: Princeton University Press, 1980), defends the view that everyone has a basic right to subsistence, and this economic right is just as important as political rights such as the right to liberty. An implication of this is that rich nations should make welfare-style transfers of food and money to poor nations. He claims that they can do this without impoverishing themselves or even causing a decline in their growth rate.

Charles B. Shuman, "Food Aid and the Free Market," in Peter G. Brown and Henry Shue, eds., *Food Policy* (New York: Free Press): 145–163, opposes Shue's approach, and advocates a free-market approach to the problem of hunger and starvation.

Nick Eberstadt, "Myths of the Food Crisis," *The New York Review of Books* (February 19, 1976): 32–37, argues that the cause of starvation is not overpopulation, but inequality in food distribution. But this inequality cannot be eliminated by welfare-style transfers of income; instead, the productivity of the world's poor must be improved.

Frances Moore Lappe, *World Hunger: Twelve Myths* (New York: Grove Press, 1986), discusses various aspects of the problem of world hunger, and argues that people in rich countries should change their diets.

C H A P T E R   E I G H T

Financial Crisis

- **Introduction**
  - Factual Background
  - The Readings
  - Philosophical Issues

INTRODUCTION

Factual Background

Market economies are subject to speculative bubbles and financial crises. Typically, speculative fever drives prices too high, and then prices crash, producing a financial crisis. This has happened over and over again throughout history. One of the first bubbles was tulip mania in Europe in the 1600s. Dutch tulips became a popular luxury item and status symbol. A wide variety of tulip bulbs were developed that would develop into beautiful flowers. As the demand for these tulip bulbs grew, so did the price. The price for tulip contracts reached a peak in 1637, and then for some reason suddenly collapsed, causing a severe shock to the economy of the Netherlands.

The stock market crash of 1929 is a famous example of the bursting of a speculative bubble. The Roaring Twenties preceded the crash; this was a time of wealth and excess, and saw a speculative boom with hundreds of thousands of Americans investing heavily in the stock market. A significant number of the investors were highly leveraged, that is, they were investing using borrowed money, a practice that is very risky. At the peak of speculation, more than $8 billion was loaned, more than the entire money supply in the United States at the time. On Black Thursday, October 24, 1929, the market dramatically turned down, and panic selling began. Eventually the stock market lost about 90 percent of its value. The Dow closed at 41.22 on July 8, 1932, the lowest the stock market had been since the nineteenth century.

The 1929 crash triggered the Great Depression of the 1930s, which is often said to have been the greatest economic and financial crisis in the history of the United States. This was a time of great suffering by workers and their families: Unemployment reached almost 40 percent, hundreds of thousands of families were evicted from their homes, more than a million families lost their farms, millions of homeless people wandered around the country, and more than 60 percent of the population was labeled poor by the federal government. The economy collapsed: Almost half the banks failed, 9 million savings accounts were wiped out, average income was reduced by 40 percent, corporate profits dropped by 90 percent, industrial production fell by nearly 45 percent, and homebuilding dropped by 80 percent.

A more recent example of the boom-and-bust cycle was the dot-com bubble that peaked in 2000 when the NASDAQ hit 5132, and then burst, driving the NASDAQ down 80 percent, to a low of 1114 in 2002. This period, from roughly 1998 to 2002, featured the creation (and failure) of new Internet-based companies commonly referred to as *dot-coms*. Some of these companies have survived and been very successful; for example, Google stock was initially offered at $85, and in 2007 it sold for $700 a share. But thousands of the dot-coms failed. At the height of the boom, a dot-com would make an initial public offering (IPO) of its stock based on an idea. (DigiScents claimed to transmit smells over the Internet. CyberRebate promised customers a 100 percent rebate if a customer bought a product at ten times the retail cost.) The stock would rise even though the company had no earnings and no business. Speculators rushed to buy these stocks; it was a "new economy," the country was going to be wired with high-speed fiber-optic cables, college students were starting up dot-coms and becoming rich overnight. But in 2000 the bubble burst. On March 13, a massive group of sell orders started a chain reaction of panic selling by nervous investors, mutual funds, and institutions. The NASDAQ went down 9 percent in a few days. By 2001, the bubble was deflating rapidly. Most of the dot-coms went bankrupt after burning through their venture capital. Many never made a profit.

The bursting of the dot-com bubble led to the U.S. housing bubble. At least, that is what the Yale economist Robert Shiller said in 2005: "Once stocks fell, real estate became the primary outlet for the speculative frenzy that the stock market had unleashed." No doubt there were other factors involved in the dramatic rise in housing prices in the early 2000s, such as low interest rates, lax lending practices, and government programs that encouraged home ownership, but the run-up of prices in hot areas such as Florida and California had all the hallmarks of speculation. Speculators were buying two or three Florida condos at a time and then "flipping" them, selling them for a profit a few weeks later. Prices peaked in the middle of 2006, but then started falling, reaching a bottom in early 2009. Houses lost about 40 percent of their value, and sometimes more (or less) depending on the location. This led to a rapid rise in default rates, particularly in the subprime market. Subprime loans were made to borrowers who did not satisfy the usual standards of creditworthiness. In other words, they did not have adequate income or assets to make the payments on the mortgage. Some of these were out-and-out "liar's loans," where nobody checked to see if the information supplied by the borrower was accurate. When prices fell, many of the houses bought at or near the peak ended up having negative equity, because the value of the house was less than the amount owed on the mortgage. Rather than make payments that added nothing to the equity of the house, some borrowers just walked away—they defaulted on their mortgages. Some could not make their mortgage payments because of reduced income or ballooning interest rates. Many of those who lost their homes had home equity loans that further reduced their equity. The increase in defaults and foreclosures led to a sharp reduction in the value of various mortgage-backed securities such as collateralized debt obligations, which were held by investment banks and other companies.

As the number of mortgage defaults and foreclosures increased, the various derivative securities tied to the mortgages lost value; in fact, nobody seemed to know how to value them. They became toxic junk that nobody would buy. Investment banks like Lehman Brothers, Goldman Sachs, and Morgan Stanley lost vast amounts of money on highly leveraged and risky investments in mortgage-backed securities and other derivatives. The problems became severe when the financial giant Lehman Brothers collapsed on September 15, 2008. Apparently Lehman had billions of dollars invested in mortgage-backed securities that it could not sell and were essentially worthless. The result was panic in the interbank loan market. Banks stopped making or receiving loans. Shortly after the bankruptcy of Lehman, on September 18, Treasury Secretary Henry Paulson and the Chairman of the Federal Reserve, Ben Bernanke, had an emergency meeting with key legislators to propose a $700 billion bailout. Bernanke reportedly told the legislators, "If we don't do this, we may not have an economy on Monday." On October 3, 2008, the $700 billion Troubled Asset Relief Program (TARP) was signed into law. This was in addition to the $400 billion bailout of Freddie Mac and Fannie Mae, the mortgage giants, which made the government accountable for $5 trillion in mortgages. In the readings, Prins and Hayes claim that the full total for the bailout and subsidization of the financial sector was an astounding $17.5 trillion.

Some economists called this financial crisis the Great Recession. Certainly it was the greatest financial crisis since the Great Depression. Most said that it began in 2008 with the Lehman bankruptcy, although others held that it began with the decline in the housing market in 2007. The consensus opinion is that it ended in 2009. The effects of the crisis were severe, although not as bad as the Great Depression. The stock market went down by about 50 percent, which reduced the value of retirement accounts, savings, and investments. The average price of housing declined by more than 20 percent, further reducing wealth. Many people with home equity loans greater than the value of their houses went bankrupt. The total decline in consumer wealth in the United States was estimated to be more than $8 trillion. Unemployment rose rapidly. If one counts discouraged workers no longer seeking employment and those working only part time in addition to those getting unemployment compensation, the number of unemployed and underemployed reached nearly 20 percent of the workforce. Many smaller banks and companies went out of business. At the same time, the federal government bailed out large banks and companies deemed "too big to fail."

The Readings

Niall Ferguson views financial institutions and crises from an evolutionary perspective. Financial ups and downs, bubbles and busts, manias and panics are perfectly natural and to be expected, from this point of view. We are doomed to be surprised by financial crises such as the meltdown in 2008, which hardly anyone predicted, because of unmeasurable uncertainty about the economy and markets, various cognitive traps that cause us to behave irrationality, and the evolutionary character of finance. Following Joseph Schumpeter, Ferguson believes that the essential feature of capitalism is *creative destruction*. This is an evolutionary process that changes the economic structure from within, destroying old companies and creating new ones. Old companies that are not fit to survive go bankrupt or disappear, and are replaced by stronger and better adapted companies. In support of this claim, Ferguson notes that of the world's 100 largest companies in 1912, 77 were bankrupt or had disappeared by 1995. In Ferguson's view, it is a mistake to interfere with the evolutionary process of creative destruction with excessive rules and regulation or by bailing out failed companies. It is undesirable to have companies that are too big to fail. Instead, we should let capitalism do its natural work of destroying firms that are not fit to live.

David McNally agrees that capitalism generates financial crises, but unlike Ferguson he does not think they do anything good. On the contrary, he argues that the 2008 financial crisis spread to a global slump with jobs lost, lower wages, toxic financial waste, and ticking time bombs ready to erupt into another crisis. In his view, the culprit is neoliberal capitalism (as he calls it), the form of capitalism followed by Alan Greenspan and his followers that reduced government control of the economy with deregulation, cut taxes for the wealthy, eliminated job protections for workers, and lowered government spending on social services.

McNally does not think that a Keynesian re-regulation of the financial markets will solve the systemic problems with capitalism. From a Marxist point of view, the basic problems with neoliberal capitalism include overaccumulation of factories, buildings, fiber-optic networks, and other goods that cannot be profitably sold; a change in the form of money to a plethora of derivatives—options, hedges, credit default swaps, and collateralized debt obligations—that are essentially fictitious capital (mere paper claims to future wealth); lower wages combined with easy credit resulting in massive consumer debt; out-of-control government deficits and debt; and reckless financial gambling. McNally concludes that neoliberal capitalism has been a colossal failure. As an alternative, he suggests we should turn to a socialism that meets people's needs for jobs, housing, food, and health care.

Paul Krugman argues that dealing with the 2008 financial crisis requires a return to "depression economics." This is more or less the regulated Keynesian economics that McNally rejects. As Krugman explains it, depression economics involves massive fiscal stimulus by the government, as much as 4 percent of gross domestic product (GDP); a new regulatory regime applied to anything that had to be rescued so that it need not be rescued again; temporary federal lending to nonfinancial institutions; and even full temporary nationalization of a significant part of the financial system, as was done in Sweden. This last proposal goes beyond just bailing out banks, which Krugman doubts will work because it does not eliminate the unregulated shadow banking system, the core of the problem. In fact, nationalization—that is, the government taking over previously private banks—fits a classic definition of socialism, which is government ownership of business. But Krugman is no socialist. He views nationalization as just a temporary measure to stabilize the banks before they are returned to private owners.

Prins and Hayes use an analogy to explain the government bailout of the banks. The banks are like a couple named Joe and Katie Hazzard who get in financial difficulty making bad bets and poor investments. The government bailout is like giving Joe money to pay off his gambling debts; it is like letting Joe sell his risky bets to other gamblers; it is like letting the Hazzards use their old junk as collateral for more loans; it is like promising to guarantee the price for their condo; it is like buying up the Hazzards' bad investments. These are just a few of the key aspects of the bank bailouts. The analogy helps us see that these bailouts were not just one mechanism, one check, but a number of different ways of propping up the financial system that added up to more than $17 trillion. Prins and Hayes think that some of this money could have been used to help people instead of banks. They note a significant lack of accountability, which means that there will be more bad bets and more financial crises in the future.

Philosophical Issues

The main issue is how to deal with the 2008 financial crisis and future crises. Ferguson seems to hold that we should do nothing: We should let capitalism do its natural work of creative destruction of companies that are not fit to survive so that new and better adapted companies can flourish. Circuit City, the large electronics company, went bankrupt and was liquidated in 2009. In Ferguson's view, the same thing should have happened to General Motors and Chrysler when they ran out of money. Instead, the government saved them. It would have been better to let GM and Chrysler go out of business and suffer through the resulting unemployment and economic hardship because then we would have new auto companies with better products—at least until the next inevitable crisis.

McNally rejects neoliberal capitalism and a laissez-faire approach to the economy as well as the leashed capitalism of Keynesian economics that tries to regulate the financial industry. He suggests a socialist alternative that focuses on people's needs rather than capitalist profits.

Krugman favors a return to depression economics. As he explains it, this involves the Keynesian measures of massive government stimulus of the economy and regulation of the financial sector designed to prevent future crises. But Krugman also recommends temporary nationalization of the banks and federal lending to nonfinancial institutions. These proposals seem to go beyond Keynesian economics to a kind of socialism.

How do we define *capitalism* and *socialism*? This is a basic question raised by the readings. Gerald Gaus (see the Suggested Readings) explains capitalism in terms of private ownership and property rights. The ideal of capitalism—that is, a pure version of capitalism—has two features. One, it extends as far as possible what can be privately owned. In principle, almost anything can be owned: land, houses, factories, highways, schools, food, rivers, lakes, forests, money, even one's own body and services. Two, ideal capitalism gives individuals the most extensive feasible property rights, including the rights to use, waste, destroy, modify, transfer, sell, or rent their property.

Gaus argues that capitalism takes different forms depending on how close it is to the ideal. American capitalism is fairly close to the ideal, but does not attain it because the American government places limits on what can be owned and what can be done with private property. Americans are not allowed to possess heroin or child pornography. They are not permitted to sell their kidneys or sexual services. There are environmental regulations, health and safety rules, and criminal laws. There are taxes to pay for social benefits such as public schools, highways, bridges, the police, the armed forces, and medical care.

The ideal of socialism, in contrast to capitalism, rejects all private ownership and property rights. But this ideal has never been practiced or even preached. Even Soviet Communism recognized personal private property such as clothes, household items, and books. Andrew Blackman (see the Suggested Readings) argues that modern socialism has evolved since the days of communism. Instead of insisting on the abolition of private ownership of land and factories (see the *Manifesto of the Communist Party* in the Suggested Readings), modern socialism holds that the rights to education, housing, health care, living wages, freedom, and democracy are all basic rights that should be guaranteed by the state. This seems to be the form of socialism McNally favors. It is compatible with at least some forms of capitalism, for example, the welfare capitalism found in Canada and Norway.

The Descent of Money

NIALL FERGUSON

Niall Ferguson is Laurence A. Tisch Professor of History at Harvard University; a Senior Research Fellow of Jesus College, Oxford University; and a Senior Fellow of the Hoover Institution, Stanford University. He is the author of *Paper and Iron* (2002), *The House of Rothschild* (1999), *The Pity of War* (2000), *The Cash Nexus* (2002), *Empire* (2004), *Colossus* (2005), and *The War of the World* (2007).

Ferguson begins with a quick tour through the history of money. It has been a roller-coaster ride of ups and downs, bubbles and busts—148 financial crises since 1870. He identifies three reasons for these crises: unmeasurable uncertainty about the financial future, as distinguished from measurable risk; cognitive traps that distort our thinking, such as availability bias, hindsight bias, confirmation bias, and bystander apathy; and most importantly, the evolutionary nature of the economy and financial institutions. Ferguson agrees with Schumpeter that the essential fact about capitalism is that it works by a process of creative destruction. Basically this is an evolutionary process whereby old companies that are no longer profitable, or otherwise not fit to survive, go bankrupt or disappear to make room for new innovative companies that are profitable. Ferguson thinks it is a mistake to interfere with this process, which is what makes capitalism work. We should not bail out companies that have gone bankrupt, but let them die. We should not allow companies to become too big to fail. We should not introduce new rules and regulations that thwart the destruction of the weakest institutions in the market, which are often gobbled up by the successful.

Today's financial world is the result of four millennia of economic evolution. Money—the crystallized relationship between debtor and creditor—begat banks, clearinghouses for ever larger aggregations of borrowing and lending. From the thirteenth century onwards, government bonds introduced the securitization of streams of interest payments; while bond markets revealed the benefits of regulated public markets for trading and pricing securities. From the seventeenth century, equity in corporations could be bought and sold in similar ways. From the eighteenth century, insurance funds and then pension funds exploited econo-mies of scale and the laws of averages to provide financial protection against calculable risk. From the nineteenth, futures and options offered more specialized and sophisticated instruments: the first derivatives. And, from the twentieth, households were encouraged, for political reasons, to increase leverage and skew their portfolios in favour of real estate.

Economies that combined all these insti-tutional innovations—banks, bond markets, stock markets, insurance and property-owning democracy—performed better over the long run than those that did not, because financial inter-mediation generally permits a more efficient allo-cation of resources than, say, feudalism or central planning. For this reason, it is not wholly sur-prising that the Western financial model tended to spread around the world, first in the guise of imperialism, then in the guise of globaliza-tion.[1] From ancient Mesopotamia to present-day China, in short, the ascent of money has been one of the driving forces behind human progress: a complex process of innovation, intermediation and integration that has been as vital as the ad-vance of science or the spread of law in mankind's escape from the drudgery of subsistence agricul-ture and the misery of the Malthusian trap. In the words of former Federal Reserve Governor Fred-eric Mishkin, 'the financial system [is] the brain of the economy. . . It acts as a coordinating mech-anism that allocates capital, the lifeblood of eco-nomic activity, to its most productive uses by businesses and households. If capital goes to the wrong uses or does not flow at all, the economy will operate inefficiently, and ultimately economic growth will be low.'[2]

Yet money's ascent has not been, and can never be, a smooth one. On the contrary, financial history is a roller-coaster ride of ups and downs, bubbles and busts, manias and panics, shocks and crashes.[3] One recent study of the available data for gross domestic product and consumption since 1870 has identified 148 cri-ses in which a country experienced a cumulative decline in GDP of at least 10 per cent and eighty-seven crises in which consumption suffered a fall of comparable magnitude, implying a probability

of financial disaster of around 3.6 per cent per year.[4] Even today, despite the unprecedented sophistication of our institutions and instru-ments, Planet Finance remains as vulnerable as ever to crises. It seems that, for all our ingenuity, we are doomed to be 'fooled by randomness'[5] and surprised by 'black swans'.[6] It may even be that we are living through the deflation of a multi-decade 'super bubble'.[7]

There are three fundamental reasons for this. The first is that too much about the future—or, rather, futures, since there is never a singular future—lies in the realm of uncertainty, as opposed to calculable risk. As Frank Knight argued in 1921, 'Uncertainty must be taken in a sense rad-ically distinct from the familiar notion of Risk, from which it has never been properly separated. . . A *measurable* uncertainty, or "risk" proper . . . is so far different from an *unmeasurable* one that it is not in effect an uncertainty at all.' To put it sim-ply, much of what happens in life isn't like a game of dice. Again and again an event will occur that is 'so entirely unique that there are no others or not a sufficient number to make it possible to tab-ulate enough like it to form a basis for any infer-ence of value about any real probability . . .'[8] The same point was brilliantly expressed by Keynes in 1937. 'By "uncertain" knowledge,' he wrote in a response to critics of his *General Theory*,

> . . . I do not mean merely to distinguish what is known for certain from what is only probable. The game of roulette is not subject, in this sense, to uncertainty. . . The expectation of life is only slightly uncertain. Even the weather is only mod-erately uncertain. The sense in which I am using the term is that in which the prospect of a Euro-pean war is uncertain, or . . . the rate of interest twenty years hence. . . About these matters there is no scientific basis on which to form any calcula-ble probability whatever. We simply do not know.*

---

*As Peter Bernstein has said, 'We pour in data from the past . . . but past data . . . constitute a sequence of events rather than a set of independent observations, which is what the laws of probability demand. History provides us with only one sample of the . . . capital markets, not with thousands of separate and randomly distributed numbers.' The same problem—that the sample size is effectively one—is of course inherent in geol-ogy, a more advanced historical science than financial history, as Larry Neal has observed.

Keynes went on to hypothesize about the ways in which investors 'manage in such circumstances to behave in a manner which saves our faces as rational, economic men':

(1) We assume that the present is a much more serviceable guide to the future than a candid examination of past experience would show it to have been hitherto. In other words we largely ignore the prospect of future changes about the actual character of which we know nothing.
(2) We assume that the *existing* state of opinion as expressed in prices and the character of existing output is based on a *correct* summing up of future prospects . . .
(3) Knowing that our own individual judgment is worthless, we endeavor to fall back on the judgment of the rest of the world which is perhaps better informed. That is, we endeavor to conform with the behavior of the majority or the average.[9]

Though it is far from clear that Keynes was correct in his interpretation of investors' behaviour, he was certainly thinking along the right lines. For there is no question that the heuristic biases of individuals play a critical role in generating volatility in financial markets.

This brings us to the second reason for the inherent instability of the financial system: human behaviour. As we have seen, all financial institutions are at the mercy of our innate inclination to veer from euphoria to despondency; our recurrent inability to protect ourselves against 'tail risk'; our perennial failure to learn from history. In a famous article, Daniel Kahneman and Amos Tversky demonstrated with a series of experiments the tendency that people have to miscalculate probabilities when confronted with simple financial choices. First, they gave their sample group 1,000 Israeli pounds each. Then they offered them a choice between either a) a 50 per cent chance of winning an additional 1,000 pounds or b) a 100 per cent chance of winning an additional 500 pounds. Only 16 per cent of people chose a); everyone else (84 per cent) chose b). Next, they asked the same group to imagine having received 2,000 Israeli pounds each and confronted them with another choice: between either c) a 50 per cent chance of losing 1,000 pounds or b) a 100 per cent chance of losing 500 pounds. This time the majority (69 per cent) chose a); only 31 per cent chose

b). Yet, viewed in terms of their payoffs, the two problems are identical. In both cases you have a choice between a 50 per cent chance of ending up with 1,000 pounds and an equal chance of ending up with 2,000 pounds (a and c) or a certainty of ending up with 1,500 pounds (b and d). In this and other experiments, Kahneman and Tversky identify a striking asymmetry: risk aversion for positive prospects, but risk seeking for negative ones. A loss has about two and a half times the impact of a gain of the same magnitude.[10]

This 'failure of invariance' is only one of many heuristic biases (skewed modes of thinking or learning) that distinguish real human beings from the *homo oeconomicus* of neoclassical economic theory, who is supposed to make his decisions rationally, on the basis of all the available information and his expected utility. Other experiments show that we also succumb too readily to such cognitive traps as:

1. *Availability bias*, which causes us to base decisions on information that is more readily available in our memories, rather than the data we really need;
2. *Hindsight bias*, which causes us to attach higher probabilities to events after they have happened (*ex post*) than we did before they happened (*ex ante*);
3. *The problem of induction*, which leads us to formulate general rules on the basis of insufficient information;
4. *The fallacy of conjunction* (or disjunction), which means we tend to overestimate the probability that seven events of 90 per cent probability will *all* occur, while underestimating the probability that *at least one* of seven events of 10 per cent probability will occur;
5. *Confirmation bias*, which inclines us to look for confirming evidence of an initial hypothesis, rather than falsifying evidence that would disprove it;
6. *Contamination effects*, whereby we allow irrelevant but proximate information to influence a decision;
7. *The affect heuristic*, whereby preconceived value-judgements interfere with our assessment of costs and benefits;

8. *Scope neglect*, which prevents us from proportionately adjusting what we should be willing to sacrifice to avoid harms of different orders of magnitude;

9. *Overconfidence in calibration*, which leads us to underestimate the confidence intervals within which our estimates will be robust (e.g. to conflate the 'best case' scenario with the 'most probable'); and

10. *Bystander apathy*, which inclines us to abdicate individual responsibility when in a crowd.[11]

If you still doubt the hard-wired fallibility of human beings, ask yourself the following question. A bat and ball, together, cost a total of £1.10 and the bat costs £1 more than the ball. How much is the ball? The wrong answer is the one that roughly one in every two people blurts out: 10 pence. The correct answer is 5 pence, since only with a bat worth £1.05 and a ball worth 5 pence are both conditions satisfied.[12]

If any field has the potential to revolutionize our understanding of the way financial markets work, it must surely be the burgeoning discipline of behavioural finance.[13] It is far from clear how much of the body of work derived from the efficient markets hypothesis can survive this challenge.[14] Those who put their faith in the 'wisdom of crowds'[15] mean no more than that a large group of people is more likely to make a correct assessment than a small group of supposed experts. But that is not saying much. The old joke that 'Macroeconomists have successfully predicted nine of the last five recessions' is not so much a joke as a dispiriting truth about the difficulty of economic forecasting.[16] Meanwhile, serious students of human psychology will expect as much madness as wisdom from large groups of people.[17] A case in point must be the near-universal delusion among investors in the first half of 2007 that a major liquidity crisis could not occur (see Introduction). To adapt an elegant summation by Eliezer Yudkowsky:

> People may be overconfident and over-optimistic. They may focus on overly specific scenarios for the future, to the exclusion of all others. They may not recall any past [liquidity crises] in memory. They may overestimate the predictability of the past, and hence underestimate the surprise of the future. They may not realize the difficulty of preparing for [liquidity crises] without the benefit of hindsight. They may prefer . . . gambles with higher payoff probabilities, neglecting the value of the stakes. They may conflate positive information about the benefits of a technology [e.g. bond insurance] and negative information about its risks. They may be contaminated by movies where the [financial system] ends up being saved. . . Or the extremely unpleasant prospect of [a liquidity crisis] may spur them to seek arguments that [liquidity] will *not* [dry up], without an equally frantic search for reasons why [it should]. But if the question is, specifically, 'Why aren't more people doing something about it?', one possible component is that people are asking that very question—darting their eyes around to see if anyone else is reacting . . . meanwhile trying to appear poised and unflustered.[18]

Most of our cognitive warping is, of course, the result of evolution. The third reason for the erratic path of financial history is also related to the theory of evolution, though by analogy. It is commonly said that finance has a Darwinian quality. 'The survival of the fittest' is a phrase that aggressive traders like to use; as we have seen, investment banks like to hold conferences with titles like 'The Evolution of Excellence'. But the American crisis of 2007 has increased the frequency of such language. US Assistant Secretary of the Treasury Anthony W. Ryan was not the only person to talk in terms of a wave of financial extinctions in the second half of 2007. Andrew Lo, director of the Massachusetts Institute of Technology's Laboratory for Financial Engineering, is in the vanguard of an effort to re-conceptualize markets as adaptive systems.[19] A long-run historical analysis of the development of financial services also suggests that evolutionary forces are present in the financial world as much as they are in the natural world.[20]

The notion that Darwinian processes may be at work in the economy is not new, of course. Evolutionary economics is in fact a well-established sub-discipline, which has had its own dedicated journal for the past sixteen years.[21] Thorstein Veblen first posed the question 'Why is Economics Not an Evolutionary Science?'

(implying that it really should be) as long ago as 1898.[22] In a famous passage in his *Capitalism, Socialism and Democracy*, which could equally well apply to finance, Joseph Schumpeter characterized industrial capitalism as 'an evolutionary process':

> This evolutionary character . . . is not merely due to the fact that economic life goes on in a social and natural environment which changes and by its change alters the data of economic action; this fact is important and these changes (wars, revolutions and so on) often condition industrial change, but they are not its prime movers. Nor is this evolutionary character due to quasi-autonomic increase in population and capital or to the vagaries of monetary systems of which exactly the same thing holds true. The fundamental impulse that sets and keeps the capitalist engine in motion comes from the new consumers' goods, the new methods of production or transportation, the new markets, the new forms of industrial organization that capitalist enterprise creates. . . The opening up of new markets, foreign or domestic, and the organizational development from the craft shop and factory to such concerns as US Steel illustrate the same process of industrial mutation—if I may use the biological term—that incessantly revolutionizes the economic structure *from within*, incessantly destroying the old one, incessantly creating a new one. This process of Creative Destruction is the essential fact about capitalism.[23]

A key point that emerges from recent research is just how much destruction goes on in a modern economy. Around one in ten US companies disappears each year. Between 1989 and 1997, to be precise, an average of 611,000 businesses a year vanished out of a total of 5.73 million firms. Ten per cent is the average extinction rate, it should be noted; in some sectors of the economy it can rise as high as 20 per cent in a bad year (as in the District of Columbia's financial sector in 1989, at the height of the Savings and Loans crisis).[24] According to the UK Department of Trade and Industry, 30 per cent of tax-registered businesses disappear after three years.[25] Even if they survive the first few years of existence and go on to enjoy great success, most firms fail eventually. Of the world's

100 largest companies in 1912, 29 were bankrupt by 1995, 48 had disappeared, and only 19 were still in the top 100.[26] Given that a good deal of what banks and stock markets do is to provide finance to companies, we should not be surprised to find a similar pattern of creative destruction in the financial world. We have already noted the high attrition rate among hedge funds. (The only reason that more banks do not fail, as we shall see, is that they are explicitly and implicitly protected from collapse by governments.)

What are the common features shared by the financial world and a true evolutionary system? Six spring to mind:

- 'Genes', in the sense that certain business practices perform the same role as genes in biology, allowing information to be stored in the 'organizational memory' and passed on from individual to individual or from firm to firm when a new firm is created.
- The potential for spontaneous mutation, usually referred to in the economic world as innovation and primarily, though by no means always, technological.
- Competition between individuals within a species for resources, with the outcomes in terms of longevity and proliferation determining which business practices persist.
- A mechanism for natural selection through the market allocation of capital and human resources and the possibility of death in cases of under-performance, i.e. 'differential survival'.
- Scope for speciation, sustaining biodiversity through the creation of wholly new species of financial institutions.
- Scope for extinction, with species dying out altogether.

Financial history is essentially the result of institutional mutation and natural selection. Random 'drift' (innovations/mutations that are not promoted by natural selection, but just happen) and 'flow' (innovations/mutations that are caused when, say, American practices are adopted by Chinese banks) play a part. There can also be 'co-evolution', when different financial species work and adapt together (like hedge funds and their prime brokers). But market selection is the main driver. Financial organisms are in competition with one another for finite resources. At certain times and in certain places, certain species may become dominant. But innovations by competitor species, or the emergence of altogether new species, prevent any permanent hierarchy or monoculture from emerging. Broadly speaking, the law of the survival of the fittest applies. Institutions with a 'selfish gene' that is good at self-replication and self-perpetuation will tend to proliferate and endure.[27]

Note that this may not result in the evolution of the perfect organism. A 'good enough' mutation will achieve dominance if it happens in the right place at the right time, because of the sensitivity of the evolutionary process to initial conditions; that is, an initial slim advantage may translate into a prolonged period of dominance, without necessarily being optimal. It is also worth bearing in mind that in the natural world, evolution is not progressive, as used to be thought (notably by the followers of Herbert Spencer). Primitive financial life-forms like loan sharks are not condemned to oblivion, any more than the microscopic prokaryotes that still account for the majority of earth's species. Evolved complexity protects neither an organism nor a firm against extinction—the fate of most animal and plant species.

The evolutionary analogy is, admittedly, imperfect. When one organism ingests another in the natural world, it is just eating; whereas, in the world of financial services, mergers and acquisitions can lead directly to mutation. Among financial organisms, there is no counterpart to the role of sexual reproduction in the animal world (though demotic sexual language is often used to describe certain kinds of financial transaction). Most financial mutation is deliberate, conscious innovation, rather than random change. Indeed, because a firm can adapt within its own lifetime to change going on around it, financial evolution (like cultural evolution) may be more Lamarckian than Darwinian in character. Two other key differences will be

discussed below. Nevertheless, evolution certainly offers a better model for understanding financial change than any other we have.

Ninety years ago, the German socialist Rudolf Hilferding predicted an inexorable movement towards more concentration of ownership in what he termed finance capital.[28] The conventional view of financial development does indeed see the process from the vantage point of the big, successful survivor firm. In Citigroup's official family tree, numerous small firms—dating back to the City Bank of New York, founded in 1812—are seen to converge over time on a common trunk, the present-day conglomerate. However, this is precisely the wrong way to think about financial evolution over the long run, which *begins* at a common trunk. Periodically, the trunk branches outwards as new kinds of bank and other financial institution evolve. The fact that a particular firm successfully devours smaller firms along the way is more or less irrelevant. In the evolutionary process, animals eat one another, but that is not the driving force behind evolutionary mutation and the emergence of new species and subspecies. The point is that economies of scale and scope are not always the driving force in financial history. More often, the real drivers are the process of speciation—whereby entirely new types of firm are created—and the equally recurrent process of creative destruction, whereby weaker firms die out.

Take the case of retail and commercial banking, where there remains considerable biodiversity. Although giants like Citigroup and Bank of America exist, North America and some European markets still have relatively fragmented retail banking sectors. The cooperative banking sector has seen the most change in recent years, with high levels of consolidation (especially following the Savings and Loans crisis of the 1980s), and most institutions moving to shareholder ownership. But the only species that is now close to extinction in the developed world is the state-owned bank, as privatization has swept the world (though the nationalization of Northern Rock suggests the species could make a comeback). In other respects, the story is one of speciation, the proliferation of new types of financial institution, which is just what we would expect in a truly evolutionary system. Many new 'mono-line' financial services firms have emerged, especially in consumer finance (for example, Capital One). A number of new 'boutiques' now exist to cater to the private banking market. Direct banking (telephone and Internet) is another relatively recent and growing phenomenon. Likewise, even as giants have formed in the realm of investment banking, new and nimbler species such as hedge funds and private equity partnerships have evolved and proliferated. And, . . . the rapidly accruing hard currency reserves of exporters of manufactured goods and energy are producing a new generation of sovereign wealth funds.

Not only are new forms of financial firm proliferating; so too are new forms of financial asset and service. In recent years, investors' appetite has grown dramatically for mortgage-backed and other asset-backed securities. The use of derivatives has also increased enormously, with the majority being bought and sold 'over the counter', on a one-to-one bespoke basis, rather than through public exchanges—a tendency which, though profitable for the sellers of derivatives, may have unpleasant as well as unintended consequences because of the lack of standardization of these instruments and the potential for legal disputes in the event of a crisis.

In evolutionary terms, then, the financial services sector appears to have passed through a twenty-year Cambrian explosion, with existing species flourishing and new species increasing in number. As in the natural world, the existence of giants has not precluded the evolution and continued existence of smaller species. Size isn't everything, in finance as in nature. Indeed, the very difficulties that arise as publicly owned firms become larger and more complex—the diseconomies of scale associated with bureaucracy, the pressures associated with quarterly reporting—give opportunities to new forms of private firm. What matters in evolution is not your size or (beyond a certain level) your complexity. All that matters is that you are good at surviving and reproducing your genes. The financial equivalent is being good at generating returns on equity and generating imitators employing a similar business model.

In the financial world, mutation and speciation have usually been evolved responses to the environment and competition, with natural selection determining which new traits become widely disseminated. Sometimes, as in the natural world, the evolutionary process has been subject to big disruptions in the form of geopolitical shocks and financial crises. The difference is, of course, that whereas giant asteroids (like the one that eliminated 85 per cent of species at the end of the Cretaceous period) are exogenous shocks, financial crises are endogenous to the financial system. The Great Depression of the 1930s and the Great Inflation of the 1970s stand out as times of major discontinuity, with 'mass extinctions' such as the bank panics of the 1930s and the Savings and Loans failures of the 1980s.

Could something similar be happening in our time? Certainly, the sharp deterioration in credit conditions in the summer of 2007 created acute problems for many hedge funds, leaving them vulnerable to redemptions by investors. But a more important feature of the recent credit crunch has been the pressure on banks and insurance companies. Losses on asset-backed securities and other forms of risky debt are thought likely to be in excess of $1 trillion. At the time of writing (May 2008), around $318 billion of write-downs (booked losses) have been acknowledged, which means that more than $600 billion of losses have yet to come to light. Since the onset of the crisis, financial institutions have raised around $225 billion of new capital, leaving a shortfall of slightly less than $100 billion. Since banks typically target a constant capital/assets ratio of less than 10 per cent, that implies that balance sheets may need to be shrunk by as much as $1 trillion. However, the collapse of the so-called shadow banking system of off-balance-sheet entities such as structured investment vehicles and conduits is making that contraction very difficult indeed.

It remains to be seen whether the major Western banks can navigate their way through this crisis without a fundamental change to the international accords (Basel I and II)* governing capital adequacy. In Europe, for example, average bank capital is now equivalent to significantly less than 10 per cent of assets (perhaps as little as 4), compared with around 25 per cent towards the beginning of the twentieth century. The 2007 crisis has dashed the hopes of those who believed that the separation of risk origination and balance sheet management would distribute risk optimally throughout the financial system. It seems inconceivable that this crisis will pass without further mergers and acquisitions, as the relatively strong devour the relatively weak. Bond insurance companies seem destined to disappear. Some hedge funds, by contrast, are likely to thrive on the return of volatility.† It also seems likely that new forms of financial institution will spring up in the aftermath of the crisis. As Andrew Lo has suggested: 'As with past forest fires in the markets, we're likely to see incredible flora and fauna springing up in its wake.'[29]

There is another big difference between nature and finance. Whereas evolution in biology takes place in the natural environment, where change is essentially random (hence Richard Dawkins's image of the blind watchmaker), evolution in financial services occurs within a regulatory framework where—to borrow a phrase from anti-Darwinian creationists—'intelligent design' plays a part. Sudden changes to the regulatory environment are rather different from sudden changes in the macroeconomic environment,

which are analogous to environmental changes in the natural world. The difference is once again that there is an element of endogeneity in regulatory changes, since those responsible are often poachers turned gamekeepers, with a good insight into the way that the private sector works. The net effect, however, is similar to climate change on biological evolution. New rules and regulations can make previously good traits suddenly disadvantageous. The rise and fall of Savings and Loans, for example, was due in large measure to changes in the regulatory environment in the United States. Regulatory changes in the wake of the 2007 crisis may have comparably unforeseen consequences.

The stated intention of most regulators is to maintain stability within the financial services sector, thereby protecting the consumers whom banks serve and the 'real' economy which the industry supports. Companies in nonfinancial industries are seen as less systemically important to the economy as a whole and less critical to the livelihood of the consumer. The collapse of a major financial institution, in which retail customers lose their deposits, is therefore an event which any regulator (and politician) wishes to avoid at all costs. An old question that has raised its head since August 2007 is how far implicit guarantees to bail out banks create a problem of moral hazard, encouraging excessive risk-taking on the assumption that the state will intervene to avert illiquidity and even insolvency if an institution is considered too big to fail— meaning too politically sensitive or too likely to bring a lot of other firms down with it. From an evolutionary perspective, however, the problem looks slightly different. It may, in fact, be undesirable to have any institutions in the category of 'too big to fail', because without occasional bouts of creative destruction the evolutionary process will be thwarted. The experience of Japan in the 1990s stands as a warning to legislators and regulators that an entire banking sector can become a kind of economic dead hand if institutions are propped up despite under-performance, and bad debts are not written off.

Every shock to the financial system must result in casualties. Left to itself, natural selection

---

*Under the Basel I rules agreed in 1988, assets of banks are divided into five categories according to credit risk, carrying risk weights ranging from zero (for example, home country government bonds) to 100 per cent (corporate debt). International banks are required to hold capital equal to 8 per cent of their risk-weighted assets. Basel II, first published in 2004 but only gradually being adopted around the world, sets out more complex rules, distinguishing between credit risk, operational risk and market risk, the last of which mandates the use of value at risk (VaR) models. Ironically, in the light of 2007–8, liquidity risk is combined with other risks under the heading 'residual risk.' Such rules inevitably conflict with the incentive all banks have to minimize their capital and hence raise their return on equity.

† In Andrew Lo's words: 'Hedge funds are the Galapagos Islands of finance. . . The rate of innovation, evolution, competition, adaptation, births and deaths, the whole range of evolutionary phenomena, occurs at an extraordinarily rapid clip.'

should work fast to eliminate the weakest institutions in the market, which typically are gobbled up by the successful. But most crises also usher in new rules and regulations, as legislators and regulators rush to stabilize the financial system and to protect the consumer/voter. The critical point is that the possibility of extinction cannot and should not be removed by excessively precautionary rules. As Joseph Schumpeter wrote more than seventy years ago, 'This economic system cannot do without the *ultima ratio* of the complete destruction of those existences which are irretrievably associated with the hopelessly unadapted.' This meant, in his view, nothing less than the disappearance of 'those firms which are unfit to live'.[30]

In writing this book, I have frequently been asked if I gave it the wrong title. *The Ascent of Money* may seem to sound an incongruously optimistic note (especially to those who miss the allusion to Bronowski's *Ascent of Man*) at a time when a surge of inflation and a flight into commodities seem to signal a literal descent in public esteem and purchasing power of fiat moneys like the dollar. Yet it should by now be obvious to the reader just how far our financial system has ascended since its distant origins among the moneylenders of Mesopotamia. There have been great reverses, contractions and dyings, to be sure. But not even the worst has set us permanently back. Though the line of financial history has a saw-tooth quality, its trajectory is unquestionably upwards.

Still, I might equally well have paid homage to Charles Darwin by calling the book *The Descent of Finance*, for the story I have told is authentically evolutionary. When we withdraw banknotes from automated telling machines, or invest portions of our monthly salaries in bonds and stocks, or insure our cars, or remortgage our homes, or renounce home bias in favour of emerging markets, we are entering into transactions with many historical antecedents.

I remain more than ever convinced that, until we fully understand the origin of financial species, we shall never understand the fundamental truth about money: that, far from being 'a monster that must be put back in its place', as the German president recently complained,[31]

financial markets are like the mirror of mankind, revealing every hour of every working day the way we value ourselves and the resources of the world around us.

It is not the fault of the mirror if it reflects our blemishes as clearly as our beauty.

NOTES

1. For some fascinating insights into the limits of globalization, see Pankaj Ghemawat, *Redefining Global Strategy: Crossing Borders in a World Where Differences Still Matter* (Boston, 2007).
2. Frederic Mishkin, Weissman Center Distinguished Lecture, Baruch College, New York (12 October 2006).
3. Larry Neal, 'A Shocking View of Economic History', *Journal of Economic History*, 60, 2 (2000), pp. 317–34.
4. Robert J. Barro and José F. Ursúa, 'Macroeconomic Crises since 1870', *Brookings Papers on Economic Activity* (forthcoming). See also Robert J. Barro, 'Rare Disasters and Asset Markets in the Twentieth Century', Harvard University Working Paper (4 December 2005).
5. Nassim Nicholas Taleb, *Fooled by Randomness: The Hidden Role of Chance in Life and in the Markets* (2nd edn., New York, 2005).
6. *Idem, The Black Swan: The Impact of the Highly Improbable* (London, 2007).
7. Georges Soros, *The New Paradigm for Financial Markets: The Credit Crash of 2008 and What It Means,* (New York, 2008), pp. 91 ff.
8. See Frank H. Knight, *Risk, Uncertainty and Profit* (Boston, 1921).
9. John Maynard Keynes, 'The General Theory of Employment', *Economic Journal*, 51, 2 (1937), p. 214.
10. Daniel Kahneman and Amos Tversky, 'Prospect Theory: An Analysis of Decision under Risk', *Econometrica*, 47, 2 (March 1979), p. 273.
11. Eliezer Yudkowsky, 'Cognitive Biases Potentially Affecting Judgment of Global Risks', in Nick Bostrom and Milan Cirkovic (eds.), *Global Catastrophic Risks* (Oxford University Press, 2008), pp. 91–119. See also Michael J. Mauboussin, *More Than You Know: Finding Financial Wisdom in Unconventional Places* (New York/Chichester, 2006).
12. Mark Buchanan, *The Social Atom: Why the Rich Get Richer, Cheaters Get Caught, and Your Neighbor Usually Looks Like You* (New York, 2007), p. 54.

13. For an introduction, see Andrei Shleifer, *Inefficient Markets: An Introduction to Behavioral Finance* (Oxford, 2000). For some practical applications see Richard H. Thaler and Cass R. Sunstein, *Nudge: Improving Decisions About Health, Wealth, and Happiness* (New Haven, 2008).

14. See Peter Bernstein, *Capital Ideas Evolving* (New York, 2007).

15. See for example James Surowiecki, *The Wisdom of Crowds* (New York, 2005); Ian Ayres, *Supercrunchers: How Anything Can Be Predicted* (London, 2007).

16. Daniel Gross, 'The Forecast for Forecasters is Dismal', *New York Times*, 4 March 2007.

17. The classic work, first published in 1841, is Charles MacKay, *Extra-ordinary Popular Delusions and the Madness of Crowds* (New York, 2003 [1841]).

18. Yudkowsky, 'Cognitive Biases', pp. 11off.

19. For an introduction to Lo's work, see Bernstein, *Capital Ideas Evolving*, ch. 4. See also John Authers, 'Quants Adapting to a Darwinian Analysis', *Financial Times*, 19 May 2008.

20. The following is partly derived from Niall Ferguson and Oliver Wyman, *The Evolution of Financial Services: Making Sense of the Past, Preparing for the Future* (London/New York, 2007).

21. *The Journal of Evolutionary Economics*. Seminal works in the field are A. A. Alchian, 'Uncertainty, Evolution and Economic Theory', *Journal of Political Economy*, 58 (1950), pp. 211–22, and R. R. Nelson and S. G. Winter, *An Evolutionary Theory of Economic Change* (Cambridge, MA, 1982).

22. Thorstein Veblen, 'Why is Economics Not an Evolutionary Science?' *Quarterly Journal of Economics*, 12 (1898), pp. 373–97.

23. Joseph A. Schumpeter, *Capitalism, Socialism and Democracy* (London, 1987 [1943]), pp. 80–4.

24. Paul Ormerod, *Why Most Things Fail: Evolution, Extinction and Economics* (London, 2005), pp. 18off.

25. Jonathan Guthrie, 'How the Old Corporate Tortoise Wins the Race', *Financial Times*, 15 February 2007.

26. Leslie Hannah, 'Marshall's "Trees" and the Global "Forest": Were "Giant Redwoods" Different?', in N. R. Lamoreaux, D. M. G. Raff and P. Temin (eds.), *Learning by Doing in Markets, Firms and Countries* (Cambridge, MA, 1999), pp. 253–94.

27. The allusion is of course to Richard Dawkins, *The Selfish Gene* (2nd edn., Oxford, 1989).

28. Rudolf Hilferding, *Finance Capital: A Study of the Latest Phase of Capitalist Development* (London, 2006 [1919]).

29. 'Fear and Loathing, and a Hint of Hope', *The Economist*, 16 February 2008.

30. Joseph Schumpeter, *The Theory of Economic Development* (Cambridge, MA, 1934), p. 253.

31. Bertrand Benoit and James Wilson, 'German President Complains of Financial Markets "Monster"', *Financial Times*, 15 May 2008.

♔ REVIEW QUESTIONS

1. How does Ferguson describe the nature and ascent (the financial history) of money?
2. According to Ferguson, why are our financial institutions subject to frequent crises?
3. Ferguson lists ten cognitive traps. What are they?
4. Explain Schumpeter's concept of creative destruction.
5. According to Ferguson, what are the common features shared by the financial world and an evolutionary system? How has banking evolved?
6. In Ferguson's view, what is the big difference between nature and finance?
7. How would Ferguson deal with the financial crisis of 2008? Why is he opposed to bailing out banks?

♔ DISCUSSION QUESTIONS

1. Ferguson claims that uncertainty about financial markets is unmeasurable. Do you agree? Why or why not?
2. Using your own experience, give examples to illustrate the cognitive traps.
3. Does evolution provide a good model for understanding the financial world? Why or why not?
4. "Financial crises are endogenous to the financial system." Is this true? Why or why not?
5. Should banks be bailed out when they go bankrupt? Should they be allowed to be too big to fail? Explain your view.

From Financial Crisis to World Slump

DAVID MCNALLY

David McNally is professor of political science at York University in Toronto, Ontario. He is the author of *Against the Market* (1993), *Bodies of Meaning* (2000), and *Another World Is Possible* (2007).

McNally gives a Marxist analysis and critique of the financial crisis. He argues that the U.S. crisis has spread to the rest of the world producing a global economic slump. The basic cause of the crisis and the slump is neoliberal capitalism. Roughly, this is the ideological view that the economy should be privatized by deregulating markets, removing labor protections (including unions), lowering taxes, and reducing public spending on social services such as health care. The rise of this form of capitalism occurred during Alan Greenspan's tenure as President of the Federal Reserve (1987–2005). The result was a wave of overaccumulation of goods that could not be profitably sold (e.g., cars); a mutation of money into fictitious capital (e.g., the astounding $450 trillion in derivatives contracts); lower wages along with increased social inequality; easy credit leading to massive private and public debt; and reckless financial gambling. McNally thinks more trouble is ahead: defaults in credit card debt and commercial paper, lower wages and unemployment, a declining dollar, immigrant-bashing, and more financial crises. McNally concludes that capitalism has been a colossal failure. But what is the alternative? McNally opts for socialism. He calls for specific reforms that include saving jobs, building social housing, investing in ecologically sustainable industries, and feeding the poor.

FROM US FINANCIAL CRISIS TO WORLD SLUMP

As the International Monetary Fund observed some months ago, we are living through "the largest financial crisis in the United States since the Great Depression." But that was to understate things in two ways. First, the financial crisis is no longer largely about the US. It has gone global, rocking the UK, the Eurozone, Japan, and the so-called "emerging market economies." A wave of devastating national and regional crises is just getting started, having already hit Iceland, Hungary, the Ukraine, and Pakistan. Secondly, this is no longer simply a financial crisis; a global economic slump is now sweeping through the so-called "real economy," hammering the construction, auto and consumer goods sectors, and clobbering growth rates in China and India. Manufacturing output is sharply down in the US, Europe, Japan and China. The Detroit Three automakers, reeling from losses of $28.6 billion in the first half of

this year, are teetering on the verge of collapse. World trade is in a stunning free fall.

Catastrophic forecasts of the sort that only handfuls of leftists indulged in, often all too glibly, have now become standard fare, with the chairman and CEO of Merrill Lynch and the former chairman of Goldman Sachs both talking of a global slowdown comparable to the Great Depression. Extreme (and misleadingly ahistorical) as such predictions are, it is easy to see why world bankers are so shaken.

Over the past year, global stock markets have dropped by 50 per cent, wiping out perhaps $25 trillion in paper assets and plunging us into "the worst bear market since the 1930s." All five of Wall Street's investment banks are gone—caput. More than 250,000 jobs have evaporated in the US financial services industry. And now, as noted above, the effects of global over-accumulation are turning financial crisis into world economic slump. Problems of over-accumulation—more factories, machines, buildings, fibre optic networks,

Source: Marx and the financial crisis of 2008. blogspot.com. David McNally.

and so on than can be operated profitably, and piles of goods that cannot profitably be sold—can only be resolved via bankruptcies, plant closings and mass layoffs. One analyst at Merrill Lynch, for instance, suggests that, to remain viable, GM will have to shut five of 12 North American car assembly plants and slash output of trucks, sports utility vehicles and cross-over utility vehicles by two-thirds. Altogether, these moves would eliminate the jobs of 59,000 out of 123,000 GM employees in the US, Mexico and Canada. The ripple effects, in the auto parts industries and beyond, would be dramatic. Indeed, the Center for Automotive Research predicts that a 50 per cent contraction of Ford, Chrysler and GM would wipe out nearly two and a half million US jobs. So, if the first phase of the global crisis centered on the financial sector, with a stunning series of bank collapses, the second phase will be dominated by failure, bailouts and/or massive downsizing of non-financial corporations. But those will then trigger big drops in global demand (as laid off workers cut back consumption and corporate demand retrenches), which in turn will hit firms in services (such as hotels and business assistance) and spark further problems for banks.

As world demand and sales dive, the effects of overcapacity (factories, machines, buildings that cannot be profitably utilized), which have been masked by credit creation over the past decade, will thus kick in with a vengeance. Experts are already predicting that US vehicle sales will plummet by at least three million in 2009, and quite possibly by twice that much, imperilling the very future of the US-based auto makers. World sales of personal computers, mobile phones, and semiconductors are collapsing by 10 per cent and more, inducing frantic price-cutting in order to generate corporate revenues. In Japan industrial production dropped three percent in October, with government officials forecasting that November will see a sharp 6.4 per cent drop in factory output. Having tried to export its way back to economic health after its "lost decade," Japan now faces relapse into a downward economic spin as world markets contract. And contract they will, as October's one per cent drop in US consumer spending, just the seventh drop in half a century, indicates.

And just as China was the center of the wave of accumulation of the past 25 years, so it will be at the center of the over-accumulation storm. According to some predictions, Chinese industry is running at only 50 per cent of capacity, as huge numbers of factories and machines sit idle. Sitting in Chinese warehouses are stockpiles of refrigerators equal to three years of world demand. Not surprisingly, steel output dropped 17 per cent in October, signalling a deepening slump in the appliance and machinery industries in particular. But most ominous was the 2.2 per cent drop in Chinese exports in November, the first such contraction in more than seven years. At the same time as it cannot export its way to growth, China's domestic markets are dramatically contracting: car sales fell by more than 10 per cent in November, while imports plummeted by almost 18 per cent. Trying to manage an economy that needs economic growth rates of eight per cent a year just to absorb the massive flows of rural migrants into industrial centers, Chinese officials describe the employment situation as "grim" and worry openly about social unrest.

The downturn in China is part of a larger recession sweeping East Asia and India. South Korea experienced a staggering 18 per cent drop in exports in November, while Taiwan's exports fell off the table, plunging 23 per cent. India too is feeling the crunch, with exports plummeting 12 per cent in October and the Commerce Secretary predicting that half a million jobs will be lost in textiles by April of next year. With global overcapacity in play, the spectre that haunted Japan throughout the 1990s—deflation—has emerged; indeed, core prices in the US fell one per cent in October, the biggest drop since 1947, when records began. Over-accumulation, asset deflation and price-cutting now threaten a downward spiral in prices and profits that would spell a seriously prolonged global slump.

And we are very far from the endpoint. Despite a stunning series of bailouts of the banking system in the Global North approaching $10 trillion, or 15 per cent of world GDP, the international financial system continues to stagger. Hundreds of billions more in losses will have to be written off by world banks. More banks will fail, more countries will be forced to turn to the IMF in order to stay afloat. Indeed, the global economy is now enmeshed in a classic downward feedback loop: financial meltdown having triggered a recession, a slump in the real economy will now spark a new round of banking crises, putting very big institutions at risk. In the wake of $65 billion in writedowns (with more to come), for instance, Citigroup, the second-largest bank in America has been kept afloat only thanks to a whopping $300 billion US government bailout.

The current crisis is unlike all the others of the past decade in terms of scope and depth. While previous financial shocks in the US were contained—the Savings and Loan meltdown of the early 1990s, the collapse of Long Term Capital Management (1998) or the bursting of the dotcom bubble (2000–1)—this one has moved from a financial meltdown to a generalized economic crisis. And unlike crises that were regionally confined—East Asia (1997), Russia (1998), Argentina (2000–1)—this is a globalizing crisis at the heart of the system. We confront, in other words, a *generalized global crisis* in specific forms for organizing the relations between capitals and the relations between capital and global labour that have characterized the neoliberal period. In short, the neoliberal reorganization of world capitalism is now systemically shaken.

And like any systemic crisis, it has produced an ideological one. Consider, for instance, the pronouncement from Alan Greenspan, who headed the Federal Reserve Bank of the US for 18 years, declaring that he is in "a state of shocked disbelief" as to how a system based on "the self-interest of lending institutions" could have found itself in this pickle. Or think about the report published by the Institute for Policy Analysis at the University of Toronto that bears the title, "We don't have a clue and we're not going to pretend we do." Neoliberal claims for the magical properties of self-regulating markets are rapidly losing traction, even among their advocates.

In this context, the Left has an enormous opportunity to provide critical analysis, strategic vision, and mobilizational proposals. This paper largely restricts itself to the first of these: critical analysis of the crisis.

CAPITAL ACCUMULATION AND THE QUESTION OF FINANCIALIZATION

On the Left, most analyses of the crisis have tended to fall into one of two camps. On the one hand, we find a series of commentators who view the financial meltdown as just the latest manifestation of a crisis of profitability that began in the early 1970s, a crisis that has effectively persisted since that time. In another camp is a large number of commentators who see the crisis as essentially caused by an explosion of financial transactions and speculation that followed from de-regulation of financial markets over the past quarter-century.

Those interpretations that focus principally on the de-regulation of financial markets suffer from a failure to grasp the deep tendencies at the level of capital accumulation and profitability that underpin this crisis. They are unable to explain why this crisis has not been restricted to financial markets, or to probe its interconnection with problems of global over-accumulation. As a result, they are prone to describe the problem in terms of neoliberalism, rather than capitalism, and to advocate a return to some sort of Keynesian re-regulation of financial markets. Socialist politics remain effectively absent from these perspectives, displaced by arguments for "a renewed leashed capitalism" of the sort that is said to have prevailed after 1945.

Those analyses that effectively read the current crisis in terms of a decline in the rate of profitability in the early 1970s at least focus on deeper problems at the level of capitalist accumulation. But they tend for the most part to be amazingly static, ignoring the specific dynamics of capitalist restructuring and accumulation in the neoliberal period. After all, across the recessions of 1974–75 and 1981–82 and the ruling class offensive against unions and the Global South that ran through this period, severe capitalist restructuring did generate a new wave of capitalist growth. As analysts like Fred Moseley have shown, after 1982 a significant restoration of profitability took place, and this underpinned major processes of expanded capitalist reproduction (particularly in China). It is true that profit rates did not recover to their peak levels of the 1960s, and that overall growth rates were not as robust. But there was a dynamic period of growth, centered on industrial expansion in East Asia, which enabled capitalism to avoid a world crisis for twenty-five years. And this process of growth, and the unique financial forms that have underpinned it, have determined many of the specific features of the current crisis.

Inattention to the specific forms of industrial, monetary and financial reorganization that have characterized the neoliberal period, or the patterns of sustained capital accumulation that have taken place over the past quarter-century, prevents us from explaining how and why capitalism managed to avoid a generalized economic and financial slump for the quarter century after the two recessions (1974–75 and 1981–82) that followed upon the sharp decline in profitability at the end of the 1960s. It will not do to say that for 25 years crisis was "postponed" because credit was pumped into the system. If this was the whole answer, if everything had simply been credit-driven, a massive global financial crisis of the sort we are witnessing today ought to have occurred *much* earlier. There is simply no way that priming the pump of credit could have staved off crisis for 25 years after the recession of 1981–82. We need, therefore, to be able to explain the partial but real successes of capital in restoring profit rates throughout the 1980s; the generation of new centers of global accumulation, such as China and the creation of huge new labour reserves (by means of ongoing "primitive accumulation"); and the associated metamorphoses in financial markets, all of which enabled neoliberal capitalism to avoid a generalized economic and financial slump for a quarter of a century—only to lay the grounds for new crises of over-accumulation and financial dislocation. In doing so we will be able to better make sense of the unique forms and patterns of this crisis by relating them to specific changes in the neoliberal organization of capitalism—and the fault lines inherent in it.

As I shall suggest below, the partial recovery in profit rates in the early 1980s sustained a wave of capitalist expansion that began to falter in 1997, with the crisis in East Asia. After that regional crisis (and particularly after the bursting of the dotcom bubble in 2000–1) a massive expansion of credit *did* underpin rates of growth, concentrating profound sources of instability in the financial sector. So, while the entire period after 1982 cannot be explained in terms of credit creation, the postponement of a general crisis *after 1997* can. A decade long credit explosion delayed the day of reckoning. But as the credit bubble burst, beginning in the summer of 2007, it generated a major financial crisis. And because of underlying problems of over-accumulation that had first manifest[ed] themselves in 1997, this financial crisis necessarily triggered a profound global economic slowdown.

To summarize, then, as well to anticipate some details, my argument rests on the following claims: 1) the neoliberal offensive succeeded in raising the rate of exploitation and profits, thereby inducing a new wave of global accumulation (1982–2007); 2) this expansion took place in the framework of transformations in money and finance that enabled financial service industries to double their share of total corporate profits, creating increasingly "financialized" relations between capitals; 3) when the first signs of a new phase of over-accumulation set in, with the Asian Crisis of 1997, massive credit-expansion, fuelled after 2001 by record-low interest rates, postponed the day of reckoning, while greatly "financializing" relations between capital and labour; 4) but when financial markets started to seize up in the summer of 2007, the underlying weaknesses of accumulation and profitability meant that financial meltdown would trigger global slump; and 5) neoliberal transformations in money and finance have given this crisis a number of unique features, which the Left ought to be able to explain.

It is with this in mind that I want to clarify the idea of financialized capitalism. For there are deep and important reasons why this crisis began in the financial system, and why it has taken unique forms—and these must be explained if we wish to illuminate the concrete features of this slump. However, in many respects, the term *financialization* can be, and has been, highly misleading. To the degree to which it suggests that finance capitalists and their interests dominate contemporary capitalism, it is especially so. And where it has been taken to imply that late capitalism rests on the *circulation* rather than the production of goods—as if we could have one without the other—it has contributed to absurd depictions of the world economy today. Moreover, the lines between industrial and financial capital are in practice often quite blurred, with giant firms engaging in both forms of profit-making. General Electric, for instance, is as much a bank as it is a manufacturing corporation, while General Motors and Ford have increasingly relied on their finance divisions in order to make a profit. Prior to its collapse, Enron was essentially a derivative trading company, not an energy firm. All of these firms financialized themselves to important degrees in response to the rising profitability of the financial sector during the neoliberal period—a point to which I return.

What the term "financialization" ought to capture, in my view, is that set of transformations through which *relations between capitals and between capital and wage labour have been increasingly financialized*—i.e. increasingly embedded in interest-paying financial transactions. Understanding this enables us to grasp how it is that financial institutions have appropriated ever larger shares of surplus value. It is as a way of capturing these structural shifts that I intend to use the term financialization. In order to avoid misunderstanding—and to close off bad theorizing often associated with the concept— I will identify it specifically with the complex interconnections among three key phenomena of the neoliberal period that have underpinned the dizzying growth—and now the stunning collapse—of the financial sector. The three phenomena at issue are:

1. the mutation in the form of world money that occurred in the early 1970s;
2. the financial effects of neoliberal wage compression over the past 30 years; and
3. the enormous global imbalances (revolving around the US current account deficit) that have flooded the world economy with US dollars.

Let me now briefly explore each of these in turn.

A MUTATION IN THE FORM OF WORLD MONEY

Commentators have rarely noted the curious conjunction that has defined capitalist globalization in the neoliberal era. On the one hand, globalizing capital has involved an intensification of capitalist value logics—removal of extra-market protections designed to subsidize prices of subsistence goods (e.g. food or fuel); weakening of labour market protections for workers; privatization of state-owned enterprises; deep cuts to non-market provision of healthcare and other social goods. On the other hand, this intensification of value logics has occurred through the medium of more unstable and volatile forms of money. As a result, *value forms have been extended at the same time as value measures (and predictions) have become more volatile.* This has given neoliberal globalization a number of distinct characteristics and a propensity to enormous credit bubbles and financial meltdowns of the sort we are witnessing at the moment. The following bullet points trace this second, and largely neglected side of the process.

- The breakdown of Bretton Woods saw not only liberalization of capital flows, but also globalization alongside a weakening in the world money properties of the US dollar. Under Bretton Woods, the dollar was considered equivalent to 1/35th of an ounce of gold, and major currencies were fixed in proportion to the dollar. Changes in these currency proportions (exchange rates) were infrequent and generally small. But with the end of dollar-gold convertibility in 1971 and the move to floating exchange rates (rates that literally fluctuate all day each and every day according to values determined on world markets), currency values, especially for the dollar, became much more volatile. As a result, the formation of values at the world level became much more uncertain and less predictable.
- With the end of convertibility, the dollar became a full-fledged international credit money—grounded in fictitious capital (the

US national debt), and lacking any substantive grounding in past labour (in this case, gold). As we shall see, this produced fertile ground for financial speculation.

- As a result of the de-commodification of the dollar and the moving from fixed to floating exchange rates for currencies, the *measure of value* property of money—the capacity of money to express the socially necessary (abstract) labor times inherent in commodities—was rendered highly unstable.

- With increased uncertainty in value relations, the importance of risk assessment and hedging against risk became a crucial activity for all capitals, especially for those whose business activities required moving in and through multiple currencies (all of whose values were fluctuating more widely). It is in this context that markets for derivatives exploded. In the first instance, derivatives are instruments designed to hedge risk. They allow, for instance, a corporation to enter a contract that provides an option to buy a currency (dollars, yens, euros or whatever) at a set price. While this option contract costs a fee, it also provides greater financial predictability for the firm.

- But while this aspect of derivatives follows conventional business logic, there has been an amazing proliferation of such instruments to cover just about every imaginable risk. And, huge numbers of such derivative contracts represent nothing more than financial gambling. This is because I can buy insurance against "risks" to assets I don't own. I can, for instance, purchase a derivative known as a Credit Default Swap (discussed further below) against the risk of GM defaulting—and I can do this even if I own none of GM's stocks or bonds. Rather than protecting my investment, then, in this case I am buying a CDS as a bet that GM *will* fail, hoping then to collect in the event of the company's failure. It is as if I could take out an insurance policy on someone I suspect to be dying, and then wait to collect. Thus, while their explosion follows on the new volatility of money since 1971, derivatives have

also evolved as speculative bets on the movements of specific currencies, interest rates, stocks or bonds, even when I don't own any of these assets. I can thus buy a derivative contract simply as a bet on the weather pattern or the result of a sports event. Derivatives also create opportunities for speculators to exploit value gaps between markets (arbitrage), when currency movements make some asset relatively cheaper or pricier in one national market compared to another.

- This volatile regime of world money thus gave an enormous impetus to foreign exchange trading and to a whole plethora of options, hedges and swaps related to it. In fact, foreign exchange trading is now far and away the world's largest market, with an average daily turnover above $4 trillion according to the Bank for International Settlements, which represents an 800 per cent increase since 1988. To that market must be added a currency derivatives market of more than half that much again.

- Meanwhile, derivatives markets have come to massively eclipse markets in stocks and bonds. In 2006, for instance, more than $450 trillion in derivative contracts were sold. That compares with $40 trillion for global stock markets, and about $65 trillion of world bond markets in the same year. And the profits that can be made on selling derivatives are much higher than on selling stocks and bonds, thereby fuelling the growth of financial markets and the profits of the financial sector.

- The heightened instability of world money, the explosion in foreign exchange trading, and the rise of instruments designed to hedge risk (derivatives) and, finally, the speculative activities associated with these have all encouraged a whole range of practices designed to financially capture *future values*, i.e. shares of surplus value that have not yet been produced. The result has been a proliferation of *fictitious capitals*, such as mortgage-backed securities and Collateralized Debt Obligations (which are discussed further below).

All of these developments, which are structurally related to the mutation in the form of world money that took place in the early 1970s, as any commodity basis to world money was abandoned and exchange rates were allowed to float, constitute an essential basis of financialization in the neoliberal period.

NEOLIBERAL WAGE COMPRESSION, SOCIAL INEQUALITY AND THE CREDIT EXPLOSION

It follows from this analysis that the financialization that defines capitalism in its neoliberal form consists in structural transformations that corresponds to a particular conjuncture, not a financial coup or the rebirth of the *rentier*.

In the first instance, this is manifest in the doubling of the share of US corporate profits going to the financial sector compared to its share during the 1970s and 1980s. While the proportion of profits going to finance doubled to more than 28 percent by 2004, the share going to the broader financial (interest-bearing) services sector—Finance, Real Estate and Insurance (FIRE)—also doubled to nearly 50 per cent of all US corporate profits.

The growth of financial markets and prefitability is tied to processes of neoliberal wage compression that also underwrote the significant partial recovery of the rate of profit between 1982 and 2007. Wage compression—which is a key component of the increase in the rate of surplus value in the neoliberal period—was accomplished by way of social and spatial reorganization of labour markets and production processes. Five dynamics figure especially prominently here: 1) the geographic relocation of production, with significant expansion of manufacturing industries in dramatically lower wage areas of East Asia and, to a lesser degree, India, Mexico and so on; 2) the downward pressure on wages triggered by a huge expansion in the reserve army of global labour resulting from massive dispossession of peasants and agricultural labourers, particularly in China and India; 3) the increase in relative surplus value brought about by the boosts to labour productivity (output per worker per hour) resulting from the combined effects of lean production techniques and new technologies; 4) increases in absolute surplus value triggered by an increase in work hours, particularly in the United States; 5) sharp cuts to real wages brought about by union-busting, two-tiered wage systems, and cuts to the "social wage" in the form of a reduction in non-wage social benefits, such as health care, food and fuel subsidies, pensions and social assistance programs.

Where successful, all of these strategies have reduced the living standards of working class people while spectacularly concentrating wealth at the top of the economic ladder. Data from the United States are especially instructive in this regard. According to detailed studies, which may if anything underestimate the polarization, between 1973 and 2002, average real incomes for the bottom 90 per cent of Americans fell by nine percent. Incomes for the top one per cent rose by 101 per cent, while those for the top 0.1 per cent soared by 227 percent. These data have recently been updated to show additional increases in household inequality in the US all the way through 2006. And a recent report from the Organization for Economic Cooperation and Development charts similar trends for most major capitalist societies.

Inevitably, even more unequal relations appear once we look beyond income to the ownership of corporate wealth. Whereas in 1991 the wealthiest one percent of Americans owned 38.7 percent of corporate wealth, by 2003 their share had soared to 57.5 per cent. And similar effects are evident at the global level. According to the Boston Consulting Group, for example, since 2000, "the 16.5 per cent of global households with at least $100,000 to invest have seen their assets soar 64 percent in value, to $84.5 trillion." The vast bulk of that wealth resides in the portfolios of millionaire households. Although they comprise just 0.7 percent of the globe's total households, these millionaire households now hold over a third of the world's wealth. And it is these households, particularly in the conditions of renewed over-accumulation of capital since the late 1990s, who have enormously boosted demand for interest-bearing financial assets.

Just as the wealthiest households demanded a plethora of financial instruments in which to invest, large numbers of working class people turned to credit markets—particularly in the context of dramatically lowered interest rates after 2001—in order to sustain living standards. And the provision of greater amounts of credit to such working class people—in the forms of mortgage and credit card debt in particular—was underpinned by the provision of "cheap money" (low interest rates) designed to prevent the deepening of the slump that began in 1997 and was reactivated in 2001, and by growing demand from wealthy investors for "securitized" debt instruments (i.e. mortgage and credit card debt packaged like securities for purchase) that offered higher rates of return. The process of securitization of debt—repacking it as a purchasable income-generating "security"— enabled working class debt to comprise a significant source of new financial instruments for banks, pension funds, financialized corporations, wealthy investors and the like.

All of these trends led to a quadrupling of private and public debt in the US, from slightly more than $10 trillion to $43 trillion, during the period of Alan Greenspan's tenure as President of the Federal Reserve (1987–2005). And the great acceleration in this debt build-up came after 1997, as the recessionary dynamics of global over-accumulation became more evident. Moreover, as I discuss below, since 2000 the rate of credit creation in many economies has been much faster than that in the highly indebted US and UK, presaging a series of local crises of the sort we have already seen in Iceland, Hungary, the Ukraine and Pakistan.

GLOBAL IMBALANCES, PROLONGED SLUMP

As I have suggested, a new wave of global capitalist expansion began in 1982, as two recessions (1974–75, 1981–82) coupled with mass unemployment, cuts to the social wage, an employers' offensive against unions, and the accelerated introduction of lean production methods all raised the rate of surplus value and general levels of profitability. Spatial restructuring of capital to take advantage of low wages, particularly in labour-intensive manufacturing and assembly, had the same effects. The center of the new wave of accumulation was East Asia. And it was there, fifteen years into the new cycle of growth, that the first symptoms of a new crisis of over-capacity manifested themselves.

While many commentators treated the Asian crisis of 1997 as simply a matter of global flows of finance (which exited the region *en masse* at the time), the regional financial outflows reflected severe pressures of over-accumulation of capital, as I argued at the time. The investment boom in East Asia created enormous excess capacity in computer chips, autos, semi-conductors, chemicals, steel, and fibre optics. One key indicator of this overcapacity is the *consumption deflator*, which measures prices in consumer goods. That index demonstrates that US prices for consumer durables–electronics, appliances, cars and more—began to decline in the autumn of 1995. This signal of rising productivity and over-production offers the best clues as to the structural underpinnings of the crisis that broke out in East Asia (the center of the manufacturing boom of the neoliberal era). Equally important, the consumption deflator shows that prices for consumer durables continued to fall from 1995 right into 2008, one of the reasons the rate of inflation was relatively low, though still positive, and a clear indication that problems of over-accumulation have not been resolved.

It is at this point—after the Asian crisis of 1997 and the slide back toward recession following the bursting of the dotcom bubble in 2000–1—that two interconnected phenomena become crucial to postponing a general slump: massive growth of debt loads; and the US current account deficit (its shortfall in trade in goods and services and interest payments with the rest of the world), which operated as the "Keynesian engine" of the global economy over the past decade. And here too, as we shall see, the new form of world money played a central role.

Although it may seem paradoxical, it was the recently-hammered East Asian economies (plus China) that drove the next decade of growth

(1998–2007). Obeying the logic of capitalism, these economies were forced to cut exchange rates of local currencies, shed labor, reduce costs and dramatically restructure industry. Soon they were exporting their way back to growth, developing huge trade surpluses and soaring international reserves (mainly dollars). But this export-led growth was sustained overwhelmingly by the growing trade and current account deficits in the US. As commentators have noted, the American economy effectively became "the consumer of last resort." From 1980 to 2000, for instance, US imports rose 40 per cent, accounting for almost one-fifth of world exports, and four per cent of world gross domestic product. But by 2006, this level of consumption of foreign goods could only be sustained at the cost of an $857 billion US current account deficit (the shortfall in trade in goods and services and in interest payments with the rest of the world). The recovery after 1997, in other words, was built on the pillars of exceptionally low US interest rates, particularly from 2001; steady growth in consumer indebtedness; and a swelling US current account deficit. Absent those, there would have been no sustained recovery after 1997—and across the related crises in Russia (1998), at Long Term Capital Management (1998), Brazil (1999) and Argentina (2000–1).

No other country but the US could have run sustained current account deficits of this magnitude for so long. And, had it not broken convertibility with gold, it would have been confronted by another run on US gold supplies. But operating now as inconvertible world money, dollars had to be accepted by those governments with whose economies the US was running a deficit. And because the euphoria of a "boom" built on asset bubbles, particularly in real estate, created real investment opportunities—even if these were increasingly built on sand—foreign investors kept pouring funds into US markets. Foreign central banks, particularly in East Asia and the OPEC nations, did the same, recycling the dollars used to cover American current account deficits into the US, therein subsidizing the credit-driven consumer boom. Because the US dollar is the main form of world money, it remained attractive, so long as the American economy looked vibrant,

despite sustained—and unsustainable—current account deficits and a massive decline in US international net worth.

But—and this is a point that has eluded many analysts—as soon as the US bubble-driven boom showed signs of faltering, a flight from the dollar and the US economy was inevitable. And precisely this is what happened in 2007. First, US profits peaked in the third quarter of 2006, entering a period of decline. By the first half of 2007, private investors saw the writing on the wall. *Private capital flows into the US turned sharply negative in the third quarter of 2007, with an annualized outflow of $234 billion*—a stunning drop of $1.1 trillion from the previous quarter (when flows were positive to the tune of $823 billion). A reversal of this sort was absolutely without precedent. And it indicated that, contrary to some pundits, capital could flee the US economy and its currency as readily as anywhere else. What saved the US economy from a dizzying collapse of the dollar and an even more brutal seizure of credit markets was continued investment (particularly in Treasury bills and bonds) by central banks in East Asia and oil-producing Middle Eastern states. Tellingly, if Chinese reports are to be believed, this was provided only after US president George Bush begged his Chinese counterpart, Hu Jintao, to keep up purchases of US bonds.

But foreign capital had spoken. Belief in the US "boom" was evaporating. The real estate bubble began to deflate, mortgage-backed securities entered their free fall, hedge funds (first at Bear Stearns) collapsed, followed by investment banks. The rout was on—and it is far from over. In the process, the capacity of whopping US current account deficits, underpinned by debt-fuelled consumer spending, to buoy the world economy appears to be exhausted. Yet, to rebalance the global economy, to eliminate huge US deficits and enormous East Asian surpluses, means to destroy the source of demand that enabled growth in a period of over-accumulation (and it would also mean much larger falls in the US dollar). For this reason, short of a long slump that destroys massive amounts of capital, it will be extremely difficult for the world economy to find a new source of demand sufficient to restart sustained growth.

FICTITIOUS CAPITAL, CONTINUING FINANCIAL CRISES

Meanwhile, we will continue to be treated to a great destruction of capitals, both real and fictitious. The concept of fictitious capital is developed by Marx with two key features in mind. First, fictitious capitals are paper claims to wealth that exist alongside the actual means of production, stocks of goods and reserves of labour-power that capitals mobilize. Yet, they can be bought and sold many times over as if they were that wealth itself (this is why the prices of stocks can come to bear an absurdly inflated relation to the actual value and profitability of a firm). Secondly, fictitious capitals lay claim to future wealth, i.e. to shares of profits or wages that have not yet come into existence. So, when a bank creates a financial asset that provides the right to the principal and interest payments from my credit card debt—a process, as we have seen, known as *securitization*—it is not selling an existing asset but a claim to income that *may* be created in the future. Should I lose my job, however, and default on my credit card debt, then the "asset" sold by the bank is revealed to be totally fictitious, a mere piece of paper—nothing more than an IOU that will never be repaid.

And during the neoliberal period, for the three reasons I have outlined, we have seen an extraordinary build-up of fictitious capitals (paper claims to future wealth) within the system. A key structural underpinning for this is the mutation in the form of world money that produced massive new industries devoted to currency trading, and the related derivative instruments—futures, options, swaps and the like—that have proliferated over the neoliberal era. As much as there are sound structural reasons for a proliferation of risk-hedging derivatives in an era of floating exchange rates, derivatives have also provided a huge field for purely speculative activity—for financial gambling, as speculators make bets as to which currencies, commodities or national interest rates will rise or fall, and reap profits or losses according to the accuracy of their bets. Of course, the profits on the trading of such instruments have to come from somewhere—and that somewhere has been

the non-financial corporate sector, whose share of total profits has systematically fallen across the neoliberal era, while the financial share has soared, as we have seen. Secondly, the massive polarization of incomes produced both a huge demand from the wealthy for interest-paying financial instruments, which was eventually met by the extension of massive amounts of credit (particularly for mortgages, housing-backed loans, and credit cards) to working class households desperate to sustain living standards. Since 2000, mortgage-backed "securities" have been the flavour of the month, often in the form of Collateralized Debt Obligations (CDOs), that is, debts backed up by collateral (in this case houses). But if the value of the underlying asset (houses) plummets, no longer equal to the paper debts themselves, then the "collateral" is largely fictitious. And that is exactly what has happened. As housing prices have fallen off a cliff in the US, Ireland, UK, Spain, and elsewhere, the actual values of CDOs have collapsed, forcing banks to write off billions of dollars in assets. At the moment, billions worth of CDOs are actually trading at prices between 20 and 40 cents on the dollar.

This is what it means when Marx says a crisis involves a destruction of capital. The "values" of fictitious capitals—stocks, bills and all kinds of paper assets—which were previously treated as if they were real assets (and against which financial institutions borrowed), enter a freefall. At the same time, real capital is destroyed, as factories are mothballed, corporations go bust and sell off their buildings, machines, land, customer lists and so on at bargain basement prices. And what is particularly troubling for the ruling class is that, even after something approaching $10 trillion in bailouts, the destruction of capital is still in the early innings.

It is quite clear that huge global companies, of the scale of GM and Chrysler, are going to collapse or be merged. The same will happen in the electronics industry. Factories will be permanently closed, millions of jobs will be eviscerated (the OECD estimates eight million additional job losses in the major economies next year, and so far every mainstream prediction as to the severity of this slump has under-estimated). And the earthquakes in the financial sector are far from over, meaning that more bank meltdowns are in store.

There are, after all, a lot more ticking time bombs in the financial system. Consider, for instance, the rising defaults on credit card debt. And then contemplate the mountain of commercial paper, much of which was sold to finance Leveraged Buy Outs (LBOs), i.e. corporate takeovers made possible by borrowing funds and issuing IOUs. As corporate profits plummet, it gets harder and harder for firms that floated such paper to meet their payments. Many will go under. For that reason, LBO commercial paper now trades at between 60 and 70 cents on the dollar. Consider also the coming decline in commercial mortgages, as businesses, faced with falling sales and disappearing profits, can't keep up their mortgage payments on lands and buildings. Those losses will wobble more banks. But perhaps the biggest fault-line runs through the market in Credit Default Swaps. As we have seen, a CDS is essentially an insurance policy taken by a creditor as a protection against default by a debtor. When all is well in the economy, it is a nice source of revenues for the insuring party. But in a crisis, it can be deadly. It is as if a life insurance company all of a sudden had to pay out on a rapidly rising percentage of its policies. But, whereas death rates are relatively constant, in the midst of a financial crisis, default rates are not. To make matters worse, as noted above, any investor can buy a Credit Default Swap, even if they do not own a single share of the company in question. This encourages speculators to literally bet on the failure of a particular company. If you think GM will default on its debt, for instance, buying a CDS on GM debt is a great way to get a payout many times higher than what the CDS costs. As a result, as speculative bets build up, the insuring party (the seller of CDSs) is on the hook for a growing number of claims in the event of default. In crisis conditions, however, the insurer can quickly go under, unable to pay out to every claimant. But in that event, nobody is protected any longer against default of the toxic waste they might be holding. And that means complete and total financial market panic. That's the secret behind the US government bailout of AIG, the world's largest insurance company. AIG

holds about $1 trillion in CDSs. In the early fall of 2008, it defaulted on just $14 billion in Credit Default Swaps. That was enough to wobble the market. The government had no real option, if it wanted to avoid a devastating panic cycle, but to bail out AIG. Yet, a mere five weeks after having injected $85 billion into the giant insurer, the US Treasury had to pump in $65 billion more, taking the total to $150 billion, the largest such bailout in history. Tellingly, of the government funds AIG has drawn, fully 95 per cent have been used to cover losses in a single sector of the Credit Default Swap market. And there are likely to be bigger CDS losses to come, both at AIG and elsewhere, as there is another $54 trillion in CDSs out there, default on a small fraction of which could induce another major financial market collapse.

And here, questions of market regulation and transparency become important. Because most derivatives, including CDSs, are sold outside regulated markets, nobody really knows who holds what, or how much. That is why banks have become so leery of lending to one another. Some institutions are sitting on time bombs, trying to conceal massive amounts of financial toxic waste. But no one knows exactly who it might be. As bankers at Lehman Brothers said to US government officials when the two groups reviewed Lehman's books, "We have no idea of the details of our derivatives exposure and neither do you."

That's why, despite massive injections of liquidity into the banking system, credit markets are still stuck in low gear. There are very large financial crises yet to unfold. All parties involved know it. Until all of that junk is washed out of the system—which means the booking of massive losses of the sort Citigroup recently took—the financial crisis will not be over. . . .

LOOKING FORWARD

We are, in sum, entering the second stage of a profound systemic crisis of neoliberal capitalism. The first stage involved a staggering financial shock that toppled major banks and elicited a multi-trillion dollar bailout of the global financial system. The second stage will entail the collapse, merger, and/or effective nationalization of major corporations, especially in the auto and electronics industries. Unemployment will ratchet higher— much higher. And the ongoing collapse of sales and profits will topple more financial institutions.

It is impossible to predict exactly how this crisis will play out and how long the slump will last, though there is a strong possibility that it will be deep and protracted. Some things, however, are clear.

First, the crisis will induce massive centralization of capital. Already, banks have been merged on a huge scale. In Japan, the crisis of the 1990s saw three national banks emerge from a field that once boasted more than ten. In Britain, the merger of Lloyds bank with the Halifax Bank of Scotland (HBOS) will create a single institution with 40 per cent of all retail banking in the UK. Bank mergers in Brazil have produced one of the 20 largest banks in the world and the largest in Latin America. Meanwhile, pressure is growing for a merger of General Motors and Chrysler or for their merger with other firms, moves which would close large numbers of plants and axe tens of thousands of jobs. And in Asia, a merger of electronics giants Panasonic and Sanyo is also being mooted. As they centralize, combining former rivals under one corporate owner, capitals try simultaneously to get a leg up on their competitors and to concentrate their power over labour, so as to drive down wages, benefits and total employment.

Second, this crisis will also pose again the question of the balance of global economic power and the role of the dollar. One of the key problems making for financial instability is the diminished capacity of the US dollar to act as a stable form of world money. In fact, despite its recent rise as a "safe haven" in the midst of financial panic, the dollar is likely to resume its downward movement in the near future, creating more instability for the world economy. This has prompted economists at the UN to advocate reforms to the international monetary system that would move towards a multi-currency regime of world money. Notwithstanding the impressive rise of the euro in less than a decade—to the point that it exceeds the dollar in international bond markets and nearly equals it as a means of payment in cross-border transactions—there is no rival currency with the economic depth to displace the dollar. As a result, the world economy is likely to drift toward a more fractured regime of world money, with two or more currencies pushing for larger shares of global financial transactions. This could lead to pressures to develop an Asian currency bloc capable of rivalling the dollar and euro zones. It could also indicate new forms of competition between rival imperial projects— not the forms of territorial and military rivalry of the nineteenth and first half of the twentieth centuries, but competition between blocs for greater control of financial markets and global monetary privileges. Interestingly, elements of this have been grasped by the US National Intelligence Council, whose *Global Trends 2025* predicts a world order characterized by "multipolarity," rather than simple US dominance.

Third, centralization of capital and competition between blocs will also be played out by way of attempts to spatially reorganize capital, so that economies in the Global North can displace the effects of crisis onto those in the South. There has been a major build up of credit in a whole number of "emerging market" economies in recent years, and these debt loads will produce a variety of crises. Especially vulnerable will be countries like Turkey and South Africa, where economic growth has been driven by huge inflows of foreign capital. At some point during this crisis, if investors become wary of the prospects of these economies in the midst of a world slump, capital outflows will trigger major financial and currency crises. Those economies may then encounter their own version of the Asian crisis. And if the IMF is called in, western governments will press to buy up assets on the cheap, as was done to South Korea in particular in 1997, after IMF loan conditions facilitated perhaps "the biggest peacetime transfer of assets from domestic to foreign owners in the past fifty years anywhere in the world." As sharp regional crises unfold, therefore, major conflicts between governments in the North and South may emerge (over loan repayment, IMF conditions requiring greater liberalization and privatization and so on), with the capacity to ignite powerful social struggles. In Latin America, where a number of governments—Bolivia, Venezuela,

Ecuador and Argentina—already strike an oppositional stance towards the US-dominated economic order, such struggles may well assume an anti-imperial form. Campaigns for debt repudiation, bank nationalizations and the like could become part of significant social upheavals.

Fourth, just as nations at the top of the imperial order will try to inflict greater hardship on the South, so we can anticipate moves toward even more draconian restrictions on the movement of migrant labour. At the same time as they press for "free movement" of capital, governments at the core of the system also demand tighter control and regulation of the movement of labour. With the deepening of the economic crisis, many have already started to play the anti-immigrant card. Britain, in particular, has signalled a tightening up of immigration policy, and others will surely follow. As businesses fail, factories close and unemployment mounts, immigrant-bashing is likely to become more widespread. Moreover, government officials and parties on the right are likely to fan xenophobic sentiments of the sort that were on display earlier this year in countries like South Africa, where migrants from Zimbabwe in particular suffered violent assaults, or in South Korea, where undocumented migrants from the Philippines have been subjected to mass deportation. This crisis will thus put a premium on a Left for which anti-racism and defence of migrant workers are absolutely central to a politics of resistance.

Finally, this crisis also puts a premium on Left responses that are clearly *socialist* in character. The notion of calling for a "leashed capitalism" in the face of such a colossal failure of the capitalist market system represents an equally colossal failure of socialist imagination. If ever there was a moment to highlight the systemic failings of capitalism and the need for a radical alternative, it is now. True, the Left must be able to do this in a meaningful and accessible language, by way of formulating concrete socialist demands and strategies that speak eloquently and powerfully to real and compelling needs and interests of oppressed people. And this will certainly involve fighting for specific reforms—to save jobs, build social housing, cancel Third World debts, invest in ecologically sustainable industries, feed the poor. But, as Rosa Luxemburg pointed out more than a century ago, while Marxists have a duty to fight for social reforms, they ought to do so in a way that builds the revolutionary capacities of the world's workers to remake the world. And one crucial part of this involves popular education and agitation for socialism. Not to advance the critique of capitalism as a system, and not to highlight the need for a systemic transformation that will break the hold of the capitalist value form over human life is to squander an opportunity that lurks within this moment of crisis. This is a moment that calls out for bold, thoughtful socialist responses, a moment when socialist theory, joined to practical struggles, can become "a material force" for changing the world. But this requires insisting, in the face of capitalist crisis, that another world really is possible.

♔ REVIEW QUESTIONS

1. According to McNally, why is the U.S. financial crisis turning into a global slump? What are the two phases of the slump?
2. Why doesn't McNally accept the explanation that deregulation of financial markets caused the crisis?
3. In McNally's view, what is wrong with the analysis of the crisis that looks at declining profits?
4. As McNally explains it, financialized capitalism involves three phenomena. What are they and how do they come about?
5. What caused wage compression (lower wages) and a lower standard of living for the working class,

according to McNally? Why did this increase both private and public debt?
6. Why did the American economy boom and then bust, in McNally's view?
7. How does McNally explain Marx's concept of fictitious capital? How does it lead to financial gambling?
8. McNally sees some ticking time bombs in the financial system. What are they?
9. How does McNally think the crisis will play out in the future?

⚜ DISCUSSION QUESTIONS

1. Does McNally convince you that the U.S. financial crisis produced a global slump? Why or why not?
2. Is his explanation of the crisis plausible? What do you think?
3. McNally concludes that we have seen a colossal failure of the capitalist market system. Do you agree? Explain your answer.
4. In concluding, McNally suggests a radical socialist alternative to capitalism that involves saving jobs, building housing, investing in sustainable industries, and feeding the poor. Should we work toward these socialist goals? What is your view?

The Return to Depression Economics

PAUL KRUGMAN

Paul Krugman is professor of economics and international affairs at Princeton University. He is the author or editor of twenty books and more than 200 journal articles. He writes a column for *The New York Times* and a daily blog ("The Conscience of a Liberal"). In 2008 he won the Nobel Prize in Economics.

Krugman believes that the current financial crisis will not cause a depression, but it requires a return to depression economics, which focuses on demand-side economics rather than supply-side economics. There has been insufficient demand, that is, private spending. The obvious solution, Krugman thinks, is to put more capital into the economy. Giving the failed banks $700 billion to recapitalize is not enough. Instead, he thinks we may need a full temporary nationalization of the banks, as Sweden did in the early 1990s. The Fed should lend directly to the nonfinancial sector. The government should use good old Keynesian fiscal stimulus, as much as 4 percent of GDP. Finally, there has to be serious financial reform. For one thing, any essential financial institution that has to be rescued during a financial crisis should be regulated when there isn't a crisis so that it will not take excessive risks and get into trouble again.

The world economy is not in depression; it probably won't fall into depression, despite the magnitude of the current crisis (although I wish I was completely sure about that). But while depression itself has not returned, depression economics—the kinds of problems that characterized much of the world economy in the 1930s but have not been seen since—has staged a stunning comeback. Fifteen years ago hardly anybody thought that modern nations would be forced to endure bone-crushing recessions for fear of currency speculators, and that major advanced nations would find themselves persistently unable to generate enough spending to keep their workers and factories employed. The world economy has turned out to be a much more dangerous place than we imagined.

How did the world become this dangerous? More important, how do we get out of the current crisis, and what can we do to prevent such crises from happening in the first place? In this book I have told many stories; now it is time to try to draw some morals.

WHAT IS DEPRESSION ECONOMICS?

What does it mean to say that depression economics has returned? Essentially it means that for the first time in two generations, failures on the demand side of the economy—insufficient private spending to make use of the available productive capacity—have become the clear and present limitation on prosperity for a large part of the world.

We—by which I mean not only economists but also policymakers and the educated public at large—weren't ready for this. The specific set of foolish ideas that has laid claim to the name "supply-side economics" is a crank doctrine that would have had little influence if it did not appeal to the prejudices of editors and wealthy men. But over the past few decades there has been a steady drift in emphasis in economic thinking away from the demand side to the supply side of the economy.

This drift was partly the result of theoretical disputes within economics that—as they so often do—gradually filtered out, in somewhat garbled form, into wider discourse. Briefly, the source of the theoretical disputes was this: in principle, shortfalls of overall demand would cure themselves if only wages and prices fell rapidly in the face of unemployment. In the story of the depressed baby-sitting co-op, one way the situation could have resolved itself would have been for the price of an hour of baby-sitting in terms of coupons to fall, so that the purchasing power of the existing supply of coupons would have risen, and the co-op would have returned to "full employment" without any action by its management. In reality prices don't fall quickly in the face of recession, but economists have been unable to agree about exactly why. The result has been a series of bitter academic battles that have made the whole subject of recessions and how they happen a sort of professional minefield in which ever fewer economists dare to tread. And the public has understandably concluded either that economists don't understand recessions or that demand-side remedies have been discredited. The truth is that good old-fashioned demand-side macroeconomics has a lot to offer in our current predicament—but its defenders lack all conviction, while its critics are filled with a passionate intensity.

Paradoxically, if the theoretical weaknesses of demand-side economics are one reason we were unready for the return of depression-type issues, its practical successes are another. During all the decades that economists have argued with one another over whether monetary policy can actually be used to get an economy out of a recession, central banks have repeatedly gone ahead and used it to do just that—so effectively in fact that the idea of a prolonged economic slump due to insufficient demand became implausible. Surely the Federal Reserve and its counterparts in other countries could always cut interest rates enough to keep spending high; except in the very short run, then, the only limitation on economic performance was an economy's ability to produce—that is, the supply side.

Even now, many economists still think of recessions as a minor issue, their study as a faintly disreputable subject. Robert Lucas's presidential address, which I quoted in Chapter 1, explicitly made the case that the business cycle was no longer an important subject, and that economists should shift their attention to technological progress and long-run growth. These are fine, important issues, and in the long run they are what really matter—but as Keynes pointed out, in the long run we are all dead.

Meanwhile, in the short run the world is lurching from crisis to crisis, all of them crucially involving the problem of generating sufficient demand. Japan from the early 1990s onward, Mexico in 1995, Mexico, Thailand, Malaysia, Indonesia, and Korea in 1997, Argentina in 2002, and just about everyone in 2008—one country after another has experienced a recession that at least temporarily undoes years of economic progress, and finds that the conventional policy responses don't seem to have any effect. Once again, the question of how to create enough demand to make use of the economy's capacity has become crucial. Depression economics is back.

WHAT TO DO: DEALING WITH THE EMERGENCY

What the world needs right now is a rescue operation. The global credit system is in a state of paralysis, and a global slump is building momentum as I write this. Reform of the weaknesses that made this crisis possible is essential, but it can wait a little while. First, we need to deal with the clear and present danger. To do this, policymakers around the world need to do two things: get credit flowing again and prop up spending.

The first task is the harder of the two, but it must be done, and soon. Hardly a day goes by without news of some further disaster wreaked by the freezing up of credit. As I wrote this draft, for example, reports were coming in of the collapse of letters of credit, the key financing method for world trade. Suddenly, buyers of imports, especially in developing countries, can't carry through on their deals, and ships are standing idle: the Baltic Dry Index, a widely used measure of shipping costs, has fallen 89 percent this year.

What lies behind the credit squeeze is the combination of reduced trust in and decimated capital at financial institutions. People and institutions, including the financial institutions, don't want to deal with anyone unless they have substantial capital to back up their promises, yet the crisis has depleted capital across the board.

The obvious solution is to put in more capital. In fact, that's a standard response in financial crises. In 1933 the Roosevelt administration used the Reconstruction Finance Corporation to recapitalize banks by buying preferred stock—stock that had seniority over common stock in terms of its claims on profits. When Sweden experienced a financial crisis in the early 1990s, the government stepped in and provided the banks with additional capital equal to 4 percent of the country's GDP—the equivalent of about $600 billion for the United States today—in return for a partial ownership. When Japan moved to rescue its banks in 1998, it purchased more than $500 billion in preferred stock, the equivalent relative to GDP of around a $2 trillion capital injection in the United States. In each case, the provision of capital helped restore the ability of banks to lend, and unfroze the credit markets.

A financial rescue along similar lines is now underway in the United States and other advanced economies, although it was late in coming, thanks in part to the ideological tilt of the Bush administration. At first, after the fall of Lehman Brothers, the Treasury Department proposed buying up $700 billion in troubled assets from banks and other financial institutions. Yet it was never clear how this was supposed to help the situation. (If the Treasury paid market value, it would do little to help the banks' capital position, while if it paid above-market value it would stand accused of throwing taxpayers' money away.) Never mind: after dithering for three weeks, the United States followed the lead already set first by Britain and then by continental European countries, and turned the plan into a recapitalization scheme.

It seems doubtful, however, that this will be enough to turn things around, for at least three reasons. First, even if the full $700 billion is used for recapitalization (so far only a fraction has been committed), it will still be small, relative to GDP, compared with the Japanese bank bailout—and it's arguable that the severity of the financial crisis in the United States and Europe now rivals that of Japan. Second, it's still not clear how much of the bailout will reach the shadow banking system, the core of the problem. Third, it's not clear whether banks will be willing to lend out the funds, as opposed to sitting on them (a problem encountered by the New Deal seventy-five years ago).

My guess is that the recapitalization will eventually have to get bigger and broader, and that there will eventually have to be more assertion of government control—in effect, it will come closer to a full temporary nationalization of a significant part of the financial system. Just to be clear, this isn't a long-term goal, a matter of seizing the economy's commanding heights: finance should be reprivatized as soon as it's safe to do so, just as Sweden put banking back in the private sector after its big bailout in the early nineties. But for now the important thing is to loosen up credit by any means at hand, without getting tied up in ideological knots. Nothing could be worse than failing to do what's necessary out of fear that acting to save the financial system is somehow "socialist."

The same goes for another line of approach to resolving the credit crunch: getting the feds, temporarily, into the business of lending directly to the nonfinancial sector. The Federal Reserve's willingness to buy commercial paper is a major step in this direction, but more will probably be necessary.

All these actions should be coordinated with other advanced countries. The reason is the globalization of finance. . . . Part of the payoff to U.S. rescues of the financial system is that they help loosen up access to credit in Europe; part of the payoff to European rescue efforts is that they loosen up credit here. So everyone should be doing more or less the same thing; we're all in this together.

And one more thing: the spread of the financial crisis to emerging markets makes a global rescue for developing countries part of the solution to the crisis. As with recapitalization, parts of this were already in place at the time of writing: the International Monetary Fund was providing loans to countries with troubled economies like Ukraine, with less of the moralizing and demands for austerity that it engaged in during the Asian crisis of the 1990s. Meanwhile, the Fed provided swap lines to several emerging-market central banks, giving them the right to borrow dollars as needed. As with recapitalization, the efforts so far look as if they're in the right direction but too small, so more will be needed.

Even if the rescue of the financial system starts to bring credit markets back to life, we'll still face a global slump that's gathering momentum. What should be done about that? The answer, almost surely, is good old Keynesian fiscal stimulus.

Now, the United States tried a fiscal stimulus in early 2008; both the Bush administration and congressional Democrats touted it as a plan to "jump-start" the economy. The actual results were, however, disappointing, for two reasons. First, the stimulus was too small, accounting for only about 1 percent of GDP. The next one should be much bigger, say, as much as 4 percent of GDP. Second, most of the money in the first package took the form of tax rebates, many of which were saved rather than spent. The next plan should focus on sustaining and expanding government spending—sustaining it by providing aid to state and local governments, expanding it with spending on roads, bridges, and other forms of infrastructure.

The usual objection to public spending as a form of economic stimulus is that it takes too long to get going—that by the time the boost to demand arrives, the slump is over. That doesn't seem to be a major worry now, however: it's very hard to see any quick economic recovery, unless some unexpected new bubble arises to replace the housing bubble. (A headline in the satirical newspaper *The Onion* captured the problem perfectly: "Recession-Plagued Nation Demands New Bubble to Invest In.") As long as public spending is pushed along with reasonable speed, it should arrive in plenty of time to help—and it has two great advantages over tax breaks. On one side, the money would actually be spent; on the other, something of value (e.g., bridges that don't fall down) would be created.

Some readers may object that providing a fiscal stimulus through public works spending is what Japan did in the 1990s—and it is. Even in Japan, however, public spending probably prevented a weak economy from plunging into an actual depression. There are, moreover, reasons to believe that stimulus through public spending would work better in the United States, if done promptly, than it did in Japan. For one thing, we aren't yet stuck in the trap of deflationary expectations that Japan fell into after years of insufficiently forceful policies. And Japan waited far too long to recapitalize its banking system, a mistake we hopefully won't repeat.

The point in all of this is to approach the current crisis in the spirit that we'll do whatever it takes to turn things around; if what has been done so far isn't enough, do more and do something different, until credit starts to flow and the real economy starts to recover.

And once the recovery effort is well underway, it will be time to turn to prophylactic measures: reforming the system so that the crisis doesn't happen again.

FINANCIAL REFORM

We have magneto trouble, said John Maynard Keynes at the start of the Great Depression: most of the economic engine was in good shape, but a crucial component, the financial system, wasn't working. He also said this: "We have involved ourselves in a colossal muddle, having blundered in the control of a delicate machine, the working of which we do not understand." Both statements are as true now as they were then.

How did this second great colossal muddle arise? In the aftermath of the Great Depression, we redesigned the machine so that we *did* understand it, well enough at any rate to avoid big disasters. Banks, the piece of the system that malfunctioned so badly in the 1930s, were placed under tight regulation and supported by a strong safety net. Meanwhile, international movements of capital, which played a disruptive role in the 1930s, were also limited. The financial system became a little boring but much safer.

Then things got interesting and dangerous again. Growing international capital flows set the stage for devastating currency crises in the 1990s and for a globalized financial crisis in 2008. The growth of the shadow banking system, without any corresponding extension of regulation, set the stage for latter-day bank runs on a massive scale. These runs involved frantic mouse clicks rather than frantic mobs outside locked bank doors, but they were no less devastating.

What we're going to have to do, clearly, is relearn the lessons our grandfathers were taught by the Great Depression. I won't try to lay out the details of a new regulatory regime, but the basic principle should be clear: anything that has to be rescued during a financial crisis, because it plays an essential role in the financial mechanism, should be regulated when there *isn't* a crisis so that it doesn't take excessive risks. Since the 1930s commercial banks have been required to have adequate capital, hold reserves of liquid assets that can be quickly converted into cash, and limit the types of investments they make, all in return for federal guarantees when things go wrong. Now that we've seen a wide range of non-bank institutions create what amounts to a banking crisis, comparable regulation has to be extended to a much larger part of the system.

We're also going to have to think hard about how to deal with financial globalization. In the aftermath of the Asian crisis of the 1990s, there were some calls for long-term restrictions on international capital flows, not just temporary controls in times of crisis. For the most part these calls were rejected in favor of a strategy of building up large foreign exchange reserves that were supposed to stave off future crises. Now it seems that this strategy didn't work. For countries like Brazil and Korea, it must seem like a nightmare: after all that they've done, they're going through the 1990s crisis all over again. Exactly what form the next response should take isn't clear, but financial globalization has definitely turned out to be even more dangerous than we realized.

THE POWER OF IDEAS

As readers may have gathered, I believe not only that we're living in a new era of depression economics, but also that John Maynard Keynes—the economist who made sense of the Great Depression—is now more relevant than ever. Keynes concluded his masterwork, *The General Theory of Employment, Interest and Money*, with a famous disquisition on the importance of economic ideas: "Soon or late, it is ideas, not vested interests, which are dangerous for good or evil."

We can argue about whether that's always true, but in times like these, it definitely is. The quintessential economic sentence is supposed to be "There is no free lunch"; it says that there are limited resources, that to have more of one thing you must accept less of another, that there is no gain without pain. Depression economics, however, is the study of situations where there *is* a free lunch, if we can only figure out how to get our hands on it, because there are unemployed resources that could be put to work. The true scarcity in Keynes's world—and ours—was therefore not of resources, or even of virtue, but of understanding.

We will not achieve the understanding we need, however, unless we are willing to think clearly about our problems and to follow those thoughts wherever they lead. Some people say that our economic problems are structural, with no quick cure available; but I believe that the only important structural obstacles to world prosperity are the obsolete doctrines that clutter the minds of men.

♔ REVIEW QUESTIONS

1. According to Krugman, what is depression economics?

2. How does Krugman think we should deal with the current economic crisis?

3. In Krugman's view, why didn't the fiscal stimulus in 2008 work?

4. What kind of financial reform does Krugman recommend?

♔ DISCUSSION QUESTIONS

1. Is the full nationalization of most of the financial system a good idea? Why or why not?

2. Krugman thinks that rescuing developing countries is part of the solution to the crisis. Do you agree? Why or why not?

3. Krugman suggests a large fiscal stimulus—4 percent of GDP. Is massive government spending going to help? What is your view?

4. Krugman thinks it is clear that any firm that has to be rescued during a financial crisis should be regulated when there isn't a crisis. Is he right about this? Why or why not?

Meet the Hazzards

NOMI PRINS AND CHRISTOPHER HAYES

Nomi Prins was a managing director at Goldman Sachs. Currently she is a senior fellow at Demos, a nonpartisan public think tank. She is the author of *Other People's Money* (2006), *Jacked* (2006), and *It Takes a Pillage* (2009).

Christopher Hayes is a fellow at the New American Foundation. He is the author of numerous essays, articles, and reviews in magazines including *The New York Times Magazine*, *The Nation*, *The American Prospect*, and *The New Republic*.

Prins and Hayes explain the government bailout of the banks using an analogy. The banks are like the Hazzards, a couple about to go bankrupt because of bad bets and investments. Prins and Hayes admit that their analogy is not perfect: Some of the banks did not get bailed out, and households do not lend money or borrow to bet. But the analogy helps reveal all the ways the government helped the banks. It was not just one loan, but a huge amount of money—$17.5 trillion, money the Fed created out of thin air. Prins and Hayes think that some of the money should have been used to bail out people instead of banks, and they note the lack of accountability. Rewarding people for acting recklessly and compulsively makes them continue this behavior. Without serious reform, more bailouts will be needed and the money that has already been poured into the current bailout will be wasted.

Source: "Meet the Hazzards" by Nomi Prins and Christopher Hayes from THE NATION, October 2009.

As we mark the end of the first year of the financial bailout, the public seems to regard the government's actions with a toxic combination of rage and confusion. People are pissed off but too bewildered to know what to do with that anger. The confusion isn't an accident. The government hasn't exactly been forthcoming about how it's made buckets of money available to the banking sector. When it does disclose some information—such as in July's SIGTARP report from the Treasury or the Federal Reserve's weekly balance sheet—it's in the form of intimidating descriptions, accounting mumbo jumbo and technical reports that do little to illuminate just what the hell is going on.

What's worse, banks and the establishment press have portrayed TARP as the sum of the banking industry's federal subsidies. An August 30 *New York Times* article, "As Banks Repay Bailout Money, U.S. Sees a Profit," gives the impression that taxpayers should be happy to have made $4 billion on the deal, as if our checks were in the mail. But when the government became Wall Street's bank, it wasn't just $700 billion of TARP money that flew north to Wall Street. TARP was but a small fraction (roughly 4 percent) of the full $17.5 trillion bailout and subsidization of the financial sector. The details of this total bailout are complicated, but the basic mechanisms aren't beyond the average citizen's grasp. We're going to walk you through it.

FIVE EASY PIECES: THE TALE OF JOE AND KATIE

There are five ways the Treasury, the Fed and other government entities have propped up the banking sector. In order to understand how each of these works, let's consider how this assistance might have looked had it been directed at a household, rather than a bank, teetering on the edge of bankruptcy. The analogy isn't exact, but considering the bailout in this manner helps make the whole thing a lot clearer.

Imagine a couple living in a three-bedroom house outside the Twin Cities. Call them Joe and Katie Hazzard. The Hazzards own a small off-track-betting (OTB) business and have some investments and a mortgage on their house. But business is terrible (no one has extra money to make bets); Katie recently lost her job; their investments have hemorrhaged value; and they can't make their mortgage, car or credit card payments. So they ask their local bank for a loan. "No dice," says the bank. "We can't give you money to pay your debts because you're no longer a good credit risk for us." That's more or less what happened to the banks last fall: they couldn't and wouldn't lend to one another.

CAPITAL INJECTIONS AND DIRECT LOANS

So the Hazzards go to the Federal Bailout Bank, which says, "Here's some money. Do with it what you want, and someday down the road, if and when you're out of the woods, you'll have to pay us back with a little bit of interest." That's roughly what the $700 billion TARP was: a direct injection of capital to purchase preferred shares, which is really more like extending a loan than making the investment the government said it was, with some very light strings attached.

But then Joe says that the handout isn't enough. It turns out that not only does he own a gambling business; he has a bit of a gambling habit. Joe made big money in previous years betting on the New England Patriots to win the Super Bowl and figured he couldn't go wrong placing the same wager again. But then Tom Brady injured his knee last year, and Joe got creamed. Inveterate gambler that he is, he's doubled down on the Patriots this year, but he won't be paid off (if, that is, the Patriots win) until later in the year. But Joe has a boatload of outstanding gambling debts he needs to pay now.

So the Federal Bailout Bank decides it'll help out. To cover the truly pressing debts (the bookie is about to send over some goons with baseball bats), the bank will just write a check. That's what the Fed did to back the losses of AIG's credit default swaps and other businesses, and what the Fed and Treasury did together by providing protection to Citigroup in the event that more of its toxic assets lost value. The money—$1.4 trillion—was structured as a loan, but it's a bit unclear how it will ever be paid back.

In addition to his bets on the Patriots, it turns out, Joe's been making bets on just about anything, the outcomes of which have yet to be determined. The Hazzards are scared that a lot of these bets don't look too promising (e.g., Joe's wager that Kanye West will win this year's Nobel Peace Prize). What they want is to unload their positions in those bets, to have some other gambler pay them the original sum they put down and take on the risk. If the bet makes good, the new gambler would get the rewards. If it doesn't, he would take the loss. But they can't find anyone to do that because so many of Joe's wagers were so reckless.

Once again, the Bailout Bank steps in to sweeten the deal, telling would-be gamblers it will put in $6 for every $1 they put up. That means Joe's Kanye West bet for $100 (at very long odds) can now be purchased by a fellow gambler for just $14.28. If Kanye does, in fact, win the Nobel, then this lucky gambler will get paid as if he had put up the whole $100. If not, he's only out fourteen bucks. That's the crux of Tim Geithner's $1 trillion Public-Private Investment Fund, which would bring the full amount of capital injections and direct loans to $2.4 trillion.

INDIRECT LOANS AND GUARANTEES

The Hazzards come back and claim that wasn't enough; they're still screwed. So the bank says, "We can give you some more short-term, thirty-day loans to get you through (even longer-term ones if that doesn't work), but you have to post collateral. It doesn't have to be very valuable: your old bicycles in the garage, your basement sofa-bed, maybe that baseball card collection you planned to use to pay for your kids' college educations. And if you still need more at the end of the thirty days, you can post some more junk from your attic as collateral."

This more or less corresponds to the newly established Federal Reserve facilities (think: credit unions for banks), which provide money to banks in exchange for various assets as collateral. Both the Federal Reserve and the Federal Reserve Bank of New York administer these facilities. They run the gamut from the $1.8 trillion Commercial Paper Funding Facility, created to provide more credit for households and businesses (which, to be fair, did help calm the markets; but it didn't get to households or to most small businesses), to the $540 billion Money Market Investor Funding Facility, created to back private funds owned by banks, insurance companies or investment advisory companies.

Joe comes back again to Bailout Bank and says that he's still short, but he has a proposal. "I'm not going to ask you for any more loans. Promise. Instead, I'm going to see if someone else will lend me money. The problem is, I'm such a terrible credit risk I need someone to back me up. Maybe instead of me asking for a loan, I could kind of use your name to ask?" That's the role the FDIC played for Goldman Sachs and other firms, which took advantage of $940 billion in FDIC guarantees to raise cheap money for themselves and another $684 billion of backing for their trading accounts as an additional perk.

All in all, these kinds of guarantees, along with the indirect collateral loans for the banking industry, total $6.7 trillion, and there is precious little transparency coming from the Fed regarding most of it. In fact, Ben Bernanke told Congress in November that too much transparency about which banks got which loans and for what collateral would be "counterproductive."

GENERAL BACKING AND SUBSIDIZATION

Bailout Bank isn't done helping the Hazzards. It turns out that the couple also has a vacation condo that's lost some value. As part of propping up their balance sheet, the Bailout Bank promises to guarantee the price of the condo. In other words, if Joe and Katie are forced to sell the condo for less than its value before the housing crisis, the Bailout Bank will write them a check for the difference in price.

This is considered "general backing," and in the bailout economy it applies to all kinds of things that weren't supposed to lose value but did and might continue to do so in the future—most important, money market funds. About $4.4 trillion was set aside for general backing of financial firms, including $3.7 trillion to mitigate any future problems with money market funds and an extra $700 billion for the FDIC to continue to back depositor funds. (The banks didn't want to pony up more premiums to do it themselves. Can you imagine just deciding you don't want to pay your insurance premiums, yet receiving insurance anyway? Well, it's like that.)

GOVERNMENT-SPONSORED ENTITIES HELP

Another part of what's putting the hurt on the Hazzards is the plummeting value of their big investment in what had been the rock-solid, blue-chip ABC Corp. This was supposed to be one of their safest investments, but now they can't sell the stock without taking a massive loss. So the Bailout Bank steps in. It starts buying tons of ABC stock, flooding it with capital and creating an inflated price for the stock in the process. This in turn raises the value of the Hazzards' investment. Bailout Bank even goes so far as to start buying ABC's products, hoping to increase its sales and thus its stock price.

Though a bit imprecise, this is basically how the Fed and Treasury propped up Fannie Mae and Freddie Mac and in the process helped the banks. The Treasury bought Fannie and Freddie stock and also the mortgages that the two enterprises sell, plus it gave them some extra money to lend. All the government's financial assistance to prop up entities that were considered safe at one point comes to $2.2 trillion.

GLOBAL MARKET AND CREDIT EXPANSIONS

Finally, just to make sure the Hazzards can get by, the Bailout Bank decides to help everyone who might use their business with some capital of their own. Since the couple runs an OTB business, when the bank gives a shot of money to everyone in town, a few people start gambling with the Hazzards again. In effect, that's what the Fed did when it dumped $905 billion into international markets to move things along and another $881 billion into domestic ones. Throwing cash here and there into the markets is the Fed's job; throwing the amounts it did was an act of desperation, although almost certainly needed.

It's important to remember that not everything the government did was solely bank-friendly. The Fed and Treasury extended $1.82 trillion in fiscal support, including about $1 trillion in direct consumer assistance (including the Recovery Act, the Cash for Clunkers program and first-time homebuyer tax breaks). It gave another $881 billion to help guarantee various federal home mortgage programs, which really did help homeowners. But this help is dwarfed by the mountains of dollars thrown at Wall Street.

Our Joe and Katie Hazzard parable is inexact. Not every bank took advantage of every kind of assistance (though some, like Citigroup, pretty much did). And households aren't structured like banks; they don't lend money or borrow big to bet big. But that's why cheap credit is a much bigger boon to banks than to households. Borrowing at a lower rate than they lend is how banks make money. Getting to borrow for next to nothing almost guarantees massive profits.

The Hazzards' tale does illuminate a few key aspects of the bailout that tend to be obscured by acronyms and decimal places. It shows the extraordinary measures the government took to prop up the banks and the financial system. It's not just one mechanism, one check or one loan. It's concentric circles of support, from "Here's some money to cover your losses" (AIG) to "We're gonna make sure there's money flowing through all the neighborhoods near you so you keep having customers" (international assistance).

It also shows how hard it is to answer the question, How much did it all cost? The amount of money that's been floated, injected and dispersed in the ways we've listed above is $17.5 trillion. But what the final cost will be is not yet clear. A lot depends on how the Hazzards do. They might pay back a lot of the loans (perhaps even with interest) and not use up the guarantees.

Their condo may rise in value, or they might have to sell it at a loss and rely on the Bailout Bank's price guarantee. The baseball card collection taken as collateral may end up in the bank's hands, and then the total loss will depend on what the card collection turns out to be worth. In short, while we can add up the total exposure of the bailouts, we can't yet tally their cost.

Finally, our tale shows how fully the banking industry has relied on the government to keep it afloat. This is a crucial point because many banks want to argue that once they've paid back their TARP money, they have discharged their obligations and are private entities again, unbeholden in any way to taxpayers.

Another question our parable doesn't answer is, Where does all the money come from? Most of it has been "printed" by the Fed, which expanded its balance sheet and, in so doing, created money out of thin air. There's nothing wrong with printing money for the sake of keeping us from another Great Depression. In fact, not taking this step would have been disastrous. But the problem is how the money has been channeled. All that money was funneled through the banks; the real Joe and Katies—the actual households facing foreclosure and declining assets—haven't gotten much help. In fact, foreclosures are at an all-time high (7.5 million US homes are in foreclosure), and there have been 1.25 million personal bankruptcies this year through June (up 34 percent from last year). Unemployment continues to climb. The FDIC continues to take over failing banks. Credit has tightened, not loosened as all the pre-bailout rhetoric promised.

A fraction of the $17.5 trillion bailout could have been used to cut the principal of homeowners' mortgages (using homes, even devalued ones, as collateral) and cover student loans at zero percent interest. Rather than pouring it into the top layers—the banks—a people's bailout would have cost less and been more humane. And it likely would have prevented the ongoing increase in defaults, foreclosures and general economic anxiety.

The banks would have hated that, of course. Even in their degraded state they have a lot of friends in Washington. Imagine if the Hazzards started using some of their easy money to hire lobbyists to make sure the Bailout Bank maintained its pro-Hazzard policies. Because that's what's going on. Banks are lobbying Congress very hard to maintain their setup. Just one year after the crisis, boasting record profits and on track for record bonuses, they are darkly warning that any new regulation could hamper growth.

Given the banks' newfound publicly sponsored financial health, Washington has little incentive to rock the boat by proposing serious reforms. True, some necessary steps are being discussed by Congress: it's important to have a Consumer Financial Protection Agency to counteract the damage caused by lax oversight, and higher capital requirements so that banks can pay for their own risk fallout. But the Fed should not be the premier risk regulator, nor should we believe that it will cap extreme bonuses—President Obama doesn't even support a cap. Parts of the media are already reporting the end of the recession; Obama has moved to reappoint Bernanke, crediting him with keeping the country from a Great Depression, and has given tacit approval to the free flow of bank subsidies. The Treasury, headed by the man who was at the helm of the New York Fed when it nearly went down, is no less culpable for bad decisions.

Such lack of accountability seems to be something of a theme. Despite conducting themselves recklessly, compulsively, almost sociopathically, our fictional Joe and Katie Hazzard got a lot of money to help maintain their lifestyle and assets. But what happens when they take all that money and double down on the wrong bet? Will they be back for another helping? Why wouldn't they be? Given everything our government has said and done so far, and the meager reform ideas on the table, it's very likely there will be another bad bet coming from the entire industry—and with it, the vaporizing of much of the assistance doled out to avoid that very occurrence.

♔ REVIEW QUESTIONS

1. Prins and Hayes describe five ways the government has helped the banking sector. How does each work for the banks and for the Hazzards?

2. Why do Prins and Hayes think the Hazzards-banks analogy is inexact but still illuminating?

♔ DISCUSSION QUESTIONS

1. Would a people's bailout have been better than a bank's bailout? Why or why not?

2. Prins and Hayes suggest that the banking industry should be subject to serious reforms. Do you agree? If so, what reforms do you recommend?

PROBLEM CASES

1. Government Bailouts

As we have seen, the U.S. federal government allocated more than a trillion dollars to bail out troubled companies during the Great Recession. By 2009, a total of $573 billion in taxpayer money had been given or promised to 719 companies and 12 programs. (For a complete list of these companies and programs, see http://bailout.propublica.org.) Banks received more than $173 billion; Bank of America got $45 billion, and Citigroup $50 billion. Fannie Mae and Freddie Mac received more than $95 billion. General Motors got $50 billion. Some companies quickly returned the money. Goldman Sachs returned the $10 billion it received, but remained the subject of controversy.

By far the largest amount of money was given to American International Group, Inc. (AIG). The government initially gave AIG an $85 billion credit line from the Federal Reserve (the Fed), but later this was increased to about $182 billion. In March 2009, AIG reported a $62 billion loss for the fourth quarter of 2008. This was the largest quarterly loss by any company in U.S. history. At the same time, AIG announced that it was awarding a lavish $198 million in retention and bonus payments to members of its Financial Products Subsidiary, the trading unit that was principally responsible for the firm's meltdown by making reckless and highly leveraged investments. The top recipient received more than $6.4 million, and the top

seven received bonuses of more than $4 million each. Another hundred traders received bonuses of $1 to $2 million. In June 2008, CEO Martin Sullivan left the firm with a payout package worth $68 million. This was his reward for guiding AIG to several quarters of gigantic losses. During his tenure as CEO, AIG's stock went from a high of more than $70 a share to a low of $1.25 on September 16, 2008.

An interesting feature of this bailout was the behavior of the AIG employees. After the government bailout, they continued to treat themselves to vacations at company (or taxpayer) expense. A week after the initial bailout, AIG employees spent $444,000 at a California retreat for spa treatments, banquets, and golfing. Later there was an English hunting trip costing $86,000 and $343,000 spent on a trip to a luxury resort in Phoenix, Arizona.

The justification for the government bailout of this failed company was that it was just too big to fail. In other words, AIG's bankruptcy would produce bad consequences, at least in the short term. Jobs would be lost and credit markets would be negatively affected. Critics pointed out that the main beneficiary of the AIG bailout was Goldman Sachs, the firm that was the largest recipient of public funds from AIG— nearly $13 billion that was owed because of credit default swap contracts. AIG's transfer of this money to

Goldman allowed the investment bank to return the $10 billion it had received from the government. In other words, critics complained that the AIG bailout was really a backdoor bailout of Goldman Sachs. In 2009, Goldman announced it was planning to give more than $23 billion in bonuses to its employees after three profitable quarters. In 2008, Goldman gave its employees $11 billion, about the same amount as it received from the government.

Another controversial bailout was the government takeover of General Motors (GM). GM is the world's second largest automaker. (Toyota is now the world's largest automaker; it passed GM in 2008.) GM makes cars and trucks in 34 countries and employs 244,500 people around the world. GM filed for Chapter 11 bankruptcy on June 1, 2009, after several years of losing money. According to the filing, GM had $82.3 billion in assets and $172.8 billion in liabilities. One reason for the company's failure was decline in sales. During the 1990s, GM profits were based on sales of gas-guzzling sport utility vehicles (SUVs) such as the Chevrolet Tahoe, the Suburban, and the GMC Yukon. For each SUV sold, GM made as much as $15,000 profit. But rising gas prices resulted in fewer sales. It did not help that GM vehicles acquired a reputation of inferior quality. In 2008, GM sales in the United States dropped 45 percent.

GM emerged from Chapter 11 bankruptcy on July 10, 2009. It is now majority-owned by the U.S. and Canadian governments. GM plans an initial stock offering in 2010, but in 2009 no shares were available to the public.

A common objection to these bailouts is that they create a moral hazard. By rescuing AIG, the government allowed AIG executives and employees to escape responsibility for making bad investments. This makes it likely that they will continue to make bad investments in the future. In fact, it appears that they were rewarded by the taxpayer for losing money. Rewarding failure encourages more failure. As for GM, it has escaped the consequences of making unwanted and low-quality vehicles. This makes it likely that the company will continue to make undesirable vehicles in the future. For example, how many people are going to buy a Chevrolet Volt for $40,000 when they can get a Honda Insight for much less? (A Toyota Prius is another cheaper car,

but some of them had problems with sudden acceleration and braking.)

After being bailed out, Goldman quickly returned to making huge profits by speculating in markets—stocks, bonds, and currencies. They became a bank holding company, which allowed the firm to borrow money cheaply. But instead of loaning money, the traditional role of a bank holding company, Goldman continued to engage in profitable but risky speculation. This makes it likely that it will get into trouble again.

Another problem is that the bailouts seem arbitrary and unfair. Why did the government let Lehman Brothers fail and save Goldman Sachs? Many critics thought the answer was favoritism on the part of Treasury Secretary Henry Paulson, a former chairman and CEO of Goldman; he was helping his friends, and at the same time eliminating Lehman, Goldman's chief rival. Certainly Goldman has prospered with Lehman out of the picture.

Then there is the general complaint, coming from free-market economists, that these government bailouts amount to socialism, which they view as a discredited economic system. In a competitive free market, better companies replace failed companies. Saving failed companies blocks the creative development of better companies, which are necessary for a healthy economy. It makes it likely that there will be another financial crisis down the road. Periodic unemployment and bankrupt companies are the price paid for a growing economy. After all, a free-market economy does not guarantee employment or profits.

What is your view? Should the government bail out private companies? Why or why not?

Socialists are not happy with the bailouts either. If companies need to be bailed out by the government, then why shouldn't the government just take over the companies? Companies that are essential to the economy should be nationalized. The government can do a better job of running these companies than executives who have proven themselves to be greedy and incompetent. That, at least, is one socialist view. Do you agree? Why or why not?

Are some companies too big to fail? If so, then the logical thing to do is to break them up and make them smaller. But the government did just the opposite with the banks; they got bigger. JP Morgan took over Bear Stearns and Washington Mutual. Bank of America bought Merrill Lynch. Wells Fargo acquired Wachovia. Now we have even bigger banks, which will have to be bailed out again when they get into trouble. Wouldn't it be better to break up banks and companies that are too big to fail and limit the growth of companies in the future? Explain your view.

2. Executive Compensation

(There is much discussion of this. For example, see "Bonus Babies," *Vanity Fair*, February 2, 2009.) One striking feature of the Great Recession was the excessive compensation paid to the CEOs and executives of the big companies responsible for the crisis.

Lloyd Blankfein, the CEO of Goldman Sachs, which received $10 billion in bailout money, set the record. In 2007 he took home $68.5 million in cash and equity. (By comparison, a full-time minimum-wage worker makes $15,080 a year.) His two co-presidents, Gary D. Cohn and Jon Winkelried, got $67.5 million each. Blankfein's total compensation from 2003 to 2007 was $210,169,732 according to Equilar, the compensation-tracking firm. Only a year after being bailed out by the taxpayer, Goldman planned to pay its employees more than $23 billion in bonuses. Some of the top executives would get stock rather than cash.

Like Goldman, Morgan Stanley received $10 billion in taxpayer money. John Mack, the CEO at Morgan Stanley, has been awarded $69,565,233 since he started with the company in 2005. In 2007, Morgan Stanley handed out $9.9 billion in bonuses, almost the same amount it received from TARP.

Merrill Lynch also got a $10 billion bailout. E. Stanley O'Neal was the CEO until he left in 2007. His compensation for five years was $87 million. His successor, John Thain, got a $15 million signing bonus and a multiyear pay package worth about $120 million. Later, Merrill Lynch was sold to Bank of America. On December 8, 2009, Thain asked for a $10 million bonus, but the directors balked at the idea of giving Thain such a generous bonus when Merrill's losses for three quarters had come to $11.67 billion. Then Bank of America CEO Ken Lewis fired Thain for failing to disclose $4 billion in bonuses that Merrill Lynch paid out before the deal with Bank of America was closed.

Thomas K. Montag began working at Merrill shortly before it was sold to Bank of America. He received a signing bonus of more than $39 million plus $50 million for his Goldman stock. Peter S. Kraus worked for Merrill for only three months. He left when Merrill was sold to Bank of America. He received $25 million for three months' work.

Bank of America CEO Ken Lewis gets $20 million a year. (In April 2009, Lewis was fired as chairman of the board of directors but remained as the CEO.) According to New York Attorney General Andrew Cuomo, Bank of America issued more than $3 billion in cash and stock bonuses to executives in 2008, despite receiving $25 billion in bailout funds. On January 16, 2009, Bank of America received an additional $20 billion from TARP, bringing the total to $45 billion. In addition, Bank of America received $5.2 billion in bailout money channeled through AIG.

Citigroup has received $45 billion in government money, while CEO Vikram Pandit was paid over $213 million for taking over the troubled company. Pandit had already received about $165 million in connection with the sale of Old Land Partners, an investment firm that Citigroup bought in 2008. In addition, he was given a sign-on grant of stock and options worth more than $48 million. Other executives at the firm received multimillion dollar bonuses. Michael Klein, the co-head of Citigroup's investment bank, was awarded more than $19 million. Lewis Kaden, a vice chairman, added more than $8 million to his salary in 2007. At the same time, Citigroup's shares declined 47 percent, and the bank had more than $20 billion in losses.

As we have noted, Lehman Brothers went bankrupt in 2008. In 2007, Lehman CEO Richard S. Fuld received more than $34 million in compensation, and in 2006 he took home upwards of $40 million. During his tenure he collected about half a billion dollars in total compensation. In 2009 the state of New Jersey began a lawsuit against Fuld and other Leman executives for fraud and misrepresentation. The lawsuit seeks compensatory damages of $118 million in addition to punitive damages.

It is hard to see how this excessive compensation is justified. It bears no relation to good performance. Poor performance is rewarded too. This means there is no disincentive for taking major risks and losing money. If a Wall Street executive can lose billions and still get a $2 or $3 million bonus, why not take a chance on making millions and getting an even bigger bonus? There is no danger of the firm going bankrupt because the government is there to bail it out (except in the case of Lehman).

One proposal is for the government to "claw back" money from companies getting TARP money. Executive compensation would be limited to $500,000 a year. Any compensation over that would be returned to the government. Is this a good idea? Why or why not?

Another proposal is to require the executives of companies getting pubic money to give up their bonuses until the company has returned the money. This would encourage them to return the company to profitability. Why shouldn't the government require this? Explain your view.

In October 2009, the Obama administration announced that it planned to reduce the total compensation for twenty-five of the top earners at seven of the bailed-out companies. The executives at AIG, Citigroup, Bank of America, GM, and Chrysler will take about a 50 percent cut in total compensation. However, the plan still allows multimillion-dollar pay packages; for example, 14 of Citigroup's executives will get between $5 and $9 million. Moreover, the plan does not cover the banks that returned government loans, namely Goldman Sachs, JP Morgan, and Morgan Stanley. Is this plan acceptable? Why or why not?

3. Shadow Banking

Five major players were involved in the financial crisis of 2008: Goldman Sachs, Morgan Stanley, Lehman Brothers, Bear Stearns, and Merrill Lynch. They were investment banks that traded in securities and managed corporate mergers and acquisitions. Unlike depository banks (such as the Bank of America), the investment banks were not subject to many safety regulations. They were allowed to operate with a very high level of financial leverage, that is, with a high ratio of debt relative to the liquid assets available to pay immediate claims. Before the crisis, these banks had leverage ratios as high as 35 to 1. In other words, for each dollar available to pay claims, they had thirty-five dollars of debt. High leverage magnifies profits during boom periods but magnifies losses during downturns. To finance the debt, the banks relied on short-term liquid markets such as money market funds, meaning they had to frequently borrow and repay. When the housing market began declining, the market in mortgage-backed securities declined too, with the result that the banks had huge losses. Investors stopped providing funds via the short-term markets, and the banks were unable to pay claims when investors demanded their money. They went bankrupt and were either bailed out or sold.

Bear Stearns was one of the first to get into trouble. The bank had been a pioneer in mortgage-backed securities. In 2007 Bear had about $13 trillion in derivative financial instruments (at least that was the notational value) and only $11 billion in liquid assets. This was a highly leveraged balance sheet with many illiquid and possibly worthless assets. Investors lost confidence and stopped loaning money. In March 2008, the Fed provided an emergency loan to avert the sudden collapse of the company, but it could not be saved. Bear was sold to JP Morgan Chase for $10 a share (Bear's stock had been as high as $133 a share before the crisis). The collapse of this company was the beginning of the meltdown of the Wall Street investment banking industry. Lehman Brothers went bankrupt. Merrill Lynch was sold to Bank of America. Both Morgan Stanley and Goldman Sachs became traditional bank holding companies, which meant that they were subject to more regulation by the government.

Economists have described the investment banking system as *shadow banking* because it was unregulated. In his book *The Return of Depression Economics and the Crisis of 2008*, Paul Krugman argues that the collapse of the shadow banking system was the primary cause of the financial crisis. He thinks the government should have regulated the investment banks. He proposes a simple rule: Anything that does what a bank does, and has to be rescued in crises the way banks are, should be regulated like a bank. Do you agree? Why or why not?

4. The Invisible Hand and the Prisoner's Dilemma

The basic assumption of free-market capitalism is that the individual's pursuit of rational self-interest benefits everyone. This is often explained in terms of Adam Smith's metaphor of the invisible hand. When an individual seeks his own benefit, there is an invisible hand that promotes the general welfare. The hand is an invisible process because the individual does not intend to help others and there is no explicit agreement to do so. But how exactly does it work in the marketplace? Free-market economists assume that a rational consumer will choose to buy at the lowest available price, and that entrepreneurs will choose to sell at a price that gives them a profit. The resulting market price reflects the self-interest of both the consumer and the entrepreneur and so both benefit. The consumer buys a valued good or service at an acceptable price and the entrepreneur makes a profit. Furthermore, the market price corrects itself. If the consumer will not buy at a certain price, the rational entrepreneur lowers the price. If the price goes too low, so that the entrepreneur does not make a profit, then she raises the price.

Does the invisible hand really work to maximize the general welfare? The Prisoner's Dilemma, a famous puzzle in game theory, seems to give us a situation or set of situations in which it does not work, where the rational pursuit of self-interest does not produce the best possible outcome.

Suppose that two people are being held prisoner in separate cells so they cannot communicate with each other. They are accused of burglary. The police interrogate each prisoner. They tell both that if neither confesses to the crime, they will each be sentenced to two years in jail. If one confesses and the other does not, then the one who confesses will go free, and the one who did not confess will get a sentence of five years. If they both confess, they will each get a sentence of three years.

What should a prisoner do in this situation? Suppose the other prisoner does not confess. In that case,

the best choice is to confess and go free. Suppose the other prisoner does confess. In that case, the best choice is still to confess and get the three-year sentence instead of the five-year sentence. If both prisoners reason in this way, then they will both confess and end up serving the three-year sentences. This is called the "dominant strategy." But this dominant strategy does not produce the best outcome, for if they had both refused to confess they would both have received two-year sentences.

Although it may not be obvious, the Prisoner's Dilemma has implications for economic behavior. Suppose GM and Toyota are deciding on auto prices. If they cooperate and keep their prices high, then they will each make a profit of $10 million a month. This strategy produces the best outcome. (It is akin to both prisoners refusing to confess.) If Toyota competes by setting a lower price, and GM keeps its price high, then Toyota's profit rises to $12 million, and GM's profit goes down to $6 million. If both set their prices low, the profits for both are $8 million. (This is akin to both prisoners confessing.) What should GM do? If Toyota keeps its price high, then GM should lower its price and make a higher profit. If Toyota lowers its price, then GM should do the same, so it at least gets the same profit as Toyota. If both GM and Toyota reason in this way, then they both lower their prices. This is the dominant strategy even though it does not produce the best outcome for the auto companies.

Or consider the situation of the investment banks deciding whether or not to invest in highly leveraged, high-risk securities. Let's call this the dangerous bet. If both Lehman Brothers and Goldman Sachs do not make the dangerous bet, then both avoid bankruptcy. This is the best outcome. (This is akin to both prisoners refusing to confess.) If Goldman makes the dangerous bet, and Lehman does not, then Goldman has higher profits and Lehman has lower profits. If they both make the dangerous bet, then they both have higher profits in the short term but risk going bankrupt. (This is akin to both prisoners confessing.) What should Lehman do? If Goldman makes the dangerous bet, then Lehman should too in order to get higher profits. (I assume that Lehman cannot accept lower profits than its rival Goldman.) If Goldman does not make the dangerous bet, then Lehman should make this bet in order to have higher profits than Goldman. (I assume that Lehman will seek higher profits than its rival Goldman.) If both Lehman and Goldman reason along these lines, then they will both make the dangerous bet, even though it carries the risk of going bankrupt. This is the dominant strategy, but as we know, it did not produce the best outcome.

Does the Prisoner's Dilemma describe what happened to the investment banks? Why or why not?

Does it also describe the behavior of greedy individual investors? What do you think?

Does this puzzle pose a serious problem for free-market capitalism? Explain your view.

☙ SUGGESTED READINGS

For factual information, see *The New York Times* website (www.nytimes.com). More useful information can be found at the *Financial Times* (www.ft.com/home/us), and the *Monthly Review* (www.monthlyreview.org), an independent socialist magazine. Specific facts can often be found or checked on Google.com.

Adam Smith, *An Inquiry into the Nature and Causes of the Wealth of Nations* (Oxford: Clarendon Press, 1976), is the classic statement of the case for laissez-faire capitalism, the view that the government should not interfere with economic activity. The pursuit of self-interest benefits everyone by a magical process famously called the invisible hand, which he implies is the hand of God.

Ayn Rand, *The Virtue of Selfishness* (New York: Penguin Group, 1989), is a collection of essays by Rand and Nathaniel Branden, beginning with "The Objectivist Ethics." Rand advocates selfishness, which she understands to be the rational concern for one's own well-being, as distinguished from the self-sacrifice required by altruism. The only role of the government is to protect the rights to life, liberty, and property. The best economic system is capitalism—"full, pure, uncontrolled, unregulated laissez-faire capitalism."

John Hospers, *Libertarianism* (Los Angeles: Nash Publishing, 1971), explains and defends libertarianism, a view that emphasizes individual freedom and condemns government interference. In the chapter on "Profits and Liberty," Hospers defends profits and high compensation in a capitalist free-market economy.

Karl Marx, *Capital: A Critique of Political Economy*, translated by Ben Fowkes (New York: Vintage Book, 1977), gives a famous critique of capitalism.

Marx argues that capitalism alienates and exploits workers; it is unjust because it favors those who own property; it creates cycles of boom and bust because markets are inherently unstable; it leads to monopolies and oligarchies and cartels; it pits the owning class against the working class; it fosters greed and envy; it has built-in contradictions, such as surpluses with shortages and poverty in the midst of riches; it requires a permanent army of the unemployed; and it encourages consumption of trivial luxury items while neglecting basic needs like health care.

Karl Marx and Frederick Engels, *Manifesto of the Communist Party* (www.marxist.org/archieve/marx/works/1848/communist-manifesto), explain how the proletarians (the workers) can overcome domination and exploitation by the bourgeoisie (the capitalists). They state ten conditions for the transition from capitalism to communism, including the abolition of private ownership of land, the abolition of inheritance, a progressive income tax, nationalization of banks, public ownership of factories, free education in public schools, and abolition of child labor.

Andrew Blackman, "What is the Soul of Socialism?" (www.monthlyreview.org), maintains that modern socialism is inspired by leaders such as Emilio Zapata rather than Marx and Engels. Followers of Zapata emphasize the basic rights to education, housing, health care, food, land, good pay for useful work, liberty, and democracy.

David C. Korten, *Agenda for a New Economy* (San Francisco: Berrett-Koehler Publishers, 2009), argues that the financial crisis was caused by Wall Street creating phantom wealth and profits that quickly disappeared. His agenda for a new economy calls for communities devoted to producing real wealth from real resources that meet the real needs of the people.

Gerald Gaus, "The Idea and Ideal of Capitalism," forthcoming in *The Oxford Handbook of Business Ethics*, edited by Tom Beauchamp and George Brenkert, explains the ideal of capitalism in terms of private ownership and property rights. In its ideal form, capitalism extends private ownership to as many things as possible, and allows the most extensive feasible property rights over what is privately owned.

Joseph Schumpeter, *Capitalism, Socialism, and Democracy* (New York: Harper, 1950), argues that creative destruction is the essence of capitalism. This process is compared to a gale that destroys old companies and creates new innovative companies that are better adapted to survive economic conditions. It is an evolutionary process that allows capitalism to survive financial crises such as recessions. Even though Schumpeter is often cited as a defender of capitalism, he actually predicts that pure capitalism will not survive because democratic societies will vote for a welfare state, which he views as socialism.

John Maynard Keynes, *The General Theory of Employment, Interest, and Money* (New York: Macmillan, 1964), is a classic that deals with recessions and depressions. Keynes recommends a mixed economy where problems of the private sector, such as runs on banks, are addressed by the government. In particular, he argues that the solution to economic depressions or recessions is to stimulate the economy by reducing interest rates and increasing government spending. This is what the Obama administration did in response to the financial crisis of 2008.

Paul Krugman, *The Return of Depression Economics and the Crisis of 2008* (New York: W.W. Norton, 2009), argues that the financial crisis of 2008 requires a return to depression economics that includes nationalization of the financial system, the Fed lending to the nonfinancial sector, good old Keynesian fiscal stimulus (as he puts it), and a new regulatory regime that prevents high-risk speculation by financial institutions.

Milton Friedman, *Capitalism and Freedom* (Chicago: University of Chicago Press, 1962), gives an influential defense of free-market capitalism as distinguished from welfare capitalism. Friedman rejects the Keynesian use of fiscal policy to relieve unemployment, and opposes the current Federal Reserve System. The banks should not be subject to detailed regulation, and private monopolies should be left alone. Social security is not necessary because people can save for retirement themselves.

Alan Greenspan, *The Age of Turbulence: Adventures in a New World* (New York: Penguin Press, 2007) argues (in the second half of the book) that free-market capitalism is better than communism or socialism. Basically, his view is that allowing financial institutions to pursue their own interest without government regulation will produce the best result. His faith in this view was shattered in the wake of the financial crisis of 2008. In testimony before Congress, he admitted to being in a state of shocked disbelief that the self-interest of the banks failed to protect their own shareholders and equity.

Naomi Klein, *The Shock Doctrine: The Rise of Disaster Capitalism* (New York: Metropolitan Books/ Henry Holt, 2007), argues that free-market capitalists influenced by Milton Friedman and his followers have used natural disasters, wars, and economic upheavals to implement their economic policies such as privatization, free trade, and reduced social spending. The result has been economic disaster: recessions, poverty, unemployment, and looting of public money by private corporations.

John Cassidy, "Rational Irrationality," *The New Yorker*, October 5, 2009, argues that the real causes of the financial crisis were not greed and stupidity. The root problem was rational irrationality—behavior that is reasonable at the individual level, but disastrous when aggregated in the marketplace. He shows how this worked in the subprime mortgage meltdown.

Dean Baker, *Plunder and Blunder* (Sausalito, CA: PoliPoint Press, 2009), explains the origin and collapse of the 2001 stock bubble. He argues that the people responsible should be held accountable.

Nomi Prins, *It Takes a Pillage: Behind the Bailouts, Bonuses, and Backroom Deals from Washington to Wall Street* (Hoboken, NJ: John Wiley & Sons, 2009), explains the financial crisis of 2008 and the bailout. Wall Street financiers converted loans into assets that allowed excessive borrowing and risk taking. The bailout gave the bankers $5 billion in bonuses without any oversight and presented big finance with a $10 trillion gift.

Nomi Prins, *Other People's Money* (New York: New Press, 2004), is an insider's account of high finance during the boom years. Among other things, she explains how Enron and other companies gamed the financial system using shell companies, political maneuvering, and fraud to make their executives rich while leaving others to foot the bill.

Andrew Ross Sorkin, *Too Big to Fail* (New York: Viking, 2009), describes the attempts to save Lehman Brothers and its eventual collapse.

Slavoj Zizek, "To Each According to His Greed," *Harper's Magazine*, October 2009, pp. 15–18, notes some of the ironies of the bailouts. They helped the rich rather than the poor, and the lenders instead of the borrowers. Both conservative Republicans and socialists shared contempt for big speculators, and both opposed the bailouts.

CHAPTER NINE

War and Terrorism

INTRODUCTION

Factual Background

The history of humans is a sad chronicle of war and terrorism. Almost every year there has been a war or an act of terrorism somewhere in the world. Thus far there have been no nuclear or biological wars, but the weapons are there ready to be used. India and Pakistan have been fighting over a disputed area of Kashmir for more than fifty years, and continue to do so. Israel has fought several wars, and continues to fight the Palestinians on a daily basis. The Palestinians respond with suicide bombers. A war in Bosnia was generated by ethnic differences. Saddam Hussein invaded Kuwait and the result was the Gulf War. A short list of the major wars in the twentieth century includes World Wars I and II, the Korean War, the Vietnam War, and a bitter struggle in Afghanistan when Russian forces tried to invade. Iran and Iraq fought a bloody war, with Iraq being armed and supported by the United States.

Constant war continues in the twenty-first century. In 2001, U.S. and British forces invaded Afghanistan in order to capture Osama bin Laden and remove the Taliban regime, which had supported the al-Qaeda terrorist organization responsible for the 9/11 attacks. After nine years of fighting, U.S. troops were still looking for bin

Laden, and battling Taliban insurgents who remained in mountain strongholds. In 2003, U.S., British, and other troops invaded and occupied Iraq, claiming that Iraq had weapons of mass destruction and ties to al Qaeda. (In 2009, the United Kingdom ended combat operations and the U.S. began withdrawing its troops, though the conflict was far from over.) In 2006, Israel fought a short war in Lebanon that killed more than a thousand people, damaged Lebanese infrastructure, and displaced more than 900,000 Lebanese.

Terrorist attacks have dramatically increased in the twenty-first century. Suicide bombings, missile strikes, shootings, and other attacks have become frequent occurrences. Sometimes soldiers or police officers are killed, but many times it is civilians who die. In 2004, Israeli missiles killed Sheik Ahmed Yassin, the spiritual leader of the militant group Hamas, which Israel claimed was responsible for terrorist bombings in Israel. In 2004, ten bombs ripped through four commuter trains in Madrid during the morning rush hour, killing nearly 200 and wounding more than 1,400. This was the deadliest terrorist attack on a European target since World War II. On September 11, 2001, nineteen terrorists hijacked four airplanes. They crashed two of the planes into the World Trade Center in New York City, destroying the twin towers. It is estimated that 3,000 people were killed. A third plane hit the Pentagon, killing nearly 200 workers. The fourth plane crashed in rural southwest Pennsylvania after the passengers overpowered the terrorists. A total of 266 people were killed on the four planes. This was the most devastating terrorist attack in U.S. history. Some compared it to the Japanese attack on Pearl Harbor that resulted in war with Japan, a war that ended shortly after Hiroshima and Nagasaki were destroyed with nuclear bombs in August 1945.

The United States produced convincing evidence that Osama bin Laden and his al-Qaeda network of terrorists were responsible for the 9/11 attacks. On September 23, 2001, bin Laden issued a statement urging his followers to remain steadfast on the path of jihad against the infidels—that is, the United States and her allies. In 2010, bin Laden had still not been captured, and he continued to issue videos promoting war against the infidels.

The 9/11 attacks were only the latest and most shocking of a series of terrorist attacks on U.S. citizens and service members. On October 12, 2000, a terrorist bombing killed 17 U.S. sailors aboard the *U.S.S. Cole* as it refueled in Yemen's port of Aden. The United States said that bin Laden was the prime suspect. On August 7, 1998, there were car bombings of U.S. embassies in Nairobi, Kenya, and Dar es Salaam, Tanzania. More than 5,500 people were injured and 224 were killed. Once again the prime suspect was Osama bin Laden. In June 1996, a truck bomb exploded outside the Khobar Towers in Dharan, Saudi Arabia, killing 19 U.S. servicemen and wounding hundreds of other people. Members of a radical Lebanese terrorist group, Hezbollah, were indicted for the attack. On February 26, 1993, a bomb exploded in a parking garage below the World Trade Center, killing 6 people and wounding more than 1,000. Six radical Muslim terrorists were convicted and sentenced to life in prison. On April 19, 1995, a federal building in Oklahoma City was destroyed by a truck bomb. There were 168 deaths. Timothy J. McVeigh was executed for the attack and Terry L. Nichols was sentenced to life in prison. On December 21, 1998, Pam Am flight 103 exploded over Lockerbie, Scotland, killing 270 people onboard. Two Libyan intelligence officers were accused of planting a suitcase containing the bomb. One was convicted in February 2001 and the other was set free.

The Readings

A traditional and important position on war and terrorism is pacifism. Pacifism can take different forms, and Douglas P. Lackey distinguishes between four of them: (1) the view that all killing is wrong; (2) the view that all violence is wrong; (3) the view that personal violence is always wrong, but political violence is sometimes morally right; and (4) the view that personal violence is sometimes morally permissible, but war is always morally wrong. Albert Schweitzer's position is an example of the first type of pacifism; he held that all killing is wrong because all life is sacred. Mohandas Gandhi's pacifism is an example of the second type because he opposed all violence. According to Lackey, a problem with both of these views is that sometimes killing or violence is required to save lives. For example, shouldn't a terrorist airplane hijacker be killed or restrained to prevent the hijacker from crashing the plane and killing all the passengers? The third view that condemns personal violence but allows political violence is attributed to St. Augustine. But this view raises a problem with personal self-defense. Most people would agree that personal violence is justified in defense of one's life, as in the case of the terrorist airplane hijacker. The kind of pacifism that Lackey supports is the fourth view, which condemns all war as morally wrong but allows some personal violence. But this antiwar pacifism has a problem, too. Why can't some wars be justified by appealing to some great moral good, such as political freedom? Certainly the Revolutionary War in America (to use Lackey's own example) could be defended in this way.

After the 9/11 attacks, pacifism did not seem to be an option for most people. Now just war theory dominates discussions of war and terrorism. The theory was originally formulated by medieval Christian theologians called Scholastics, and it has been discussed ever since. The theory distinguishes between two questions about war. First, there is the question about the right to go to war, called *jus ad bellum*, or "right to war": What are the conditions that justify going to war? Second, there is the question about right conduct in war, called *jus in bello*, or "right in war": How should combatants conduct themselves while fighting a war?

Michael W. Brough, John W. Lango, and Harry van der Linden explain the basic principles of traditional just war theory in the second reading. They note that there are disagreements about how the principles are to be understood and applied. They list eight principles: six *jus ad bellum* principles (just cause, legitimate authority, right intention, last resort, reasonable chance of success, and proportionality) and two *jus in bello* principles (discrimination and proportionality). They also note that some just war theorists hold that the conclusion of the war should be guided by a third set of principles, which they call *jus post bellum* principles. One such principle is order, that is, the end of the war should produce a stable post-conflict environment. Another principle concerns punishment for crimes. For example, after World War II, the Nuremberg trials were conducted to try German leaders for war crimes and genocide.

Besides stating the basic principles of just war theory, Brough, Lango, and van der Linden mention some important controversies raised by each principle. Is humanitarian intervention or protecting citizens from human rights violations a just cause for war? Can insurgent or terrorists groups have the legitimate authority to engage in warfare? Can motives such as economic gain or access to resources be accepted as motivations for war? Is the killing of noncombatants allowed by the principle of discrimination? How can the use of nuclear weapons or landmines be justified when they indiscriminately kill innocent civilians?

Pacifism and just war theory developed in the tradition of Christianity. Another important doctrine about war comes from Islam, and is used to justify both war and terrorism: the Islamic doctrine of *jihad*. Although the term *jihad* is often translated as "holy war," this is not exactly what the term means. According to Michael G. Knapp (see the Suggested Readings), the jihad means struggle or striving in the path of God for a noble cause. The classic view of jihad allowed defensive war against the enemies of Islam, but it did not sanction the killing of all non-Muslims or even their conversion by force. Knapp quotes the Koran (2:256): "There is no compulsion in religion." Killing of other Muslims could be justified only by classifying them as non-Muslims (e.g., as apostates or rebels). He notes that the Islamic law tradition was very hostile toward terrorism and severely punished rebels who attacked innocent victims.

Osama bin Laden (see the Suggested Readings) has tried to justify attacks on the United States by appealing to the doctrine of jihad, which he interprets as allowing attacks on enemies of Islam. He says that he and his followers are attacking America "because you attacked us and continue to attack us." He gives a long list of places where the alleged U.S. attacks have occurred, including Palestine, Somalia, Chechnya, Lebanon, Iraq, and Afghanistan. He says that the Palestinians are fighting to regain the land taken away from them by Israel. American infidels are occupying holy places in Saudi Arabia, namely the cities of Mecca and Medina; and fighting a war of annihilation against Iraq, which for 500 years was the heart of an Islamic empire. He goes on to morally condemn American society as a cesspool of usury, sexual debauchery, drug addiction, gambling, prostitution, and so on. He concludes by arguing that the United States violates human rights while claiming to uphold them.

In response to the 9/11 attacks, the United States attacked Afghanistan and then Iraq. Many commentators have called these *preventive wars*, that is, wars justified by the possibility of a future attack by terrorists or rogue states. By contrast, a *preemptive war* is one justified by the imminent threat of attack, not just the chance of an attack in the future.

In the third reading, Neta C. Crawford argues that a slippery slope leads from defensive preemptive war to offensive preventive war. In her view, a morally legitimate preemptive attack must meet four necessary conditions. The "self" to be defended is lives, not other national interests such as a need for oil or world domination. War should be inevitable and likely in the near future, and not something that might happen in the distant future. The preemptive attack should be likely to succeed. Military force must be necessary, and no other measures available, to counter the threat. When an attack does not meet one or more of these necessary conditions, then the line between preemptive war and preventive war has been crossed. Crawford warns that aggressive preventive war has risks. It increases instability and insecurity. It makes states arm themselves defensively because of fear of attack. It increases resentment. At its worst, it is a recipe for constant conflict.

In the fourth reading, Laurie Calhoun applies just war theory to terrorism, focusing on political and moral/religious terrorists. She does not argue that terrorism is morally wrong. Rather, she wants to show how just war theory can be used by terrorists to defend their actions, at least to themselves and their followers, using the very same theory that democratic nations use to justify their military campaigns, which kill innocent civilians. To see how terrorists can do this, we need to look more closely at just war theory, and particularly the doctrine of double effect. How can a nation justify dropping bombs on another nation when this act results in the killing of innocent civilians? If the principle of discrimination is understood as absolutely forbidding the killing of innocents, then no modern war could be justified. Lackey and others make this point. To justify killing innocents, just war theorists appeal to the Catholic doctrine of double effect (already discussed in the introduction to Chapter 3). This doctrine distinguishes between two effects of an action: an intended effect; and one that is foreseen but not intended, that is, a side effect. The doctrine says that as long as the intended consequence of an act is good (for example, winning a war or saving lives), then a bad foreseen consequence (for example, the death of innocents) is morally allowed, provided this bad consequence is not intended. Calhoun argues that terrorists can use this sort of reasoning to justify their actions, as Timothy McVeigh did when he characterized the deaths of innocent people in the Oklahoma City bombing as "collateral damage." In other words, she argues, "just war" rationalizations are available to everyone, bin Laden as well as President Obama. Terrorists can present themselves to their followers as warriors for justice, and not as mere murderers or vigilantes.

Unlike Calhoun, Louise Richardson (see the Suggested Readings) gives us a precise definition of *terrorism*. It simply means deliberately and violently targeting civilians for political purposes. The point of doing this is to send a political message to an audience that is not the same as the victims. To do this, the act and the victim usually have symbolic significance. To use her example, the Twin Towers and the Pentagon targeted in the 9/11 attacks were seen as icons of America's economic and military power, and this symbolism enhanced the shock value of the attacks. She denies that terrorists are irrational or insane. In fact, they attempt to justify their actions in various ways.

In the fifth reading, Thomas Nagel explains why terrorism is wrong. The condemnation of terrorism does not require rejecting the terrorists' ends. Rather, terrorism is wrong because of the means used by the terrorists. They *aim* directly at noncombatants and this violates the basic moral principle that aiming at (intending) the death of a harmless person is morally wrong. However, Nagel allows that killing innocent people in war does not violate this principle as long as the victims are killed as a side effect of an attack on a legitimate military target, and are not deliberately or intentionally killed.

Claudia Card (see the Suggested Readings) has no difficulty seeing the 9/11 attacks as terrorist and evil, but she doubts that the war on terrorism is the appropriate response. Terrorism is not an identifiable agent, and it is not clear what kinds of terrorists count as legitimate targets. For example, is a war on terrorism a justifiable response to domestic battering? If not, then similar objections may apply to the war on public terrorism. A more appropriate response, in her view, would be to hunt down those responsible for the planning and support of the attacks, and bring them to trial by international tribunals.

In the last reading for the chapter, David Luban discusses more problems with the war on terrorism. Luban agrees with Card that the current fight against terrorism does not fit the traditional model of a just war. Instead, the war on terrorism uses a new hybrid war-law model that combines features of the war model with the law model. The new war model allows the use of lethal force, the foreseen but unintended killing of innocents, and the capture and killing of suspected terrorists. These are features of war. But in traditional war, the enemy can legitimately fight back, other nations can opt for neutrality, and enemy soldiers have certain rights under the Geneva Convention. The war on terrorism rejects these features by appealing to a law model. Terrorists are criminals, so they cannot legitimately fight back. Other nations cannot be neutral when it comes to illegal murder; if they harbor or aid terrorists, they are against us. Finally, terrorists are treated as enemy combatants rather than as soldiers or ordinary criminals, and as such they have no rights, neither the rights of ordinary criminals nor the rights of soldiers under the Geneva Convention. There is no presumption of innocence, they have no right to a hearing, and they can be detained indefinitely. Even torture is allowable. So, according to Luban, the war on terrorism puts an end to international human rights because anyone identified as a terrorist has no rights. (For an example of the treatment of suspected terrorists, see the case of Jose Padilla in the Problem Cases.)

Philosophical Issues

The readings in the chapter raise some very important issues. Can war be justified? If so, how? Pacifists such as Schweitzer and Gandhi, who were opposed to all killing or all violence, hold that no war is ever justified. The problem with these absolutist views is that there seems to be an obvious exception, namely, killing or violence in the defense of one's life. Lackey's antiwar pacifism is not so easily dismissed. If one agrees that the killing of soldiers and civilians is a very great evil, one that cannot be balanced by goods such as political freedom, then it seems very difficult, if not impossible, to justify modern wars.

Just war theorists such as William V. O'Brien (see the Suggested Readings) try to justify modern wars such as World War II, but to do so they have to modify or interpret the principles of the theory. The most troublesome principle is the one about discrimination. As O'Brien says, if this principle is understood to forbid absolutely the killing of noncombatants, then it is hard to see how any modern war could have been justified, since they all involved killing noncombatants. Perhaps the most graphic example was the atomic bombing of Hiroshima and Nagasaki, which killed more than 200,000 innocent noncombatants.

There are various ways to get around the problem. One is to deny that there are any innocent noncombatants in war; everyone in an enemy nation is a legitimate target. (Some terrorists take this position, too.) The most common way of justifying the killing of innocents, as we have seen, is to appeal to the Catholic doctrine of double effect.

There is debate about how to formulate and apply the doctrine of double effect. O'Brien admits that the distinction between the two effects—one that is directly intended and the other an unintended side effect—is often difficult to accept. Consider President Harry Truman's decision to bomb Hiroshima and Nagasaki. At the time, he said that his decision was based on the fact that an invasion of Japan would cost the lives of thousands of American soldiers, and he wanted to save those lives. But he surely knew that using atomic bombs on these undefended cities would result in the deaths of thousands of innocent Japanese noncombatants. Did he directly intend the killing of innocents, or merely foresee this killing as an unintended consequence? Can we make the distinction in this case? If we do, then what is the basis for the distinction?

Are acts of terrorism ever justified? As we have seen, Calhoun argues that terrorists can and do appeal to the just war theory, the very theory that others use to demonstrate that terrorism is wrong. How can just war theory be used to defend terrorism? Calhoun argues that terrorists can appeal to the doctrine of double effect. To see how this might be done, let's take another look at the doctrine as stated by Father Richard McCormick and quoted by O'Brien. McCormick says, "It is immoral directly to take innocent human life except with divine authorization." Why is the killing of innocents allowed if there is divine authorization? One explanation is that just war theory was developed by Catholic theologians to defend the holy crusades against infidels, crusades that were believed to be commanded by God. But of course fundamentalist Muslim terrorists also believe they have divine authorization; they believe they are engaged in a holy war commanded by Allah against infidels. Thus, both Christians and Muslims claim divine authorization for war and terrorism.

Now let us turn to the distinction between direct and indirect killing, which is at the heart of the doctrine of double effect. As McCormick explains it, "Direct taking of human life implies that one performs a lethal action with the intention that death should result for himself or another. Death is therefore deliberately willed as the effect of one's action." But Muslim terrorists may sincerely believe that all things happen by Allah's will, and they do not will anything, much less the death of others. They are merely submitting to the will of Allah, and Allah commands them to jihad. Hence, they can claim that the deaths that result from their actions are not positively willed, but merely foreseen as a consequence of following Allah's commands. In other words, they are only indirectly killing innocents. It appears, then, that terrorists can attempt to justify their actions by appealing to the Catholic doctrine of double effect, at least as it is stated by McCormick.

How do we define terrorism? This is another issue discussed in the readings. Calhoun argues that there is no satisfactory definition of terrorism. The moral definition, which defines terrorism as killing or threatening to kill innocent people, is unsatisfactory because it seems to apply to every nation that has engaged in bombing campaigns resulting in the deaths of innocent children. The legal definition, which defines terrorism as illegal acts of killing or harming people, is defective because it would not apply to the reign of terror imposed by the Third Reich in Nazi Germany.

Richardson asserts that *terrorism* simply means deliberately and violently targeting civilians for political purposes. She admits that this simple definition applies to some actions of democratic states. She mentions the Allied bombing campaign in World War II, which targeted cities in Germany, and the nuclear bombing of Hiroshima and Nagasaki. Current examples are not hard to find. In the Lebanon War, Israel used unguided cluster bombs to attack civilian targets. In 1986, the United States tried to kill Colonel Gaddafi, the Libyan leader, and succeeded in killing his fifteen-month-old daughter and fifteen other civilians. Richardson's solution to the problem of state terrorism is to stipulate, for the sake of "analytic clarity," that terrorism is the act of substate groups, not states. She adds, however, that when states deliberately target civilian populations, as they did in World War II, this is the moral equivalent of terrorism.

Card adopts Carl Wellman's definition of terrorism as political violence with two targets: a direct but secondary target that suffers the harm and an indirect but primary target that gets a political message. By this definition, the 9/11 attacks were clearly terrorist attacks. They were also evil, indeed paradigmatically evil, because the harms were intolerable, planned, and foreseeable.

Finally, how should we deal with terrorists? Do we treat them as enemy soldiers who have rights under the Geneva Convention, such as the right not to be tortured and the right to be fed, clothed, given medical treatment, and released when hostilities are over? In Card's view, terrorists should be treated as criminals, not soldiers. We should hunt down those responsible for the terrorist attacks like 9/11, including those who planned and supported the attacks. When captured, they should be charged with crimes against humanity and given an international trial. But if they are criminals, do they have the legal rights accorded to ordinary criminals in the United States, such as the presumption of innocence, the right to a fair trial, the right to be defended by a lawyer, the right not to testify against themselves, and the right not to be held without charges? Luban argues that the war on terrorism treats suspected terrorists as neither soldiers nor criminals but as enemy combatants with no rights at all, and this amounts to the end of international human rights.

Pacifism

DOUGLAS P. LACKEY

Douglas P. Lackey is professor of philosophy at Baruch College and the Graduate Center of the City University of New York. He is the author of *Moral Principles and Nuclear Weapons* (1984); *The Ethics of War and Peace* (1989); *God, Immortality, Ethics* (1990); and *Ethics and Strategic Defense* (1990). Our reading is taken from *The Ethics of War and Peace* (1989).

Lackey distinguishes between four types of pacifism. There is the universal pacifist view that all killing is wrong, the universal pacifist view that all violence is wrong, private pacifism that condemns personal violence but not political violence, and antiwar pacifism that allows personal violence but condemns all wars. Lackey discusses objections to all of these views, but he seems to defend antiwar pacifism. At least, he answers every objection to antiwar pacifism, leaving the reader with the impression that he supports this view.

1. VARIETIES OF PACIFISM

Everyone has a vague idea of what a pacifist is, but few realize that there are many kinds of pacifists. (Sometimes the different kinds quarrel with each other!) One task for the student of international ethics is to distinguish the different types of pacifism and to identify which types represent genuine moral theories.

Most of us at some time or other have run into the "live and let live" pacifist, the person who says, "I am absolutely opposed to killing and violence—but I don't seek to impose my own code on anyone else. If other people want to use violence, so be it. They have their values and I have mine." For such a person, pacifism is one life-style among others, a life-style committed to gentleness and care, and opposed to belligerence and militarism. Doubtless, many people who express such commitments are sincere and are prepared to live by their beliefs. At the same time, it is important to see why "live and let live" pacifism does not constitute a moral point of view.

Source: Douglas P. Lackey, "Pacifism," from *The Ethics of War and Peace* by Douglas P. Lackey, pp. 6–24. Prentice Hall, Inc. Copyright 1989. Electronically reproduced by permission of Pearson Education, Inc., Upper Saddle River, NJ.

When someone judges that a certain action, A, is morally wrong, that judgment entails that no one should do A. Thus, there is no way to have moral values without believing that these values apply to other people. If a person says that A is morally wrong but that it doesn't matter if other people do A, than that person either is being inconsistent or doesn't know what the word "moral" means. If a person believes that killing, in certain circumstances, is morally wrong, that belief implies that no one should kill, at least in those circumstances. If a pacifist claims that killing is wrong in *all* circumstances, but that it is permissible for other people to kill on occasion, then he has not understood the universal character of genuine moral principles. If pacifism is to be a moral theory, it must be prescribed for all or prescribed for none.

Once one recognizes this "universalizing" character of genuine moral beliefs, one will take moral commitments more seriously than those who treat a moral code as a personal life-style. Since moral principles apply to everyone, we must take care that our moral principles are correct, checking that they are not inconsistent with each other, developing and adjusting them so that they are detailed and subtle enough to deal with a variety of circumstances, and making sure that they are defensible against the objections of those who do not accept them. Of course many pacifists do take the business of morality seriously and advance pacifism as a genuine moral position, not as a mere life-style. All such serious pacifists believe that *everyone* ought to be a pacifist, and that those who reject pacifism are deluded or wicked. Moreover, they do not simply endorse pacifism; they offer arguments in its defense.

We will consider four types of pacifist moral theory. First, there are pacifists who maintain that the central idea of pacifism is the immorality of killing. Second, there are pacifists who maintain that the essence of pacifism is the immorality of violence, whether this be violence in personal relations or violence in relations between nation-states. Third, there are pacifists who argue that personal violence is always morally wrong but that political violence is sometimes morally right: for example, that it is sometimes morally permissible for a nation to go to war. Fourth and finally, there are pacifists who believe that personal violence is sometimes permissible but that war is always morally wrong.

Albert Schweitzer, who opposed all killing on the grounds that life is sacred, was the first sort of pacifist. Mohandas Gandhi and Leo Tolstoy, who opposed not only killing but every kind of coercion and violence, were pacifists of the second sort: I will call such pacifists "universal pacifists." St. Augustine, who condemned self-defense but endorsed wars against heretics, was a pacifist of the third sort. Let us call him a "private pacifist," since he condemned only violence in the private sphere. Pacifists of the fourth sort, increasingly common in the modern era of nuclear and total war, I will call "antiwar pacifists."

2. THE PROHIBITION AGAINST KILLING

(a) The Biblical Prohibition

One simple and common argument for pacifism is the argument that the Bible, God's revealed word, says to all people "Thou shalt not kill" (Exod. 20:13). Some pacifists interpret this sentence as implying that no one should kill under any circumstances, unless God indicates that this command is suspended, as He did when He commanded Abraham to slay Isaac. The justification for this interpretation is the words themselves, "Thou shalt not kill," which are presented in the Bible bluntly and without qualification, not only in Exodus but also in Deuteronomy (5:17).

This argument, however, is subject to a great many criticisms. The original language of Exodus and Deuteronomy is Hebrew, and the consensus of scholarship says that the Hebrew sentence at Exodus 20:23, "Lo Tirzach," is best translated as "Thou shalt do no murder," not as "Thou shalt not kill." If this translation is correct, then Exodus 20:13 does not forbid all killing but only those killings that happen to be murders. Furthermore, there are many places in the Bible where God commands human beings to kill in specified circumstances. God announces 613 commandments in all, and these include "Thou shalt not suffer a witch to live" (Exod. 22:18); "He that blasphemeth the name of the Lord . . . shall surely be put to death, and all the congregation shall stone him" (Lev. 24:16); "He that killeth any man shall surely be put to death" (Lev. 24:17); and so forth. It is difficult to argue that these instructions are like God's specific instructions to Abraham to slay Isaac: these are general commandments to be applied by many people, to many people, day in and day out. They are at least as general and as divinely sanctioned as the commandment translated "Thou shalt not kill."

There are other difficulties for pacifists who pin their hopes on prohibitions in the Hebrew Bible. Even if the commandment "Thou shalt not kill," properly interpreted, did prohibit all types of killing, the skeptics can ask whether this, by itself, proves that all killing is immoral. First, how do we know that statements in the Hebrew Bible really are God's word, and not just the guesses of ancient scribes? Second, even if the commandments in the Bible do express God's views, why are we morally bound to obey divine commands? (To say that we will be punished if we do not obey is to appeal to fear and self-interest, not to moral sentiments.) Third, are the commandments in the Old Testament laws for all people, or just laws for the children of Israel? If they are laws for all people, then all people who do not eat unleavened bread for Passover are either deluded or wicked. If they are laws only for the children of Israel, they are religious laws and not moral laws, since they lack the universality that all moral laws must have.

Finally, the argument assumes the existence of God, and philosophers report that the existence of God is not easy to demonstrate. Even many religious believers are more confident of the truth of basic moral judgments, such as "Small children should not be tortured to death for purposes of amusement," than they are confident of the existence of God. For such people, it would seem odd to try to justify moral principles by appeals to religious principles, since the evidence for those religious principles is weaker than the evidence for the moral principles they are supposed to justify.

(b) The Sacredness of Life

There are, however, people who oppose all killing but do not seek justification in divine revelation. Many of these defend pacifism by appeal to the sacredness of life. Almost everyone is struck with wonder when watching the movements and reactions of a newborn baby, and almost everyone can be provoked to awe by the study of living things, great and small. The complexity of the mechanisms found in living bodies, combined with the efficiency with which they fulfill their functions, is not matched by any of the processes in nonliving matter. People who are particularly awestruck by the beauty of living things infer [from] these feelings that life is sacred, that all killing is wrong.

Different versions of pacifism have been derived from beliefs about the sacredness of life. The most extreme version forbids the killing of any living thing. This view was allegedly held by Pythagoras, and presently held by members of the Jain religion in India. (Those who think that such pacifists must soon starve to death should note that a life-sustaining diet can easily be constructed from milk, honey, fallen fruit and vegetables, and other items that are consumable without prior killing.) A less extreme view sanctions the killing of plants but forbids the killing of animals. The most moderate view prohibits only the killing of fellow beings.

There is deep appeal in an argument that connects the sacredness of life with the wrongfulness of taking life. Even people who are not pacifists are often revolted by the spectacle of killing, and most Americans would be unable to eat meat if they had to watch how the animals whose flesh they consume had been slaughtered, or if they had to do the slaughtering themselves. Most people sense that they do not own the world they inhabit and recognize that they are not free to do with the world as they will, that the things in it, most especially living things, are worthy of respect and care. Seemingly nothing could violate the respect living things deserve more than killing, especially since much of the taking of human and nonhuman life is so obviously unnecessary.

But with the introduction of the word "unnecessary" a paradox arises. Sometimes—less often than we think, but sometimes—the taking of some lives will save other lives. Does the principle that life is sacred and ought to be preserved imply that nothing should ever be killed, or does it imply that as much life should be preserved as possible? Obviously pacifists take the former view; nonpacifists, the latter.

The view that killing is wrong because it destroys what is sacred seems to imply that killing is wrong because killing diminishes the amount of good in the world. It seems to follow that if a person can save more lives by killing than by refusing to kill, arguments about the sacredness of life would not show that killing in these circumstances is wrong. (It might be wrong for other reasons.) The more lives saved, the greater the quantity of good in the world.

The difficulty that some killing might, on balance, save lives, is not the only problem for pacifism based on the sacredness of life. If preserving life is the highest value, a value not comparable with other, non-life-preserving goods, it follows that any acts which place life at risk are immoral. But many admirable actions have been undertaken in the face of death, and many less heroic but morally impeccable actions—driving on a road at moderate speed, authorizing a commercial flight to take off, and so forth—place life at risk. In cases of martyrdom in which people choose death over religious conversion, life is just as much destroyed as it is in a common murder. Yet, on the whole, automobile drivers, air traffic controllers, and religious martyrs are not thought to be wicked. Likewise, people on life-sustaining machinery sometimes request that the machines be turned off, on the grounds that quality of life matters more than quantity of life. We may consider such people mistaken, but we hardly think that they are morally depraved.

In answering this objection, the pacifist may wish to distinguish between *killing other people* and *getting oneself killed*, arguing that only the former is immoral. But although there is a genuine distinction between killing and getting killed, the distinction does not entail that killing other people destroys life but getting oneself killed does not. If life is sacred, life, including one's own life, must be preserved at all cost. In many cases, people consider the price of preserving their own lives simply too high.

(c) The Right to Life

Some pacifists may try to avoid the difficulties of the "sacredness of life" view by arguing that the essential immorality of killing is that it violates the *right to life* that every human being possesses. If people have a right to life, then it is never morally permissible to kill some people in order to save others, since according to the usual interpretation of rights, it is never permissible to violate a right in order to secure some good.

A discussion of the logic of rights in general and the right to life in particular is beyond the scope of this book. But a number of students of this subject are prepared to argue that the possession of any right implies the permissibility of defending that right against aggression: if this were not so, what would be the point of asserting the existence of rights? But if the possession of a right to life implies the permissibility of defending that right against aggression—a defense that may require killing the aggressor—then the existence of a right to life cannot by itself imply the impermissibility of killing. On this view, the right to life implies the right to self-defense, including violent self-defense. It does not imply pacifism.

3. UNIVERSAL PACIFISM

(a) Christian Pacifism

Universal pacifists are morally opposed to all violence, not just to killing. Many universal pacifists derive their views from the Christian Gospels. In the Sermon on the Mount, Christ taught:

> Ye have heard that it hath been said, An eye for an eye, a tooth for a tooth:
>
> But I say unto you, that ye resist not evil: but whosoever shall smite thee on the right cheek, turn to him the other also. . . .
>
> Ye have heard it said, thou shalt love thy neighbor, and hate thine enemy. But I say unto you, Love your enemies, bless them that curse you, do good to them that hate you . . . . that ye may be the children of your father which is in heaven: for he maketh the sun to rise on the evil and on the good, and sendeth the rain on the just and the unjust. (Matt. 5:38–45)

In the early centuries of the Christian era, it was widely assumed that to follow Christ and to obey His teaching meant that one should reject violence and refuse service in the Roman army. But by the fifth century, after the Roman Empire had become Christian and after barbarian Goths in 410 sacked Rome itself, Church Fathers debated whether Christ really intended that the Empire and its Church should remain undefended. The Church Fathers noticed passages in the Gospels that seem to contradict pacifism:

> Think not that I am come to send peace on earth: I came not to send peace, but a sword.
>
> For I am come to set a man at variance against his father, and the daughter against her mother, and the daughter-in-law against her mother-in-law. (Matt. 10:34–35)

And there are several instances in the Gospels (for instance, Matt. 8:5–10) in which Jesus encounters soldiers and does not rebuke them for engaging in an occupation that is essentially committed to violence. Rather, he argues, "Render unto Caesar the things which are Caesar's; and unto God the things that are God's" (Matt. 22:21). This would seem to include military service, or at least taxes to pay for the army.

A thorough analysis of whether the Gospels command pacifism is beyond the scope of this book. The passages in the Sermon on the Mount seem to be clearly pacifist; yet many eminent scholars have denied the pacifist message. A more interesting question, for philosophy, if not for biblical scholarship, is this: If Jesus did preach pacifism in the Sermon on the Mount, did He preach it as a *moral* doctrine?

Jesus did not view his teaching as replacing the moral law as he knew it:

> Think not that I am come to destroy the law, or the prophets: I am come not to destroy, but to fulfill. . . .
>
> Till heaven and earth pass, one jot or one tittle shall in no wise pass from the law, till all be fulfilled. (Matt. 5:17–18)

Perhaps, then, the prescriptions of the Sermon on the Mount should be interpreted as rules that one must obey in order to follow Christ, or rules that one must follow in order to obtain salvation. But it does not follow from this alone that everyone has an obligation to follow Christ, and it does not follow from this alone that everyone has an obligation to seek salvation. Even Christians will admit that some people have refused to become Christians and have led morally admirable lives nonetheless; and if salvation is a good, one can nevertheless choose to reject it, just as a citizen can neglect to hand in a winning lottery ticket without breaking the law. If so, the prescriptions of the Sermon on the Mount apply only to Christians seeking a Christian salvation. They are not universally binding rules and do not qualify as moral principles.

(b) The Moral Exemplar Argument

Many people and at least one illustrious philosopher, Immanuel Kant, believe that morally proper action consists in choosing to act in such a way that your conduct could serve as an example for all mankind. (It was Kant's genius to recognize that moral conduct is *essentially* exemplary.) Some universal pacifists appeal to this idea, arguing that if everyone were a pacifist, the world would be a much better place than it is now. This is an argument that Leo Tolstoy (1828–1910) used to support the Gospel prescription not to resist evil:

> [Christ] put the proposition of non-resistance to evil in such a way that, according to his teaching, it was to be the foundation of the joint life of men and was to free humanity from the evil that is inflicted on itself. (*My Religion*, Ch. 4) Instead of having the whole life based on violence and every joy obtained and guarded through violence; instead of seeing each one of us punished or inflicting punishment from childhood to old age, I imagined that we were all impressed in word and deed by the idea that vengeance is a very low, animal feeling; that violence is not only a disgraceful act, but also one that deprives man of true happiness. . . .
>
> I imagined that instead of those national hatreds which are impressed on us under the form of patriotism, instead of those glorifications of murder, called wars . . . that we were impressed with the idea that the recognition of any countries, special laws, borders, lands, is a sign of grossest ignorance. . . .
>
> Through the fulfillment of these commandments, the life of men will be what every human

heart seeks and desires. All men will be brothers and everybody will always be at peace with others, enjoying all the benefits of the world. (*My Religion*, Ch. 6)

Few would deny that if everyone were a pacifist, the world would be a better place, perhaps even a paradise. Furthermore, since the argument is essentially hypothetical, it cannot be refuted (as many nonpacifists believe) by pointing out that not everyone will become a pacifist. The problem is whether this argument can establish pacifism as a moral imperative.

One difficulty with the argument is that it seems to rely on a premise the truth of which is purely verbal. In what way would the world be a better place if people gave up fighting? The most obvious way is that the world would be better because there would be no war. But the statement "If everyone gave up fighting, there would be no war" is true by definition, since "war" implies "fighting." It is difficult to see how a statement that simply relates the meanings of words could tell us something about our moral obligations.

A deeper problem with Tolstoy's argument is that "resist not evil" is not the only rule that would yield paradise if everyone obeyed it. Suppose that everyone in the world subscribed to the principle "Use violence, but only in self-defense." If everyone used violence only in self-defense, the same consequences would follow as would arise from universal acceptance of the rule "Never use violence." Consequently, pacifism cannot be shown to be superior to nonpacifism by noting the good consequences that would undeniably ensue if everyone were a pacifist.

(c) Gandhian Pacifism

Certainly the most interesting and effective pacifist of the twentieth century was Mohandas Gandhi (1869–1948). Though a devout Hindu, Gandhi developed his doctrine of nonviolence from elementary metaphysical concepts that are by no means special to Hinduism:

> Man as an animal is violent, but as spirit, nonviolent. The moment he awakes to the spirit he cannot remain violent. Either he progresses towards *ahimsa* [nonviolence] or rushes to his doom. (*Nonviolence in Peace and War*, I, p. 311)

The requirement not to be violent seems wholly negative; sleeping people achieve it with ease. But for Gandhi the essential moral task is not merely to be nonviolent but to use the force of the soul (*satyagraha*, "truth grasping") in a continual struggle for justice. The methods of applied *satyagraha* developed by Gandhi—the weaponless marches, the sit-downs and sit-ins, strikes and boycotts, fasts and prayers—captured the admiration of the world and have been widely copied, most notably by Martin Luther King, Jr., in his campaigns against racial discrimination. According to Gandhi, each person, by engaging in *satyagraha* and experiencing suffering on behalf of justice, purifies the soul from pollution emanating from man's animal nature:

> A *satyagrahi* is dead to his body even before his enemy attempts to kill him, i.e. he is free from the attachments of his body and lives only in the victory of his soul. (*Nonviolence in Peace and War*, I, p. 318) Nonviolence implies as complete self-purification as is humanly possible. (*Nonviolence in Peace and War*, I, p. 111)

By acting nonviolently, pacifists not only purify their own souls but also transform the souls of their opponents: "A nonviolent revolution is not a program of seizure of power. It is a program of transformation of relationships, ending in peaceful transfer of power." (*Nonviolence in Peace and War*, II, p. 8)

Though in most places Gandhi emphasizes the personal redemption that is possible only through nonviolent resistance to evil, the spiritually positive effect of nonviolence on evil opponents is perhaps equally important, since "The soul of the *satyagrahi* is love." (*Nonviolence in Peace and War*, II, p. 59)

Gandhi, then, is far from preaching the sacredness of biological life. What matters is not biological life but the condition of the soul, the natural and proper state of which is *ahimsa*. The evil of violence is that it distorts and disrupts this natural condition of the soul. The basic moral law (*dharma*) for all people is to seek the restoration of their souls to the harmony of *ahimsa*. This spiritual restoration cannot be achieved by violence, but only by the application of *satyagraha*.

Disharmony cannot produce harmony; violence cannot produce spiritual peace.

The "sacredness of life" defense of pacifism ran into difficulties analyzing situations in which taking one life could save many lives. For Gandhi, this is no problem at all: taking one life may save many biological lives, but it will not save souls. On the contrary, the soul of the killer will be perverted by the act, and that perversion—not the loss of life—is what matters morally.

The system of values professed by Gandhi—that the highest human good is a harmonious condition of soul—must be kept in mind when considering the frequent accusation that Gandhi's method of nonviolent resistance "does not work," that nonviolence alone did not and could not force the British to leave India, and that nonviolent resistance to murderous tyrants like Hitler will only provoke the mass murder of the innocent. Perhaps the practice of nonviolence could not "defeat" the British or "defeat" Hitler, but by Gandhi's standard the use of military force would only produce a greater defeat, perverting the souls of thousands engaged in war and intensifying the will to violence on the opposing side. On the other hand, the soul of the *satyagrahi* will be strengthened and purified by nonviolent struggle against British imperialism or German Nazism, and in this purification the Gandhian pacifist can obtain spiritual victory even in the face of political defeat.

India did not adopt the creed of nonviolence after the British left in 1948, and it is hardly likely that any modern nation-state will organize its international affairs along Gandhian lines. But none of this affects the validity of Gandhi's arguments, which indicate how things ought to be, not how they are. We have seen that Gandhi's principles do not falter in the face of situations in which taking one life can save lives on balance. But what of situations in which the sacrifice of spiritual purity by one will prevent the corruption of many souls? Suppose, for example, that a Gandhian believes (on good evidence) that a well-timed commando raid will prevent a nation from embarking on an aggressive war, a war that would inflame whole populations with hatred for the enemy. Wouldn't a concern with one's own spiritual purity in such a situation show an immoral lack of concern for the souls of one's fellow men?

Another problem for Gandhi concerns the relationship between violence and coercion. To coerce people is to make them act against their will, for fear of the consequences they will suffer if they do not obey. Coercion, then, is a kind of spiritual violence, directed against the imagination and will of the victim. The "violence" most conspicuously rejected by Gandhi—pushing, shoving, striking with hands, the use of weapons, the placing of bombs and explosives—is essentially physical violence, directed against the bodies of opponents. But if physical violence against bodies is spiritually corrupting, psychological violence directed at the will of opponents must be even more corrupting.

In his writings Gandhi condemned coercion. Yet in practice he can hardly be said to have renounced *psychological* coercion. Obviously he would have preferred to have the British depart from India of their own free will, deciding that it was in their own best interest, or at least morally necessary, to leave. But if the British had decided, in the absence of coercion, to stay, Gandhi was prepared to exert every kind of nonviolent pressure to make them go. And when Gandhi on occasion attempted to achieve political objectives by a "fast unto death," his threat of self-starvation brought enormous psychological pressure on the authorities, who, among other things, feared [that] riots would ensue should Gandhi die.

The Gandhian pacifist, then, must explain why psychological pressure is permissible if physical pressure is forbidden. One possible answer is that physical pressure cannot transform the soul of the opponents, but psychological pressure, since it operates on the mind, can effect a spiritual transformation. Indeed, Gandhi characterized his terrifying fasts as acts of education, not coercion. But the claim that these fasts were not coercive confuses the noncoercive intention behind the act with its predictable coercive effects; and if education is the name of the game, the nonpacifists will remark that violence has been known to teach a few good lessons in its day. In many spiritual traditions, what matters essentially is not the kind of pressure but that the right pressure be applied at the right time and in the right way. Zen masters have brought students to enlightenment by clouting them on the ears, and God helped St. Paul to see the light by knocking him off his horse.

In addition to these technical problems, many people will be inclined to reject the system of values from which Gandhi's deductions flow. Many will concede that good character is important and that helping others to develop moral virtues is an important task. But few agree with Gandhi that the development of moral purity is the supreme human good, and that other goods, like the preservation of human life, or progress in the arts and sciences, have little or no value in comparison. If even a little value is conceded to these other things, then on occasion it will be necessary to put aside the project of developing spiritual purity in order to preserve other values. These acts of preservation may require physical violence, and those who use violence to defend life or beauty or liberty may indeed be corrupting their souls. But it is hard to believe that an occasional and necessary act of violence on behalf of these values will totally and permanently corrupt the soul, and those who use violence judiciously may be right in thinking that the saving of life or beauty or liberty may be worth a small or temporary spiritual loss.

4. PRIVATE PACIFISM

Perhaps the rarest form of pacifist is the pacifist who renounces violence in personal relations but condones the use of force in the political sphere. Such a pacifist will not use violence for self-defense but believes that it is permissible for the state to use judicial force against criminals and military force against foreign enemies. A private pacifist renounces self-defense but supports national defense.

(a) Augustine's Limited Pacifism

Historically, private pacifism developed as an attempt to reconcile the demands of the Sermon on the Mount with the Christian duty to charity. The Sermon on the Mount requires Christians to "resist not evil"; the duty of charity requires

pity for the weak who suffer the injustice of the strong. For St. Augustine (354–430), one essential message of the Gospels is the good news that this present life is as nothing compared with the life to come. The person who tries to hold on to earthly possessions is deluded as to what is truly valuable: "If any man will sue thee at the law, and take away thy coat, let him have thy cloak also" (Matt. 5:40). What goes for earthly coats should go for earthly life as well, so if any man seeks to take a Christian life, the Christian should let him have it. On this view, the doctrine "resist no evil" is just an expression of contempt for earthly possessions.

But according to Augustine there are some things in this world that do have value: justice, for example, the relief of suffering, and the preservation of the Church, which Augustine equated with civilization itself. To defend these things with necessary force is not to fall prey to delusions about the good. For Augustine, then, service in the armed forces is not inconsistent with Christian values.

One difficulty for theories like Augustine's is that they seem to justify military service only when military force is used in a just cause. Unfortunately, once in the service, the man in the ranks is not in a position to evaluate the justice of his nation's cause; indeed, in many modern nations, the principle of military subordination to civilian rule prevents even generals from evaluating the purposes of war declared by political leaders. But Augustine argues that the cause of justice cannot be served without armies, and armies cannot function unless subordinates follow orders without questioning the purposes of the conflict. The necessary conditions for justice and charity require that some men put themselves in positions in which they might be required to fight for injustice.

(b) The Problem of Self-Defense

Many will agree with Augustine that most violence at the personal level—the violence of crime, vendetta, and domestic brutality, for example—goes contrary to moral principles. But most are prepared to draw the line at personal and collective self-defense. Can the obligation to be charitable justify participation in military service but stop short of justifying the use of force by private citizens, if that force is exercised to protect the weak from the oppression of the strong? Furthermore, the obligation to be charitable does not exclude acts of charity toward oneself. For Augustine, violence was a dangerous tool, best kept out of the hands of the citizens and best left strictly at the disposal of the state. Beset with fears of crime in the streets, the contemporary American is less inclined to worry about the anarchic effects of private uses of defensive force and more inclined to worry about the protection the police seem unable to provide.

For these worried people, the existence of a right to self-defense is self-evident. But the existence of this right is not self-evident to universal or private pacifists; and it was not self-evident to St. Augustine. In the Christian tradition, no right to self-defense was recognized until its existence was certified by Thomas Aquinas in the thirteenth century. Aquinas derived the right to self-defense from the universal tendency to self-preservation, assuming (contrary to Augustine) that a natural tendency must be morally right. As for the Christian duty to love one's enemy, Aquinas argued that acts of self-defense have two effects—the saving of life and the taking of life—and that self-defensive uses of force intend primarily the saving of life. This makes the use of force in self-defense a morally permissible act of charity. The right to self-defense is now generally recognized in Catholic moral theology and in Western legal systems. But it can hardly be said that Aquinas's arguments, which rely heavily on assumptions from Greek philosophy, succeed in reconciling the claims of self-defense with the prescriptions of the Sermon on the Mount.

5. ANTIWAR PACIFISM

Most people who believe in the right to personal self-defense also believe that some wars are morally justified. In fact, the notion of self-defense and the notion of just war are commonly linked; just wars are said to be defensive wars, and the justice of defensive war is inferred from the right of personal self-defense, projected from the individual to the national level. But some people reject this projection: they endorse the validity of personal self-defense, but they deny that war can be justified by appeal to self-defense or any other right. On the contrary, they argue that war always involves an inexcusable violation of rights. For such anti-war pacifists, all participation in war is morally wrong.

(a) The Killing of Soldiers

One universal and necessary feature of wars is that soldiers get killed in them. Most people accept such killings as a necessary evil, and judge the killing of soldiers in war to be morally acceptable. If the war is fought for the just cause, the killing of enemy soldiers is justified as necessary to the triumph of right. If the war is fought for an unjust cause, the killing of enemy soldiers is acceptable because it is considered an honorable thing to fight for one's country, right or wrong, provided that one fights well and cleanly. But the antiwar pacifist does not take the killing of soldiers for granted. Everyone has a right to life, and the killing of soldiers in war is intentional killing, a deliberate violation of the right to life. According to the standard interpretation of basic rights, it is never morally justifiable to violate a basic right in order to produce some good; the end, in such cases, does not justify the means. How, then, can the killing of soldiers in war be morally justified—or even excused?

Perhaps the commonest reply to the challenge of antiwar pacifism is that killing in war is a matter of self-defense, *personal* self-defense, the right to which is freely acknowledged by the antiwar pacifist. In war, the argument goes, it is either kill or be killed—and that type of killing is killing in self-defense. But though the appeal to self-defense is natural, antiwar pacifists believe that it is not successful. First of all, on the usual understanding of "self-defense," those who kill can claim the justification of self-defense only if (a) they had no other way to save their lives or preserve themselves from physical harm except by killing, and (b) they did nothing to provoke the attack to which they are subjected. Antiwar pacifists point out that soldiers on the battlefield do have a way of saving themselves from death or harm without killing anyone: they can surrender. Furthermore, for soldiers fighting for an unjust cause—for example, German soldiers fighting in the invasion of Russia in 1941—it is difficult to argue that they "did nothing to provoke" the deadly force directed at them. But if the German army provoked the Russians to stand and fight on Russian soil, German soldiers cannot legitimately claim self-defense as a moral justification for killing Russian soldiers.

To the nonpacifist, these points might seem like legalistic quibbles. But the antiwar pacifist has an even stronger argument against killing soldiers in war. The vast majority of soldiers who die in war do not die in "kill or be killed" situations. They are killed by bullets, shells, or bombs directed from safe launching points—"safe" in the sense that those who shoot the bullets or fire the shells or drop the bombs are in no immediate danger of death. Since those who kill are not in immediate danger of death, they cannot invoke "self-defense" to justify the deaths they cause.

Some other argument besides self-defense, then, must explain why the killing of soldiers in war should not be classified as murder. Frequently, nonpacifists argue that the explanation is found in the doctrine of "assumption of risk," the idea, common in civil law, that persons who freely assume a risk have only themselves to blame if the risk is realized. When a soldier goes to war, he is well aware that one risk of his trade is getting killed on the battlefield. If he dies on the field, the responsibility for his death lies with himself, not with the man who shot him. By assuming the risk—so the argument goes—he waived his right to life, at least on the battlefield.

One does not have to be a pacifist to see difficulties in this argument. First of all, in all substantial modern wars, most of the men on the line are not volunteers, but draftees. Only a wealthy nation like the United States can afford an all-volunteer army, and most experts believe that the American volunteer ranks will have to be supplemented by draftees should the United States become involved in another conflict on the scale of Korea or Vietnam. Second, in many cases in which a risk is realized, responsibility for the bad outcome lies not with the person who assumed

the risk but with the person who created it. If an arsonist sets fire to a house and a parent rushes in to save the children, dying in the rescue attempt, responsibility for the parent's death lies not with the parent who assumed the risk, but with the arsonist who created it. So if German armies invade Russia, posing the risk of death in battle, and if Russian soldiers assume this risk and fight back, the deaths of Russians are the fault of German invaders, not the fault of the defenders who assumed the risk.

These criticisms of German foot soldiers will irritate many who served in the armed forces and who know how little political and military decision making is left to the men on the front lines, who seem to be the special target of these pacifist arguments. But antiwar pacifists will deny that their aim is to condemn the men on the battlefield. Most antiwar pacifists feel that soldiers in war act under considerable compulsion and are excused for that reason from responsibility for the killing they do. But to say that battlefield killings are *excusable* is not to say that they are morally *justified*. On the contrary, if such killings are excusable, it must be that there is some immorality to be excused.

(b) The Killing of Civilians

In the chronicles of ancient wars, conflict was total and loss in battle was frequently followed by general slaughter of men, women, and children on the losing side. It has always been considered part of the trend toward civilization to confine the destruction of war to the personnel and instruments of war, sparing civilians and their property as much as possible. This civilizing trend was conspicuously reversed in World War II, in which the ratio of civilian deaths to total war deaths was perhaps the highest it had been since the wars of religion in the seventeenth century. A very high ratio of civilian deaths to total deaths was also characteristic of the war in Vietnam. Given the immense firepower of modern weapons and the great distances between the discharges of weapons and the explosions of bullets or shells near the targets, substantial civilian casualties are an inevitable part of modern land war. But it is immoral to kill civilians, the antiwar pacifist argues, and from this it follows that modern land warfare is necessarily immoral.

Few nonpacifists will argue that killing enemy civilians is justifiable when such killings are avoidable. Few will argue that killing enemy civilians is justifiable when such killings are the *primary* objective of a military operation. But what about the deaths of civilians that are the unavoidable results of military operations directed to some *other* result? The pacifist classifies such killings as immoral, whereas most nonpacifists call them regrettable but unavoidable deaths, not murders. But why are they not murder, if the civilians are innocent, and if it is known in advance that some civilians will be killed? Isn't this an intentional killing of the innocent, which is the traditional definition of murder?

The sophisticated nonpacifist may try to parry this thrust with analogies to policies outside the arena of war. There are, after all, many morally acceptable policies that, when adopted, have the effect of killing innocent persons. If the Congress decides to set a speed limit of 55 miles per hour on federal highways, more people will die than if Congress sets the speed limit at 45 miles per hour. Since many people who die on the highway are innocent, the Congress has chosen a policy that knowingly brings death to the innocent, but no one calls it murder. Or suppose, for example, that a public health officer is considering a national vaccination program to forestall a flu epidemic. He knows that if he does not implement the vaccination program, many people will die from the flu. On the other hand, if the program is implemented, a certain number of people will die of allergic reactions to the vaccine. Most of the people who die from allergic reactions will be people who would not have died of the flu if the vaccination program had not been implemented. So the vaccination program will kill innocent people who would otherwise be saved if the program were abandoned. If the public health officer implements such a program, we do *not* think that he is a murderer.

Nonpacifists argue that what makes the action of Congress and the action of the public health officer morally permissible in these cases is that the deaths of the innocent, although foreseen, are not the intended goal of these policies. Congress does not want people to die on the highways; every highway death is a regrettable death. The purpose of setting the speed limit at 55 miles per hour is not to kill people but to provide a reasonable balance between safety and convenience. Likewise, it is not the purpose of the public health officer to kill people by giving them vaccine. His goal is to save lives on balance, and every death from the vaccine is a regrettable death. Likewise, in war, when civilians are killed as a result of necessary military operations, the deaths of the civilians are not the intended goal of the military operation. They are foreseen, but they are always regretted. If we do not accuse Congress of murder and the Public Health Service of murder in these cases, consistency requires that we not accuse military forces of murder when they cause civilian deaths in war, especially if every attempt is made to keep civilian deaths to a minimum.

Antiwar pacifists do not condemn the Congress and the Public Health Service in cases like these. But they assert that the case of war is different in a morally relevant way. To demonstrate the difference, antiwar pacifists provide an entirely different analysis of the moral justification for speed limits and vaccination programs. In their opinion, the facts that highway deaths and vaccination deaths are "unintended" and "regretted" is morally irrelevant. The real justification lies in the factor of consent. In the case of federal highway regulations, the rules are decided by Congress, which is elected by the people, the same people who use the highways. If Congress decides on a 55-mile-an-hour limit, this is a regulation that, in some sense, highway drivers have imposed upon themselves. Those people who die on the highway because of a higher speed limit have, in a double sense, assumed the risks generated by that speed limit: they have, through the Congress, created the risk, and by venturing onto the highway, have freely exposed themselves to the risk. The responsibility for these highway deaths, then, lies either on the drivers themselves or on the people who crashed into them—not on the Congress.

Likewise, in the case of the vaccination program, if people are warned in advance of the risks of vaccination, and if they nevertheless choose to be vaccinated, they are responsible for their own deaths should the risks be realized. According to the antiwar pacifist, it is this consent given by drivers and vaccination volunteers that justifies these policies, and it is precisely this element of consent that is absent in the case of the risks inflicted on enemy civilians in time of war.

Consider the standard textbook example of allegedly justifiable killing of civilians in time of war. Suppose that the destruction of a certain bridge is an important military objective, but if the bridge is bombed, it is very likely that civilians living close by will be killed. (The civilians cannot be warned without alerting the enemy to reinforce the bridge.) If the bridge is bombed and some civilians are killed, the bombing victims are not in the same moral category as highway victims or victims of vaccination. The bombing victims did not order the bombing of themselves through some set of elected representatives. Nor did the bombing victims freely consent to the bombing of their bridge. Nor was the bombing in any way undertaken as a calculated risk in the interest of the victims. For all these reasons, the moral conclusions regarding highway legislation and vaccination programs do not carry over to bombing of the bridge.

Nonpacifists who recognize that it will be very difficult to fight wars without bombing bridges may argue that the victims of this bombing in some sense assumed the risks of bombardment by choosing to live close to a potential military target. Indeed, it is occasionally claimed that all the civilians in a nation at war have assumed the risks of war, since they could avoid the risks of war simply by moving to a neutral country. But such arguments are strained and uncharitable, even for those rare warring nations that permit freedom of emigration. Most people consider it a major sacrifice to give up their homes, and an option that requires such a sacrifice cannot be considered an option open for free choice. The analogy between the unintended victims of vaccination and the unintended civilian victims of war seems to have broken down.

(c) The Balance of Good and Evil in War

It is left to the nonpacifist to argue that the killing of soldiers and civilians in war is in the end justifiable in order to obtain great moral goods that can be obtained only by fighting for them. Civilians have rights to life, but those rights can be outweighed by the national objectives, provided those objectives are morally acceptable and overwhelmingly important. Admittedly, this argument for killing civilians is available only to the just side in a war, but if the argument is valid, it proves that there can *be* a just side, contrary to the arguments of antiwar pacifism.

Antiwar pacifists have two lines of defense. First, they can continue to maintain that the end does not justify the means, if the means be murderous. Second, they can, and will, go on to argue that it is a tragic mistake to believe that there are great moral goods that can be obtained only by war. According to antiwar pacifists, the amount of moral good produced by war is greatly exaggerated. The Mexican War, for example, resulted in half of Mexico being transferred to American rule. This was a great good for the United States, but not a great moral good, since the United States had little claim to the ceded territory, and no great injustice would have persisted if the war had not been fought at all.

The Revolutionary War in America is widely viewed as a war that produced a great moral good; but if the war had not been fought, the history of the United States would be similar to the history of Canada (which remained loyal)—and no one feels that the Canadians have suffered or are suffering great injustices that the American colonies avoided by war. Likewise, it is difficult to establish the goods produced by World War I or the moral losses that would have ensued if the winning side, "our side," had lost. Bertrand Russell imagined the results of a British loss in World War I as follows:

> The greatest sum that foreigners could possibly exact would be the total economic rent of the land and natural resources of England. [But] the working classes, the shopkeepers, manufacturers, and merchants, the literary men and men

of science—all the people that make England of any account in the world—have at most an infinitesimal and accidental share in the rental of England. The men who have a share use their rents in luxury, political corruption, taking the lives of birds, and depopulating and enslaving the rural districts. It is this life of the idle rich that would be curtailed if the Germans exacted tribute from England. (*Justice in War Time*, pp. 48–49)

But multiplying examples of wars that did little moral good will not establish the pacifist case. The pacifist must show that *no* war has done enough good to justify the killing of soldiers and the killing of civilians that occurred in the war. A single war that produces moral goods sufficient to justify its killings will refute the pacifist claim that *all* wars are morally unjustifiable. Obviously this brings the antiwar pacifist head to head with World War II.

It is commonly estimated that 35 million people died as a result of World War II. It is difficult to imagine that any cause could justify so much death, but fortunately the Allies need only justify their share of these killings. Between 1939 and 1945 Allied forces killed about 5.5 million Axis soldiers and about 1 million civilians in Axis countries. Suppose that Britain and the United States had chosen to stay out of World War II and suppose Stalin had, like Lenin, surrendered to Germany shortly after the invasion. Does avoiding the world that would have resulted from these decisions justify killing 6.5 million people?

If Hitler and Tojo had won the war, doubtless they would have killed a great many people both before and after victory, but it is quite likely that the total of *additional* victims, beyond those they killed in the war that *was* fought, would have been less than 6.5 million and, at any rate, the responsibility for those deaths would fall on Hitler and Tojo, not on Allied nations. If Hitler and Tojo had won the war, large portions of the world would have fallen under foreign domination, perhaps for a very long time. But the antiwar pacifist will point out that the main areas of Axis foreign domination—China and Russia—were not places in which the citizens enjoyed a high level of

freedom *before the war began*. Perhaps the majority of people in the conquered areas would have worked out a *modus vivendi* with their new rulers, as did the majority of French citizens during the German occupation. Nor can it be argued that World War II was necessary to save six million Jews from annihilation in the Holocaust, since in fact the war did *not* save them.

The ultimate aims of Axis leaders are a matter for historical debate. Clearly the Japanese had no intention of conquering the United States, and some historians suggest that Hitler hoped to avoid war with England and America, declaring war with England reluctantly, and only after the English declared it against him. Nevertheless, popular opinion holds that Hitler intended to conquer the world, and if preventing the conquest of Russia and China could not justify six and one-half million killings, most Americans are quite confident that preventing the conquest of England and the United States does justify killing on this scale.

The antiwar pacifist disagrees. Certainly German rule of England and the United States would have been a very bad thing. At the same time, hatred of such German rule would be particularly fueled by hatred of foreigners, and hatred of foreigners, as such, is an irrational and morally unjustifiable passion. After all, if rule by foreigners were, by itself, a great moral wrong, the British, with their great colonial empire, could hardly consider themselves the morally superior side in World War II.

No one denies that a Nazi victory in World War II would have had morally frightful results. But, according to antiwar pacifism, killing six and one-half million people is also morally frightful, and preventing one moral wrong does not obviously outweigh committing the other. Very few people today share the pacifists' condemnation of World War II, but perhaps that is because the dead killed by the Allies cannot speak up and make sure that their losses are properly counted on the moral scales. Antiwar pacifists speak on behalf of the enemy dead, and on behalf of all those millions who would have lived if the war had not been fought. On this silent constituency they rest their moral case.

⚜ REVIEW QUESTIONS

1. Characterize universal pacifists (there are two types), private pacifists, and antiwar pacifists.
2. Why doesn't Lackey accept the appeal to the Bible, or the sacredness of life, or the right to life as a good reason for accepting pacifism?
3. What is Christian pacifism and Tolstoy's argument used to defend it? Why doesn't Lackey accept Tolstoy's argument?
4. Explain Gandhi's pacifism, including *satyagraha*. What problems does Lackey raise for this view?
5. Explain Augustine's so-called limited pacifism. What problems does this view have according to Lackey?
6. State the position of antiwar pacifism. Why do antiwar pacifists believe that all wars are wrong? According to Lackey, what are the objections to antiwar pacifism, and how can antiwar pacifists reply?

⚜ DISCUSSION QUESTIONS

1. Is Gandhi's view a defensible one? Why or why not?
2. Does the antiwar pacifist have a good reply to all the objections Lackey discusses? Are there any good objections that Lackey does not discuss?
3. Many people think that World War II was morally justified. What does the antiwar pacifist say? What do you think?
4. According to Lackey, no great moral good was produced by the Revolutionary War in America. If America had lost this war and remained under British rule, then its history would be like that of Canada—and Canada has not suffered, he says. Do you agree? Explain your answer.

Just War Principles

MICHAEL W. BROUGH, JOHN W. LANGO, HARRY VAN DER LINDEN

Michael W. Brough is a major in the U.S. Army, and was an assistant professor of philosophy at the U.S. Military Academy at West Point before being deployed to Iraq.

John W. Lango is professor of philosophy at Hunter College of the City University of New York. He is the author of *Whitehead's Ontology* (1972), and articles on war, ethics, and metaphysics.

Harry van der Linden is professor of philosophy at Butler University. He is the author of *Kantian Ethics and Socialism* (1988) and other writings on Kant and Marx. His most recent articles are on global poverty, economic migration, humanitarian intervention, and preventive war.

Brough, Lango, and van der Linden state and explain the basic principles of traditional just war theory. The first set of principles concern what justifies going to war. They are called *jus ad bello* (justice in the resort to war) principles. These principles include the just cause for war, legitimate authority for war, and the right intention for war. Also, the war must be a last resort with a reasonable chance of success, and the anticipated goods must be commensurate with the expected evils. These principles are seen as the responsibility of the political leaders of a state. The second set of principles, called *jus in bello* (justice in the conduct of war) principles, is thought to be the responsibility of the military. They are concerned with how the war is fought. They say that soldiers should target combatants and not civilians, and that force should be used in proportion to the end pursued, and not beyond what is necessary.

Source: Appendix, Just War Principles: An Introduction with Further Reading from Rethinking the Just War Tradition by Michael W. Brough, John W. Lango and Harry Van Der Linden. Copyright © 2007. NY: State University of New York Press.

JUST WAR PRINCIPLES

The just war tradition is based on two highly contested ideas: that there are norms on the basis of which one can conclude that in some situations the resort to war is just, and that there are norms that enable war to be conducted in a just manner. What makes the first idea controversial, and especially disconcerting to pacifists, is the claim that the massive and systematic killing and maiming of human beings can sometimes be just. What makes the second idea controversial—and naive or unacceptable to the realist who holds that only self-preservation, national interest, and seeking power motivate conduct between states—is the belief that wars with all their horrors and unanticipated consequences can be fought in a morally constrained manner. Traditionally, the first set of norms, the *jus ad bellum* (justice in the resort to war) principles, is thought to be the responsibility mainly of the political leadership of a country, while the second set of norms, the *jus in bello* (justice in the conduct of war) principles, is viewed as the primary responsibility of military commanders and soldiers. This traditional understanding is not without controversy. It may be questioned, for example, whether soldiers in a war of aggression can be honored for killing in accordance with *jus in bello* principles. And, it may be argued that, since citizens in a democratic society are to some degree responsible for the wars fought in their name, just war thinking is their civic duty.

Not all contemporary just war theorists offer the same list of just war principles, and instead of the term *principles* some authors use other terms, such as *criteria* or *norms*. More importantly, there is disagreement about how the various principles are to be articulated or comprehended. And there are other disagreements—for example, concerning how (and even whether) *jus ad bellum* principles are to be weighed in the resort to war decision. Our view is that much philosophical work remains to be done in terms of clarifying the individual principles and elucidating their rationale, their relative weight, and their connection to international law. This task—which is central to the project of rethinking the just war tradition—is an ongoing one, since (among other reasons) just war thinking should evolve with the changing nature of warfare caused by broader economic, cultural, technological, and political developments.

The list of just war principles stated here is widely accepted. The accounts of the different principles include some controversies about their interpretation and significance, which illustrate the need to rethink the principles. It should be noted that some recent just war theorists have argued that the conclusion of war must be guided by a third set of just war norms, *jus post bellum* principles. These principles are not included here. . . .

We have added an annotated list of writings pertinent to the theme of this book. It is not a comprehensive bibliography but rather a list of suggestions for further reading, especially for readers less familiar with the just war tradition. For lack of space, we had to leave out equally valuable writings. We have not included writings by our contributors. Joan T. Philips of Air University Library, Maxwell Air Force Base, Alabama, maintains a detailed online bibliography of current publications on just war theory at http://www.au.af.mil/au/aul/bibs/just/justwar.htm.

JUS AD BELLUM PRINCIPLES

1. Just cause. A war is justified only if waged for one or more just causes. Just war theorists generally agree that defense against an unjust attack is a just cause. Similarly, although this might be contested, assisting an ally against an unjust attack is a just cause. More controversial just causes include protecting civilians from massive basic human rights violations committed by their own government or by other parties in a civil war (humanitarian intervention), the imminent threat of aggression (preemptive war), and, especially, future threats—notably, as posed by the possible use of weapons of mass destruction by terrorists or "rogue" states (preventive war).

2. Legitimate authority. The use of military force is permissible only if it is authorized by a political body that is widely recognized as having this power. This principle is also referred to as the *proper, right,* or *competent authority principle.* It is matter of some controversy whether governments irrespective of their moral status or credibility have legitimate authority. There is also disagreement about whether non-state actors, such as guerrilla, insurgent groups, or terrorist groups, can have legitimate authority. And there is dispute about whether an international body—in particular, the United Nations, but also regional organizations, such as NATO or the African Union—can have legitimate authority and what the scope of this authority might be vis-à-vis states.

3. Right intention. A war must be waged with the pursuit of its just cause as its sole (or primary) motive. For instance, if the just cause is stopping genocide, then the sole (or primary) motive guiding the armed humanitarian intervention must be to stop the genocide. As signaled by the parenthetical word *primary*, it is controversial whether there may be other motives. Thus it is controversial whether armed intervention with a primary humanitarian motive may also be secondarily motivated by national self-interest. Clearly, some secondary motives, such as access to resources, economic gain, territorial expansion, increased international influence and power, or ethnic hatred, may weaken or undermine the moral legitimacy of a war.

4. Last resort. Nonmilitary alternatives, including diplomacy, negotiations, sanctions, and legal adjudication, must be pursued—within reasonable limits—prior to resorting to military force. Delaying the use of military force, or threat thereof, too long may be morally objectionable in that it may stimulate aggression or allow for the escalation of a humanitarian disaster. Crucial to a correct explication of this principle is determining what is meant by *within reasonable limits.*

5. Reasonable chance (hope) of success. A war should be fought only if there is a reasonable hope that the goals embedded in its just cause will be realized. It is objectionable to demand great sacrifices of combatants—or inflict serious harms on noncombatants—if military victory seems a very remote possibility. On a broader and more controversial account, a just war entails a possibility of creating an enduring peace.

6. Proportionality. The anticipated goods of waging a war must be proportionate or commensurate to its expected evils. On the common interpretation, this means that the anticipated benefits of war must outweigh its harms, but on a less demanding account it requires only that the expected harms do not greatly exceed the benefits. The principle of proportionality is also referred to as the *principle of macro-proportionality*, so as to distinguish it from the *jus in bello* proportionality principle, which is then referred to as the principle of micro-proportionality. The benefits and costs for one's own people of resorting to war should definitely be counted, but how much weight should be given to the goods and evils that the war imposes upon the enemy or non-warring countries is a matter of debate. Whether goods should be counted resulting from war but not related to its just cause is also a matter of dispute. In light of the history of controversies about how to measure utility, it is not surprising that some just war theorists have contested whether the proportionality principle provides significant moral guidance.

JUS IN BELLO PRINCIPLES

7. Discrimination. Soldiers should discriminate between combatants and noncombatants and target only the former. This principle is also called the *principle of noncombatant immunity*. Just war theorists offer differing accounts of who is to be counted as noncombatants and why. Harm to noncombatants is typically seen as an acceptable result of a military action if it is not intentionally inflicted and is proportionate to the importance of the goals of the military action. A more stringent—and contested—view of how much "collateral damage" is morally acceptable is to demand of soldiers that they seek to minimize noncombatant casualties even at the risk of greater costs to themselves. It is morally impermissible to destroy targets that have primarily civilian purposes. It is a matter of controversy whether structures with both weighty military and civilian significance may be directly targeted. Some weapons, such as nuclear weapons, biological weapons, and (more controversially) landmines, are morally objectionable due to their indiscriminate impact.

8. Proportionality. Force should be used in proportion to the end pursued, and destruction beyond what is necessary to reach a military objective is morally suspect. It might be claimed that the laws of war allow the killing of enemy soldiers without limit, but such a claim is objectionable in terms of the principle of proportionality. Weapons that cause injuries to people long after they have ceased to be combatants, such as nuclear and biological weapons, are disproportionate. Additionally, as with the *jus ad bellum* proportionality principle, there are disputes about which benefits and costs are to be counted, and how they are to be weighted.

⚜ FURTHER READING

Chatterjee, Deen K., and Scheid, Don E., eds. *Ethics and Foreign Intervention*. Cambridge: Cambridge University Press, 2003.

A collection of essays exploring the ethics and legality of secession and humanitarian intervention. A few essays offer qualified support for humanitarian intervention on the basis of the just war tradition. Several contributions articulate a normative and pragmatic "critique of interventionism," concluding that "altruistic wars" are seldom, if ever, justified.

Childress, James F. "Just War Theories: The Bases, Interrelations, Priorities, and Functions of Their Criteria." *Theological Studies* 39 (1978). Revised as chapter 3 in his *Moral Responsibility in Conflicts: Essays on Nonviolence, War, and Conscience*. Baton Rouge: Louisiana State University Press, 1982.

Instead of simply presupposing just war principles, the author attempts to ground them in W. D. Ross's conception of prima facie duties, especially the duty of nonmaleficence. In terms of such a grounding, he discusses the order, strength, and function of the principles.

Coates, A. J. *The Ethics of War*. Manchester: Manchester University Press, 1997.

The book offers chapter-length discussions of just war principles, paying attention to their historical roots but focusing on their contemporary significance and interpretive controversies. Many historical illustrations are provided.

Coppieters, Bruno, and Fotion, Nick, eds. *Moral Constraints on War: Principles and Cases*. Lanham, MD: Lexington Books, 2002.

Scholars from Belgium, China, Russia, and the United States analyze each of the just war principles in a separate chapter with a wide range of historical examples. The book also offers five case studies, all involving American resort to war except for a study of the First Chechen War.

Evans, Mark, ed. *Just War Theory: A Reappraisal*. Edinburgh: Edinburgh University Press, 2005.

A collection of essays, mainly by political scientists, that are distributed among parts entitled "Just Cause," "Justice in the Conduct of War," and "Justice and the End of War." The essays are on such topics as preventive war, proportionality, supreme emergency, and *jus post bellum*.

Held, Virginia. "Legitimate Authority in Non-State Groups Using Violence." *Journal of Social Philosophy* 36 (2005): 175–193.

The author argues that non-state groups using violence and even terrorism may represent their people and meet the requirement of legitimate authority.

Hurka, Thomas. "Proportionality in the Morality of War." *Philosophy and Public Affairs* 33 (2005): 34–66.

With respect to both the *jus ad bellum* and *jus in bello* principles of proportionality, this article discusses which goods and evils fall within their scope and how they should be weighted against one another. Hurka argues that only goods included in the sufficient and contributing just causes of a war should be counted in macroproportionality.

Johnson, James Turner. *Morality and Contemporary Warfare*. New Haven: Yale University Press, 1999.

This book offers an introduction to the just war tradition and covers such topics as humanitarian intervention, noncombatant immunity and modern war, and reconciliation after war. Johnson draws from his influential historical studies of the just war tradition.

Luban, David. "Just War and Human Rights." *Philosophy and Public Affairs* 9 (1980): 160–181.

The author argues that only wars in defense of "socially basic human rights" are just, so that self-defensive wars by corrupt regimes may be unjust and an attack on such regimes may be just.

Lucas, George R., Jr., *Perspectives on Humanitarian Military Intervention*. Berkeley: Berkeley Public Policy Press, 2001.

On analogy with just war theory's *jus ad bellum* and *jus in bello* principles, the author advocates principles for just humanitarian military intervention, which are termed *jus ad interventionem* and *jus in interventione* criteria.

———. "The Role of the 'International Community' in Just War Tradition—Confronting the Challenges of Humanitarian Intervention and Preemptive War." *Journal of Military Ethics* 2 (2003): 122–144.

The author describes important similarities between preemptive war and humanitarian intervention, including that both in their justification appeal to a poorly defined notion of the "international community." Criteria for just resort to force in both cases are proposed with special attention to the issue of international authorization.

McMahan, Jeff. "The Ethics of Killing in War." *Ethics* 114 (2004): 693–733.

The author challenges the principle of noncombatant immunity and the common view that soldiers in an unjust war do not act wrongly as long as they uphold the *jus in bello* principles.

Orend, Brian. *War and International Justice: A Kantian Perspective*. Waterloo: Wilfrid Laurier University Press, 2000.

Orend makes the controversial claim that Kant had a just war theory and was the first thinker to maintain that just war theory should be completed by a category of *jus post bellum*. The book articulates a list of Kantian principles of justice after war. See also Orend, "Justice after War," *Ethics and International Affairs* 16 (2002): 43–56.

Rodin, David. *War and Self-Defense*. Oxford: Oxford University Press, 2002.

This book contests the commonly accepted idea that war is justified in case of national self-defense and carefully argues that the domestic analogy of individual self-defense fails. Rodin proposes that the use of armed force may be justified as a police action against enemy soldiers involved in an aggressive war. His view is commented upon in "Symposium: War and Self-Defense," *Ethics and International Affairs* 18 (Winter 2004).

Sterba, James P., ed. *Terrorism and International Justice*. Oxford: Oxford University Press, 2003.

A collection of essays focused on 9/11 and its aftermath. Several contributors argue that 9/11 was a criminal act, requiring a legal response. The U.S. war against the Taliban is also assessed on the basis of "just war pacifism" and more traditional just war criteria. Attention is also paid to whether weaker parties in asymmetric conflict may rightfully loosen *jus in bello* criteria.

Walzer, Michael. *Just and Unjust Wars: A Moral Argument with Historical Illustrations*, third edition with a new preface by the author. New York: Basic Books, 2000. First edition appeared in 1977.

Even almost three decades after its publication it remains a reference point for much current just war thinking. At the occasion of its twentieth year of publication, *Ethics and International Affairs* 11 (1997) published a handful of critical essays with a response by Walzer.

———. *Arguing About War*. New Haven: Yale University Press, 2004.

A collection of Walzer's essays written after his classic *Just and Unjust War* (1977). Topics include military responsibility, humanitarian intervention, and terrorism. The very recent essays are all applications of just war criteria, covering Kosovo, the Israel-Palestine conflict, 9/11, and the Iraq war, with the exception of an essay that proclaims the triumph of just war theory and poses the question of what is still left to be done for just war theorists.

Zupan, Daniel S. *War, Morality, and Autonomy: An Investigation in Just War Theory*. Burlington, VT: Ashgate, 2003.

The author argues that autonomy, based on a Kantian notion of humanity, provides a better theoretical underpinning for the war convention or *jus in bello* principles than consequentialist or rights-based theories. The analysis is applied to the supreme emergency doctrine and the war on terrorism.

✢ REVIEW QUESTIONS

1. According to Brough, Lango, and van der Linden, the just war tradition is based on two controversial ideas. What are they and why are they controversial?

2. State and explain the *jus ad bellum* principles.
3. State and explain the *jus in bello* principles.

✢ DISCUSSION QUESTIONS

1. Do the wars in Iraq and Afghanistan satisfy the just war principles? Defend your answer.
2. Can insurgents or rebels have the legitimate authority to fight a war? For example, did the I.R.A. have the legitimate authority to fight the British

rule of Ireland? What about the American revolutionaries who fought the British to achieve independence?
3. Do nuclear weapons violate the discrimination principle? Why or why not?

The Slippery Slope to Preventive War

NETA C. CRAWFORD

Neta C. Crawford is professor of political science and African American studies at Boston University. She is the author of *Argument and Change in World Politics* (2002), and articles on intervention, prevention, and U.S. military strategy.

Crawford argues that the preemption doctrine of the Bush administration is flawed and can slide into a morally unacceptable practice of preventive war. The problem with the preemptive doctrine is that it makes no distinction between terrorists who want to harm us and rogue states that do not want to harm us and pose no imminent threat. Preemption is legitimate only if lives are threatened, war is inevitable in the immediate future, the preemption is likely to succeed, and military force is necessary. Preemption is not legitimate to protect other national interests, such as economic well-being, or because of fear of future attack. In such cases, defensive preemption becomes offensive preventive war that makes things worse by producing more war and increasing resentment.

The Bush administration's arguments in favor of a preemptive doctrine rest on the view that warfare has been transformed. As Colin Powell argues, "It's a different world . . . it's a new kind of threat."[1] And in several important respects, war has changed along the lines the administration suggests, although that transformation has

been under way for at least the last ten to fifteen years. Unconventional adversaries prepared to wage unconventional war can conceal their movements, weapons, and immediate intentions and conduct devastating surprise attacks.[2] Nuclear, chemical, and biological weapons, though not widely dispersed, are more readily available

Source: The Slippery Slope to Preventive War by Neta C. Crawford from Ethics & International Affairs, Volume 17, No 1, Spring 2003. NY: Carnegie Council for Ethics in International Affairs.

than they were in the recent past. And the everyday infrastructure of the United States can be turned against it as were the planes the terrorists hijacked on September 11, 2001. Further, the administration argues that we face enemies who "reject basic human values and hate the United States and everything for which it stands."[3] Although vulnerability could certainly be reduced in many ways, it is impossible to achieve complete invulnerability.

Such vulnerability and fear, the argument goes, means the United States must take the offensive. Indeed, soon after the September 11, 2001, attacks, members of the Bush administration began equating self-defense with preemption:

> There is no question but that the United States of America has every right, as every country does, of self-defense, and the problem with terrorism is that there is no way to defend against the terrorists at every place and every time against every conceivable technique. Therefore, the only way to deal with the terrorist network is to take the battle to them. That is in fact what we're doing. That is in effect self-defense of a preemptive nature.[4]

The character of potential threats becomes extremely important in evaluating the legitimacy of the new preemption doctrine, and thus the assertion that the United States faces rogue enemies who oppose everything about the United States must be carefully evaluated. There is certainly robust evidence to believe that al-Qaeda members desire to harm the United States and American citizens. The National Security Strategy makes a questionable leap, however, when it assumes that "rogue states" also desire to harm the United States and pose an imminent military threat. Further, the administration blurs the distinction between "rogue states" and terrorists, essentially erasing the difference between terrorists and those states in which they reside: "We make no distinction between terrorists and those who knowingly harbor or provide aid to them."[5] But these distinctions do indeed make a difference.

Legitimate preemption could occur if four necessary conditions were met. First, the party contemplating preemption would have a narrow conception of the "self" to be defended in circumstances of self-defense. Preemption is not justified to protect imperial interests or assets taken in a war of aggression. Second, there would have to be strong evidence that war was inevitable and likely in the immediate future. Immediate threats are those which can be made manifest within days or weeks unless action is taken to thwart them. This requires clear intelligence showing that a potential aggressor has both the capability and the intention to do harm in the near future. Capability alone is not a justification. Third, preemption should be likely to succeed in reducing the threat. Specifically, there should be a high likelihood that the source of the military threat can be found and the damage that it was about to do can be greatly reduced or eliminated by a preemptive attack. If preemption is likely to fail, it should not be undertaken. Fourth, military force must be necessary; no other measures can have time to work or be likely to work.

A DEFENSIBLE SELF

On the face of it, the self-defense criteria seem clear. When our lives are threatened, we must be able to defend ourselves using force if necessary. But self-defense may have another meaning, that in which our "self" is expressed not only by mere existence, but also by a free and prosperous life. For example, even if a tyrant would allow us to live, but not under institutions of our own choosing, we may justly fight to free ourselves from political oppression. But how far do the rights of the self extend? If someone threatens our access to food, or fuel, or shelter, can we legitimately use force? Or if they allow us access to the material goods necessary for our existence, but charge such a high price that we must make a terrible choice between food and health care, or between mere existence and growth, are we justified in using force to secure access to a good that would enhance the self? When economic interests and vulnerabilities are understood to be global, and when the moral and political community of democracy and human rights are defined more broadly than ever before, the self-conception of great powers tends to enlarge. But a broad conception of self is not necessarily legitimate and neither are the values to be defended completely obvious.

For example, the U.S. definition of the self to be defended has become very broad. The administration, in its most recent Quadrennial Defense Review, defines "enduring national interests" as including "contributing to economic well-being," which entails maintaining "vitality and productivity of the global economy" and "access to key markets and strategic resources." Further, the goal of U.S. strategy, according to this document, is to maintain "preeminence."[6] The National Security Strategy also fuses ambitious political and economic goals with security: "The U.S. national security strategy will be based on a distinctly American internationalism that reflects the fusion of our values and our national interests. The aim of this strategy is to help make the world not just safer but better." And "today the distinction between domestic and foreign affairs is diminishing."[7]

If the self is defined so broadly and threats to this greater "self" are met with military force, at what point does self-defense begin to look like aggression? As Richard Betts has argued, "When security is defined in terms broader than protecting the near-term integrity of national sovereignty and borders, the distinction between offense and defense blurs hopelessly. . . . Security can be as insatiable an appetite as acquisitiveness—there may never be enough buffers."[8] The large self-conception of the United States could lead to a tendency to intervene everywhere that this greater self might conceivably be at risk of, for example, losing access to markets. Thus, a conception of the self that justifies legitimate preemption in self-defense must be narrowly confined to immediate risks to life and health within borders or to the life and health of citizens abroad.

THRESHOLD AND CONDUCT OF JUSTIFIED PREEMPTION

The Bush administration is correct to emphasize the United States' vulnerability to terrorist attack. The administration also argues that the

United States cannot wait for a smoking gun if it comes in the form of a mushroom cloud. There may be little or no evidence in advance of a terrorist attack using nuclear, chemical, or biological weapons. Yet, under this view, the requirement for evidence is reduced to a fear that the other has, or might someday acquire, the means for an assault. But the bar for preemption seems to be set too low in the Bush administration's National Security Strategy. How much and what kind of evidence is necessary to justify preemption? What is a credible fear that justifies preemption?

As Michael Walzer has argued persuasively in *Just and Unjust Wars*, simple fear cannot be the only criterion. Fear is omnipresent in the context of a terrorist campaign. And if fear was once clearly justified, when and how will we know that a threat has been significantly reduced or eliminated? The nature of fear may be that once a group has suffered a terrible surprise attack, a government and people will, justifiably, be vigilant. Indeed they may, out of fear, be aware of threats to the point of hypervigilance—seeing small threats as large, and squashing all potential threats with enormous brutality.

The threshold for credible fear is necessarily lower in the context of contemporary counterterrorism war, but the consequences of lowering the threshold may be increased instability and the premature use of force. If this is the case, if fear justifies assault, then the occasions for attack will potentially be limitless since, according to the Bush administration's own arguments, we cannot always know with certainty what the other side has, where it might be located, or when it might be used. If one attacks on the basis of fear, or suspicion that a potential adversary may someday have the intention and capacity to harm you, then the line between preemptive and preventive war has been crossed. Again, the problem is knowing the capabilities and intentions of potential adversaries.

There is thus a fine balance to be struck. The threshold of evidence and warning cannot be too low, where simple apprehension that a potential adversary might be out there somewhere and may be acquiring the means to do the United States harm triggers the offensive use of force.

This is not preemption, but paranoid aggression. We must, as stressful as this is psychologically, accept some vulnerability and uncertainty. We must also avoid the tendency to exaggerate the threat and inadvertently to heighten our own fear. For example, although nuclear weapons are more widely available than in the past, as are delivery vehicles of medium and long range, these forces are not yet in the hands of dozens of terrorists. A policy that assumes such a dangerous world is, at this historical juncture, paranoid. We must, rather than assume this is the present case or will be in the future, work to make this outcome less likely.

On the other hand, the threshold of evidence and warning for justified fear cannot be so high that those who might be about to do harm get so advanced in their preparations that they cannot be stopped or the damage limited. What is required, assuming a substantial investment in intelligence gathering, assessment, and understanding of potential advisories, is a policy that both maximizes our understanding of the capabilities and intentions of potential adversaries and minimizes our physical vulnerability. While uncertainty about intentions, capabilities, and risk can never be eliminated, it can be reduced.

Fear of possible future attack is not enough to justify preemption. Rather, aggressive intent, coupled with a capacity and plans to do immediate harm, is the threshold that may trigger justified preemptive attacks. We may judge aggressive intent if the answer to these two questions is yes: First, have potential aggressors said they want to harm us in the near future or have they harmed us in the recent past? Second, are potential adversaries moving their forces into a position to do significant harm?

While it might be tempting to assume that secrecy on the part of a potential adversary is a sure sign of aggressive intentions, secrecy may simply be a desire to prepare a deterrent force. After all, potential adversaries may feel the need to look after their own defense against their neighbors or even the United States. We cannot assume that all forces in the world are aimed offensively at the United States and that all want to broadcast their defensive preparations—especially if that means

they might become the target of a preventive offensive strike by the United States.

The conduct of preemptive actions must be limited in purpose to reducing or eliminating the immediate threat. Preemptive strikes that go beyond this purpose will, reasonably, be considered aggression by the targets of such strikes. Those conducting preemptive strikes should also obey the *jus in bello* limits of just war theory, specifically avoiding injury to noncombatants and avoiding disproportionate damage. For example, in the case of the plans for the September 11, 2001, attacks, on these criteria—and assuming intelligence warning of preparations and clear evidence of aggressive intent—a justifiable preemptive action would have been the arrest of the hijackers of the four aircraft that were to be used as weapons. But, prior to the attacks, taking the war to Afghanistan to attack al-Qaeda camps or the Taliban could not have been justified preemption.

THE RISKS OF PREVENTIVE WAR

Foreign policies must not only be judged on grounds of legality and morality, but also on grounds of prudence. Preemption is only prudent if it is limited to clear and immediate dangers and if there are limits to its conduct—proportionality, discrimination, and limited aims. If preemption becomes a regular practice or if it becomes the cover for a preventive offensive war doctrine, the strategy then may become self-defeating as it increases instability and insecurity.

Specifically, a legitimate preemptive war requires that states identify that potential aggressors have both the capability and the intention of doing great harm to you in the immediate future. However, while capability may not be in dispute, the motives and intentions of a potential adversary may be misinterpreted. Specifically, states may mobilize in what appear to be aggressive ways because they are fearful or because they are aggressive. A preemptive doctrine which has, because of great fear and a desire to control the international environment, become a preventive war doctrine of eliminating potential threats that may materialize at some point in the future is likely to create more of both fearful and aggressive states. Some states may defensively arm because they are afraid of the preemptive-preventive state; others may arm offensively because they resent the preventive war aggressor who may have killed many innocents in its quest for total security.

In either case, whether states and groups armed because they were afraid or because they have aggressive intentions, instability is likely to grow as a preventive war doctrine creates the mutual fear of surprise attack. In the case of the U.S. preemptive-preventive war doctrine, instability is likely to increase because the doctrine is coupled with the U.S. goal of maintaining global preeminence and a military force "beyond challenge."[9]

Further, a preventive offensive war doctrine undermines international law and diplomacy, both of which can be useful, even to hegemonic powers. Preventive war short-circuits nonmilitary means of solving problems. If all states reacted to potential adversaries as if they faced a clear and present danger of imminent attack, security would be destabilized as tensions escalated along already tense borders and regions. Article 51 of the UN Charter would lose much of its force. In sum, a preemptive-preventive doctrine moves us closer to a state of nature than a state of international law. Moreover, while preventive war doctrines assume that today's potential rival will become tomorrow's adversary, diplomacy or some other factor could work to change the relationship from antagonism to accommodation. As Otto von Bismarck said to Wilhelm I in 1875, "I would . . . never advise Your Majesty to declare war forthwith, simply because it appeared that our opponent would begin hostilities in the near future. One can never anticipate the ways of divine providence securely enough for that."[10]

One can understand why any administration would favor preemption and why some would be attracted to preventive wars if they think a preventive war could guarantee security from future attack. But the psychological reassurance promised by a preventive offensive war doctrine is at best illusory, and at worst, preventive war is a recipe for conflict. Preventive wars are imprudent because they bring wars that might not happen and increase resentment. They are also unjust because they assume perfect knowledge of an adversary's ill intentions when such a presumption of guilt may be premature or unwarranted. Preemption can be justified, on the other hand, if it is undertaken due to an immediate threat, where there is no time for diplomacy to be attempted, and where the action is limited to reducing that threat. There is a great temptation, however, to step over the line from preemptive to preventive war, because that line is vague and because the stress of living under the threat of war is great. But that temptation should be avoided, and the stress of living in fear should be assuaged by true prevention—arms control, disarmament, negotiations, confidence-building measures, and the development of international law.

NOTES

1. Colin Powell, "Perspectives: Powell Defends a First Strike as Iraq Option," interview, *New York Times*, September 8, 2002, sec. 1, p. 18.
2. For more on the nature of this transformation, see Neta C. Crawford, "Just War Theory and the U.S. Counterterror War," *Perspectives on Politics* 1 (March 2003), forthcoming.
3. "The National Security Strategy of the United States of America September 2002," p. 14; available at www.whitehouse.gov/nsc/nss.pdf.
4. Donald H. Rumsfeld, "Remarks at Stakeout Outside ABC TV Studio," October 28, 2001; available at www.defenselink.mil/news/Oct2001/t10292001_t1028sd3.html.
5. "National Security Strategy," p. 5.
6. Department of Defense, "Quadrennial Defense Review" (Washington, D.C.: U.S. Government Printing Office, September 30, 2001), pp. 2, 30, 62.
7. "National Security Strategy," pp. 1, 31.
8. Richard K. Betts, *Surprise Attack: Lessons for Defense Planning* (Washington, D.C.: Brookings Institution, 1982), pp. 14–43.
9. Department of Defense, "Quadrennial Defense Review," pp. 30, 62; and "Remarks by President George W. Bush at Graduation Exercise of the

United States Military Academy, West Point, New York," June 1, 2002; available at www.whitehouse.gov/news/releases/2002/06/20020601-3.html.

10. Quoted in Gordon A. Craig, *The Politics of the Prussian Army, 1640–1945* (Oxford: Oxford University Press, 1955), p. 255.

⚜ REVIEW QUESTIONS

1. How has war changed, according to Crawford?
2. What is the new preemption doctrine? How does Crawford criticize it?
3. Crawford claims that legitimate preemption requires four conditions. What are they?
4. Why does Crawford think that the Bush administration set the bar too low for preemption?
5. When does preemption turn into paranoid aggression, in Crawford's view?

⚜ DISCUSSION QUESTIONS

1. What does Crawford mean by a broad conception of self, as distinguished from a narrow conception? Should this broad self be defended? Why or why not?
2. Suppose Iran is developing nuclear weapons in secret. Does that justify a preventive attack? What is Crawford's view? What do you think?

The Terrorist's Tacit Message[*]

LAURIE CALHOUN

Laurie Calhoun is the author of *Philosophy Unmasked: A Skeptic's Critique* (1997) and many essays on ethics, rhetoric, and war.

    Calhoun applies just war theory to terrorism. Terrorism is condemned by the governments of democratic nations, who continue to engage in "just wars." But when the assumptions involved in the "just war" approach to group conflict are examined, it emerges that terrorists merely follow these assumptions to their logical conclusion. They see themselves fighting "just wars," as "warriors for justice." That is their tacit message. Accordingly, unless the stance toward war embraced by most governments of the world transforms radically, terrorism can be expected to continue over time. As groups proliferate, so will conflicts, and some groups will resort to deadly force, reasoning along "just war" lines. Because terrorists are innovative strategists, it is doubtful that measures based upon conventional military operations will effectively counter terrorism.

Source: Reprinted from *The Peace Review*, vol. 14, no. 1 (2002). Reprinted with permission from Taylor & Francis Ltd.

[*] Editor's Note: This article was written before 9/11.

The refusal to "negotiate with terrorists" is a common refrain in political parlance. It is often accepted as self-evident that terrorists are so far beyond the pale that it would be morally reprehensible even to engage in discourse with them. But the term "terrorist" remains elusive, defined in various ways by various parties, albeit always derogatorily. Judging from the use of the term by the government officials of disparate nations, it would seem to be analytically true that, whoever the speakers may be, they are not terrorists. "Terrorists" refers exclusively to *them*, a lesser or greater set of political actors, depending ultimately upon the sympathies of the speaker.

Government leaders often speak as though terrorists are beyond the reach of reason, but particular terrorists in particular places believe that they are transmitting to the populace a message with concrete content. The message invariably takes the following general form: *There is something seriously wrong with the world in which we live, and this must be changed.* Terrorists sometimes claim to have as their aim to rouse the populace to consciousness so that they might at last see what the terrorists take themselves to have seen. However, the members of various terrorist groups together transmit (unwittingly) a more global message. The lesson that we ought to glean from terrorists is not the specific, context-dependent message that they hope through their use of violence to convey. Terrorists are right that there is something seriously wrong with the world in which we and they live, but they are no less a party to the problem than are the governments against which they inveigh.

That the annihilation of human life is sometimes morally permissible or even obligatory is embodied in two social practices: the execution of criminals and the maintenance of military institutions. This suggests that there are two distinct ways of understanding terrorists' interpretations of their own actions. Either they are attempting to effect "vigilante justice," or else they are fighting "just wars." Because their victims are typically non-combatants, terrorist actions more closely resemble acts of war than vigilante killings. There are of course killers who do not conceive of their own crimes along these lines, having themselves no political agenda or moral mission. Unfortunately, the tendency of governments to conflate terrorists with ordinary murderers (without political agendas) shrouds the similarity between the violent activities of factional groups and those of formal nations.

Attempts to identify "terrorists" by appeal to what these people do give rise to what some might find to be embarrassing implications. For example, to specify "terrorism" as necessarily *illegal* leads to problems in interpreting the reign of terror imposed by the Third Reich in Nazi Germany and other governmental regimes of ill repute. One might, then, propose a moral rather than a legal basis, for example, by delineating "terrorists" as *ideologically or politically motivated actors who kill or threaten to kill innocent people bearing no responsibility for the grievances of the killers*. This would imply that every nation that has engaged in bombing campaigns resulting in the deaths of innocent children has committed acts of terrorism. Faced with this proposed assimilation of nations and factions that deploy deadly force, most people will simply back away, insisting that, though a precise definition is not possible, certain obvious examples of terrorists can be enumerated, and so "terrorist" can be defined by ostension.

The governments of democratic nations harshly condemn "terrorists," but when the assumptions involved in any view according to which war is sometimes just are carefully examined, it emerges that terrorists merely follow these assumptions to their logical conclusion, given the situations in which they find themselves. While nations prohibit the use of deadly force by individuals and sub-national factions, in fact, violent attacks upon strategic targets can be understood straightforwardly as permitted by "just war" rationales, at least as interpreted by the killers. Small terrorist groups could not, with any chance of success, attack a formal military institution, so instead they select targets for their shock appeal.

While secrecy is often thought to be of the very essence of terrorism, the covert practices of terrorist groups are due in part to their illegality. The members of such groups often hide their identities (or at least their own involvement in particular acts of terrorism), not because they believe that their actions are wrong, but because it would be imprudent to expose themselves. Clearly, if one is subject to arrest for publicly committing an act, then one's efficacy as a soldier for the cause in question will be short-lived. Committing illegal acts in the open renders an actor immediately vulnerable to arrest and incarceration, but it is precisely because factional groups reject the legitimacy of the reigning regime that they undertake secretive initiatives best understood as militarily strategic. "Intelligence agencies" are an important part of modern military institutions, and secrecy has long been regarded as integral to martial excellence. Sun Tzu, author of the ancient Chinese classic *The Art of War*, observed nearly three thousand years ago that "All warfare is based on deception."

It is perhaps often simply terrorists' fervent commitment to their cause that leads them to maximize the efficacy of their campaigns by sheltering themselves from vulnerability to the laws of the land, as any prudent transgressor of the law would do. At the other extreme, suicide missions, in which agents openly act in ways that lead to their personal demise, are undertaken only when such martyrdom appears to be the most effective means of drawing attention to the cause. Far from being beyond rational comprehension, the actions of terrorists are dictated by military strategy deployed in the name of what the actors believe to be justice. The extreme lengths to which terrorists are willing to go, the sacrifices that they will make in their efforts to effect a change in the *status quo*, evidence their ardent commitment to their cause.

The common construal of war as a sometimes "necessary evil" implies that war may be waged when the alternative (not waging war) would be worse. If the military could have achieved its objectives without killing innocent people, then it would have done so. Military spokesmen have often maintained that unintended civilian deaths, even when foreseen, are permissible, provided the situation is sufficiently grave. In the just war tradition, what matters, morally speaking, is whether such "collateral damage" is intended by the actors. Equally integral to defenses of the moral permissibility of collateral damage is the principle of last resort, according to which nonbelligerent means must have been attempted and failed. If war is not a last resort, then collateral damage is avoidable and therefore morally impermissible. Few would deny that, if there exist ways to resolve a conflict without destroying innocent persons in the process, then those methods must, morally speaking, be pursued. But disputes arise, in specific contexts, regarding whether in fact nonbelligerent means to conflict resolution exist. To say that during wartime people *resort* to deadly force is to say that they have a reason, for it is of the very nature of justification to advert to reasons. Defenders of the recourse by nations to deadly force as a means of conflict resolution are willing to condone the killing of innocent people under certain circumstances. The question becomes: When have nonbelligerent means been exhausted?

Perhaps the most important (though seldom acknowledged) problem with just war theory is its inextricable dependence upon the interpretation of the very people considering recourse to deadly force. Human fallibility is a given, so in owning that war is justified in some cases, one must acknowledge that the "facts" upon which a given interpretation is based may prove to be false. And anyone who affirms the right (or obligation) to wage war when *they believe* the tenets of just war theory to be satisfied, must, in consistency, also affirm this right (or obligation) for all those who find themselves in analogous situations. But throughout human history wars have been characterized by their instigators as "just," including those retrospectively denounced as grossly unjust, for example, Hitler's campaign. People tend to ascribe good intentions to their own leaders and comrades while ascribing evil intentions to those stigmatized by officials as "the enemy."

The simplicity of its intuitive principles accounts for the widespread appeal of the "just war" paradigm. Throughout human history appeals to principles of "just cause" and "last resort" have been made by both sides to virtually every violent conflict. "Just war" rationalizations are available to everyone, Hussein as well as Bush, Milosevic as well as Clinton. To take a recent example, we find Timothy McVeigh characterizing the deaths of innocent people in the Oklahoma City bombing as "collateral damage." The public response to McVeigh's "preposterous" appropriation of just war theory suggests how difficult it is for military supporters to admit that they are not so very different from the political killers whose actions they condemn.

The received view is that the intention of planting bombs in public places such as the Federal Building in Oklahoma City or the World Trade Center in New York City is to terrorize, and the people who do such things are terrorists. According to the received view, though some innocent people may have been traumatized and killed during the Vietnam War, the Gulf War, and NATO's 1999 bombing campaign in Kosovo, whatever the intentions behind those actions may have been, they certainly were not to *terrorize* people. Nations excuse as regrettable though unavoidable the deaths of children such as occurred during the Gulf War, the Vietnam War, and in Kosovo during NATO's bombing campaign against the regime of Slobodan Milosevic. "Terrorists" are the people who threaten or deploy deadly force for causes of which we do not approve.

Political organizations have often engaged in actions intended to instill fear in the populace and thus draw attention to their cause. But the groups that engage in what is typically labeled "terrorism" are motivated by grievances no less than are nations engaged in war. Were their grievances somehow alleviated, dissenting political groups would no longer feel the need to engage in what they interpret to be "just wars." In appropriating military rationales and tactics, terrorists underscore the obvious, that nations are conventionally assembled groups of people who appoint their leaders just as do sub-national factions. The problem with the received view is that it exercises maximal interpretive charity when it comes to nations (most often, the interpreter's own), while minimal interpretive charity when it comes to sub-national groups. The intention of a terrorist act, *as understood by the terrorist*, is not the immediate act of terrorism, but to air some grave concern, which the terrorist is attempting to bring to the public's attention. In reality, the requirement of "last resort" seems far simpler to fulfill in the cases of smaller, informal factional groups than in those involving a first-world super power such as the United States, the economic policies of which can, with only minor modifications, spell catastrophe for an offending regime. According to the just war tradition, the permissible use of deadly force is a last resort, deployed only after all pacific means have proven infeasible, and the terrorist most likely reasons along precisely these lines. Indeed, the urgency of the terrorist's situation (to his own mind) makes his own claims regarding last resort all the more compelling. A terrorist, no less than the military spokesmen of established nations, may regret the deaths of the innocent people to which his activities give rise. But, applying the "just war" approach to "collateral damage," terrorists may emerge beyond moral reproach, since were their claims adequately addressed by the powers that be, they would presumably cease their violent activities. It is because they believe that their rights have been denied that groups engage in the activities identified as "terrorism" and thought by most people to be morally distinct from the military actions of states.

Once one grants the possibility of a "just war," it seems to follow straightforwardly that political dissidents convinced of the unjust practices of the government in power ought to engage in violent acts of subversion. Factions lack the advantage of currently enshrined institutions that naturally perpetuate the very *status quo* claimed by dissidents to be unjust. Accordingly, so long as nations continue to wage wars in the name of "justice," it seems plausible that smaller groups and factions will do so as well. Many terrorist groups insist that their claims have been squelched or ignored by the regime in power. But if formal nations may wage war to defend their own integrity and sovereignty, then why not separatist groups? And if such a group lacks a nationally funded and sanctioned army, then must not the group assemble its own?

The terrorist is not a peculiar type of creature who nefariously resorts to deadly force in opposition to the demands of morality upheld by all civilized nations. Rather, the terrorist merely embraces the widely held view that deadly military action is morally permissible, while delimiting "nations" differently than do those who uncritically accept the conventions which they have been raised to believe. The nations in existence are historically contingent, not a part of the very essence of things. The terrorist recognizes that current nations came into being and transformed as a result of warfare. Accordingly, agents who, in the name of justice, wield deadly force against the society in which they live conceive of themselves as civil warriors. Terrorist groups are smaller armies than those of established nations funded by taxpayers and sanctioned by the law, but for this very reason they may feel compelled to avail themselves of particularly drastic methods. No less than the military leaders of most countries throughout history, terrorists maintain that the situations which call for war are so desperate as to require the extremest of measures.

That a terrorist is not *sui generis* can be illustrated as follows: Imagine the commander-in-chief of any established nation being, instead, the leader of a group dissenting from the currently reigning regime. The very same person's acts of deadly violence (or his ordering his comrades to commit such acts) do not differ in his own mind merely because he has been formally designated the commander-in-chief in one case but not in the other. Both parties to every conflict maintain that they are right and their adversaries wrong, and terrorist factions are not exceptional in this respect. When we look carefully at the situation of terrorists, it becomes difficult to identify any morally significant distinction between what they do and what formal nations do in flying planes over enemy nations and dropping bombs,

knowing full well that innocent people will die as a result of their actions.

Most advanced nations with standing armies not only produce but also export the types of deadly weapons used by factions in terrorist actions. If we restrict the use of the term "terrorist" to those groups that deploy deadly violence "beyond the pale" of any established legal system, then it follows that terrorists derive their weapons from more formal (and legal) military institutions and industries. The conventional weapons trade has proven all but impossible to control, given the ease with which stockpiled arms are transferred from regime to regime and provided by some countries to smaller groups that they deem to be politically correct. And even when scandals such as Iran-Contra are brought to light, seldom are the culpable agents held more than nominally accountable for their actions. Leniency toward military personnel and political leaders who engage in or facilitate patriotic though illegal weapons commerce results from the basic assumption on the part of most people, that they and their comrades are good, while those who disagree are not.

In some cases, terrorists develop innovative weapons through the use of materials with nonmilitary applications, for example, sulfuric acid or ammonium nitrate. Given the possibility for innovative destruction by terrorist groups, it would seem that even more instrumental to the perpetuation of terrorism than the ongoing exportation of deadly weapons is the support by national leaders of *the idea* that killing human beings can be a mandate of justice. Bombing campaigns serve as graphic illustrations of the approbation by governments of the use of deadly force. It is simple indeed to understand what must be a common refrain among members of dissenting groups who adopt violent means: "If they can do it, then why cannot we?"

Political groups have agendas, and some of these groups deploy violence strategically in attempting to effect their aims. Terrorists are not "beyond the pale," intellectually and morally speaking, for their actions are best understood through appeal to the very just war theory invoked by nations in defending their own military campaigns. Terrorists interpret their own wars as just, while holding culpable all those who benefit from the policies of the government with which they disagree. The groups commonly identified as "terrorists" disagree with governments about not whether there can be a just war, nor whether morality is of such paramount importance as sometimes to require the killing of innocent people. Terrorist groups and the military institutions of nations embrace the very same "just war" schema, disagreeing only about facts.

Thus we find that the terrorist conveys two distinct messages. First, and this is usually the only claim to truth recognized by outsiders, the terrorist alleges injustices within the framework of society. In many cases there may be some truth to the specific charges made by terrorist groups, and this would be enough to turn against them all those who benefit from the regime in power. But a second and more important type of truth is highlighted by the very conduct of the terrorist. Perhaps there is something profoundly misguided about not only some of the specific policies within our societies, but also the manner in which we conceptualize the institutionalized use of deadly force, the activity of war, as an acceptable route to dispute resolution.

The connotations associated with "terrorist" are strongly pejorative and, although terrorists clearly operate from within what they take to be a moral framework, they are often subject to much more powerful condemnation than nonpolitical killers. But murderers who reject the very idea of morality would seem to be worse enemies of society than are political terrorists, who are motivated primarily by moral considerations. Why is it, then, that people fear and loathe terrorists so intensely? Perhaps they recognize, on some level, that terrorists are operating along lines that society in fact implicitly condones and even encourages. Perhaps people see shadows of themselves and their own activities in those of terrorists.

If it is true that terrorists view themselves as warriors for justice, then unless the stance toward war embraced by most governments of the world transforms radically, terrorism should be expected to continue over time. To the extent to which groups proliferate, conflicts will as well, and some subset of the parties to conflict will resort to deadly force, buoyed by what they, along with most of the populace, take to be the respectability of "just war." Military solutions are no longer used even by stable nations merely as "last resorts." Tragically, the ready availability of deadly weapons and the widespread assumption that the use of such weapons is often morally acceptable, if not obligatory, has brought about a world in which leaders often think first, not last, of military solutions to conflict. This readiness to deploy deadly means has arguably contributed to the escalation of violence in the contemporary world on many different levels, the most frightening of which being to many people those involving the unpredictable actions of factional groups, "the terrorists." But the leaders of established nations delude themselves in thinking that they will quell terrorism through threats and weapons proliferation. Terrorists "innovate" by re-defining what are commonly thought of as non-military targets as military. There is no reason for believing that terrorists' capacity for innovation will be frustrated by the construction of an anti-ballistic missile system or the implementation of other initiatives premised upon conventional military practices and strategies.

♔ RECOMMENDED READINGS

Arendt, Hannah. 1979. *The Origins of Totalitarianism.* New York: Harcourt Brace.

Calhoun, Laurie. 2002. "How Violence Breeds Violence: Some Utilitarian Considerations," *Politics,* vol. 22, no. 2, pp. 95–108.

Calhoun, Laurie. 2001. "Killing, Letting Die, and the Alleged Necessity of Military Intervention," *Peace and Conflict Studies,* vol. 8, no. 2, pp. 5–22.

Calhoun, Laurie. 2001. "The Metaethical Paradox of Just War Theory," *Ethical Theory and Moral Practice,* vol. 4, no. 1, pp. 41–58.

Calhoun, Laurie. 2002. "The Phenomenology of Paid Killing," *International Journal of Human Rights*, vol. 6, no. 1, pp. 1–18.

Calhoun, Laurie. 2001. "Violence and Hypocrisy," and "Laurie Calhoun replies [to Michael Walzer]," *Dissent*, (winter) vol. 48, no. 1, pp. 79–87. Reprinted in *Just War: A Casebook in Argumentation*, eds. Walsh & Asch, Heinle/Thomson, 2004.

Cerovic, Stanko. 2001. *Dans les griffes des humanistes*, trans. Mireille Robin. Paris: Éditions Climats.

Colson, Bruno. 1999. *L'art de la guerre de Machiavel à Clausewitz*. Namur: Bibliothèque Universitaire Moretus Plantin.

Cooper, H. H. A. 2001. "Terrorism: The Problem of Definition Revisited," *American Behavioral Scientist*, vol. 44, no. 6, pp. 881–893.

Gibbs, Jack P. 1989. "Conceptualization of Terrorism," *American Sociological Review*, vol. 54, no. 3, pp. 329–340.

Grossman, Lt. Colonel Dave. 1995. *On Killing: The Psychological Cost of Learning to Kill in War and Society*. Boston: Little Brown.

Harman, Gilbert. 2000. *Explaining Value*. Oxford: Oxford University Press.

Harman, Gilbert. 1977. *The Nature of Morality*. New York: Oxford University Press.

Holmes, Robert L. 1989. *On War and Morality*. Princeton: Princeton University Press.

Le Borgne, Claude. 1986. *La Guerre est Morte . . . mais on ne le sait pas encore*. Paris: Bernard Grasset.

Rapoport, David C. 1984. "Fear and Trembling: Terrorism in Three Religious Traditions," *The American Political Science Review*, vol. 78, no. 3, pp.

⚜ REVIEW QUESTIONS

1. According to Calhoun, what is the concrete message of terrorists? What is the more global message, the "tacit message"?
2. What problems does Calhoun see with the legal and moral definitions of the term *terrorists*?
3. How do terrorists view their actions, according to Calhoun?
4. How do military justify "collateral damage," or the killing of innocent people, according to Calhoun?
5. What role does interpretation play in just war theory, in Calhoun's view? Why does she think that "just war" rationalizations are available to everyone, from Hussein to Bush?
6. According to Calhoun, what is the intention of the terrorist act, as understood by the terrorist?
7. Why does Calhoun believe that terrorism is best understood by appealing to the very just war theory invoked by nations defending their wars?

⚜ DISCUSSION QUESTIONS

1. Calhoun argues that anyone can rationalize war or terrorism by appealing to just war theory. Is this true? Why or why not?
2. Calhoun says, "Terrorists are people who threaten or deploy deadly force for causes of which we do not approve." Do you agree? Why or why not?
3. Calhoun claims that there is hardly any moral difference between what the terrorists do and what nations such as the United States do when they drop bombs on enemy nations knowing full well that innocent people will die. Do you agree? Why or why not?

What Is Wrong with Terrorism?

THOMAS NAGEL

Thomas Nagel is university professor, professor of law, and professor of philosophy at New York University. He is the author of *The Possibility of Altruism* (1970), *Mortal Questions* (1979), *The View from Nowhere* (1986), *What Does It All Mean* (1987), *Equality and Partiality* (1991), *Other Minds* (1995), *The Last Word* (1997), *The Myth of Ownership*: *Taxes and Justice* (with Liam Murphy, 2002), and *Concealment and Exposure* (2002).

To explain what is wrong with terrorism, Nagel makes a distinction between means and ends. It is not the ends or goals of the terrorist that make terrorism wrong, but the means used, namely the deliberate killing of harmless persons. This violates the basic moral principle that aiming at the death of a harmless person is morally wrong. In his view, killing in self-defense does not violate this moral prohibition. Also, killing harmless persons in warfare is morally allowed as long this occurs as an unintended side effect of an attack on a legitimate military target.

People all over the world react with visceral horror to attacks on civilians by Al Qaeda, by Palestinian suicide bombers, by Basque or Chechen separatists, or by IRA militants. As there now seems to be a pause in the spate of suicide bombings and other terrorist acts—if only momentary—perhaps now is a moment to grapple with a fundamental question: What makes *terrorist* killings any more worthy of condemnation than other forms of murder?

The special opprobrium associated with the word "terrorism" must be understood as a condemnation of means, not ends. Of course, those who condemn terrorist attacks on civilians often also reject the ends that the attackers are trying to achieve. They think that a separate Basque state, or the withdrawal of US forces from the Middle East, for example, are not aims that anyone should be pursuing, let alone by violent means.

But the condemnation does not depend on rejecting the aims of the terrorists. The reaction to the attacks of September 11, 2001 on New York and Washington and their like underscores that such means are outrageous whatever the end; they should not be used to achieve even a good end—indeed, even if there is no other way to achieve it. The normal balancing of costs against benefits is not allowable here.

This claim is not as simple as it appears because it does not depend on a general moral principle forbidding all killing of non-combatants. Similarly, those who condemn terrorism as beyond the pale are usually not pacifists. They believe not only that it is all right to kill soldiers and bomb munitions depots in times of war, but that inflicting "collateral damage" on non-combatants is sometimes unavoidable—and morally permissible.

But if that is permissible, why is it wrong to aim *directly* at non-combatants if killing them will have a good chance of inducing the enemy to cease hostilities, withdraw from occupied territory, or grant independence? Dying is bad, however one is killed. So why should a civilian death be acceptable if it occurs as a side effect of combat that serves a worthy end, whereas a civilian death that is inflicted deliberately as a means to the *same* end is a terrorist outrage?

The distinction is not universally accepted—certainly not by the major belligerents in World

---

Source: What's Wrong with Terrorism by Thomas Nagel from Project-Syndicate.org, 2002.

War II. Hiroshima is the most famous example of terror bombing, but the Germans, the Japanese, and the British as well as the Americans deliberately slaughtered civilian non-combatants in large numbers. Today, however, terrorism inspires widespread revulsion, which in turn helps to justify military action against it. So it is essential that the reason for that revulsion become better understood.

The core moral idea is a prohibition against *aiming* at the death of a harmless person. Everyone is presumed to be inviolable in this way until he himself becomes a danger to others; so we are permitted to kill in self-defense, and to attack enemy combatants in war. But this is an exception to a general and strict requirement of respect for human life. So long as we are not doing any harm, no one may kill us just because it would be useful to do so. This minimal basic respect is owed to *every* individual, and it may not be violated even to achieve valuable long-term goals.

However, there are some activities, including legitimate self-defense or warfare, that create an unavoidable risk of harm to innocent parties. This is true not only of violent military or police actions but also of peaceful projects like major construction in densely populated cities. In those cases, if the aim is important enough, the activity is not morally prohibited provided due care is taken to minimize the risk of harm to innocent parties, consistent with the achievement of the aim.

The moral point is that we are obliged to do our best to avoid or minimize civilian casualties in warfare, even if we know that we cannot avoid them completely. Those deaths do not violate the strictest protection of human life—that we may not *aim* to kill a harmless person. On the contrary, our aim is if possible to avoid such collateral deaths.

Of course, the victim ends up dead whether killed deliberately by a terrorist or regrettably as the side effect of an attack on a legitimate military target. But in our sense of what we are owed morally by our fellow human beings, there is a huge difference between these two acts, and the attitudes they express toward human life.

So long as it remains an effective means for weak parties to exert pressure on their more powerful enemies, terrorism cannot be expected to disappear. But we should hope nonetheless that the recognition of its special form of contempt for humanity will spread, rather than being lost as a result of its recent successes.

♔ REVIEW QUESTIONS

1. What is it about terrorist killing that makes it worse than other forms of murder, according to Nagel?

2. What exactly makes terrorism wrong in Nagel's view?

♔ DISCUSSION QUESTIONS

1. Is terrorism always wrong? What if it produces a good result such as the elimination of apartheid in South Africa or the overthrow of an oppressive government?

2. Nagel says that the atomic bombing of Hiroshima is an example of morally prohibited "terror bombing" rather than an attack on a legitimate military target. Do you agree? Why or why not?

3. Nagel thinks there is a "huge difference" between being deliberately killed by a terrorist and being killed as the side effect of an attack on a military target. But in both cases a harmless person is killed. Is there really such a huge difference? What is your view?

The War on Terrorism and the End of Human Rights

DAVID LUBAN

David Luban is the Frederick J. Hass Professor of Law and Philosophy at the Georgetown University Law Center. He is the author of *Lawyers and Justice* (1988), *Legal Modernism* (1994), *Legal Ethics and Human Dignity* (2007), and numerous journal articles and book chapters.

Luban argues that the current War on Terrorism combines a war model with a law model to produce a new model of state action, a hybrid war-law model. This hybrid model selectively picks out elements of the war and law models to maximize the use of lethal force while eliminating the rights of both adversaries and innocent bystanders. The result is that the War on Terrorism means the end of human rights.

In the immediate aftermath of September 11, President Bush stated that the perpetrators of the deed would be brought to justice. Soon afterwards, the President announced that the United States would engage in a war on terrorism. The first of these statements adopts the familiar language of criminal law and criminal justice. It treats the September 11 attacks as horrific crimes—mass murders—and the government's mission as apprehending and punishing the surviving planners and conspirators for their roles in the crimes. The War on Terrorism is a different proposition, however, and a different model of governmental action—not law but war. Most obviously, it dramatically broadens the scope of action, because now terrorists who knew nothing about September 11 have been earmarked as enemies. But that is only the beginning.

THE HYBRID WAR-LAW APPROACH

The model of war offers much freer rein than that of law, and therein lies its appeal in the wake of 9/11. First, in war but not in law it is permissible to use lethal force on enemy troops regardless of their degree of personal involvement with the adversary. The conscripted cook is as legitimate a target as the enemy general. Second, in war but not in law "collateral damage," that is, foreseen but unintended killing of noncombatants, is permissible. (Police cannot blow up an apartment building full of people because a murderer is inside, but an air force can bomb the building if it contains a military target.) Third, the requirements of evidence and proof are drastically weaker in war than in criminal justice. Soldiers do not need proof beyond a reasonable doubt, or even proof by a preponderance of evidence, that someone is an enemy soldier before firing on him or capturing and imprisoning him. They don't need proof at all, merely plausible intelligence. Thus, the U.S. military remains regretful but unapologetic about its January 2002 attack on the Afghani town of Uruzgan, in which 21 innocent civilians were killed, based on faulty intelligence that they were al Qaeda fighters. Fourth, in war one can attack an enemy without concern over whether he has done anything. Legitimate targets are those who in the course of combat *might* harm us, not those who *have* harmed us. No doubt there are other significant differences as well. But the basic point should be clear: Given Washington's mandate to eliminate the danger of future 9/11s, so far as humanly possible, the model of war offers important advantages over the model of law.

There are disadvantages as well. Most obviously, in war but not in law, fighting back is a *legitimate* response of the enemy. Second, when nations fight a war, other nations may opt for neutrality. Third, because fighting back is legitimate, in war the enemy soldier deserves special regard once he is rendered harmless through injury or surrender. It is impermissible to punish him for his role in fighting the war. Nor can he be harshly interrogated after he is captured. The Third Geneva Convention provides: "Prisoners of war who refuse to answer [questions] may not be threatened, insulted, or exposed to unpleasant or disadvantageous treatment of any kind." And, when the war concludes, the enemy soldier must be repatriated.

Here, however, Washington has different ideas, designed to eliminate these tactical disadvantages in the traditional war model. Washington regards international terrorism not only as a military adversary, but also as a criminal activity and criminal conspiracy. In the law model, criminals don't get to shoot back, and their acts of violence subject them to legitimate punishment. That is what we see in Washington's prosecution of the War on Terrorism. Captured terrorists may be tried before military or civilian tribunals, and shooting back at Americans, including American troops, is a federal crime (for a statute under which John Walker Lindh was indicted criminalizes anyone regardless of nationality, who "outside the United States attempts to kill, or engages in a conspiracy to kill, a national of the United States" or "engages in physical violence with intent to cause serious bodily injury to a national of the United States; or with the result that serious bodily injury is caused to a national of the United States"). Furthermore, the U.S. may rightly demand that other countries not be neutral about murder and terrorism. Unlike the war model, a nation may insist that those who are not with us in fighting murder and terror are against us, because by not joining our operations they are providing a safe haven for terrorists or their bank accounts. By selectively combining elements of

the war model and elements of the law model, Washington is able to maximize its own ability to mobilize lethal force against terrorists while eliminating most traditional rights of a military adversary, as well as the rights of innocent bystanders caught in the crossfire.

A LIMBO OF RIGHTLESSNESS

The legal status of al Qaeda suspects imprisoned at the Guantanamo Bay Naval Base in Cuba is emblematic of this hybrid war-law approach to the threat of terrorism. In line with the war model, they lack the usual rights of criminal suspects—the presumption of innocence, the right to a hearing to determine guilt, the opportunity to prove that the authorities have grabbed the wrong man. But, in line with the law model, they are considered *unlawful* combatants. Because they are not uniformed forces, they lack the rights of prisoners of war and are liable to criminal punishment. Initially, the American government declared that the Guantanamo Bay prisoners have no rights under the Geneva Conventions. In the face of international protests, Washington quickly backpedaled and announced that the Guantanamo Bay prisoners would indeed be treated as decently as POWs—but it also made clear that the prisoners have no right to such treatment. Neither criminal suspects nor POWs, neither fish nor fowl, they inhabit a limbo of rightlessness. Secretary of Defense Rumsfeld's assertion that the U.S. may continue to detain them even if they are acquitted by a military tribunal dramatizes the point.

To understand how extraordinary their status is, consider an analogy. Suppose that Washington declares a War on Organized Crime. Troops are dispatched to Sicily, and a number of Mafiosi are seized, brought to Guantanamo Bay, and imprisoned without a hearing for the indefinite future, maybe the rest of their lives. They are accused of no crimes, because their capture is based not on what they have done but on what they might do. After all, to become "made" they took oaths of obedience to the bad guys. Seizing them accords with the war model: they are enemy foot soldiers. But they are foot soldiers out of uniform; they lack a "fixed distinctive emblem," in the words of The Hague Convention. That makes them unlawful combatants, so they lack the rights of POWs. They may object that it is only a unilateral declaration by the American President that has turned them into combatants in the first place—he called it a war, they didn't—and that, since they do not regard themselves as literal foot soldiers it never occurred to them to wear a fixed distinctive emblem. They have a point. It seems too easy for the President to divest anyone in the world of rights and liberty simply by announcing that the U.S. is at war with them and then declaring them unlawful combatants if they resist. But, in the hybrid war-law model, they protest in vain.

Consider another example. In January 2002, U.S. forces in Bosnia seized five Algerians and a Yemeni suspected of al Qaeda connections and took them to Guantanamo Bay. The six had been jailed in Bosnia, but a Bosnian court released them for lack of evidence, and the Bosnian Human Rights Chamber issued an injunction that four of them be allowed to remain in the country pending further legal proceedings. The Human Rights Chamber, ironically, was created under U.S. auspices in the Dayton peace accords, and it was designed specifically to protect against treatment like this. Ruth Wedgwood, a well-known international law scholar at Yale and a member of the Council on Foreign Relations, defended the Bosnian seizure in war-model terms. "I think we would simply argue this was a matter of self-defense. One of the fundamental rules of military law is that you have a right ultimately to act in self-defense. And if these folks were actively plotting to blow up the U.S. embassy, they should be considered combatants and captured as combatants in a war." Notice that Professor Wedgwood argues in terms of what the men seized in Bosnia were *planning to do*, not what they *did*; notice as well that the decision of the Bosnian court that there was insufficient evidence does not matter. These are characteristics of the war model.

More recently, two American citizens alleged to be al Qaeda operatives (Jose Padilla, a.k.a.

Abdullah al Muhajir, and Yasser Esam Hamdi) have been held in American military prisons, with no crimes charged, no opportunity to consult counsel, and no hearing. The President described Padilla as "a bad man" who aimed to build a nuclear "dirty" bomb and use it against America; and the Justice Department has classified both men as "enemy combatants" who may be held indefinitely. Yet, as military law expert Gary Solis points out, "Until now, as used by the attorney general, the term 'enemy combatant' appeared nowhere in U.S. criminal law, international law or in the law of war." The phrase comes from the 1942 Supreme Court case *Ex parte Quirin*, but all the Court says there is that "an enemy combatant who without uniform comes secretly through the lines for the purpose of waging war by destruction of life or property" would "not . . . be entitled to the status of prisoner of war, but . . . [they would] be offenders against the law of war subject to trial and punishment by military tribunals." For the Court, in other words, the status of a person as a non-uniformed enemy combatant makes him a criminal rather than a warrior, and determines *where* he is tried (in a military, rather than a civilian, tribunal) but not *whether* he is tried. Far from authorizing open-ended confinement, *Ex parte Quirin* presupposes that criminals are entitled to hearings: without a hearing how can suspects prove that the government made a mistake? *Quirin* embeds the concept of "enemy combatant" firmly in the law model. In the war model, by contrast, POWs may be detained without a hearing until hostilities are over. But POWs were captured in uniform, and only their undoubted identity as enemy soldiers justifies such openended custody. Apparently, Hamdi and Padilla will get the worst of both models—open-ended custody with no trial, like POWs, but no certainty beyond the U.S. government's say-so that they really are "bad men." This is the hybrid war-law model. It combines the *Quirin* category of "enemy combatant without uniform," used in the law model to justify a military trial, with the war model's practice of indefinite confinement with no trial at all.

THE CASE FOR THE HYBRID APPROACH

Is there any justification for the hybrid war-law model, which so drastically diminishes the rights of the enemy? An argument can be offered along the following lines. In ordinary cases of war among states, enemy soldiers may well be morally and politically innocent. Many of them are conscripts, and those who aren't do not necessarily endorse the state policies they are fighting to defend. But enemy soldiers in the War on Terrorism are, by definition, those who have embarked on a path of terrorism. They are neither morally nor politically innocent. Their sworn aim—"Death to America!"—is to create more 9/11s. In this respect, they are much more akin to criminal conspirators than to conscript soldiers. Terrorists will fight as soldiers when they must, and metamorphose into mass murderers when they can.

Furthermore, suicide terrorists pose a special, unique danger. Ordinary criminals do not target innocent bystanders. They may be willing to kill them if necessary, but bystanders enjoy at least some measure of security because they are not primary targets. Not so with terrorists, who aim to kill as many innocent people as possible. Likewise, innocent bystanders are protected from ordinary criminals by whatever deterrent force the threat of punishment and the risk of getting killed in the act of committing a crime offer. For a suicide bomber, neither of these threats is a deterrent at all—after all, for the suicide bomber one of the hallmarks of a *successful* operation is that he winds up dead at day's end. Given the unique and heightened danger that suicide terrorists pose, a stronger response that grants potential terrorists fewer rights may be justified. Add to this the danger that terrorists may come to possess weapons of mass destruction, including nuclear devices in suitcases. Under circumstances of such dire menace, it is appropriate to treat terrorists as though they embody the most dangerous aspects of both warriors and criminals. That is the basis of the hybrid war-law model.

THE CASE AGAINST EXPEDIENCY

The argument against the hybrid war-law model is equally clear. The U.S. has simply chosen the bits of the law model and the bits of the war model that are most convenient for American interests, and ignored the rest. The model abolishes the rights of potential enemies (and their innocent shields) by fiat—not for reasons of moral or legal principle, but solely because the U.S. does not want them to have rights. The more rights they have, the more risk they pose. But Americans' urgent desire to minimize our risks doesn't make other people's rights disappear. Calling our policy a War on Terrorism obscures this point.

The theoretical basis of the objection is that the law model and the war model each comes as a package, with a kind of intellectual integrity. The law model grows out of relationships within states, while the war model arises from relationships between states. The law model imputes a ground-level community of values to those subject to the law—paradigmatically, citizens of a state, but also visitors and foreigners who choose to engage in conduct that affects a state. Only because law imputes shared basic values to the community can a state condemn the conduct of criminals and inflict punishment on them. Criminals deserve condemnation and punishment because their conduct violates norms that we are entitled to count on their sharing. But, for the same reason—the imputed community of values—those subject to the law ordinarily enjoy a presumption of innocence and an expectation of safety. The government cannot simply grab them and confine them without making sure they have broken the law, nor can it condemn them without due process for ensuring that it has the right person, nor can it knowingly place bystanders in mortal peril in the course of fighting crime. They are our fellows, and the community should protect them just as it protects us. The same imputed community of values that justifies condemnation and punishment creates rights to due care and due process.

War is different. War is the ultimate acknowledgment that human beings do not live in a single community with shared norms. If their norms conflict enough, communities pose a physical danger to each other, and nothing can safeguard a community against its enemies except force of arms. That makes enemy soldiers legitimate targets; but it makes our soldiers legitimate targets as well, and, once the enemy no longer poses a danger, he should be immune from punishment, because if he has fought cleanly he has violated no norms that we are entitled to presume he honors. Our norms are, after all, our norms, not his.

Because the law model and war model come as conceptual packages, it is unprincipled to wrench them apart and recombine them simply because it is in America's interest to do so. To declare that Americans can fight enemies with the latitude of warriors, but if the enemies fight back they are not warriors but criminals, amounts to a kind of heads-I-win-tails-you-lose international morality in which whatever it takes to reduce American risk, no matter what the cost to others, turns out to be justified. This, in brief, is the criticism of the hybrid war-law model.

To be sure, the law model could be made to incorporate the war model merely by rewriting a handful of statutes. Congress could enact laws permitting imprisonment or execution of persons who pose a significant threat of terrorism whether or not they have already done anything wrong. The standard of evidence could be set low and the requirement of a hearing eliminated. Finally, Congress could authorize the use of lethal force against terrorists regardless of the danger to innocent bystanders, and it could immunize officials from lawsuits or prosecution by victims of collateral damage. Such statutes would violate the Constitution, but the Constitution could be amended to incorporate anti-terrorist exceptions to the Fourth, Fifth, and Sixth Amendments. In the end, we would have a system of law that includes all the essential features of the war model.

It would, however, be a system that imprisons people for their intentions rather than their actions, and that offers the innocent few protections against mistaken detention or inadvertent

death through collateral damage. Gone are the principles that people should never be punished for their thoughts, only for their deeds, and that innocent people must be protected rather than injured by their own government. In that sense, at any rate, repackaging war as law seems merely cosmetic, because it replaces the ideal of law as a protector of rights with the more problematic goal of protecting some innocent people by sacrificing others. The hypothetical legislation incorporates war into law only by making law as partisan and ruthless as war. It no longer resembles law as Americans generally understand it.

THE THREAT TO INTERNATIONAL HUMAN RIGHTS

In the War on Terrorism, what becomes of international human rights? It seems beyond dispute that the war model poses a threat to international human rights, because honoring human rights is neither practically possible nor theoretically required during war. Combatants are legitimate targets; noncombatants maimed by accident or mistake are regarded as collateral damage rather than victims of atrocities; cases of mistaken identity get killed or confined without a hearing because combat conditions preclude due process. To be sure, the laws of war specify minimum human rights, but these are far less robust than rights in peacetime—and the hybrid war-law model reduces this schedule of rights even further by classifying the enemy as unlawful combatants.

One striking example of the erosion of human rights is tolerance of torture. It should be recalled that a 1995 al Qaeda plot to bomb eleven U.S. airliners was thwarted by information tortured out of a Pakistani suspect by the Philippine police—an eerie real-life version of the familiar philosophical thought-experiment. The *Washington Post* reports that since September 11 the U.S. has engaged in the summary transfer of dozens of terrorism suspects to countries where they will be interrogated under torture. But it isn't just the

United States that has proven willing to tolerate torture for security reasons. Last December, the Swedish government snatched a suspected Islamic extremist to whom it had previously granted political asylum, and the same day had him transferred to Egypt, where Amnesty International reports that he has been tortured to the point where he walks only with difficulty. Sweden is not, to say the least, a traditionally hard-line nation on human rights issues. None of this international transportation is lawful—indeed, it violates international treaty obligations under the Convention against Torture that in the U.S. have constitutional status as "supreme Law of the Land"—but that may not matter under the war model, in which even constitutional rights may be abrogated.

It is natural to suggest that this suspension of human rights is an exceptional emergency measure to deal with an unprecedented threat. This raises the question of how long human rights will remain suspended. When will the war be over?

Here, the chief problem is that the War on Terrorism is not like any other kind of war. The enemy, Terrorism, is not a territorial state or nation or government. There is no opposite number to negotiate with. There is no one on the other side to call a truce or declare a ceasefire, no one among the enemy authorized to surrender. In traditional wars among states, the war aim is, as Clausewitz argued, to impose one state's political will on another's. The *aim* of the war is not to kill the enemy—killing the enemy is the *means* used to achieve the real end, which is to force capitulation. In the War on Terrorism, no capitulation is possible. That means that the real aim of the war is, quite simply, to kill or capture all of the terrorists—to keep on killing and killing, capturing and capturing, until they are all gone.

Of course, no one expects that terrorism will ever disappear completely. Everyone understands that new anti-American extremists, new terrorists, will always arise and always be available for recruitment and deployment. Everyone understands that even if al Qaeda is destroyed

or decapitated, other groups, with other leaders, will arise in its place. It follows, then, that the War on Terrorism will be a war that can only be abandoned, never concluded. The War has no natural resting point, no moment of victory or finality. It requires a mission of killing and capturing, in territories all over the globe, that will go on in perpetuity. It follows as well that the suspension of human rights implicit in the hybrid war-law model is not temporary but permanent.

Perhaps with this fear in mind, Congressional authorization of President Bush's military campaign limits its scope to those responsible for September 11 and their sponsors. But the War on Terrorism has taken on a life of its own that makes the Congressional authorization little more than a technicality. Because of the threat of nuclear terror, the American leadership actively debates a war on Iraq regardless of whether Iraq was implicated in September 11; and the President's yoking of Iraq, Iran, and North Korea into a single axis of evil because they back terror suggests that the War on Terrorism might eventually encompass all these nations. If the U.S. ever unearths tangible evidence that any of these countries is harboring or abetting terrorists with weapons of mass destruction, there can be little doubt that Congress will support military action. So too, Russia invokes the American War on Terrorism to justify its attacks on Chechen rebels, China uses it to deflect criticisms of its campaign against Uighur separatists, and Israeli Prime Minister Sharon explicitly links military actions against Palestinian insurgents to the American War on Terrorism. No doubt there is political opportunism at work in some or all of these efforts to piggy-back onto America's campaign, but the opportunity would not exist if "War on Terrorism" were merely the codename of a discrete, neatly-boxed American operation. Instead, the War on Terrorism has become a model of politics, a world-view with its own distinctive premises and consequences. As I have argued, it includes a new model of state action, the hybrid war-law model, which depresses human rights from their peace-time standard to the war-time standard, and indeed even further. So long as it continues, the War on Terrorism means the end of human rights, at least for those near enough to be touched by the fire of battle.

Sources: On the January 2002 attack on the Afghani town of Uruzgan, see: John Ward Anderson, "Afghans Falsely Held by U.S. Tried to Explain; Fighters Recount Unanswered Pleas, Beatings—and an Apology on Their Release," *Washington Post* (March 26, 2002); see also Susan B. Glasser, "Afghans Live and Die With U.S. Mistakes; Villagers Tell of Over 100 Casualties," *Washington Post* (Feb. 20, 2002). On the Third Geneva Convention, see: Geneva Convention (III) Relative to the Treatment of Prisoners of War, 6 U.S.T. 3317, signed on August 12, 1949, at Geneva, Article 17. Although the U.S. has not ratified the Geneva Convention, it has become part of customary international law, and certainly belongs to the war model. Count One of the Lindh indictment charges him with violating 18 U.S.C. 2332(b), "Whoever outside the United States attempts to kill, or engages in a conspiracy to kill, a national of the United States" may be sentenced to 20 years (for attempts) or life imprisonment (for conspiracies). Subsection (c) likewise criminalizes "engag[ing] in physical violence with intent to cause serious bodily injury to a national of the United States; or with the result that serious bodily injury is caused to a national of the United States." Lawful combatants are defined in the Hague Convention (IV) Respecting the Laws and Customs of War on Land, Annex to the Convention, 1 Bevans 631, signed on October 18, 1907, at The Hague, Article 1. The definition requires that combatants "have a fixed distinctive emblem recognizable at a distance." Protocol I Additional to the Geneva Conventions of 1949, 1125 U.N.T.S. 3, adopted on June 8, 1977, at Geneva, Article 44(3) makes an important change in the Hague Convention, expanding the definition of combatants to include non-uniformed irregulars. However, the United States has not agreed to Protocol I. The source of Ruth Wedgwood's remarks: Interview with Melissa Block, National Public Radio program, "All Things Considered" (January 18, 2002); Gary Solis, "Even a 'Bad Man' Has Rights," *Washington Post* (June 25, 2002); *Ex parte Quirin*, 317 U.S. 1, 31 (1942). On the torture of the Pakistani militant by Philippine police: Doug Struck et al., "Borderless Network of Terror; Bin Laden Followers Reach Across Globe," *Washington Post* (September 23, 2001): "'For weeks, agents hit him with a chair and a long piece of wood, forced water into his mouth, and crushed lighted cigarettes into his private parts,' wrote journalists Marites Vitug and Glenda Gloria in 'Under the Crescent Moon,' an acclaimed book on Abu Sayyaf. 'His ribs were almost totally broken and his captors were surprised he survived.'" On U.S. and Swedish transfers of Isamic militants to countries employing torture: Rajiv Chandrasakaran and Peter Finn, "U.S. Behind Secret Transfer of Terror Suspects," *Washington Post* (March 11, 2002); Peter Finn, "Europeans Tossing Terror Suspects Out the Door," *Washington Post* (January 29, 2002); Anthony Shadid, "Fighting Terror/Atmosphere in Europe, Military Campaign/Asylum Bids; in Shift, Sweden Extradites Militants to Egypt," *Boston Globe* (December 31, 2001). Article 3(1) of the Convention against Torture provides that "No State Party shall expel, return ('*refouler*') or extradite a person to another State where there are substantial grounds for believing that he would be in danger of being subjected to torture." Article 2(2) cautions that "No exceptional circumstances whatsoever, whether a state of war or a threat of war, internal political instability or any other public emergency, may be invoked as a justification of torture." But no parallel caution is incorporated into Article 3(1)'s non-*refoulement* rule, and a lawyer might well argue that its absence implies that the rule may be abrogated during war or similar public emergency. *Convention against Torture and Other Cruel, Inhuman or Degrading Treatment or Punishment*, 1465 U.N.T.S. 85. Ratified by the United States, Oct. 2, 1994. Entered into force for the United States, Nov. 20, 1994. (Article VI of the U.S. Constitution provides that treaties are the "supreme Law of the Land.")

☙ REVIEW QUESTIONS

1. According to Luban, what is the traditional model of war? What are its four main features? What are its disadvantages?

2. How does Luban describe the law model? How is it combined with the war model to produce a hybrid war-law approach to terrorism?

3. In Luban's view, what is the legal status of al-Qaeda suspects? Do they have any rights?

4. Describe the case of the al-Qaeda suspects seized in Bosnia.

5. How does Luban explain the concept of enemy combatant? How is this concept applied to Jose Padilla and Yasser Esam Harudi?

6. According to Luban, what is the case for the hybrid war-law model? What is the case against it?

7. In Luban's view, what becomes of human rights in the War on Terrorism?

🎗 DISCUSSION QUESTIONS

1. In January 2002, the U.S. military killed twenty-one innocent civilians in an attack on the Afghani town of Uruzgan. Was this attack justified? Why or why not?
2. Should the Guantánamo prisoners have rights? If so, what are they? If not, why not?
3. Is it acceptable to confine suspected terrorists indefinitely with no trial?
4. Is the hybrid war-law model of the War on Terrorism acceptable? Why or why not?
5. Should torture be used to fight terrorism? Why or why not?

PROBLEM CASES

1. The Draft

According to the U.S. Selective Service System (www.sss.gov), if you are a man aged eighteen to twenty-five, you are legally required to register with the Selective Service System. You can register online or at any U.S. post office.

Congress passed the law requiring registration in 1980, but currently it is not being enforced. Since 1986, no one has been prosecuted for failure to register, but this could change if the Selective Service starts drafting men—that is, calling men up for mandatory military service. (No one has been drafted since 1973, when conscription ended.) The mission of the Selective Service System is to "serve the emergency manpower needs of the Military by conscripting untrained manpower, or personnel with professional health care skills, if directed by Congress and the President in a national crisis." The national crisis could be the ongoing wars in Iraq and Afghanistan, a war with Iran, or some other conflict.

During the Vietnam War, many young men were drafted to fight in this unpopular war. There were many ways to avoid the draft. One way was to get a college deferment. This was how Dick Cheney and Paul Wolfowitz, the advocates of the Iraq war, avoided military service. President Bill Clinton also had a college deferment. President George W. Bush used his family connections to get into the National Guard, which involved low-risk duty in the United States. Another avoidance tactic was to get a medical rejection by claiming to be suicidal or a homosexual. Men with criminal records were rejected, as well as those saying they were communists. As a last resort, some men went to Canada, which did not support the Vietnam War.

Perhaps the most famous draft resister was boxer Muhammad Ali. In 1967, he refused induction into the armed forces. He maintained that fighting in the Vietnam War was against his Muslim religion and famously said, "I ain't got no quarrel with those Vietcong." He was convicted of refusing induction, sentenced to five years in prison, and not allowed to box professionally for more than three years. In late 1971, the Supreme Court reversed his conviction.

The Iraq war and the war in Afghanistan have produced enormous strain in the U.S. voluntary army. Soldiers are suffering from extended and repeated tours of duty. Many soldiers and officers are not reenlisting. As a result, some leaders are calling for a reinstatement of the draft. U.S. Representative Charles Rangel (D-N.Y.) has argued that poor men and women are far more likely to enlist for military service, and that this is unfair. The draft would ensure that the rich and the poor equally share military service in Iraq and other wars. Also, he argues that a country with conscription would be less likely to engage in military adventures like the one in Iraq.

In December 2006, President Bush announced that he was sending more troops to Iraq, and the next day the Selective Service System announced that it was getting ready to test the system's operations. Should the draft be reinstated? Under what circumstances, if any, would you be willing to be drafted? The question applies to women as well as men.

If we draft men for military service, why not draft women too? Other countries such as Israel draft women. Women now serve in the U.S. military with distinction; they fly jets and command troops in combat. There are plenty of young women who are just as capable as young men. Why shouldn't women be drafted?

As we have seen, during the Vietnam War many men avoided the draft by getting a college deferment. The Selective Service System has since modified this rule. Now a deferment lasts only to the end of the semester, although if a man is a senior, he can defer until the end of the academic year. Should there be college deferments? Is this fair?

During the Vietnam War, a man who claimed to be homosexual was not drafted. Currently, the armed forces discharge any person who is openly gay or lesbian. Should gay men or lesbians be drafted? Why or why not?

Why limit the draft to citizens aged eighteen to twenty-five? Why not draft older and younger people too? Is this a good idea? Why or why not?

2. War in Afghanistan

(For information and opinions on the war, see the Institute for the Study of War (www.understandingwar.org), the Center for a New American Security (www.cnas.org), and Peace Direct (www.peacedirect.org). The war began in 2001 as a response to the 9/11 attacks. The United States launched an invasion (called Operation Enduring Freedom) together with British forces. The United Nations did not approve the invasion. The initial goal was to find Osama bin Laden and other al-Qaeda members responsible for planning the 9/11 attacks and to remove the Taliban regime, which had provided a safe haven for bin Laden and the al-Qaeda organization.

In 2010, after nine years of fighting and some initial success, the U.S. and coalition forces had failed to find bin Laden and had not defeated the Taliban, who continued to fight with suicide bombers and improvised explosive devices. Bin Laden continued to issue statements from his hideout in Pakistan.

The Afghan President Hamid Karzai requested more U.S. troops in 2009, and President Obama responded by sending 30,000 additional troops in 2010, bringing the total to nearly 100,000. U.S. General Stanley A. McChrystal said that the defeat of the Taliban would require 500,000 troops and at least 5 more years of fighting, but President Obama was committed to withdrawing troops after a year or so.

According to the website www.causalities.org, there have been a total of 1,713 coalition military fatalities, including 1,034 American deaths. It is estimated that about 3,000 U.S. troops have been seriously injured in the war, and about 2,000 coalition troops seriously injured. No official estimates have been given for Afghan casualties and injuries, but a conservative estimate is that more than 8,000 Afghan troops have been killed, and about 25,000 seriously injured. It is estimated that at least 10,000 Afghan civilians have died in the fighting, and 15,000 have been seriously injured.

So far the war in Afghanistan has cost U.S. taxpayers more than $200 billion, and it is projected to cost at least half a trillion dollars when future occupation and veterans' benefits are taken into account. It is likely that U.S. troops will be based in the country for years, perhaps indefinitely. By comparison, Britain has spent about $6 billion and Canada $7 billion on the war.

Afghanistan is the world's leading producer of opium. The country makes about 90 percent of the world's opium, which is processed into heroin and sold in Europe and Russia. Heroin is one of the main sources of income in this poor country, and U.S. efforts to stop the drug trade have repeatedly failed. It is suspected that many of the top officials in the Karzai government are in the drug business. The Karzai government is widely perceived as corrupt and illegitimate. Apparently there was widespread fraud in Karzai's election. Furthermore, Karzai himself seems to be mentally unstable, having recently suggested that he was going to join the Taliban.

Should the United States continue to support the Karzai government? If not, what is the alternative?

Critics of the war point out that the Soviets also committed 100,000 troops in Afghanistan and were defeated after suffering huge loses. Does the same fate await the U.S. campaign? What do you think?

The international community has offered a billion dollars to support negotiations with the Taliban, including the leadership in Pakistan. Is this a good idea? Why or why not?

It was the al-Qaeda organization that attacked the United States, not the Taliban. The Taliban never posed a threat to the security of the United States. Now that al-Qaeda has shifted its operations to Pakistan, defeating the Taliban will not shut down al-Qaeda. If this is true, then is continuing to fight in Afghanistan justified? Explain your position.

3. The Iraq War

For information, books, and articles on the Iraq war, see the Suggested Readings.) After a long buildup, U.S. and British troops invaded Iraq in March 2003. The war continued for at least seven years. On February 27, 2009, President Obama announced that the U.S. combat mission would end by August 31, 2010, but he also said that 50,000 troops would remain until the end of 2011. It seems likely that U.S. troops will be in Iraq for a long time.

At least two goals were accomplished by the war: First, Saddam Hussein, the brutal dictator of Iraq, was captured, given a trial, found guilty, and executed. Second, a democratically elected government, led by Prime Minister Nouri al-Maliki, took power in 2006. In an election in 2010, Maliki was defeated by Ayad Allawi, a former interim prime minister. During the election, 37 people were killed in 136 attacks using bombs, rockets, and small-arms fire. The attacks continued after the election, with nearly 60 people killed and more than 200 injured. Iraqi political experts predict a long period of political uncertainty and violence.

The war produced casualties and it was expensive. More than 4,300 U.S. troops were killed, and more than 30,000 injured. More than half of those injured returned to duty, but about 15,000 have serious injuries such as spinal cord injury or brain damage that will require life-long treatment. It is estimated that more than 300,000 troops have some level of brain damage caused by explosions from roadside bombs and other explosions. No reliable data exists for Iraqi casualties. One estimate is that the total number of deaths for all Iraqi civilians, military personnel, and insurgents is at least 70,000 and may be as high as 655,000. Another estimate is that 753,209 Iraqi civilians have been killed, and 1,355,776 have been seriously injured. About 2 million people, including many professional people, have left Iraq, and another 2 million have been displaced inside Iraq's borders. By 2010, only 15 percent of those who left Iraq had returned.

From 2003 to 2010, the war cost the United States more than $700 billion. It is estimated that the total cost to the U.S. economy will be about $3 trillion. The massive spending was conducive to bribes, fraud, and theft. For example, the U.S. Congress appropriated about $53 billion for reconstruction projects, and another $100 billion for rebuilding came from Iraqi assets. The use of cash payments and weak oversight allowed people to take bribes and steal cash. By 2010, there had been fifty-eight convictions for fraud and theft in various forms. In some cases, people simply mailed themselves money or carried it out of the country in duffel bags or suitcases. Millions of dollars were moved by wire transfer. There were about 16 million reports of suspicious financial activity involving cash deposits of more than $10,000.

What was the justification for this war? First, there was the prevention argument. In its most basic form, this is the argument that if one nation threatens another, or might be able to threaten another, then the threatened nation is justified in attacking the nation that poses the actual or possible threat. The Bush administration claimed that Iraq was possibly a threat to the United States and its allies, and that was the reason for attacking. In the words of President Bush's National Security Statement, the United States must "stop rogue states and their terrorist clients before they are able to threaten or use weapons of mass destruction against the United States and our allies and friends."

One problem with this statement is that Iraq did not have the weapons of mass destruction it was alleged to have, nor the programs to develop them. According to Hans Blix, the head of the UN inspection team, the UN inspections had been effective in eliminating the weapons or the programs to develop them. The Iraq Study Group came to similar conclusions. There was no solid evidence of the existence of the weapons or programs.

Another problem with President Bush's statement is that there was no credible evidence that Saddam Hussein was connected to either the 9/11 attacks or to the al-Qaeda organization. Richard A. Clark, the counterterrorism czar in both the Clinton and Bush administrations, claimed that President Bush was eager to attack Iraq from the beginning of his administration, and used the 9/11 attacks as an excuse to link Hussein and al Qaeda in the war on terrorism. Furthermore, it has been claimed that the Muslim terrorists hated the secular government of Saddam Hussein and welcomed its demise. The al-Qaeda organization was happy to see Hussein executed; it encouraged the violence in Iraq because it created more militants to fight the United States and its allies.

The main problem with the prevention argument is that it makes it too easy to justify war. Iraq was not an actual threat, but might have been "able to threaten," and that was enough justification for war, at least according to President Bush's statement. But, according to just war theory, war should be the last resort, not the first thing considered. Even Henry Kissinger, surely no peacenik, acknowledged this problem when he warned against using the appeal to prevention as a universal principle available to every nation. For example, during the Cold War, the USSR was actually threatened by the United States, which had thousands of missiles with nuclear warheads targeting Russian cities and military bases. Even today the United States has at least 15,000 nuclear warheads, which could be launched in a crisis or because of an accident; also, the United States reserves the right to strike first. The United States is a certainly an actual threat to Russia. Does that justify a Russian first strike?

North Korea is a rogue state that actually has nuclear weapons, and may be selling them to other countries. Are we justified in attacking North Korea? (The fact that we have not makes a good case for having nuclear weapons; they are an effective deterrent.) Iran is probably developing nuclear weapons. Should we attack Iran before it is able to produce them? This is not merely a hypothetical question. In 2010, war plans were being made to attack Iran in the event that it developed nuclear weapon capability.

A second argument used to justify the Iraq war was the humanitarian argument that Saddam Hussein was a brutal dictator—comparable to Hitler, no less—and needed to be removed from power. No doubt Hussein was an evil man, having launched aggressive wars against Iran and Kuwait; gassed thousands of Kurds; killed numerous rivals; and at least attempted to develop chemical, biological, and nuclear weapons before this was stopped by the UN inspections. These facts, however, constitute an argument for assassination, not war. The CIA tried to kill Fidel Castro several times because he was perceived to be evil, but the United States has not launched a massive invasion of Cuba. Why not? (The Bay of Pigs operation was not an all-out military operation with "shock and awe" like the Iraq war.) Besides, like the prevention argument, the humanitarian argument makes it too easy to justify war. Should we go to war against any and all countries ruled by evil persons?

A third argument used to justify the war is the legalistic argument that war with Iraq was necessary to enforce the United Nations resolutions in the face of Iraqi defiance. But France, Germany, and other member nations of the UN argued that more inspections would do the job, since Iraq was allowing them. They also contended that in the event war was necessary, it should have been undertaken by a genuine coalition of member nations, and not just by the United States and Britain with token forces contributed by other nations.

As the occupation continued through 2009, with civilian and military casualties continuing every day, pundits, analysts, and journalists offered various other justifications for war and permanent occupation by U.S. forces. One was the nation-building argument: the view that turning despotic regimes in the Middle East into secular democracies would be a good thing. This view was attributed to Bush former administration officials such as Paul Wolfowitz. However, there was the possibility that Iraq would end up being a fundamentalist Islamic state like Iran. Critics of the war maintained that the real reason for the war was President Bush getting back at his father's enemy. European critics thought the war was really about oil—America wanted to control one of the world's largest oil reserves. They pointed to President Bush's connection to the oil industry, and to the fact that Halliburton, the company run by Dick Cheney before he became vice president, was immediately given the contract to rebuild Iraq's oil industry.

All things considered, was the Iraq war justified or not? Can it be justified using just war theory? Can it be justified in some other way? Explain your position.

4. Jose Padilla

Mr. Padilla, age thirty-six, was born in Brooklyn and raised in Chicago. He served prison time for a juvenile murder in Illinois and for gun possession in Florida. He converted to Islam in prison and took the name Abdullah al Muhijir when he lived in Egypt. According to the U.S. government, he also spent time in Saudi Arabia, Pakistan, and Afghanistan.

The FBI arrested Mr. Padilla in May 2002 when he arrived from overseas at Chicago's O'Hare International Airport. Then he was held incommunicado at a Navy brig in Charleston, South Carolina, for three and one-half years, during which time he was denied counsel. No formal charges were brought against Mr. Padilla during this time, but not long after his arrest, Attorney General John Ashcroft claimed that Mr. Padilla was part of a plot by al Qaeda to explode a radiological dirty bomb.

On December 18, 2003, a federal appeals court in Manhattan ruled (2 to 1) that the president does not have the executive authority to hold American citizens indefinitely without access to lawyers simply by declaring them to be enemy combatants. The decision said that the president does not have the constitutional authority as Commander-in-Chief to detain as enemy combatants American citizens seized on American soil, away from the zone of combat. Furthermore, the ruling said, citing a 1971 statute, that Congress did not authorize detention of an American citizen under the circumstances of Mr. Padilla's case. The court ordered the government to release Mr. Padilla from military custody.

On the same day as the court's decision, the Department of Justice issued a statement on the case. The government's statement said that Mr. Padilla was associated with senior al-Qaeda leaders, including Osama bin Laden, and that he had received training from al-Qaeda operatives on wiring explosive devices and on the construction of a uranium-enhanced explosive device. The statement concluded that Mr. Padilla "is an enemy combatant who poses a serious and continuing threat to the American people and our national security."

Mr. Padilla appealed his case to the U.S. Supreme Court, but the court declined to take the case because it was moot. In November 2005, as the court challenge to his status was pending, the Bush administration suddenly announced that criminal charges had been filed against Padilla in Miami. He was moved out of military custody in Miami, where he was held without bail. Instead of being charged as an enemy combatant, he was accused of being part of a cell of Islamic terrorists. His lawyers moved to have the charges against him dismissed on the ground that the psychological damage he suffered during his long confinement from abuse and isolation left him incompetent to stand trial. The motion was denied and the trial went ahead. On August 16, 2007, he was found guilty of conspiring to kill people and supporting terrorism. Six months later, he was sentenced to 17 years and 4 months in prison.

This case raises some troubling questions. Does the government have the legal power to imprison American citizens indefinitely without bringing any charges and denying access to counsel? Is this constitutional? Do citizens charged with a crime have a right to a speedy trial?

In addition to Mr. Padilla, some 600 men of varying nationalities are being held at the Guantánamo Bay naval base in Cuba. These men were captured in Afghanistan and Pakistan during the operations against the Taliban. Like Mr. Padilla, they are deemed by the U.S. government to be enemy combatants having no legal rights. They are not being allowed to contest their detention through petitions for habeas corpus, the ancient writ which for centuries has been used in the English-speaking world to challenge the legality of confinement.

The basic issue is whether or not the president should have the power to deny basic rights in the name of fighting terrorism. What is your view of this?

5. Fighting Terrorism

What can the United States do to prevent terrorist attacks like the September 11 assault on the World Trade Center and the Pentagon? One proposal is national identity cards, discussed by Daniel J. Wakin in *The New York Times*, October 7, 2001. According to polls taken after the attacks, about 70 percent of

Americans favor such cards, which are used in other countries. French citizens are required to carry national ID cards, and they may be stopped by the police for card inspection at any time. Such cards are also required in Belgium, Greece, Luxembourg, Portugal, and Spain. Privacy International, a watchdog group in London, estimates that about one hundred countries have compulsory national IDs. Some, like Denmark, issue ID numbers at birth, around which a lifetime of personal information accumulates.

It is not clear if required ID cards would violate the U.S. Constitution. One objection is that a police demand to see the card would constitute a "seizure" forbidden by the Fourth Amendment. Another objection is that illegal immigrants would be targeted rather than terrorists. In contrast, proponents of the cards argue that they could be used to identify terrorists and protect travelers. Larry Ellison, the chief executive of the software maker Oracle, claims that people's fingerprints could be embedded on the cards and police or airport guards could scan the cards and check the fingerprints against a database of terrorists. The cards could protect airline travelers at check-in and guard against identity theft. Advocates of the cards argue that a great deal of personal information is already gathered by private industry, so any invasion of privacy occasioned by the ID cards would not matter much. What do you think? Are national ID cards a good way to fight against terrorism?

Another proposal is to allow suspicionless searches. In Israel, the police can search citizens and their belongings at any time without any particular cause or suspicion. These searches are conducted at shopping centers, airports, stadiums, and other public places. Citizens are also required to pass through metal detectors before entering public places. The U.S. Constitution requires police to have an objective suspicion or "probable cause" to search you, your belongings, or your car, but the Supreme Court has granted exceptions such as border searches and drunk-driving

checkpoints. Why not allow suspicionless searches at public places like shopping centers, airports, and football stadiums?

Even more controversial is racial profiling. Israeli authorities single out travelers and citizens for questioning and searches based on racial profiling. Experts cite vigorous racial profiling as one of the reasons Israeli airplanes are not hijacked. The U.S. Supreme Court has not ruled on whether racial profiling violates the equal protection clause of the U.S. Constitution and has declined to hear cases on the practice. Opinions differ on what counts as racial profiling and when or if it is unconstitutional. Advocates of the practice claim that police already practice racial profiling and that it is effective in preventing crime. Critics object that it is nothing more than racism. Is racial profiling justified in the fight against terrorism?

In Canada, police are allowed to arrest and hold suspected terrorists without charges and without bail for up to ninety days. In France, suspects can be held for questioning for nearly five days without being charged and without having any contact with an attorney. Britain's antiterrorist legislation allows suspicious individuals to be detained for up to seven days without a court appearance. The new antiterrorist legislation proposed by the U.S. Congress would allow authorities to hold foreigners suspected of terrorist activity for up to a week without charges. Is this indefinite holding without charges and without bail acceptable?

Finally, in the fight against terrorism Israel has condoned assassinations or "judicially sanctioned executions," that is, killing of terrorist leaders such as Osama bin Laden. The United States does not currently permit assassination, but this prohibition stems from an executive order (which could be repealed), not because it is forbidden by the Constitution. Should the United States reconsider its position on assassination?

In general, are these methods of fighting terrorism acceptable to you? Why or why not?

6. *National Missile Defense*

National Missile Defense (NMD) is the controversial $8.3-billion missile defense shield championed by President George W. Bush and his Secretary of Defense, Donald Rumsfeld. It is an updated version of President Reagan's Strategic Defense Initiative. More

than $60 billion has already been spent on the missile defense program in the last two decades.

The basic idea of NMD is appealing. Instead of ensuring peace by relying on the Cold War strategy of mutual assured destruction (MAD), where neither the

United States nor Russia can defend against nuclear attack but can destroy the other if attacked, NMD would protect the United States from missile attack with a defensive umbrella of antimissile missiles. This would give the United States an advantage over Russia or other nuclear powers not having any missile defense.

Russia is no longer seen as the main threat, even though Russia still has thousands of long-range missiles left over from the Cold War arms race. According to President Bush, the main threat to the United States comes from so-called rogue nations unfriendly to the United States, such as North Korea and Iraq. In view of the September 11 attacks, the al-Qaeda terrorist network of Osama bin Laden also should be considered a threat. Bin Laden has promised more terrorist attacks on the United States and has proclaimed a jihad against the United States. Even though these terrorists do not possess nuclear weapons or missiles at present (at least, as far as we know, they don't), it seems likely that they will acquire them in the future. Then they could hold America hostage by threatening a nuclear attack, or they might launch a surprise attack on an undefended American city such as New York City or Los Angeles.

Even though it seems like a good idea, NMD has problems. There is a good chance that it would not work in an actual attack. Two out of four major missile

defense tests conducted so far have failed. Critics say that trying to hit a missile with another missile is like trying to shoot down a bullet with another bullet. It is difficult, to say the least. Countermeasures such as dummy missiles or balloons could fool the defense system. Low-tech missiles, the most likely to be used, do not follow a predictable path, so they would probably be missed by antimissile missiles.

Even if the defensive system worked perfectly, it would defend only against long-range missiles and not against nuclear weapons delivered by other means. For example, a short-range missile could be launched from a submarine just off the coast, or a weapon could be taken to its target by truck or a private shipper. The most likely scenario is that terrorists would assemble a nuclear weapon at the target and then explode it. Obviously, NMD is no defense against such terrorist attacks.

Finally, there are political problems. NMD violates the 1972 Antiballistic Missile Treaty with Russia. The treaty limits the testing and deployment of new defense systems. Russian President Vladimir Putin contends that violating the 1972 treaty will upset nuclear stability and result in a new arms race.

Given these problems and how much it will cost, is NMD a good idea? What is your position?

7. Mini-Nukes

(For more details, see Fred Kaplan, "Low-Yield Nukes," posted November 21, 2003, on http://www.slate.msn.com.)

In 1970, the United States signed the Non-Proliferation Treaty. This treaty involved a pact between nations having nuclear weapons and nations not having them. Nations not having them promised not to develop nuclear weapons, and nations already having them promised to pursue nuclear disarmament. In 1992, the United States unilaterally stopped nuclear testing, on orders of the first President Bush, and then formalized this in 1995 by signing the Comprehensive Test Ban Treaty. This latter treaty prohibits the testing and development of nuclear weapons indefinitely, and it was signed by 186 other nations.

In 2003, the second Bush administration insisted that Iran and North Korea halt their nuclear weapons programs, and argued that the invasion and

occupation of Iraq were justified because Iraq had weapons of mass destruction (WMD), that is, chemical, biological, and nuclear weapons (or at least a nuclear weapons program). Yet, at the same time, the second Bush administration was actively developing a new generation of exotic nuclear weapons, including low-yield mini-nukes and earth-penetrating nukes, despite the fact that the country already had 7,650 nuclear warheads and bombs. Specifically, the fiscal year 2004 defense bill, passed by both houses of Congress in November 2003, did four things. First, it repealed the 1992 law banning the development of low-yield nuclear weapons. Second, the bill provided $15 million to develop an earth-penetrating nuclear weapon, a bunker buster. Third, it allocated $6 million to explore special-effects bombs, for example, the neutron bomb that enhances radiation. Finally, the bill provided $25 million for underground nuclear tests.

This renewed development of nuclear weapons and testing violated the 1970 and 1995 treaties, but the second Bush administration argued that it was necessary to do this for self-defense. The old warheads mounted on intercontinental missiles were designed to wipe out industrial complexes or destroy whole cities. Such weapons were never used, and it appeared that they no longer had any utility. Certainly they were not effective against suicide bombers or other terrorist attacks. What was needed, it was argued, was smaller warheads that could destroy underground bunkers or WMD storage sites.

Critics argued that the U.S. development of more nuclear weapons undermined the attempt to stop similar development in other nations. If the United States needed nuclear weapons for self-defense, then why didn't other nations need them too? The fact that the United States did not attack North Korea (which had nuclear weapons) seemed to support the view that nations needed these weapons to deter attacks.

Furthermore, critics argued that mini-nukes or bunker busters were not necessary. Conventional weapons could do the job. The United States already had at least two non-nuclear smart bombs that could penetrate the earth before exploding. There was the GBU-24, a 2000-pound laser-guided bomb, and the BLU-109 JDAM, a 2000-pound satellite-guided bomb. Both of these bombs could be filled with incendiary explosive that would burn whatever biological or chemical agents might be stored in an underground site.

So why did the United States need to develop more nuclear weapons? Was this necessary or effective for self-defense? Explain your answer. Why did the United States continue to keep 7,650 nuclear warheads and bombs? Was it ever necessary to have so many weapons? Is it necessary now? What is your view?

8. The Gulf War

(For a book-length treatment of the Gulf War, including the view of it as jihad, see Kenneth L. Vaux, *Ethics and the Gulf War* [Boulder, CO: Westview Press, 1992].) In August 1990, the Iraqi army invaded and occupied Kuwait. Although the United States had received warnings, officials did not take them seriously. Saddam Hussein believed the United States would not intervene and apparently had received assurances to that effect. Hussein claimed that the invasion was justified because Kuwait had once been part of Iraq and because the Kuwaitis were exploiting the Rumalla oilfield, which extended into Iraq. The immediate response of the United States and its allies was to begin a ship embargo against Iraq. President George Bush, citing atrocities against the Kuwaitis, compared Hussein to Hitler. For his part, Hussein declared the war to be jihad and threatened the mother of all battles (as he put it) if the Americans dared to intervene. Iran's Ayatollah Khomeini, certainly no friend of the United States, seconded the claim of jihad, adding that anyone killed in battle would be a martyr and immediately go to paradise, the Islamic heaven.

In the months that followed, Iraq ignored repeated ultimatums to leave Kuwait. But Iraq did try to stall for time, following the Koranic teaching of "withholding your hand a little while from war" (Vaux, 1992, p. 71). Thousands of foreign prisoners were released, and Iraq responded positively to French and Soviet peace initiatives. At the same time, Saddam Hussein continued to call it a holy war, saying that the United States was a satanic force attacking the religious values and practices of Islam.

On January 16, 1991, after a UN deadline had passed, the allied forces (American, British, French, Saudi, and Kuwaiti) launched a massive day-and-night air attack on military targets in Iraq, including the capital city of Baghdad. The forty days of air war that followed were very one-sided. The allied forces were able to bomb targets at will using advanced technical weapons such as radar-seeking missiles, laser-guided bombs, stealth fighters that avoided radar detection, and smart cruise missiles that could adjust their course. The Iraqi air force never got off the ground, but hid or flew to Iran. Iraqi Scud missiles killed twenty-two American soldiers sleeping in Saudi Arabia and civilians in Israel, but were mostly unreliable and ineffective. Finally, the ground war (Operation Desert Storm) lasted only 100 hours before the allied forces liberated Kuwait City. The Iraqis suffered more than 200,000 casualties (according to American estimates), whereas the allied forces sustained fewer than 200 casualties.

Can this war be justified using the just war theory? Carefully explain your answer. Keep in mind that some religious leaders at the time said that it was not a just war.

Was this really a jihad, as Saddam Hussein and the Ayatollah Khomeini said? Remember that Kuwait and Saudi Arabia are also Muslim countries.

Oil presented another consideration. Kuwait had about 20 percent of the world's known oil reserves at the time. Some said the war was really about the control and price of oil and argued that if Kuwait had not had valuable resources, the United States would not have intervened. (For example, the United States did nothing when China invaded and occupied a defenseless Tibet in 1949.)

👑 SUGGESTED READINGS

Several U.S. government websites post information and news about the ongoing wars and terrorism. See those of the Department of Defense (www.defense.gov), the CIA (www.cia.gov), the Department of Homeland Security (www.dhs.gov), the FBI (www.fbi.org), and the White House (www.whitehouse.gov). For antiwar and pacifist views, see www.antiwar.com and www.nonviolence.org. The Arab perspective is presented at www.iwpr.net.

Michael G. Knapp, "The Concept and Practice of Jihad in Islam," *Parameters*, Spring (2003): 82–84, surveys the concept of jihad in Islam. In the classical view, jihad was restricted to defensive war against non-Muslims. Modern militant Islam changed the concept to include wars of aggression. The movement reached an extreme with Osama bin Laden, who declared jihad, war, against the United States and its allies.

Louise Richardson, *What Terrorists Want: Understanding the Enemy, Containing the Threat* (New York: Random House, 2007), explains the causes of terrorism, proposes a definition, and discusses the proper response.

Claudia Card, "Questions Regarding a War on Terrorism," *Hypatia*, Vol. 18, No. 1 (Winger 2003): 164–169, critically examines the so-called *war on terrorism*.

William V. O'Brien, *The Conduct of Just and Limited War* (Westport, CT: Greenwood Publishing Group, 1981), gives an exhaustive and detailed explanation of traditional just war theory.

Michael W. Brough, John W. Lango, and Harry van der Linden, eds., *Rethinking the Just War Tradition* (Albany, NY: State University of New York Press, 2007), is a valuable collection of articles on just war theory, the distinction between combatants and noncombatants, and preventive war.

Timothy Shanahan, ed., *Philosophy 9/11* (Peru, IL: Open Court Publishing, 2005), is a collection of articles on terrorism, just war theory, terrorists, the war on terrorism, and counterterrorism.

Uwe Steinhoff, *On the Ethics of War and Terrorism* (Oxford: Oxford University Press, 2007), examines war and terrorism using just war theory. There are chapters on legitimate authority, just cause and right intention, innocents, double effect, and proportionality.

Seamus Miller, *Terrorism and Counter-Terrorism* (Oxford: Blackwell Publishing, 2009), critically examines various issues about terrorism. There are chapters on the varieties of terrorism, defining terrorism, terrorism and collective responsibility, terrorism-as-crime, and terrorism in war.

Pierre Allan and Alexis Keller, eds., *What Is a Just Peace?* (Oxford: Oxford University Press, 2008), is a collection of readings on the problem of determining a just peace. For example, what would be a just peace plan for ending the Israeli-Palestinian conflict?

Osama bin Laden, "To the Americans," in *Messages to the World*, ed. B. Lawrence (London: Verso, 2005), 162–172. This letter gives bin Laden's reasons for the 9/11 attacks. It was published in the *London Observer* on November 24, 2002. An al-Qaeda document that attempts to justify the 9/11 attacks is available in English translation at www.mepc.org.

Hans Blix, *Disarming Iraq* (New York: Pantheon Books, 2004), concludes that every claim made by the Bush administration about Iraq's weapons programs—the mobile biological labs, the yellowcake, the aluminum tubes—has proven to be false and that the Iraq war was unnecessary.

Richard A. Clarke, *Against All Enemies* (New York: Free Press, 2004). Clarke was the counterterrorism coordinator in both the Clinton and the second Bush administrations. He claims that President George W. Bush was obsessed with Iraq after the 9/11 attacks and eager to blame Iraq even though there was overwhelming evidence that al Qaeda was responsible and Saddam Hussein was not.

Christopher Hitchens, *A Long Short War* (London: Plume, 2003), is an enthusiastic supporter of the Iraq war. He claims that it liberated the Iraqis from oppression and prevented Iraq from attacking the United States with nuclear weapons.

Robert Kagan and William Kristol, "The Right War for the Right Reasons," in *The Right War*, ed. Gary Kosen (Cambridge: Cambridge University Press, 2005), 18–35, defend the Iraq war. They claim that Saddam Hussein had "undeniable ties" to terrorists, was a brutal dictator, and was pursuing weapons of mass destruction.

Jan Narveson, "Regime Change," in *A Matter of Principle*, ed. Thomas Cushman (Berkeley: University of California Press, 2005), 58–75, presents the case for regime change in Iraq. He argues that military intervention in Iraq was justified because it produced a decent regime "at modest cost to the Iraqis" and "at quite modest cost in lives to the Coalition" (p. 74).

C. A. J. Coady, "Terrorism and Innocence," *Journal of Ethics* 8 (2004): 37–58, discusses problems with defining terrorism and deciding who is innocent.

Burleigh Taylor Wilkins, *Terrorism and Collective Responsibility* (London: Routledge, 1992), argues that terrorism can be morally justified in certain circumstances. For example, terrorism aimed at defeating Hitler would have been justified.

Whitley R. P. Kaufman, "Terrorism, Self-Defense, and the Killing of the Innocent," *Social Philosophy Today* 20 (2004): 41–52, argues that terrorism violates the moral prohibition against harming the innocent, and as such is always morally impermissible.

Andrew Valls, "Can Terrorism Be Justified?" in *Ethics in International Affairs*, ed. Andrew Valls (Lanham, MD: Roman & Littlefield, 2000), 65–79, argues that if war can be justified using just war theory, then terrorism can be justified as well.

Virginia Held, "Legitimate Authority in Non-state Groups Using Violence," *Journal of Social Philosophy* 36, no. 2 (Summer 2005): 175–193, argues that in actual circumstances, such as the struggle to gain independence in South Africa, some uses of violence may be justified, and terrorism may be as justified as war.

Steve Coll, *Ghost Wars* (London: Penguin Press, 2004), explains the history of al Qaeda in Afghanistan, including how Saudi Arabia aided the rise of Osama bin Laden and Islamic extremism.

Ahmed Rashid, *Taliban: Militant Islam, Oil, and Fundamentalism in Central Asia* (New Haven, CT: Yale University Press, 2000), presents the history of the Taliban and explains their version of Islam. They believe they are God's invincible soldiers fighting an unending war against unbelievers.

Anthony H. Cordesman, *Terrorism, Asymmetric Warfare, and Weapons of Mass Destruction* (Westport, CT: Praeger, 2001), discusses previous commissions on terrorism, the details of homeland defense, and the risk of chemical and biological attacks.

Yossef Bodansky, *Bin Laden: The Man Who Declared War on America* (New York: Random House, 2001). This book is by a well-known expert on terrorism; it covers bin Laden's life and his pursuit of chemical, biological, and nuclear weapons.

Paul R. Pillar, *Terrorism and U.S. Foreign Policy* (Washington, DC: Brookings Institution, 2001), explains the causes of modern terrorism in countries such as Pakistan and Afghanistan and examines the new war against terrorism.

Peter Partner, *God of Battles: Holy Wars of Christianity and Islam* (Princeton, NJ: Princeton University Press, 1998), explains the doctrines of war in Christianity and Islam.

James Turner Johnson, *Mortality and Contemporary Warfare* (New Haven, CT: Yale University Press, 1999), presents the history and development of just war theory and its application in the real world.

Bryan Brophy-Baermann and John A. C. Conybeare, "Retaliating against Terrorism," *American Journal of Political Science* 38, no. 1 (February 1994): 196–210, argue that retaliation against terrorism produces a temporary deviation in attacks but no long-term effect.

Dilip Hiro, *Holy Wars: The Rise of Islamic Fundamentalism* (London: Routledge, 1989), explains the development of Islamic fundamentalism found today in Iran and Afghanistan, where Islam has emerged as a radical ideology of armed warfare.

Ayatollah Ruhollah Khomeini, "Islam Is Not a Religion of Pacifists," in *Holy Terror*, ed. Amir Taheri (Bethesda, MD: Adler & Adler, 1987), gives a clear statement of the Islamic doctrine of holy war. According to the Ayatollah Khomeini, Islam says, "Kill all the unbelievers just as they would kill you all!"

R. Peters, "Jihad," in *The Encyclopedia of Religion* (New York: Macmillan, 1989), gives a scholarly account of the Islamic concept of jihad and its application to war.

A. Mallory, *The Crusaders through Arab Eyes* (New York: Schocken Books, 1985), covers two centuries of hostility and war between Muslim Arabs and Christian Crusaders from the West (called Franks), starting with the fall of Jerusalem in 1099. It is a depressing history of invasion, counterinvasion, massacres, and plunder.

Michael Walzer, *Just and Unjust Wars: A Moral Argument with Historical Illustrations* (New York: Basic Books, 1977), develops and defends just war theory and applies the theory to numerous historical cases, such as the Six-Day War, the Vietnam War, the Korean War, and World War II. He argues that the Vietnam War can be justified as assistance to the legitimate government of South Vietnam.

Robert L. Phillips, *War and Justice* (Norman: University of Oklahoma Press, 1984), defends just war theory. He accepts two principles of the theory, the principle of proportionality and the principle of discrimination. The latter principle, however, in turn rests on the doctrine of double effect, which distinguishes between intending to kill and merely foreseeing that death will occur as an unintended consequence of an action.

James Johnson, *The Just War Tradition and the Restraint of War* (Princeton, NJ: Princeton University Press, 1981), explains the historical development of just war theory from the Middle Ages to the present.

Paul Ramsey, *The Just War: Force and Political Responsibility* (New York: Charles Scribner's Sons, 1968). This book is a collection of articles on just war theory, all written by Ramsey. He is a Christian who defends a version of the theory that has an absolute principle of discrimination against killing noncombatants. Yet having accepted this principle, he goes on to claim that the war in Vietnam was justified though it involved killing many noncombatants.

Paul Christopher, *The Ethics of War and Peace* (Englewood Cliffs, NJ: Prentice Hall, 1994). This textbook covers the just war tradition, the international laws on war, and moral issues such as war crimes; reprisals; and nuclear, biological, and chemical weapons.

Immanuel Kant, *Perpetual Peace* (New York: Liberal Arts Press, 1957). In a classic discussion, Kant maintains that war must not be conducted in a way that rules out future peace. Perpetual peace results when democratic countries let the people decide about going to war. Kant believes that the people will always vote for peace.

Albert Schweitzer, *The Teaching of Reverence for Life*, trans. Richard and Clara Masters (New York: Holt, Rinehart & Winston, 1965), argues that all taking of life is wrong because all life is sacred.

Leo Tolstoy, *The Law of Love and the Law of Violence*, trans. Mary Koutouzow Tolstoy (New York: Holt, Rinehart & Winston, 1971), explains his Christian pacifism.

Mohandas K. Gandhi, "The Practice of Satyagraha," in *Gandhi: Selected Writings*, ed. Ronald Duncan (New York: Harper & Row, 1971), presents his view of nonviolent resistance as an alternative to war.

T. R. Miles, "On the Limits to the Use of Force," *Religious Studies* 20 (1984): 113–120, defends a version of pacifism that is opposed to all war but not to all use of force. This kind of pacifism would require one to refuse to serve in the military but would not rule out serving as a police officer.

William Earle, "In Defense of War," *The Monist* 57, no. 4 (October 1973): 561–569 attacks pacifism (defined as the principled opposition to all war) and then gives a justification for the morality and rationality of war.

Jan Narveson, "In Defense of Peace," in *Moral Issues*, ed. Jan Narveson (Oxford: Oxford University Press, 1983), 59–71, replies to Earle. He does not defend pacifism; instead, he argues that whenever there is a war, at least one party is morally unjustified.

Jan Narveson, "Morality and Violence: War, Revolution, Terrorism," in *Matters of Life and Death: New Introductory Essays in Moral Philosophy*, ed. Tom Regan (New York: McGraw Hill, 1993), pp. 121–159. In this survey article, Narveson covers many different issues, including the nature and morality of violence, the right of self-defense, pacifism, just war theory, and terrorism.

Richard A. Wasserstrom, ed., *War and Morality* (Belmont, CA: Wadsworth, 1970), is a collection of articles on the morality of war and other issues. Elizabeth Anscombe discusses the doctrine of double effect as it applies to war. Wasserstrom argues that modern wars are very difficult to justify because innocents are inevitably killed.

Jean Bethke Elshtain, *Women and War* (New York: Basic Books, 1987). What is the feminist view of war? According to Elshtain, some feminists are pacifists working for world peace, whereas others want to reject the traditional noncombatant role of women and become warriors. As a result of the second position, the United States now has a higher percentage of women in the military than any other industrialized nation.

Sebastian Junger, *War* (New York: Hachette Book Group, 2010), gives a vivid account of the U.S. military operations in the Korengal Valley, the valley in Afghanistan where the Soviets were defeated. In 2010 the U.S. military abandoned its bases and withdrew from the valley.

Torture

- **Introduction**
  - Factual Background
  - The Readings
  - Philosophical Issues

INTRODUCTION

Factual Background

Humans have been torturing each other for a long time. Throughout the ages, the most common method has been beating. The Romans used the cat-of-nine-tails, a whip having nine tips embedded with lead, nails, and glass; it was used to flog people to extract information. The Chinese used bamboo sticks to beat people. During the Spanish Inquisition, torture was used to get confessions or religious conversions. One common method was called the *strappado*: The hands were bound behind the back, and the victim was suspended until the joints in the arms and shoulders dislocated. Other torture methods included the rack, the iron maiden, the thumbscrew, the boot, and red-hot pincers applied to the toes, ears, nose, or nipples. In modern times, electricity has become one of the most popular and painful tools of torturers. Prisoners are poked with electric cattle prods or have car battery leads attached to their bodies. Stun weapons are used to deliver shocks up to 75,000 volts. Psychological torture is common and includes prolonged solitary confinement, hooding, stress positions, withholding food and water, sleep deprivation, loud noise, bright light, hot and cold temperatures, nakedness, rape and sexual humiliation, mock executions, water boarding, and the use of dogs. Another method is to inject drugs such as sodium pentothal, which depresses the central nervous system and is supposed to make the subject easier to interrogate.

There are international agreements that prohibit torture. The United Nations Universal Declaration of Human Rights, Article 5, says, "No one shall be subjected to torture or cruel, inhuman, or degrading treatment or punishment." The Geneva Convention, Article 3, prohibits "cruel treatment and torture." It also bans "outrages upon personal dignity, in particular, humiliating and degrading treatment." (See the Problem Case.)

American soldiers at Abu Ghraib prison outside Baghdad, Iraq, violated these prohibitions. According to a 2003 report by Major General Antonio M. Taguba, there were numerous instances of "sadistic, blatant, and wanton criminal abuses," including pouring cold water or phosphoric liquid on naked detainees, threatening them with rape or death, sodomizing them with broomsticks, and using military dogs to bite them. There is the well-known picture of a hooded man forced to stand on a box with wires attached to his hands and neck. Reportedly, he was told that he would be electrocuted if he stepped or fell off the box. Former prisoners tell stories of U.S. soldiers beating prisoners, sometimes to death. Mohammed Unis Hassan says that he was cuffed to bars of his cell and then a female soldier poked his eye with her fingers so hard that he couldn't see afterward. Now his left eye is gray and glassy and his vision is blurred. He says he saw an old man forced to lie naked on his face until he died. Other naked prisoners were threatened and bitten by attack dogs.

Some of the mistreatment at Abu Ghraib involved sexual humiliation. There are photographs of naked Iraqi prisoners forced to simulate oral or anal sex. Private Lynndie England is shown giving a thumbs-up sign and pointing to the genitals of a naked and hooded Iraqi as he masturbates. In another picture, Private England is shown with Specialist Charles A. Graner, both grinning and giving the thumbs-up sign in front of a pile of naked Iraqis. Another picture shows Private England leading a naked man around on a dog leash.

Another place where prisoners have been tortured is the U.S. naval base at Guantánamo Bay, Cuba. FBI agents, Red Cross inspectors, and numerous released detainees have alleged that prisoners were chained in a fetal position on the floor or in a baseball catcher's position, subjected to extremes of temperature, made to walk on broken glass or barbed wire, subjected to loud music and flashing lights, given electrical shocks, chained and hanged from the ceiling, and beaten. One of the more bizarre acts was throwing the Koran in the toilet.

The revelation of torture at Abu Ghraib and Guantánamo Bay produced outrage among human rights activists. The response of the Bush administration was a Justice Department memo in 2002 asserting that inflicting moderate pain is not torture. According to the memo, mistreatment is torture only if it produces suffering "equivalent in intensity to the pain accompanying serious physical injury, such as organ failure, impairment of bodily function, or even death." On his talk show, Rush Limbaugh said that the sexual humiliation at Abu Ghraib was just harmless fun, similar to what goes on in college fraternities or secret societies.

In 2006, President Bush signed the McCain Detainee Amendment into law. It prohibits "cruel, inhuman or degrading" treatment of prisoners by U.S. officials or agents, but it is not clear what torture methods are prohibited. The amendment requires that military interrogations follow the U.S. Army's *Field Manual on Interrogation*, but this document is being rewritten and the section on interrogation techniques is classified. The McCain amendment authorizes any method on the highly classified list of techniques, no matter what they are.

The interrogation methods used by the United States are secret, and they have also been outsourced to other countries. The CIA has been operating covert prisons in eight countries, including Egypt, Thailand, Afghanistan, and several democracies in Eastern Europe. The existence and locations of these facilities, called "black sites," were classified, but President Bush revealed their existence in September 2006. He said in a speech that fourteen prisoners had been moved from the CIA's secret prisons in Europe to Guantánamo Bay. The prisoners included Khalid Sheik Mohammed, who confessed to planning the 9/11 attacks. (See the Problem Case.) President Bush said the fourteen prisoners were the last ones remaining in CIA custody, but Manfred Nowak, the UN special investigator on torture, said, "Of course there are many others." In his speech, President Bush said, "The United States does not torture," but he refused to say what specific methods had been used to get confessions from the prisoners.

The Readings

Alan Dershowitz defends the use of nonlethal torture to get lifesaving information from a terrorist. He gives two examples of instances in which torture can be morally justified. The examples are hypothetical, but they are based on actual situations. First, suppose the FBI tortured Zacarias Moussaoui before the 9/11 attacks and used the information gained from his torture to prevent the attacks. Dershowitz is confident that everyone will agree the torture was justified. Second, suppose a stolen Russian nuclear weapon is going to be detonated in New York City. The detonation of this "ticking bomb" can be prevented if we torture a terrorist and find out where it is located. Again, Dershowitz is sure that people will agree the torture was justified. In both cases, the justification is basically a simple appeal to costs and benefits; that is, to act utilitarianism. The pain of torture is bad, but the good produced, namely saving thousands of lives, makes the torture morally justified.

It can be objected that allowing torture in these cases turns it into a social practice or institution. This is undesirable because it leads to torture in other cases in which it is not justified. Dershowitz's reply to this slippery-slope objection is that principled lines have to be drawn between justified and unjustified torture. But whom can we trust to do this? Dershowitz proposes that judges issue "torture warrants" making torture legal in cases in which it is justified. Torture warrants are better than allowing secret torture because they protect the rights of the suspect and provide the open accountability and visibility that is important in a democracy.

David Luban does not agree that torture is morally justified in a ticking-bomb case like the one described by Dershowitz. He claims the ticking-bomb story is intellectual fraud that tricks us into thinking that torture can be justified and that the torturer is not a sadistic brute but a heroic public servant trying to save innocent lives. Luban claims that the story cheats by assuming too much—that officials know there is a bomb, that they have captured the one who planted it or knows where it is, that torture will make him talk, and so on. None of this is certain in the real world. Also, the story assumes that it is rational to choose between the certainty of torture versus the uncertainty of saving lives and that a decision can be made by calculating costs and benefits. All this is so remote from the real world that the wise course is to deny the possibility. It is a waste of time, insane, or frivolous to try to make a moral decision in this case. Besides, back in the real world, once it is granted that torture is permitted in the imaginary ticking-bomb case, we end up with a torture culture with torture practices, training, and institutions.

Uwe Steinhoff has a different position. Unlike Luban, he thinks torture is clearly justified in rare cases. There is the Dirty Harry case, where Harry saves an innocent girl's life by torturing the guilty kidnapper. As for the ticking-bomb case, Steinhoff argues that interrogative torture of a terrorist is morally justified even if we are not certain about the relevant facts—that we have the right person, that he knows where the bomb is located, and so on. Torturing a suspect who might be guilty of planting a bomb is like shooting a man who seems ready to kill the president. We have to act even if we are not certain. Steinhoff also attacks Dershowitz's proposal for torture warrants. Torture may be morally justified in rare cases, but that does not mean it should be legal. It can remain illegal and be excused in the rare cases in which it is justified. It is unnecessary to have torture warrants if torture is rarely used. Furthermore, torture warrants result in the institutionalization of torture, and this conflicts with the general prohibition of torture. Finally, torture warrants lead to a brutalization of the enforcers, which includes the state.

Heather MacDonald (see the Suggested Readings) defends the U.S. military's treatment of enemy combatants. She argues that the actual interrogational techniques used by the military are light-years away from real torture and are controlled by bureaucratic safeguards. The illegal acts at Abu Ghraib were not the result of any official decisions, but rather were caused by the anarchy of war. As for the alleged torture at Guantánamo, the interrogational techniques used there were not torture at all, in her view. They were merely stress techniques that included isolation, sleep deprivation, loud noise, prolonged standing, poking, grabbing, and so on. She admits, however, that the water boarding of Khalid Sheik Mohammed (see the Problem Case) arguably crossed the line into torture, and she notes that the CIA's behavior remains a "black box." She insists that to succeed in the war on terrorism, interrogators must be allowed to use these stress techniques on terrorists.

Philosophical Issues

What is torture? There is disagreement about how to define *torture* and what treatment is considered torture. MacDonald quotes a famous 2002 memo by Assistant Attorney General Jay S. Bybee, which interprets the 1984 Convention Against Torture as forbidding only physical pain equivalent to that "accompanying serious physical injury, such as organ failure, impairment of bodily function or even death," or mental pain resulting in "significant psychological harm of significant duration, e.g., lasting for months or even years." Following Luban, we can call this "torture heavy." Most people would classify water boarding, electrocution, and severe beating as torture heavy.

MacDonald and others argue that the interrogation techniques used at Guantánamo and other secret locations were not torture, or at least not torture heavy. What should we call being chained in a fetal position, or given electrical shocks, or being chained and hanged from the ceiling? Most people would say these treatments are a form of torture. Following Luban, we can call such treatment "torture lite."

Luban also discusses deceptive techniques designed to elicit emotions such as fear, hate, and love. He does not think they amount to torture, but they do create an environment of mind control. Then there is abuse, which seems to be a milder form of torture lite.

Dershowitz mentions inserting a needle under the fingernails to produce unbearable pain without any threat to life or health and drilling an unanesthetized tooth. These techniques seem to be torture heavy even though they are not lethal.

In contrast to the Bybee memo, the Human Rights Watch statement (also quoted by MacDonald) includes among the effects of torture "long-term depression, post-traumatic stress disorder, marked sleep disturbances and alterations in self-perceptions, not to mention feelings of powerlessness, of fear, guilt and shame." If those are the effects of torture, then all the techniques described by MacDonald, and certainly the techniques used by the CIA (see the Problem Case), count as torture.

What techniques should be allowed when interrogating terrorists? MacDonald's position is that torture lite should be permitted but not torture heavy. Dershowitz and Steinhoff seem to allow anything short of killing the terrorist. The Human Rights Watch position is that prisoners should not be tortured, and torture includes both torture lite and heavy. Luban argues that if we allow torture lite it will turn into torture heavy. In other words, there is a slippery slope where deception slides into abuse, abuse slides into torture lite, and torture lite slides into torture heavy. To avoid the slippery slope, we need to draw bright lines prohibiting abuse and torture.

Is torture morally wrong? Luban says that reverence for human rights and dignity makes torture morally unacceptable. Dershowitz and Steinhoff agree that it is usually morally wrong, but they both argue that it can be morally justified in some cases, for example, in the ticking-bomb case. Steinhoff says that cases of justified torture are very rare, while Dershowitz is willing to let a judge decide when torture is morally justified. It seems safe to say that all three would agree that sadistic torture—that is, torture done merely to cause suffering—is obviously wrong, even if the torturer enjoys it. (Kant famously gave sadistic torture as a counterexample to utilitarianism.) They would agree that torture done to punish a criminal is wrong as well. For one thing, it violates the Eighth Amendment prohibition of cruel and unusual punishment. They would condemn torturing a prisoner to produce a confession. Besides being cruel, torturing to produce a confession is worthless because people will confess to anything under torture. (See the book by William Sampson in the Suggested Readings.)

The debate about the morality of torture in the readings centers around interrogation torture and, specifically, whether torture is morally justified in a ticking-bomb case. This case was first discussed by Henry Shue (see the Suggested Reading). Shue argued that torture is permitted in this case, but like Steinhoff he had reservations. Even if it is permitted in this unusual case, this does not mean torture should be legalized. As we have seen, Dershowitz not only thinks torture is morally justified in cases in which lives can be saved, it also should be legal when authorized by a judge. Luban does not agree that torture is morally permitted in the ticking-bomb case, or in any other case for that matter. He characterizes the ticking-bomb case as a fraud, a picture that bewitches us. His position is that torture, whether heavy or lite, should be absolutely prohibited.

The Case for Torturing the Ticking Bomb Terrorist

ALAN DERSHOWITZ

Alan Dershowitz is the Felix Frankfurter Professor of Law at Harvard Law School. He is the author of 25 books and more than 100 articles. His most recent book is *The Case for Moral Clarity: Israel, Hamas and Gaza* (2009).

Dershowitz makes the case for torturing terrorists in cases in which many lives can be saved, for example, to prevent a nuclear bomb from being detonated in New York City. A simple cost-benefit analysis makes it obvious that torture is justified in such cases. It is better to torture a guilty terrorist than to allow millions of innocent victims to die. In reply to the slippery-slope objection that allowing torture in such cases will lead to unjustified torture, Dershowitz argues that clear lines must be drawn. To do this, he proposes that torture warrants (like search warrants) be issued by a judge. These warrants would help secure the safety of citizens, and at the same time recognize civil liberties and human rights. They would ensure the open accountability required in a democracy, and be preferable to secret, off-the-books torture because they would actually reduce the mistreatment of suspects and protect their rights.

The arguments in favor of using torture as a last resort to prevent a ticking bomb from exploding and killing many people are both simple and simple-minded. Bentham constructed a compelling hypothetical case to support his utilitarian argument against an absolute prohibition on torture:

> Suppose an occasion were to arise, in which a suspicion is entertained, as strong as that which would be received as a sufficient ground for arrest and commitment as for felony—a suspicion that at this very time a considerable number of individuals are actually suffering, by illegal violence inflictions equal in intensity to those which if inflicted by the hand of justice, would universally be spoken of under the name of torture. For the purpose of rescuing from torture these hundred innocents, should any scruple be made of applying equal or superior torture, to extract the requisite information from the mouth of one criminal, who having it in his power to make known the place where at this time the enormity was practising or about to be practised, should refuse to do so? To say nothing of wisdom, could any pretence be made so much as to the praise of blind and vulgar humanity, by the man who to save one

criminal, should determine to abandon 100 innocent persons to the same fate?[1]

If the torture of one guilty person would be justified to prevent the torture of a hundred innocent persons, it would seem to follow—certainly to Bentham—that it would also be justified to prevent the murder of thousands of innocent civilians in the ticking bomb case. Consider two hypothetical situations that are not, unfortunately, beyond the realm of possibility. In fact, they are both extrapolations on actual situations we have faced.

Several weeks before September 11, 2001, the Immigration and Naturalization Service detained Zacarias Moussaoui after flight instructors reported suspicious statements he had made while taking flying lessons and paying for them with large amounts of cash.[2] The government decided not to seek a warrant to search his computer. Now imagine that they had, and that they discovered he was part of a plan to destroy large occupied buildings, but without any further details. They interrogated him, gave him immunity from prosecution, and offered him large cash rewards and a new identity. He refused to talk. They then threatened him, tried to trick him, and employed every lawful technique available. He still refused. They even injected him with sodium pentothal and other truth serums, but to no avail. The attack now appeared to be imminent, but the FBI still had no idea what the target was or what means would be used to attack it. We could not simply evacuate all buildings indefinitely. An FBI agent proposes the use of nonlethal torture—say, a sterilized needle inserted under the fingernails to produce unbearable pain without any threat to health or life, or the method used in the film *Marathon Man*, a dental drill through an unanesthetized tooth.

The simple cost-benefit analysis for employing such nonlethal torture seems overwhelming: it is surely better to inflict nonlethal pain on one guilty terrorist who is illegally withholding information needed to prevent an act of terrorism than to permit a large number of innocent victims to die.[3] Pain is a lesser and more remediable harm than death; and the lives of a thousand innocent people should be valued more than the bodily integrity of one guilty person. If the variation on the Moussaoui case is not sufficiently compelling to make this point, we can always raise the stakes. Several weeks after September 11, our government received reports that a ten-kiloton nuclear weapon may have been stolen from Russia and was on its way to New York City, where it would be detonated and kill hundreds of thousands of people. The reliability of the source, code named Dragonfire, was uncertain, but assume for purposes of this hypothetical extension of the actual case that the source was a captured terrorist—like the one tortured by the Philippine authorities—who knew precisely how and where the weapon was being brought into New York and was to be detonated. Again, everything short of torture is tried, but to no avail. It is not absolutely certain torture will work, but it is our last, best hope for preventing a cataclysmic nuclear devastation in a city too large to evacuate in time. Should nonlethal torture be tried? Bentham would certainly have said yes.

The strongest argument against any resort to torture, even in the ticking bomb case, also derives from Bentham's utilitarian calculus. Experience has shown that if torture, which has been deemed illegitimate by the civilized world for more than a century, were now to be legitimated—even for limited use in one extraordinary type of situation—such legitimation would constitute an important symbolic setback in the worldwide campaign against human rights abuses. Inevitably, the legitimation of torture by the world's leading democracy would provide a welcome justification for its more widespread use in other parts of the world. Two Bentham scholars, W. L. Twining and P. E. Twining, have argued that torture is unacceptable even if it is restricted to an extremely limited category of cases:

> There is at least one good practical reason for drawing a distinction between justifying an isolated act of torture in an extreme emergency of the kind postulated above and justifying the *institutionalisation* of torture as a regular practice. The circumstances are so extreme in which most of us would be prepared to justify resort to torture, if at all, the conditions we would impose would be so stringent, the practical problems of devising and enforcing adequate safeguards so difficult and the risks of abuse so great that it would be unwise and dangerous to entrust any government, however enlightened, with such a power. Even an out-and-out utilitarian can support an absolute prohibition against institutionalised torture on the ground that no government in the world can be trusted not to abuse the power and to satisfy in practice the conditions he would impose.[4]

Bentham's own justification was based on *case* or *act* utilitarianism—a demonstration that in a *particular case*, the benefits that would flow from the limited use of torture would outweigh its costs. The argument against any use of torture would derive from *rule* utilitarianism—which considers the implications of establishing a precedent that would inevitably be extended beyond its limited case utilitarian justification to other possible evils of lesser magnitude. Even terrorism itself could be justified by a case utilitarian approach. Surely one could come up with a singular situation in which the targeting of a small number of civilians could be thought necessary to save thousands of other civilians—blowing up a German kindergarten by the relatives of inmates in a Nazi death camp, for example, and threatening to repeat the targeting of German children unless the death camps were shut down.

The reason this kind of single-case utilitarian justification is simple-minded is that it has no inherent limiting principle. If nonlethal torture of one person is justified to prevent the killing of many important people, then what if it were necessary to use lethal torture—or at least torture that posed a substantial risk of death? What if it were necessary to torture the suspect's mother or children to get him to divulge the information? What if it took threatening to kill his family, his friends, his entire village?[5] Under a simple-minded quantitative case utilitarianism, anything goes as long as the number of people tortured or killed does not exceed the number that would be saved. This is morality by numbers, unless there are other constraints on what we can properly do. These other constraints can come from rule utilitarianisms or other principles of morality, such as the prohibition against deliberately punishing the innocent. Unless we are prepared to impose some limits on the use of torture or other barbaric tactics that might be of some use in preventing terrorism, we risk hurtling down a slippery slope into the abyss of amorality and ultimately tyranny. Dostoevsky captured the complexity of this dilemma in *The Brothers Karamazov* when he had Ivan pose the following question to Alyosha: "Imagine that you are creating a fabric of human destiny with the object of making men happy in the end, giving them peace at least, but that it was essential and inevitable to torture to death only one tiny creature—that baby beating its breast with its fist, for instance—and to found that edifice on its unavenged tears, would you consent to be the architect [under] those conditions? Tell me the truth."

A willingness to kill an innocent child suggests a willingness to do anything to achieve a necessary result. Hence the slippery slope.

It does not necessarily follow from this understandable fear of the slippery slope that we can never consider the use of nonlethal infliction of pain, if its use were to be limited by acceptable principles of morality. After all, imprisoning a witness who refuses to testify after being given immunity is designed to be punitive—that is painful. Such imprisonment can, on occasion, produce more pain and greater risk of death than nonlethal torture. Yet we continue to threaten and use the pain of imprisonment to loosen the tongues of reluctant witnesses.[6]

It is commonplace for police and prosecutors to threaten recalcitrant suspects with prison rape. As one prosecutor put it: "You're going to be the boyfriend of a very bad man." The slippery slope is an argument of caution, not a debate stopper, since virtually every compromise with an absolutist approach to rights carries the risk of slipping further. An appropriate response to the slippery slope is to build in a principled break. For example, if nonlethal torture were legally limited to convicted terrorists who had knowledge of future massive terrorist acts, were given immunity, and still refused to provide the information, there might still be objections to the use of torture, but they would have to go beyond the slippery slope argument.[7]

The case utilitarian argument for torturing a ticking bomb terrorist is bolstered by an argument from analogy—an *a fortiori* argument. What moral principle could justify the death penalty for past individual murders and at the same time condemn nonlethal torture to prevent future mass murders? Bentham posed this rhetorical question as support for his argument. The death penalty is, of course, reserved for convicted murderers. But again, what if torture was limited to convicted terrorists who refused to divulge information about future terrorism? Consider as well the analogy to the use of deadly force against suspects fleeing from arrest for dangerous felonies of which they have not yet been convicted. Or military retaliations that produce the predictable and inevitable collateral killing of some innocent civilians. The case against torture, if made by a Quaker who opposes the death penalty, war, self-defense, and the use of lethal force against fleeing felons, is understandable. But for anyone who justifies killing on the basis of a cost-benefit analysis, the case against the use of nonlethal torture to save multiple lives is more difficult to make. In the end, absolute opposition to torture—even nonlethal torture in the ticking bomb case—may rest more on historical and aesthetic considerations than on moral or logical ones.

In debating the issue of torture, the first question I am often asked is, "Do you want to take us back to the Middle Ages?" The association between any form of torture and gruesome death is powerful in the minds of most people knowledgeable of the history of its abuses. This understandable association makes it difficult for many people to think about nonlethal torture as a technique for *saving* lives.

The second question I am asked is, "What kind of torture do you have in mind?" When I respond by describing the sterilized needle being shoved under the fingernails, the reaction is visceral and often visible—a shudder coupled with a facial gesture of disgust. Discussions of the death penalty on the other hand can be conducted without these kinds of reactions, especially now that we literally put the condemned prisoner "to sleep" by laying him out on a gurney and injecting a lethal substance into his body. There is no breaking of the neck, burning of the brain, bursting of internal organs, or gasping for breath that used to accompany hanging, electrocution, shooting, and gassing. The executioner has been replaced by a paramedical technician, as the aesthetics of death have become more acceptable. All this tends to cover up the reality that death is forever while nonlethal pain is temporary. In our modern age death is underrated, while pain is overrated.

I observed a similar phenomenon several years ago during the debate over corporal punishment that was generated by the decision of a court in Singapore to sentence a young American to medically supervised lashing with a cane. Americans who support the death penalty and who express little concern about inner-city prison conditions were outraged by the specter of a few welts on the buttocks of an American. It was an utterly irrational display of hypocrisy and double standards. Given a choice between a medically administered whipping and one month in a typical state lockup or prison, any rational and knowledgeable person would choose the lash. No one dies of welts or pain, but many inmates are raped, beaten, knifed, and otherwise mutilated and tortured in American prisons. The difference is that we don't see—and we don't want to see—what goes on behind their high walls. Nor do we want to think about it. Raising the issue of torture makes Americans think about a brutalizing and unaesthetic phenomenon that has been out of our consciousness for many years.[8]

THE THREE—OR FOUR—WAYS

The debate over the use of torture goes back many years, with Bentham supporting it in a limited category of cases, Kant opposing it as part of his categorical imperative against improperly using people as means for achieving noble ends, and Voltaire's views on the matter being "hopelessly confused."[9] The modern resort to terrorism has renewed the debate over how a rights-based society should respond to the prospect of using nonlethal torture in the ticking bomb situation. In the late 1980s the Israeli government appointed a commission headed by a retired Supreme Court justice to look into precisely that situation. The commission concluded that there are "three ways for solving this grave dilemma between the vital need to preserve the very existence of the state and its citizens, and maintain its character as a law-abiding state." The first is to allow the security services to continue to fight terrorism in "a twilight zone which is outside the realm of law." The second is "the way of the hypocrites: they declare that they abide by the rule of law, but turn a blind eye to what goes on beneath the surface." And the third, "the truthful road of the rule of law," is that the "law itself must insure a proper framework for the activity" of the security services in seeking to prevent terrorist acts.[10]

There is of course a fourth road: namely to forgo any use of torture and simply allow the preventable terrorist act to occur.[11] After the Supreme Court of Israel outlawed the use of physical pressure, the Israeli security services claimed that, as a result of the Supreme Court's decision, at least one preventable act of terrorism had been allowed to take place, one that killed several people when a bus was bombed.[12] Whether this claim is true, false, or somewhere in between is difficult to assess.[13] But it is clear that if the preventable act of terrorism was of the magnitude of the attacks of September 11, there would be a great outcry in any democracy that had deliberately refused to take available preventive action, even if it required the use of torture. During numerous public appearances since September 11, 2001, I have asked audiences for a show of hands as to how many would support the use of nonlethal torture in a ticking bomb case. Virtually every hand is raised. The few that remain down go up when I ask how many believe that torture would actually be used in such a case.

Law enforcement personnel give similar responses. This can be seen in reports of physical abuse directed against some suspects that have been detained following September 11, reports that have been taken quite seriously by at least one federal judge.[14] It is confirmed by the willingness of U.S. law enforcement officials to facilitate the torture of terrorist suspects by repressive regimes allied with our intelligence agencies. As one former CIA operative with thirty years of experience reported: "A lot of people are saying we need someone at the agency who can pull fingernails out. Others are saying, 'Let others use interrogation methods that we don't use.' The only question then is, do you want to have CIA people in the room?" The real issue, therefore, is not whether some torture would or would not be used in the ticking bomb case—it would. The question is whether it would be done openly, pursuant to a previously established legal procedure, or whether it would be done secretly, in violation of existing law.[15]

Several important values are pitted against each other in this conflict. The first is the safety and security of a nation's citizens. Under the ticking bomb scenario this value may require the use of torture, if that is the only way to prevent the bomb from exploding and killing large numbers of civilians. The second value is the preservation of civil liberties and human rights. This value requires that we not accept torture as a legitimate part of our legal system. In my debates with two prominent civil libertarians, Floyd Abrams and Harvey Silverglate, both have acknowledged that they would want nonlethal torture to be used if it could prevent thousands of deaths, but they did not want torture to be officially recognized by our legal system. As Abrams put it: "In a democracy sometimes it is necessary to do things off the books and below the radar screen." Former presidential candidate Alan Keyes took the position that although torture might be *necessary* in a given situation it could never be *right*. He suggested that a president *should* authorize the torturing of a ticking bomb terrorist, but that this act should not be legitimated by the courts or incorporated into our legal system. He argued that wrongful and indeed unlawful acts might sometimes be necessary to preserve the nation, but that no aura of legitimacy should be placed on these actions by judicial imprimatur.

This understandable approach is in conflict with the third important value: namely, open accountability and visibility in a democracy. "Off-the-book actions below the radar screen" are antithetical to the theory and practice of democracy. Citizens cannot approve or disapprove of governmental actions of which they are unaware. We have learned the lesson of history that off-the-book actions can produce terrible consequences. Richard Nixon's creation of a group of "plumbers" led to Watergate, and Ronald Reagan's authorization of an off-the-books foreign policy in Central America led to the Iran-Contra scandal. And these are only the ones we know about!

Perhaps the most extreme example of such a hypocritical approach to torture comes—not surprisingly—from the French experience in Algeria. The French army used torture extensively in seeking to prevent terrorism during a brutal colonial war from 1955 to 1957. An officer who supervised this torture, General Paul Aussaresses, wrote a book recounting what he had done and seen, including the torture of dozens of Algerians. "The best way to make a terrorist talk when he refused to say what he knew was to torture him," he boasted. Although the book was published decades after the war was over, the general was prosecuted—but not for what he had done to the Algerians. Instead, he was prosecuted for *revealing* what he had done, and seeking to justify it.[16]

In a democracy governed by the rule of law, we should never want our soldiers or our president to take any action that we deem wrong or illegal. A good test of whether an action should or should not be done is whether we are prepared to have it disclosed—perhaps not immediately, but certainly after some time has passed. No legal system operating under the rule of law should ever tolerate an "off-the-books" approach to necessity. Even the defense of necessity must be justified lawfully. The road to tyranny has always been paved with claims of necessity made by those responsible for the security of a nation. Our system of checks and balances requires that all presidential actions, like all legislative or military actions, be consistent with governing law. If it is necessary to torture in the ticking bomb case, then our governing laws must accommodate this practice. If we refuse to change our law to accommodate any particular action, then our government should not take that action.[17]

Only in a democracy committed to civil liberties would a triangular conflict of this kind exist. Totalitarian and authoritarian regimes experience no such conflict, because they subscribe to neither the civil libertarian nor the democratic values that come in conflict with the value of security. The hard question is: which value is to be preferred when an inevitable clash occurs? One or more of these values must inevitably be compromised in making the tragic choice presented by the ticking bomb case. If we do not torture, we compromise the security and safety of our citizens. If we tolerate torture, but keep it off the books and below the radar screen, we compromise principles of democratic accountability. If we create a legal structure for limiting and controlling torture, we compromise our principled opposition to torture in all circumstances and create a potentially dangerous and expandable situation.

In 1678, the French writer Francois de La Rochefoucauld said that "hypocrisy is the homage that vice renders to virtue." In this case we have two vices: terrorism and torture. We also have two virtues: civil liberties and democratic

accountability. Most civil libertarians I know prefer hypocrisy, precisely because it appears to avoid the conflict between security and civil liberties, but by choosing the way of the hypocrite these civil libertarians compromise the value of democratic accountability. Such is the nature of tragic choices in a complex world. As Bentham put it more than two centuries ago: "Government throughout is but a choice of evils." In a democracy, such choices must be made, whenever possible, with openness and democratic accountability, and subject to the rule of law.[18]

Consider another terrible choice of evils that could easily have been presented on September 11, 2001—and may well be presented in the future: a hijacked passenger jet is on a collision course with a densely occupied office building; the only way to prevent the destruction of the building and the killing of its occupants is to shoot down the jet, thereby killing its innocent passengers. This choice now seems easy, because the passengers are certain to die anyway and their somewhat earlier deaths will save numerous lives. The passenger jet must be shot down. But what if it were only *probable*, not certain, that the jet would crash into the building? Say, for example, we know from cell phone transmissions that passengers are struggling to regain control of the hijacked jet, but it is unlikely they will succeed in time. Or say we have no communication with the jet and all we know is that it is off course and heading toward Washington, D.C., or some other densely populated city. Under these more questionable circumstances, the question becomes *who* should make this life and death choice between evils—a decision that may turn out tragically wrong?

No reasonable person would allocate this decision to a fighter jet pilot who happened to be in the area or to a local airbase commander—unless of course there was no time for the matter to be passed up the chain of command to the president or the secretary of defense. A decision of this kind should be made at the highest level possible, with visibility and accountability.

Why is this not also true of the decision to torture a ticking bomb terrorist? Why should that choice of evils be relegated to a local policeman,

FBI agent, or CIA operative, rather than to a judge, the attorney general, or the president?

There are, of course, important differences between the decision to shoot down the plane and the decision to torture the ticking bomb terrorist. Having to shoot down an airplane, though tragic, is not likely to be a recurring issue. There is no slope down which to slip.[19] Moreover, the jet to be shot down is filled with our fellow citizens—people with whom we can identify. The suspected terrorist we may choose to torture is a "they"—an enemy with whom we do not identify but with whose potential victims we do identify. The risk of making the wrong decision, or of overdoing the torture, is far greater, since we do not care as much what happens to "them" as to "us."[20] Finally, there is something different about torture—even nonlethal torture—that sets it apart from a quick death. In addition to the horrible history associated with torture, there is also the aesthetic of torture. The very idea of deliberately subjecting a captive human being to excruciating pain violates our sense of what is acceptable. On a purely rational basis, it is far worse to shoot a fleeing felon in the back and kill him, yet every civilized society authorizes shooting such a suspect who poses dangers of committing violent crimes against the police or others. In the United States we execute convicted murderers, despite compelling evidence of the unfairness and ineffectiveness of capital punishment. Yet many of us recoil at the prospect of shoving a sterilized needle under the finger of a suspect who is refusing to divulge information that might prevent multiple deaths. Despite the irrationality of these distinctions, they are understandable, especially in light of the sordid history of torture.

We associate torture with the Inquisition, the Gestapo, the Stalinist purges, and the Argentine colonels responsible for the "dirty war." We recall it as a prelude to death, an integral part of a regime of gratuitous pain leading to a painful demise. We find it difficult to imagine a benign use of nonlethal torture to save lives.

Yet there was a time in the history of Anglo-Saxon law when torture was used to save life, rather than to take it, and when the limited administration of nonlethal torture was supervised by judges, including some who are well remembered in history.[21] This fascinating story has been recounted by Professor John Langbein of Yale Law School, and it is worth summarizing here because it helps inform the debate over whether, if torture would in fact be used in a ticking bomb case, it would be worse to make it part of the legal system, or worse to have it done off the books and below the radar screen.

In his book on legalized torture during the sixteenth and seventeenth centuries, *Torture and the Law of Proof*, Langbein demonstrates the trade-off between torture and other important values. Torture was employed for several purposes. First, it was used to secure the evidence necessary to obtain a guilty verdict under the rigorous criteria for conviction required at the time—either the testimony of two eyewitnesses or the confession of the accused himself. Circumstantial evidence, no matter how compelling, would not do. As Langbein concludes, "no society will long tolerate a legal system in which there is no prospect in convicting unrepentant persons who commit clandestine crimes. Something had to be done to extend the system to those cases. The two-eyewitness rule was hard to compromise or evade, but the confession invited 'subterfuge.'" The subterfuge that was adopted permitted the use of torture to obtain confessions from suspects against whom there was compelling circumstantial evidence of guilt. The circumstantial evidence, alone, could not be used to convict, but it was used to obtain a torture warrant. That torture warrant was in turn used to obtain a confession, which then had to be independently corroborated—at least in most cases (witchcraft and other such cases were exempted from the requirement of corroboration).[22]

Torture was also used against persons already convicted of capital crimes, such as high treason, who were thought to have information necessary to prevent attacks on the state.

Langbein studied eighty-one torture warrants, issued between 1540 and 1640, and found that in many of them, especially in "the higher cases of treasons, torture is used for discovery, and not for evidence." Torture was "used to protect the state" and "mostly that meant preventive torture to identify and forestall plots and plotters." It was only when the legal system loosened its requirement of proof (or introduced the "black box" of the jury system) and when perceived threats against the state diminished that torture was no longer deemed necessary to convict guilty defendants against whom there had previously been insufficient evidence, or to secure preventive information.[23]

The ancient Jewish system of jurisprudence came up with yet another solution to the conundrum of convicting the guilty and preventing harms to the community in the face of difficult evidentiary barriers. Jewish law required two witnesses and a specific advance warning before a guilty person could be convicted. Because confessions were disfavored, torture was not an available option. Instead, the defendant who had been seen killing by one reliable witness, or whose guilt was obvious from the circumstantial evidence, was formally acquitted, but he was then taken to a secure location and fed a concoction of barley and water until his stomach burst and he died. Moreover, Jewish law permitted more flexible forms of self-help against those who were believed to endanger the community.[24]

Every society has insisted on the incapacitation of dangerous criminals regardless of strictures in the formal legal rules. Some use torture, others use informal sanctions, while yet others create the black box of a jury, which need not explain its commonsense verdicts. Similarly, every society insists that, if there are steps that can be taken to prevent effective acts of terrorism, these steps should be taken, even if they require some compromise with other important principles.

In deciding whether the ticking bomb terrorist should be tortured, one important question is whether there would be less torture if it were done as part of the legal system, as it was in sixteenth- and seventeenth-century England, or off the books, as it is in many countries today. The Langbein study does not definitively answer this question, but it does provide some suggestive insights. The English system of torture was more visible and thus more subject to public accountability, and it is likely that torture was employed less frequently in England than in France.

"During these years when it appears that torture might have become routinized in English criminal procedure, the Privy Council kept the torture power under careful control and never allowed it to fall into the hands of the regular law enforcement officers," as it had in France. In England "no law enforcement officer . . . acquired the power to use torture without special warrant." Moreover, when torture warrants were abolished, "the English experiment with torture left no traces." Because it was under centralized control, it was easier to abolish than it was in France, where it persisted for many years.[25]

It is always difficult to extrapolate from history, but it seems logical that a formal, visible, accountable, and centralized system is somewhat easier to control than an ad hoc, off-the-books, and under-the-radar-screen nonsystem. I believe, though I certainly cannot prove, that a formal requirement of a judicial warrant as a prerequisite to nonlethal torture would decrease the amount of physical violence directed against suspects. At the most obvious level, a double check is always more protective than a single check. In every instance in which a warrant is requested, a field officer has already decided that torture is justified and, in the absence of a warrant requirement, would simply proceed with the torture. Requiring that decision to be approved by a judicial officer will result in fewer instances of torture even if the judge rarely turns down a request. Moreover, I believe that most judges would require compelling evidence before they would authorize so extraordinary a departure from our constitutional norms, and law enforcement officials would be reluctant to seek a warrant unless they had compelling evidence that the suspect had information needed to prevent an imminent terrorist attack. A record would be kept of every warrant granted, and although it is certainly possible that some individual agents might torture without a warrant, they would have no excuse, since a warrant procedure would be available. They could not claim "necessity," because the decision as to whether the torture is indeed necessary has been taken out of their hands and placed in the hands of a judge. In addition, even if torture were deemed totally illegal without any exception, it would still occur, though the public would be less aware of its existence.

I also believe that the rights of the suspect would be better protected with a warrant requirement. He would be granted immunity, told that he was now compelled to testify, threatened with imprisonment if he refused to do so, and given the option of providing the requested information. Only if he refused to do what he was legally compelled to do—provide necessary information, which could not incriminate him because of the immunity—would he be threatened with torture. Knowing that such a threat was authorized by the law, he might well provide the information.[26] If he still refused to, he would be subjected to judicially monitored physical measures designed to cause excruciating pain without leaving any lasting damage.

NOTES

1. Quoted in W.L. Twining and P.E. Twining, "Bentham on Torture," *Northern Ireland Legal Quarterly*, Autumn 1973, p. 347. Bentham's hypothetical question does not distinguish between torture inflicted by private persons and by governments.

2. David Johnston and Philip Shenon, "F.B.I. Curbed Scrutiny of Man Now a Suspect in the Attacks," *New York Times*, 10/6/2001.

3. It is illegal to withhold relevant information from a grand jury after receiving immunity. See *Kastigar v. U.S.* 406 U.S. 441 (1972).

4. Twining and Twining, "Bentham on Torture," pp. 348–49. The argument for the limited use of torture in the ticking bomb case falls into a category of argument known as "argument from the extreme case," which is a useful heuristic to counter arguments for absolute principles.

5. To demonstrate that this is not just in the realm of the hypothetical: "The former CIA officer said he also suggested the agency begin targeting close relatives of known terrorists and use them to obtain intelligence. 'You get their mothers and their brothers and their sisters under your complete control, and then you make that known to the target,' he said. 'You imply or you directly threaten [that] his family is going to pay the price if he makes the wrong decision,'" Bob Drogin and Greg Miller, "Spy Agencies Facing Questions of Tactics," *Los Angeles Times*, 10/28/2001.

6. One of my clients, who refused to testify against the mafia, was threatened by the government that if he persisted in his refusal the government would "leak" false information that he was cooperating, thus exposing him to mob retaliation.

7. *USA v. Cobb.*

8. On conditions in American prisons, see Alan M. Dershowitz, "Supreme Court Acknowledges Country's Other Rape Epidemic," *Boston Herald*, 6/12/1994.

   The United States may already be guilty of violating at least the spirit of the prohibition against torture. In a recent case the Canadian Supreme Court refused to extradite an accused person to the United States because of threats made by a judge and a prosecutor regarding the treatment of those who did not voluntarily surrender themselves to the jurisdiction of the U.S. court. First, as he was sentencing a co-conspirator in the scheme, the American judge assigned to their trial commented that those fugitives who did not cooperate would get the "absolute maximum jail sentence." Then, the prosecuting attorney hinted during a television interview that uncooperative fugitives would be subject to homosexual rape in prison:

   > Zubrod [prosecutor]: I have told some of these individuals, "Look, you can come down and you can put this behind you by serving your time in prison and making restitution to the victims, or you can wind up serving a great deal longer sentence under much more stringent conditions," and describe those conditions to them.
   >
   > MacIntyre [reporter]: How would you describe those conditions?
   >
   > Zubrod: *You're going to be the boyfriend of a very bad man if you wait out your extradition.*
   >
   > MacIntyre: And does that have much of an impact on these people?
   >
   > Zubrod: Well, out of the 89 people we've indicted so far, approximately 55 of them have said, "We give up."

   After reading the transcripts, the Supreme Court of Canada held: "The pressures were not only inappropriate but also, in the case of the statements made by the prosecutor on the eve of the opening of the judicial hearing in Canada, unequivocally amounted to an abuse of the process of the court. We do not condone the threat of sexual violence as a means for one party before the court to persuade any opponent to abandon his or her right to a hearing. Nor should we expect litigants to overcome well-founded fears of violent reprisals in order to be participants in a judicial process. Aside from such intimidation itself, it is plain that a committal order requiring a fugitive to return to face such an ominous climate—which was created by those who would play a large, if not decisive role in determining the fugitive's ultimate fate—would not be consistent with the principles of fundamental justice." *USA v. Cobb*, 1 S.C.R. 587 (2001). (Thanks to Craig Jones, a student, for bringing this matter to my attention.)

9. John Langbein, *Torture and the Law of Proof* (Chicago: University of Chicago Press, 1977), p. 68. Voltaire generally opposed torture but favored it in some cases.

10. A special edition of the *Israel Law Review* in 1989 presented a written symposium on the report on the Landau Commission, which investigated interrogation practices of Israel's General Security Services from 1987 to 1989.

11. A fifth approach would be simply to never discuss the issue of torture—or to postpone any such discussion until after we actually experience a ticking bomb case—but I have always believed that it is preferable to consider and discuss tragic choices before we confront them, so that the issue can be debated without recriminatory emotions and after-the-fact finger-pointing.

12. "The Supreme Court of Israel left the security services a tiny window of opportunity in extreme cases. Citing the traditional common-law defense of necessity, the Supreme Court left open the possibility that a member of the security service who honestly believed that rough interrogation was the only means available to save lives in imminent danger could raise this defense. This leaves each individual member of the security services in the position of having to guess how a court would ultimately resolve his case. That is extremely unfair to such investigators. It would have been far better had the court required any investigator who believed that torture was necessary in order to save lives to apply to a judge. The judge would then be in a position either to authorize or refuse to authorize a 'torture warrant.' Such a procedure would require judges to dirty their hands by authorizing torture warrants or bear the responsibility for failing to do so. Individual interrogators should not have to place their liberty at risk by guessing how a court might ultimately decide a close case. They should be able to get an advance ruling based on the evidence available at the time.

"Perhaps the legislature will create a procedure for advance judicial scrutiny. This would be akin to the warrant requirement in the Fourth Amendment to the United States Constitution. It is a traditional role for judges to play, since it is the job of the judiciary to balance the needs for security against the imperatives of liberty. Interrogators from the security service are not trained to strike such a delicate balance. Their mission is single-minded: to prevent terrorism. Similarly, the mission of civil liberties lawyers who oppose torture is single-minded: to vindicate the individual rights of suspected terrorists. It is the role of the court to strike the appropriate balance. The Supreme Court of Israel took a giant step in the direction of striking that balance. But it—or the legislature—should take the further step of requiring the judiciary to assume responsibility in individual cases. The essence of a democracy is placing responsibility for difficult choices in a visible and neutral institution like the judiciary." Dershowitz, *Shouting Fire*, pp. 476–77.

13. Charles M. Sennott, "Israeli High Court Bans Torture in Questioning; 10,000 Palestinians Subjected to Tactics," *Boston Globe*, 9/7/1999.

14. Osama Awadallah, a green-card holder living in San Diego, has made various charges of torture, abuse, and denial of access to a lawyer. Shira Scheindlin, a federal district court judge in New York, has confirmed the seriousness and credibility of the charges, saying Awadallah may have been "unlawfully arrested, unlawfully searched, abused by law enforcement officials, denied access to his lawyer and family." Lewis, "Taking Our Liberties."

15. Drogin and Miller, "Spy Agencies Facing Questions of Tactics." Philip Heymann is the only person I have debated thus far who is willing to take the position that no form of torture should ever be permitted—or used—even if thousands of lives could be saved by its use. Philip B. Heymann, "Torture Should Not Be Authorized," *Boston Globe*, 2/16/2002. Whether he would act on that principled view if he were the responsible government official who was authorized to make this life and death choice—as distinguished from an academic with the luxury of expressing views without being accountable for their consequences—is a more difficult question. He has told me that he probably would authorize torture in an actual ticking bomb case, but that it would be wrong and he would expect to be punished for it.

16. Suzanne Daley, "France Is Seeking a Fine in Trial of Algerian War General," *New York Times*, 11/29/2001.

17. The necessity defense is designed to allow interstitial action to be taken in the absence of any governing law and in the absence of time to change the law. It is for the nonrecurring situation that was never anticipated by the law. The use of torture in the ticking bomb case has been debated for decades. It can surely be anticipated. See Dershowitz, *Shouting Fire*, pp. 474–76.

    Indeed, there is already one case in our jurisprudence in which this has occurred and the courts have considered it. In the 1984 case of *Leon v. Wainwright*, Jean Leon and an accomplice kidnapped a taxicab driver and held him for ransom. Leon was arrested while trying to collect the ransom but refused to disclose where he was holding the victim. At this point, several police officers threatened him and then twisted his arm behind his back and choked him until he told them the victim's whereabouts. Although the federal appellate court disclaimed any wish to "sanction the use of force and coercion by police officers," the judges went out of their way to state that this was not the act of "brutal law enforcement agents trying to obtain a confession." "This was instead a group of concerned officers acting in a reasonable manner to obtain information they needed in order to protect another individual from bodily harm or death." Although the court did not find it necessary to invoke the "necessity defense," since no charges were brought against the policemen who tortured the kidnapper, it described the torture as having been "motivated by the immediate *necessity* to find the victim and save his life."

Leon v. *Wainwright*, 734 F.2d 770, 772–73 (11th Circuit 1984) (emphasis added). If an appellate court would so regard the use of police brutality—torture—in a case involving one kidnap victim, it is not difficult to extrapolate to a situation in which hundreds or thousands of lives might hang in the balance.

18. Quoted in Twining and Twining, "Bentham on Torture," p. 345.

19. For an elaboration of this view, see Dershowitz, *Shouting Fire*, pp. 97–99.

20. The pilot who would have been responsible for shooting down the hijacked plane heading from Pennsylvania to Washington, D.C., on September 11, 2001, has praised the passengers who apparently struggled with the hijackers, causing the plane to crash. These brave passengers spared him the dreadful task of shooting down a plane full of fellow Americans. The stakes are different when it comes to torturing enemy terrorists.

21. Sir Edward Coke was "designated in commissions to examine particular suspects under torture." Langbein, *Torture and the Law of Proof*, p. 73.

22. Ibid., p. 7.

23. Ibid., p. 90, quoting Bacon.

24. Din Rodef, or Law of the Pursuer, refers to the halachic principle that one may kill a person who is threatening someone else's life. This rule was set forth in the twelfth century by Moses Maimonides, a great Talmudic scholar.

25. Langbein, *Torture and the Law of Proof*, pp. 136–37, 139.

26. When it is known that torture is a possible option, terrorists sometimes provide the information and then claim they have been tortured, in order to be able to justify their complicity to their colleagues.

♔ REVIEW QUESTIONS

1. Dershowitz discusses three cases in which torture can be justified. What are they?

2. According to Dershowitz, what is the strongest argument against any resort to torture? How does he reply?

3. Explain Dershowitz's argument from analogy for torturing a ticking-bomb terrorist.

4. In what four ways can a state respond to terrorism, according to Dershowitz? Why does he reject forgoing any use of torture?

5. What are the important values involved in the debate about allowing torture, according to Dershowitz? Why does he not object to secret torturing by the state?

6. Explain Dershowitz's proposal for torture warrants. Why does he think they will decrease the amount of violence directed at suspects and protect their rights?

1. Does rule utilitarianism provide a good argument for the absolute prohibition of torture? Why or why not?
2. Would you torture a baby to death if this would make all men happy? Explain your answer.
3. Would torture be justified to prevent the 9/11 attacks? What does Dershowitz say? What do you think?
4. Are torture warrants a good idea? Why or why not?

Liberalism, Torture and the Ticking Bomb

DAVID LUBAN

For biographical information on David Luban, see his reading in Chapter 9.

Luban attacks what he calls the liberal ideology of torture, which on its surface seems to respect human rights and prohibit torture, but at a deeper level accepts torture in hypothetical ticking-bomb cases and ends up creating a torture culture. In Luban's view, the ticking-bomb story rests on so many assumptions that it amounts to an intellectual fraud. The story unrealistically assumes that the authorities know there is a bomb, that they have captured the man who planted it, that the man will talk when tortured, that lives will be saved, and so on. But this is all uncertain in the real world. We are asked to decide between the certainty of cruel torture and the mere possibility of saving lives, by totting up costs and benefits.

Trying to make a decision in the ticking-bomb case is just a mistake. The wise course is to deny that it is possible or at least so unlikely that trying to make a decision is insane and frivolous. Furthermore, once we grant the permissibility of torture in a hypothetical case, we end up in the real world with a torture culture that includes trained torturers and prisons like Abu Ghraib.

INTRODUCTION

Torture used to be incompatible with American values. Our Bill of Rights forbids cruel and unusual punishment, and that has come to include all forms of corporal punishment except prison and death by methods purported to be painless. Americans and our government have historically condemned states that torture; we have granted asylum or refuge to those who fear it. The Senate ratified the Convention Against Torture, Congress enacted anti-torture legislation, and judicial opinions spoke of "the dastardly and totally inhuman act of torture."

Then came September 11. Less than one week later, a feature story reported that a quiz in a university ethics class "gave four choices for the proper U.S. response to the terrorist attacks: A.) execute the perpetrators on sight; B.) bring them back for trial in the United States; C.) subject the perpetrators to an international tribunal; or D.) torture and interrogate those involved." Most students chose A and D—execute them on sight and torture them. Six weeks after September 11, the press reported that frustrated FBI interrogators were considering harsh interrogation tactics; a few weeks after that, the *New York Times* reported that torture had become a topic of conversation "in bars, on commuter trains, and at dinner tables." By mid-November 2001, the *Christian Science Monitor* found that thirty-two percent of surveyed Americans favored torturing terror suspects. Alan Dershowitz reported

Source: "Liberalism, Torture and the Ticking Bomb" by David Luban from VIRGINIA LAW REVIEW, October 2005. Reprinted by permission of Virginia Law Review via Copyright Clearance Center.

in 2002 that "[d]uring numerous public appearances since September 11, 2001, I have asked audiences for a show of hands as to how many would support the use of nonlethal torture in a ticking-bomb case. Virtually every hand is raised." American abhorrence to torture now appears to have extraordinarily shallow roots.

To an important extent, one's stance on torture runs independent of progressive or conservative ideology. Alan Dershowitz suggests that torture should be regulated by a judicial warrant requirement. Liberal Senator Charles Schumer has publicly rejected the idea "that torture should never, ever be used." He argues that most U.S. senators would back torture to find out where a ticking time bomb is planted. By contrast, William Safire, a self-described "conservative . . . and card-carrying hard-liner," expresses revulsion at "phony-tough" pro-torture arguments, and forthrightly labels torture "barbarism." Examples like these illustrate how vital it is to avoid a simple left-right reductionism. For the most part, American conservatives belong no less than progressives to liberal culture, broadly understood. Henceforth, when I speak of "liberalism," I mean it in the broad sense used by political philosophers from John Stuart Mill on, a sense that includes conservatives as well as progressives, so long as they believe in limited government and the importance of human dignity and individual rights. . . .

On its surface, liberal reverence for individual rights makes torture morally unacceptable; at a deeper level, the same liberal ideas seemingly can justify interrogational torture in the face of danger. These ideas allow us to construct a liberal ideology of torture, by which liberals reassure themselves that essential interrogational torture is detached from its illiberal roots. The liberal ideology of torture is expressed perfectly in so-called "ticking-bomb hypotheticals" designed to show that even perfectly compassionate liberals (like Senator Schumer) might justify torture to find the ticking bomb.

I will criticize the liberal ideology of torture and suggest that ticking-bomb stories are built on a set of assumptions that amount to intellectual fraud. Ticking-bomb stories depict torture as

an emergency exception, but use intuitions based on the exceptional case to justify institutionalized practices and procedures of torture. In short, the ticking bomb begins by denying that torture belongs to liberal culture, and ends by constructing a torture culture. . . .

THE TICKING BOMB

Suppose the bomb is planted somewhere in the crowded heart of an American city, and you have custody of the man who planted it. He won't talk. Surely, the hypothetical suggests, we shouldn't be too squeamish to torture the information out of him and save hundreds of lives. Consequences count, and abstract moral prohibitions must yield to the calculus of consequences.

Everyone argues the pros and cons of torture through the ticking time bomb. Senator Schumer and Professor Dershowitz, the Israeli Supreme Court and indeed every journalist devoting a think-piece to the unpleasant question of torture, begins with the ticking time bomb and ends there as well. The Schlesinger Report on Abu Ghraib notes that "[f]or the U.S., most cases for permitting harsh treatment of detainees on moral grounds begin with variants of the 'ticking time-bomb' scenario." At this point in my argument, I mean to disarm the ticking time bomb and argue that it is the wrong thing to think about. If so, then the liberal ideology of torture begins to unravel.

But before beginning these arguments, I want to pause and ask why this jejune example has become the alpha and omega of our thinking about torture. I believe the answer is this: The ticking time bomb is proffered against liberals who believe in an absolute prohibition against torture. The idea is to force the liberal prohibitionist to admit that yes, even he or even she would agree to torture in at least this one situation. Once the prohibitionist admits that, then she has conceded that her opposition to torture is not based on principle. Now that the prohibitionist has admitted that her moral principles can be breached, all that is left is haggling about the price. No longer can the prohibitionist claim the moral high ground; no longer can she put the burden of proof on her opponent. She is down in the mud with them, and the only question left is how much further down she will go. Dialectically, getting the prohibitionist to address the ticking time bomb is like getting the vegetarian to eat just one little oyster because it has no nervous system. Once she does that—*gotcha!*

The ticking time-bomb scenario serves a second rhetorical goal, one that is equally important to the proponent of torture. It makes us see the torturer in a different light—one of the essential points in the liberal ideology of torture because it is the way that liberals can reconcile themselves to torture even while continuing to "put cruelty first." Now, he is not a cruel man or a sadistic man or a coarse, insensitive brutish man. The torturer is instead a conscientious public servant, heroic the way that New York firefighters were heroic, willing to do desperate things only because the plight is so desperate and so many innocent lives are weighing on the public servant's conscience. The time bomb clinches the great divorce between torture and cruelty; it placates liberals, who put cruelty first.

Wittgenstein once wrote that confusion arises when we become bewitched by a picture. He meant that it's easy to get seduced by simplistic examples that look compelling but actually misrepresent the world in which we live. If the subject is the morality of torture, philosophical confusions can have life-or-death consequences. I believe the ticking time bomb is the picture that bewitches us.

I don't mean that the time-bomb scenario is completely unreal. To take a real-life counterpart: in 1995, an al Qaeda plot to bomb eleven U.S. airliners and assassinate the Pope was thwarted by information tortured out of a Pakistani bomb-maker by the Philippine police. According to journalists Marites Dañguilan Vitug and Glenda M. Gloria, the police had received word of possible threats against the Pope. They went to work. "For weeks, agents hit him with a chair and a long piece of wood, forced water into his mouth, and crushed lighted cigarettes into his private parts. . . . His ribs were almost totally broken that his captors were surprised that

he survived. . . . Grisly, to be sure—but if they hadn't done it, thousands of innocent travelers might have died horrible deaths.

But look at the example one more time. The Philippine agents were surprised he survived—in other words, they came close to torturing him to death *before* he talked. And they tortured him *for weeks*, during which time they didn't know about any specific al Qaeda plot. What if he too didn't know? Or what if there had been no al Qaeda plot? Then they would have tortured him for weeks, possibly tortured him to death, for nothing. For all they knew at the time, that is exactly what they were doing. You cannot use the argument that preventing the al Qaeda attack justified the decision to torture, because *at the moment the decision was made* no one knew about the al Qaeda attack.

The ticking-bomb scenario cheats its way around these difficulties by stipulating that the bomb is there, ticking away, and that officials know it and know they have the man who planted it. Those conditions will seldom be met. Let us try some more realistic hypotheticals and the questions they raise:

1. The authorities know there may be a bomb plot in the offing, and they have captured a man who may know something about it, but may not. Torture him? How much? For weeks? For months? The chances are considerable that you are torturing a man with nothing to tell you. If he doesn't talk, does that mean it's time to stop, or time to ramp up the level of torture? How likely does it have to be that he knows something important? Fifty-fifty? Thirty-seventy? Will one out of a hundred suffice to land him on the waterboard?

2. Do you really want to make the torture decision by running the numbers? A one-percent chance of saving a thousand lives yields ten statistical lives. Does that mean that you can torture up to nine people on a one-percent chance of finding crucial information?

3. The authorities think that one out of a group of fifty captives in Guantanamo might know where Osama bin Laden is hiding, but they do not know which captive. Torture them all? That is: Do you torture forty-nine captives with

nothing to tell you on the uncertain chance of capturing bin Laden?

4. For that matter, would capturing Osama bin Laden demonstrably save a single human life? The Bush administration has downplayed the importance of capturing bin Laden because American strategy has succeeded in marginalizing him. Maybe capturing him would save lives, but how certain do you have to be? Or does it not matter whether torture is intended to save human lives from a specific threat, as long as it furthers some goal in the War on Terror? This last question is especially important once we realize that the interrogation of al Qaeda suspects will almost never be employed to find out where the ticking bomb is hidden. Instead, interrogation is a more general fishing expedition for any intelligence that might be used to help "unwind" the terrorist organization. Now one might reply that al Qaeda is itself the ticking time bomb, so that unwinding the organization meets the formal conditions of the ticking-bomb hypothetical. This is equivalent to asserting that any intelligence that promotes victory in the War on Terror justifies torture, precisely because we understand that the enemy in the War on Terror aims to kill American civilians. Presumably, on this argument, Japan would have been justified in torturing American captives in World War II on the chance of finding intelligence that would help them shoot down the Enola Gay; I assume that a ticking-bomb hardliner will not flinch from this conclusion. But at this point, we verge on declaring all military threats and adversaries that menace American civilians to be ticking bombs whose defeat justifies torture. The limitation of torture to emergency exceptions, implicit in the ticking-bomb story, now threatens to unravel, making torture a legitimate instrument of military policy. And then the question becomes inevitable: Why not torture in pursuit of any worthwhile goal?

5. Indeed, if you are willing to torture forty-nine innocent people to get information from the one who has it, why stop there? If suspects will not break under torture, why not torture their loved ones in front of them? They are no more innocent than the forty-nine you have already shown you are prepared to torture. In fact, if only the numbers matter, torturing loved ones is almost a no-brainer if you think it will work. Of course, you won't know until you try whether torturing his child will break the suspect. But that just changes the odds; it does not alter the argument.

The point of the examples is that in a world of uncertainty and imperfect knowledge, the ticking-bomb scenario should not form the point of reference. The ticking bomb is the picture that bewitches us. The real debate is not between one guilty man's pain and hundreds of innocent lives. It is the debate between the certainty of anguish and the mere possibility of learning something vital and saving lives. And, above all, it is the question about whether a responsible citizen must unblinkingly think the unthinkable and accept that the morality of torture should be decided purely by totaling up costs and benefits. Once you accept that only the numbers count, then anything, no matter how gruesome, becomes possible. "Consequentialist rationality," as Bernard Williams notes sardonically, "will have something to say even on the difference between massacring seven million, and massacring seven million and one."

I am inclined to think that the path of wisdom instead lies in Holocaust survivor David Rousset's famous caution that normal human beings do *not* know that everything is possible. As Williams says, "there are certain situations so monstrous that the idea that the processes of moral rationality could yield an answer in them is insane" and "to spend time thinking what one would decide if one were in such a situation is also insane, if not merely frivolous."

TORTURE AS A PRACTICE

There is a second, insidious, error built into the ticking-bomb hypothetical. It assumes a single, ad hoc decision about whether to torture, by officials who ordinarily would do no such thing except in a desperate emergency. But in the real world of interrogations, decisions are not made on-off. The real world is a world of policies, guidelines, and directives. It is a world of *practices*, not of ad hoc emergency measures. Therefore, any responsible discussion of torture must address the practice of torture, not the ticking-bomb hypothetical. I am not saying anything original here; other writers have made exactly this point. But somehow, we always manage to forget this and circle back to the ticking time bomb. Its rhetorical power has made it indispensable to the sensitive liberal soul, and we would much rather talk about the ticking bomb than about torture as an organized social practice.

Treating torture as a practice rather than as a desperate improvisation in an emergency means changing the subject from the ticking bomb to other issues like these: Should we create a professional cadre of trained torturers? That means a group of interrogators who know the techniques, who learn to overcome their instinctive revulsion against causing physical pain, and who acquire the legendary surgeon's arrogance about their own infallibility. It has happened before. Medieval executioners were schooled in the arts of agony as part of the trade: how to break men on the wheel, how to rack them, and even how to surreptitiously strangle them as an act of mercy without the bloodthirsty crowd catching on. In Louis XVI's Paris, torture was a hereditary family trade whose tricks were passed on from father to son. Who will teach torture techniques now? Should universities create an undergraduate course in torture? Or should the subject be offered only in police and military academies? Do we want federal grants for research to devise new and better techniques? Patents issued on high-tech torture devices? Companies competing to manufacture them? Trade conventions in Las Vegas? Should there be a medical sub-specialty of torture doctors, who ensure that captives do not die before they talk? The questions amount to this: Do we really want to create a torture culture and the kind of people who inhabit it? The ticking time bomb distracts us from the real issue, which is not about emergencies, but about the normalization of torture.

Perhaps the solution is to keep the practice of torture secret in order to avoid the moral corruption that comes from creating a public culture of torture. But this so-called "solution" does not reject the normalization of torture. It accepts it, but layers on top of it the normalization of state secrecy. The result would be a shadow culture of torturers and those who train and support them, operating outside the public eye and accountable only to other insiders of the torture culture.

Just as importantly: Who guarantees that casehardened torturers, inured to levels of violence and pain that would make ordinary people vomit at the sight, will know where to draw the line on when torture should be used? They rarely have in the past. They didn't in Algeria. They didn't in Israel, where in 1999, the Israeli Supreme Court backpedaled from an earlier consent to torture lite because the interrogators were running amok and torturing two-thirds of their Palestinian captives. In the Argentinian Dirty War, the tortures began because terrorist cells had a policy of fleeing when one of their members had disappeared for forty-eight hours, leaving authorities two days to wring the information out of the captive. Mark Osiel, who has studied the Argentinean military in the Dirty War, reports that many of the torturers initially had qualms about what they were doing, until their priests reassured them that they were fighting God's fight. By the end of the Dirty War, the qualms were gone, and, as John Simpson and Jana Bennett report, hardened young officers were placing bets on who could kidnap the prettiest girl to rape and torture. Escalation is the rule, not the aberration.

There are two fundamental reasons for this: one rooted in the nature of bureaucracy and the other in social psychology. The liberal ideology of torture presupposes a torturer impelled by the desire to stop a looming catastrophe, not by cruelty. Implicitly, this image presumes that the interrogator and the decisionmaker are the same person. But the defining fact about real organizations is the division of labor. The person who decides whether this prisoner presents a genuine ticking-bomb case is not the interrogator. The decision about what counts as a ticking-bomb case—one where torture is the lesser evil—depends on complex value judgments, and these are made further up the chain of command. The interrogator simply executes decisions made elsewhere.

Interrogators do not inhabit a world of loving kindness, or of equal concern and respect for all human beings. Interrogating resistant prisoners non-violently and non-abusively still requires a relationship that in any other context would be morally abhorrent. It requires tricking information out of the subject, and the interrogator does this by setting up elaborate scenarios to disorient the subject and propel him into an alternative reality. The subject must be deceived into thinking that his high-value intelligence has already been revealed by someone else, so that it is no longer of any value. He must be fooled into thinking that his friends have betrayed him or that the interrogator is his friend. The interrogator disrupts his sense of time and place, disorients him with sessions that never take place at predictable times or intervals, and manipulates his emotions. The very names of interrogation techniques show this: "Emotional Love," "Emotional Hate," "Fear Up Harsh," "Fear Up Mild," "Reduced Fear," "Pride and Ego Up," "Pride and Ego Down," "Futility." The interrogator may set up a scenario to make the subject think he is in the clutches of a much-feared secret police organization from a different country ("False Flag"). Every bit of the subject's environment is fair game for manipulation and deception, as the interrogator aims to create the total lie that gets the subject talking.

Let me be clear that I am not objecting to these deceptions. None of these practices rises to the level of abuse or torture lite, let alone torture heavy, and surely tricking the subject into talking is legitimate if the goals of the interrogation are legitimate. But what I have described is a relationship of totalitarian mind-control more profound than the world of Orwell's *1984*. The interrogator is like Descartes' Evil Deceiver, and the subject lives in a false reality reminiscent of *The Matrix*. The liberal fiction that interrogation can be done by people who are neither cruel nor tyrannical runs aground on the fact that regardless of the interrogator's character off the job, on the job, every fiber of his concentration is devoted to dominating the mind of the subject.

Only one thing prevents this from turning into abuse and torture, and that is a clear set of bright-line rules, drummed into the interrogator

with the intensity of a religious indoctrination, complete with warnings of fire and brimstone. American interrogator Chris Mackey reports that warnings about the dire consequences of violating the Geneva Conventions "were repeated so often that by the end of our time at [training school] the three syllables 'Leaven-worth' were ringing in our ears."

But what happens when the line is breached? When, as in Afghanistan, the interrogator gets mixed messages about whether Geneva applies, or hears rumors of ghost detainees, of high-value captives held for years of interrogation in the top-secret facility known as "Hotel California," located in some nation somewhere? Or when the interrogator observes around him the move from deception to abuse, from abuse to torture lite, from torture lite to beatings and waterboarding? Without clear lines, the tyranny innate in the interrogator's job has nothing to hold it in check. Perhaps someone, somewhere in the chain of command, is wringing hands over whether this interrogation qualifies as a ticking-bomb case; but the interrogator knows only that the rules of the road have changed and the posted speed limits no longer apply. The liberal fiction of the conscientious interrogator overlooks a division of moral labor in which the person with the fastidious conscience and the person doing the interrogation are not the same.

The fiction must presume, therefore, that the interrogator operates only under the strictest supervision, in a chain of command where his every move gets vetted and controlled by the superiors who are actually doing the deliberating. The trouble is that this assumption flies in the face of everything that we know about how organizations work. The basic rule in every bureaucratic organization is that operational details and the guilty knowledge that goes with them get pushed down the chain of command as far as possible. As sociologist Robert Jackall explains,

[i]t is characteristic . . . that details are pushed down and credit is pulled up. Superiors do not like to give detailed instructions to subordinates. . . . [O]ne of the privileges of authority is the divestment of humdrum intricacies.

. . . Perhaps more important, pushing details down protects the privilege of authority to declare that a mistake has been made. . . . Moreover, pushing down details relieves superiors of the burden of too much knowledge, particularly guilty knowledge.

We saw this phenomenon at Abu Ghraib, where military intelligence officers gave military police vague orders like: "'Loosen this guy up for us.' 'Make sure he has a bad night.' 'Make sure he gets the treatment.'" Suppose that the eighteen-year-old guard interprets "[m]ake sure he has a bad night" to mean, simply, "keep him awake all night." How do you do that without physical abuse? Furthermore, personnel at Abu Ghraib witnessed far harsher treatment of prisoners by "other governmental agencies" (OGA), a euphemism for the Central Intelligence Agency. They saw OGA spirit away the dead body of an interrogation subject, and allegedly witnessed a contract employee rape a youthful prisoner. When that is what you see, abuses like those in the Abu Ghraib photos will not look outrageous. Outrageous compared with what?

This brings me to the point of social psychology. Simply stated, it is this: we judge right and wrong against the baseline of whatever we have come to consider "normal" behavior, and if the norm shifts in the direction of violence, we will come to tolerate and accept violence as a normal response. The psychological mechanisms for this re-normalization have been studied for more than half a century, and by now they are reasonably well understood. Rather than detour into psychological theory, however, I will illustrate the point with the most salient example—one that seems so obviously applicable to Abu Ghraib that the Schlesinger Commission discussed it at length in an appendix to its report. This is the famous Stanford Prison Experiment. Male volunteers were divided randomly into two groups who would simulate the guards and inmates in a mock prison. Within a matter of days, the inmates began acting like actual prison inmates—depressed, enraged, and anxious. And the guards began to abuse the inmates to such an alarming degree that the researchers had to halt the two-week experiment after just seven days. In the words of the experimenters:

The use of power was self-aggrandising and self-perpetuating. The guard power, derived initially from an arbitrary label, was intensified whenever there was any perceived threat by the prisoners and this new level subsequently became the baseline from which further hostility and harassment would begin. . . . [T]he absolute level of aggression as well as the more subtle and "creative" forms of aggression manifested, increased in a spiralling function.

It took only five days before a guard, who prior to the experiment described himself as a pacifist, was forcing greasy sausages down the throat of a prisoner who refused to eat; and in less than a week, the guards were placing bags over prisoners' heads, making them strip, and sexually humiliating them in ways reminiscent of Abu Ghraib.

My conclusion is very simple. Abu Ghraib is the fully predictable image of what a torture culture looks like. Abu Ghraib is not a few bad apples—it is the apple tree. And you cannot reasonably expect that interrogators in a torture culture will be the fastidious and well-meaning torturers that the liberal ideology fantasizes.

This is why Alan Dershowitz has argued that judges, not torturers, should oversee the permission to torture, which in his view must be regulated by warrants. The irony is that Jay S. Bybee, who signed the Justice Department's highly permissive torture memo, is now a federal judge. Politicians pick judges, and if the politicians accept torture, the judges will as well. Once we create a torture culture, only the naive would suppose that judges will provide a safeguard. Judges do not fight their culture—they reflect it.

For all these reasons, the ticking-bomb scenario is an intellectual fraud. In its place, we must address the real questions about torture—questions about uncertainty, questions about the morality of consequences, and questions about what it does to a culture and the torturers themselves to introduce the practice. Once we do so, I suspect that few Americans will be willing to accept that everything is possible.

✿ REVIEW QUESTIONS

1. What happened to the American view of torture after 9/11, according to Luban?
2. How does Luban define "liberalism"? Who is a liberal on his definition?
3. Explain Luban's view of the "liberal ideology of torture."
4. What is the basic ticking-bomb story? According to Luban, what assumptions does the story make? What questions are left unanswered?
5. Besides being unrealistic, what second error is built into the ticking-bomb story?
6. What is Luban's point about the Stanford Prison Experiment?

✿ DISCUSSION QUESTIONS

1. Does the ticking-bomb story amount to intellectual fraud, as Luban says? Or does it describe a situation that could actually happen? What is your view?
2. Should we train professional torturers so that we will be able to effectively torture terrorists to get information about possible or actual attacks?

Torture—The Case for Dirty Harry and against Alan Dershowitz

UWE STEINHOFF

Uwe Steinhoff is Senior Associate in the Oxford University Leverhulme Programme on the Changing Character of War. He is the author of *On the Ethics of War and Terrorism* (2007).

Steinhoff begins with an attack on the absolute moral prohibition of torture. He argues that there are two cases in which interrogative torture is morally justified. First, there is the Dirty Harry case: Harry saves an innocent girl's life by torturing the guilty kidnapper. Second, there is the ticking-bomb case. Steinhoff's view is in sharp contrast to Luban's position. Steinhoff argues that interrogative torture of a terrorist is morally justified even if we are not certain about the reliability of the information or sure that we have the right person. It is morally justified even if the terrorist has not planted the bomb and does not know where it is. In Steinhoff's view, there is no relevant moral difference between shooting a man who seems ready to shoot the president and torturing a terrorist who might have planted a bomb. However, just because torture is morally justified in these rare cases does not mean that it should be legal. It can be excused in the rare cases even if it is illegal. Steinhoff goes on to critically examine Alan Dershowitz's proposal to make torture legal by introducing legal torture warrants. Steinhoff thinks this is a bad idea. We do not need torture warrants because the cases in which torture is morally justified are rare. Also, the institutionalizing of torture with torture warrants undermines the general prohibition of torture and leads to a brutalization of the enforcer.

Consider the Dirty Harry case. In the Don Siegel movie *Dirty Harry* someone kidnaps a female child and puts her in a place where she will suffocate if not rescued in time. There is not much time left, according to the very claims of the kidnapper. The police officer Harry

(Clint Eastwood) is to deliver the ransom to the kidnapper. When they finally meet at night in a park, the kidnapper knocks Harry down with his gun and tells him that he will let the girl die anyway. He also tells Harry that he wants him to know that before he kills him too. In the moment he is about to shoot Harry, who lies defenceless and badly beaten to his feet, Harry's partner interferes (and is shot). The kidnapper can escape, wounded. Harry pursues him. Finally he corners him, and the kidnapper raises his arms to surrender. Harry shoots him in the leg. The kidnapper is frightened to death, tells Harry not to kill him and that he has rights. Harry asks him where the girl is. The kidnapper talks only about his rights. Harry sees the kidnapper's leg wound and puts his foot on it, torturing the kidnapper. The camera retreats. In the next scene, the girl is saved.

The Dirty Harry case, it seems to me, is a case of morally justified torture. But isn't the kidnapper right? Does not even he have rights? Yes, he has, but in these circumstances he does not have the right not to be tortured. Again, the situation is analogous to self-defence. The aggressor does not lose all of his rights, but his right to life weighs less than the innocent defender's right to life. The aggressor culpably brings about a situation where one of the two—he or the defender—will die. It is only just and fair that the harm that will befall in this situation upon one of the two is diverted to the person who is responsible for the harm—the aggressor. In the Dirty Harry case, the kidnapper brings about a situation where a person is tortured or will continue to be tortured until death (being slowly suffocated in a small hole *is* torture). It is only just and fair that this harm befalls the person responsible for the situation—the kidnapper. Moreover, the choice is made even easier by the fact that being tortured for a small period of time is better than being tortured until death. Harry made the right decision.

Two replies might be made at this point. The first one—repeated like a litany by certain opponents of torture—is that interrogative torture simply does not work. That, however, is simply wrong. Sometimes interrogative torture does work, and the torturer gets the information he was looking for.[1]

Well, one might say, but at least interrogative torture is not very reliable. Apart from the fact that even that is not so clear, it would not even help. Consider the following case: An innocent person is being attacked by an aggressor, who fires a deadly weapon at him (and misses him at first but keeps firing). The attacked person's only possibility to save his life is by using the One-Million-Pains-To-One-Kill-Gun that he happens to have with him. On average, you have to pull the trigger of this gun one million times in order to have one immediately incapacitating projectile come out of it (it incapacitates through the infliction of unbearable pain). All the other times it fires projectiles that only ten seconds after hitting a human target cause the target unbearable pain. Thus, firing this gun at the aggressor will certainly cause the aggressor unbearable pain, but the probability that it will save the life of the defender is only 1:1,000,000. I must admit that I cannot even begin to make sense of the suggestion that, given these odds, the defender should not use the gun against the aggressor. Yes, the pain inflicted by the weapon on the aggressor is extremely unlikely to secure the survival of the defender, but there still *is* a chance that it will, so why should the *defender* forgo this chance for the benefit of the *aggressor*? Obviously, there is no reason (at least none that I could see). Again, the application to the torture of ticking bomb terrorists and Dirty Harry kidnappers is obvious.

What is the second reply? Richard H. Weisberg takes issue with the example of the ticking bomb case:

> . . . the hypothetical itself lacks the virtues of intelligence, appropriateness, and especially sophistication. Here, as in *The Brothers Karamazov*—*pace* Sandy Levinson—it is the complex rationalizers who wind up being more naive than those who speak strictly, directly, and simply against injustice. 'You can't know whether a person knows where the bomb is', explains Cole in a recent piece in the *Nation*, 'or even if they're telling the truth. Because of this, you wind up sanctioning torture in general'.[2]

To begin with, by allowing torture in the ticking bomb case one does *not* necessarily wind up sanctioning it in general. Killing (of certain people) is sanctioned in war but not in general. The actual second reply I was referring to, however, is *that you do not know whether you have the right person.* (That you do not know whether the person speaks the truth is simply the first reply. We have already dealt with it.) But what does it mean: 'You don't know'? Does it mean you do not know for certain? If not knowing for certain whether you have the right person would be sufficient reason not to harm that person, we would not only have to abstain from self-defence but also from punishment. You *never* know for certain!

Take the example of a man who draws a gun in front of a head of states and aims at him. The bodyguards simply cannot know (for certain) whether this person wants to shoot, they cannot even know whether it is a real gun. Maybe the 'attacker' is only a retard with a water pistol. So the bodyguards of the head of state (whom we want to assume innocent) should not shoot at such a person who, for all they *can* know, seems to be attacking the person they are to protect? Actually, if shooting (and probably killing) him is the only way to make sure that he is not able to pull the trigger, they *should* shoot him.

One might say that this person, even if he does not really want to shoot and has no real gun, at least *feigns* an attack, and this makes him liable to counter-attack. Whoever credibly feigns an attack on another person cannot later, after having suffered from severe countermeasures, complain that he 'only' feigned it. He shouldn't have feigned it at all. We can, however, have a comparable situation with a terrorist. If a person says to other persons that he is going to build a powerful bomb to blow up a kindergarten and has the necessary skills and buys the necessary chemicals, he had better not, when the security service storms his hideout where he is surrounded by his bomb-making equipment, sneeringly say: 'You are too late. I have already planted the bomb. It will go off in 12 hours and kill hundreds of children'. If he then is tortured by the security service, which wants to find out where the bomb is, he is not, it seems, in a particularly good position to complain about that *even if he has not planted a bomb.*[3] Moreover, even if a real or supposed terrorist has

not made that particularly threatening statement, hanging around with the wrong people in the wrong situations can also make you liable to attack. Suppose an innocent woman is hunted by a mob. Maybe they do not like her skin colour, her ethnic group, her religion or whatever. The mob has already killed other people for the same reason. She hides with the hand grenade she fortunately has, behind a bush. Suddenly one of the group sees her, points his finger at her, shouts 'There she is', and the armed members of the group raise their guns to shoot at her. Not all members of the group have guns. Some are unarmed and shout: 'Kill her, kill her!' Others do not even shout but sneer, foaming at the mouth (I am not talking about completely innocent people, who just 'happen' to be there for no fault of their own). The only way she can save herself is to throw the grenade at the mob, which will kill all of them, including the unarmed ones. Is she justified in doing so? I would think so. Being a member of certain groups that collectively undertake aggressive acts or intentionally pose a threat to innocent people makes one liable to severe countermeasures. Consequently, a member of a terrorist group might be liable to torture in the ticking bomb case, even if he does not know were the bomb is.

It helps, by the way, very little to aver at this point that torture is simply not compatible with liberalism. David Luban, for example, claims that torture aims 'to strip away from its victim all the qualities of human dignity that liberalism prizes' and that 'torture is a microcosm, raised to the highest level of intensity, of the tyrannical political relationships that liberalism hates the most'.[4] However, prisons are also 'microcosms' of tyranny; yet, most liberals do not find them incompatible with liberalism. Where is the difference? Maybe it lies in the fact that in torture tyranny is 'raised to the highest level'. But, first, it is far from clear that one hour of torture is more tyrannical than 15 years of prison. Second, even if torture were more tyrannical than prison, and liberalism abhorred tyranny, there remained still the fact that liberalism can accommodate quite intense forms of tyranny, such as incarceration for life (or for a decade and more). Why should it not also be able to accommodate the most extreme form of tyranny? 'Because it is the most extreme form' is in itself no answer to this question.

More importantly, liberalism is not so much about 'dignity'—which is a quite elusive concept, anyway (in particular, I deny that the dignity of the culpable aggressor is violated by Dirty Harry's action any more than it would be violated by Dirty Harry's killing him in self-defence)—but about liberty. It is called liberalism, not 'dignism'. It is also not about just anybody's liberty. It is about the liberty of the innocent. This is why there is no particular problem in liberalism to kill aggressors or to deprive them of their liberty if this is the only way to protect innocent people from these aggressors. The core value of the liberal state is the protection of the liberty and the rights of *innocent* individuals against *aggressors*. The state can be such an aggressor, but the state can and must also protect against other aggressors. To keep Dirty Harry in the situation described from torturing the kidnapper, therefore, would run against the liberal state's own *raison d'être*. The state would help the aggressor, not the victim; it would help the aggressor's tyranny over the innocent and therefore actually abet the relationship it hates the most.

Since my description of the core value of liberalism, as I submit, is at least as plausible as Luban's (and I think it is historically much more plausible), the appeal to liberalism cannot help absolute opponents of torture. To claim that liberalism 'correctly understood' absolutely prohibits torture simply engages in an attempt of persuasive definition and begs the question. Besides, why could liberalism, 'correctly understood', not be wrong?

But—speaking about the innocent—what about the risk of torturing a completely *innocent* person, a person that made itself *not* liable? Yes, that risk exists, as it does in the case of punishment. In the latter case, the risk of punishing innocent persons has to be weighed against the risk of not at all punishing the non-innocent and of not at all deterring potential criminals. In the case of interrogative torture in the context of a ticking bomb situation, the risk of torturing an innocent person has to be weighed against

the risk of letting other innocent persons die in an explosion. If the weighing process in the former case can justify punishment, it is unclear why the weighing process in the latter case could not sometimes justify torture. If the odds are high enough, it does. In fact, the justification in the latter case might even be easier—easier at least than justifying capital punishment, for death, as already noted, is worse than torture (at least for most people who are confronted with a decision between their death and being tortured for a limited time). It might even be easier than justifying incarceration for one or two decades, for it is not clear that many persons would not prefer some hours or even days of torture to that alternative.

To sum up the discussion so far: A compelling argument for an absolute *moral* prohibition of torture cannot be made. Under certain circumstances torture can be justified. *Justified*, not only excused. I emphasise this because some philosophers claim that situations of so-called necessity or emergency can only *excuse* torture (and some other extreme measures). But there is nothing in the meaning of the terms 'necessity' or 'emergency' themselves that could warrant that view. For example, the German penal code distinguishes between 'justifying emergency' and 'excusing emergency'. § 34 reads:

> Whosoever, in order to avert a not otherwise avoidable present danger to life, body, freedom, honour, property, or another legally protected interest, acts so as to avert the danger to himself or others, does not act illegally if, upon consideration of the conflicting interests, namely of the threatened legally protected interests and of the degree of the threatened danger, the protected interest substantially outweighs the infringed interest. This, however, is true only if the act is an adequate [in the sense of means-end rationality ('angemessen')] means to avert the danger.[5]

He does not act illegally, and that means his act is legally justified. If the protected interests do not substantially outweigh the infringed interest, however, he can at best be excused. The moral case is not different. There can be situations where torture is an instrumentally adequate and the only means to avert a certain danger from certain morally protected interests and where the protected interests substantially outweigh the infringed ones. Therefore, if the odds are high enough, torture can be not only excused but morally justified.

No doubt, an absolutist opponent of torture will not be particularly impressed by the argument offered so far. In fact, absolutists normally (although perhaps not always) do not even try to refute the arguments adduced against their absolutist positions; they tend to just persistently and dramatically reaffirm their positions. The writer and poet Ariel Dorfman is a good example:

> I can only pray that humanity will have the courage to say no, no to torture, no to torture under any circumstance whatsoever, no to torture, no matter who the enemy, what the accusation, what sort of fear we harbor; no to torture no matter what kind of threat is posed to our safety; no to torture anytime, anywhere; no to torture anyone; no to torture.[6]

Moral absolutism is a dangerous and mistaken view. If, for example, humanity would face the choice (maybe posed by some maniac with the ultimate weapon or by an alien race, or what have you) between being exterminated or torturing one particularly bad man (let us say Idi Amin) for an hour or a day, it is far from clear why any person in his right mind—both intellectually *and* morally—should pray that humanity said 'no to torture'.[7] And what, by the way, if the choice is between all human beings (that includes children) being *tortured* by the alien race or only one particularly bad man being tortured by some humans? Consequences count; they cannot simply be ignored for the benefit of some allegedly absolute rule, especially if they might be catastrophic. *Fiat justitia, pereat mundus* is an irrational and immoral maxim.

To say it again: A compelling argument for an absolute *moral* prohibition of torture cannot be made. But what about the legal prohibition of torture? If torture can be morally justified under certain circumstances, should it also be legalised?

It could seem that torture is already legal under the German penal code. For if, as I claimed, the interests which are protected by torturing a terrorist can substantially outweigh the infringed interests (most notably of the terrorist), then torture must be legal. However, the fact that this outweighing can occur from a moral perspective does not yet mean that it can also occur from the legal perspective of a certain penal code. Each system of laws is in principle free to stipulate an *absolute* prohibition of torture. The German law does this in so far as it accepts certain international absolute prohibitions of torture as binding. That is, according to German law *nothing* can (legally) outweigh the interest of not being tortured (or at least of not being tortured by state officials or agents acting on behalf of a state). That torture is illegal under all circumstances in a given system of law, however, does not exclude the possibility that the practice might under some circumstances be excused by the law. It seems to me that it would be reasonable to excuse it under some circumstances.[8] I shall, however, say nothing further on this topic here. . . .

Instead, I shall say something about the proposal to *justify torture before the act* (rather than excusing it *ex post*). The lawyer Alan Dershowitz made the infamous suggestion to introduce legal 'torture warrants', issued by judges.

. . . it is important to ask the following question: if torture is being or will be practiced, is it worse to close our eyes to it and tolerate its use by low-level law enforcement officials without accountability, or instead to bring it to the surface by requiring that a warrant of some kind be required as a precondition to the infliction of any type of torture under any circumstances?[9]

And he states:

> My own belief is that a warrant requirement, if properly enforced, would probably reduce the frequency, severity, and duration of torture. I cannot see how it could possibly increase it, since a warrant requirement simply imposes an additional level of prior review . . . here are two examples to demonstrate why I think there would be less torture with a warrant requirement than without one. Recall the case of the alleged national security wiretap being placed on the phones of Martin Luther King by the Kennedy administration in the early 1960s. This was in the days when the attorney general could authorize a national

security wiretap without a warrant. Today no judge would issue a warrant in a case as flimsy as that one. When Zacarias Moussaoui was detained after trying to learn how to fly an airplane, without wanting to know much about landing it, the government did not even seek a national security wiretap because its lawyers believed that a judge would not have granted one.[10]

A few things must be said concerning this argument. First, closing one's eyes to the practice of torture is not the only alternative to the introduction of torture warrants. Unfortunately, Dershowitz seems to have difficulties grasping the difference between closing one's eyes on the one hand and exposing and condemning on the other. To wit, he criticises William Schulz, the executive director of Amnesty International USA, who asks whether Dershowitz would also favour brutality warrants and prisoner rape warrants. (Dershowitz answers with a 'heuristic yes', whatever that is supposed to be.)[11] And he quotes himself saying: 'My question back to Schulz is do you prefer the current situation in which brutality, testilying and prisoner rape are rampant, but we close our eyes to these evils?'[12] Who is 'we'? Certainly not Schulz or Amnesty International.[13]

Second, Dershowitz admits that he 'certainly cannot prove . . . that a formal requirement of a judicial warrant as prerequisite to nonlethal torture would decrease the amount of physical violence directed against suspects'.[14] It seems, however, that Dershowitz should offer something more than his personal 'belief' and two examples to back the quite grave proposal to legalise torture. That he does not displays a lightness about the matter which is out of place. To be sure, he also adduces John H. Langbein's historical study of torture,[15] and although he concedes that it 'does not definitely answer' 'whether there would be less torture if it were done as part of the legal system', he thinks that it 'does provide some suggestive insights'.[16] Yet, before drawing 'suggestive insights' from Langbein's study and from history, one should get both straight. Dershowitz does not.[17] In fact, Langbein leaves no doubt that torture was *not* part of the judicial system in England. Not only 'law enforcement officers' but

also the courts (and judges) could not warrant torture. Langbein even states:

> The legal basis, such as it was, for the use of torture in the eighty-one known cases appears to have been the notion of sovereign immunity, a defensive doctrine that spared the authorities from having to supply justification for what they were doing.[18]

The facts, then, are that torture was never part of the English judicial system (if it was ever legal in England at all) whereas it *was* part of the Continental legal system. Extensive (not to say epidemic) use was made of torture on the Continent but not in England. Obviously, these facts suggest insights quite different from the ones Dershowitz comes up with.

Moreover, it is also funny that Dershowitz thinks that his two examples *support* his case. What his examples show (if they show anything) is that an attorney general who is *authorised* to put a wiretap without judicial warrant is more likely to put a wiretap than an attorney general who does need a warrant. However, the question to be answered is whether torture would be less likely under a requirement of a judicial warrant than *under a total ban*. To suggest a positive answer to this question by way of an analogy, Dershowitz would have to compare a legal arrangement in which the attorney general is *prohibited* from putting a wiretap with a legal arrangement where he is authorised to do so if he has a warrant. Dershowitz does not do that. It is he who engages in 'tortured reasoning', to use his term,[19] not his critics.

Finally, why shouldn't state agents who do not get a warrant torture anyway? They do not get a warrant today, and some of them torture anyway. Dershowitz answers that:

> . . . the current excuse being offered—we had to do what we did to get information—would no longer be available, since there would be an authorized method of securing information in extraordinary cases by the use of extraordinary means.[20]

First, people who escape detection are not in need of excuses to wriggle out of punishment in the first place. Besides, the excuse *would* be available. It would be: 'Since the judge didn't give us the warrant—he did not realise the seriousness of the situation (or there wasn't enough time)—we just had to torture under these circumstances without a warrant in order to get the information and to avoid a great evil'.

In short, Dershowitz has not offered the slightest bit of evidence—not even anecdotal—for his bold claim that the introduction of torture warrants would reduce torture or as much as increase accountability. Yet there is very good evidence to the contrary. Since Dershowitz invited us to draw suggestive insights from history, especially on the basis of Langbein's study, it might be worthwhile to note what Langbein himself has to say:

'Another insight from history is the danger that, once legitimated, torture could develop a constituency with a vested interest in perpetuating it.'[21]

And that, to draw the conclusion Dershowitz isn't able to draw, would hardly help to reduce torture or to increase accountability.

But why *should* we try to reduce torture? After all, in the first part of this paper I have argued that no compelling argument for an absolute moral prohibition of torture can be made; yes, not even for a prohibition in the Dirty Harry cases. I have also argued that torture is not worse than death and probably not worse than a decade of incarceration. So since we have legal incarceration, why shouldn't we have legal torture too?

One very straightforward answer is: because we don't need it. The ticking bomb case or the Dirty Harry case is a very rare case. In fact, it is safe to assume that all the torture that happened or happens in Abu Ghraib, Afghanistan and Guantanamo simply has nothing to do with ticking bombs or hostages who are about to die. The same holds for the overwhelming majority of all other cases of torture. Ticking bomb and Dirty Harry cases are *exceptions*. An emergency or necessity paragraph along the lines of § 35 of the German penal code can deal with such exceptions, and perhaps not even that is needed. If the stakes are high enough and no other option is available, police officers or other state agents will probably use torture even if they face prosecution if caught (that is, incidentally, what Dershowitz himself

claims). Besides, if punished, they might still be allowed the benefit of mitigating circumstances.

Second, that being tortured (or torturing someone) is not necessarily worse than being killed or incarcerated for a long time (or than killing someone or incarcerating him for a long time) does not imply that introducing a *wider practice* of torture is not worse than introducing or maintaining a wider practice of incarceration or killing. Dershowitz, for example, acknowledges:

Experience has shown that if torture, which has been deemed illegitimate by the civilized world for more than a century, were now to be legitimated—even for limited use in one extraordinary type of situation—such legitimation would constitute an important symbolic setback in the worldwide campaign against human rights abuses.[22]

However, he thinks:

It does not necessarily follow from this understandable fear of the slippery slope that we can never consider the use of nonlethal infliction of pain, if its use were to be limited by acceptable principles of morality. After all, imprisoning a witness who refuses to testify after being given immunity is designed to be punitive—that is painful. Such imprisonment can, on occasion, produce more pain and greater risk of death than nonlethal torture.[23]

It does indeed not follow that we can never consider the use of non-lethal infliction of pain, but it does follow that *institutionalising* torture—for example with torture warrants—is a bad idea. In particular, the analogy with the practice of coercing witnesses through imprisonment into testifying is misleading. The practice is designed to be punitive, yes, but that is not the same as being designed to be *painful*. Not every aversive treatment causes pain. It is important not to blur the distinctions. Further, the very fact that imprisonment produces only *on occasion* more pain and greater risk of death than non-lethal torture (although I suppose that non-lethal imprisonment would carry no risk of death) shows that it is not designed to produce pain and death. After all, being released can, on occasion, also produce more pain and greater risk of death than non-lethal torture. But how is that supposed to support the case for torture or for torture warrants? Thus, by using imprisonment as a method of punishment we are *not* already on the slippery slope.

Even if legalising torture puts us on a slippery slope, couldn't we stop the slide downwards? Dershowitz proposes a 'principled break':

> For example, if nonlethal torture were legally limited to convicted terrorists who had knowledge of future massive terrorist acts, were given immunity, and still refused to provide the information, there might still be objections to the use of torture, but they would have to go beyond the slippery slope argument.[24]

Actually, one argument that could be made here is that a *convicted* terrorist will hardly be a ticking bomb terrorist, unless, of course, he has set the time fuse on a few months or even years in the future *or* his conviction was made without due process. Giving up due process, however, does not look very much like a 'principled break', at least if the principle is supposed to be compatible with the rule of law. That notwithstanding, it has to be admitted that 'massive terrorist acts' will have to be planned long enough in advance so that a convicted terrorist might have knowledge of them. Consequently, torturing him might be a means to thwart the attacks.

However, Dershowitz's talk about a 'principled break' does, in fact, not address the problem of an 'important symbolic setback in the worldwide campaign against human rights abuses' at all. The symbolic setback consists precisely in undermining the *absolute* prohibition on torture and cannot be compensated, probably not even mitigated, by recourse to alleged 'principled breaks'. Moreover, the whole idea of a 'principled break' in connection with 'security laws' that cut down on civil liberties and individual rights is rather naïve. (I put 'security laws' in quotation marks because cutting down on civil liberties and individual rights hardly increases an individual's security from the state—the political entity, it should be remembered, that has slaughtered more people than any other political entity in history and is certainly more dangerous than any subnational terrorist organisation.) Experience shows that measures introduced against putative terrorists in alleged conditions of emergency tend to be doubly extended, namely, beyond the emergency and to crimes or offences of lesser seriousness. In the UK, for example, emergency anti-terrorist measures, such as limitations on the right to silence, admissibility of confession evidence and extended periods of pre-judicial detention, have infiltrated ordinary criminal law and procedure.[25] Once advertised as being targeted only against terrorists, they can now befall any citizen who gets involved in criminal procedure.

It is to be expected, then, that the legalisation of torture for certain specific circumstances will, just like other so-called security laws, come with an inherent 'metastatic tendency'[26] that in time extends it beyond those circumstances. Apart from this dangerous tendency of 'security laws' in general there is, in addition, something very *special* about torture. Jeremy Waldron has argued that the prohibition of torture is archetypical of the idea:

> . . . that even where law has to operate forcefully, there will not be the connection that has existed in other times or places between law and brutality. People may fear and be deterred by legal sanctions . . . they may even on occasion be forced . . . to do things or go places against their will. But even when this happens, they will not be herded like cattle or broken like horses; they will not be beaten like dumb animals or treated as bodies to be manipulated. Instead, there will be an enduring connection between the spirit of law and respect for human dignity—respect for human dignity even in extremis, where law is at its most forceful and its subjects at their most vulnerable.[27]

That the prohibition of torture is a legal *archetype* means that it has 'a significance stemming from the fact that it sums up or makes vivid to us the point, purpose, principle, or policy of a whole area of law'.[28] For example, Waldron shows that decisive court rulings against lesser forms of police brutality—lesser, that is, than torture—were made with reference to torture. The similarities with torture were invoked to reject those other brutalities. This, of course, would not be possible if torture itself became regularised and justified by law, for the similarity with a regular legal practice could hardly count against some other practice. As Waldron puts it:

> The idea is that our confidence that what lies at the bottom of the slope (torture) is wrong informs and supports our confidence that the lesser evils that lie above torture are wrong too.[29]

Thus, by undermining the archetype of the prohibition of torture one also undermines the prohibition of lesser forms of brutality. The whole set of injunctions against brutality would unravel and the character of the legal system would be corrupted.[30]

What is so frightening about such a brutalisation of the legal system is that it is also the brutalisation of its *enforcer*—which, in modern societies, is ultimately the *state*. It is one thing to grant to an individual in a certain situation the moral justification to torture another individual; it is a completely different thing to allow the state to legally institutionalise torture in certain circumstances. Dirty Harry has to justify himself not only morally but also legally. He might face legal charges, and that might make him think twice before he tortures someone. This, in fact, ensures that the slope of the moral permission of torture in certain cases does not become too slippery to be acceptable. Dirty Harry takes his decision as an individual, not as an agent of the state. The state is not behind him. But if law enforcers can resort to torture knowing in advance that the state is behind them, the worst has to be expected—on a large and inevitably growing scale. Here it is worth noting that the argument that the prohibition of torture is an archetype and the argument that the legal introduction of torture would have a metastatic tendency reinforce each other. The further the practice of torture extends, the more it will undermine the archetypical character of the prohibition; the more that happens, the further the practice will extend. It is not only a slippery slope but also a slope that on its way down gets exponentially steeper. One of the functions of the rule of law is to keep the power of the state under control. But this doesn't work with *any* law. It doesn't work with a brutal or brutalised one. Torture warrants are indeed a 'stunningly bad idea'.[31]

NOTES

1. See S. Levinson, 'Contemplating torture: an introduction' in Levinson (2004) op. cit. (see n. 1), pp. 23–43, at pp. 33ff., and the further references there.

2. R. H. Weisberg, 'Loose professionalism' in Levinson (2004) op. cit, pp. 299–305, at p. 304.

3. Jeff McMahan agrees that this person cannot complain under the circumstances but thinks that this still does not make him liable to be tortured, the reason being that 'torturing him serves no purpose under the circumstances'. (Personal communication) However, if he cannot complain, he cannot be being wronged (for then he obviously could complain); and I think that the only possible reason why someone is not wronged by an attack (for example in the form of torture) is that he is liable to the attack. In fact, this seems to be pretty much the meaning of 'liable to attack'. Besides, if someone unjustly shoots at me and I shoot back, hitting him in the shoulder, and he continues shooting and kills me, then my counterattack has served no purpose under the circumstances (if it had, I would not be dead). That makes my counterattack hardly unjust or the attacker not liable to be shot at (otherwise every unsuccessful defender would also be an unjust defender, which is absurd).

4. D. Luban, (2005) 'Liberalism and the unpleasant question of torture', http://ethics.stanford.edu/newsletter/_old/december, accessed on 2 October 2005, electronic resource. A comparable argument is put forward by K. Seth, 'Too close to the rack and the screw: constitutional constraints on torture in the war on terror', *University of Pennsylvania Journal of Constitutional Law* 6 (2003–2004): 278–325.

5. The translation is mine.

6. A. Dorfman, 'The tyranny of terror: is torture inevitable in our century and beyond?' in Levinson (2004) op. cit., pp. 3–18, at p. 17.

7. Torturing this person would, of course, be a case of self-preservation and not of self- or other-defence (or something close to it) as in the Dirty Harry case.

8. That seems to be the position of Shue op. cit., pp. 58f., and R. A. Posner, 'Torture, terrorism, and interrogation' in Levinson (2004) op. cit., pp. 291–298, at pp. 297f.; and it is the position of O. Gross, 'The prohibition on torture and the limits of the law' in Levinson (2004) op. cit., pp. 229–253, esp. at pp. 231 and 239–250.

9. A. Dershowitz, 'Tortured reasoning' in Levinson (2004) op. cit., pp. 257–280, at p. 257. He emphasises that *that* was his question and not the 'old, abstract' one 'over whether torture can ever be justified', and he complains about 'misleading' descriptions of his proposals. *Ibid.*, p. 266. Maybe the next time he addresses the former question instead of the latter he could help to avoid 'misleading' descriptions of his intentions by not using titles like 'Should the Ticking Bomb Terrorist Be Tortured?' See A. Dershowitz, *Why Terrorism Works: Understanding the Threats, Responding to the Challenge* (New Haven, CT: Yale University Press, 2002) p. 131.

10. Dershowitz (2004) op. cit., pp. 270f.

11. *Ibid.*, pp. 266f.

12. *Ibid.*, p. 267, '"Testilying" is a term coined by New York City police to describe systematic perjury regarding the circumstances that led to a search, seizure, or interrogation'. *Ibid.*, p.278, n. 13.

13. Compare E. Scarry, 'Five errors in the reasoning of Alan Dershowitz' in Levinson (2004) op. cit., pp. 281–290, at p. 288.

14. Dershowitz (2002) op. cit., p. 158.

15. J. H. Langbein, *Torture and the Law of Proof: Europe and England in the Ancien Régime* (Chicago, IL: University of Chicago Press, 1977).

16. Dershowitz (2002) op. cit., p. 158.

17. On Dershowitz's misreading of Langbein see also J. Waldron, 'Torture and positive law: jurisprudence for the White House', *Columbia Law Review* 105 (2005): 1739, n. 250.

18. J. H. Langbein, 'The legal history of torture' in Levinson (2004) op. cit., pp. 93–103, at p. 100.

19. Dershowitz (2004) op. cit., p. 257.

20. *Ibid.*, p. 276.

21. Langbein (2004) op. cit., p. 101.

22. Dershowitz (2002) op. cit., p. 145.

23. *Ibid.*, p. 147.

24. *Ibid.*

25. P. Hillyard, 'The normalization of special powers from Northern Ireland to Britain' in N. Lacey (ed.) *A Reader on Criminal Justice* (Oxford: Oxford University Press, 1994); O. Gross, 'Cutting down trees: law-making under the shadow of great calamities' in R. J. Daniels, P. Macklem and K. Roach (eds.), *The Security of Freedom: Essays on Canada's Anti-Terrorism Bill* (Toronto: Toronto University Press, 2001), pp. 39–61, esp. at 47ff. I owe the references to these articles to L. Zedner, 'Securing liberty in the face of terror: reflections from criminal justice', pp. 7 and 15, and to C. Warbrick, 'Terrorism, counter-terrorism, international law', p. 9, unpublished papers held at the colloquium *Moral and Legal Aspects of Terrorism*, Corpus Christi College, Oxford, 5 March 2005.

26. Shue op. cit., p. 58.

27. Waldron op. cit., pp. 1726f.

28. *Ibid.*, p. 1723.

29. *Ibid.*, p. 1735.

30. *Ibid.*, p. 1728-1739.

31. J. B. Elshtain, 'Reflections on the problem of "dirty hands"' in Levinson (2004) op. cit., pp. 77–89, at p. 83. I owe thanks to patrick Lenta, Jeff McMahan and David Rodin for helpful comments on an earlier draft of this paper.

♛ REVIEW QUESTIONS

1. Why does Steinhoff think that interrogative torture is morally justified in the Dirty Harry case?

2. How does Steinhoff reply to the objection that torture does not work?

3. What is Steinhoff's reply to the objection that interrogative torture is not reliable? How does this reply apply to the ticking-bomb case?

4. What is Weisberg's criticism of the ticking-bomb case? How does Steinhoff reply?

5. What is Luban's objection to torture? How does Steinhoff respond?

6. Why does Steinhoff think that interrogative torture is justified in the ticking-bomb case?

7. Why does Steinhoff hold that moral absolutism is dangerous and mistaken?

8. Explain Alan Dershowitz's proposal. Why does Steinhoff reject it as a bad idea?

⚜ DISCUSSION QUESTIONS

1. Are you convinced that Harry is morally justified in torturing the kidnapper? Should this behavior be legal? Explain your answers.
2. Unlike Luban, Steinhoff thinks torturing terrorists is morally justified even given various uncertainties. Do you agree? Why or why not?
3. Is moral absolutism always dangerous and mistaken? What is your view?
4. Is Dershowitz's proposal really a bad idea? What do you think?

PROBLEM CASES

1. A Nuclear Bomb

Al Qaeda terrorists have planted a small nuclear device in an apartment building in London, and it is set to go off in two hours. If it goes off, it will kill thousands of people and injure thousands more. It will destroy a large part of the city. The terrorist group that planted the bomb has been under surveillance by the police. The police suspect that a devastating terrorist act has been planned; they have been monitoring telephone conversations and e-mails for months. They decide to bring in one of the terrorists for questioning. They know he has planned terrorist attacks in the past, and they have good evidence that a nuclear attack is going to happen in London and that he knows about it. The terrorist has been questioned before, and he knows the routine. If he refuses to talk, then the bomb will go off as he planned; his terrorist mission will be accomplished. Time is running out. There is not enough time to evacuate the city. The police are reasonably confident that the suspect knows where the bomb is and when it is set to go off. One of the policemen happens to have experience in torturing, although torture is illegal and not normally used. The policeman believes the terrorist will talk if tortured.

Should the terrorist be tortured or not? If he does not talk, the bomb will go off as planned and thousands will die or be injured. But if he does reveal the location of the bomb, experts will rush to the location and they will be able to prevent it from detonating. Is torture justified in this situation? Why or why not?

2. The Extraordinary Rendition Program

(See Jane Mayer, "Outsourcing Torture," *The New Yorker*, February 14, 2005.) The extraordinary rendition program began as far back as 1995. Originally, it was directed at suspects having outstanding foreign arrest warrants, but after 9/11, the program was expanded to target suspected terrorists. Suspicious "enemy combatants" were captured and confined and interrogated in secret CIA prisons called "black sites" outside the United States. President Bush admitted the existence of such prisons in a September 2006 speech. The most common destinations for suspects are Egypt, Jordan, Syria, and Morocco; all are known to practice torture and have been cited for human rights violations by the State Department. An estimated 150 people have been rendered since 2001.

The legal status of the rendering program is controversial. In 1998, Congress passed legislation saying that the policy of the United States is not to expel, extradite, or otherwise affect the involuntary return of any person to a country where the person would be in danger of being subjected to torture. The American Civil Liberties Union claims that the United States is violating federal and international law by engaging in secret abductions and torture. But Alberto Gonzales, the U.S. attorney general, argues that U.S. and international laws and prohibitions against torture do not apply to "enemy combatants" and do not apply to American interrogations of confined suspects overseas. In this view, suspected terrorists are basically outside the scope of the law. They can be detained indefinitely, without counsel, without charges of wrongdoing, and interrogated using CIA methods.

CIA sources have described six "Enhanced Interrogation Techniques" that are used to interrogate al-Qaeda suspects confined in the secret prisons. The CIA interrogators are supposed to be trained and authorized to use these techniques:

1. Attention Grab: The interrogator forcefully grabs the shirt front of the prisoner and shakes him. Violent shaking can cause whiplash injuries.

2. Attention Slap: The prisoner is slapped in the face with the aim of causing pain and fear.

3. Belly Slap: The naked prisoner is slapped hard in the stomach to cause pain. A punch to the stomach can produce permanent internal damage.

4. Long Time Standing: This technique is very effective. Prisoners are forced to stand handcuffed with their feet shackled to an eyebolt in the floor for more than forty hours. They become exhausted and sleep deprived.

5. The Cold Cell: The naked prisoner is made to stand in a cell kept below fifty degrees and is regularly doused with cold water. The prisoner can die of hypothermia.

6. Water Boarding: The prisoner is bound to an inclined board with the feet raised and the head slightly below the feet. Cellophane is wrapped over the face. Water is poured on the face from a hose or a bucket. The gag reflex quickly kicks in with a terrifying fear of drowning. After a short time, the victim pleads for the treatment to stop.

Are these CIA methods torture or not? Suppose that these methods produce valuable information about al-Qaeda terrorists and their future plans for attacks. If so, are these methods justified? What is your view? Should the United States continue the rendering program? Why or why not?

3. Khalid Sheik Mohammed

(See the Wikipedia article with links to news reports.) According to a transcript released by the military on March 15, 2007, Mr. Mohammed confessed to directing the 9/11 attacks and thirty-one other terrorist attacks and plans. He testified at the Guantánamo Bay detention facility that he was "responsible for the 9/11 attacks from A to Z." He described himself as al Qaeda's military operational commander for foreign operations. He claimed that he personally decapitated Daniel Pearl, the American journalist who was kidnapped and murdered in 2002 in Pakistan. He said he was responsible for several other operations, including the 2001 Richard Reid shoe-bomber attempt to blow up an airliner, the 2002 Bali nightclub bombing in Indonesia, and the 1993 World Trade Center attack. He said he was involved in more than two dozen uncompleted terrorist plots, including ones that targeted offices in New York City, Los Angeles, and Chicago. He plotted to blow up nuclear power plants. He planned assassination attempts of several U.S. presidents. He planned to explode London's Big Ben tower and destroy the Panama Canal.

Mr. Mohammed was arrested in Pakistan in 2003 and "disappeared" to a semisecret prison in Jordan where he was interrogated by the CIA. His confession came after four years of captivity, including six months at Guantánamo Bay. CIA officials told ABC news that Mr. Mohammed's interrogation included water boarding. The technique involves strapping a prisoner on an inclined board with the head below the feet. The face is wrapped in cellophane and water poured over it. This produces an intense gag reflex and fear of drowning, but it is not supposed to result in permanent physical damage. The CIA officers who subjected themselves to the procedure lasted an average of fourteen seconds before giving up. Mr. Mohammed impressed the interrogators when he was able to last between two and two-and-a-half minutes before begging to confess.

The Human Rights Watch says that Mr. Mohammed was tortured. Do you agree? Should water boarding be acknowledged as torture? Why or why not?

The CIA officials admit that confessions resulting from torture or mistreatment may not be reliable. For example, Ibn al Shaykh al Libbi was water boarded and then made to stand naked in a cold cell overnight where he was regularly doused with cold water. After two weeks of "enhanced interrogation," his confessions became the basis for the Bush administration claim that Iraq trained al-Qaeda members to use biochemical weapons. Later, it was established that he had no knowledge of such training or weapons and had fabricated the statements to avoid further harsh treatment.

Some commentators are skeptical about Mr. Mohammed's rambling and wide-ranging confessions. For example, Michigan Representative Mike Rogers, a Republican on the terrorism panel of the House Intelligence Committee, found the confessions to be exaggerated or self-promotional. He doubted that Mr. Mohammed had a role in so many terrorist acts and plans. One CIA official admitted that some of Mr. Mohammed's claims during interrogation were "white noise" designed to send the interrogators on "wild goose chases" or to "get him through the day's interrogation sessions."

If Mr. Mohammed's confessions were not useful or reliable, then was the CIA interrogation justified?

Suppose that the confessions in question produced useful information that prevented terrorist attacks.

Would that fact justify the treatment Mr. Mohammed received at the hands of the CIA interrogators?

Now that he has confessed to crimes including murder, what should be done with Mr. Mohammed? The Bush administration position was that he is an "enemy combatant" without any legal rights. This means that he could be executed without a trial. Is this the right thing to do?

The Obama administration has announced that it expects Mohammed to be given a trial, found guilty, and executed. But there was confusion about how to do this. In 2010, all charges against Mohammed by military commissions were withdrawn without prejudice, which allows officials to try Mohammed and the other suspects in a civilian court. But where should he be tried? The plan to have the trial in New York City was abandoned after a wave of protests. Another problem is that confessions or evidence based on torture are not admissible in U.S. civilian courts. In the meantime, he is being held at Guantánamo Bay.

Should Mohammed be given a trial or not? If so, should he be found guilty and executed? Another option is to hold him indefinitely without a trial at Guantánamo Bay. What should be done with him?

4. *The Geneva Convention and the UN Convention*

The United States ratified the Geneva Convention relative to the Treatment of Prisoners of War in 1955. It prohibits "cruel treatment and torture." It also prohibits "outrages upon personal dignity, in particular, humiliating and degrading treatment."

The United Nations Convention Against Torture and Other Cruel, Inhuman or Degrading Treatment or Punishment was adopted by the UN General Assembly in 1984. To date, 142 nations have ratified it, including the United States.

Article 1 defines torture (in part) as "any act by which severe pain or suffering, whether physical or mental, is intentionally inflicted on a person for such purposes as obtaining from him or a third person information or a confession."

Article 2 requires each state to take "effective legislative, administrative, judicial or other measures to

prevent acts of torture." It also says that no circumstances whatever, whether a state of war or a threat of war or any other public emergency, may be used to justify torture.

Article 3 prohibits a state from extraditing a person to another state to be tortured.

Article 16 states that each state that is a party to the agreement "shall undertake to prevent in any territory under its jurisdiction other acts of cruel, inhuman or degrading treatment or punishment which do not amount to torture as defined in Article 1."

Should the United States follow these conventions or not? Are violations of these conventions war crimes? What is your position?

☙ SUGGESTED READINGS

The *Stanford Encyclopedia of Philosophy* (http://plato.stanford.edu) has an excellent article on torture written by Seamus Miller. The CIA website (www.cia.gov) has detailed information on torture, including personal anecdotes, methods used, and information gained. The World Organization Against Torture (www.omct.org) is a global network fighting against torture and other human rights violations. The Human Rights Watch (www.hrw.org) has reports on the use of torture around the world.

Heather MacDonald, "How to Interrogate Terrorists," *City Journal*, Winter 2005: 1–8, argues that to succeed in the war on terror, the U.S. military must be allowed to use stress techniques on unlawful combatants, including sleep deprivation, loud noise, prolonged kneeling or standing, and so on. These techniques are not torture in her view, but she admits that water boarding may cross the line into torture.

Henry Shue, "Torture," *Philosophy and Public Affairs* 7, no. 2 (Winter 1978): 124–143, argues that torture is morally worse than killing in a just war because it violates the prohibition against assaulting the defenseless, but he suggests that there is at least one imaginable case in which interrogational torture might be justified: the now-famous ticking-bomb case. As Shue describes the case, there is a fanatic who has hidden a nuclear bomb set to explode in Paris, and the only way to prevent the destruction of Paris is to torture the fanatic to find out where the bomb is hidden so that it can be found and deactivated.

Bob Brecher, *Torture and the Ticking Bomb* (London: Wiley-Blackwell, 2007), gives a detailed critique of the ticking-bomb story used by Dershowitz and others to justify torture.

Kenneth Roth and Minky Worden, eds., *Torture* (New York: New Press, 2005). This is a collection of twelve articles on torture, including Michael Ignatieff on justifying torture, Jean Mendez on the victim's perspective, Jamie Feiner on torture in U.S. prisons, and David Rieff on the inadequacies of the human rights view.

Sanford Levison, ed., *Torture* (Oxford: Oxford University Press, 2006). This is a useful collection of seventeen essays covering the morality, legality, and practice of torture.

Fritz Allhoff, "Terrorism and Torture," *International Journal of Applied Philosophy* 17, no. 1 (2003): 105–118, supports the use of torture to get information about imminent and significant threats but not to force confession or to deter crime.

Fritz Allhoff, "A Defense of Torture," *International Journal of Applied Philosophy* 19, no. 2 (Fall 2005): 243–264, argues for the permissibility of torture in ticking-bomb cases.

Michael Davis, "The Moral Justification of Torture and Other Cruel, Inhuman, or Degrading Treatment," *International Journal of Applied Philosophy* 19, no. 2 (2005): 161–178, argues that the ticking-bomb case proves nothing because it relies on intuition, which is unreliable and fails to provide any justification.

Christopher W. Tindale, "Tragic Choices," *International Journal of Applied Philosophy* 19, no. 2 (Fall 2005): 209–222, defends an absolute prohibition of interrogational torture; he argues that the ticking-bomb scenarios are ill considered.

Larry May, "Torturing Detainees During Interrogation," *International Journal of Applied Philosophy* 19, no. 2 (Fall 2005): 193–208, argues that our humanity demands that suspected terrorists not be subject to torture when they are captured and imprisoned.

David Sussman, "What's Wrong with Torture?" *Philosophy and Public Affairs* 33 (December 2005): 1–33, defends the intuition that torture is a special type of wrong, and this explains why we find it more morally offensive than other ways of inflicting harm.

Seamus Miller, "Is Torture Ever Morally Justified?" *International Journal of Applied Philosophy* 19, no. 2 (2005): 179–192, argues that torture is morally justified in extreme emergencies, but it ought not to be legalized.

Jeremy Waldron, "Torture and Positive Law," *Columbia Law Review* 105, no. 6 (2005): 1681–1750, defends the legal prohibition of torture. This prohibition is not just one rule among others; it is a legal archetype that is emblematic of a basic commitment to nonbrutality in the legal system.

Alan M. Dershowitz, *Why Terrorism Works* (New Haven, CT: Yale University Press, 2002), devotes a chapter to defending the use of torture on terrorists to get information about imminent attacks.

Howard J. Curzer, "Admirable Immorality, Dirty Hands, Ticking Bombs, and Torturing

Innocents," *Southern Journal of Philosophy* 44, no. 1 (Spring 2006): 31–56, argues that torturing is morally required and should be done when it is the only way to avert disasters. He admits that it is odd to hold that a vicious act like torture is morally required.

Jessica Wolfendale, "Training Torturers," *Social Theory and Practice* 322, no. 2 (April 2006): 269–287, argues that ticking-bomb arguments ignore the fact that permitting torture requires training torturers. This fact casts doubt on the arguments.

Karen J. Greenberg and Joshua L. Drafel, eds., *The Torture Papers* (Cambridge: Cambridge University Press, 2006), documents the abuse of prisoners at Abu Ghraib and Guantánamo.

Mark Danner, *Torture and Truth* (New York: New York Review of Books, 2004), argues that torture is part of a planned policy of the Bush administration.

Karen J. Greenberg, ed., *The Torture Debate in America* (Cambridge: Cambridge University Press, 2006), presents different perspectives on torture, from absolute prohibition to a useful weapon in the war on terrorism.

Colin Dayan, *The Story of Cruel and Unusual* (Boston: MIT Press, 2007), argues that recent Supreme Court decisions have dismantled the Eighth Amendment protection against "cruel and unusual" punishment. The result is the abuse and torture of prisoners at Abu Ghraib and Guantánamo.

William Sampson, *Confession of an Innocent Man* (Toronto: McClellan & Stewart, 2005). This is the horrifying story of an innocent Canadian man arrested, imprisoned, and tortured into confessing to car bombings he did not commit. Later, he was officially exonerated of the crimes.

Alfred McCoy, *A Question of Torture* (New York: Owl Books, 2006), describes the development of the torture methods used by the CIA.

Susan Sontag, "Regarding the Torture of Others," *The New York Times Magazine*, May 24, 2004, discusses the implications and meaning of the famous photographs of prisoners at Abu Ghraib.

Assassination

- **Introduction**
  - Factual Background
  - The Readings
  - Philosophical Issues

INTRODUCTION

Factual Background

Assassination (or *targeted killing*) is the killing of a political or military leader or other public figure. There have been numerous assassinations throughout recorded history. On the Ides of March (March 15) 44 BCE, the Roman dictator Julius Caesar was stabbed to death by members of the Senate. The event is famously presented in Shakespeare's play *Julius Caesar*. In the Middle Ages, the French kings Henry III and Henry IV were assassinated. In Russia, four emperors were killed within 200 years. In modern times, the assassination of Franz Ferdinand is blamed for starting World War I. In 1948, an assassin shot and killed India's Mohandas K. Gandhi. In the United States, four presidents have been assassinated: Abraham Lincoln, James Garfield, William McKinley, and John F. Kennedy. An assassin also killed Robert Kennedy. Martin Luther King, Jr., the civil rights leader, was shot and killed by James Earl Ray in 1968.

Assassination is prohibited in international law. Article 23b of the Hague Regulations prohibits "assassination, proscriptions, or outlawry of an enemy, or putting a price upon an enemy's head, as well as offering a reward of an enemy 'dead or alive.'" U.S. law also makes assassination illegal. In 1976, President Ford issued an executive order that states: "No employee of the United States Government shall engage in, or conspire to engage in, political assassination." President Carter reaffirmed the prohibition. In 1981, President Reagan reiterated the prohibition in almost the same language: "No person employed by or acting on behalf of the United States Government shall engage in, or conspire to engage in, assassination."

Despite the legal prohibition of assassination, both Israel and the United States have assassinated political leaders and others, or tried to do so. In 1986, the Reagan administration dropped bombs on Libyan leader Muammar Qaddafi's home in retaliation for the bombing of a Berlin discotheque that killed a U.S. soldier. The attack killed Qaddafi's adopted infant daughter and fifteen others but not Qaddafi. According to Mark Bowden (see the Suggested Readings), a U.S. Delta Force sniper shot and killed Colombian drug lord Pablo Escobar in 1993. The CIA tried for nearly half a century to assassinate Fidel Castro, using bizarre methods such as an exploding cigar (see the Problem Case). In 2003, the U.S. military hit a Baghdad restaurant with Tomahawk missiles in an attempt to kill Saddam Hussein and his sons. The explosions killed fourteen civilians but not Hussein and his sons. The Israeli military has targeted and killed several Hamas leaders, including Salah Shehada (2002; see the Problem Case), Ahmed Yassin (2004; see the Problem Case), Abdel Aziz al-Rantissi (2004), and Adman al-Ghoul (2004). In 2009, Israel used a one-ton bomb to flatten the home of Hamas leader Nizar Rayan, killing him and four of his children and two of his wives. During the war in Iraq, CIA or Blackwater hit teams armed with sawed-off M-4 automatic weapons with silencers made nightly raids to kill or capture suspected insurgents.

After the 9/11 attacks, President George W. Bush authorized "lethal covert actions" without formally rescinding the executive orders of Presidents Ford, Carter, and Reagan making assassination illegal. He said that bin Laden was wanted "dead or alive." Later, "wanted" posters were put up in Afghanistan promising $25 million for information leading to the capture of bin Laden. In June 2009, CIA director Leon Panetta revealed a secret CIA assassination program. Teams of assassins were to be deployed around the world to track down and kill suspected terrorist leaders. Members of Congress were angry because they had not been informed of the program. The furor grew when it was learned that the CIA had outsourced the program to Blackwater (now called Xe Services), the controversial private contractor. Panetta claimed that he had cancelled the program, but left open the possibility of reviving it.

In addition to assassins, bombs, and cruise missiles, the U.S. government uses Predator and Reaper drones for assassination. (The U.S. military prefers to call it "targeted killing" to avoid the negative connotations of "assassination.") The Predator is an unmanned aerial vehicle or plane that can fire two Hellfire missiles. The Reaper is four times heavier than the Predator and carries four Hellfire missiles and two 500-pound bombs. These unmanned drones have been frequently used in Pakistan and Afghanistan to target al-Qaeda and Taliban leaders. According to Pakistani authorities, there were more than sixty Predator or Reaper strikes in Pakistan between January 14, 2006, and April 8, 2009. Only ten were able to hit their actual targets, killing fourteen al-Qaeda leaders. The other 50 attacks went wrong because of faulty intelligence information, and thus killed 687 innocent civilians, including women and children. To give one example, in 2006 a Predator aircraft attacked the northern Pakistani village of Damadola and two other villages. The target was Ayman al-Zawahiri, al Qaeda's second in command after bin Laden. It is believed that he was killed but this has not been officially confirmed. Pakistani intelligence claimed that Abu Khabab al-Masri, al Qaeda's chief bomb maker and chemical weapons expert, was killed in the attacks. Pakistani officials also said the attacks killed eighteen civilians, including five children. According to a United Nations report issued in February 2009, targeted air strikes have killed more than 800 civilians in Afghanistan.

About 160 innocent civilians have been killed in Afghanistan since President Obama took office in January 2009.

In 2010, the number of drone strikes in the North Waziristan area of Pakistan increased dramatically. The drones, operated by the CIA, were flying twenty-four hours a day looking for targets, as compared to one flight a week in 2009. The fleet of Reaper aircraft was doubled. This increase in strikes and aircraft was in response to the suicide bombing of seven Americans in Afghanistan on December 30, 2009. According to Pakistani news reports, about ninety suspected terrorists were killed in January 2010.

Thus far we have discussed the use of Predators or Reapers by the U.S. military, which is publicly acknowledged. According to Jane Mayer (see the Suggested Readings), there is also a secret private program, run by Xe Services, aimed at terrorists around the world. The program is classified as covert, meaning that the CIA does not reveal where it operates, how it selects a target, who is in charge, or how many people have been killed. (Still, it is not exactly secret; see Scott Shane in the Suggested Readings.) Nevertheless, the CIA reported the assassination of Taliban leader Baitullah Mehsud by a missile strike in August 2009. He was hit while he was on a drip infusion for his kidney disease. The attack also killed Mehsud's wife and his parents-in-law. According to a study completed by the New American Foundation, a policy group in Washington, the Obama administration has sanctioned at least 41 CIA missile strikes in Pakistan that killed about 500 people, many of them innocent bystanders and including children. (In response to this report, CIA spokesman Paul Gimigliano said that there have been only twenty civilian deaths from Predator strikes.)

The Readings

Whitley R. P. Kaufman uses the term *assassination* to mean targeted killing without reference to treachery. He is primarily concerned about the morality of the premeditated, extrajudicial killing of individuals in positions of political or military leadership. He addresses the issue using just war doctrine. In that doctrine, the use of violence is justified only if it meets the requirements of necessity, proportionality, noncombatant immunity, and right motive. Revenge, punishment, or maximization of good consequences cannot provide a legitimate basis for violence. He argues that assassination is justified in just war theory only if the targeted individual is an aggressor and poses an imminent threat. Thus, just war doctrine generally prohibits assassination. It is legitimate only in very limited circumstances.

Daniel Statman uses the term *targeted killing* rather than *assassination*. He finds it puzzling that people are willing to accept the morality and legality of killing in a conventional war, such as the Falkland Islands War, and yet reject it when it comes to the targeted killing of terrorist leaders. After all, the threat to the United States posed by al Qaeda is greater than the threat the Argentinean invasion of the Falkland Islands posed to the British. In his view, the war on terror is analogous to conventional war. Both are responses to threats, and in both it is legitimate to target aggressors in self-defense. If one accepts the moral legitimacy of large-scale killing of combatants in conventional wars, then one should accept the moral legitimacy of targeted killing of terrorist leaders in wars against terror. Unlike Kaufman, Statman also accepts retribution as a moral justification for the targeted killing of Palestinian terrorists. In fact, he believes that the killing of activist terrorists is more justified than the killing of enemy combatants in conventional wars.

Philosophical Issues

What is assassination? There is disagreement about what counts as an assassination or how to define the term *assassination*. As Whitley R. P. Kaufman uses the term, the targeted killing of a political or military leader is an assassination. An assassination does not essentially involve the use of treachery; rather, it is the premeditated, extra-judicial killing of leaders.

Daniel Statman chooses to use the term *targeted killing* rather than *assassination* to avoid the negative moral connotation of the latter term, that is, the presumption that assassination is morally wrong. If assassination is murder, then by definition it is morally wrong. *Targeted killing* is a more neutral term that leaves open the question of whether it is morally wrong. As we have seen, Statman argues that targeted killing is not always morally wrong.

Amnesty International (see the Suggested Readings) refers to the targeted killing of political or military leaders by governments such as Israel or the United States as *state* assassination, as distinguished from assassinations done by private individuals. Jane Mayer (see the Suggested Readings) speaks of *targeted* assassinations of terrorists. Others call the targeted killing of suspected terrorists extrajudicial executions.

The main issue raised in the readings is whether assassination or targeted killing can be morally justified. Kaufman argues that it is generally unjustified if one adheres to the principles of just war doctrine. As he understands those principles, the targeted assassination or killing of a military or political leader could be justified only if it were done to prevent an imminent unjust attack with the motive of protecting oneself or others from death or serious harm. The force must be necessary, such that there is no less violent means of preventing attack (such as capturing the target). It must be proportionate, in the sense that the harm produced is proportionate to the harm prevented. With those restrictions in mind, it seems that targeted killing that results in the deaths of innocent bystanders is not morally justified. This means that almost all of the targeted killing done by the United States and Israel is not morally justified.

Statman defends targeted killing. It is not only morally justified, it is even more defensible than the killing that goes on in all-out conventional wars. If one accepts the large-scale killing of combatants and noncombatants in conventional wars, then it is hard to see why the targeted killing of guilty terrorists is not morally justified, too. Furthermore, killing terrorists satisfies the desire for revenge or retribution. This consideration provides further support for the moral justification of targeted killing.

Steven de Wijze (see the Suggested Reading) offers a third alternative to the moral complexity of targeted killing. Unlike Statman, he does not think that targeted killing is entirely morally justified, but he does not believe it should be un-equivocally condemned, either. Instead, he suggests that the government and agents who engage in such actions end up having "dirty hands." They have done something wrong in order to do right. They have chosen the lesser of two evils, and par-adoxically this is morally justified and at the same time morally reprehensible. The moral emotion produced is "tragic remorse," the anguish produced by necessary wrongdoing.

Rethinking the Ban on Assassination

WHITLEY R. P. KAUFMAN

Whitley R. P. Kaufman is chair and associate professor of philosophy at the University of Massachusetts, Lowell. He is the author of *Justified Killing: The Paradox of Self-Defense* (2009) and about twenty articles, many of them on the topic of self-defense, punishment, and just war doctrine.

Kaufman argues that assassination or targeted killing is generally impermissible under just war doctrine, but may be legitimate in certain limited circumstances. He distinguishes between a punishment rationale, a self-defense rationale, and a consequentialist rationale for assassination. In just war theory, only the self-defense rationale can morally justify assassination: Assassination is morally justified if the target is an aggressor and poses an imminent threat. Even if the target is a combatant, there remain serious concerns about the morality of assassination: the fact that it is premeditated, the duty to use minimum harm, the danger of misuse, and the problem of a slippery slope of killing.

The September 11, 2001, terrorist attacks appear to have undermined, at least in the United States, what had previously been a firm moral and legal consensus against the use of political assassination. Though it is banned under international law[1] and has been prohibited as a matter of U.S. policy since 1976 when President Ford signed an executive order banning assassination, U.S. policy appears to have reversed course in response to the increase in terrorist attacks. President Clinton revealed at a news conference in 2001 following the Trade Center attacks that his administration in 1998, following the bombing of U.S. embassies, had authorized the "arrest and, if necessary, the killing of Osama bin Laden," though a lack of intelligence prevented the successful completion of the mission. In October 2001 George Bush authorized the CIA to carry out missions to assassinate Osama bin Laden and his supporters (and indeed publicly declared that bin Laden "was wanted, dead or alive"). In addition, Israel has increasingly resorted to the use of assassination of terrorist leaders among the Palestinians to prevent suicide bombing attacks. Vigorous debates have also arisen over the question of the potential assassination of political leaders such as Saddam Hussein or Muammar Qaddafi. More fundamentally, these actions have taken place in a shifting moral environment, in which the earlier assumption that assassination is morally impermissible no longer seems convincing in an age of terrorism.

In this essay I will analyze the ethics of political assassination from within the context of the just war tradition. Just war doctrine involves a strong presumption against the use of violence or killing (in peacetime or in war) outside of certain limited contexts, specifically the punishment of the guilty, defense against an unjust attacker, and the enforcement of natural justice or law. Even in those contexts, the use of violence is subject to the just war requirements including last resort (aka necessity), proportionality, noncombatant immunity, and right motive. Crucially, just war doctrine rejects the Realist/consequentialist position that an action can be justified merely because it leads to good overall results (though of course consequences are morally relevant in just war doctrine). Given that the most commonly stated rationale for assassination is consequentialist in nature—that is, that assassination would be the most efficient means of achieving one's goals—the practice of assassination would then seem to be ruled out in just war doctrine. But is this in fact the case, and even if it is, does the rise of terrorism and weapons of mass destruction require a modification of the tradition? On one extreme is the view that assassination is never morally permissible, no matter the circumstances; at the other extreme is the position that the conditions of the present day are so dangerous that traditional moral constraints must be sacrificed where necessary. I will argue here that neither position is correct; assassination is not automatically prohibited by just war doctrine, though it will be morally permissible only under very limited circumstances.

A first issue is, of course, the problem of defining *assassination*, a concept which is very difficult to pin down. Traditionally, the term *assassination* was held to refer to killing by means of treachery, betrayal, or perfidy. Some commentators have argued that this prohibition reflected a concern for honor or chivalry, and that it was not meant to prohibit targeting military or political leaders per se. Thus Caspar Weinberger has argued that when assassination is forbidden in the law of armed conflict, what is meant is "murder by treacherous means,"[2] and that therefore there is nothing wrong with assassination per se, so long as it does not involve "treachery." This argument however is a red herring. Whatever the concerns about the use of treachery in war, the central moral issue at stake is not the betrayal of trust, but rather the morality of premeditated, extrajudicial killing of specific individuals (i.e., those in leadership positions). Such an action would seem far removed from the paradigmatic case of justified killing: the soldier on the battlefield with a weapon in hand. Alberico Gentili, for example, allowed for seeking out the leader on the battlefield, but disapproved of the killing of the leader if he were "remote from arms and happened to be swimming in the Tiber," for this is killing an "unarmed man remote from war."[3] Such actions would ordinarily be considered simply murder, and the question is whether there is sufficient moral basis for permitting such a prima

facie wrongful act. Some commentators have adopted the term *targeted killing* so as to avoid any connotations of treachery associated with the term *assassination*.[4] However, in this essay I will use the terms *assassination* and *targeted killing* interchangeably, whether or not "treachery" is involved. The moral question is then whether assassinations—the premeditated, extrajudicial killings of a named individual—are permissible or not under just war doctrine.

A second issue we will have to examine is whether there is an essential difference between military and political leaders as regards the legitimacy of assassination. It is often assumed that military leaders, as they are obviously combatants under just war principles, are legitimate targets in wartime, and therefore it is permissible to assassinate them. Political leaders such as Saddam Hussein or Fidel Castro, some have argued, are different: they are not obviously combatants, even where they have ultimate control over the military. Similar difficult questions concern countries where the commander of the military is a civilian, as in the United States. The question is of course further complicated by the problem of assigning combatant status at all when there is not a state of war, especially as regards the problem of terrorism, which takes place in what William Banks calls the "twilight zone between war and peace."[5] But even within terrorist groups one can distinguish between political and military leaders. Israel's policy to date has been to accept just such a distinction within terrorist organizations such as Hamas, so that it does not try to kill political leaders who do not direct suicide bombers. This Israeli policy may however be breaking down currently, and many advocates of assassination reject the political/military distinction as artificial.

The question to be faced then is the following: is there a moral basis for a policy of premeditated, extrajudicial killing, and does it depend on whether the target is a military or merely political leader? Discussion of this question is often muddled by a failure to clearly distinguish the punishment rationale from the self-defense rationale for assassination. Indeed, the idea of justifying a policy of assassination under the rubric of punishment would seem to run into intractable moral problems, for a policy of summary execution without trial or any significant procedural constraints would not ordinarily be considered a legitimate form of punishment. Consider for example Caspar Weinberger's discussion: he begins with a just war defensive rationale for targeting leaders (on the grounds that they are combatants), then switches to a punishment argument ("there is every reason to punish the leaders for the acts that brought on the war"), and ends with a consequentialist rationale for assassination ("killing leaders may end a war with a big saving of soldiers' lives").[6] He concludes that if killing the leaders would not violate the laws of armed conflict, "then clearly the taking of any enemy commander (without any treachery) and holding him for trial conducted under normal national rules would not violate any moral or legal prohibition."[7] But the confusions in this argument are legion. The just war tradition, as I have said, does not obviously dictate that heads of state are combatants, and in any case Weinberger's invocation of consequentialist justifications are clearly ruled out under just war doctrine. More importantly, the syllogism with which Weinberger concludes his essay—that if killing the leader is permissible, then trying him is permissible—is not to the point. What is clear is that capturing an enemy commander and placing him on trial is morally and legally permissible. What is not clear is whether intentionally killing him—without benefit of trial—is permissible.

Given that the punishment rationale for extrajudicial assassination seems so obviously inapt, and given that most commentators do not want to resort to the Realist/consequentialist reasoning that Weinberger invokes, it is no surprise that most defenders of the assassination policy invoke a self-defense rationale. Thus, for example, Secretary of Defense Donald Rumsfeld reportedly told CNN that "the US would be acting in self-defense" in carrying out missions to assassinate bin Laden and other terrorists.[8] Yet even this line of argument is repeatedly conflated with nondefensive justifications. Brenda Godfrey, for example, defends Rumsfeld's position, and correctly distinguishes self-defense from backward-looking motives of reprisal or retaliation.[9] Yet she too

fails to clearly distinguish defense from forward-looking consequentialist or punishment motives. When there is an imminent threat of a terrorist attack, she argues, force is justified "in order to prevent the attack or to deter further attacks."[10] But the deterrence rationale is not obviously part of the doctrine of self-defense. Rather, deterrence belongs to the sphere of punishment and of consequentialist reasoning. Godfrey also appears to conflate the preventive use of force with the consequentialist justification that whatever leads to the best results is thereby morally permissible, as evidenced by her claim that "use of force should include the covert killing of the terrorist because it is the most efficient means of averting future harm."[11] Thomas Wingfield similarly invokes deterrence, consequentialist, and punishment rationales for assassination: "The proportionality doctrine of international law supports a conclusion that it is wrong to allow the slaughter of 10,000 relatively innocent soldiers and civilians if the underlying aggression can be brought to an end by the elimination of one guilty individual."[12] So, too, does Louis Beres confuse self-defense with consequentialism, arguing that the right of self-defense in Article 51 of the United Nations Charter authorizes assassination, given that a "utilitarian or balance-of-harms criterion could surely favor assassination" over large-scale uses of defensive force.[13]

Beres further asserts that in certain circumstances, the resort to assassination would be "decidedly rational and humane."[14] It is important to acknowledge just how tempting the idea of assassination is even from a moral standpoint. It offers a trade of a single death to avoid the death of millions, and as former White House press secretary Ari Fleischer put it, "The cost of one bullet, if the Iraqi people take it on themselves, is substantially less" than going to war.[15] The televangelist Pat Robertson recently on his television program called for the assassination of Venezuelan President Hugo Chavez, on the grounds that assassination is "a whole lot cheaper than starting a war."[16] Perhaps more pertinently, it appears to vindicate our moral sense, in that assassination goes directly after the responsible, indeed morally guilty, parties rather than after the "innocent" soldiers who in most cases are merely following orders, often under duress (as for instance in the Iraqi army). Jeff McMahan, for example, far too quickly assumes that morality favors targeting the guilty in war rather than those presenting a direct threat: "morality concedes that certain morally noninnocent noncombatants, like the political leader who initiates an unjust war, may be attacked."[17]

However, as tempting as these arguments sound, they do not in fact provide a moral basis for killing in war. Under just war doctrine, the primary justification for killing in war is defensive; it follows that neither of the aforementioned factors is morally relevant. The rationale of self-defense, as we have said, is distinct from the consequentialist or Realist rationale that aims to minimize overall costs and permits adopting any means so long as the ultimate end is permissible. Equally important, moral guilt, while it is the basis for the justification of punishment, is not the rationale for the use of defensive force. Defensive force in general is justified by the fact of aggression, not by the guilt of the aggressor. Hence soldiers may be killed even if they are not morally guilty of any wrong. "Innocence" in just war doctrine (and in self-defense doctrine generally) is a term of art, meaning one who is not presently threatening harm (from the Latin *nocere* = to harm). Thus it is crucial to understand the nature of the justification for killing and avoid conflating incompatible moral theories.

Thus we may conclude that the just war rationale for killing enemies in conflict is that the enemy poses a direct, unjust threat that can be countered by no other means than violence. While this rationale is often described as *defensive*, this term must be understood in a broad sense. That is, it is not necessarily limited to imminent or immediate threats, but can include preventive force against potential future threats. Thus the just war tradition has long recognized the legitimacy of *preventive* force against a potential future threat (assuming one has also satisfied the conditions of last resort, proportionality, and other requirements for going to war).[18] One is legitimately entitled to act so as to protect oneself against an unjust threat, even if that threat is in the future and not

yet imminent. However, it is crucial to note the distinction between the preventive rationale and the consequentialist justification. For the consequentialist, any use of force is justified so long as it leads to a net balance of good results. The just war preventive rationale, in contrast, insists that one is also constrained by a moral duty only to use harm against unjust threats. It is this distinction that accounts for why terrorism (intentionally targeting civilians for political or military purposes) is prohibited under just war doctrine, whereas terrorism in principle would be morally permissible for consequentialism. For just war doctrine, the preventive or defensive use of force must be targeted only against an unjust attacker.

Hence the question facing us, in order to determine whether assassination is permissible, is whether political or military leaders are legitimate military targets, that is, whether they are unjust attackers. It is often taken as uncontroversial and unproblematic that military leaders are legitimate military targets, given their presence in the chain of command—and sometimes this is extended to political leaders, too, so long as they direct the military. Thomas Wingfield, for instance, approvingly cites Schmitt: "lawful targeting in wartime has never required that the individual actually be engaged in combat. Rather, it depends on combatant status. The general directing operations miles from battle is as valid a target as the commander leading his troops in combat. The same applies to Saddam Hussein. Once he became a combatant, the law of war clearly permitted targeting him."[19] But, even apart from the logical leap between military commanders and heads of state, the chief error in this passage is what we might call the *formalist fallacy*. Just war doctrine indeed is often accused of formalism (sometimes called *essentialism*), of making combatancy simply determined by one's formal role, as if one can simply read off one's combatant status by identifying the essence of one's role. But this is I think a mischaracterization of just war doctrine.

Stephen Kershnar, for example, accuses the just war doctrine of holding that certain roles have "essences" that in turn determine one's status as combatant or noncombatant.[20] A doctor's essential role is to heal, a farmer's essential role is to grow food; hence they are not combatants. But a soldier's—and a military leader's—essential role is to fight, thus making him a combatant. The question of whether a political leader is a legitimate target then comes down to the question of whether his role is essentially one connected to aggression. Kershnar rightfully criticizes this view as clumsy and unconvincing. Indeed, it is not even clear in this view whether the political leader is a combatant or not. Is the nature of his role political leadership or military leadership? The formalist doctrine is also unhelpful in its application to terrorism, where there is no war and thus no combatancy in the technical sense. But it is also wrong, I would argue, because it mischaracterizes just war doctrine.

In the just war doctrine, combatancy is not determined by one's formal status, but rather by one's current and ongoing actions: that is, whether they constitute aggression or not. A soldier who lays down his weapons, or is no longer a threat, is no longer a combatant for purposes of exercising one's right to use deadly force. He may be captured, but he may not be shot. Correspondingly, a civilian who takes up arms and attempts aggressive action is a legitimate target, despite not being a combatant in the formal or essential sense. In other words, there is no avoiding a substantive analysis of the notion of combatancy. One is a combatant to the extent one is engaging in unjustified aggression; one is a noncombatant to the extent one is not a present or imminent threat. The paradigm of the combatant, then, is the soldier with the weapon pointed at you. On this view, it is not automatically true that a military leader is a combatant in the strict sense, and it is even more difficult to say whether a political leader—who is typically unarmed and not a fighter, nor himself an imminent threat—constitutes a combatant. Thus law professor Abram Chayes, appearing on *Nightline*, argued that "if Saddam was out leading his troops and he got killed in the midst of an engagement, well, that's one thing. But if he is deliberately and selectively targeted, I think that's another."[21] Chayes goes too far, for surely actual presence on the battlefield is not the only way one can constitute a direct threat. The problem, of course, is to say

just under what circumstances a leader is himself a direct threat sufficient to justify making him a legitimate military target.

But how can we answer such a question? What I would suggest is that we must resort to the substantive criteria for aggression. Jeffrie Murphy's definition of aggression provides a good starting point: "What I mean by this [i.e., aggression] is that the links of the chain (like the links between motives and actions) are held together logically and not merely causally, i.e., all held together, in this case, under the notion of who it is that is engaged in an attempt to destroy you."[22] The idea here is that the criteria are more than merely causal (or else doctors and farmers would be aggressors), but have to do with the nature of one's agency. Is one a direct agent in the unjustified aggression? Thomas Wingfield concedes that merely being a "regime elite" does not render one a legitimate target; this only applies to those members "participating in or taking an active role in directing military operations."[23] But even this is too weak. The further away we get from this paradigm case of the soldier wielding a weapon, the more suspect must be the use of force against someone. With those in a supervisory role, the presumption must be against killing them, unless their role is immediate and direct in the act of aggression. It is more plausible to consider them aggressors where it is they who are actually initiating the acts, that is, issuing orders to subordinates to carry out specific acts of violence. (It should be noted that *aggression* can refer either to external and internal violence: attacks on other countries, or unjustified attacks on one's own people, as say Hitler's policy of genocide or Hussein's use of chemical weapons on the Kurds.)

Clearly, military leaders will be far more likely to qualify as part of the direct chain of aggression than will political leaders. On this analysis, there can be no simple answer as to whether a given political leader is an aggressor, and hence a legitimate target in war. The answer will depend on the extent of involvement with the waging and oversight of the aggression, including, importantly, the extent to which he provides the initiative for the war itself, or for particular acts of aggression within it. The political structure of the society will obviously be relevant; in a dictatorship, there is far more centralized control of state functions, and thus a much stronger presumption of direct responsibility on the part of the ruler. In a democracy, in contrast, the leader may be acting as the agent of the legislature or the people in general. Even having the ultimate responsibility for giving the green light to war does not necessarily constitute the leader as an aggressor— this will depend on such factors as whether he is the initiator of the aggression or merely a figurehead. But it seems that in general political leaders are sufficiently different from military leaders such that the ordinary presumption of combatancy does not apply to the former category. Arguably Saddam Hussein was a legitimate target in that he appeared to maintain "operational control over military action"[24] and was himself directly responsible for the immediate or future potential harm. This would be even more justifiable where a leader is on the verge of ordering a nuclear strike, or authorizing an act of terrorism—assuming that he is genuinely the initiator and motivating force of the action, not merely a bureaucrat providing formal approval. It is true that in the age of modern warfare, the traditional paradigm of the target as one who is on the battlefield or even wielding a weapon is less useful, given the capacity of a political leader to order the launching of weapons of mass destruction from behind the lines (though this is not so much due to terrorism, but to the development of high technology, especially WMD). But of course the standard must be set very high here; the further removed a person is from direct control over the attack, the stronger the presumption must be against treating him as a direct threat and therefore a legitimate target.

Nonetheless, there remain serious concerns about the idea of assassination even if we decide that the leader is a legitimate target; these concerns apply to the assassination of military leaders as well as political leaders. The fact of premeditation is troublesome; in any case of homicide, premeditation often indicates a motive to kill whether or not such killing is strictly necessary. A primary moral duty with respect to any use of force is to use the minimum necessary harm. An assassination order, or a bounty offered for the target "dead or alive," is in itself not morally permissible, because it violates this duty. Any planned assassination must be one in which killing is only a last resort; the order must be to capture alive if at all possible. (Some questions were raised, for example, about the killing of Hussein's sons: was every reasonable effort made to capture them alive?) This is to say, a premeditated killing is always suspect; the aim must be to capture if at all possible, and to kill only to prevent the target from escaping and carrying out further harm.[25]

A second concern is the danger of the slippery slope: if assassinations are permitted, will this undermine the just war limits on killing? The worry here is about breaking down the barrier between legitimate killing in self-defense or prevention of future harm (or, more controversially, punishment in the context of war crimes tribunals) versus the sort of illegitimate killing of which terrorism is a prime example, and which can simply be called *murder*. Assassination, given its premeditated character, is uncomfortably close to the side of illegitimacy. This is not necessarily a reason to reject the legitimacy of all assassinations, but it is a reason to reiterate the strict limitations on the policy. To the extent a person is in a role distant from the actual aggression itself (i.e., a supervisory role), there must be a direct connection between him and the acts of violence. A mere figurehead leader, as Wingfield suggests, is not a legitimate target, nor ordinarily is a civilian commander in a democratic state. The ordinary assumption must be that one may use defensive force only against those who are the agents threatening unjust violence. In just war doctrine, targeting of political leaders should be especially avoided. The Israeli policy of assassination of Hamas terrorist leaders has been defended on the grounds that it is designed to prevent imminent unjust attacks on civilians, that these leaders are directly responsible for planning and authorizing attacks, and that all reasonable alternatives have been exhausted (including issuing arrest warrants to Palestinian authorities, requesting extradition, etc.). To the extent these claims are true, they would seem to constitute a legitimate case of justifiable assassination.

In conclusion, it appears that the policy of assassination or targeted killing, though it raises serious moral concerns, can in some circumstances be a legitimate tool of war. However, the justification for such acts cannot be consequentialist in nature, aiming at a more "efficient" victory or at waging war "on the cheap." Much of the recent shift in opinion in favor of the use of assassination can be revealed for what it is: a newly emboldened effort of the Realists and the consequentialists to make inroads into the just war doctrine.[26] Nonetheless, the targeting of military or political leaders can in certain circumstances be a morally legitimate tool of war, justified as a preventive use of force against the initiator or controlling force of unjust aggression (even where there is not an imminent threat). Indeed, a murderous tyrant such as Hussein would seem to provide just such a case: where the political leader exerts near-total control over military and political decisions, where he is clearly the initiator of the unjust aggression, and where his capture or prevention is not possible other than by killing him. While we must reject the Realist idea that assassination is simply another tool of war to be used wherever effective, we must also reject the view that assassination is wholly prohibited under just war doctrine. It is only under very limited circumstances that the assassination of a political leader will be morally permissible.

NOTES

1. Article 23b, Annex to the Hague Convention IV (1907), prohibits "assassination, proscription, or outlawry of an enemy, or putting a price upon an enemy's head, as well as offering a reward for an enemy 'dead or alive.'"
2. Weinberger, "When Can We Target the Leaders?" *Strategic Review* (Spring 2001): 21–24, p. 23. See also Thomas Wingfield, "Taking Aim at Regime Elites," *Maryland Journal of International Law and Trade* 22 (1999): 287–317, p. 287.
3. *De Jure Belli Libri Tres* (1612), Book II Chapter VIII, in *The Classics of International Law*, trans. J. Rolfe (Oxford: Oxford University Press, 1950), 171.
4. See, e.g., Williams Banks, "Targeted Killing and Assassination: The U.S. Legal Framework," *University of Richmond Law Review* 37 (March 2003): 667–749, p. 671.
5. Ibid.
6. Weinberger, "When Can We Target the Leaders?," 22.
7. Ibid., 24.
8. Quoted in Brenda Godfrey, "Authorization to Kill Terrorist Leaders," *San Diego International Law Journal* 4 (2003): 491–512, p. 491.
9. Ibid., 501.
10. Ibid., 504.
11. Ibid.
12. Wingfield, "Taking Aim at Regime Elites," 312. Note the two distinct errors in this claim: (1) a conflation of self-defense with the punishment-based notions of guilt and innocence, and (2) a misunderstanding of the proportionality constraint as a consequentialist provision.
13. Beres, "On International Law and Nuclear Terrorism," *Georgia Journal of International and Comparative Law* 24 (1994): 1–36, p. 33.
14. Ibid.
15. See http://www.whitehouse.gov/news/releases/2002/10/20021001-4.html.
16. See, e.g., "A Call for Assassination Brings a Cry of Outrage," *Los Angeles Times*, 24 August 2005, 1.
17. McMahan, "Realism, Morality, and War," in *The Ethics of War and Peace*, ed. Terry Nardin (Princeton: Princeton University Press, 1996). 90.
18. See my "What's Wrong with Defensive War?" *Ethics and International Affairs* 19:3 (2005), for a discussion on the legitimacy of the use of preventive force in war.
19. Wingfield, "Taking Aim at Regime Elites," 314.
20. "The Moral Argument for a Policy of Assassination," paper delivered at APA Central Division Meeting, 2003. This paper has since been published in *Reason Papers* 27 (Fall 2004): 45–67.
21. Program on 4 February 1991. Wingfield dismisses Chayes's example too quickly (see Wingfield, "Taking Aim at Regime Elites," 314).
22. Murphy, "The Killing of the Innocent," in *War, Morality, and the Military Profession*, ed. Malham Wakin (Boulder: Westview Press, 1986), 346.
23. Wingfield, "Taking Aim at Regime Elites," 311.
24. Sebastien Jodoin, "The Legality of Saddam Hussein's Assassination," Part II, 3 (available at http://www.law.mcgill.ca/quid/archive/2003/03040805.html).
25. One might argue that the "dead or alive" idea means that the ultimate goal is to get the target, however necessary. Still, it implies indifference as between the two, even a veiled preference for "dead." Clearly, the moral rule requires the aim of capturing alive if at all possible.

26. See, for example, John Yoo's assertion that "a nation at war may use force against members of the enemy at any time, regardless of their proximity to hostilities or their activity at the time of attack." Yoo is believed to have authorized a Justice Department opinion justifying the use of assassinations in wartime. See Paul Barrett, "Opinion Maker: A Young Lawyer Helps Chart Shift in Foreign Policy," *Wall Street Journal*, 12 September 2005, A1.

⚜ REVIEW QUESTIONS

1. How does Kaufman describe just war doctrine?
2. How does he use the term *assassination*?
3. Kaufman distinguishes between a punishment rationale, a self-defense rationale, and a consequentialist rationale for assassination. Why does he reject both the punishment rationale and the consequentialist rationale?
4. According to Kaufman, what is the formalist fallacy? Why does it mischaracterize just war theory?
5. According to Kaufman, what two questions must be answered in the affirmative to morally justify assassination?
6. Kaufman says there are serious concerns about the idea of assassination even if the target is a combatant. What are they?
7. State and explain Kaufman's conclusion.

⚜ DISCUSSION QUESTIONS

1. Does revenge or punishment justify the assassination of Osama bin Laden? What is your view? What if killing him had good consequences, such as stopping al-Qaeda attacks on the United States? Would that morally justify killing him? Why or why not?
2. Would the assassination of Hitler have been justified at the start of World War II? Explain your position.
3. Kaufman claims that an assassination order, or a bounty offered, for a target like bin Laden "dead or alive" is not morally permissible. Do you agree? Why or why not?

Targeted Killing

DANIEL STATMAN

Daniel Statman is professor of philosophy at the University of Haifa in Haifa, Israel. He is the author of *Moral Dilemmas* (1995) and *Religion and Morality* (1995) with Avi Sagi. He is also the author of more than thirty articles in ethics.

Statman argues that targeted killing is analogous to conventional war. If a conventional war such as the British attack on the Falkland Islands is morally justified, then so is the targeted killing of al-Qaeda or Hamas leaders. In Statman's view, targeted killing is morally preferable to conventional war because fewer civilians are killed. The gravity of the terrorist threat posed by al Qaeda and Hamas, and the lack of any other option for the community to defend itself from the threat, gives the community a moral license to kill in self-defense. In addition to self-defense, Statman endorses retribution as justifying targeted killing terrorists with blood on their hands.

INTRODUCTION

The threat of terror has found the West widely unprepared to deal with it. The standard means of waging war are irrelevant to contending with this threat; tanks, jets, and submarines are helpful when confronting other tanks, jets, and submarines, not hijackers carrying knives or terrorists wearing explosive belts. The standard means of fighting crime also seem unaccommodating in the face of this threat; the chances of Interpol capturing Bin Laden and his followers and bringing them to justice are remote, as are the chances of the Israeli police arresting and trying the leaders of the Hammas and Islamic Jihad. Hence, to effectively stop terror, a different model must be sought, not the model of conventional war with its machines and tools, nor that of the police and court activities conducted against ordinary criminals. Rather, the wars against terror must adopt methods that are less common, or altogether uncommon, in conventional wars. One such method, whose legitimacy I wish to defend here, is that of targeted killings.

In choosing the term "targeted killing" rather than "assassination," I have sought to avoid the negative moral connotation that is almost inherent in the latter. If the argument of this paper is sound, then not all acts of assassination are morally wrong or, alternatively, not all acts of targeted killing are assassinations. Prior to September 11, 2001, Israel was the only country openly employing this tactic in its fight against terror, and it was strongly condemned for doing so by most of the international community, including the U.S. But since the September 11th attacks, the U.S. itself has adopted this policy in its war against Al Qaeda. In November 2002, an American Predator UAV (Unmanned Aerial Vehicle) targeted and killed an Al Qaeda activist in Yemen[1] using a technique similar to that used by the Israeli army against Hammas or Islamic Jihad activists. Furthermore, in December 2002,

The New York Times reported that "[t]he CIA is authorized to kill individuals described as 'terrorist leaders' on a list approved by the White House."[2] However, some commentators continue to believe that there is a moral difference between the Israeli and the American positions, and I will address their argument later on.

The main thesis of this article is that acceptance of the legitimacy of the killing and destruction in a conventional war necessarily entails accepting the legitimacy of targeted killings in the war against terror. In other words, a principled objection to targeted killings necessarily entails a pacifist approach to conventional war. I present this thesis and defend it in Section I. In Section II, I explore the possibility of justifying targeted killings on the basis of retribution, which, I argue, might play a more significant role in this context than usually assumed. Section III rejects a sophisticated philosophical argument against targeted killings, namely, that based on the alleged problematic implications of "named killing" for war ethics. In Section IV, I turn to the effectiveness of targeted killings and, in Section V, analyze the moral status of targeted killings in the context of conventional war. The final section summarizes the conclusions of the discussion regarding the legitimacy of targeted killing.

I. MORALITY AND WAR

I mentioned at the outset two general models for dealing with threats to vital interests: the war model and the non-war (i.e., criminal law and individual self-defense) model. In war, goes the common wisdom, soldiers of all sides are permitted to kill any soldier of the adversary, unless the latter surrenders or in limited exceptional circumstances. This permission to kill is not contingent on establishing that the soldier being killed poses any significant threat to the other side or, even assuming that he does pose such a threat, that he is morally responsible for doing so. Moreover,

---

[1]Walter Pincus, *U.S. Strike Kills Six in Al Qaeda; Missile Fired by Predator Drone; Key Figure in Yemen Among Dead,* Wash. Post, Nov. 5, 2002, at A1.

[2]*C.I.A. Expands Authority To Kill Qaeda Leaders,* N.Y. Times, Dec. 15, 2002, at A2.

under the principle of *jus ad bellum*, states are not required to establish the imperativeness of the interests threatened in order to justify going to war. Usually a violation of territorial sovereignty will be considered a just cause for going to war, a *casus belli*, even if the consequences of that violation for human lives and dignity might be relatively insignificant. Many believe that the British attack on the Falkland Islands was not only legally justified but also morally justified, despite the fact that the Argentinean invasion most likely would not have led to the killing of British citizens or acts of oppression. Thus: (1) states can go to war for the sake of formal sovereignty with no need to show that, beyond that formal sovereignty, any vital interests are in clear and imminent danger, and (2) once they actually do wage war, they can kill any enemy soldier, regardless of the personal danger posed by or responsibility of those being killed. Following McMahan, I shall call this view the "Orthodox View."[3]

Things are, of course, totally different, both morally and legally, in the context of the relations between individuals under criminal law and accepted rules of self-defense. To kill in self-defense, one is required to verify that the perceived attacker poses a clear and imminent danger to one's vital interests and that the attacker bears responsibility for this danger. And, of course, with respect to punishment, it can be imposed only after establishing beyond reasonable doubt that the accused did commit the alleged crime with the required *mens rea*.

It is truly puzzling that most people who endorse the strongest restrictions on killing in self-defense and the most stringent procedures and application of criminal law, often including an objection to capital punishment, subscribe to the Orthodox View with regard to the morality and legality of killing in the context of war. What is puzzling is that not only do they accept this view, but they do so with almost no reservation and with no awareness of the tension that exists between the blanket license to kill (enemy soldiers)

in war and the strict limitations on killing in a non-war context. This seems another instance of the human ability to compartmentalize, a capacity that is probably advantageous from an evolutionary point of view, but still startling whenever we face it. I am referring to the cognitive ability to allocate different judgments to the different "compartments" within which we function: home, work, politics, etc. Thus, people generally fail to notice the moral problem with many instances of killings in war even when they are fierce objectors to the death penalty, because they view the situation of war as different from the non-war context. They see war as constituting a separate sphere with its own set of rules, which are, after all, almost universally accepted. Jurists are especially vulnerable to this kind of thinking, because since international law recognizes the legitimacy of large-scale killing in war (of soldiers), it fosters the line of thought that wars are simply different than regular conflicts between individuals and are governed by different rules.

Let me leave the psychology of these conflicting attitudes to others and focus instead on the relevant normative issues. The contention that war *qua* war is simply "different" and, hence, governed by a different set of rules is merely a sophisticated (albeit more moderate) version of the realist view, according to which "*Inter arma silent leges*" ("In time of war the laws are silent"). We need to understand why this is so, how it is that human life, held so sacred in domestic law, is held in such light regard by the laws of war. Killing in war can be justified only on the basis of the same fundamental principles that guide relations between individuals outside the sphere of war. If these principles fail to provide the justification for killing in war, then the Orthodox View can be maintained only at the cost of inconsistency and with the aid of psychological mechanisms such as compartmentalization and self-deception.

Discussing the tenability of the Orthodox View is far beyond the scope of the present paper. It is, however, crucial to note that most philosophers who have addressed this topic over the last two decades have taken for granted what may be called the unity of our moral and legal thought—i.e., that the same general justifications for killing

---

[3]Jeff McMahan, *Innocence, Self-Defense, and Killing in War*, 2 J. Pol. Phil. 193 (1994).

people in non-war situations must apply to war situations as well. This assumption has led some philosophers to call into question the validity of the Orthodox View and to suggest that some modifications are, in any event, warranted. I will offer two examples of such modifications, one relating to *jus ad bellum*, the other to *jus in bello*.

The first example is in the context of the previously mentioned Falkland Islands War. The common view holds that the Argentinean invasion of the Falkland Islands was a *casus belli*; hence the U.K. was morally and legally justified in going to war. Yet, according to Richard Norman, the war was unjustified as it was waged for the sake of formal sovereignty alone.[4] Just as in the case of individual self-defense, the mere formal violation of rights (for example, property rights) is not sufficient to justify killing another human being. Violation of territorial sovereignty can justify going to war only if it threatens substantive values such as life, dignity, or the survival of a culture and, of course, when there is no other way of protecting such values. Thus, the common view regarding the conditions that justify going to war tends to be overly lax.

The second example is the stance taken by Jeff McMahan. Arguing against the Orthodox View, he defends what he calls the "Moral View," under which a combatant's moral innocence or guilt is determined, in part, by whether or not he is fighting in a just war. If his war is unjust and if he is not forced to take part in it, he cannot claim a moral right to kill enemy soldiers on the basis of self-defense.[5] This conclusion, which makes a lot of moral sense, runs counter to a widespread convention of *jus in bello*, namely, that all combatants are "morally equal."

These two examples illustrate what happens to the ethics of war once one takes seriously the requirement to square the moral rules concerning war with those regulating relations in non-war situations. If the moral rationale for going to war is self-defense, then the same conditions that govern self-defense on the individual level must do so at the level of nations too, in particular: (1) the rule that what is defended is either one's life or something close to it in value and (2) the rule that the attacker's responsibility is highly relevant in making him the object of killing in self-defense.

With this brief introduction in mind, we can now move to wars against terror.[6] Let me start by asking, What entitles the U.S. to define its campaign against Al Qaeda as war, with the loosening of various moral prohibitions implied by such a definition, rather than as a police enforcement action aimed at bringing a group of criminals to justice? The answer here—as with conventional war—lies in: (a) the gravity of the threat posed by Al Qaeda and (b) the impracticality of coping with this threat by conventional law-enforcing institutions and methods. The threat posed by Al Qaeda to the U.S. is enormous. It is not only a threat to the lives of thousands of people, Americans and others, but also the threat of the terrorizing results of such mass killing on the entire country in terms of the economy and the quality of day-to-day life. A war of terror does not mean that all citizens are under actual attack all the time, but that such attacks are frequent enough and devastating enough to make life unbearable. As Hobbes observed, being in a state of war does not mean that there are battles all the time, but, rather, a miserable condition in which

> there is no place for industry; because the fruit thereof is uncertain: and consequently no culture of the earth; no navigation, nor use of the commodities that might be imported by sea . . . no account of time; no arts; no letters; no society; and which is worst of all, continual fear, and danger of violent death; and the life of man, solitary, poor, nasty, brutish, and short.[7]

Clearly enough, condition (a) applies *a fortiori* to the situation to which Israel is subject in what the Palestinians call the *Alaqsa Intifada*, whose main characteristic is almost daily attempts

---

[4]Richard Norman, *Ethics, Killing and War*, 156–58 (1995).
[5]McMahan, *supra* note 3. *Cf.* Norman, *supra* note 4, at 172–73.

[6]I say "wars against terror" rather than "the war against terror" because I see no reason to regard the various actual or potential wars against terror as part of one big war against one defined enemy.
[7]Thomas Hobbes, *Leviathan*, pt. 1, ch. 13, at 84 (J.C.A. Gaskin ed., Oxford Univ. Press 1996) (1651).

at murdering Jews across Israel, in buses, restaurants, nightclubs, universities, wherever possible. If ever there could be a *casus belli* on grounds of self-defense, it is such a terror campaign launched against a country or some other collective. From a moral point of view, the values under threat in such cases are far more important than those involved in cases of a mere formal violation of sovereignty, which, under the common view, justify waging war. To make the point as clear as possible, if the United Kingdom was morally justified in waging war to regain control over the Falkland Islands when there was no threat to the lives of British citizens and no significant threat to their security or economy, then surely the U.S. is morally justified in going to war against Bin Laden to prevent another attack against it, an attack that could cause the loss of many innocent lives and have catastrophic effects on the life of the nation. And if the U.S. is justified in going to war after only one (awful) day of terror, Israel certainly has the right to do so after so many dark days of terror.

The second condition mentioned above for regarding a situation as war rather than as a law-enforcement operation, namely, the impracticality of coping with the threat by means of conventional law-enforcing institutions and methods, is met in the case of the U.S. campaign against Al Qaeda as well as in the case of the Israeli struggle with the Palestinian terror organizations. The proposition that Al Qaeda members could be prevented from carrying out further terror attacks by issuing an arrest order to the governments harboring them, is, at best, naïve, and the same is true with regard to the thousands of Palestinians involved in planning and executing murderous actions in Israel. Things might have been different had the Palestinian Authority and its police cooperated with Israel in capturing the criminals and bringing them to justice. But this, of course, is pure wishful thinking. The Palestinian Authority not only refrained from arresting terrorists and, in general, from taking action against terror; it actually supported it in various ways.[8]

If we are to accept that the struggle against Al Qaeda and, likewise, that against the Palestinian armed organizations can be described as war, it follows that just as the U.S. can use lethal means to kill Al Qaeda members, so Israel can do so to kill Hammas or Tanzim members—just like in conventional war. Yet, while in conventional wars, enemy combatants are identified by their uniform and are located in camps, bases, and bunkers separate from the civilian population, in wars of terror, the fighters hide amongst the civilian population, which shelters them and supports them by various means. Hence, the latter wars do not take the conventional form of soldiers from one side of the conflict fighting directly against soldiers from the other side in an open space—in trenches, in the air, or at sea, remote from civilian life. Indeed, they take a rather different form. If we are to continue to adhere to the fundamental idea of just war theory, namely, that wars are fought between combatants only and should avoid targeting non-combatants, we must conclude that in wars against terror, too, the combatants of the terrorized country may direct their weapons only at members and activists in the terror organizations against which they are fighting.

To complete the analogy between conventional wars and wars against terror, we can assume that just as all soldiers (but only soldiers) are legitimate targets in the former, regardless of their individual roles, the threat they pose as individuals, or their personal responsibility in the waging or conducting of the war, so in the latter all members of the relevant terror organizations are legitimate targets and can be killed by the terrorized side on the basis of the latter's right to self-defense. Moreover, members of terrorist organizations bear far greater moral responsibility for their actions than soldiers in conventional wars, because many of the latter are conscripts forced to participate in the war, whereas joining a terror organization is usually a more voluntary act.

The problem, of course, is that terrorists do not come out into the open to fight against the armed forces of the other side, but, rather, hide amongst the civilian population and use the homes of families and friends as bases in planning

---

[8]For the deep involvement of the Palestinian Authority in terror, see, e.g., Ronen Bergman, Authority Given (2002) (Hebrew).

and executing their attacks. But the fact that civilians are the shield behind which terrorists hide should not be grounds for granting the latter some sort of immunity from attack. If they use their homes as terror bases, they cannot claim that these bases must be regarded as innocent civilian buildings. If soldiers in a conventional war hide in a residential building and shoot through its windows at enemy soldiers, there is no dispute that the latter are justified in using snipers to target and kill the former. Thus, if in a war against terror, terrorists establish their base in a residential area from where they launch murderous attacks (dispatching suicide terrorists or firing artillery), the other side is justified in using snipers, helicopters, and other methods to target and kill the terrorists.

Targeted killing, then, emerges as the most natural manifestation of *jus in bello* in wars on terror, for under *jus in bello*, even if a war is unjust, it should be directed (to as great an extent as possible) only at combatants. This implies that wars against terror should be directed (to as great an extent as possible) only at terrorists. However, unlike enemy soldiers in conventional wars, terrorists are embedded amidst the civilian population and can be hit only (or mainly) in their homes, cars, and so forth. Thus, targeted killing is the most natural application of the principles of *jus in bello* in wars against terror.[9]

The moral legitimacy of targeted killing becomes even clearer when compared to the alternative means of fighting terror—that is, the massive invasion of the community that shelters and supports the terrorists in an attempt to catch or kill the terrorists and destroy their infrastructure. This mode of operation was adopted, for example, by the U.S. and Britain in Afghanistan and by Israel in its "Operation Defensive Shield" carried out after the terrorist Passover massacre in March 2002. While many claim this method to be morally preferable to targeted killing—likely because it bears more of a resemblance to "real" war—I believe the opposite to be true. First, invading a civilian area inevitably leads to the deaths and injury of far more people, mostly innocent people, than careful use of targeted killing. Second, such actions bring death, misery, and destruction to people who are only minimally involved (if at all) in, or responsible for, terror or military attacks, whereas with targeted killing, collateral damage is significantly reduced (though not prevented altogether). Hence, targeted killing is the preferable method not only because, on a utilitarian calculation, it saves lives—a very weighty moral consideration—but also because it is more commensurate with a fundamental condition of justified self-defense, namely, that those killed are responsible for the threat posed. Members of the Hammas in Gaza are far more responsible for the threat of terror to Israel than their non-activist neighbors are; hence it is preferable from a moral standpoint to target the former directly rather than invade Gaza and inevitably cause great injury to the latter and to the general population.

Let me press this last point a bit further. Suppose that Arafat were to call a special meeting of the Palestinian government and formally declare war on Israel by all means available. Suppose further that in the wake of this declaration, Israel were to face a wave of terror identical to that it faced in the months preceding Operation Defensive Shield. Surely no one would question Israel's right to wage war in return, that is, to invade the Gaza Strip and the West Bank and fight against its enemy, though such an operation would claim the lives of many people bearing no, or only minimal, responsibility for the terror wreaked on Israel. How could such an operation be considered

---

[9]Some critics totally deny the fundamental distinction made by just war theory and international law between combatants and non-combatants and, hence, see nothing wrong in principle with acts of terrorism. A notorious example is Ted Honderich, *After the Terror* 151 (2002), who explicitly states that "the Palestinians have exercised a moral right in their terrorism against the Israelis . . . those who have killed themselves in the cause of their people have indeed sanctified themselves." Obviously, if indiscriminate killing of children is a legitimate means of achieving political aims, then targeting killing is even more so. Hence, targeted killing cannot be morally objected to on the ground of constituting an illegitimate means of warfare. Views such as Honderich's thus *reduce* the arguments available to opponents of targeted killing. For a critical analysis of his view, see Tamar Meisels, *The Trouble With Terror* (2003) (unpublished manuscript, on file with author).

morally justified, yet the measure of killing fewer people and only those more active in and responsible for the terror (namely, targeted killing) be less justified or even unjustified?

To conclude, it is my claim that there is a profound inconsistency in, on the one hand, accepting the legitimacy of killing in conventional war but, on the other, making a moral objection to targeted killing in wars against terror. If, as Georg Nolte emphasizes, "the right to life must be protected most strictly,"[10] it is, indeed, understandable that he would have qualms with regard to the killing of terrorist leaders or activists. However, it is then puzzling how he can accept large-scale killing in a war of human beings, i.e., soldiers (e.g., in Afghanistan[11]), whose personal responsibility for the waging of the war and whose direct threat to the other side are, at best, uncertain.

II. TARGETED KILLING AND RETRIBUTION

In a recent article on targeted killing, Steven David argues that the best moral justification for Israel's policy of targeted killing is retribution.[12] The argument is a simple and straightforward one: Those people targeted committed terrible crimes. Evildoers deserve to suffer in response and in a way suited to their crimes. Palestinian terrorists with blood on their hands therefore deserve death, the ultimate punishment for their crimes. Hence, the targeted killing of these terrorists is justified.

One could object to this argument by claiming that acts of retribution can be imposed only by a court of justice, within whose authority it is to punish and only after establishing the relevant facts of the case and the blameworthiness of the defendant. Retribution cannot be imposed by private individuals, nor by governments, but only by legal institutions.

But this objection must be wrong. First, for those who accept the idea of retribution,[13] the legal institution of punishment is the best means of achieving it, but not a necessary condition for its possibility. For retribution to apply, evildoers need to suffer, and this can be imposed by God, by Nature—or by some human being. No doubt there are powerful social and moral reasons for making the courts the only body that administers retribution in society, but these reasons bear no relevance on the justification of retribution per se, which, in principle, can be achieved outside the courtroom too. In the case of terrorists, the problem that arises is that retribution through the legal system is not an option with regard to most of them, because the countries that harbor them hardly ever bring them to trial within their territories, nor do they extradite them to be tried in a foreign domestic or international court. Since in such cases, retribution through the legal system is unfeasible, and if we take seriously the idea that evildoers deserve punishment, the inevitable conclusion is that retribution can, or must,[14] be imposed by some other entity, such as the army of the injured country.

Second, the role of courts in establishing the facts of the matter and the blameworthiness of the alleged criminal seems less significant in the context of terrorists because many of them are only too happy to admit their participation in the

---

[10]Georg Nolte, *Preventive Use of Force and Preventive Killings: Moves into a Different Legal Order*, 5 Theoretical Inquiries L. 111 (2004).

[11]*Id.* at [9–10], where Nolte concedes that "Taliban and Al Qaeda fighters could be killed by U.S. and other troops in Afghanistan as long as the United States was exercising its right of self-defence against organized and identified resistance in Afghanistan." Yet that this was a case of exercising the right of self-defense is exactly what needs to be established, and in any case, it does not imply that each individual Taliban fighter was a legitimate target.

[12]Steven R. David, *Israel's Policy of Targeted Killing*, 17 J. Ethics & Int'l Aff. 111 (2003).

[13]Needless to say, not everybody does. *See, e.g.*, David Dolinko, *Three Mistakes of Retributivism*, 39 UCLA L. Rev. 1623 (1992).

[14]I wish to take a neutral stance between the "hard" and "soft" views of retributivism. Under the former view, we have a moral duty to impose upon evildoers what they deserve, while under the latter, we are merely allowed to do so. For the purpose of the present argument, the weaker version is sufficient, because my central aim is to show that targeted killing is morally acceptable, not that it is morally mandatory.

relevant crimes or their active membership and roles in the relevant organizations.

In conventional wars, when the enemy upholds the conventions of war, retribution is irrelevant with regard to individual soldiers, and hence self-defense provides the only framework for justifying killing them. In wars against terror, retribution offers a justificatory framework that complements and bolsters the self-defense justification. Thus, killing enemy combatants in wars on terror—namely, activists in the terror organizations—is, if anything, more, and not less, justified than killing enemy combatants in conventional wars. . . .

SUMMARY AND CONCLUSIONS

The purpose of this paper is to provide a philosophical defense of targeted killing in wars against terror. It argues that if one accepts the moral legitimacy of the large-scale killing of combatants in conventional wars, one cannot object on moral grounds to the targeted killing of members of terrorist organizations in wars against terror. If one rejects this legitimacy, one must object to all killing in war, targeted and non-targeted alike, and thus not support the view, which is criticized here, that targeted killing is particularly disturbing from a moral point of view.

Defining a conflict as war, with the moral license to kill entailed thereby, is not an arbitrary decision. It has to do with the gravity of the threat to the vital interests of a given community and the absence of any other option for this community to defend itself against this threat. Under this understanding, certain conventional wars, such as the Falkland Islands War, do not justify the above license to kill, whereas certain unconventional wars, such as that waged against Al Qaeda, do. Moreover, the perception of a conflict as war and the legitimacy of using lethal measures in that conflict do not depend on the nature of the aggressor's motivation, be it national, religious, or otherwise, unless that motivation happens to affect the severity of the threat or the availability of non-war methods for coping with it.

Regarding the effectiveness of targeted killing in wars against terror, here, too, we can draw an analogy to conventional wars. Fighting armies do their best to choose effective measures, i.e., measures that will contribute to the defeat of their enemy. But very rarely will they be criticized, prospectively or retrospectively, on the grounds that ineffective actions caused the unnecessary deaths of enemy soldiers. Applied to targeted killing, this means that its effectiveness should concern us morally no more than the effectiveness of methods used or actions taken in conventional wars. At any rate, in most cases and in the long run, there is no convincing evidence that targeted killing is an ineffective means in fighting terror.

Finally, objectors to targeted killing (and to other anti-terrorism methods) often warn of overestimating the danger posed by terror and of hastening to use violent solutions instead of seeking a peacefully diplomatic solution. They urge the attacked country or collective to "understand" the roots of terror, implying that once these roots are understood and dealt with in a peaceful and constructive manner, the terror will vanish with no need for war. There is something to be said for these warnings. Yet, just as there is a danger of overestimating threats of terror, there is also a danger of underestimating them. Just as there is a danger of overlooking possible peaceful solutions and rushing to use force, there is also a danger of over-delaying the use of force due to false hopes for peaceful avenues. The atrocities in the former Yugoslavia in the 1990s provide us with a painful reminder of the toll in innocent lives that hesitation to use force to counter aggression can take.[15] The argument developed in this paper contends that with organizations such as Al Qaeda and the Hammas, the danger of over-delaying the use of force is more alarming than the prospect of missing out on peaceful solutions. Those who hold the opposite view and are more optimistic about human nature than I am are, of course, to be respected. But—one last time—I think their view applies, *a fortiori*, to conventional wars too.

---

[15]See, for example, Jonathan Glover, *Humanity: A Moral History of the 20th Century* at ch. 16, at 133–40 (2001), who argues that "the UN would have been more effective from the start if it had come closer to wielding Leviathan's power." *Id.* at 140.

⚜ REVIEW QUESTIONS

1. Statman distinguishes between two models for dealing with threats. What are they?
2. According to Statman, what is the Orthodox View of war? Why does he find this view puzzling?
3. How do Richard Norman and Jeff McMahan modify the Orthodox View?
4. Why does Statman think that the U.S. campaign against al Qaeda and Israel's attacks on Hamas are justified wars rather than police actions?
5. In what ways are conventional wars and wars against terror analogous, according to Statman? How are they not analogous?
6. Why does Statman think that targeted killing is morally legitimate? Why does he think it is morally preferable to conventional war?
7. What is Steven David's moral justification for targeted killing? Why does he accept it?

⚜ DISCUSSION QUESTIONS

1. Statman says that the threat posed by al Qaeda to the United States is enormous. Do you agree? If so, then why have there been no attacks on the United States since 2001?
2. Are wars against terror analogous to conventional wars? Why or why not?
3. Statman claims that targeted killing is morally preferable to conventional war. Do you agree? Why or why not?
4. Does retribution justify the targeted killing of Palestinian terrorists? Why or why not?

PROBLEM CASES

1. Osama bin Laden

In 1998 the CIA identified bin Laden as the leader of the al-Qaeda terrorist organization responsible for suicide bombing attacks on the U.S. embassies in Tanzania and Kenya. There were hundreds of casualties. A few days after the attacks, the CIA learned that bin Laden was scheduled to visit a terrorist training camp in Afghanistan. President Clinton ordered missile strikes to assassinate bin Laden and other leaders in retaliation. On August 20, 1998, about seventy-five cruise missiles hit four terrorist training camps in or near Khost, a city in eastern Afghanistan. The Khost camp, Zawhar Kili, was believed to be a meeting place for terrorist leaders, including bin Laden. After the attack, the CIA found out that bin Laden had indeed been at the Zawhar Kili camp, but had left an hour or so before the missiles hit. According to Pakistani journalist Ahmed Rashid, the air strikes killed twenty Afghans, seven Pakistanis, and seven others.

Ten years later, on August 20, 2008, newly declassified government documents were posted on the National Security Archive (www.nsarchive.org), which suggest that the 1998 air strikes not only failed to kill bin Laden but also helped al Qaeda and the Taliban in some ways. In particular, it is claimed that the attacks "provoked a new round of terrorist bombing plots," added to bin Laden's reputation "as an underdog standing firm in the face of bullying aggression," and resulted in the United States losing the moral high ground by imitating bin Laden's strategy of bombing in retaliation for grievances. Also, the attacks did not destroy or disrupt al Qaeda or the Taliban; they became even stronger and more effective after the attacks. Nevertheless, the attacks demonstrated U.S. military might and resolve to fight against terrorism. Also, the attacks may have deterred some terrorists and nations harboring terrorists.

All things considered, were these air strikes morally justified? Why or why not?

For the sake of argument, suppose the missile strikes had killed bin Laden. Three years later, maybe the attacks of 9/11 would not have happened. Bin Laden was central in planning the attacks. He came up with the plan to use commercial planes. He chose Muhammad Atta to be the leader of the terrorist attack team. He selected the targets, and he micromanaged the timing. However, if bin Laden had been killed in 1998, Ayman al-Zawahiri, his second-in-command, might have taken over the planning with the result that the 9/11 attacks would still have happened. We cannot be sure about the consequences of bin Laden's death.

If bin Laden had been killed in 1998 by the missile strikes, would those attacks have been morally acceptable? What is your view?

2. Ahmed Yassin

In 2004, Israeli helicopters killed Ahmed Yassin (age sixty-seven) with a missile strike. Yassin was leaving a mosque in Gaza city in his wheelchair when he was hit. The first missile hit him directly, leaving his body severely disfigured. Seven other people were killed in the attack, and another seventeen were injured, including two of Yassin's sons.

Yassin was a founder and leader of Hamas, the Palestinian organization that rules the Gaza portion of the Palestinian Territories. (In 2007, it won a large majority in the Palestinian parliament, and it has popular support in the Gaza Strip.) Hamas was created in 1987 by Yassin and two others at the beginning of the First Intifada, the popular uprising against Israeli rule in the Palestinian Territories. At the time of the assassination of Yassin, the United States and other countries classified Hamas as a terrorist organization because of its responsibility for numerous suicide bombings against Israelis.

The assassination of Yassin was condemned by Yasser Arafat, the Palestinian leader, as a "barbaric crime." In London, prime minister Tony Blair also condemned the killing. Hamas and other militant groups warned of more violence in retaliation. An estimated 200,000 mourners turned out for Yassin's funeral procession in Gaza.

Was Yassin's assassination by Israel morally justified? Why or why not?

3. Fidel Castro

(See Fabian Escalante, *Executive Action: 638 Ways to Kill Castro* [New York: Ocean Press, 2006].) Fabian Escalante was the head of the Cuban secret service. In his book he describes more than 600 ways in which the CIA tried to assassinate Fidel Castro, the Cuban dictator. The assassination attempts began in 1959 after the Cuban revolution and continued for nearly half a century. Perhaps the most famous was the loaded-cigar plot, in which the CIA planned to treat a box of cigars with a chemical that would explode when the cigar was lit. Another scheme was to give Castro a skin-diving suit dusted with a fungus that would produce a disabling skin disease and to contaminate the breathing apparatus with the bacterium that causes tuberculosis. Another idea was to booby-trap a seashell that would explode when the seashell was lifted; it was to be planted in an area where Castro was known to frequently skin-dive. Still another plot was to have poison pills delivered to a restaurant where Castro liked to eat. This plot involved Mafia figures Sam Giancani, Santos Trafficante, and Jonny Rosseli, who had contacts in Havana from the pre-Castro days.

These assassination attempts became public knowledge in 1975 when Senator Frank Church conducted hearings on "Alleged Assassination Plots Involving Foreign Leaders." In addition to the attempts to assassinate Castro, the hearings revealed attempts to assassinate other foreign leaders, including Patrice Lumumba of the Congo, Rafael Trujillo of the Dominican Republic, and Rene Schneider of Chile. As chair of the commission, Church famously described the CIA as a "rogue elephant rampaging out of control."

The assassination attempts on Castro were illegal. Were they morally justified? Explain your answer.

4. Salah Shehada

Hamas leader Salah Shehada (age forty) was killed in July 2002 when an Israeli F-16 jet dropped a one-ton bomb on an apartment building in the Gaza Strip where Shehada was living. The explosion caused the building to collapse and damaged several buildings nearby. Shehada was killed, along with fourteen other Palestinians, including several children. Palestinian doctors claimed that 154 civilians were injured as well.

Shehada was on Israel's most-wanted list at the time of his assassination. Israel claimed that he was directly responsible for hundreds of attacks on Israeli citizens and security forces. He was one of the founders of Hamas (along with Ahmed Yassin) and had spent some fifteen years as a Palestinian military leader.

Hamas reacted to the attack by calling it a massacre and vowing to take revenge against Israeli targets. President George W. Bush denounced the hit as "heavy-handed." Human rights organizations around the world criticized the attack, saying that intentionally dropping a one-ton bomb in the middle of the night on a crowded civilian neighborhood amounted to a war crime.

In 2005, a lawsuit was filed by the Center for Constitutional Rights. It alleged that Avraham Dichter, the military commander in charge of the operation against Shehada, had planned the assassinations of more than 300 Palestinian leaders and caused the deaths or injuries of hundreds of innocent bystanders. The lawsuit noted that assassination is illegal under international law.

In 2008, an Israeli commission said that the attack on Shehada did not involve the premeditated intention to kill civilians, and that the commanders did not know innocent people were in the building that was hit. If this is true, was the attack morally justified? Explain your answer.

It seems unlikely that the building occupied by Shehada in the middle of the night housed no one else. It seems safe to assume that there were innocent people in the building, and that the commanders of the attack knew this. Was the dropping of a one-ton bomb on the apartment building still morally justified? Why or why not?

⚜ SUGGESTED READINGS

Storming Media (www.stormingmedia.us) has abstracts of Pentagon reports on targeted killing defending it as legitimate military action against unlawful enemy combatants. The Federation of American Scientists (www.fas.org) has reports on assassinations and defenses of targeted killing by members of the military. The Brookings website (www.brookings.edu) has reports and articles on assassination and targeted killing. The Hoover Institute (www.hoover.org) has reports on assassination and targeted killing. The CIA website (www.cia.gov) has information on drones, missiles, and terrorists. Amnesty International (www.amnesty.org) has reports on assassinations by Israel and others; they are condemned as illegal and immoral. Assassinology (www.assassinology.org) examines assassination in detail—facts, people killed, conspiracies, and news. The *Stanford Encyclopedia of Philosophy* (http://plato.stanford.edu) has an interesting article on "The Problem of Dirty Hands" by Tony Coady.

Mark Bowden, *Killing Pablo* (New York: Atlantic Monthly Press, 2001), describes the assassination of cocaine trafficker Pablo Escobar on December 2, 1993, by a Delta Force sniper. The Delta Force is an elite Department of Defense group engaged in covert missions.

Stephen de Wijze, "Targeted Killing: A 'Dirty Hands' Analysis,'" *Contemporary Politics* 15, no. 3 (September 2009): 305–320, argues that targeted killing is neither entirely morally justified nor completely wrong. Rather, those who do it have "dirty hands," that is, they have done something wrong in order to do right.

Steven de Wijze, "Tragic Remorse—The Anguish of Dirty Hands," *Ethical Theory and Moral Practice* 7, no. 5 (January 2005): 453–471, explains and defends the moral emotion of tragic remorse that results from unavoidable wrongdoing.

Peter M. Cullen, "The Role of Targeted Killing in the Campaign against Terror," *Joint Force Quarterly* 48 (2008, 1st Quarter): 22–29, gives a careful discussion of the legality and morality of targeted killing of terrorists. He concludes that it is an effective tactic in the campaign against terror.

Ward Thomas, "Norms and Security," *International Security* 25, no. 1 (Summer 2000): 105–133, makes a case against international assassination, especially when the target is a national leader.

Jane Mayer, "The Predator War," *New Yorker* 85, no. 34 (October 26, 2009): 36–45, discusses the risks of the CIA covert drone program, noting that the program has carried out targeted assassinations without arousing controversy.

Scott Shane, "CIA Expanding Drone Assaults Inside Pakistan," *The New York Times*, December 4, 2009, reports on the increased CIA drone or Predator attacks inside Pakistan's tribal areas. Included are quotes from the CIA defending the covert program, which is described as one of Washington's "worst-kept secrets."

Harold Zeller, ed., *Assassination* (Cambridge, MA: Schenkman Publishing, 1974). This is a collection of articles on assassination by well-known philosophers. James Rachels defends the hypothetical assassination of Hitler, while Douglas Lackey argues that it would not have been morally justified because we cannot be sure of the consequences.

Michael L. Gross, "Assassination and Targeted Killing," *Journal of Applied Philosophy* 23, no. 3 (2006): 323–335, discusses the attempt to justify targeted killing by appealing to self-defense and law enforcement. He argues that the only possible way to justify named killing is self-defense.

Paul McGeough, *Kill Khalid* (New York: New Press, 2009), describes the attempted assassination of Hamas leader Kalid Mishal by Mossad, the Israeli secret service. They tried to poison him in 1997 when he was taking his sons for a haircut. Mishal became a Hamas hero, the martyr who did not die.

David Kretzmer, "Targeted Killing of Suspected Terrorists," *European Journal of International Law* 16, no. 2 (2005): 171–212, discusses the legality of targeted killing of suspected terrorists under international human rights law and international humanitarian law. Under the former system, such killings are lawful only if done to prevent an imminent attack. Under the latter system, the killings may be lawful if the suspected terrorists are viewed as combatants.

Steven R. David, "Israel's Policy of Targeted Killing," *Ethics and International Affairs* 17, no. 1 (Spring 2003): 111–126, argues that Israel's policy of hunting down and killing alleged Palestinian terrorists is legal, but raises doubts about its effectiveness because it exacerbated murderous retaliation against Israeli civilians, unmasked several informers, diverted intelligence resources, and drew international condemnation. The benefits include deterring some attacks and satisfying the desire for revenge and retribution.

Yael Stein, "By Any Name Illegal and Immoral: Response to 'Israel's Policy of Targeted Killing,'" *Ethics and International Affairs* 17, no. 1 (Spring 2003): 127–137, argues that the Israeli policy of killing suspected terrorists is illegal and immoral. The targets are civilians, not combatants. Revenge and retribution can serve to justify acts that are both illegal and immoral.

Steven R. David, "If Not Combatants, Certainly Not Civilians," *Ethics and International Affairs* 17, no. 1 (Spring 2003): 138–140, replies to Stein. Stein sees Palestinian terrorists as civilian noncombatants not engaged in war. David thinks they are combatants who seek to kill as many Israeli civilians as possible, and that Israel has the right and obligation to defend itself.

INDEX